Naum Gabo Retrospective

Organized by the Dallas Museum of Art
and the Kunstsammlung Nordrhein-Westfalen, Düsseldorf

Dallas Museum of Art
September 29 – November 17, 1985

Art Gallery of Ontario, Toronto
December 13, 1985 – February 9, 1986

The Solomon R. Guggenheim Museum, New York
March 6 – April 27, 1986

Akademie der Künste, Berlin-West
September 7 – October 19, 1986

Kunstsammlung Nordrhein-Westfalen, Düsseldorf
November 20, 1986 – January 11, 1987

The Tate Gallery, London
February 11 – April 20, 1987

Naum Gabo

Sixty Years of Constructivism

Edited by
Steven A. Nash
and Jörn Merkert

Including
Catalogue Raisonné
of the Constructions and Sculptures

Prestel-Verlag

This book was published on the occasion of the exhibition ›Naum Gabo: Sixty Years of Constructivism‹ at the Dallas Museum of Art (September 29 – November 17, 1985), the Art Gallery of Ontario, Toronto (December 13, 1985 – February 9, 1986), The Solomon R. Guggenheim Museum, New York (March 6 – April 27, 1986), the Akademie der Künste, Berlin-West (September 7 – October 20, 1986), the Kunstsammlung Nordrhein-Westfalen, Düsseldorf (November 20, 1986 – January 11, 1987) and The Tate Gallery, London (February 11 – April 20, 1987).

The tour of this exhibition in North America was generously supported by a grant from the National Endowment for the Arts, a U.S. federal agency, an indemnity from the Federal Council on the Arts and Humanities, and additional funding from Akin, Gump, Strauss, Hauer and Feld and Knoll International, Inc.

Front cover: Constructed Head No. 2, 1916 (cat. 2)
Back cover: Linear Construction in Space No. 3, with Red, 1952/57 – 58 (cat. 47)
Frontispiece: Naum Gabo on his 80th birthday, August 5, 1970

The essay of Jörn Merkert was translated by Michael Foster.

ISBN 3 7913 0742 8 (hardcover edition; Distribution in the U.S.A. by te Neues Publishing Company, 15 East 76 Street, New York, N.Y. 10021)

ISBN 0 9609622 7 1 (softcover edition)

Type set and printed by Dr. C. Wolf und Sohn, München
Offset Lithography by Brend'Amour, Simhardt GmbH & Co., München
Bound by R. Oldenbourg Graphische Betriebe GmbH, München

Printed in Germany

Table of Contents

Lenders to the exhibition

Family Collection
Albright—Knox Art Gallery, Buffalo
Art Institute of Chicago
Berlin, Staatliche Museen Preußischer Kulturbesitz, Nationalgalerie
Dallas Museum of Art
The Solomon R. Guggenheim Museum, New York
The Jeffrey H. Loria Collection, New York
Collection of Mr. and Mrs. Raymond D. Nasher, Dallas
Collection of Marion and Nathan Smooke, Los Angeles
The Tate Gallery, London
Collection of Thomas P. Whitney
Yale University Art Gallery, New Haven

Preface

The extraordinary talents of pioneer constructivist Naum Gabo have too long been overlooked in view of his major contributions to twentieth century art and his sixty years of active work produced in Russia, Germany, England and finally America. Gabo's innovative sculptural evolution inspired countless other artists, painters as well as sculptors, and his profound legacy, though limited in number of works, remains as a testament to his visionary imagination and creative energy and skills.

The Dallas Museum of Art is extremely proud of its role in organizing the first truly comprehensive exhibition devoted to Gabo and of the international cooperation it represents. After premiering in Dallas, *Naum Gabo: Sixty Years of Constructivism* will travel to Toronto, New York, Berlin, Düsseldorf, and London. The exhibition's scholarly importance and its impressive tour represent a realization of the Dallas Museum's expressed goal to originate major international exhibits and signals the beginning of a new era in our museum's history.

Credit for the exhibition's concept, content, and organization is due to Steven A. Nash, Deputy Director/Chief Curator of the Dallas Museum of Art, whose study of Naum Gabo spans both his academic and professional careers, and without whose unflagging interest, museum diplomacy, and ongoing contact with heirs to the Gabo estate, this significant exhibition would not have been possible. The exhibition has additional relevance to the Dallas Museum, because of Dr. Nash's continuing research on the artist and his guidance in a DMA acquisition of an important early Gabo sculpture (*Constructed Head No. 2,* 1916). I should also like to recognize the efforts of Robert V. Rozelle, Chairman, DMA Publications, who helped to edit part of the catalogue's manuscript and arranged a publishing agreement.

Of course, an exhibition with so complex a tour as that of *Naum Gabo* requires extensive international cooperation on many different levels. We gratefully acknowledge the significant support provided by the National Endowment for the Arts in making possible the exhibition's North American tour. We are appreciative of the special collegial relationships which have grown out of the exhibition in working with the professional staffs of the Art Gallery of Ontario, The Solomon R. Guggenheim Museum, Akademie der Künste, and The Tate Gallery, and we are particularly grateful to Düsseldorf's Kunstsammlung Nordrhein-Westfalen, whose curator Jörn Merkert organized the show's European tour. Lastly, we are greatly indebted to Miriam Gabo and Nina and Graham Williams, the artist's widow and daughter and her husband, whose rich and representative private collection provides the nuclear basis of this exhibition tribute to Naum Gabo.

Harry S. Parker III
Director, Dallas Museum of Art

Note on illustration captions:

Works included in the exhibition are accompanied
by a reference to the catalogue section (cat. no.)
and to the Catalogue Raisonné by Colin Sanderson
and Christina Lodder at the back of the book
(S.–L. no.).
Sculptures by Gabo not included in the exhibition
carry only the Catalogue Raisonné number.

Introduction and Acknowledgements

Steven A. Nash

This exhibition and its catalogue comprise the most comprehensive survey ever presented of the art of Naum Gabo. Although long recognized as a pioneer of modern sculpture and a leader in the Constructivist movement, knowledge of Gabo's life and work has remained surprisingly incomplete. This is due not to a lack of interest but rather, to a conjoining of several historical factors: The turbulent years through which Gabo lived as a youth left little documentary trace of his activities. Several key works disappeared at early dates, and others (including a great many drawings) were retained by Gabo and rarely if ever publically displayed. He was never, at any rate, a prolific artist, and conservation problems afflicting his fragile constructions have taken several of those in public collections out of exposure and made his work in general difficult to borrow for exhibitions. Moreover, Gabo himself was not always sympathetic with art historical interpretation and discouraged certain scholarly projects.

Now, however, thanks primarily to the extreme generosity and cooperation of the Gabo family, a thorough examination of his achievements is possible. Over a hundred works of art, most of them lent by Gabo's family, have been assembled to form a survey stretching from his very earliest to his very last creations. Of these, many have rarely or never been exhibited. Indeed, several of the early sculptures, newly reassembled from pieces found in Gabo's studio after his death, have long been considered lost. The display of these works coincides with the publication of a comprehensive catalogue raisonné of Gabo's sculpture prepared by Colin Sanderson and Christina Lodder, which sheds much new light on complex issues of dating, provenance, publication histories, materials utilized, etc., and which we are proud to include in the exhibition catalogue. This impressive study will instantly become an indispensable tool for anyone interested in Gabo or Constructivist art. Also of great importance in tracing Gabo's development is the emergence of new documentary information from family archives. These heretofore unpublished references inform our catalogue and the catalogue raisonné throughout and allow for a more complete biographical picture than ever before presented. Because the previous scholarly literature on Gabo is so limited (the last major study on him was published in 1957 and contains no in-depth critical essays), a need was felt for extensive interpretative analysis, resulting in the several essays at the beginning of our book. Through these various means, an important chapter in the history of modern art has been greatly expanded and revised.

What emerges is a much more continuous, well-rounded, and accurate record of Gabo's work and contributions, which were many. By accepting the Cubist revolution as a challenge to reform completely the way sculpture was made, and its ability to express contemporary life, Gabo helped open a dominant vein of modernist thought, the ramifications of which are still strongly felt today. Through his delicate and radiant constructions, he gave new meaning to light, time, and space as sculptural elements. His exploration of new materials and scientific perspectives opened paths for many other artists, and he constantly sought to expand the boundaries of sculpture and its environmental role. His life, in the ideas and changes he fought for, was a constant affirmation of the Constructive values embodied in his art.

This exhibition, and its ability to present that art in a new light, would simply not have been possible without the close cooperation of the Gabo family. Miriam Gabo and Nina Williams (née Gabo) have been a constant source of information, encouragement, generosity and support, and Graham Williams has also assisted the whole undertaking in myriad ways. It has been a great pleasure working with all of them.

Our European collaborator, Jörn Merkert, shared conscientiously a major part of the organizational burden, and I also wish to thank for their cooperation our colleagues at museums on the North American tour, specifically Alan Wilkinson of the Art Gallery of Ontario and Diane Waldman of the Guggenheim Museum.

A considerable amount of the information presented in my catalogue essay and the chronology can be credited to the diligent research of Natalie Lee, volunteer research assistant. She painstakingly tracked down obscure sources and historical details but shares no blame for any faulty interpretations based on those facts. Charles Wilson, who worked with Gabo for many years as an assistant and probably knows his work better than anyone else, assisted freely with information and restored a number of objects in the exhibition. Christina Lodder and Colin Sanderson generously shared their extensive knowledge of Gabo's development, and among the many other scholars and artists who have kindly answered questions I want to acknowledge specially the following: Helga Kliemann, John Bowlt, Arthur Drexler, Judith Wolin, Anthony Hill, George Rickey, Willy Rotzler, Linda Henderson, and William Jack. My initial research on Gabo six years ago was supported by a Fellowship for Museum Professionals from the National Endowment for the Arts, and that same agency helped make possible the exhibition's North American tour with a sizeable grant. The tour was also greatly aided by the National Indemnification Program.

For their help with translations, we are indebted to Paul Pickering, Annette Schlagenhauff, the Rev. Moses N. Nagy, and Ilya Mamantov. Many librarians assisted our research efforts, including most notably Donna Rhein and Amy Schaffner of the Dallas Museum of Art but also staff members at the Dallas Public Library, Beinecke Rare Book and Manuscript Library at Yale University, the Museum of Modern Art Library, the Guggenheim Museum Library, and the Henry Clay Frick Fine Arts Library, University of Pittsburg. Harry Parker, Director of the Dallas Museum of Art, was supportive of the project from its inception, and other staff members have contributed importantly, including Irene Martin, Katherine Wagner, Elizabeth Simon, Anna McFarland and Deb Richards. Robert Rozelle helped oversee catalogue production, working closely with Prestel-Verlag, with whom we are pleased to have been associated. Lee Clockman, of the Dallas Museum, and John Webb, of London, provided beautiful photography, and Barbara Woodcock did a wonderful job of matting and framing the drawings.

To the lenders, all of whom made special concessions to allow their delicate works by Gabo to travel, we are particularly grateful. Our deep appreciation goes out to Jeffrey Loria, Thomas Whitney, Mr. and Mrs. Nathan Smooke, Raymond and Patsy Nasher, James Wood and James Speyer of The Chicago Art Institute, Douglas Schultz at the Albright-Knox Art Gallery, Alan Bowness at The Tate Gallery, Diane Waldman and Thomas Messer of the Guggenheim Museum, and Alan Shestack formerly of the Yale University Art Gallery.

Finally, for all her support of the Gabo project and her other profound contributions to the Dallas Museum of Art, we dedicate this catalogue to the memory of Betty Marcus.

Naum Gabo: Sculptures of Purity and Possibility

Steven A. Nash

1. Gabo put it explicitly: »Artists of the future must be universal, they must know the spirit of their time . . .« (*Studio International* 171, no. 876 [April 1966]: 130.) The artist attempts to project »Not only what he himself feels and looks forward to as an individual, but what the collective human mind of his time feels and aspires towards, but cannot yet express.« (*Three Lectures on Modern Art,* Trowbridge Lectures [New York, 1949], p. 68.)
2. From »Art and the Proletariat« in *Izobrazitelnoe iskusstvo,* no. 1 (1918); quoted by A. Nakov, *2 Stenberg 2* (London and Toronto, 1975), p. 14.
3. *Three Lectures,* p. 83.
4. From *Backward Glances;* quoted by Will Grohmann, *Wassily Kandinsky: Life and Work* (New York, 1958), p. 54.
5. »The Constructive Idea in Art,« *Circle: International Survey of Constructive Art* (London, 1937), p. 5.
6. Gabo's dependence on science is not infrequently overestimated. He is sometimes referred to misleadingly as a »scientific« or »mathematical« artist, reducing the complexity of his creative process to an overly simplified formula. Or his work is seen as relying singlemindedly on scientific models. Rosalind Krauss, for example, has written: »[Max] Bill's work, like that of Gabo and Pevsner, elaborates models for mathematical concepts into sculptural form« (*Passages in Modern Sculpture* [New York, 1977], p. 65), and William Tucker notes (erroneously): »Gabo, trained as an engineer, used sculpture as a means of illustrating scientific principles« (»Space/Illusion/Sculpture,« *Tracks* 1, pt. 3 [Fall 1975]: 12). It must be stressed that subjective and intuitive responses played as central a role in Gabo's work as scientific insight. Gabo continually asserted that reality is revealed not just scientifically but also through inner perception. Hence, he could assert that »Our works are not to be understood, they are to be felt.« See »Constructive Art,« *The Listener* 16, no. 408 (November 4, 1936): 846–48; reprinted in *Circle.*
7. Later in life, even Gabo reconciled himself with the broader, more popular usage of the term Constructivism, as applied to the multifarious tradition of geometric abstraction deriving out of Russian and Dutch models.

Gabo's art, throughout its long evolution of context and form, always reflected the revolutionary period in which it was born. Associated even as a youth with anarchistic causes, schooled in Munich in one of Europe's leading scientific centers, nurtured as an artist by the breakthroughs of Cubism during years of war and revolution, Gabo was to absorb from this climate of political and intellectual upheaval a fervent social idealism and a belief in art as an active, productive force. A new age was dawning and art was to play a critical role in the re-ordering of modern life. Gabo had already articulated such ideals by 1920 in his *Realistic Manifesto,* and he remained committed to them for the rest of his long career.

Basic to the mission he assigned to art in general and sculpture in particular was the creation of new images to express the collective consciousness of the era and to produce a deeper understanding of modern reality. To be of one's own time artistically took on renewed meaning.[1] Sculpture carried an ontological function, reminiscent of Punin's definition of art as »a means of knowing.«[2] As Gabo put it, he sought new images »not for the sake of their novelty but for the sake of finding an expression of the new outlook on the world around me and the new insight into the forces of life and nature in me.«[3] Recent discoveries in science had profoundly affected perceptions of natural law, stretching the modern imagination in new directions, and Gabo was among those artists who responded with a search for visual modes to help understand these emerging realities. The impact of such changes was registered, for example, by Kandinsky's famous statement, »The disintegration of the atom was to me like the disintegration of the whole world.«[4]

Art, too, was undergoing profound changes. Cubism, Gabo wrote, had left artistic tradition in ruins.[5] It was up to the new generation to build upon these ruins by devising visual languages appropriate to a vastly changed world. His personal response to this challenge involved a marriage between art and science. Contrary to what is sometimes presumed, however, he never sought merely to illustrate scientific principles.[6] Rather, he found in science a model of analytical thought and a basis of disciplined form. By expanding subjectively upon these sources, he could create his own new geometries which, absolute unto themselves, also elucidate external processes and forces.

In his pursuit of these lofty ambitions, Gabo's fascinating life took him from Russia and Germany before World War I, to Norway, back to Revolutionary Russia, then on to Germany, Paris, England during World War II, and finally America. His sustained, 60-year artistic development is marked by a continuity which, in its emphasis on universals, managed to transcend the extreme personal and cultural disruptions he experienced. The terminology he himself chose for his art and philosophy was »Constructive« (as differentiated from the narrower label of »Constructivism« as it applied to the Productivist movement in post-Revolutionary Russia, which Gabo found abhorrent for its elevation of political over spiritual values).[7] In the dual metaphors offered by this term – real, positive contribution and the actual processes of building – we find a summation of Gabo's whole outlook.

The historical survey that follows attempts to trace Gabo's long development and the major forces and concerns that gave it direction. As well known as Gabo's work in general now is, much about the particulars of its evolution remain ill-defined. Important questions still exist, for example, regarding the sources behind his earliest sculptures, the degree and character of his interaction with the Russian avant-garde, the relationship of his theoretical work to other theoretical writings of the period, the nature of the scientific element in his development, and his attitude toward issues of scale, materials, and the public role of sculpture. One must ask to what degree his aspirations and ideals were fulfilled, and perhaps most importantly, a closer reading of individual works is necessary to try to come to grips with their enduring imaginative force.

I. Early Development: Russia, Germany, Norway

Within his own family Gabo found stimulation for the two central pursuits of his life; art and science.[8] His father, Boris Pevsner, was a metallurgist and owner of a metals factory and rolling mill. Continuing this tradition, his two eldest brothers, Mark and Jeremy, chose scientific careers in metallurgy and engineering. His brother Antoine, however, decided to become an artist. He studied at the art school in Kiev from 1902 to 1909 and then briefly attended the Academy of Art at St. Petersburg before moving to Paris in 1911 to pursue his career. Although the direction of influence would be reversed in later years, Antoine's example must have been significant for Gabo, who as a child was inclined toward literary and artistic interests.

Despite these leanings, Gabo's father decided that, since two sons were already engineers and one an artist, the fourth should become a doctor. Accordingly, Gabo was enrolled in the medical curriculum at the University of Munich. In 1910 he traveled first to Berlin then on to Munich to begin his studies.

Unfortunately, information on the chronology and content of Gabo's studies in Munich is minimal.[9] We know that after beginning in the medical faculty he shifted (probably in 1911) into mathematics and natural sciences and subsequently (c. 1912) took up applied sciences and civil engineering, transferring to the Technische Hochschule, or Polytechnical School. At this time, William Konrad Röntgen, winner of the Nobel Prize in physics, and the great organic chemist Adolf von Baeyer, another Nobel Prize winner, were both on the physical science faculty at the University, indicating the advanced level of instruction available.[10] Since the sciences were part of the larger Philosophische Fakultät, it is natural that Gabo should have rounded out his studies with courses in philosophy, including lectures from Heinrich Wölfflin in art history. Out of this broad background and the period's heady atmosphere of discovery and debate, Gabo developed extremely wideranging interests in such theorists as Bergson, Einstein, Worringer, Lipps, Kandinsky, and even Frank Lloyd Wright.[11] For example, he later mentioned attending about 1911 or 1912 a gathering of scientists and students at which one of the professors spoke about Einstein's Theory of Relativity. »I myself was then studying physics. There was a sharp discussion. I grasped the idea, though I couldn't say exactly what it was about. But there was an elation in the air.«[12] Although he never completed his degree, the scientific learning and methodology which Gabo absorbed in Munich permanently influenced his way of thinking and outlook on the world.

Simultaneously, his interests in art were developing. He found Wölfflin's lectures particularly stimulating, and he had for some time been making watercolors and drawings, described by Alexei as swift, impetuous, »romantic and expressive.«[13] During a visit back to Briansk in 1911 he executed one such drawing that supposedly prompted Antoine to declare that he no longer knew which of them was the artist.[14] Works that survive from this period (e.g. cat. nos. 67–70) show a natural fluency of draughtsmanship in a style heavily influenced by Art Nouveau and the progressive Russian artist Mikhail Vrubel, later acknowledged by Gabo as an early source of inspiration. In the pastel *Christmas* from c. 1910–12 (cat. no. 67) the example of Matisse seems to come into play, indicating that by this period Gabo may have already visited the famous Shchukin collection in Moscow which contained the similarly flattened and patterned *Harmony in Red*.[15] More expressionist in feeling was a sculpture he made the winter of 1912–13 (now lost) of the head of a sad-eyed Black he had seen in the streets of Munich (catalogue raisonne no. 1). Both the subject and style of this sculpture suggest that he was becoming familiar with work by the German Expressionists.

8. Most of the available information on Gabo's childhood comes from Alexei Pevsner, *A Biographical Sketch of My Brothers Naum Gabo and Antoine Pevsner* (Amsterdam, 1964), supplemented by Christina Lodder's biographic essay in this catalogue.
9. More thorough notes are found in Lodder's accompanying essay.
10. Justus Bier (»Der Glasplastiker Gabo,« *Glastechnische Berichte*, 10 [1932] reported that Gabo studied under Röntgen, Baeyer, and also the physicist Leo Graetz, but it is not known if this assertion is based on direct evidence or conjecture.
11. Alexei Pevsner reported verbally to Miriam Gabo, the artist's widow, that Gabo had greatly admired Bergson in his early years of study. On Gabo's knowledge of Einstein, see below in the text. On his knowledge of Worringer there is conflicting information: Gabo wrote to Werner Hofmann in 1960 that he did not know of Worringer while a student (see Christina Lodder, *Russian Constructivism* [New Haven and London, 1983], p. 272, n. 106), while he indicated in notes for a letter to Herbert Read of Jan. 25, 1966 (Gabo papers, Beinecke Rare Book and Manuscript Library, Yale University) that he was familiar with Worringer's theories but didn't actually own his book until the 20s. In that same letter he stated that he first met Kandinsky in Moscow in 1917 but had read *On the Spiritual in Art* sometime around 1913. In the above-mentioned letter to Werner Hofmann he wrote that Professor Lipp's ideas were well known in Munich at that time. For a statement by Gabo about his early excitement over the architecture and the ideas of F. L. Wright, see *Focus* (London), no. 4 (1939): 51.
12. »Naum Gabo talks about his work,« *Studio International*, 171, no. 876 (April 1966): 128.
13. Alexei Pevsner, p. 6.
14. Ibid., p. 6.
15. Another possible instance of Matisse's influence can be seen in Gabo's *Girl with Roses* (ibid., p. 10), which Alexei Pevsner says was made in Zurich in 1912 and which compares to Matisse's *Girl with Tulips* (1910) in the Shchukin collection and the *Girl with a Black Cat* (1910), shown in Zurich in the summer of 1912.
16. »Gabo talks about his work,« p. 127.
17. For example, Cubist artists had shown at the invitation of the New Artist's Federation in 1910; Picasso took part in a large exhibition at the Tannhauser gallery in February 1913, and again in a group show with other Cubists at the Hans Goltz gallery in summer 1914; Blaue Reiter exhibitions appeared in January and February 1912; Kandinsky had a one-man show in September 1912; large avant-garde exhibitions appeared at Hans Goltz's gallery in October 1912 and August 1913; and the *Neue Münchener Secession* held its first exhibition in May–October 1914.
18. In an unpublished interview with Kenneth Frampton and S. Frederick Starr in 1970 (ms. in Gabo papers, Beinecke Library; hereafter referred to as Starr-Frampton interview), Gabo noted that he saw the Morozov collection as

a youth but didn't actually meet Morozov until after the Revolution when his collection was joined with Shchukin's under the control of the state. He also said that both he and Pevsner worked with the collections as helpers at that later time, as did Rodchenko. Olson and Chanin (in *Naum Gabo/Antoine Pevsner*. [Museum of Modern Art, New York, 1948]) report that Gabo visited both collections during his student days, but their documentation must be used cautiously since it contains identifiable errors, despite being based in part on interviews with Gabo.

19. In the above-cited notes by Gabo for a letter to Herbert Read of Jan. 25, 1966 (Gabo papers, Beinecke Library), he states that the trips to Paris took place in 1912 and 1913. Several secondary sources give the date of the second as 1914, but this seems unlikely given other travels by Gabo in the spring of that year. The dates for the Salon des Indépendants in 1912 and 1913 were March 20–May 16 and March 19–May 18, respectively.

20. Letter to Read, ibid., and »Gabo talks about his work,« p. 127.

21. »Gabo talks about his work,« p. 129.

22. Alexei Pevsner, pp. 10–11. Also see p. 14 for a description of Gabo's first sculptural experiments in Norway.

23. For an in-depth analysis of the importance of n-dimensional geometries in the development of modern art, see Linda D. Henderson, *The Fourth Dimension and Non-Euclidian Geometry in Modern Art* (Princeton, 1983).

A walking trip to Italy in 1913 along an itinerary provided by Wölfflin, although reaching only Florence rather than the original destination of Rome, opened Gabo's eyes to the glories of Renaissance art and also touched off notions about new possibilities in sculpture.[16] Munich itself provided exposure to much progressive art activity,[17] and at some point early in life Gabo was able to visit the Morozov collection of modern art in Moscow and, perhaps, the Shchukin collection as well.[18] Even more important for an introduction to contemporary artistic currents, however, were the trips he made to Paris to visit Antoine and tour the galleries and museums. Different dates have been given for these trips, but Gabo himself remembered them as 1912 and 1913.[19] Since Antoine's work from this period shows a receptivity to Cubist influence, conversation between the brothers undoubtedly delved into this revolutionary new movement, and Gabo is known to have attended at least one of the large Salons des Indépendants and to have seen works by Cubist painters including Lhote, Gleizes, Metzinger, Léger, and Delaunay. He is often said to have also met Archipenko, who was a friend of Antoine's and was already beginning his work in *sculpto-peinture,* and while Gabo later denied that such a meeting took place, he did acknowledge seeing works by Archipenko at the Indépendants.[20] The legacy of these experiences would soon become apparent.

The outbreak of war in August 1914 closed this early student chapter of Gabo's life, as he and his brother Alexei, who had joined him in Munich, fled first to Copenhagen then Christiania (Oslo). Alexei was eligible for military service in Russia, and Gabo's father had sent money so they could stay in Oslo and Alexei could attend the university. In a 1966 interview Gabo commented on the fortuitous nature of this disruption: »[It] freed me from my last exams. I knew I wasn't going to be an engineer; I thought the teaching methods were idiotic . . .«[21] He now had the time and freedom to concentrate on what had become his primary aspiration – sculpture. According again to Alexei, Gabo was:

specially keen to find a place of seclusion from the war, where he would have a chance to concentrate on executing some of the ideas he was having for sculptures. . . . It was precisely here (Norway) that he set to work and here that he announced to me that he would have no other profession but sculpture.[22]

By winter of 1915 Gabo had begun work on the *Constructed Head No. 1* (fig. 5), initiating a series of constructions that signal his sudden emergence as a significant artist. Considering that he never received formal training and that we know of no sculptural efforts (other than a few experimentations referred to by Alexei) intervening between the amateurish *Head of a Negro* and the *Head No. 1*, this abrupt leap forward is all the more remarkable. Clearly it was predicated in large degree on his scientific background as well as reaction to works of a geometric vocabulary he had seen in Paris and possibly Munich. From engineering he had gained a respect for economy of materials and form and for innovative methods of construction. Thus was born the important premise, basic to his work and theoretical stance as articulated later in the *Realistic Manifesto,* that volume and strength are independent of mass. Just as open systems of beams, trusses, and planes provide the engineer with an efficient vocabulary of structure (fig. 1), so too are they relevant to new methods of sculpture. Concomitantly, Gabo had begun to see space and time through the eyes of science as the basic elements of life. Whether manifested in Rutherford's model of the atom (published in 1909–11), popularized notions of the fourth dimension with geometric diagrams disintegrating solids into linear webs (e.g. fig. 2),[23] or Bergson's theories of constant transition (well known by 1910), recent developments had thoroughly discredited concepts of solid and static matter. Space invades and links all matter, as does time, as change or inner rhythm. Any sculpture that was truly responsive to modern existence would reflect these new perceptions, and Gabo's quest, therefore, centered on a means of expressing his concepts of space, structure, and the energy of motion as well as the general technological ethos which characterized the era.

How much these aims may have been influenced by his knowledge of Cubism and Futurism is difficult to determine. Boccioni, for example, in his widely read *Technical Manifesto of Futurist Sculpture* of 1912, wrote with conviction about similar

Fig. 1 Eiffel Tower under construction, Paris, c. 1888

concerns: We »proclaim the absolute and complete abolition of finite lines and the contained statue. Let's split open our figures and place the environment inside them. We declare that the environment must form part of the plastic whole.« Sculpture must »give an adequate sense of rhythmic movement to planes and lines,« while »transparent planes, glass, strips of metal sheeting, wire, streetlamps or house-lights may all indicate planes – the shapes, tones and semitones of a new reality.«[24] Gabo's early drawings reveal an interest in Cubism, and he had seen how Cubist sculptors introduced space and time into form by creating a positive play of spatial voids, excavating shapes with angular planes that catch the light, and shuffling perspective and anatomical sequence. Certainly such objectives would have reinforced his own observations, although Gabo, as we will see, eventually criticized Cubism and Futurism as only halfway, essentially anachronistic measures. His early sculptures must be understood partially as critiques of their approach.

That he was initially receptive to Cubist influence, however, is proven by a drawing of a kneeling figure that can be dated to his early years in Norway or slightly before (fig. 4). Executed on a rough piece of cardboard, it shows the artist experimenting with the flattening and faceting of solids, the manipulation of sequence, and the African motifs associated with Analytic Cubism in its earliest manifestations. It is one of Gabo's most pictorial graphic works, with its shadings and variations of linear weight, and contrasts with the lean, »technological« aspect that his drawing style assumed thereafter. But most importantly, it provides an early look at Gabo's analysis of the figure through intersecting planes that still describe anatomy but allow it to be re-engineered in depth.

His next step in solving the problems of expression he had set for himself was to appropriate from solid geometry the so-called stereometric method for the measurement of volume and other metrical elements of form.[25] The cellular structure associated with this system, now well known through Gabo's many explanations (fig. 3), allowed him to introduce space into sculpture as a primary element and also, through its reduction of form into interlocking planes, represents a renunciation of mass, solidity, and density as essential conditions of volume. Its many associations – mathematical, technological, n-dimensional – all pertain in Gabo's attempts to image modernity. It has been suggested that he may have known and been influenced by earlier planar and cellular techniques, such as those applied by the 19th century artist Barthélemy Menn in his anatomical models,[26] but no direct points of contact can be documented. Moreover, planar construction was an innovative idea deriving out of Cubism and the constructive »tesserae« of Cezanne that was very much in the

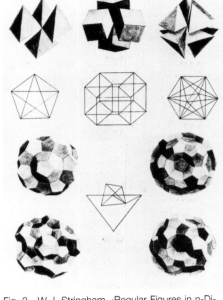

Fig. 2   W. I. Stringham, ›Regular Figures in n-Dimensional Space‹, *American Journal of Mathematics,* 1880, pl.l.

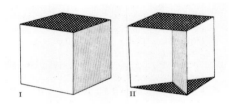

Fig. 3   Diagram of geometric cube and a cube constructed according to the stereometric system.

24. *Futurist Manifestos,* The Documents of 20th-Century Art, ed. Umbro Apollonio (New York, 1973), pp. 63, 64.
25. Stereometry in general concerns the measuring of volumetric and solid properties, as distinguished from planimetry. As a mathematical discipline it dates back to Johannes Kepler, whose book *Nova Stereometria doliorum vinariorum* of 1615 describes computation of the volume of wine casks, and seems to have been commonly a separate mathematical course at European universities in the 19th century. Gabo's transformation of the

Fig. 4   Gabo, *Kneeling Figure,* c. 1915, pencil and charcoal, Family Collection (cat. no. 71).

Fig. 5   Gabo, *Constructed Head No. 1,* 1915/reassembled 1985, plywood, Family Collection (cat. no.1, *S.–L. 3.2*).

»stereometric system« into an assemblage of interlocked planes for sculptural usage must have been prompted by the kinds of diagrams, dividing solid forms into planar and linear constituents, that are commonly found in early textbooks on solid geometry and stereometry, e.g. George B. Halsted, *Metrical Geometry, An Elementary Treatise on Mensuration* (Boston, 1881).

26. This connection was first posited by Willy Rotzler in his introduction to *Constructivism and the Geometric Tradition: Selections from the McCrory Corporation Collection* (Albright-Knox Art Gallery, Buffalo, 1979), p.7.

27. Margit Rowell's exhibition and catalogue *The Planar Dimension, Europe, 1912–1932* (The Solomon R. Guggenheim Museum, New York, 1979) still stand as the leading study of trends in early modern sculpture utilizing the plane as a critically new basic module of structure.

28. Gabo told Ronald Alley that he had considered *Head No. 1* only partially successful due in particular to insufficient concavity, especially in the lower sections. Ronald Alley, *Catalogue of the Tate Gallery's Collection of Modern Art other than works by British Artists* (London, 1981), p. 263.

29. Ibid., p. 263.

30. Vollard had published an edition of casts of the *Head of a Woman* soon after Picasso completed the plaster, and Archipenko's *Head* was published in Apollinaire's *Les Soirées de Paris,* June 15, 1914.

31. Gabo, »The Concepts of Russian Art, *»World Review* (London, 1942). Several early drawings by Gabo show a mother and child motif in a simplified linear style that could have been influenced by icon paintings. See also Naum Gabo, *Of Divers Arts,* Bollingen Series XXXV (Princeton and London, 1962), esp. pp. 172–73.

Fig. 6 Gabo, *Constructed Head No. 2,* 1916, galvanized iron, Family Collection (cat. no. 2, S.–L. 4.2).

air but was not developed by any artists prior to Gabo in so rigorous and rationalized a fashion.[27]

In successive works, his application of the stereometric method became more sophisticated and complex. The first work in his series of heads and torsos, *Constructed Head No. 1* (fig. 5), exemplifies the working method for the whole group. He first made cardboard models prior to finished versions in plywood (in the case of *Head No. 1*) or sheetmetal. Flat or curved planes were cut and then slotted together or assembled with hinges, glue, or solder, depending on the material. The result is a light, honeycombed structure that opens the depths of the sculpture to light and space and only implies an outer skin through the edges of planes and gaps between members. Mass is renounced, and the object is no longer understood from its surfaces. In *Head No. 1*, which is publicly displayed in this exhibition for the first time in more than 50 years, the long neck and tipped head give a somewhat quixotic aspect to Gabo's android-like vision of the future, half human and half scientific diagram.

If this work still seems a bit experimental or tentative, *Head No. 2* from one year later is a fully realized statement of the stereometric method at its most intricate, and would rapidly become an icon of the Constructivist movement in general (fig. 6).[28] The honeycombing of structure is more elaborate, the underlying figural motif more thoroughly rethought, and the whole expression given a more architectonic nature. Several surviving drawings (e.g. cat. nos. 73–75) trace the transformation from *Head No. 1* (one notes again the somewhat primitivizing stylization of the head in certain of these studies). Gabo had been particularly dissatisfied with the lower section of the earlier work due to its relatively naturalistic structure. In drawings and then in the sculpture itself, he introduced the folded hands which are fully integrated into the dynamism of form in the chest, shoulders, and head. The interplay of light and shadow has become so complex as to change constantly under different illumination and as one moves around the piece. Different compositional aspects of the figure emerge from different points-of-view. And an active dialogue of inward and outward movement, line and plane, highlight and depth, representation and abstraction mitigates against any sense of stasis and seems to define an object in a perpetual state of becoming. Gabo himself felt that *Head No. 2* embodied completely his objectives at that time.[29] Made from sheets of galvanized iron, he painted the original version in order to protect it, but in the 1960s he stripped it down to the bare metal, with its rugged industrial look, after a miraculous and somewhat mysterious retrieval of the sculpture, apparently from Russia.

Head No. 2 is sometimes compared to Cubist sculptures such as Picasso's *Head of a Woman* of 1909 or Archipenko's *Head* of 1913 (figs. 7 and 8), both of which Gabo could possibly have known,[30] as a proposition of direct connections. Precedents such as these, in which modern artists isolate the human head to invest it with personal meanings, may well have prompted Gabo's concentration on the motifs of head and torso, although another possible influence, that of Russian icons, should also be noted (compare figs. 6 and 9). Gabo would later analyze the ancient tradition of icon painting, which had such far-reaching implications for the formation of Russian abstract art, in terms of continuities with the modern movement.[31] This kinship could account to some degree for the intensity that Gabo's figures manage to convey, despite their industrial nature.

That his early drawings relate more to Cubist painting than sculpture is significant. Despite its aggressive reformations, Picasso's bronze *Head of a Woman* maintains a closed surface that shortchanges the propositions of space and time opened up in Cubist painting. Against Cubist sculpture in general Gabo always leveled the charge that it never fundamentally broke with the massiveness and stasis of earlier work, and even Archipenko's planar *Head* of 1913 seems heavy and solid compared to the thinly membraned *Head No. 2*. Furthermore, Gabo felt, like Mondrian, that Cubism never realized its own full potential after its revolutionary beginnings and that, by remaining tied to visual appearance, it constituted an essentially superficial graphic reorganization.[32] In structure Gabo's early work is actually much closer to Picasso's sheetmetal *Guitar* of 1911–12 with its discontinuous surfaces and implied rather

 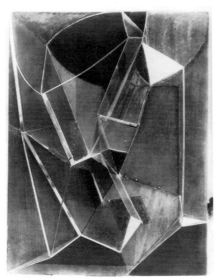 

It would appear that after settling in Moscow Gabo's first major efforts were centered on constructing in metal the large *Torso,* already begun in Norway, and he may also have been working on a celluloid version of *Head in a Corner Niche,* although the dating of this version is problematic and can be argued to have been considerably later.[39] Keeping in mind that other sculptures may have been lost and undocumented, the next recorded three-dimensional work is the missing *Construction en creux* of 1919, made from painted cardboard (fig. 11).[40] This relief is often associated as a preliminary version with the plastic and wood *Construction en creux* of 1921 (fig. 12; also lost), although the internal syntax of forms is quite different. Together with the related *Space Construction C* of 1919–21 (fig. 13) and *Square Relief* of 1920–21 (cat. no. 12), these works signal Gabo's arrival at a new stage of development, one of total abstraction. A never-before examined series of drawings allows one to trace the step-by-step conceptualization behind this emergence from a figurative to an abstract mode.

The transition has its start in a heavily worked pencil and pastel *Study of a Head* (fig. 15), that must date from c. 1917–18 or slightly earlier.[41] The general motif

Fig. 11   Gabo, *Construction en creux,* 1919, painted cardboard, destroyed (*S.–L. 7.1*).

Fig. 12   Gabo, *Construction en creux,* 1920–21, plastic and wood, presumed destroyed (*S.–L. 7.2*).

Fig. 13   Gabo, *Space Construction C,* 1919–21, plastic, destroyed (*S.–L. 8*).

39. See the accompanying catalogue raisonné by Sanderson and Lodder, no. 5, for evidence dating the celluloid version to c. 1917–20, based primarily on a not altogether clear statement Gabo made in 1948. It seems to this writer more probable that Gabo first made a cardboard and then a metal version, as was his usual practice at this time, and that the metal version was the one exhibited in Germany in 1922 (photographs of the in-stallation seem to confirm that it was indeed a metal piece that was shown). It is fairly certain that Gabo made the celluloid construction of *Head No. 2* after the metal version of this work was mistakenly returned to Russia following the appearance of the First Russian Exhibition in Berlin and Amsterdam. Since the celluloid version of *Head in a Corner Niche* is executed from a similar material, it seems probable that it was made at the same time, i.e. c. 1923, under the same circumstances, and that the contrary datings are the result of confusion between versions.
40. This work is dated 1919 both by Alexei Pevs-ner (p. 26) and an article in the Hungarian journal *Egyśeg* (no. 2, 1922, p. 8) in which a translation of the *Realistic Manifesto* appears.

 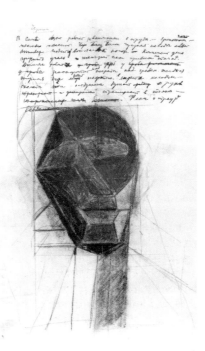

Fig. 14   Vladimir Burliuk, *Portrait of Benedict Liv-shits,* 1911, oil on canvas, whereabouts unknown.

Fig. 15   Gabo, *Study of a Head,* c. 1917–18, pencil and pastel, Family Collection (cat. no. 87).

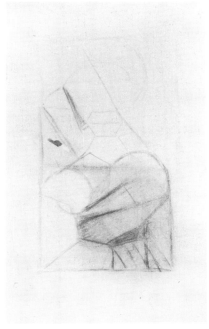

Fig. 16   Gabo, *Study for a Relief,* c. 1917–19, pencil, Family Collection.

Fig. 17   Gabo, *Study for a Relief,* inscribed 1914, but here dated to c. 1917–19, pencil, Family Collection (cat. no. 88).

Fig. 18   Gabo, *Study for a Relief,* inscribed 1916, but here dated to c. 1917–19, pencil, Family Collection.

41. The long inscription on this drawing is very difficult to decipher but seems to be a story entitled »Black« about a mine or factory filled with smoke, according to Christina Lodder. Although the head pictured could be interpreted as that of a Black, there is no evidence linking it with Gabo's sculpture *Head of a Negro,* of 1912–13, and a strong stylistic case exists for dating it considerably later.
42. Both drawings belong to the family of the artist. The one shown in fig. 16 is pencil on thin paper and measures 20.3 x14 cm. The drawing in fig. 17 is included in the exhibition as cat. no. 88. The theory of dating presented here is based on internal formal evidence and the logic of relationship to sculptures of known date.
43. Collection of the artist's family, pencil and charcoal on heavy paper, 50 × 39 cm, dated anachronistically on one side to 1916.

recalls to some degree both *Constructed Head No. 1* and *Constructed Head No. 2,* although the blocky faceting of planes and overall density are unusual and relate most clearly to a sculpturally-oriented Cubist style found several years earlier in the work of numerous artists and typified, for example, by Vladimir Burliuk's *Portrait of Benedict Livshits* of 1911 (fig. 14). In succeeding drawings of the same motif, done probably over a lengthy period of time, Gabo proceeded to redefine the head and shoulders into an increasingly autonomous pattern of lines and planes that are structured into a surrounding frame, giving the suggestion of either a forward-projecting relief or a construction recessed in a niche. Progressive stages are seen in figs. 16 and 17, the latter drawing carrying an inscribed date of 1914 which, however, was probably added much later and is probably inaccurate.[42] Figs. 18 and 19 show two drawings on the front and reverse of a single sheet that take the variations further.[43] In all of these works, as they become progressively more abstract, the strong diagonal of the nose is preserved as are a curve for the skull, lines for the eyes and mouth, and a curve or angle for the shoulder.

Fig. 19   Gabo, *Study for a Relief,* c. 1917–19, pencil, Family Collection (verso of fig. 18).

Fig. 20   Gabo, *Sketch for a Relief Construction,* c. 1917–19, pencil, The Tate Gallery (cat. no. 89). Illustrated here upside down.

At this point in his experimentations, Gabo seems oddly enough to have decided to *flip over* the design, as is apparent from the *upside down* illustration of the drawing in fig. 20, which continues the same evolution of design (compare especially to fig.17).[44] Closely related to this study is another drawing in the Tate Gallery (#T.2152), which must also be read upside down to unterstand its continuities with the rest of the group.[45] Keeping in mind the earlier drawings it is still possible to detect elements of the head and shoulders, but these features have been distilled and absorbed into an overall design of intersecting geometric components that, at first acquaintance, seems to be totally abstract. To show the direct bearing on Gabo's 1919 *Construction en creux*, this work is also illustrated upside down (fig. 21). Gabo's earliest documented abstract sculpture, *Construction en creux* emerges as the final product of this lengthy evolution, one which liberated Gabo forever from dependence on natural appearance.

Other Russian artists, of course, had moved into the realm of pure abstraction as early as five or six years before. It was undoubtedly Gabo's exposure to these developments in both painting and sculpture when he moved back to Russia that prompted him to explore similar directions. The work of Vladimir Tatlin, with whom Gabo later would differ on several issues, must have had particular impact, either directly or through its widespread influence. Tatlin's geometric reliefs (e.g. fig. 22) were well known from 1915–16 and offered a compelling example of aggressive manipulation of space through raw materials and nonreferential shapes. His experiments created a sensation in both Moscow and Petrograd and spurred other artists in the same direction. Parallel explorations of collage-inspired geometric assemblages are found in the work of such artists as Puni, Kliun, and Bruni, although generally not carrying the same intense interplay with surrounding space typical of the work of Tatlin. Free-standing spatial constructions, often drawing upon Tatlin's ideas of *faktura* through their dissonant mixture of diverse materials including wood, metal, glass, and cloth, also had become relatively widespread in Russia in the years 1917–20.[46]

Gabo's first reliefs (figs. 11–13) demonstrate his reactions to these developments and his maintenance of a personal approach. While now fully abstract, they continue certain preoccupations of his constructions from 1915–17, particularly *Head in a Corner Niche.* The angulation of planes and use of thin sheets of material open the objects to an interpenetration of light and space that is even more dynamic than before, despite the anchoring role of a background plane. Line in sculpture was

44. Tate Gallery, no. T2151, included in the exhibition as cat. no. 89.

45. This drawing has been titled *Design for a Construction in a Niche.* It measures 24.5 x 19.4 cm. and is inscribed »N. Gabo 1918.« See Alley, p. 232.

46. For a particularly good selection of illustrations of both reliefs and freestanding sculptures from this period, see Lodder, *Russian Constructivism,* chaps. 1 and 2.

Fig. 21   Gabo, *Construction en creux,* 1919, painted cardboard, destroyed. Illustrated here upside down (*S.–L. 7.1*).

Fig. 22   Vladimir Tatlin, *Corner Counter-Relief,* 1914–15, metal and wire, whereabouts unknown. (From A. Nakov, *L'Avant-Garde Russe,* Paris 1984).

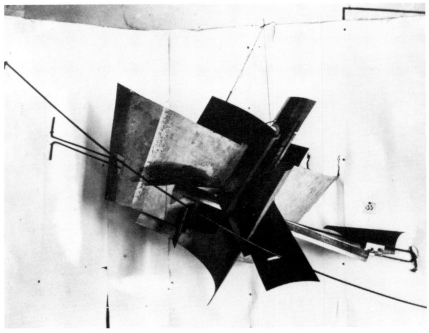

47. Albert Elsen, *Modern European Sculpture 1918–1945* (New York, 1979), p. 114.

48. For a brief survey of the role of such pioneering architects and theorists as Bruno Taut, Paul Scheerbart, and Hermann Muthesius in the »glass dream,« see Reyner Banham, »The Glass Paradise,« *Architectural Review* (February 1959), pp. 87–89.

49. »In the art of sculpture every material has its own aesthetical properties. The emotions aroused by materials are caused by their intrinsic properties and are as universal as any other psychological reaction determined by nature.« *Circle, p. 105.*

50. As general sources on the *Kinetic Construction* and its subsequent influence see Frank Popper, *Origins and Development of Kinetic Art* (Greenwich, 1968), esp. p. 124f. and also Jack Burnham, *Beyond Modern Sculpture* (New York, 1968), pp. 230–32.

51. Gabo's account of how he made the *Kinetic Construction* has been published in *Techne*, I, no. 1 (April 14, 1969); *Studio International*, 178, no. 914 (September 1969), p. 89; and Alley, p. 235.

conceived by Gabo as marking a path of motion, tension, or inner rhythm. These rhythms, now liberated from description, had become more free-flowing and self-sufficient. In addition, the introduction of plastic as the primary material provides both reflectivity and transparency, adding substantially to the dynamics of light and furthering Gabo's longstanding quest for a dematerialization of solids. Only the *Square Relief* of 1921 still survives, but judging from photos of *Construction in Relief* and *Construction en creux*, all these works displayed a lightness and linear dynamism that are unique (in the *Square Relief,* a slit in the background plane emits light from another direction to activate even further the sharply defined movements of form). As Albert Elsen has noted, »Gabo's reliefs brought to the medium a beauty, optical complexity and elegance that, like his freestanding sculptures, permitted a new tangibility of light and space.«[47]

Although Gabo took transparency as a formal principle to new heights, it was an idea with numerous precedents. As we have seen, Boccioni in his *Technical Manifesto of Futurist Sculpture* (1912) included glass among the nontraditional materials he proposed for an assertively new plastic art. Archipenko started using glass the same year for some of his *Medrano* constructions; Tatlin used it in his relief *The Bottle* of 1913; and other artists such as Bruni and the Stenbergs followed suit. At the same time, plastics were becoming more widely available and offered the dual assets of transparency and workability. In materials-starved Moscow, they also had the advantage of being considerably less expensive than glass. Whether glass or plastic, these new sculptural materials allowed the transformation of a solid plane into a more immaterial, virtual plane, giving birth even to metaphysical suggestions of transfiguration or superimposed layers of meaning. Their use went considerably beyond the creation of *implied* transparency in contemporary Cubist sculpture and the *suggestion* of transparency in Russian abstract painting, and can also be compared with a new plastic imagination then emerging in modern architecture's exploitation of glass for structural and ideological purpose connected with the so-called ›glass dream‹.[48]

For Tatlin, the incorporation of glass grew from his ideas on a »culture of materials,« that is, an exploitation of the inherent, expressive qualities of different materials. Gabo, who also believed in the differing psychological effects of various substances,[49] was concerned with something quite different from physical facts. Increasingly, his sculptures were to subvert their own physicality and, through the use of light and space, break down their actual metric limits. Accordingly, they lack the rugged, unpolished, and highly differentiated look of Tatlin's reliefs and strive instead for delicacy and clarity, for a conspicuously fabricated and technological appearance. While never slavishly imitating machines, the machine aesthetic had more stimulation for him than the call for »real materials in real space.«

The dematerialization process that we have traced as so important to Gabo's development finds consummation in a work from 1920 which, despite Gabo's feelings that it was an unfulfilled experiment, stands as a landmark in modern sculpture – the famous *Kinetic Construction* (cat. no. 8). Much has been written about this work as a precursor of motorized kinetic art.[50] The story of how Gabo made it in a workshop at the Polytechnicum Museum in Moscow from discarded parts and the electromagnet from a large bell has also become well known.[51] Gabo related:

> . . . standing waves had attracted my attention since my student days, in particular the fact that when you look at a standing wave, the image becomes three-dimensional. In order to show what I meant by calling for the introduction of kinetic rhythms into a constructed sculpture, I chose that standing wave as a good illustration . . .

By attaching two carefully positioned weights at the bottom and top of a steel rod that is set into vibration by a motor concealed in a base-like box, Gabo was able to create a standing wave that seems to describe an elliptical volume bowing out, then in, then out again.

Other artists of the period were also interested in mechanized movement. Duchamp, for example, used a motor to turn the blades in his *Rotary Glass Plate* of 1920. Tatlin dreamed of revolving chambers in his huge *Monument to the Third*

International. And the Futurists called for and to some degree were able to incorporate actual dynamism in their sculptures. Gabo's construction, however, has a combination of complexity and purity that caught the imagination of other artists such as Moholy-Nagy and became influential in an extended history of kinetic experiments.[52] He himself expressed dissatisfaction with the cumbersome mechanics involved, claiming that the design was »more an explanation of the idea of a kinetic sculpture than a kinetic sculpture itself,«[53] and he never returned again to motorized movement except for the occasional use of a revolving base or revolving picture panel. The importance of this work in his development, however, lies not just in the introduction of actual movement, an element stressed in his forthcoming *Realistic Manifesto,* but also in the consummation of a tendency to replace solidity with space and time. The stereometric method had been his first step, followed by a further reduction of mass through transparency, and finally, the creation of *illusory* volume through the standing wave. Sculpture thereby becomes purely a relationship of forces, a concept so advanced that it could only be retreated from.[54] Drawings of mechanical constructions from the same period (e.g. cat. no. 94) show ideas for more complex orchestrations of parts and movement which, however, were far beyond the mechanical possibilities of the times.

Concurrent with his work in these other areas, Gabo was also experimenting with visionary notions of architecture and towers, an activity confined at first to drawings but then expressed in sculptures which, while complete in themselves, can also be considered models for monumental structures. The iconography of the tower was a potent one in Russian art of the period. It drew upon a family of associations with, for example, electrical and radio towers, conning platforms, and the engineering innovations of the Eiffel Tower, and in general it carried connotations of energy, progress, and social responsibility. Variations were endless as artists and architects designed towers in purely imaginary terms, or attempted practical solutions in designs for kiosks, stage sets, and public celebrations (compare figs. 23 and 24).[55] Gabo's well known *Design for a Radio Station* (now lost) and a series of drawings included in the present exhibition (cat. nos. 84–86) illustrate some of his early thinking in this vein. Highly improbable as architecture, such works would later be criticized by Gabo as overly romantic but show nevertheless an excitement and conceptual daring.[56] The Eiffel Tower was never far removed as a source of inspiration, and indeed, numerous sketches of this structure exist among Gabo's sketchbooks and drawings. But his concern was more with ideological and emotional

52. On Moholy-Nagy's interest, see Burnham, p. 237. Lissitzky gave the work begrudging credit in his *A. and Pangeometry* of 1925 but characterized it as a stylization of the pendulum movement of a metronome (Sophie Lissitzky-Küppers, *El Lissitzky,* Greenwich, 1968), p. 352.

53. *Circle,* p. 109.

54. For an insightful analysis of the meaning of the *Kinetic Construction* in Gabo's development see Andrei Nakov, introduction to the exhibition catalogue *The First Russian Show* (Annely Juda Fine Art, London, 1983), p. 32.

55. This element of visionary design is dealt with at length in Kestutis Paul Zygas, *Form Follows Form: Source Imagery of Constructivist Architecture 1917–1925* (Ann Arbor, 1981) including a section on Gabo's *Project for a Radio Station.* A good source on Russian architecture of the period in general is Selim O. Chan-Magomedow, *Pioniere der sowjetischen Architektur* (Dresden, 1983).

56. In recounting his negative criticism of Tatlin's tower, Gabo noted that he »had already designed my ›Project for a Radio Tower,‹ and had come to the conclusion that Tatlin and I were following a romantic and fantastical course, with no real understanding of the strength of materials or construction.« Quoted by Judith Wolin, »VKHUTEMAS,« *Chicago Architectural Journal,* I (1981), p. 24; source of the quotation identified in correspondence with the Dallas Museum as a personal interview with Gabo in 1970. Similar sentiments were voiced by Gabo in the Starr-Frampton interview (Beinecke Library).

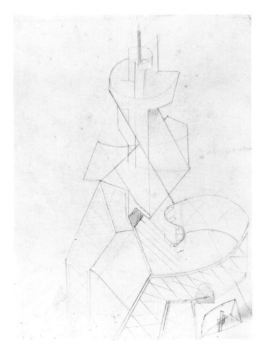

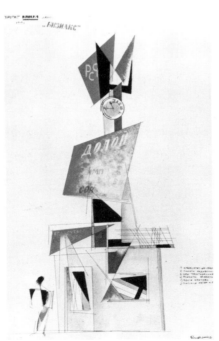

Fig. 23   Gabo, *Study for a Tower,* c. 1917, pencil, Family Collection (cat. no. 86).

Fig. 24   Alexander Rodchenko, *News Kiosk,* 1919, ink and watercolor on paper, Rodchenko Archive, Moscow.

Fig. 25 Alexander Rodchenko, *White Nonobjective Sculpture,* 1918, painted metal and cardboard, whereabouts unknown.

Fig. 26 Gabo, *Column,* 1922–23/rebuilt 1937, glass, plastic, metal, and wood, Solomon R. Guggenheim Museum, New York (*S.–L.10.2*).

 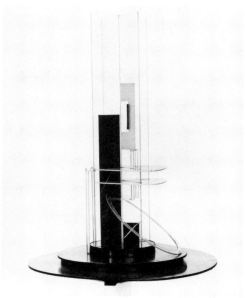

57. Quoted from Nikolai Ladovsky by Judith Wolin, ibid., p. 28; also in *Art and Architecture USSR – 1917–32,* exhibition cat. (New York, 1971), pp. 13–16 (Ladovsky's contribution to *Izvestiia ASNOVA,* Moscow, 1926).

58. Chan-Magomedow, pl. 516.

59. Read and Martin, pls. 20–29.

60. Gabo's statement is found in Read and Martin, opp. pls. 24–26. As examples of early critics commenting on the merger of art and architecture in his work see Ernst Kallai, »Der Plastiker Gabo«, *i 10, internationale revue* (Amsterdam), I, no. 7 (1927), pp. 245–49; Lewis Mumford, »The Moderns,« *The New Republic* (Jan. 12, 1927), p. 222; and Justus Bier, »Der Glasplastiker Gabo,« *Glastechnische Berichte,* 10, no. 1 (1932).

Fig. 27   Mies van der Rohe, model for a glass skyscraper, 1921–22.

expression than practicality, typifying Russian attempts to join revolutionary and artistic aims. As one architect of the period noted:

> All those who worked in the architectural offices of that time remember that almost every project, important or not, was expressed in plan or elevation by an impetuous spiral, that asymmetry ruled supreme, that undulating planes and volumes were the rage, and that every building had, at all costs, to be »inflated« into a gigantic edifice capable, by sheer size and scale alone, of communicating the revolutionary emotion that consumed the young architects.[57]

The occasional building of a Constructivist kiosk or exhibition tower or an exciting industrial form such as V. G. Shukov's radio mast of 1922 must have encouraged a hope for influencing practical applications.[58].

The inventiveness of these drawings was harnessed by Gabo into a series of tower-like sculptures that bridge the period 1920 to 1925, overlapping his move to Germany.[59] All have a technical or science-fiction orientation that finds its closest parallels in the work of the Stenberg brothers and the metallic structures of Rodchenko and Klutsis (e. g. fig. 25). Most were too fragile to survive except in parts, but the small *Tower* from Yale (cat. no. 13), the newly restored *Model for a Fountain* (cat. no. 14), and the various versions of the *Column* (fig. 26 and cat. nos. 9–11) all show their ability to achieve a sense of scale far beyond their actual size. Early critics writing on Gabo frequently praised the merger of architectural and sculptural thinking in these works and Gabo himself acknowledged such intentions:

> From the very beginning of the Constructive Movement it was clear to me that a constructed sculpture, by its very method and technique, brings sculpture very near to architecture. . . . My works of this time, up to 1924, are all in the search for an image which would fuse the sculptural element with the architectural element into one unit. I consider my Column the culmination of that search.[60]

These towers display certain characteristic features of design. The underlying structure is generally rectilinear, with intersecting vertical planes or angular frame-like pieces forming a skeleton into which interlock smaller vertical, horizontal, or sometimes diagonal planes along with curvilinear elements (circles, arcs, spirals) or thin guy-lines. A bilateral symmetry is enforced, and themes of open structure and transparent and reflective surfaces are continued from earlier works. Through the intricacy of fit and design, sometimes even involving small spinning or revolving parts, together with the modern materials and general shapes, correspondences are invoked with laboratory equipment. The delicately assembled *Monument for an Observatory,* for example, with its projecting angle and sequence of circles (fig. 28) reminds one of a microscope or certain kinds of telescope (fig. 29), while the *Monument for an Institute of Physics and Mathematics* recalls other instruments of celestial measurement. Such relationships were certainly conscious but never literal.

Column, the best known of these works because of its survival in several versions, summarizes the concepts behind the entire group. As a harbinger of architectural possibilities it can be compared with Mies van der Rohe's designs for glass towers of approximately the same date (see fig. 27).[61] Indeed, *Column* was later used by Gabo for the instruction of architecture students. In the 1970s Gabo finally was able to obtain the large sheets of perfectly clear, untinted glass that he had always wanted in order to construct this work on a monumental scale. The result (cat. no. 11) shows the easy receptivity of *Column* and, by implication, the other tower models of the 20s, to major enlargement. In this work the conjunction of vertical planes creates an apparent or virtual volume. The sense of depth is continuous, allowing the exchange between inner and outer space that writers on glass architecture spoke of so approvingly. The dynamism of movement and sequence within an open structure, with a seeming suspension of parts, creates a visual and spatial experience which would have been even more powerful in the huge variation on the *Column* that Gabo envisioned for a fountain in 1924 (cat. no. 98). In this drawing as in the actual models, his treatment of bases is an important part of the overall design. Linked to the upper forms by congeniality of shape and material, the bases tend to minimize attention on the function of support and thus assist the sense of upward movement or levitation. Other artists of the period (e. g. Kobro and Rodchenko) took this concept a step further by rejecting the sculptural base and asserting the primacy of autonomous space by suspending their sculptures in air.

These works, together with the series of reliefs from 1919–21 and the *Kinetic Construction,* are the fruits of Gabo's development in Russia. Inherent in their making was Gabo's abiding belief in the experimental, spiritual nature of art, a concept central to the theoretical positions he articulated and defended amid the ideological struggles of the period. The primary document of these views is, of course, the *Realistic Manifesto,* written by Gabo, signed by him and Pevsner, and distributed at the time of their outdoor exhibition on Tverskoi Boulevard in August 1920.[62] This exhibition, the only public display of Gabo's works in Russia, also included works by Klutsis and several students. It seems to have excited considerable attention, as did also the *Manifesto,* posted around the city and attracting through the word »realistic« in its title the unsuspecting attention of audiences not otherwise interested in abstract art. As the initial expression of the theoretical concepts behind his sculptures, the *Realistic Manifesto* must be considered here in greater depth.

The polemical background behind the birth of the *Manifesto* was summarized by Gabo in 1956:

> At the end of the third year [the three years of intense artistic explorations from the Revolution in 1917 to 1920] two opposing ideologies had emerged, one group around Tatlin and the other around my brother Antoine Pevsner and myself. . . . There was another event which also happend at that time when the Suprematistic group was dissolved. . . . As far as Tatlin's group is concerned, they gradually developed an ideology of a purely Marxist and political kind. . . . We were politically neutral, but this group around Tatlin followed a trend to join the communist party and based their ideology on Marxism. The Government, as I said before, was only tolerating all of us. There was a very strong opposition in the Government against our art. The conflict in our ideologies, between Tatlin's group, who called themselves productivists, and our group only accelerated the open break and forced us to make a public declaration.[63]

Evolving out of articles in *Art of the Commune* beginning in December 1918 and debates at INKhUK (the Institute of Artistic Culture, founded in March 1920), the Productivist credo to which Gabo refers had posited a unity between technological production, artistic creativity, and Communist ideology.[64] Formulated by such artists and critics as Punin, Brik, Rodchenko, Popova, and Stepanova, it proclaimed an exhaustion of »pure« formal art and called for »artist-engineers« to insert artistic creativity into the production process as »a weapon to be used in the struggle for the building of socialism.« An ideal of »communistic expression of material structures« mandated utilitarian rather than aesthetic objects and found promotion through slogans such as »Down with Art« and »Long live the Constructivist technician.«

Although the material results of this movement were limited, and while its reconciliation of formal art and Communist doctrine did not long forestall governmental

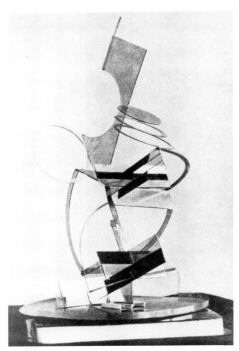

Fig. 28 Gabo, *Model for a Monument for an Observatory,* 1922, celluloid, metal, and wood, Family Collection (fragments only, *S.–L.16*).

61. Evidence now points to dates for Mies' Friedrichstrasse skyscraper and his second glass skyscraper as 1921 and 1921–22 respectively. Both were published in the periodical *Frühlicht* in 1922 (I, pp. 122–24). I am indebted to Arthur Drexler of the Museum of Modern Art for this information. Mies' concerns in these projects for skeletal structure, the transparency and reflectivity of glass, and strict clarity of design are all paralleled in Gabo's work.

62. Surviving examples of the *Realisticheskii manifest* are now extremely rare. Two translations are available: the one most frequently quoted is by Gabo himself (Read and Martin, pp. 151–52); a second was published by Camilla Gray (*The Structurist,* no. 8 (1968), pp. 43–47), although Gabo objected to certain elements of this version (see *The Structurist,* no. 9 [1969], p. 64) For a modern Soviet discussion, see V. Tasalov, *Prometei ili Orfei* (Prometheus or Orpheus) (Moscow, 1967), pp. 237–45.

63. Read and Martin, p. 157.

64. The best single source on this doctrinal evolution is Lodder, *Russian Constructivism* pp. 73f.

Fig. 29 Brass compound monocular microscope, by Bleuler, 18th century.

65. Ibid., pp. 83 and 281, n. 102.
66. Read and Martin, p. 158.
67. Even among artists who endorsed the Productivist credo there survived a belief in the
exploratory or »laboratory« purposes of art.
Aleksandr Vesnin, who became one of the
leading architects of the period, argued for
the psychological factor in art and the useful-
ness of laboratory work for solving problems
of contemporary form. See C. Lodder, »Constructivist Theater as a Laboratory for an Architectural Aesthetic, »*Architectural Association Quarterly,* 11, no. 2 (1979), pp. 27–28.
Similar points-of-view were expressed by
Medunetsky, the Stenberg brothers, and
Lissitzky. See A. Nakov, *2 Stenberg 2* (London and Toronto, 1975), pp. 13–14, and
Vesch, no. 1–2 (March–April 1922).
68. John Bowlt has pointed out similarities, for
example, with the use of the term by Larionov
in his *Rayonist Painting* and by Puni and Bo-
guslavskaya in their *Supremetist Manifesto.*
See Bowlt, *Russian Art of the Avant-Garde:
Theory and Criticism 1902–1934* (New York,
1976), p. 209.
69. For a fascinating and detailed examination of
the impact of concepts of the fourth dimension on early modern art, see Henderson, *The
Fourth Dimension.* Malevich was particularly
interested in ramifications of hyperspace
philosophy. See Henderson esp. pp. 25f.;
and Susan Compton, »Malevich's Suprematism
ism – The Higher Intuition,« *Burlington
Magazine,* 118, no. 881 (August 1976),
pp. 577–85.

suppression, it provided for several years a strong rallying point for many of the avant-garde. It resulted in the formation in March 1921 of the First Working Group of Constructivists which soon published a position program,[65] and in books most notably by Aleksei Gan (*Constructivism,* 1922), Nikolai Tarabukin (*From the Easel to the Machine,* 1923) and Moisei Ginzburg (*Style and the Epoch,* 1924) exploring its foundations and ramifications.

It is against the extreme functionalism and political dedication of the Productivist movement that we must understand Gabo's claim in his *Realistic Manifesto* that art »should attend us everywhere that life flows and acts . . . in order that the flame to live should not extinguish in mankind«. As he later explained it, »The most important idea in the manifesto was the assertion that art has its absolute, independent value and a function to perform in society whether capitalistic, socialistic, or communistic – art will always be alive as one of the indispensable expressions of human experience and as an important means of communication.«[66] Against collective endeavor, he affirmed individual creative spirit; against utilitarian aims, he defended the higher spiritual function of art. Although Gabo fought throughout his life for social applications of progressive art in monuments, architecture, and industrial design, he struggled equally against the co-opting of art for political or materialistic purposes.[67]

Further analysis of the *Realistic Manifesto* reveals a body of formalist ideas which, to a considerable extent, draw upon widespread theoretical currents. We have seen how Gabo's critique of Cubism fed his earliest constructions in Norway. The *Realistic Manifesto* proclaims a revolutionary art based on new values and new forms of life and concludes that, for the »demands of the renascent spirit of our time,« the artistic answers of Cubism and Futurism are inadequate. Nothing short of the »realization of our perceptions of the world in the forms of space and time« will do, and with this goal in mind, an inspiring analogue for artistic activity can be found in the world of science and engineering. In the actual construction of art works, several principles must obtain. Color is illusory and is renounced in favor of natural tone. Line must not serve a descriptive function, but rather, act as a delineator of forces and rhythm. Depth, rather than volume, is asserted as the »only pictorial and plastic form of space.« Mass is renounced as a sculptural element: strength and form do not depend upon mass. And finally, time is a basic ingredient of art which is perceived through kinetic rhythm.

Certain of the basic precepts found here are familiar from the many other manifestos and declarations of the period. The very use of the term »realistic« in the title, connoting reality in its truest, most elemental form, reflects an interpretation common in Russian avant-garde circles.[68] The espousal of a revolutionary art to express a new, revolutionary era was hardly unique, nor was the reference to engineering as an exemplum for artistic production. Gabo's ideas on space and time as the primary elements of life and art, so fundamental to his whole outlook, also invoke other sources. He was familiar with Bergson's theories on the relationship between time and consciousness, and by 1920, Einstein's notions of time as the fourth dimension and the inseparability of time and space were becoming popularized.[69] Indeed, the Russian mathematician Alexander V. Vasiliev had published in 1913 his *New Ideas in Mathematics,* including in its second volume (entitled »Space and Time«) extensive discussion of both Einstein and Minkowsi. Space, time, and movement as issues for the modern artist had become explicit ingredients in the theory and criticism of both Cubism and Futurism. And Georges Vantongerloo's *Réflexions,* published in *De Stijl* in 1918 (vol. I, no. 9) contain observations remarkably similar to some of Gabo's: »Time and space are the natural laws of nature and art. Time and space are the instruments of sound and volume. . . . Volume has void as its complement. . . .«

Moreover, discussions of time and space, with myriad shadings of both scientific and metaphysical interpretation, were commonplace within the Russian avant-garde from early in the teens. Interest in outer space, in the fourth dimension and hence in the ideas of such hyperspace philosophers as Hinton and Ouspensky, and in the new spatial postulates of Cubism, had helped stimulate thinking about cosmic space, »higher space consciousness,« and the interaction of movement and time with spatial representation.

Gabo spoke of his incorporation of movement into sculpture as an introduction of the fourth dimension.[70] His interpretation of time and space, however, was neither scientific nor imbued with the metaphysics found, for example, in Malevich's writings. He had a more basic and concrete understanding, and made it clear, in different writings, that his was a nonabstract notion based on sensory awareness and an extrapolation outward through intuition. Time equals movement and can be conveyed through either actual or implied kinetics. Space also is a concrete reality: »In our sculpture space has ceased to be for us a logical abstraction or a transcendental idea and has become a malleable material element.«[71] A function of sculpture is to sharpen the perception of space and time, which are both seen as real graspable elements.[72]

Further parallels could be cited between Gabo's denunciation of applied color and Boccioni's praise of the »tones and semitones of a new reality« found in modern materials,[73] between Gabo's notion of line as a path of force and Popova's assertion that line »directs the forces of construction,«[74] or between his affirmation of dynamic rhythm and the kinetics proclaimed by Boccioni or Malevich.[75] One can only speculate on particular lines of influence behind Gabo's theoretical thinking. Important to note, however, is the fact that the *Manifesto* recapitulates ideas he had addressed in his sculpture even before his return to Russia in 1917. It is a cogently reasoned document that integrates certain widespread concepts with other more personally developed principles regarding dematerialization, spatial continuity, and rhythm, all with a pragmatic concern for the actual realization of sculpture. The fact that it has long held an important position in the history of western artistic thought is testimony to its conceptual rigor. Gabo himself would elaborate upon it in later writings but never deviate from its core philosophy.

The *Manifesto,* reprinted in the Hungarian journal *Egység* in 1922 and also cited with the outdoor exhibition in Lissitzky's *Veshch/Gegenstand/Object* of the same year, was Gabo's primary introduction to western audiences, to be followed soon by his triumph at the First Russian Art Exhibition in Berlin. It was also the uncredited source for a more synoptic manifesto published by Alfred Kemeny and Lazlo Moholy-Nagy in *Der Sturm* in March 1922.[76] Gabo was at a productive highpoint, but just at this time, opposition from the Productivist group and a growing reactionary trend against the avant-garde in general had begun to make his position in Russia untenable. Tolerance of abstraction diminished as a cessation of civil war allowed the government to focus more on domestic and economic issues, fostering demands for a more publicly understandable art through which to promote socialist ideals. With the reorganization of IZO in 1921, avant-garde artists lost prominent positions and were faced with a resurgence of influence from the academic right, a group that had never completely disappeared from view. Although Gabo maintained faith in the principles of the Communist revolution until much later in life,[77] the realities of the political situation in Russia in the 20s forced a decision on his part to leave.[78] From Lunacharsky (Commissar of Enlightenment) he was able to obtain a passport, and Shterenberg helped by suggesting he could join his staff in Berlin for the organization of a major Russian art exhibition.

Gabo left by train early in 1922. His experience within the Russian avant-garde had strenthened the conceptual fiber of his art and inspired him to cross the threshold of abstraction. It nurtured his ideas on art in the service of society but also sharpened his notion of the ultimate spirtuality of artistic enterprise. His subsequent development built naturally upon the foundations thus established.

III. Berlin and Paris: International Constructivism

Soon after arriving in Berlin, Gabo made contact with Shterenberg again and was put to work organizing the three rooms of abstract art for the First Russian Art Exhibition, opening at the Galerie van Diemen on Unter den Linden in October of that year.[79] After the First World War, Berlin had become a busy crossroads of interna-

70. Read and Martin, p. 160.

71. *Circle*, p. 107.

72. Gabo wrote in 1937: »I do not hesitate to affirm that the perception of space is a primary natural sense which belongs to the basic sense of our psychology.« (*Circle*, p. 107.) And he later explained: »[Space] is not what is in the minds of scientists today. In science it's a formula. But for me it is a real element of vision; it is as material as any concrete material.« (Kuh, p. 102).

73. In his *Technical Manifesto of Futurist Sculpture,* 1912.

74. Statement in the catalogue of the Tenth State Exhibition: Nonobjective Creation and Suprematism, Moscow, 1919 (see Bowlt, p. 147).

75. Malevich touches on speed and movement in his *From Cubism to Futurism to Suprematism: The New Painterly Realism,* 1915 (see Bowlt, p. 123).

76. On these reappearances of the *Realistic Manifesto,* see Lodder, *Russian Constructivism* pp. 96, 227–28, 236, 282 note 116.

77. Later correspondence between Gabo and Herbert Read (Gabo papers, Beinecke Library) evidence the abiding faith of both men in socialist revolution and the validity, if necessary, of anarchism for political purposes. It was only with Gabo's trip to Russia in 1962 that he became convinced that the principles of the Revolution in Russia had been permanently corrupted.

78. The often-repeated story that Gabo was locked out of his studio and that this helped persuade him to leave the country seems to have no factual basis.

79. In the Starr-Frampton interview (Beinecke Library), Gabo recounted his discussions with Shterenberg concerning emigration to Germany and work on the First Russian Show: »And that was that. I left for Berlin. But I was no longer employed, not officially, although some have since written that I was. When Shterenberg arrived in Berlin six months later, he told me, ›Now you are here and will join my staff; and will organize the three galleries of abstract art.‹« On the exhibition staff, he reported: »I have a folder listing the whole staff there which I have never published. Shterenberg was the head, with Nathan Altman under him. Marianov from the Cheka was also there, officially to look after me. He came from the government to watch Shterenberg.« Although Lissitzky is sometimes credited with a major organizational role, Gabo claimed that his participation was limited to that of an exhibitor (his contention that the catalogue cover was actually designed by Altman rather than Lissitzky, however, can be proven to be incorrect). See *Studio International,* 182, no. 938 (Nov. 1971), p. 171.

80. The large, politically diverse, and mainly un-assimilated Russian population in Berlin after WWI is discussed by John Bowlt in »Art in Exile: The Russian Avant-Garde and the Emigration,« *Art Journal* (Fall 1981), esp. pp. 217f. He points out that by 1922 the Russian population in Berlin was estimated at 100,000. An often cited source on the Russian intellectual and artistic colonies in Germany is Robert Williams‹ *Culture in Exile: Russian Emigrés in Germany 1881–1941* (Ithaca, 1972) which, however, must be used with caution due to factual errors (including a number regarding Gabo and Pevsner). See also Eberhard Steneberg, *Russische Kunst: Berlin 1919–1932* (Berlin, 1969) and John Willett, *Art and Politics in the Weimar Period* (New York, 1978).

81. Bowlt, »Art in Exile,« p. 218.

82. *Hans Richter by Hans Richter,* ed. Cleve Gray (New York, 1971), p. 56. See also Richter's *Köpfe und Hinterköpfe* (Zurich, 1967), pp. 97–98. Among critics who singled out Gabo for praise are Lajos Kassak in *MA* (VIII, nos. 2 and 3 [Dec. 1922]); Maurice Raynal in *l'Intransigeant* (Nov. 1, 1922); and Curt Bauer, *Der Cicerone* (Leipzig, 14, no. 4 [1922]).

83. Willet, pp. 78–79.

84. On the patronage and friendship that Dreier afforded Gabo, see Robert Herbert *et al., The Société Anonyme and the Dreier Bequest at Yale University* (New Haven, 1984), esp. pp. 281–82: »After including Gabo's work in a Société Anonyme exhibition in New York in 1924, [Dreier] began, in 1926, to give him a special place in her canon of preferred artists.«

85. One can only conjecture that the other two *Raumkonstruktions* were the *Construction en creux* of 1921 and the *Square Relief* of 1921.

Fig. 30   Installation at First Russian Art Exhibition, Berlin, 1922 (showing three works by Gabo).

tional culture – in Nicolas Nabokov's words, a »sort of caravanserai where everybody met«[80] – and Gabo wasted no time in establishing contact with a wide range of important artists and architects. Among other artistic movements vying for attention, Germany provided fertile ground for the growth of Constructivism, now divorced from the sense of urgency and moral imperative that informed it in Russia and therefore susceptible to a more aestheticized interpretation, but providing nevertheless a vital force attracting artists of divergent background and approaches. Gabo, for one, did not waver in his hopes for social contribution. Indeed, his participation lent to the various Constructivist manifestations in Germany a sense of historical continuity and mission.

Constructivist affiliations existed around the two magazines *Veshch* and *G*, around the Bauhaus and the Dada-De Stijl axis, and within the short-lived art congresses at Weimar and Düsseldorf. Informal contact at studios and cafés also stimulated artistic exchange, including the often heated discussions at the Café Léon (the so-called *Haus der Künste*). Gabo contributed to many of these forums, even exhibiting with the more rightwing, expressionist-oriented *Novembergruppe,* but remained steadfastly independent of any group identification. He pursued his own path, buoyed by the spirit of Weimar optimism, until the economic and political disruptions of the early 30s drove him to Paris and then on to England. Emigration did not adversely affect his development as it did with certain other Russian artists. During this period, he continued and consolidated his progress from the Russian years through work on the tower constructions and architectural designs, always seeking opportunities for monumental realization. At the same time, he evolved a different concept of spatial expression that would substantially change his art.

The main factor establishing Gabo's presence in the west was the Russian Exhibition. This show was arranged ostensibly to benefit the Committee to Help the Starving of the 1921–22 famine in Russia, and while it has been pointed out that ulterior political motives existed concerning the need to strengthen German investment in Russia,[81] it provided western audiences with their first truly expansive look at Russian nonobjective art and received a welcome reception. In all, more than 600 objects were shown, covering a full spectrum of styles from the traditional to the modern but with a sizeable representation of the avant-garde, including works by Malevich, Popova, Rodchenko, Rozanova, Klutsis, Tatlin, the Stenbergs, Gabo, Pevsner and several others. Attendance was not particularly high, and some critics attacked the eclecticism of the selection and the fact that the modernist contributions seemed to deal more in art problems than resolutions. But reaction among artists and the more progressive art press was enthusiastic, and one of the individuals who stood out most in terms of impact was Gabo (fig. 30). Hans Richter's response was not uncharacteristic: »Gabo was, for me, the great sensation at the Van Diemen Exhibition of New Russian Art in Berlin, 1922. The middle of the first room contained a large sculpture of a reclining woman [the *Torso,* actually] in front of a woman's head – both made from sheet metal. I met the author and we became friends for forty years.«[82] Attending the show at Lissitzky's invitation, Kurt Schwitters appears from the notes he made in the catalogue to have been particularly impressed with the work of Gabo and also Altman, Malevich, Rodchenko, and Medunetskii.[83] Katherine Dreier, already assembling her famous Société Anonyme collection, also visited the show and was so taken by it that she bought Gabo's *Construction in Relief* along with several other works, thus beginning his first relationship with a patron and a friendship that would last until Dreier's death many years later. She would visit him in Berlin in 1926 and in the fall of that year included three of his sculptures in the Société Anonyme show at Brooklyn.[84]

Eight sculptures by Gabo are listed in the exhibition catalogue (plus one drawing of an electrical station): *Constructed Head No. 2, Head in a Corner Niche, Torso, Kinetic Construction,* three works entitled *Raumkonstruktion* including the *Construction in Relief* that Dreier bought,[85] and a *Relief en creux* (possibly the cardboard *Construction en creux* of 1919). He may also have exhibited other works ex-catalogue. The particularly heavy representation of his work certainly is attributable to the role he played in organizing the show, and it had the salutary effect of allowing visitors to see a cross-sectional sampling of his art, thus promoting understanding. Several critics responded with sensitive interpretations, focusing their remarks alternately on the implications of the stereometric system in the earlier works and the dialogue of light and space in the more recent plastic pieces.[86]. A negative aftermath occurred, however, when most of the exhibition contents, after a second showing in Amsterdam (Stedelijk Museum, April-May 1923), were mistakenly returned to Russia. Gabo thus lost possession of several major works, of which he was later to retrieve only one, *Constructed Head No. 2.* This loss occasioned his re-construction of *Head No. 2* in celluloid, and possibly also the re-construction of *Head in a Corner Niche.*[87]

On the personal side, we know that when Pevsner joined Gabo in Berlin for a brief period in 1923–24, the two of them together with Pevsner's wife Virginia lived on the Steglitzerstrasse. After Pevsner's departure, Gabo relocated to the nearby suburb of Lichterfelde. During a serious illness he was attended by Richter's ex-wife Lilly, and the two of them struck up a liaison that lasted until Lilly's death several years later.

Gabo was working at the time on his tower models, culminating in 1923–25 in such distinctive achievements as *Column, Model for a Fountain,* and *Monument for an Institute of Physics and Mathematics,* with their heroic architectural implications. These, together with works like *Construction in a Hemisphere* and *Circular Relief* of 1925, have an airiness that contrasts with the metallic sculptures exhibited at the First Russian Exhibition. In this regard, Richter noted that during Gabo's early years in Germany, »his metallic, heavy sculptures had transformed themselves into transparent planes. In this transparency the spatial play became even more distinct, even more multi-layered.«[88] This transformation, of course, was initiated in Russia but now received wider exposure and further development in a lengthy series of works. High points in this series are represented by the *Construction in Space with Balance on Two Points* (1924–25; fig. 31 and cat. nos. 15 and 16), *Construction in Space: Sliding* (or »Gliding«) (1924; now lost),[89] *Monument for an Airport* (1924–26; cat. no. 17), *Construction in Space: Two Cones* (1927; cat no. 18), *Torsion* (1929; later metal version, cat. no. 61), and Gabo's ballet sets for *La Chatte* (1926–27).

The first three of these works form a distinctive sub-group with features of its own. All have an internal architecture of angled rectilinear planes that are black, white, or clear, anchored to which are large external planes of glass. Inner structure is thus suspended within transparent »wings«. All the elements have a sharp-edged clarity

86. In addition to remarks by the critics cited above, see also V. Poljanski, »Kroz rusku izlozbu u Berlinu,« *Zenit,* Zagreb, no. 22 (March 1923), pp. 4–5.

87. On the dating of the celluloid version of this work, see the discussion in chapter II.

88. Richter, *Köpfe und Hinterköpfe,* p. 98.

89. The German word *gleitend* in the title of this sculpture can be translated either »sliding« or »gliding«. Sanderson and Lodder (catalogue rainsonné, no. 20) prefer »sliding,« but the alternative seems to this author more poetic and more in keeping with the sculpture's associative implications.

Fig. 31   Gabo, *Construction in Space with Balance on Two Points,* 1924–25, enamelled brass, glass, and plastic, Yale University Art Gallery, Gift of H. Wade White (*S.–L. 22.3*).

Fig. 32   Gabo, *Construction in Space: Sliding* (or *Gliding),* 1924, glass and metal, destroyed (*S.–L. 20.2*).

90. See the discussion in Alley, pp. 243–44.
91. For information on the early history of the project, see Richard Buckle, *Diaghilev* (New York, 1979), pp. 483f. Much of Buckle's information is based on interviews with Gabo.
92. In the same year as *La Chatte* he would also produce *Le Pas d'acier* with sets by Georges Yakulov and music by Serge Prokofiev. Not long after, however, Diaghilev would turn his back on Constructivism as that which »will and does lead our generation away. Its reign . . . is now approaching its end. . . .« See S. Lifar, *Serge Diaghilev,* reprint (New York, 1976), pp. 237–38.

which aggressively slices and shapes space, and the angular junctures and back-and-forth play of transparency sets up a rapid rhythm which is heightened by the stark contrasts of black and white. All three objects have the look of mechanisms involving flight, rapid motion, or hovering, freed however from specific functionalism.

In *Gliding,* (fig. 32) the central, downward-slanted plane provides support and contact with the ground. In *Balance on Two Points* (fig. 31), the curving glass »wings« seem to lift the whole assembly into the air. Reinforced with two small vertical sleeves, the point of contact with the base is minimized to produce an anti-gravitational, suspended effect. In this work, the intersection of metal and glass planes, the various spatial vectors, and the play of transparency are so complex that one has to circle the sculpture to see them unfold and to grasp the structure. This and the other works like it speak a modern language not just by virtue of their abstractness, but through their ability to invoke modern realities such as the conquering of space, mechanized flight, and new frontiers of velocity.

In *Monument for an Airport,* newly restored for this exhibition (cat. no. 17), the parallelogram is utilized for an effect of sleekness. Here, all the planes are strictly rectilinear, assembled somewhat in the configuration of an aircraft's tail section. The simplified structure and abrupt transitions between parts add to its distinctly streamlined nature. Gabo entertained hopes of building this, or his second *Airport* model (c. 1932, cat. no. 21), on a large scale outdoors as an emblematic airport structure, but after intitial encouragement, plans eventually collapsed (in England during the 30s).[90]

The painting of metallic parts black and white in these works seems to contradict Gabo's own proscription against applied color in sculpture as stated in the *Realistic Manifesto.* He had already used colored materials, however, in the missing *Construction in Relief* of 1921 and in *Column* had employed small red, black, and white plastic pieces to help differentiate planes in space and to add compositional accent. The stark contrasts of black and white in *Balance on Two Points, Gliding,* and *Monument for an Airport* may owe something to the elemental palette of the De Stijl group. In turn, and in combination with transparent materials, they had lasting effect on the work of Moholy-Nagy and other Bauhaus artists.

There followed in close order several works which incorporate the movement of curves and spirals into this syntax of planar transparency. Curving movement had been featured in several earlier works and actually planned as literal motion in Gabo's drawings for motorized assemblages. In the *Circular Relief* and *Construction in a Hemisphere* of 1925 he emphasized the spiral, but in the stage set for *La Chatte* and in *Construction in Space: Two Cones* of 1926–27 and 1927 respectively, the dynamics of curving rhythm became still more assertive.

The full, involved story of *La Chatte* cannot be told here in detail. Gabo's radical stage sets, however, belong as much to the history of sculpture as that of set design, and therefore must be considered in the context of his sculptural development. His participation along with Pevsner in this project derived from their joint exhibition at the Galerie Percier in Paris in 1924.[91] Diaghilev, then at the height of his fame as director of the Ballets Russes, apparently saw the exhibition or was told of it. Although he had never involved a Constructivist artist in his long list of innovatively modern stage productions, he was aware of developments in Russian set design and choreography, having seen Tairov's Kamerny Theater in Paris in 1923.[92] He visited Gabo in Lichterfelde in the autumn of 1924 and again in the winter of 1925–26 and broached the subject of designing a ballet. Gabo, mindful of exciting precedents of Constructivist design in Russian theater, must have looked upon the opportunity with enthusiasm. He insisted on including Pevsner as a collaborator. A contract was signed, and during the summer of 1926 he lived at Pevsner's flat in Paris, making a model out of plastics he had brought from Berlin.

La Chatte, with book by Boris Kochno (pseudonym of Sobeka) based on a fable by Aesop, had been chosen by Diaghilev as a vehicle for the famous dancer Olga Spessivtseva. In its ancient theme of transformation, a young man, danced by Serge Lifar, falls in love with a cat who is changed by Aphrodite into a woman but then, after chasing a mouse maliciously loosed by Aphrodite, is transformed again into a

Fig. 33 Gabo and Pevsner, *Stage Set for »La Chatte«*, 1926–27.

cat, causing the young man to die of a broken heart. For this rather simple scenario, Henri Sauguet provided the music and Georges Balanchine the choreography. After the opening performances, Spessivtseva either broke her ankle or, feeling distressed over sharing the limelight not only with Lifar but also Gabo's unusual sets, feigned an ankle injury. She was replaced alternately by Alice Nikitina and Alicia Markova.

Gabo was responsible for all the design work except the mechanistic figure of Aphrodite that stood high in the center of the set. Refusing to make any figurative sculpture, he left this element to Pevsner. His overall conception involved a severe environment of geometry and light to act as a foil for the ancient theme, rather sweet music, and athletic grace of the dancers. Two drawings (cat. nos. 102 and 103) show his early thoughts on the design. The first involves a series of receding frame-like structures that provide a deep perspective and a scaffolding for the installation of smaller-scale geometric forms, including a prominent arc that spirals down from the ceiling. In the second sketch, the set is greatly simplified and comes closer to its final form, with platforms, cubicles, and masts arranged in a roughly pyramidal grouping and the spiral »ramp« now running from mid-stage out into the foreground. Numerous drawings (e.g. cat nos. 104–107) record simultaneous work on the costumes and show Gabo looking for a clean, geometric, rather »sci-fi« appearance, that sometimes rivals in ingenuity the contemporaneous costume designs of Oskar Schlemmer. Unfortunately, only a few pieces of the model still survive, and even the final set is known only from a handful of documentary photographs (see figs. 33–35). What is clear, however, are the gleaming effects Gabo achieved from his sharply cut forms, reflective and transparent materials, and strong spotlighting.

The primary material for the sets was Cellon, a cellulose acetate preferable to celluloid because it was less flammable (available at the time in Germany from its manufacturer, Celonwerke).[93] This possibly was interspersed with other kinds of plastic in the costumes, which consisted of small plastic helmets and tight, athletic outfits made from silvercloth and plastic panels.[94] Large sheets of black oilcloth formed a backdrop and floor surface.

Gabo and Pevsner fabricated the sets themselves, which involved welding metal supports and cutting and assembling the plastic panels. Boris Kochno provides a humorous recollection of the two brothers descending on the small hotels of Monaco and sending other guests into panic with their blow torches, safety masks, and hellish noises.[95] Apparently the various units were equipped with pins and sockets that allowed for easy erection and disassembly.[96]

La Chatte opened in Monte Carlo in April, 1927, and later played in Paris and London. It was a tremendous success, with credit due equally to the dancing and

93. Due partly to confusion over the terminology of contemporary plastics, different identifications of the material from which the sets were made have been given, including talc, mica, and celluloid.

94. A helmet and costume, heavily restored, were recently sold at auction with other items from the Serge Lifar collection (Sotheby Parke Bernet, London, May 9, 1984, lot no. 51).

95. *Diaghilev and the Ballets Russes* (New York, 1970), pp. 248–53.

96. See Cyril Beaumont, *The Diaghilev Ballet in London* (London, 1940), pp. 273–4.

Fig. 34   Dancers in *La Chatte,* with costumes by Gabo, 1927.

Fig. 35   Alice Nikitina and Serge Lifar in costumes by Gabo for *La Chatte,* 1927.

sets. In their reflective costumes, the dancers crawled, jumped, and spun around Gabo's transparent forms, sometimes carrying large geometric shapes painted black and white and always highlighted with intense illumination. The grace and beauty of the leads played excitingly against the background and, as one observer noted, they »were further enhanced and almost deified whenever the [plastic] in their costumes caught the light and reflected it back in a myriad flashes.«[97] Another observer wrote that »the lights as they flickered on [the set] had made the whole place shine with a quicksilver radiance.«[98]

The roots of Gabo's composition are found in earlier Russian set design, and even the use of plastic can be traced to Exter's costumes for the 1924 film *Aelita,* but no predecessor had carried the partnership of geometry, transparency, and light to such dazzling heights. Gabo was able to create an environment of shifting, fluid states, with materials fusing into space. Integrated with movement and drama, the whole ensemble would have been truly a visual and sensual adventure. The importance accorded Gabo's stage set as an evironmental statement is evidenced by its early publication in Arthur Korn's *Glas im Bau und als Gebrauchsgegenstand* of 1929 and Moholy-Nagy's *Von Material zu Architektur* of the same year.

Another feature of the set design central to Gabo's development is the use of strong circular rhythms initiated by the spiral ramp in the foreground and carried out and echoed by various curves and arcs above. This tendency to define space curvilinearly, so distinct from the angular structuring in *Balance on Two Points, Gliding,* and *Monument for an Airport,* is even more pronounced in the *Construction in Space: Two Cones* of 1927 (cat. no. 18). Evidenced here is the beginning of a trend that would reach fruition in the *Spheric Theme* of 1936. In describing that work, Gabo reported that he was seeking a way to indicate his perceptions that space is both continuous and curved, a concept undoubtedly influenced by Einstein's notions of spatial curvature.[99] »Instead of indicating space by an angular intersection of planes, I enclose the space in one curved continuous surface.« This intuition seems already to be at work in *Two Cones,* where a constant flow of looping and curving movement engulfs the central nucleus. The rims of the two cones, the linear arms that sweep up to the tops of the cones, and the two elliptically curved planes at the apex all establish orbits of different directions and speeds. The incorporation through transparency of orbits in the back adds further to the complexity of implied motion. Very little of the structure is static. Emerging is a sense of form as energy and time, constantly turning in and around itself to reveal inner

97. Ibid., p. 276.
98. W. A. Propert, *The Russian Ballet* (New York, 1932), p. 55.
99. Read and Martin, opp. pl. 64.

depth and the penetration of space. This tendency is seen not only in *Two Cones* but also *Torsion* of 1929, where the spiralling, upward movement is notable, *Construction in a Niche* of 1930, and even Gabo's design for the Palace of Soviets of 1931–32, with its opposing elliptical projections.

While working on these projects, Gabo remained active in outside areas. In 1923 he was one of the founding members of the *G* group along with Richter, Mies van der Rohe, Lissitzky, and others, and contributed to the first issue of their magazine a brief article, »*Thesen aus dem realistischen Manifest Moscow 1920.*« He lectured at the Bauhaus, despite his disapproval of some of its methods, and published in the magazine *Bauhaus* (1928, vol. II, no. 4) his important article »*Gestaltung?*«, refining his distinctions between art or »constructive will« and utilitarian design. As already mentioned, he exhibited with Pevsner at the Galerie Percier in Paris in 1924, and in 1926 he showed with the *Novembergruppe* section at the Great Berlin Exhibition, had a show with van Doesburg and Pevsner at The Little Review Gallery in New York, and was included among several artists in Lissitzky's special exhibition room at Dresden.

Architecture and public monuments remained a primary interest. Drawings of the period show him working on skyscraper designs which, compared to his Russian drawings, are more pragmatic and buildable, if less exciting (cat. nos. 99–101). The two works he exhibited with the Novembergruppe in 1926 were a *Raumkonstruktion: Projekt zu einem Denkmal* and a *Hochhaus Modell*, neither of which has been conclusively identified.[100]

Soon after moving to Germany, Gabo had met Hugo Häring, City Architect for Berlin, and the two became close friends. When a light festival was planned for the city in 1928, Häring approached Gabo for designs for a searchlight display in the Potsdamerplatz and along Unter den Linden to the Tiergarten.[101] Part of his conception is recorded in the drawing published in the magazine *Bauhaus* in 1928 (see fig. 36), showing the elaborate geometric bases that he intended to build out of plywood and the vertical spray of his searchlights. Unfortunately, Gabo's plans were ultimately rejected because his bases would have covered historical statues, but they became well known nevertheless and hold a place in the history of artificial light in art. The potentials of this new medium were an important theoretical and practical issue in Germany, from Paul Scheerbart's visions of powerful illumination as part of the futuristic glass cityscape soon to come, to the enthusiastic espousal of light in art through film in Moholy-Nagy and Kemeny's *Dynamisch-konstruktives Kraftsystem*.[102] Lucia Moholy observed that »light and motion were the slogan of the day,« and Gabo's contribution to this ethos, through his kinetic designs and light project, cannot be overestimated.[103] Other artists such as Baranoff-Rossiné and the lesser known but innovative Nikolaus Braun had worked with artificial light in one way or another,[104] but Gabo's light project was certainly one of most ambitious to date and furthered his reputation as an adventuresome designer.[105] It served as forebear to Moholy's ideas for searchlights pulled at night through the streets of a city and, ironically, Albert Speer's monumental light displays for Nazi celebrations.

Additional examples of Gabo's work on a monumental scale are found in the commission he received from Erich Mendelsohn for a large glass relief for the home Mendelsohn built for himself in 1929, and his designs for the Palace of Soviets, an open international competition in 1931. The former project Gabo was not able to complete due to the prohibitively high costs of cutting and bending glass.[106] The latter involved his most concerted architectural efforts and his invention of a novel system of roof construction. He had heard about the project from Häring and quickly produced 15 drawings for submission, all of which were sent to Russia and never returned (see the photograph in fig. 37 and the preparatory sketch, cat. no. 112).[107] His design featured two huge rooms, an auditorium and a theater, placed back-to-back as large ellipses. His solution for spanning such a width without columns involved a tetrahedral space-frame module that, at the urging of Häring, he patented in Germany and again later in England and America. This invention eventually drew praise from architectural historians but, much to Gabo's disappointment, never found an application.

100. These were cat. nos. 1535 and 1536. For information on Gabo's submissions, I am indebted to Helga Kliemann.

101. Information on this project is provided by Gabo in the Starr-Frampton interview (Bienecke Library).

102. For a partial history of the exploratory uses of light in art during this period, see Nan R. Piene, »Light Art,« *Art in America* 55, no. 3 (May–June 1967), pp. 27–48.

103. Lucia Moholy, *Moholy-Nagy, Marginal Notes* (Krefeld, 1972), p. 81. The *Kinetic Construction,* through its exhibition in the First Russian show, had a traceable impact on numerous artists including Moholy-Nagy and Lissitzky. One of Gabo's designs for a kinetic construction was published in *Jahrbuch der Jungenkunst,* 5 (1924).

104. On Braun's *Lichtbilder* and *Lichtreliefs* of the mid-20s, see *Der Sturm*, XV (June 1924); and XVII, no. 9 (Dec. 1926). Braun published with Arthur Segal in 1925 a paper entitled »*Lichtprobleme in der Bildenden Kunst.*« Moholy-Nagy's *Light Prop* or *Light-Space Modulator,* perhaps the most famous light work of the period, was conceived in 1922 but not actually executed until 1930.

105. See Justus Bier, for some interesting remarks on the potentialities of light in Gabo's work, as well as Kallai, on the same subject.

106. This project is discussed briefly in Alley, pp. 241–42. Two models connected with the project, *Double Relief in a Niche* and *Construction in a Niche*, are in the Tate. Judging from the models, this work seems labored and overly complex and would indeed have been difficult to execute in glass.

107. Information on his participation is given by Gabo in his interview with Starr and Frampton (Beinecke Library). His entry was one of more than 450. We know from a notation in one of his diaries that Gabo sent his drawings to Moscow in December 1931 (I am indebted to Christina Lodder for this information). The results of the judging of the competition's first phase were announced by March 1932, and Gabo was sorely disappointed to learn that he was not among the finalists. For the history of this important but unfulfilled competition, which began with high ideals and elicited many creative designs but finally died ignominiously, see S. O. Chan-Magomedov, *passim*, and the bibliography in S. F. Starr, *Melnikov* (Princeton, 1978), p. 156 n. 15.

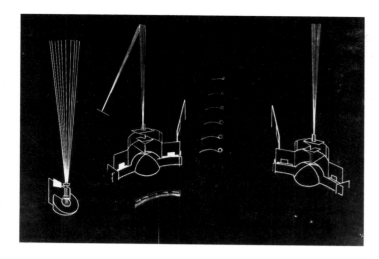

Fig. 36   Gabo, *Study for a Searchlight Project, Berlin,* 1928, whereabouts unknown.

Fig. 37   Gabo, *Design for Palace of Soviets,* 1931, whereabouts unknown.

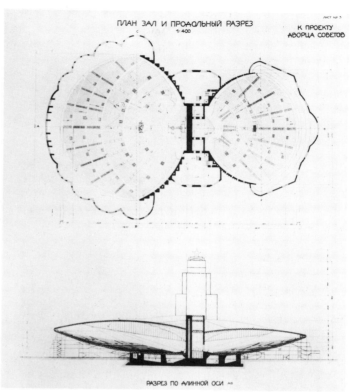

108. For an indication of early negative emotions see Michel Seuphor, *Cercle et carré* (Paris, 1971), p. 14. Ill feelings existed between the brothers until a reconciliation quite late in their lives.

109. Gabo did meet Hilla Rebay during this period (see her biography by Joan M. Lukach from 1983, *Hilla Rebay, in Search of The Spirit in Art,* p. 270), which led eventually to her purchase in 1947 and 1948 of four works for the Guggenheim collection. Gabo looked upon her as »a good colleague« and »one of the rare active friends of abstract and constructive art.« (Correspondence quoted in the biography.)

110. From the text of a lecture given by Gabo at the Albright-Knox Art Gallery in Buffalo in 1968 (ms. among his papers in the Beinecke Library).

By 1932 Gabo's international reputation was well established, assisted by the exhibitions already noted and a one-man show at the Kestner-Gesellschaft in Hannover in 1930. The effects of runaway inflation and Hitler's rise to power, however, convinced him again to move, and in 1932 he left with all of his studio contents for Paris to join Pevsner, who lately had been active with other artists working to create a more supportive environment for non-objective art. Gabo earlier was contacted by Michel Seuphor to join the newly formed *Cercle et carré* group but had declined. The organization in 1931 of a successor group, *Abstraction-Création,* provided a promising context of like-minded associates, and both he and Pevsner took part. Gabo's statement for the first issue of *Abstraction-Création, Art non-Figuratif* in 1932 stressed efforts of Constructivism to expand the role of art, to bring it into closer alignment with architecture and to explore the inner forces of nature. Excerpts were also included from the *Realistic Manifesto.* As with his various activities in Berlin, Gabo's participation in this group lent the authority of direct contact with the pioneering, socially engaged manifestations of Constructivist art in Russia, a particularly forceful tonic in an era of sometimes more decorative abstraction.

Gabo's sojourn in Paris, however, proved to be an unhappy one. After the political experiments of Russia and the Weimar Republic, he found France complacent and superficial. Tension also was mounting between him and Pevsner, springing from complicated fraternal emotions involving pride of artistic place, jealousy, and (for Gabo) a sense of betrayal.[108] His personal situation, compounded by a lack of any new patronage,[109] affected Gabo's productivity, and only one major sculpture emerged from these years, the *Stone with Collar* (cat. no. 22).

This, however, is a key work, in that it introduced Gabo's involvement with stone carving, which would continually resurface throughout his career. On first consideration, his use of stone may seem antithetical to his denial of mass and solidity in sculpture. What he attempted was to animate the stone's mass through carving, thus lightening it and creating a sense of space circulating around and through it. He wanted to show »that space even penetrates material, even solids.«[110]

In *Stone with Collar,* Gabo incorporated the stone into a general flow of materials and direction. A thin metallic band fastened to the slate base (itself dynamically shaped) sweeps up and around to the back of the stone where it meets a plastic collar that continues the circulating orbit of movement. Another over-arching band in the original work was broken off or removed by Gabo and not replaced, which clarifies and strengthens the primary rhythms. These merge into the stone, which is subtly shaped with a descending ridge that curves down and around the eccentrically ovoid mass. The slow movements effectively unify his rather audacious mixture of slate, metal, plastic, and limestone, and draw in the surrounding space, much like the linear orbits in the previous *Construction in Space: Two Cones.*

Through *Abstraction-Création* Gabo had met the British artists Ben Nicholson and Barbara Hepworth, as well as the critic-poet Herbert Read. In 1935 he visited England for the first time to discuss his role in Nicolette Gray's forthcoming exhibition *Abstract and Concrete.* He also had a letter of introduction to Miriam Isreals, whom he later would marry. England seemed to offer more possibilities than France, on many fronts, as well as greater political stability, and when he returned there in 1936, he stayed.

IV. England: New Constructive Purities

With the political situation rapidly deteriorating on the Continent, England appealed as a new home base because of its relative safety and high quotient of artistic tolerance, not just to Gabo but to numerous other leading European artists as well. Erich Mendelsohn moved to London in 1933 and was followed by Walter Gropius (1934), Marcel Breuer and Moholy-Nagy (both in 1935), Oskar Kokoschka (1938), and Piet Mondrian (1938). Efforts had been underway through, for example, the Seven and Five Society, Herbert Read's book *Art Now,* the journals *Axis* and *Unit I,* as well as exhibitions of contemporary continental and British artists at several London galleries, to contravene against indigenous aesthetic conservatism and support the cause of modern art.[111] Ben Nicholson, Barbara Hepworth, and Henry Moore were all emerging as significant native talents, while Herbert Read provided important theoretical exegesis for the different currents of British modernism. These developments plus the arrival of emissaries from the European avant-garde suddenly catapulted London into a position as one of the world's leading art centers. Many of the artists, architects, and writers lived in close proximity in the Camden Town – Hampstead area (Gabo among them) in a mutually supportive and stimulating relationship memorably described by Herbert Read as a »nest of gentle artists.« Within this milieu, united by a commitment to modernism, divergent points-of-view survived, with allegiances varying and sometimes overlapping between vitalism or Surrealism on the one hand and geometric abstraction on the other. In the latter camp, greatly strengthened by the arrival of Gabo, Mondrian and Moholy-Nagy, a natural affinity for advanced forms of architecture and design coalesced into a loose confederation given ideological expression by the 1937 publication *Circle: International Survey of Constructive Art.*

Gabo found within these developments a platform for the elaboration of his Constructive credo in both writings and sculpture. Several other factors also came into play at this time in his work. Marriage and the birth of his only child provided a happy family environment. From his friend John Sisson at ICI he was soon able to obtain the new, not readily available Perspex, far more stable than the various cellulose acetates he had used in the past.[112] An introduction into the activities of the Design Research Unit opened the way to interesting work in the design field. The influence of mathematical models, over and above the stereometric system, came to play at least a partial role in shaping new sculptural ideas, and the development of a profound mutual respect and friendship with Herbert Read provided encouragement and philosophical reinforcement.

Gabo's first major work in England, the *Kinetic Stone Carving* begun in 1936 (cat. no. 23), readdressed the problem of dematerializing a solid mass through carving, seen earlier in *Stone with Collar* (1933) and returned to again with different solutions

111. The best single source on the development of modernism in England during the first part of the century is Charles Harrison, *English Art and Modernism 1900–1939* (London, 1981).

112. Sisson was a head chemist at Imperial Chemical Industries and got to know Gabo very early during his English sojourn.

113. On Vantongerloo's use of mathematics, see Burnham, esp. pp. 134–37. Although it has not been analyzed in the Vantongerloo literature, certain of his early abstract sculptures bear strong resemblances to different mathematical models. Explanation of Kobro's use of mathematical proportion systems is found in *Constructivism in Poland 1923–1936: BLOK, Praesens, a.r.* (Museum Folkwang, Essen, and Rijksmuseum Kröller-Müller, Otterlo, 1973), esp. pp. 126–30.

114. A. Hill, »Construcitivism – the European phenomenon,« *Studio International,* 171, no. 876 (April 1966), p. 144. Hill states: »Gabo has explained that his idea was to take this complicated formula and change its realization to prove that what was basically a fantasy (the intuition of the mathematician) could be seen through the intuition of an artist. Gabo says he was attracted to this model as it was totally asymmetric and that few other models have interested him«. It is Mr Hill's recollection that this information came from conversations with Gabo (correspondence with the author, 1984).

115. Man Ray later used the photographs for a series of paintings on Shakespearian themes. The models were first brought to his attention by Max Ernst, and a selcetion was included in the Surrealist Exhibition of Objects at the Galerie Charles Ratton in Paris in May 1936. See Arturo Schwarz, *Man Ray* (New York, 1977), p. 76.

116. On Moores's use of mathematical models, see Alan Wilkinson, *The Drawings of Henry Moore* (The Tate Gallery, London, 1977), pp. 97–98. Moore responded to the idea of combining mechanical lines of force with organic forms as rhythmic and formal counterpoint and a way of defining space. For him, however, it was an idea which quickly ran its course.

Fig. 38 Gabo, *Construction in Space: Crystal*, 1937, rhodoid (now extensively deteriorated), Museum of Art, Rhode Island School of Design (*S.–L. 41.3*).

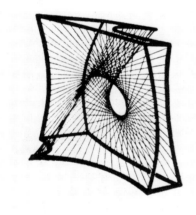

Fig. 39 Mathematical model (oscillating developable of a cubic ellipse), Institut Henri Poincaré, Paris.

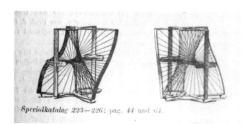

Specialkatalog 223—226: pag. 44 und 64.

Fig. 40 Mathematical model, published in Walter Dyck, *Katalog mathematischer und mathematische-physikalische Modelle, Apparate und Instrumente*, Munich, 1892.

in the later *Alabaster Carving* (1938–39), *Repose* (1953), and *Granite Carving* (1964–65). Here, the deep cuts and smoothed surfaces set up soft waves of movement that flow around the breadth of the stone in an unending rhythm. The white, purified forms of Arp and Brancusi are brought to mind, but Gabo differs from these more biologically inclined sources in his attempt to unlock spatial and fourth-dimensional qualities.

Gabo's productivity after moving to England was exceptionally high, and within three years he had also created an impressive series of works in plastic: *Construction on a Line* (1937), *Construction on a Plane* (1937), *Construction in Space: Crystal* (1937), *Construction in Space: Arch* (1937), several versions of *Spheric Theme* (1937), and *Construction in Space with Crystalline Center* (1938) (see cat. nos. 23–33). Several of these works rank among his best. That they are not generally granted greater acclaim in the histories of modern sculpture is partly due to their inaccessibility: their fragility has led to many conservation problems and the total loss of some versions, and those which Gabo retained have not been widely exhibited.

These sculptures represent a departure from the earlier transparencies. With the exception of the *Spheric Themes*, they generally have the look of standing reliefs viewable from two sides. Interweaving lines and surfaces penetrate back and forth through a literal or implied central plane. The configurations are always asymmetrical, which adds with the lightness of structure to a sense of dynamism, justifying Gabo's notion that kinetic rhythms need not involve actual motion. And while even the most transparent of earlier constructions incorporated a diversity of materials and tones, these are almost all completely clear and uniform. In sum, these works achieve a new degree of ephemerality and insubstantiality, of conceptual purity. Whereas architecture, mechanics, or scientific instruments often are metaphorically implied by earlier works, these sculptures in their purity of form are more redolent of abstract mathematics and sometimes of natural, organic rhythms. How much the latter quality may be due to the vitalistic tendencies Gabo encountered in England is hard to say. Evidence does exist, however, of a renewed interest on his part in mathematical models.

Gabo is sometimes referred to as a »mathematical artist,« as if his forms were regularly based on mathematical formulas or models in the same way that Vantongerloo's and Kobro's often were.[113] The clarity and precision of his work, however, are instinctive rather than mechanically generated, and although his stereometric system derives from solid geometry, its application was always highly subjective. Moreover, Gabo consistently denied any direct scientific dependence and disdained the tendency of some artists to mystify their work with algebraic titles. Nevertheless, during the mid-30s it can be seen that his work went beyond a *general* relationship with science through a more explicit referencing of mathematical models of the kind that physically embody algebraic formulas and developable surfaces. Anthony Hill, for example, has demonstrated how closely the *Construction in Space: Crystal* of 1937 resembles the model of a developable cubic ellipse (compare figs. 38 and 39).[114] Possibly starting from drawings such as the one shown here as cat. no. 120, he developed from the model a study of the conjunction in space of twisting and curving transparent planes. That he decided to incise some of the planes with lines for a sense of radiation and expansion may again indicate the influence of the model and its spiralling pattern of strings. This incising would soon evolve into the actual use of rods and then of thin nylon filament, in a way that resembles the stringing that was so common a feature of mathematical devices (compare figs. 39 and 40). Such objects were routinely included in geometry handbooks and had very recently been publicized in the art world through Man Ray's photographs of models at the Institut Henri Poincaré, published in *Cahiers d'Art* in 1936 (nos. 1 and 2). Also, at this same time Henry Moore was discovering mathematical models in the Science Museum in London and adapting their forms into drawings and sculptures of stringed figures (fig. 41).[116]

Mathematical implications in another of Gabo's sculptures, the *Spheric Theme* (fig. 42), were recognized by the scientist-philosopher Lancelot Whyte, who compared the endless spherical continuity in this work with investigations of spherical point distributions.[117] Such parallels of discovery in art and science, not necessarily interrelated, reinforced Gabo's concept of these two disciplines as operating in separate channels but manifesting one creative consciousness. With *Spheric Theme,* he felt he had arrived at a particularly satisfactory realization of his perception of spatial curvature, which we have traced evolving through earlier sculptures.

> I felt that the visual character of space is not angular: that to transfer the perception of space into sculptural terms, it has to be spheric. . . . I consider that in this work of mine there is a satisfactory solution to that problem. Instead of indicating space by an angular interaction of planes, I enclose the space in one curved continuous surface. . . . I have made several variations on this theme in order to show the structural possibilities. There is an immense variety of images which a constructive sculptor may conceive which can be executed with the help of this system.[118]

The variations that Gabo refers to followed over a lengthy period of time. Four models for *Spheric Theme* are included in this exhibition, made respectively out of plastic rods, clear plastic, and phosphor bronze (cat. nos. 24, 25, 27, 63). When Gabo was commissioned by Wallace Harrison to design a fountain for the General Electric Company pavillion at the New York World's Fair of 1939, he elected to use the *Spheric Theme* form (a model was prepared but the fountain was abandoned for reasons of expense). A *Bronze Spheric Theme (Variation)* made from metal with steel spring-wire dates from 1964–66, and a still larger outdoor version from 1969–76 exists in an edition of five. Gabo seems to have frequently experimented with the basic structure, as his studio contained many small »trials« in materials from paper and foil to plastic and metal. Comprised of two flat discs, each with a hole in the center, that are cut and fastened together and then twisted into three-dimensional form, the structure must have greatly appealed to Gabo for its combination of economic means and involved spatial dynamics. These dynamics were taken a step further in the lively but perhaps overly complex *Spiral Theme* of 1941 and were given a new twist through the use of stringing in works from 1942 onward.

While conveying overtones of mathematical meaning, the works of this period are far more than mechanical repetitions of models or demonstrations of mathematical principles. Their meanings lie in visual, physical and emotional experience and their ability to stimulate imaginative thinking about energy, light, space, and time. As Jack Burnham has observed, »Mathematical influence in Gabo's constructions appear more sensual than theoretical, having more to do with the optical consistency of mathematical models – in terms of their airiness, fragility, and intricacy – than with formal meaning.«[119] Models were invented to explain existing concepts and realities, while Gabo wished to create *new* realities. The advanced conceptualism of his work, on the other hand, has been criticized for its deviation from the earlier, more heroic studies for architecture and monuments, supposedly resulting in *objets d'art* for connoisseurs.[120] Gabo, however, would surely have denied any such compromise of principles. He viewed each sculpture as a communication of perceptions and thus, a learning opportunity, and even the highly purified works he regarded as sources for monumental projects, as evidenced by the later manifestations of *Spheric Theme.*

Gabo's productivity in sculpture was matched on the theoretical side by his contributions to *Circle,* representing his most important ideological statements since the *Realistic Manifesto.* Gabo's involvement in this compendium of writings and illustrations dealing with geometric abstraction was of central, if not primary, importance to its realization. He shared editorial and organizational duties with Leslie Martin and Ben Nicholson but wrote the introductory essay, and, most likely, provided much of the polemical spark behind the whole project. Margaret Gardiner recalled how the idea for *Circle* derived from reactions to the 1936 Surrealist exhibition at the New Burlington Galleries.[121] In addition to countering Surrealism, which both Nicholson and Gabo considered a negative and even destructive force, *Circle* offered an opportunity to enlighten a largely uncomprehending public on the meanings of abstract art and still more importantly, to provide an organ of expression for international artists working along similar lines. Contributions were gathered from a diverse group of artists, architects, and critics in several countries, including Mondrian, Le Corbusier, Siegfried Giedion, Henry Moore, and Jan Tschichold. Although somewhat disguised by the clean, unifying design of the book, a healthy variety of viewpoints was pre-

Fig. 41   Henry Moore, *Stringed Figure,* 1937, cherry wood and string, Collection of Mrs. Irina Moore.

Fig. 42   Gabo, *Spheric Theme: Transparent Variation.* c. 1937, celluloid and perspex, Family Collection (cat. no. 27, *S.–L. 37.8*).

117. »The Unity of Visual Experience,« *Bulletin of the Atomic Scientists,* XV, no. 2 (1959), p. 75.
118. Read and Martin, opp. pl. 64. The probable bearing of Einstein's theory of spatial continuum and curvature on Gabo's ideas is discussed in the previous chapter.
119. Burnham, p. 140.
120. David Thompson, »Outlines for a Public Art,« *Studio International,* 171, no. 876 (April 1966), p. 136: »After the thrusting and virile energy of projects that obviously would never be built, [came] the more yielding delicacy, fragility and gracefulness of what Constructivism was supposed not to be about – ›objets d'art‹ for the connoisseur.«

121. Margaret Gardiner, *Barbara Hepworth: a memoir* (Edingburgh, 1982), p. 46. She recalls that »Circle was, in fact, born in an ABC tea shop where Barbara, Ben and Gabo had gone to restore themselves one day in 1936 after viewing the Surrealist Exhibition and where they decided that they absolutely had to do something to clear the air. [They determined] to produce a book of contributions from artists whose common basis was the constructive trend in contemporary art . . .« A more detailed analysis of the birth and contents of *Circle* is found in the exhibition catalogue *Circle: constructive art in Britain 1934–40,* Jeremy Lewison ed. (Kettle's Yard Gallery, Cambridge, 1982).

122. »Constructive Art: An Exchange of Letters between Naum Gabo and Herbert Read,« *Horizon,* X, no. 55 (July 1944), pp. 57–65; reprinted in Read and Martin, pp. 171–73, among other places.

123. For a recent examination of the interaction of progressive artists in Cornwall in the 30s and 40s, see the exhibition catalogue *St Ives 1939–64,* Tate Gallery, London, 1985.

124. Gabo's wartime diary, now in his family's archive, reveals dark moods and periods of despair. Christina Lodder is working on a transcription and translation of the diary. Some of this emotion and the effect it had on Gabo's positivistic idealism is revealed in the exchange of letters with Herbert Read in 1944 (*Horizon*).

125. Illustrated in Hill, p. 140.

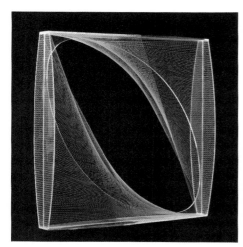

Fig. 43 Gabo, *Linear Construction in Space No. 1,* 1942/c.1945–46, Perspex with nylon monofilament, Solomon R. Guggenheim Museum, New York (*S.–L. 48.9*).

sented, demonstrating the complex evolution that geometric abstraction had undergone in its 25 year history. Gabo stated in the introduction that the organizers had »no intention of creating a particular group circumscribed by the limitations of personal manifestos.« Indeed, the importance of *Circle* lies not in any artificial attempt to define a united international ideology but in the demonstration of how widespread the Constructivist spirit had become in modern life.

Gabo's own two essays (»The Constructive Idea in Art« and »Sculpture – Carving and Construction in Space«) present themes familiar from earlier writings: the unifying, universal language of Constructive art; the function of purely spiritual or emotional explorations (»destined to stimulate or perfect the substance of material or spiritual life«); and the primacy of space and time as sculptural elements. He took up in detail, however, a subject central to his later theoretical thought, about which he wrote with conviction and feeling – the relationship between art and science. Of primary importance is his definition of the distinctions and interrelations of the two spheres. The Constructive idea »does not impose on art the function of Science.« Their cognitive bases are different: »Science teaches, Art asserts. . . . Science looks and observes, Art sees and foresees.« The basis of science is reason, while »the force of art lies in its immediate influence on human psychology . . .« Yet, the two rise »from the same creative source and flow into the same ocean of the common culture.«

These writings and others that followed reflect the compulsion Gabo felt to clarify issues surrounding his work. In 1944 he would lament that Constructive art was still bound in an »atmosphere of controversy«.[122] By then the war had blunted his idealism, but he still hoped through his art »to alleviate the pains and convulsions of our time.« If a perfected society now seemed more distant, one must nevertheless look to the »striving« and »direction« of positive change through art, relying more than ever on the Constructive process.

With the outbreak of war in 1939, Gabo and his wife were persuaded by Nicholson and Hepworth to join them at Carbis Bay near St. Ives, where they soon became friends with other members of the large colony of artists and writers in Cornwall, including Adrian Stokes and Bernard Leach as well as the younger painters Peter Lanyon and Patrick Heron. This period marks the high point of what is misleadingly called the St. Ives School.[123] Gabo's influence definitely had an impact within the group and can be detected, for example, in the work of Barbara Hepworth and certain younger artists as well, but the war took a deepening psychological toll[124] and his output during these years was limited. Between 1940 and 1946 his sculptural activity was restricted to *Linear Construction in Space No. 1* (several versions) and *Spiral Theme,* but he was also involved in certain design projects and took up painting.

Linear Construction No.. 1 (fig. 43) stands out as a breakthrough for Gabo in that it marked his transition to actual stringing from the incised lines in *Crystal* and certain versions of *Spheric Theme.* Precedents exist for the use of strings and rods in modern sculptures, including, for example, the lines of force indicated by twine in Balla's 1915 *Sculpture,*[125] the wire guy-lines in standing towers by the Stenbergs, the wire strings in Picasso's sheetmetal *Guitar* of 1912, and the welded rods in his famous *Wire Construction* of 1928. As already noted, Gabo's use of stringing derives most probably from mathematical models. Whether or not Henry Moore's stringed figures starting in 1937 formed another source of influence is difficult to determine, but it seems unlikely since the strings in his work serve so different a function, acting as accents to solid mass rather than delineating light and space.

In the first models for *Linear Construction No. 1,* thread was wound around small, square-shaped plastic frames. In larger versions Gabo used nylon filament, and the stringing became considerably more complex. Notches around the sides of a more streamlined framework keep the spacings absolutely precise and even. The taut nylon lines are all straight but converge in such a way as to form beautifully rounded curves – a strong elliptical void in the center framed by strings intersecting into concave crevasses and convex roles. What was a plastic surface in earlier works becomes a virtual plane opened up by the strings to light and air. These »surfaces«, or linear directionals, describe space folding in and out of itself and seeming, through the radial patterns, to expand outward. Systems vary with the use of double stringing, or through variations in the framework as with the steps in *Linear Construction No. 1 (Variation)*, or with a reversal of directions as with variations on the slightly later *Suspended* theme (cat. nos. 51–53). Where the strings overlap or are superimposed in different directions, a secondary image and reading of space is created.

The nylon filament is reflective, so between the delicacy and openness of the stringing and the transparent and reflective materials, these works take on an intense luminosity. They are like instruments of light, as reflections play across the warping movement of their curves and project through the plastic end-pieces. The stringing also creates a heightened sense of extension and duration, making palpable the element of time. It is a device that Gabo would use consistently, with either nylon or thin metallic spring-wire, throughout the rest of his career.

For his explorations of folding surfaces and spatial curvature, Gabo began to find it useful first to work out his ideas in paintings, often envisioning spatial convolutions which would have been impossible actually to construct (see fig. 44). Later, when asked if his paintings and drawings were conceived as studies for sculpture, he explained:

> They are works in themselves, but sometimes I paint the image so realistically that it can be taken as an image of a sculpture. However, I often turn to painting when the image of my experience becomes so involved in structure, in form and in color that there is no possible way for me to execute it in three-dimensional material.[126]

Paintings also gave Gabo an opportunity to employ color and texture as additional constructive elements, and he enjoyed the physical nature of paint, often mixing his own colors and experimenting with combinations, opacity, and densities.

To activate the forms he created in paintings and to emphasize their spatial movements, Gabo sometimes mounted his pictures on motorized revolving panels. As the painting turns, the eye grasps different spatial relationships and patterns.[127] Some of these works do give a convincing and luminous account of complex formal interactions. One must admit, however, that Gabo did not have a great sensitivity for this medium, so that many of the paintings have a heavy, labored quality at odds with his delicate three-dimensional work.

For variation and as a way of affecting actual construction, Gabo became involved during this period in several design projects. For a friend in Cornwall, Dr. John Ince,

Fig. 44   Gabo, *Blue Construction in Space (Kinetic)*, 1953, oil on panel, 91 cm in diameter, Wadsworth Atheneum, Hartford.

Fig. 45   Gabo, *Design for a Door Pull for the Queen Mary*, 1943–44, pencil and ink on paper, Family Collection.

Fig. 46   Gabo, clay model for Jowett car, 1943, destroyed.

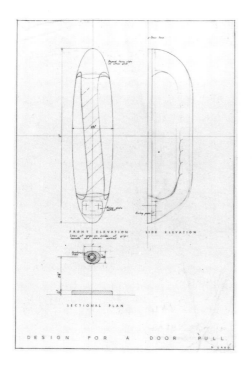

he designed a stone fireplace. He continued to experiment with his roof invention. For Grey Wornum, decoration architect of the S. S. Queen Mary, he designed a set of interior fixtures, including door handles and clothes hooks which were distinguished by their smooth, curvilinear profiles (see fig. 45) but which unfortunately were never executed due to the war. And in 1943 he became involved through Herbert Read with the Design Research Unit in London, out of which association came a commission from Jowett cars for the design of an automobile.[128] His efforts on this project stretched over two years and included first a maquette in clay (fig. 46), then one in wood, and finally the supervision of a set of detailed drawings. With its blunt-nosed body and such mechanical innovations as a rear-mounted engine, however, his car finally was judged either too radical or too costly and never reached production.[129]

During the Cornwall period, Gabo's work received only limited outside attention in terms of exhibitions and sales. Discouraged, he wrote to Herbert Read in January 1946 that he saw so little prospect of support in England that he had to look instead to the United States, finding particular promise in the idea of a show at the Museum of Modern Art.[130] Contacts with Katherine Dreier, Hilla Rebay, Wallace Harrison and various museum and gallery personnel he had met during a trip to the U.S. in 1938 were also encouraging, and later in 1946 he and his wife decided to move permanently to America.

V. America: Monumentality and the Public Eye

In the United States, Gabo at last received the opportunity to realize some of his dreams for large-scale public sculpture, for an art that would »attend us everywhere that life flows and acts. . . .« From his arrival in 1946 until his death in 1977 he lived and worked in Connecticut, first in Woodbury and then Middlebury. He became an American citizen in 1952, but his attitude toward his new country always had a degree of ambivalence; he missed the deep cultural roots of Europe and had reason to feel that his art still was not fully understood or appreciated, but he also found hope and energy in the country's youthful spirit and enjoyed the companionship of new friends such as Lewis Mumford and William Ivins. And, while hardly extensive in number, there materialized a series of commissions that drew fully upon his talents as an artist engineer and brought his work more than ever into the public arena. In certain cases he resurrected earlier, unfulfilled projects and he also finally had the means to execute some of his previous works in the large scale originally envisioned. This last period of his career, therefore, was marked by a working dialogue between the old and the new, sometimes with transferals into larger scale and new materials, and often with elaboration of themes found in earlier work. In general, we see little reaction to the styles of other artists, as Gabo steadfastly pursued his own path. An important question remains, however, as to how fully his hopes for an art of social character were fulfilled.

Gabo's first major opportunities came in 1949 and 1950, with projects for the Esso Building in Rockefeller Center and the Baltimore Museum of Art. The former proved to be a disappointment, but the latter was a success and a milestone for Gabo, thanks in part to the understanding patronage of Saidie A. May. Mrs. May, the important collector of modern art and supporter of the Baltimore Museum, had donated to the museum a new wing for children's art activities and early in 1950 commissioned from Gabo a sculpture to hang in its imposing three-story stairwell. She asked originally for a kinetic sculpture, but Gabo concluded that such a work would interfere with movement on the stairs and decided instead to incorporate that movement into a sequential reading of the sculpture. He wrote:

> In effect, the spiral movement of the ascending or descending spectator, if it is incorporated in the conception of the sculpture, would give an imaginary movement to the sculpture. . . . Apart from that, I had to take into account the fact that the observer would inevitably be looking at the work not only from a series of points on a horizontal plane, but also from all the points along the vertical axis of the spiral periphery of the stairs as well.[131]

126. Kuh, p. 96.
127. For an interesting analysis of one of these revolving paintings, see C.E.B. [uckley], »Blue Construction in Space (Kinetic),« *Wadsworth Atheneum Bulletin,* no. 47 (March 1954), p. 1.
128. In letters from Gabo to Herbert Read of August 9 and September 13, 1943 (Gabo papers, Beinecke Library) he mentions his progress on designs for the car, also mentions the possibility of working on designs for utensils and furniture, and enthuses, »You see, Herbert, I have answered the call which you made to us constructivists and I stand prepared for action.«
129. Kuh, p. 103: »It never materialized because it was considered too radical. I introduced many features that were completely new then, but that now are frequently found in automobiles. For instance, I put the engine in the back; the hood declined toward the ground and the whole design was contrary to the then prevailing streamlined style.«
130. Letter of January 15, 1946 (Gabo papers, Beinecke Library).
131. »A New Construction for Baltimore,« *Magazine of Art,* XLV (1952), pp. 71–74.

His conception of a dynamic of sequential, multiple views goes beyond the functions of hanging sculpture explored by both Rodchenko and Calder. What he decided upon was a two-part structure extending 15 feet into the stairwell, with one, more horizontal element attached to the ceiling, and, suspended on thin wires below that, a more vertical element consisting of an open »cradle« of aluminium surrounding an inner plastic core (see fig. 47). All the parts share a looping, ribbon-like movement and interact to form distinctly different patterns as one moves around and up past the sculpture. The mixture of materials – anodized aluminium, gold wire, bronze mesh, plastic – plays against surrounding colors and, with reflected highlights, gives a rich, sensuous effect. Gabo executed the work himself and supervised its installation, with an official unveiling in November 1951.[132] He noted in his speech at the opening ceremony how much it meant to him finally to complete one of his monumental designs.

The outcome of the Esso project, which he had begun in 1949, was less happy. The problem given Gabo was to adorn two large blank walls on elevator shafts in the building's lobby, one facing an entrance on 52nd Street and the other facing across a narrow corridor to the 51st Street entrance. His model, now in the Museum of Modern Art (fig. 48), was completed in 1949. For the 52nd Street side, he proposed a set of converging perspective lines that seem to break the wall into a deeper space, and within these lines, a large construction of spiralling arcs around a vertical axis. Over the flanking revolving doors were to be located two standing stringed sculptures that revolved at a slower rate than the doors. On the other wall, with its narrower frontal space, he proposed a construction which is more strongly vertical but still incorporates a swinging movement that reaches toward the side walls and draws them in. In these sculptures, the webbed or stringed construction of *Linear No. 1* is combined with particularly free-flowing linear movements. Unfortunately, we cannot judge their final effectiveness, since Esso cancelled the project, claiming prohibitive construction costs.[133] James Johnson Sweeney, writing in *Art News* in March 1951, announced that »New York City has once again unfortunately missed an opportunity to boast an important public work of contemporary art . . . what would have probably been one of the most provocative architectural sculptures in this century.«[134] And Gabo once again was denied an important public oppurtunity for supposed financial considerations.

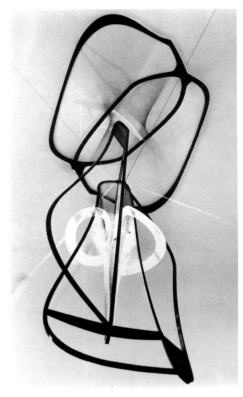

Fig. 47 Gabo, *Baltimore ›Construction Suspended in Space‹,* 1950–51, aluminum, phosphor-bronze mesh, wire, and plastic, The Baltimore Museum of Art (*S.–L. 57.3*).

Fig. 48 Gabo, model for sculptures for lobby of the Esso Building, Rockefeller Center, 1949, Collection of the Museum of Modern Art, New York (*S.–L. 56*).

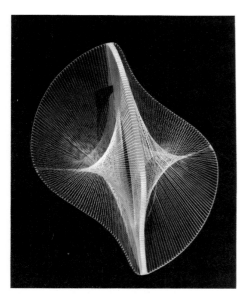

Fig. 49 Gabo, *Linear Construction in Space No. 2*, 1949/1958, plexiglass with nylon monofilament, Solomon R. Guggenheim Museum, New York, Gift of Mr. and Mrs. Marcel Breuer (*S.–L. 55.14*).

132. The formal contract had been executed on May 19, 1950, and Gabo's model was approved in November 1950. For more on this work, see *The Baltimore Museum of Art News* (Dec. 1951), pp. 3–4; Patrick Heron, *The Changing Forms of Art* (New York, 1960), pp. 44–45; Alley, p. 253.

133. In a letter to Herbert Read of January 20, 1950, Gabo reported, »Because of the unusual character of the project, the contracting firms were unwilling to cooperate and sabotaged the whole affair by demanding a price out of all proportion to the work.« (Gabo papers, Beinecke Library.)

134. »Construction unconstructible?« *Art News*, 50, no. 1 (March 1951), pp. 34f. Also see Alley, pp. 252–53.

135. Alley, p. 266.

136. The competition aroused widespread interest and a great deal of press coverage, much of it decidedly negative. For a balanced report, see Henry McBride, »Unknown Political Monument,« *Art News*, 51, no. 10 (Feb. 1953), pp. 20f.; and for a more recent overview, see Richard Calvocoressi's essay in *British Sculpture in the Twentieth Century* (Whitechapel Art Gallery, London, 1981), pp. 136f. A good example of the hostile criticism is found in John Berger's review, *The New Statesman* (March 24, 1953), pp. 337–38.

137. Gabo papers, Beinecke Library.

138. »The Unknown Political Prisoner,« *The Listener* (March 19, 1953), p. 478.

The project was not a total loss, however, since the important *Linear Construction No. 2* (fig. 49) derived from the small models for the sculptures over the revolving doors. It was fabricated by Gabo in both standing and hanging versions. Its strings are wound around two intersecting lobed planes of plastic and create even more complex three-dimensional patterns of inward and outward spatial folds than those in *Linear No. 1*, while its organic shapes call to mind analogies of the womb, seed pods, or cocoons. Its sleek and reflective forms preserve a scientific look, nevertheless, and give it far greater unity than the related but more eccentric shapes in the larger Esso constructions. Executed in several different sizes, *Linear No. 2* was a favorite work of Gabo's, and when Herbert Read died in the late 60s it was a version of this sculpture that Gabo donated to the Tate Gallery in his memory.[135]

At this same time, another major disappointment was in the offing. On January 31, 1952, the Institute of Contemporary Arts in London announced an international contest for a monument to The Unknown Political Prisoner, with a 10-person international jury and a selection process leading to a large exhibition at the Tate Gallery of all the finalists in March–April 1953.[136] Herbert Read was one of the organizers of this ill-fated competition, and Gabo obviously had heard of it earlier because on January 4, 1952, he wrote to Read about his thoughts for the project.[137] He had been struggling with an idea for a monument to victims of the Nazis and resisting the use of a figurative image. For this theme or that of the Unknown Political Prisoner, one could react either through compassion or awe, and in the latter spirit a large-scale architectural oriented image had come to him which he decided to enter in the competition. Since the early *Column*, he felt this was »the height of my thirty years striving towards an image which would combine both sculpture and architecture in one entity.«

His model shows a structure with two tall, symmetrical, bowed »wings« made of plastic and wire mesh which he must have thought of in its final form as grids of metal rods (cat. No. 45). In the center is a single vertical shaft with mesh projections, providing a solemn yet upwardly pointed and therefore hopeful note. It is difficult, however, to imagine the delicate precision of the model expanded to a monument 30 or 40 feet high, which, along with the uncompromising abstraction of the work, may have been a dissuading factor for the selection committee. Reg Butler's controversial design took first prize, and Gabo was awarded a second of £ 775 along with Mirko, Basaldella, Hepworth, and Pevsner. David Sylvester's comments typify the ambivalence of some of even the most sympathetic responses, while also alluding to problems of scale and inherent difficulties in abstract treatments of political themes:

> The Gabo, with its dual implication of confinement and freedom and its quietly impressive dignity, conveys a sense of the set theme to a degree surprisingly adequate in a purely geometric invention. On a monumental scale, though, it would register much less effectively, making us all too aware of its lack of pity and terror.[138]

One nevertheless finds in this project the seeds for Gabo's key, slightly later, Bijenkorf construction.

The history of the Bijenkorf commission is long and complex and is traced in greater detail through its various stages in the accompanying catalogue rainsonné of Gabo's sculpture. In brief, it provided an unusual opportunity for Gabo to work in concert with an important architect and an entire urban development scheme and resulted in his most significant public sculpture. He was intrigued by the city-wide plans for the rebuilding of Rotterdam after the war and the chance to match its other main public monument, a standing figure by Zadkine expressive of war's agony and destruction, with a symbol of reconstruction and hope. Marcel Breuer, architect of the new Bijenkorf department store, obtained through the planning board and store owner a commission for Gabo for a large outdoor sculpture along the store's busy Coolsingel approach, one which would match the sightlines of structures along the vista and would help ameliorate the rather severe relation between facade and streetscape.[139] Gabo signed a contract with Breuer on June 22, 1954, and sent his first model to Rotterdam by September.[140]

At first he worked with the idea of a large relief on the facade, somewhat reminiscent of his design for the Esso building. This project was abandoned, however, and in November of 1954 he and Breuer obtained permission for a freestanding sculpture to be set several yards away from the building. A new small-scale model was prepared and sent to Rotterdam in May 1955, with a large-scale version following in October. These show a sleekly narrow and bowed structure similar to Gabo's design for the Unknown Political Prisoner competition. At first he planned to set the sculpture into a curvilinear basin-like lower section. As he worked on the larger model, however, he decided to discard this element since it detracted, he felt, from the sculpture's clean lines and inner structure. Since the final work was to rise 85 feet into the air, questions of anchoring and wind resistance were crucial. Engineering solutions going back to the Eiffel Tower helped dictate the open, bowed form. Gabo visualized the whole structure somewhat like a tree, with a deep root system, and planned to sink a large section of it underground and tie it into the building's foundation. Careful scrutiny by engineers and wind-tunnel tests proved his calculations to be correct. In final form (fig. 50), the tensile, lithe superstructure consists of two pairs of curving steel shafts, coated with golden bronze, set into two bases of reinforced concrete sheathed with black granite. The cradled inner structure is made of bronze wire sprung over a stainless steel skeleton.

Gabo had hoped through this work to reaffirm »the vital role contemporary sculpture ought to play as an integrated part in contemporary architecture.«[141] And indeed, the sculpture harmonizes with its surroundings in both form and spirit to become a valuable element in the city's life. It stands out against busy pedestrian traffic and the restrained scale of surrounding structures as truly monumental. Its technological connotations seem particularly at home in modern rebuilt Rotterdam, and its message of rebirth, progress, and invention is as clear as ever. Lewis Mumford has described the festive processional that sprang up spontaneously in May 1957 as the huge sculpture was transported from the shipyard where it was built to its home on the Bijenkorf plaza,[142] where it is still regarded today with civic pride. From a critical distance we can see a formal problem involving the unified integration of inner and outer shapes, one that plagued other of Gabo's late works, but on the whole, it must be regarded as one of his major triumphs.

While working on the Bijenkorf project Gabo received another commission, from Wallace Harrison for a large relief for the lobby of the U.S. Rubber Company Building in Radio City.[143] Completed in November 1956, the sculpture consists of two outer, ribbon-like elements made in cast aluminium that are reminiscent of the curvilinear rhythms in the Baltimore project, surrounding an inner shield-shaped device fabricated from plastic and phosphor bronze and incorporating red and black surfaces. Again at work is a dialogue between inner and outer forms, here manifested as linear orbits around a suspended, more angular »nucleus«.

A much different formal approach was taken by Gabo for the last of his public commissions, the large *Revolving Torsion, Fountain*. This work was conceived, and a first model was built, in the early 60s (cat. no. 61), but it was not executed in large scale until 1972–73.[144] Knowing of Gabo's hopes to find a location and backer for his latest fountain design, Sir Norman Reid, then Director of the Tate Gallery, was able to persuade a private patron, Alistair McAlpine, to undertake the project as a gift for the Tate. Gabo collaborated with two construction and metalworking companies on the fabrication out of stainless steel of the large revolving structure, which was installed in late 1975 on the grounds of St. Thomas' Hospital on the south bank of the Thames as a permanent loan (fig. 51).

In an example of creative adaptation of earlier works, he modelled the fountain more or less exactly after the plastic *Torsion* of 1929. It is designed so that jets of water shoot from the outer edges of the ribs in a timed pattern, turning the upper section and thus actualizing the movement that was only implied in the spiral shapes of the original sculpture. As Gabo pointed out, the jets of water form lines that correspond to his use of lines and stringing in other projects of the period,[145] but they also provide a diaphanous veil around the shiny metallic center. Water, light, reflective form, and movement all act together when the fountain is operating to

Fig. 50   Gabo, *Bijenkorf Construction*, 1956–57, pre-stressed concrete, steel ribs, stainless steel, bronze wire, and marble, Rotterdam (*S.–L. 67.5*).

139. Lewis Mumford (*The Highway and the City* [New York, 1953], esp. pp. 39, 47–50) analyzes the architectural setting as part of Rotterdam's rebuilt cityscape. He explains that Dr. Cornelius van Traa, in charge of the city plan, suggested an additional bay on the Bijenkorf to counterbalance the facade of an old building on the next corner that projected farther out. As a compromise, a sculpture was instead conceived to help break up the long vista along the Bijenkorf.

140. The sequence of models is discussed in Alley, pp. 258–60. Gabo wrote to Read on November 19, 1954, that he had accepted the task of »a project for a very difficult architectural problem . . . to find the compromise in a conflict between the architects . . . and the Town Planners who have created a rigid plan for the rebuilding of the bombed parts of Rotterdam.« He was delighted by the chance to »build something on a scale on which my work and my ideas could really be tested in a larger frame of reference and therefore more conclusive than what I have to do within the four walls of my studio.« (Gabo papers, Beinecke Library.) Other good sources on this project include Kuh, p. 100; H. Read, *The*

Tenth Muse (1957), p. 57; David Lewis, »Naum Gabo's Monument for the Rotterdam ›Beehive,‹« *Arts* (June 1958), pp. 39–40; »Rotterdam's Beehive,« *Architectural Forum*, 107 (September 1957), pp. 132–35. For Gabo's interest in, and thoughts on, city planning, see his »Prepare for Design,« *World Review*, London (April 1943), pp. 43–49.

141. From an unpublished statement by Gabo on the Bijenkorf project in the Gabo papers, Beinecke Library.

142. Mumford, *Highway and the City*, p. 49.

143. Catalogue Raisonné, no. 69; illustrated in Read and Martin, pl. 101. The construction was re-sited in 1976 to the Celanese Building on the Avenue of the Americas, but remains the property of Rockefeller Center.

144. For the story of the evolution from maquette to final structure, see «Naum Gabo talks to David Thompson,» *Art Monthly*, no. 4 (February 1977), pp. 10–13, and Alley, pp. 262 and 267.

Fig. 51   Gabo, *Revolving Torsion, Fountain*, 1972–73, stainless steel, The Tate Gallery, installed outside St. Thomas' Hospital, London (*S.–L. 30.7*).

create a joyful visual experience, a suitable climax to Gabo's longstanding desires to enhance public spaces with a new breed of Constructivist fountain.[146]

The quest for monumentality also led Gabo during the 60s and 70s to execute certain earlier themes in larger scale, sometimes for placement out-of-doors. Of the *Constructed Head No. 2* he made a series of three 5½-foot versions in different metals and finishes in 1966–67 (cat. no. 4). The availability of large sheets of totally clear glass allowed him in 1975 to realize his longtime ambition of enlarging the *Column* of 1923 to monumental proportions (cat. no. 11). And following his *Bronze Spheric Theme (Variation)* of 1964–66 (cat. no. 62), which is based on the spheric composition originally explored in 1937, he produced a larger version, similar in form, in a series of five for placement out-of-doors (fig. 52). His *Vertical Construction No. 2*, an indoor work, exists in a version three meters high (cat. no. 65). An uncompleted project, his *Monument to the Astronauts*, is known only in two maquettes (cat. no. 66) but was conceived by Gabo as standing 18 or 20 feet high out-of-doors, with a central section rotated by the wind and with neon tubes lining that section's edges so that at night it would appear as a floating wave.[147] In both this project and the *Revolving Torsion, Fountain*, kinetics again entered his work as a basic principle, although the movement was no longer motorized. The fact that Gabo could freely return to earlier ideas for certain of these sculptures, or repeat compositions in later, multiple originals, indicates that he did not think of his work in terms of art historical phases. Rather, it was all part of an on-going process in which worthy ideas never lost relevance. That he could change materials for the same composition indicates not so much an indetermination as a steady sense of exploration and a tendency also to think in sequential series. His ideas on the appropriateness of

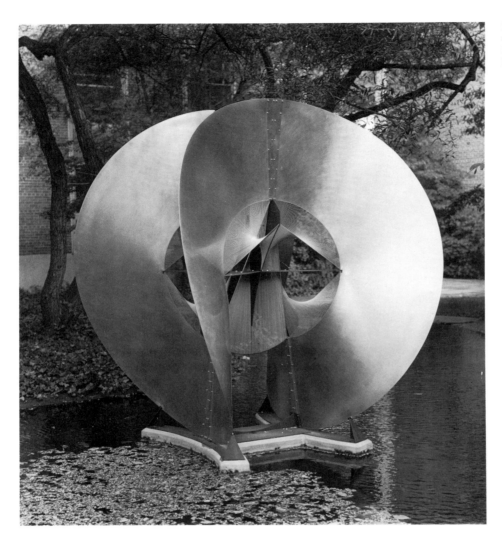

Fig. 52   Gabo, *Spheric Theme,* 1967–68/1974, stainless steel and spring-wire, The Art Museum, Princeton University, The John B. Putnam Jr. Memorial Collection (*S.–L. 42.11*).

materials for certain works were flexible, and he liked to see how sculptures reacted to such changes.

In the smaller, indoor works of this late period, Gabo pursued with logical consistency a number of themes that overlap with the larger commissions but generally speak a different language of precision and sometimes almost precious intricacy (see cat. nos. 40–44, 49–55). Those that are most effective – such as *Linear No. 2, Bronze Spheric Theme* (Variation), *Torsion Variation,* and certain versions of *Linear No. 4* – have a unity that overrides their complexity of structure and helps them make an authoritative statement. Excluding the stone pieces, these later works almost all use stringed patterns to shape space and provide a variety of curving, penetrating movements. Cut-out and twisted or intersecting planes form the ribs from which are suspended, or around which are wrapped, the nylon line or thin metal spring-wires. The basic shapes may be spherical, or tall and pointed, or multi-lobed, or aggressively spiked, as biotechnics mix with straightforward geometry in a freer variation of composition than seen before. Within these formats, a great variety of spatial effects are created by the different patterns of strings and the play of negative and positive space, solid and void, real and implied surfaces. Light is always a key partner, and materials are chosen and varied to exploit the potentials of luminosity. Indeed, many of these works give the impression of self contained, incorporeal galaxies of light and energy.

As elegant and poetic as these objects can be, it is the monumental projects which constitute the primary ambition of Gabo's late career. They eloquently summarize many of the principles and aspirations behind his entire life's work and

145. Thompson, *Art Monthly,* p. 10.
146. In a letter to Lewis Mumford of October 29, 1976, Gabo expressed great pleasure and pride in the completed fountain, noting that it fulfilled »a dream which I have been carrying with me ever since 1929 and before.« (Gabo papers, Beinecke Library.)
147. Alley, p. 265.
148. Letter to Herbert Read, January 4, 1952 (Gabo papers, Beinecke Library).

his long-standing compulsion »to dedicate myself to the task of making constructivism into a public art.«[148] The fact that he was given so few opportunities to exercise his monumental vision is society's loss and also a measure of a lasting resistance to abstract thought much greater than Gabo could have predicted in 1920. The proliferation of progressive public sculpture in Europe and the United States in the late 1970s and 80s could, however, be seen as a redemption for his efforts and dreams.

Postcript

From the standpoint of nearly a decade after Gabo's death, it is now possible to put the man and his art into clearer perspective, to grasp the wholeness and underlying unity of his accomplishments, and to assess more accurately the artist's position in the history of modernism. What emerges is Gabo's unique contribution to the enduring Constructivist tradition (still very much alive today in diversified forms) and to the broader endeavor of elucidating modern reality through visual means. Gabo's sustained development spans 60 years within the Constructivist movement, from its very inception to a point of worldwide dissemination and reinterpretation. While knowledge of many of the early pioneers of the movement was obscured for long periods, Gabo remained an active advocate, moving from country to country, diligently pursuing his work, and invigorating other artists by his example. That he never cultivated any direct followers was not a concern. He always went his own way, no matter what the prevailing contemporary trends might be, addressing problems that he hoped would eventually open windows of perception for others. Although working in stylistic conventions that stress generalization and the impersonal, Gabo's work carries a strong stamp of individualtiy. In many areas of modern sculptural concern – kinetics, the merger of sculpture and architecture, exploration of new materials, the incorporation of scientific vistas – he had a lasting impact.

Within the diversification of Constructivist-oriented trends witnessed since World War II, Gabo's influence has continued to play an important role, particularly for artists sharing an interest in the mechanistic and technological. In Europe, this influence is apparent in the work of sculptors such as Max Bill, Kenneth Martin, and François Morellet, who employ a pure, geometric vocabulary to explore mathematical concepts and dynamic structural systems. In postwar America, related concerns can be seen in the work of Kenneth Snelson, Richard Lippold, and George Rickey, among others. For artists motivated by universal values of clarity, logic, and geometric order, Gabo's art has stood as an exemplum of the eloquence achievable through geometric means. To be sure, many contemporary adaptations of Constructivist principles have taken different directions, for which Gabo's complex refinements have little relevance. Painters turning to hard-edged abstraction as a response to the emotional extremes of 50s expressionism, for example, and sculptors exploring minimalist concerns with primary objects and sequential structure, have found the severe abstractions of Mondrian and Malevich to be far more pertinent sources. In the recent resurgence of interest in fabricated geometric reliefs of diverse materials and colors, artists such as Tatlin, Puni, and Schwitters must be credited with an inspirational role. But in the field of kinetics, and for artists and critics interested in forming new bridges between art and technology, Gabo is frequently invoked as one of the most significant forerunners. As an ironic tribute, imitations of his gleaming, incorporeal structures have become almost a modernist cliché in the hands of many lesser sculptors.

It is perhaps not surprising to find that postwar reactions to Gabo's work and to Constructivism in general stress the formal over the ideological. Little of the movement's utopian positivism survived the horrors of World War II. In subsequent decades, formalistic reappraisals of the geometric tradition have allowed an antihistorical blurring of ideological distinctions, making it possible to borrow pictorial ideas without regard for extra-pictorial content.

Gabo, however, never swerved from the high idealism he articulated as early as 1920 in the *Realistic Manifesto.* Indeed, it is difficult to think of many artists who enacted their convictions with more courage and determination. Art for him was a tool of exploration and communication. A constant goal was to delve beyond phenomenological evidence to reveal essential processes, forces and structures in the world around us. Gabo's imagination focused on realities beyond empirical verification, revealed not just analytically but through subjective interpretation bordering at times on a Constructivist romanticism. Such hard to grasp concepts as the joining through light of solidity and space, the localization of invisible energies, and the activation of substance into events, find intuitive materialization in his evolving spatial constructions and their embrace of light, movement, and new structural possibilities. Even at the dawning of the Post-Machine Age, these works still stimulate the contemplation of new horizons. For Gabo, art for art's sake was a meaningless concept. To reveal, to celebrate, to integrate art and environment: these were his ambitions and the basis of his genuine humanism.

Gabo in Russia and Germany 1890–1922:
A Biographical Study

Christina Lodder

I should like to thank the Julia A. Whitney Foundation which financed my work on Naum Gabo's Russian papers; Thomas P. Whitney for his support; Miriam Gabo and Nina and Graham Williams for making their archives and their memories so generously available to me; and Dr. Schoonover and the staff of the Beinecke Rare Book and Manuscript Library, Yale University, for their help and co-operation.

1. Naum Gabo, *Of Divers Arts,* Bollingen Foundation, New York, 1962, p. 121.
2. John Read, »Naum Gabo«, 1972, Film, Transcript of the soundtrack, Roll 5, p. 8, Beinecke Rare Book and Manuscript Library, Yale University, New Haven (hereafter Yale). Gabo became an American citizen in 1952.
3. Naum Gabo, Diary, 6 August 1940, Family Archive London (hereafter London). In his Soviet Passport, issued in Paris on 14 November 1934, Gabo is entered as »Neemiya (Naum) Borisovich Gabo-Pevzner.« Yale. In Russian Pevzner is so spelt, but in accordance with established usage I have adopted the spelling Pevsner throughout the text. Apparently Gabo's father gave him the Hebrew name Neemiya in addition to the Russian Naum, to remind him that he was Jewish (Miriam Gabo, »Biographical Notes«, London).
4. Naum Gabo, »Autobiographical Fragments«, ms, 1970s, p. 150, London; Miriam Gabo, »Biographical Notes«, London; »Naum Gabo talks to David Thompson«, *Art Monthly,* No. 4, 1977, p. 12; Naum Gabo, »Kak ya stal revolutsionerom« [»How I became a Revolutionary«], ms, 1970s, p. 3, London. Gabo's birthplace is given as Bryansk in his Soviet passport (Yale). In Munich, Gabo gave his birthplace as Klimovitsch [sic] (Registration form, 1910/1911, Munich University Archive). Gabo's family in Russia have confirmed that he was born in Klimovich (conversation with author, 21 May 1985). Bryansk, situated on the River Desma was an industrial town in the district of Orel, with a population of 30,400. It had strong military connections. The Arsenal and gun foundry had been established in 1783. The Maltsov works was the largest industrial enterprise, employing 20,000 workmen. It also made railway carriages. This area supplied most of the railway stock for the construction of the Russian railway network. For Bryansk see Karl Baedeker, *Russia: Handbook for Travellers,* Leipzig, 1914, p. 376.
5. Alexei Pevsner, *A Biographical Sketch of My Brothers Naum Gabo and Antoine Pevsner* (Augustin and Schoonman, Amsterdam, 1964), p. 3.

In 1962 Naum Gabo wrote »I was born and brought up in Russia, my consciousness was moulded there . . . I was fortunate enough to get an education which enlarged that consciousness beyond the frontiers of Russian culture and helped me to absorb the influences of other cultures as well and to understand that they are all one.«[1] In 1922, after having lived through the Revolution and the Civil War, Gabo left Russia, to return only once again, in 1962, to see his recently rediscovered family. He spent the remaining fifty-five years of his life in the West: ten years in Germany where he witnessed the rise of the Third Reich, four in France, and ten in England where he spent the Second World War. He finally settled in America in 1946. As he recalled in 1972: »[It is] only now in the last perhaps twenty-five years, that I am settled more or less; all the other time I was wandering from one country to the other; I left my own country . . . hoping all the time that things would change, and I had a Soviet passport for twenty-four years«.[2] The unsettled quality of Gabo's life and the upheavals through which he lived have made it particularly difficult to reconstruct the formative years of his artistic career, especially those leading up to the publication of *The Realistic Manifesto* in 1920.

It was in Russia that Gabo as Naum [Neemia] Borisovich Pevsner was born on 5 August 1890. Even this date is subject to some confusion because Gabo was registered as being older than he was in order to avoid military service: »I have not managed to find out my exact age . . . my father always disputed the dates and never agreed with my mother . . . Transactions in Russia then, in our backwoods, must have been conducted like everything else – unthinkingly.«[3]

Gabo was born in South West Russia, apparently in the village of Klimovich, in the district of Orel, and was brought up in the village of Katnida where he lived »very near to the people«. When he was seven the family moved to Bryansk where his father, Boris Grigorevich Pevsner, owned a factory that produced various alloys and machines used in the construction of the Russian railway network.[4] The sixth of seven surviving children, Gabo had four brothers and two sisters: Jeremy, Mark, Natan (later Antoine), Alexei, Anna and Masha. In his »Biographical Sketch of My Brothers Naum Gabo and Antoine Pevsner« he described his family as »a tightly knit, loving, patriarchal unit«; they described him as »a mischievous daredevil«.[5]

Gabo started his artistic experiments while very young: »My first childish impulse was sculpture. As a child, because we lived in a village, I did not see anything that one would call sculpture. What I *did* see was the silver rouble. On one side of the rouble was a bas relief of the Tsar.«[6] When he was five Gabo tried to scratch something on »the big stone which was outside our house in the wood«.[7] A year later, when he was six, he made his first sculpture: »I loved looking at the face of my father. He was bald and had a fine chiselled profile and I liked to play with a silver coin he once gave me. On the face of that coin was the profile of the Tsar . . . and I got the idea of making the portrait of my father in the same way as the coin.«[8] »I decided to make the portrait out of clay. Not having any clay I broke two bricks, rubbed them together, mixed the dust with water, and made my portrait out of that. Then I hid it.«[9] Sadly the next day Gabo found that the relief had cracked and he admitted »I threw it away – with a broken heart.«[10]

Both of Gabo's parents were Jewish; his mother Fanny Borisovna (née Ozersky) was non-practising, but his father was a Jewish mystic, probably a Kabbalist. Despite his profound religiosity, Gabo's father did not educate his sons in Judaism. Whatever religious education Gabo did receive came from his firmly Russian Orthodox nanny. In 1952 Gabo explained: »Although my father was of the Jewish faith, I as well as my brothers were brought up as Christians.«[11] Through his nanny, Gabo became acquainted with Russian icons: »in our nursery on the wall opposite me hung an icon and in nanny's corner another icon and a lamp that was always lit . . . we went to bed and slept at night and woke up in the morning with its image.«[12] Gabo later avowed that »they made certainly the most decisive . . . impression on me. I still think and feel that in the icons there were the beginnings of my education in painting«.[13]

In 1904, having been expelled from his primary school for composing a rude poem about the headmaster, Gabo was sent to Tomsk in Siberia to stay with his eldest brother Mark who was studying at the Technical Institute there. During the eleven day journey from Bryansk to Tomsk, Gabo was educated by students returning to their studies after the summer vacation: »I learnt a lot from their conversations about various political programmes and parties. I learnt to understand a lot in the brochures that were circulating in the carriages.«[14] Gabo was in Tomsk during the 1905 Revolution and he never forgot the events that followed the publication of the Tsar's manifesto in October 1905:

> there was to be a people's meeting in the theatre. . . . I became curious about what was going on. . . . I followed a group of people to the theatre. . . . I wanted to be with the people; the empty streets frightened me . . . Inside, the whole theatre and the stage were full of people and noise, everyone was talking . . . a student on the stage suddenly warned the crowd that the police and the Black Hundreds were getting ready to approach the theatre from the cathedral and that in the small streets around the square detachments of Cossacks were standing ready to surround the theatre . . . a spasm of silence met the speaker's warning. I stood pressed against the railing surrounding the lower stage – the pressure of the crowd was so great that where I was standing a plank gave way and revealed an entrance large enough for me to see that a dark space lay beyond, and for me to feel the mustiness and the smell of a cellar or basement. I was small and it was not difficult for me to push my way into this darkness. Looking around blindly I saw daylight in the distance. . . . I groped my way towards it and came out into an open courtyard. . . . I went out onto the main street. . . . I saw a grey crowd coming out of the cathedral, led by the Bishop . . . the crowd positioned itself at the theatre's main entrances and exits and surrounded the theatre on all sides. . . . A man suddenly came out of the theatre and plunged into the crowd. I saw how they caught him, I saw how the crowd began to beat him . . . it was clear to me that they were killing him. . . . Inside they understood the danger and barricaded the theatre . . . outside the crowd stopped-up all the exits . . . they set light to the theatre . . . the Cossacks surrounded the theatre. . . . I heard the cries of the dying, the cries of those imprisoned in the burning theatre. . . . I saw how the crowd were shooting those who were standing on the roof and how they were throwing petrol onto the flames. . . . I saw a lot that day . . . but I do not know if I can convey in words the horror that oppressed me and seized my soul for many years. . . . I was fifteen years old and that day and that night I became a revolutionary.[15]

Gabo subsequently returned to Bryansk, acquiring more political education on the journey: »In the carriage of the train from Sibera to Moscow, full of exiles freed by the amnesty, I received lessons on social questions . . . from the participants in the country's revolutionary movement, from their discussions and disquisitions and even from their heated arguments.«[16] In Bryansk during 1906/7 Gabo became involved with an illegal group that was responsible for teaching literacy, distributing literature among the workers, and for »propagandising revolutionary ideas in the country and factories.«[17] The secret library of illegal social-democratic literature was installed in the cellar of an annex to the Pevsner family home where Gabo's older brothers lived (Mark, Jeremy and Antoine): »the steps that led into the cellar led nowhere but served as shelves for the books and proclamations . . . awaiting distribution.«[18] In 1907 Gabo was arrested for political subversion, but within two hours his father, as a prominent local citizen, had secured his release, on the understanding that Gabo would be sent away.

In 1907 Gabo entered the gymnasium in Kursk, graduating in 1910 with a prize for his essay on Gogol. During this period Gabo wrote poems and in 1908 he began to draw and paint: »My first real drawing was done when I had a picture of Hamlet in my mind. But I started drawing from the wrong place – I did the helmet first and there wasn't room on the paper to finish it.«[19] Gabo's early works were done under the influence of Mikhail Vrubel whose paintings and sculptures Gabo had seen in Moscow, in the Morozov Collection when he was a boy.[20]

In the summer of 1910 Gabo's father sent him to Germany to study medicine.[21] After staying two months in Berlin Gabo decided to go to Munich. At his father's

6. »Naum Gabo talks about his work«, *Studio International*, April 1966, p. 127.
7. Read, »Naum Gabo«, Roll 6, p. 7.
8. Naum Gabo, »On Sculpture and Construction in Space«, lecture delivered at Princeton University, 22 April 1975, p. 4, Yale.
9. »Naum Gabo talks about his work«, p. 127.
10. Princeton lecture, p. 4.
11. Naum Gabo, letter to Dr. Karl Schwarz, 19 February 1952, p. 1, Yale. Gabo was probably baptised (Miriam Gabo, »Biographical Notes«).
12. »Autobiographical Fragments«, p. 168.
13. Read, »Naum Gabo«, Roll 1, p. 3. In *Of Divers Arts* Gabo explained the importance of the icon for the development of abstract art in Russia.
14. Pevsner, *A Biographical Sketch*, pp. 3–4; »Autobiographical Fragments«, p. 44.
15. »How I Became a Revolutionary«, pp. 53–71. The events that Gabo described probably took place on 18 October 1905. On 17 October an Imperial Manifesto was published bestowing civil liberties on the entire Russian population, but 18–21 October the Jews and the politically active and progressive Christian elements were attacked by the Black Hundreds: the police and the Imperial troops working in unison. There were 50 attacks against Jews in Russia, and a further 20 attacks on students and intellectuals in places such as Tomsk and Tver (S. M. Dubnow, *History of the Jews in Russia and Poland from the Earliest Times until the Present Day*, Jewish Publication Society of America, Philadelphia, 1920, Vol. 3, pp. 127–131).
16. »Autobiographical Fragments«, p. 126.
17. »How I Became a Revolutionary«, pp. 16–17.
18. »How I Became a Revolutionary«, p. 15.
19. Pevsner, *A Biographical Sketch*, p. 4; Gabo later recalled how the praise of Antoine's friend, Mitaev, made a deep and »fateful« impression on him (Naum Gabo, draft of letter to Antoine Pevsner, n.d., 1946, p. 9, London).

Fig. 1   Gabo at gymnasium age c.14

Fig. 2   Gabo as a student in Munich.

20. S. Frederick Starr and Kenneth Frampton, »Russian Art in Revolution and Emigration: An Interview with Naum Gabo«, 1969, edited transcript, p. 19, Yale.

21. Gabo quoted his father as saying »I have two engineering sons and one an artist; you must be a doctor (»Naum Gabo talks about his work«, p. 127). 552 Russian students were registered at the University of Munich for the 1912–1913 academic year and about 5,000 in the whole of Germany (R. C. Williams, *Culture in Exile: Russian Emigrés in Germany 1881–1941,* University of Cornell Press, Ithaca and London, 1972, p. 25).

22. Princeton lecture, p. 3. Elsewhere Gabo stated that he had studied civil engineering at the Technische Hochschule 1910–1914 (draft letter to Desmond Bernal, [November 1946], p. 3, Yale). The Technische Hochschule's records are unavailable. Information concerning Gabo's studies at Munich University is derived from the registration forms for 1910/11, 1911, 1911/12, 1912/13, 1913/14, and 1914, University of Munich Archive. See also Colin C. Sanderson, »Gabo in Munich«, paper delivered to Association of Art Historians' Conference, London, March 1983.

23. Naum Gabo, letter to Dr. Werner Hofmann, 12 August 1960, and letter to Herbert Read, 25 Jan. 1966, Yale. There is no evidence that Gabo was taught by Theodore Lipps but Gabo did recollect attending some art history seminars by Professor Voss. Gabo did read Worringer's *Abstraction and Empathy,* but not until after 1922 (letter to H. Read, 25 Jan. 1966, Yale).

24. Naum Gabo, letter to Dr. Werner Hofmann, 12 August 1960, Yale.

25. Cleve Gray, »Naum Gabo talks about Constructivism«, *Art in America,* No. 6, 1966, p. 49.

26. Naum Gabo, postcard to Anna Gilman, 19 August 1913, Yale, reproduced in Pevsner, *A Biographical Sketch,* p. 7.

27. Dr. Owen Franklin's and Miriam Gabo's recollections. Gabo evidently did not walk all the way.

28. Pevsner, *A Biographical Sketch,* p. 8.

29. »Naum Gabo talks about his work«, p. 128.

30. Naum Gabo, letter to Professor Giovanni Lista, 31 December 1971, Yale.

insistence, Gabo immediately enrolled at the University of Munich to study medicine and subsequently followed courses in organic chemistry, physiology and anatomy. Two years later he abandoned his medical studies and enrolled for courses in civil-engineering at the Technische Hochschule, courses which he pursued until the outbreak of the First World War in 1914.[22] At the same time Gabo continued to study at the University where in 1912 he changed his registration to philosophy, and took courses in logic, logic and cognition, and Kant's *Critique of Pure Reason.* In 1914 Gabo enrolled for another course on Kant.

In 1913 while still pursuing philosophy Gabo registered for two art history courses: Dr. Wolters' on Greek vase-painting and Dr. Scherman's on Indian art and culture. Gabo recollected later that »the theory of Professor Lipps was very popular amongst the students at that time«, and that »[Worringer's] theories were discussed amongst the students . . . and made a serious impression on me . . . [but] I did not and do not agree with his treatment.«[23]

While he was in Munich Gabo also studied art history under Professor Heinrich Wölfflin. Gabo has stated that it was in 1912 or 1912/1913.[24]. This is possible because Wölfflin arrived at the University of Munich in 1912. Wölfflin's course, however, was not listed on Gabo's registration form for the winter semester of 1912/13, and unfortunately there is no registration form for the 1913 semester. Of course, Gabo could have attended Wölfflin's public lectures without registering, but these would have attracted large numbers and would have been relatively impersonal. It seems most likely that Gabo studied with Wölfflin in the summer of 1913, just before he went to Italy.

Gabo related:

> Quite often I had private meetings with Wölfflin. To a certain extent they were unofficial examinations. Wölfflin was a warm person; his lectures were profound and clear; he was always good to students. One day he said to me, ›You must now go to Italy.‹ At that time I was in conflict with my father; he found out that I was not going to be a doctor. So I said to the professor that I could not afford it. He replied ›If you have no means then you must go *ad pedes apostolorum*.‹ He intended that I should go on *foot.* It shocked me at first, then I decided I might do that. I wrote to my mother for help. I asked Wölfflin to give me an itinerary. He said ›Come back next week.‹ Next week he gave me a list – where to go and what to see. . . . From Munich to Rome, it listed every church, every museum, castle, monastery on the way. He gave me also a letter: ›Such-and-such is my student, show him what he wants to see.‹ It was an open-sesame. I was allowed in everywhere. But I failed. . . . It was too much. I knew what I saw was dead, and I couldn't go on to Rome. I was supposed to give him a report, so from Venice I wrote him a card and said, ›I don't like this town there are no horses here.‹ When I got back, I reported to him; he was at his desk, he held in his hand the card I had sent him and said, ›You think that you have seen Venice? There are horses in Venice – four of them!
>
> It took me a while to understand him. I said to him that I had the impression it was all dead, that it could not go on that way. . . . I disliked the David in Florence, for instance, and I gave him other examples . . . it was *nature* that impressed me, not art. . . . But I must say, without my knowing it, that *ad pedes apostolorum* still has left a trace. I still retain the good works I have seen there. I think their handling of the means, their apporach is valid today too. . . . I look at the masterpieces like absolute things, at the way in which they are composed – which was really what Wölfflin meant.[25]

It is difficult to reconstruct Gabo's itinerary. The trip lasted six weeks, and although he had intended to go to Rome, he only reached Florence where he stayed a week. On 19 August 1913 Gabo wrote from Florence to his sister Anna, »I am very sorry that I have to absorb such a mass of interesting impressions alone. Because of this I am now turning back.«[26] In Venice on 23 August Gabo sent Antoine a postcard without any stamps because he was short of funds. Gabo also visited Pisa and Bologna.[27] Travelling from Italy to Paris he had to stop in Villefranche and write to Alexei to send him some money.[28] Later Gabo said »visiting Italy was like a great shock, seeing Michelangelo and all those works of the Renaissance masters. ›Something has to be done in sculpture‹ I felt. What it was I did not know«.[29]

While in Italy Gabo apparently did not see any contemporary Italian painting or make contact with the Futurists: »My task was to study mainly the classics. I, of course, knew about Cubism and Futurism but at that time they did not attract my interest, and I did not meet any of the leading figures either in Italy or in Paris.«[30] In 1912 and 1913, when he visited Antoine in Paris, Gabo seems to have seen exhibitions and works by contemporary artists, including Picasso, Braque, Gris, Laurens,

Lipchitz, Duchamp-Villon and Archipenko, but he remained dissatisfied with the »unsystematic, accidental, in a sense anarchistic« nature of Cubist space.[31]

Gabo's interest in art history during his stay in Munich was accompanied by an intensification of his own artistic experimentation. While on holiday in Bryansk in 1911 Gabo had spent a lot of time drawing. By 1912 he had begun to draw, paint, and sculpt quite intensively. Alexei recalled that »during the latter years of his study in Munich, away from everyone, he studied not only what he had been sent to study, but also the fine arts, and these, moreover, he studied with even greater zeal.«[32] In the winter of 1912–13 Gabo modelled the *Head of a Negro*.[33]

Despite the increasing importance of Gabo's artistic interests, there is no evidence that he established any links with the art world of Munich during this period. Although there were Russian artists in Munich, such as Kandinsky and Jawlensky, Gabo seems to have had no direct contact with them or with the Blaue Reiter group.[34] Gabo could have visited the Blaue Reiter exhibitions of 1911 and 1912 which included works by Kandinsky, Marc, Macke, Klee, Larionov, Goncharova, and Malevich. He may also have read the *Blaue Reiter Almanach*; certainly in 1913 he did read Kandinsky's *Concerning the Spiritual in Art*.[35] Gabo was evidently aware of the artistic theories being debated in Munich. He later wrote: »artistc life in Munich was preoccupied with a new idea of art, on a deeper, more philosophical level. The idea of non-objective (abstract) art was very seriously discussed.«[36]

In Munich Gabo seems to have pursued art, philosophy and science with almost equal energy: »Up to the war it was this way: I knew it had to be sculpture, but it had to be a totally different sculpture. And it had to express a new way of looking at the universe. A new feeling was already going through the universities and among the intellectuals. There was a feeling of time and space, a movement in men's minds. For instance, I will never forget when I was present at a gathering of scientists and students, in well, about 1911 or 1912 – one of the professors was talking of Einstein's theory. I myself was then studying physics.«[37]

While in Munich Gabo also pursued his political interests and belonged to a Russian student society: »We were a group of Russian students, mainly socialist and we were inviting lecturers in all fields.«[38] Gabo was a member of the committee that organised the lectures in the small hall of a German tavern. Among the speakers they invited in the winter of 1911–12 was Lev Trotsky. Gabo had been deputised to meet and look after Trotsky, but was not particularly impressed by Trotsky's appearance or his oratory. The lecture, about ethics and revolution or terror and revolution, was unmemorable. Later Gabo recalled: »No, I would not have followed him to the barricades that evening and I shirked from my duty of taking him to the flat where he was to spend the night. . . . I was disappointed. I had expected the former president of the Committee of Worker's Deputies of the First Russian Revolution and I met an absent-minded lecturer.«[39]

In April 1914 Gabo returned to Bryansk and spent a great deal of time painting. In May he escorted his mother to Berlin and returned to Munich. Gabo had been living in Planegg, a small village just outside of Munich, since 1913 and in July 1914 Alexei joined him there.[40] Shortly afterwards, when war was declared, the brothers left Munich. They were arrested *en route* for Hamburg, but managed to secure permission to travel to Copenhagen. After receiving money from home, they left Denmark and by October 1914 had arrived in Norway.[41]

Norway represented a peaceful interlude. There Gabo was able to assimilate and synthesize the ideas and impressions that he had gained from his period in Germany. Gabo later wrote: »I spent the First World War, from its beginning in 1914 until April 1917, in Norway, in the neutral peace of its fjords, amongst a peaceful and hospitable people, in the perfect peace for me to work on my constructions.«[42] Gabo recalled that in Norway he »found the peace necessary for creativity and for my rebirth from an engineer into a sculptor«. »I stopped reading the newspapers, my aversion to the war strengthened. . . . The longer the war continued the more I immersed myself in the depths of my spatial constructions. . . . I lived as if not on the earth, but in the space above the fjords.«[43] In Christiania (now Oslo), in the winter of 1915–1916 Gabo produced his *Constructed Head No. 1*.[44] Gabo explained: »I took

31. Read, »Naum Gabo«, Roll 2, p. 1; and Herbert Read, »Introduction« in *Naum Gabo: Constructions, Paintings, Drawings,* Arts Council of Great Britain at the Tate Gallery, London, 15 March–15 April 1966, p. 3. Archipenko had become a close friend of Antoine's in Kiev but Gabo said »I never met Archipenko myself« (»Naum Gabo talks about his work«, p. 128.

32. Pevsner, *A Biographical Sketch*, pp. 6, 8.

33. Naum Gabo, letter to Ronald Johnson, 13 May 1965, Yale. See *Catalogue Raisonné of the Constructions and Sculptures of Naum Gabo,* No. 1.

34. Naum Gabo, letter to Herbert Read, 25 January 1966, Yale. In a biography prepared for Miss Dreier in 1949 Gabo stated that he had been in contact with Kandinsky and the Blaue Reiter Group, but he did not repeat this elsewhere. Gabo stated repeatedly that he first met Kandinsky in Russia in 1917 (letter to Ronald Johnson, 13 May 1965).

35. H. Read, »Introduction«, p. 3.

36. Read, »Naum Gabo«, Roll 1, p. 6.

37. »Naum Gabo talks about his work«, p. 128. Gabo attended lectures on Einstein's theory and recalled that »Einstein's principle was discussed among the dons, among the professors, and among the students.« (Read, »Naum Gabo«, Roll. 1, p. 6).

38. Read, »Naum Gabo«, Roll 3, p. 6.

39. Naum Gabo, Diary, 23 August 1940, London.

40. Pevsner, *A Biographical Sketch*, p. 9. Registration form for winter semester 1913/14, University of Munich Archive.

41. Naum Gabo, Diary, 22 April 1977, London.

42. »Autobiographical Fragments«, p. 14.

43. Ibid., p. 16.

44. Pevsner, *A Biographical Sketch*, p. 14.

Fig. 3   Naum Gabo and Alexei Pevsner in Copenhagen, August 1914.

Fig. 4 Naum Gabo and Alexei Pevsner in Norway, c. 1915.

45. Naum Gabo, letter to Willi Sandberg, 12 March 1963, Yale.
46. »Autobiographical Fragments«, pp. 25–6. By this time, Gabo stated that he had made contact with artists in Christiania.
47. Alexei Pevsner Interview with Colin Sanderson, November 1979, Transcript, Family Archive London, p. 4. See *Catalogue Raisonné*, No. 40.
48. »Autobiographical Fragments«, pp. 1–2. Elsewhere Gabo recollected: »we got a telegram from our parents telling us to come home« (Read, »Naum Gabo«, Roll 2, p. 3).
49. »Autobiographical Fragments«, p. 12.
50. »Autobiographical Fragments«, pp. 25–29.
51. »Autobiographical Fragments«, pp. 36–40.
52. »Autobiographical Fragments«, p. 73.
53. »Autobiographical Fragments«, p. 80; Read, »Naum Gabo«, Roll 2, p. 4.
54. Read, »Naum Gabo«, Roll 2, p. 41.
55. Miriam Gabo, »Biographical Notes«; and Read, »Naum Gabo.« Roll 2, p. 5.
56. Ibid. Travelling conditions were such that their clothes had to be fumigated when they arrived.
57. Read, »Naum Gabo«, Roll 2, pp. 5–6.
58. Naum Gabo, »The ›Kinetic Construction of 1920‹«, *Studio International*, September 1969, p. 89.

on the name of Gabo when I decided that art was my real vocation . . . in Norway in 1915 when I signed my name to the first *Constructed Head*. I did it in order to distinguish my work from that of my brother, Antoine, who was already a painter.[45]

The brothers (Antoine had joined them in December 1915), spent the summers at the Sogne Fjord, near Bergen, where Gabo and Antoine had a studio in the annex of the Kvickness Hotel.[46] In Christiania, while Antoine painted and Gabo worked on his constructions, Alexei studied medicine at the University. In the winter they skied on weekends. In the summer of 1916 they spent a month in Copenhagen, and after they returned to Christiania in August 1916, Gabo made his second *Head*.[47]

Gabo's artistic production was interrupted by the February Revolution of 1917. Later Gabo wrote »I returned to Russia from Norway only because the Revolution had happened. . . . From that peaceful distance the Revolution seemed to me to be some kind of heavenly radiance, a token of fate presaging a new life, a new earth, a new people in my homeland . . . nothing except the Revolution could have induced me to interrupt my work. . . . How could I stay away from my homeland when there was such rejoicing there . . . within a week we were in Petrograd.«[48] They travelled via Stockholm and the north of Sweden to the Finnish border (Haparanda) and from there to Petrograd:

> We arrived in Haparanda . . . a strange picture unfolded before us. . . . There were red banners on poles, on wagons, the whole station was in red, everyone had red arm bands on their sleeves, on their weapons, and everyone had weapons on their shoulders. . . . I had forgotten that half the world was immersed in the fire and bloodshed of a cruel war. . . . We stood there . . . with our clothes and belongings we looked so different to the military personnel walking about on the platform. . . . I remembered my youth when the image of the Revolution was for me, as for my peers, a golden dream.[49]

There was a problem about their documents and the brothers were sent under armed escort to Petrograd where Mark met them. Having been questioned by a committee, the brothers were eventually released thanks to Mark's intervention: »We left the station depressed . . . what was happening to us? A nightmare? Or a holiday?«[50] Mark explained that Antoine had been mistaken for a German spy by the name of Pevsner, who was living in Christiania. Suspicions had been aroused by Antoine's prolonged stay in Norway when ostensibly he had gone there to purchase machines for his father's factory.

The following day Gabo was awakened by noises in the street:

> It was not simply a crowd going along the street, but a demonstration densely packed with red flags and posters displaying the slogans »All Power to the Soviets« and »Down with Milyukov«. Workers in warm sheepskin jackets, soldiers in overcoats without guns, and Cossacks with guns on horseback with red flags . . . houses decorated with red flags. . . . I gazed dumbfounded. . . . The Revolution! . . . dressing quickly, without eating or drinking, I went out into the street, I plunged into the demonstration. That day was my real baptism into the Revolution. It was the first time I had taken part in a demonstration. . . . It was as if I had been born again. . . . The Revolution was in me.[51]

After a week in Petrograd during which Gabo did not have any contact with the artistic life of the city but »walked around the streets from morning until evening«, the brothers returned to Bryansk.[52] They did not stay long: Alexei had to finish his studies, Antoine wanted to return to his studio in Moscow, and Gabo wanted to find a studio there. Having fortunately failed his medical examination for the army, Gabo went to Moscow in the summer of 1917.[53] By this time »the revolution was spreading deeper into the whole life, into every sinew and fibre of the body and mind of the people.«[54] Law and order were beginning to break down and bands of brigands were roaming the countryside. Gabo took the precaution of travelling with a gun.[55]

While in Russia from 1917 to 1922 Gabo lived almost entirely in Moscow. He occasionally stayed with Anna Gilman, his sister, in Serpukhov and during the Civil War he or Antoine would go there every week to collect a sack of potatoes on which they lived for the rest of the week.[56] It was a time of immense hardships, but also of great activity: »The main character of our life was deteriorating from day to day. We were hungry, we were freezing, there was disorder, but Moscow inside lived and worked in spite of all that . . . we worked on our art.«[57] In the winter of 1919–20, at »the height of the civil war, hunger and disorder in Russia« Gabo managed to complete *Kinetic Construction*.[58]

In 1918 Gabo met Lenin. The Monument to Alexander III had been demolished and the site was being dedicated to a revolutionary statue: «We talked with Lenin and . . . he made a speech for about 10 minutes . . . a homely thing in the middle of Moscow. . . . Nobody knew about it. We were about . . . 50 people in all, maybe less . . . this is the one time I met him.«[59]

During the bitter winter of 1918–1919 Gabo and Alexei were apparently living in the Pertsov apartment house, near the Church of the Redeemer in Moscow.[60] When the government moved to Moscow the building, with the exception of the artist's studios, was commandeered by the general staff of the Red Army. Gabo recalled: »Only a few months later they began to hanker after the studios as well, trying to evict us also, which they did not manage to do thanks to our persistent petitioning of Trotsky and his favourable response to our arguments. I was one of the mediators together with Tatyshev and then with Natan Altman. That winter (it was 1918), I saw Trotsky almost every day over a period of several weeks.«[61] Gabo described his first conversation with Trotsky:

> One could say that our meeting was of a domestic nature. The house was not heated. In our studios the pipes had burst like shells. There was not one bucket, nor one uncracked pot and the ice on the floor was like a skating rink. In Trotsky's office it was no warmer. He sat, huddled up on a stool at the end of the table, half turned towards an electric fire that was standing close to his feet. . . he sat and worked in his fur coat. The cold was oppressive. . . . I think that he was glad of an opportunity to leave his work for a while, to rub his hands, to stretch his legs, to have a talk and to get warm. . . . I explained that we heated our stoves with books. . . that Leskov and Chekhov burn well . . . with a bitter smile he advised me to go to the commandant and petition for an allocation of firewood. . . . he wrote an order to the commandant on a piece of paper to leave us artists in peace and not to touch the studios. . . . Very soon after this Trotsky moved . . . leaving us to the mercy of the General Staff.[62]

Ultimately the artists lost the battle, and in early 1920 Gabo and his brother moved to Rozhdestvenskii Boulevard.

Gabo evidently identified with the Revolution quite sincerely. He stressed that »we and the leaders at the beginning of the Revolution were idealists of the highest order« and he added that »of us in the arts . . . only very few were members of the Party, but . . . [we] accepted the whole thing sympathetically.«[63] Indeed Gabo described himself as »one of the hundreds of artists in Moscow, possessed by the new vision of a new life.«[64] Gabo was immersed in the avant-garde activity that accompanied the Revolution. He knew Malevich, Tatlin, Rozanova, Udaltsova, Drevin, Popova, Rodchenko, the Vesnin brothers, Lissitzky, Melnikov and Ladovsky. Like them, he was inspired by dreams of revolution, by dreams of creating a new world, a new society and a new art. Like them, Gabo co-operated in running the artistic life of the country for the revolutionary regime: »at the beginning of the Revolution we were all working with the government.«[65] Yet it is very difficult to ascertain the precise extent of Gabo's involvement with the Department of Fine Arts (IZO) of the People's Commissariat for Enlightenment, run by Lunacharsky. Gabo's description of his work at IZO suggests a wide-ranging activity: »We did not have only to buy or sell works, we had to deal with education, changing programmes in the schools, deciding where art schools should be built . . . we had to work out some kind of a method for a relationship between the state and the artists.« And »we were also participating in work for certain festivals, 1st May . . . 17th October.«[66]

Gabo certainly had some contact with the Museums Bureau. In 1920 the Bureau purchased Gabo's *Constructed Torso* and later a brass version of *Constructed Head No. 3*.[67] Earlier, in 1919, Gabo had apparently been a member of the Bureau's purchasing commission. This body visited artists and selected works for purchase. The works were then bought and prices agreed in a meeting where, as Gabo recalled, »all the best artists got good prices.«[68] During this process Gabo was visited by Smirnov, »a sincere man and a devoted communist«, but an untalented artist. He suggested that mediocre artists should be paid more than talented artists. He reasoned: »We are the spiritual proletarians, we are deprived by Nature of the advantages you have. It is easy for you to produce excellent work, much more easy than it is for me. . . . Therefore you must be paid less and I must be paid more.«[69]

Gabo was apparently also involved in editing the journal *IZO*: »[Shterenberg, head of IZO] said, ›We are organising a journal, IZO. I am editor and would like you to be

59. Read, »Naum Gabo«, Roll 3, pp. 5–6. Such dedications were part of Lenin's Plan of Monumental Propaganda to educate the masses. The monument to Alexander III (erected 1912), was situated to the north-east of the Church of the Redeemer. Gabo did not see Lenin when he visited the VKhUTEMAS in 1921.

60. Starr and Frampton, »Russian Art«, p. 5. The Pertsov House, built 1905–7 in the Neo-Russian style, is on Soimonovskii Proezd, between Kropotkinskaya Naberezhnaya and Kursovoi Pereulok. Gabo stated that the house in question was on Lesnoi Pereulok (Gabo, letter to L. Sjoborg, 15 August 1960, Yale). It was on Lesnoi Proezd (later renamed Soimonovskii). In 1962 Gabo showed Miriam Gabo the Pertsov house as the building where he had had his studio.

61. Diary, 23 August 1940.

62. Ibid.

63. Read, »Naum Gabo«, Roll 3, p. 2 and Roll 2, p. 6.

64. Diary, 23 August 1940.

65. Read, »Naum Gabo«, Roll 5, p. 4.

66. Read, »Naum Gabo«, Roll 2, pp. 5–6.

67. The purchase of *Torso* is documented (State Archives of Literature and Art, Moscow, fond 665, ed. khr. 23, list 5v and fond 665, ed. khr. 14, list 84; information courtesy of Peter Nisbet). The purchase of *Head in a Corner Niche* is based on statements by Gabo (letter to Alfred H. Barr Jr, 20 January 1948, Yale). See *Catalogue Raisonné*, Nos. 6.3, 5.

68. Read, »Gabo«, Roll 5, p. 5.

69. Naum Gabo, letter to Herbert Read, 24 June 1958, p. 2, Yale.

70. Starr and Frampton, »Russian Art«, p. 5. It is difficult to identify this journal. It might be *Izobrazitelnoe Iskusstvo* (*Fine Art*; I issue, 1919); *Iskusstvo: Vestnik IZO* (*Art: Bulletin of IZO*; 8 issues, 1919); or *Iskusstvo* (*Art*; 6 issues, 1918, edited by Kandinsky). All of them were published by the Moscow IZO, but none of them carry Gabo's name as an editor.

71. Starr and Frampton, »Russian Art«, p. 5; Abram Lassaw and Ilya Bolotowsky, »Russia and Constructivism: An Interview with Naum Gabo«, *Gabo, Constructions, Sculpture, Paintings, Drawings, Engravings* (Lund Humphries, London, 1957), p. 157.

72. Starr and Frampton, »Russian Art« pp. 3–4. Antoine Pevsner recalled that he had 150 students in his studio. »Propos d'un sculpteur: Interview d'Antoine Pevsner par Rosamond Bernier«, *L'Oeil*, No. 23, November 1956, p. 30. Among Gabo's students were Klutsis, Menkhen, Shapiro, and Statsky (Starr and Frampton, »Russian Art« p. 11).

73. Naum Gabo, letter to James Johnson Sweeney, 8 September 1948, p. 4, Yale.

74. Lassaw and Bolotowsky, »Russia and Constructivism«, p. 158.

75. Ibid.

co-editor with me. I am also inviting Rodchenko.‹ I said fine. So we started *IZO* together; it took time, a lot of time . . . the format was big. The journal was under the Commissariat of Enlightenment. Only in this way was I connected with the government.«[70]

Gabo was active as a teacher, although he did not hold any official teaching position at the Moscow State Free Art Studios set up in 1918, nor in the Higher State Artistic and Technical Workshops, the VKhUTEMAS, organised in 1920. Shterenberg invited Gabo to take over the Sculpture and Ceramics workshop but Gabo refused unless sculpture was separated from ceramics: »I disagreed with the merging of the two departments and . . . I did not know anything about ceramics.«[71] Gabo nevertheless maintained a close relationship to the school:

> The VKhUTEMAS was a free academy . . . some had studios, but nobody got more bread and more herrings than the rest. . . . There were lectures and constant discussions in the studios. Rodchenko would come in, or someone like that, or even Tatlin . . . there were a great many students and up to a thousand people sometimes attended in the great auditorium. . . . I had no studio in the VKhUTEMAS and was not a member of it. . . . My brother had a studio and we used it as if we were one man. . . . I did some teaching . . . the students very often invited me to give lectures and what you would call seminars. And students often visited me.[72]

Gabo evidently participated quite actively in the various heated debates that punctuated and indeed flavoured the artistic life of the period. He stressed that »it was in those years from 1917 to 1920 that the Constructive movement as an ideology developed in full.«[73] In July 1920 Gabo wrote *The Realistic Manifesto* that was published in August to accompany his exhibition on Tverskoi Boulevard. In the manifesto Gabo proclaimed time and space as the backbone of constructive art and asserted »the value of art as an independent means of expression«.[74] Gabo was implicitly criticising the emerging stance of those artists, including Tatlin, who later formed the First Working Group of Constructivists and who wanted to make utilitarian objects not works of art. At the same time, Gabo was also attacking the propaganda-inspired realism advocated by the Party. Gabo did not use the term »realistic« to facilitate publication of the manifesto (although it inevitably did), but to convey the conviction »that what we were doing represented a new reality«.[75] The ideas of *The Realistic Manifesto* remained, with modifications, the basis of Gabo's »constructive« approach to art, until the end of his life.

Fig. 5 The Realistic Manifesto, Moscow, 1920.

During the Tverskoi Boulevard exhibition, the VKhUTEMAS students organised a meeting to discuss the problem of »Where to Now?«: Malevich told the meeting: »If you want to see the way we must go from here you should go and look at the exhibition by Gabo and the rest of them on Tverskoi Boulevard. You will see that those works are a step forward.«[76] At this meeting Gabo warned the productivists that »If you . . . deny the importance of art you will reach a point where . . . the working class will cut out prints from the newspaper and hang them on the wall, and you will have the academicians back.«[77]

In December 1920 the VKhUTEMAS's Cézanne Club organised a meeting to discuss Tatlin's Monument to the Third International, then on exhibition in Moscow during the Eighth Congress of the Soviets. At this meeting the difference between Gabo and Tatlin »developed into a real fight.«[78] Gabo spoke after Brik and Maya-kovsky:

> The question was whether or not the Tower should be built. I quite calmly started to say that for God's sake I would do everything to let the thing be built. ›But I should also tell you what I think about it‹, I said. Tatlin was sitting right there, not saying a word. ›Forgive me‹, I asked him, because I had already told him personally what I thought about the whole thing. I told the audience that the Tower was a medieval idea . . . [like] the Tower of Babel. . . . There was one way in which this new tower was probably different – the idea of the moving parts. But these were absolute nonsense. ›You know perfectly well‹, I said to them, ›that such a thing is technically out of the question, it is not that it cannot be built, but that it never will be built. You don't turn a six or seven or ten story building to follow the sun.‹[79]

By 1921 and the end of the Civil War, the government, which had previously toler-ated the avant-garde, was able to reassert its own ideas for a realistic art that the people would understand, an art accessible to the people, »an art of five kopecks«.[80] Gabo was disillusioned; he explained to Shterenberg and Lunacharsky that he wanted to leave. They supported his request and Shterenberg offered Gabo the job of helping to organize the Erste Russische Kunstausstellung which was to open in Berlin in October 1922. In the Spring of 1922 Gabo left Russia.[81]

> The very same day that I left Moscow in a train taking me to Riga, the capital of Latvia, on my way to Berlin, my fellow traveller in the carriage introduced himself as a journalist with a German newspaper. He declared that he knew me, who I was in Moscow, and he offered to introduce me to the editor-in-chief of the newspaper where he worked if I would agree to write a series of articles about what I knew of life in Moscow during the Revolution. . . . This would arouse a great deal of interest in Berlin‹, he assured me, ›and it would be well paid‹. Horrified, I refused and having thanked the stranger for his kindness, I retreated into the corridor where I stood all the way to Riga.[82]

For Gabo the years 1917–1922 had been rich but also »full of painful and rather tragic experiences«.[83] When Gabo did eventually put pen to paper about his life in Russia and started writing his autobiography he was 85.

76. Starr and Frampton, »Russian Art«, p. 11.
77. Ibid.
78. Ibid., p. 8. This meeting and Gabo's criticism were also recorded by N. Khardzhiev, »Maya-kovskii i Tatlin«, *Neue russische Literatur: Almanach* (Salzburg, 1978), p. 90.
79. Starr and Frampton, »Russian Art«, ibid., p. 9.
80. Ibid., p. 13.
81. Ibid., p. 14–15.
82. »Autobiographical Fragments«, p. 2.
83. Naum Gabo, letter to Norman Reid, 19 July 1973, p. 1, Yale.

Conceptions of Sculpture: Gabo and Paris in 1937

Jörn Merkert

1 The various events of 1937 are the subject of an exhibition being prepared for 1987 by the Kunstsammlung Nordrhein-Westfalen and other institutions in Düsseldorf: *50 Years Ago – Europe on the Eve of the Second World War.*
2 All quotations are from Adolf Hitler, ›Rede zur Eröffnung des Hauses der Deutschen Kunst‹, in *Führer durch die Ausstellung Entartete Kunst,* Munich, 1937.

Seen together, certain individual events of 1937, however unconnected they may at first appear, combine to give a picture of the varied intellectual, cultural and political landscape of Europe on the eve of the Second World War.[1] A few of these events will be recalled here in order to provide a wider background against which to view some aspects of Naum Gabo's life and work.

On 18 July 1937 Adolf Hitler opened the ›Haus der Deutschen Kunst‹ with a speech guaranteed to send shivers down the spines of attentive listeners. The exhibition of National Socialist painting – or what this was officially held to be – aimed at revealing, for the first time, »a cultural rebirth« through art which »can reckon with the most joyful and heartfelt approval from the healthy broad mass of the people«. Hitler's speech was equally concerned with another exhibition which stood in demagogic opposition to the first; it opened the following day in the Munich Hofgarten – the ›Degenerate Art‹ exhibition. Put together from works confiscated from German museums, this second exhibition was intended to demonstrate the »Jewification« of modern art, to denounce its practitioners as »artistic Bolshevists« and lunatics, and to »clear away the clichés from German artistic life, just as we have from the field of politics«.[2]

Following on from the signal given by the burning of books on 10 May 1933, this was another important stage (and one which was noted abroad) in a series of actions which now included systematic attacks on the visual arts. Individual artists were being hampered and persecuted, threatened and restricted in Germany even before the Nazis reached power. In 1932, for instance, Storm Troopers had visited the studio of the Russian Jew, Naum Gabo, who thereupon left the country. He fled to Paris, which he knew from previous visits and where his brother, Antoine Pevsner, had already been working for some time.

Figs. 1 and 2   The German and Soviet-Russian pavilions facing each other across the Champ de Mars – Contemporary postcards, Paris 1937

On 26 April 1937 German bombers came to the aid of the Fascists in the Spanish Civil War, destroying the small town of Guernica in the process. From 1 May to mid-June of that year Pablo Picasso, commissioned by the young Spanish Republic to contribute to the Spanish pavilion at the Paris World Fair, painted his indictment of Franco's Fascists. His vision was of the horrors of war in general and a pictorial protest against violence and destruction, suffering and death. The huge painting *Guernica* dominated the large main room of the exhibition building. Compared to other buildings at the World Fair, the Spanish pavilion, designed by José-Luis Sert, was avant-garde architecture.[3]

The Fair, which ran from the summer to the autumn of 1937 on the Champs de Mars around the Eiffel Tower, developed into a series of national demonstrations using architecture and the visual arts. It offered an international survey of the conflicting ideologies of the time.

Next to the Spanish pavilion, close to the bank of the Seine, stood the pavilion of National Socialist Germany (fig. 1) and opposite it that of Stalin's Soviet Union. Their skyscraper-like fronts, towering pompously over everything except the Eiffel Tower itself, were crowned on the one side by Schmidt-Ehmen's enormous imperial eagle, symbolising the Nazis' claims to imperial power, and on the other side with a pair of figures by the Soviet sculptor Mukhina, wielding hammer and sickle, as they stormed triumphantly upwards into the future (fig. 2).

The Aviation pavilion represented a completely different kind of architecture. In this steel-framed building of glass Robert Delaunay hung a large space and color construction of ellipses, which dominated the high dome with its encircling curves and intersections (fig. 3). A real aeroplane hovered in the middle of this ›sculpture‹, the construction of ellipses emphasizing its energy and its speed in space. When illuminated at night, this optimistic symbol of faith in the progress offered by modern technology could be seen from afar, shining through the glass architecture. Delaunay also designed the murals for the Railway pavilion.[4]

In a wider sense it is possible to connect these French pavilions on general themes of the World Fair – as well as the Norwegian, Swedish, Belgian and Spanish pavilions – with the new conceptions of architecture developed at the Bauhaus in Dessau, which had already been forced to close by the Nazis in 1933. However, one is tempted to associate the buildings commissioned by the French state for the right bank of the Seine (for example the Musée d'art Moderne and the Palais de Chaillot on the Trocadéro) with the kind of architecture which Fascism (but not only Fascism) favoured; an architectural form which seemed set to become the international style of the time.

3 Also exhibited in the Spanish pavilion were a sculpture by Picasso and works by González, Miró and Calder.

4 Delaunay's designs for the Aviation and Railway pavilions are in the Konstmuseet, Arkiv för Dekorativ Konst, Lund (Sweden).

5 See the article in the present catalogue by Steven A. Nash, ›Naum Gabo: Sculptures of Purity and Possibility‹, p. 33.

6 Gabo and Pevsner held their first independent one-man-exhibition in Paris in 1924 in the Galerie Percier, where González also exhibited.

7 All quotations are from Naum Gabo, ›The Constructive Idea in Art‹, in Naum Gabo, Leslie Martin and Ben Nicholson (eds), *Circle: International Survey of Constructive Art,* London, 1937. Italics are the present author's.

Fig. 3   The Aviation pavilion at the Paris World Fair, with Robert Delaunay's space construction, 1937

Fig. 4   Room XIV in the exhibition *Origines et Développement de l'Art International Indépendent* in the Musée du Jeu de Paume, Paris, 1937

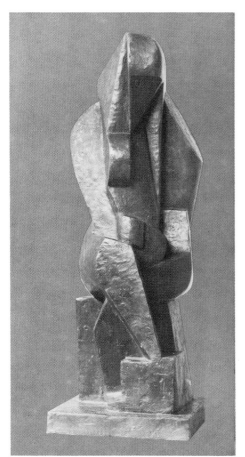

Fig. 5   Jacques Lipchitz, *Baigneuse assise,* 1916 Marlborough Gallery, New York

By 1937 Naum Gabo had already been living in London for two years. Unlike his brother Pevsner, he had not succeeded in gaining a real foothold in Paris during his three-year stay, despite his active involvement in the activities of the artistic metropolis, through membership of the group ›Abstraction – Création‹.[5] Gabo's decision to leave in 1935 was probably dictated by more than purely personal considerations. Artistic issues in the Paris of the early 1930s were dominated to a very large extent by Cubism and Surrealism, both of which had achieved a great international reputation, and by the abstract painting developing from them. These artistic avenues meant little to Gabo.

Gabo's conception of art aimed ultimately at transforming the world. In Paris he again found himself largely isolated – a lone wolf – notwithstanding the presence of Pevsner, Mondrian, Seuphor and Domela. In Paris at that time the avant-garde in sculpture consisted of Picasso, Lipchitz, Laurens and Archipenko, as well as Brancusi, Duchamp-Villon, Calder and González, although González seldom exhibited and hardly associated with the artistic circles of Montparnasse.[6] These names represent a type of sculpture which, in quite disparate ways, sought to make the formal principles of Cubism and Surrealism a fruitful source of three-dimensional art. It was far removed from the radical standpoint formulated by Gabo in the Moscow *Realistic Manifesto* of 1920, a standpoint by no means unknown in Paris since the first issue of the periodical *Abstraction – Création* had published the manifesto's most important demands in 1932. With its striving after revolutionary renewal, this view of art's possibilities and requirements certainly occupied a significant place in the artistic discussions in Paris – and hence in international debates too, promoted by the diverse nationalities of the artists listed above. Yet the views prevailing among the recognized avant-garde were diametrically opposed to Gabo's Constructivism.

In his article *The Constructive Idea in Art,* published in London in 1937, Gabo expressed this quite clearly.[7] He saw Cubism as comparable to the recent discoveries in physics, praising it as »a revolution . . . directed against the fundamental basis of art«. At the same time he declared Cubism to be insufficient, since upheavals in all fields, including the social, had led to the disintegration of *all* existing orders. With unbroken optimism he stated that »in the realm of ideas we are now entering on the period of reconstruction«. Science and art were therefore charged with the »construction of a new stable model for our apprehension of the universe«. The constructive idea seemed to him the most suitable, because it represented a general concept of the world which was valid for *all* domains of the new culture. Hence his art not merely reflected this concept of the world, but was a part of its »reality«, since content and form are one in the constructive idea.

Just how much Gabo thereby defined not only his own position, but also reflected, with critical precision, the intentions of the Cubist sculptors, is made clear by two quotations. Looking back, Jacques Lipchitz stated:

Cubism was not a school, not an aesthetic theory and on no account simply an artistic tendency: it was a new way of looking at the world. Cubism searched for a new way to depict *nature,* for a *mode of expression* appropriate to our time. The spirit of Cubism represented a search for a new formal structure.[8]

Julio González disassociated himself from the wholly non-figurative works of the Constructivists in a somewhat more polemical vein:

One will not produce great art by making perfect circles and squares with the aid of compass and ruler, or by drawing one's inspiration from New York skyscrapers. The truly novel works, which often look bizarre, are, quite simply, those which are directly inspired by *nature,* and executed with love and sincerity.[9]

The conflict between these conceptions and Gabo's were strikingly evident in an exhibition held in the Jeu de Paume at the same time as the World Fair. Under the title *Origines et Développement de l'Art International Indépendant – De Cézanne à l'Art Non Figurativ* the avant-garde exhibited its own view of itself, including those sources of modern art which it held to have influenced the development of twentieth-century art. Sculptures, masks and fetishes from Polynesia, Oceania, New Zealand and Africa were thus seen alongside works by Cézanne, van Gogh, Gauguin, Seurat and Rousseau. Contemporary sculpture occupied a surprisingly subordinate position, with the catalogue mentioning a mere nine sculptors.[10]

The exhibition unintentionally turned into an impressive counter-demonstration in celebration of the ›degenerate‹ art then being denounced in Munich. Of course it was no accident that many of the artists, of various nationalities, were represented in both exhibitions. In seeking refuge from Nazi persecution they had gravitated to Paris, the metropolis of the arts.

Whereas the introductory texts in the exhibition catalogue attempted systematic groupings according to style, in the exhibition Purism, Neo-Plasticism, Dadaism, Surrealism, Constructivism and non-figurative art were all shown together in the spacious rooms XIV and XV of the Jeu de Paume (fig. 4). Four pieces of sculpture – by Lipchitz, Pevsner, González and Gabo – dominated one of the rooms, in front of pictures by Kandinsky, Delaunay, Miró, Tanguy, Ernst and Klee. The sculptures demonstrated the variety of conceptions outlined above.

In very different ways both Lipchitz and González translated into sculpture the formal principles developed previously by Cubist painters. Lipchitz pursued the basic idea of reducing figurative forms to elementary geometric and stereometric ones. This led to an abstraction of the human figure, consisting of a structure of intersecting volumes. Individual forms slide out of or into others, in a construction of tectonic rhythms. The structure produced by the traditional sculptural methods, of adding to or removing from a central core, remains intact. Through the planar nature of its geometric elements, this sculpture in the Jeu de Paume acquired a relief-like character. It was not a work to be viewed from all sides and, significantly, was placed in front of a wall (fig. 5).[11]

A centralized repose and a statue-like severity emphasize the architectonic quality of such ›Cubist‹ sculpture which, however, works against one of Cubism's basic concerns. In Cubist painting, various angles from which an object is viewed are combined on the picture plane, producing simultaneous multiple viewpoints. Yet Lipchitz's figure is clothed in a formal framework which at many points leaves the object altogether, tending towards flatness and thus towards relief. Since the forms have been arrived at through abstraction – a formal reduction of the object – we may recognize in this the »new formal structure« and »new way of depicting nature« Lipchitz was striving for.[12]

González approached these problems from a quite different angle, especially in his *Femme au miroir* of 1937 (fig. 6). Welded wrought iron, a material he was the first sculptor to use, enabled him to introduce another Cubist discovery into sculpture – the collage. A piece of sculpture no longer needed to be carved from a block or modelled in plaster or clay but could be assembled in space from a number of components. As in a collage, *objets trouvés* could be combined with individually prepared or treated elements. The traces of such treatment remained as a particular means of expression; the creative process becoming part and parcel of a personal

Fig. 6   Julio González, *Femme au miroir,* 1937 González Estate, Paris

8 J. Johnson Sweeny, ›An Interview with Jacques Lipchitz‹, *Partisan Review,* XII, 1945, pp. 83 ff. Italics are the present author's.

9 Julio González, *Picasso sculpteur et les cathedrales,* 1931; first published as Julio González, ›Picasso sculpteur‹, *Cahiers d'Art,* Paris, 1936, and quoted here according to Josephine Withers, *Julio González, Sculpture in Iron,* New York, 1978, Appendix I, p. 136.

10 The exhibition was organized by a committee which included Georges Braque, Paul Eluard, Fernand Léger, Louis Marcoussis, Henri Matisse, Pablo Picasso and Christian Zervos. The sculptors mentioned as represented in the exhibition are Brancusi, Calder, Duchamp-Villon, Gabo, González, Laurens, Lipchitz, Pevsner and Picasso.

11 The photograph reproduced here shows what is without doubt a sculpture by Lipchitz near the door of the room. However, it cannot be identified with certainty and since the catalogue contains no detailed information I have selected a sculpture as close as possible to the one in the photograph. The catalogue, which is not always accurate in its datings, lists as no. 78 *A Bathing Woman* of 1918 by Lipchitz.

12 See Jörn Merkert, ›Jacques Lipchitz und das Problem des Kubismus in der Skulptur‹, in the exhib. cat. *Jacques Lipchitz – Skulpturen und Zeichnungen 1911–1969,* Nationalgalerie, Berlin, 1970.

13 See Jörn Merkert, »Spintisierende Eisenklitterei« oder »Die Risiken individueller Erfahrung« – Ein (nicht nur) erfundener Bericht über den Umgang mit Widersprüchen im Werk von Julio González‹, in the exhib. cat. *Julio González 1876–1942 – Plastiken, Zeichnungen, Kunstgewerbe*, Akademie der Künste, Berlin, 1983.

artistic language. A central core is thus abandoned in favour of a construction using empty space as volume. Moreover, individual elements, often linear or flat and thus lacking volume, could be viewed from different sides and angles through the pierced construction.

Moving round the figure, the beholder can experience new and unexpected combinations in the links and overlappings of individual components: surfaces become edges and are perceived as lines, while widely spaced elements sometimes close to form self-contained plastic bodies. Each detail remains abstract in itself. A single main view no longer exists. By moving round the object the beholder himself must assemble the sculpture from an infinite series of interpenetrating views. The simultaneous multiple views of Cubist painting are transferred to the third dimension by specifically sculptural means. González never forsook the object completely, however much he may have transformed it by abstraction: he extracted all the components and their combinations from his experience of visual reality, and they remain unmistakably figurative in character. The opposition between figurative and non-figurative did not exist for González; he worked on the largely ›abstract‹ *Femme au miroir* and on the completely ›realistic‹ *Montserrat* at one and the same time. *Monserrat* stood in front of the Spanish pavilion at the World Fair as a symbol of the Catalan people's determined opposition to Franco's Fascism.[13]

González developed sculpture's autonomous formal means a great deal further than Lipchitz, arriving at a synthesis of »great abstraction and great realism« (Kandinsky). This new conception of sculpture nevertheless remained within the tradition of Catalan ironwork and refused to relinquish the human figure as a subject of art. It may »look bizarre«, but it is still »directly inspired by nature«.

The works of Naum Gabo and Antoine Pevsner are totally different. They permit no figurative associations whatsoever. Pevsner's *Construction for an Airport* (1934/35; fig. 7) may not only be apprehended in time by moving around it, but the immateriality of such a sequential process is its very subject matter: energy, movement and speed, rising in circles. Like González's sculpture, this construction is pierced. It refers initially to nothing other than itself and raises a radical claim for purely artistic autonomy. It is a completely real, completely independent and completely self-contained object of reality – like an aeroplane. Through the use of plastic in its widely circling curves the construction reflects a modern feeling for life and incorporates the reality of that twentieth-century technical progress which had conquered the skies.

Gabo's *Construction in Space: Crystal* (1937; fig. 8) is also a fully autonomous object resisting figurative interpretation. It is no longer the result of abstraction, but purely abstract and thus concrete. The use of plastic – a contemporary material of the future – enabled Gabo to construct the object from closed surfaces which, because they are transparent, make visible the continual interpenetration of its space. With the greatest possible immateriality, movement as a sequence in time, crystallizes for a moment into a concentrated vibration in space.

Gabo and Pevsner pursued problems quite different from those occupying the ›traditional avant-garde‹. Their art sought the anonymity of man – made or factory processed materials rather than the familiarity of those of nature and tradition. They left no artists' handwriting, no typical texture or patina on the surface of their materials. The final appearance of their constructions seems to embrace, even to foreshadow, a new technological age. This alone seemed to them appropriate to the »period of reconstruction«. These autonomous constructions, these models which in no way reflect reality, represented the artists' »apprehension of the universe« and did indeed demonstrate that content and form are »from the constructive point of view one and the same thing«.

Gabo and Pevsner were the only representatives of Constructivism included in this exhibition. Indeed the catalogue still classified Constructivism as a »child of Cubism«. This must have awakened protests from both artists, for they were definitely no longer concerned either with »formal structures« or with being »inspired by nature« to depict reality. As a help to visitors the catalogue did, however, print an interpretation of the basic concepts listed in the *Realistic Manifesto* of 1920:

Fig. 7 Antoine Pevsner, *Construction for an Airport*, 1934/35. Museum moderner Kunst, Museum des 20. Jahrhunderts, Wien

Fig. 8 Naum Gabo, *Construction in Space: Crystal*, 1937. Rhode Island School of Design

1) Space and time are the only elements of real life. In order to correspond to life art must therefore refer to these two basic elements.

2) Volume is not the only means of expressing space.

3) Static rhythms are not the only means of expressing time. Kinetic and dynamic elements are the only means of expressing real time.[14]

The extent to which this artistic standpoint corresponded to the emotional and intellectual needs of the time, still governed by the optimistic belief in progress, only becomes clear when viewed against the background of Europe on the eve of the Second World War. Yet in the Jeu de Paume exhibition, Constructivism was clearly isolated within the artistic avant-garde. Only on his own could Gabo pursue his course unperturbed. Two years before the Jeu de Paume exhibition he had left Paris, to which he had fled only three years previously from the political upheaval in Germany. Paris had not held its dream for him, emotionally starved and artistically isolated he had been brought to the point of suicide.[15] Not for the first time he moved on, away from political restraints and artistic rejection, to keep his integrity as an artist. In England, among new friends, he developed his ideas, later moving to the USA for the last thirty years of his life.

The Fascists had an acute awareness of the rebellion, revolution and power to enlighten, that modern art, in all its styles, so forcefully represented. It was an artistic expression of new ideas that they could not control, perhaps not even comprehend. Their political violation of it stemmed from their fear — they sought to annihilate it, as they did everything else that stood in their way.

Cubism, as a sculptural concept, faded into its own obscurity; it needed no political assistance. Constructivism continued to develop throughout Gabo's lifetime, and continues as a major influence on contemporary art.

14 Anon., in the exhib. cat. *Origines et Développement de l'Art International Indépendent,* Musée du Jeu de Paume, Paris, 1937.

15 Discussions with the family.

Chronology

Natalie H. Lee and Steven A. Nash

1890

August 5: Naum (also called Neemia) Borisovich Pevsner born in Bryansk, Russia, a small, industrial town some 250 miles southwest of Moscow. He was one of nine children born to Boris Pevsner, owner of a metals factory and Agrippina-Fanny Pevsner (née Ozersky). Seven Pevsner children survived childhood: Mark, Jeremy, Mariya (or Masha), Natan (later called Antoine), Anna (or Anya), Naum, and Alexei.

1904–05

Expelled from primary school in Bryansk for writing an uncomplimentary poem about the headmaster. Tutored in Tomsk, Siberia, where oldest brother, Mark, was a student at the Institute of Technology.

1905

Returned to Bryansk due to unrest in Tomsk during the aborted First Russian Revolution.

1907

Arrested briefly in Bryansk because of involvement with an illegal group committed to spreading literacy among workers and peasants.

1907–10

Attended Kursk gymnasium, graduating with special recognition for achievement in literature and creative writing.
Experimented with drawing and painting from about 1907 onward.

1910

Went to Berlin for a brief stay, then on to Munich.
August: Matriculated in medical faculty of University of Munich.

1911

Switched from study of medicine to study of natural science.

1912

Entered Munich's Technische Hochschule (Polytechnic School) to study civil engineering.
Spring: Visited Paris, where older brother Antoine, then a painter, was living. During this or a subsequent trip to Paris, the following year, visited the Salon des Indépendants and elsewhere saw works by numerous avant-garde artists.
Summer: Visited Zurich.
In Munich, modeled clay study of the head of a Negro (his earliest sculpture for which visual documentation exists).

Fig. 1　Naum Gabo and Antoine Pevsner in Paris.

1912–13

Lived in the village of Planegg outside of Munich.
Attended art history lectures of noted Swiss scholar, Heinrich Wölfflin.

1913

Spring: Second trip to Paris.
Summer: At suggestion of Professor Wölfflin, set out on walking tour of Italy, visiting museums and churches in Bologna, Alessandria, Milan, Pisa, Venice, and Florence.

1914

April: After returning home to Bryansk early in the year, accompanied his mother on a trip back to Germany.
July: Was joined in Planegg by younger brother Alexei.
July 31: Learning that the Germans were barring the streets in preparation for war, advised Alexei that as enemy aliens they must leave Germany at once.
August 1: With Alexei, set out for Denmark. Detained briefly in Hamburg by German authorities. Continued to Copenhagen and made contact with parents, who sent money for Alexei's education and their support.
Traveled to Bergen, intending to sail to England where Alexei hoped to enter a university, but decided to return to Christiania (Oslo) because of wartime dangers in the North Sea.

1915

Was joined in Christiania by brother Antoine.

1915–16

Made first constructions. Adopted Gabo as a surname in place of Pevsner, in order to set himself apart from his artist-brother.

1917

February: At outbreak of Russian Revolution, was asked by parents to return home.
April: Together with Antoine and Alexei, left Norway for Bryansk by way of Stockholm, Finland, and Petrograd.
August: Moved to Moscow, where he shared an apartment with Antoine and Alexei in a building containing artist studios.

1918

Declined teaching position in department of ceramics and sculpture at the State Free Art Studios (which later became the VKhUTEMAS, or Higher State Art-Technical Studios) offered him by David Shterenberg, director of IZO (the Fine Arts department of the Commissariat for Enlightenment).

1918–20

Worked with Shterenberg in an unofficial capacity on various projects, including a journal published by IZO.

1919

Designed project for a radio station at Serpukhov, a textile town near Moscow, where his sister Anna was living.

Fig. 2   Gabo in Munich in front of what is now the Staatliche Antikensammlungen, between 1910 and 1914.

Fig. 3 Gabo in Lichterfelde, Berlin, in the 1920s.

1920

Moved with Alexei to Rozhdestvenskii Boulevard. Executed *Kinetic Construction.*
July: Wrote the *Realistic Manifesto,* which was also signed by Pevsner.
August 5: Five thousand copies of the *Realistic Manifesto* published in Moscow by Second State Printing House, many of which were posted in areas designated for governmental decrees.
August 6: With Antoine Pevsner, Gustav Klutsis, and several students, opened exhibition of sculpture and paintings in an open-air bandstand on Tverskoi Blvd., Moscow. This was the only public exhibition of his work in Russia and drew considerable attention, even internationally.

1922

Received permission from Commissar for Enlightenment, Anatolii Lunacharsky, to leave Russia for Germany, where he would help with installation of the abstract section of the *Erste Russische Kunstausstellung,* organized by the Soviet government at the Galerie van Diemen, Berlin. Gabo showed at least nine works at the exhibition, which opened in October, plus possibly several works ex-catalogue.
Met Katherine Dreier, who visited the van Diemen exhibition and bought one of Gabo's works, initiating a life-long friendship. Through Dreier, Gabo later met and became good friends with Marcel Duchamp.

1922–23

Lived in Steglitzerstrasse in Berlin.
Was joined in 1923 by brother Antoine and his wife, Virginia, who shared Gabo's apartment for nine months.
Moved to Lichterfelde, where he lived with Lilly Richter (former wife of Hans Richter) until her death c. 1929.

1923

July: Contributed an article to the first issue of the magazine *G* (published in Berlin by Hans Richter).

Fig. 4 Van Diemen Gallery, Berlin 1922. Left to right: David Shterenberg (commisar of the exhibition), D. Maryanov (propaganda agent), Nathan Altman (an artist), Naum Gabo and Mr. Lutz (director of the gallery).

1924

February: *Space Construction C* of 1920 included by Katherine Dreier in the Société Anonyme's Modern Russian Artists exhibition, held in New York City, marking the first occasion on which Gabo's work was exhibited in the United States.

June: Participated in *Constructivistes Russes: Gabo et Pevsner* exhibition with Pevsner at Galerie Percier, Paris.

Autumn: Was visited at studio in Lichterfelde by Sergei Diaghilev, who suggested the possibility of Gabo's designing a ballet.

1926

Signed contract with Diaghilev to create decor for the ballet, *La Chatte*.

Exhibited two works in *Novembergruppe* section of *Grosse Berliner Kunstausstellung*.

Summer: While staying at Pevsner's flat in Paris, created model for *La Chatte* and presented it to Diaghilev.

November: Was included in International Exhibition of Modern Art assembled by Société Anonyme at Brooklyn Museum.

Included among artists whose work was shown in El Lissitzky's special exhibition room in Dresden.

1927

April 30: First performance of *La Chatte* at the Casino theater in Monte Carlo, with sets, costumes, and properties designed and executed by Gabo with assistance from Pevsner. (The production traveled also to Paris, London, and Berlin.)

May: Was included in Machine Age Exposition, organized by The Little Review Gallery and others.

1928:

Lectured at Bauhaus.

Published article, »*Gestaltung?*«, in periodical *Bauhaus* (vol. 2, no. 4). Designed a searchlight display for the Berlin City Architect, Hugo Häring, as part of a city-wide light festival (not executed).

1930

November: First one-man exhibition of constructions, organized by Justus Bier, at Kestner-Gesellschaft, Hannover. Gave lecture on »The Rational and Irrational in Art« to members of the Kestner Society at the home of Herman Bode.

Designed construction for a niche in the home of Eric Mendelsohn (not executed).

Declined invitation of Michel Seuphor and Joaquín Torres-García to join their *Cercle et Carré* group in Paris.

1931

Participated in first phase of international design competition for proposed (but never built) Palace of Soviets, Moscow, submitting a set of drawings in December.

1932

Left Berlin for Paris (after Nazi storm troopers came to his studio). Joined *Abstraction-Création* and contributed to the first two issues of its journal. Through this association he later met the artists Ben Nicholson and Barbara Hepworth and the poet-critic Herbert Read, with whom he formed a particularly close and lasting relationship.

Fig. 5 Gabo, Alexei and Virginia Pevsner in Lichterfelde, c. 1928.

Fig. 6   Gabo in his studio in Lichterfelde, before 1933.

1933

Met Hilla Rebay.

1935

June: Visited England for the first time to discuss participation in forthcoming exhibition organized by Nicolette Gray.

October–November: Participated in Abstract Art exhibition with Pevsner, Domela, and Mondrian in recently opened Avery Memorial galleries for modern art in the Wadsworth Atheneum, Hartford, Connecticut.

1936

February–June: Participated in Abstract and Concrete, an international exhibition organized by Nicolette Gray, which opened in Oxford and traveled to Liverpool, London, Cambridge, and Newcastle.

Settled in London, taking a room in Bloomsbury and later, one in Lawn Road, Hampstead.

March–April: Represented by seven works in Alfred Barr's Cubism and Abstract Art exhibition at Museum of Modern Art, New York. Exhibited with Pevsner at Chicago Arts Club.

October: Set up home in Ormonde Terrace, St. John's Wood, with Miriam Israels, an American painter and grandniece of nineteenth century Dutch artist Jozef Israels (dated their marriage from this time but formalized it in December 1937). Later moved to Cholmley Gardens, West Hampstead.

c. 1936–1937

Met John Sisson of ICI, who supplied him with Perspex.

1937

January–February: Represented by two works in *Konstruktivisten* exhibition at Kunsthalle, Basel.

July–October: Participated in *Origines et développement de l'art internationale indépendant* at the Jeu de Paume, Paris.

Represented by two works in Constructive Art exhibition at London Gallery.

With Leslie Martin and Ben Nicholson, edited *Circle: International Survey of Constructive Art,* to which he also contributed two essays and much of the organizational leadership.

1938

January–May: One-man exhibition, Constructions in Space, opened at London Gallery and traveled to Wadsworth Atheneum, Hartford, Connecticut; Julien Levy Gallery, New York; and Vassar College, Poughkeepsie, New York.

With wife, Miriam, made his first trip to the United States, in conjunction with his traveling exhibition.

Met Lewis Mumford, who became a lifelong friend.

At the instigation of Wallace K. Harrison, *Spheric Theme* was purchased as model for fountain project for General Electric Company Pavilion at New York World's Fair (never realized).

1939

Worked on designs for interior fittings for ocean liner Queen Mary, commissioned by Grey Wornum (not executed).

September: Two days after outbreak of World War II, persuaded by Ben Nicholson and Barbara Hepworth to move to Carbis Bay, Cornwall, for duration of war. Took up oil painting while in Cornwall. Held position as Air Warden after USSR entered the war on Allies' side. Started writing a diary which he maintained throughout the war.

Fig. 7   Gabo and his wife Miriam in Cholmley Gardens, 1937.

September: Two days after outbreak of World War II, persuaded by Ben Nicholson and Barbara Hepworth to move to Carbis Bay, Cornwall, for duration of war. Took up oil painting while in Cornwall. Held position as Air Warden after USSR entered the war on Allies' side. Started writing a diary which he maintained throughout the war.

1940

January 15: Participated in BBC radio program, »Artist in the Witness Box« (no. 6), with painter-administrator William Coldstream and art critic Eric Newton.

Fig. 8   Gabo in his studio at Carbis Bay, c. 1941.

1941

May 26: Birth of daughter, Nina-Serafima.

1942

May–June: Participated in New Movements in Art, Contemporary Work in England exhibition at Leicester Museum and Art Gallery, and London Museum.

1943–44

Worked with Design Research Unit, London, (formed by Herbert Read, Misha Black, and Milner Grey) on various unrealized projects.
For the Jowett Company, designed an innovative automobile, which, however, did not go into production.

1946

November: With wife and daughter, left England for the United States. Arrived in New York on November 26. Settled in Woodbury, Connecticut (near Orenaug Park) in house lent to the Gabos by a close friend, until they were able to purchase their own. Rented a small store for a studio.

1947

March 2: Gave lecture-demonstration at Sinton Hotel, Cincinnati, Ohio (sponsored by Cincinnati Modern Art Society).
Became a member of board of directors of Société Anonyme, New Haven, having maintained contact even from Europe with its founder Katherine Dreier and her close adviser Marcel Duchamp.

1948

February: Exhibition with Pevsner at Museum of Modern Art, New York.
April 21: Lectured on »The Philosophy of Constructivist Art« in MoMA auditorium.
Participated in exhibition at Yale of works by past and present directors of Société Anonyme.
March: Lectured at Yale with Katherine S. Dreier and James J. Sweeney in Trowbridge Series.
Lectured to students at Institute of Design (formerly New Bauhaus), Chicago, at invitation of director Serge Chermayeff.

1949

Commissioned to design sculptures for lobbies of the Esso Building, Rockefeller Center, New York (project never carried out).
Participated in *Les Premiers maîtres de l'art abstrait* exhibition, organized by Michel Seuphor at Galerie Maeght, Paris.

Fig. 9   Gabo and his daughter Nina on the beach at Carbis Bay, St. Ives, Cornwall, c. 1942.

1950

March—April: Exhibited constructions and lectured (April 14) at the Baltimore Museum of Art.
May 19: Commissioned by Saidie A. May to make a large construction for the stairwell of the Young People's Art Center of the Baltimore Museum of Art (installed November 1951).

1951

November: One-man exhibition, Massachusetts Institute of Technology.

1952

Became an American citizen.
January—February: Exhibited with Jozef Albers at Chicago Arts Club.

1952—53

Participated in Sculpture of the Twentieth Century exhibition at the Philadelphia Museum of Art, Art Institute of Chicago, and Museum of Modern Art, New York (organized by Andrew C. Richie).

1953

Moved with family to Breakneck Hill Road, Middlebury, Connecticut.
April—May: One-man exhibition at Pierre Matisse Gallery, New York.
October—November: Exhibited with Alexander Calder at Wadsworth Atheneum, Hartford, Connecticut. Awarded second prize in international sculpture competition for a Monument to the Unknown Political Prisoner, sponsored by the Institute of Contemporary Arts in London.

1953—54

Taught at Harvard University Graduate School of Architecture, at invitation of Walter Gropius.

1954

First trip back to England.
Awarded Guggenheim Fellowship.
Awarded Mr. and Mrs. Frank G. Logan Medal, Art Institute of Chicago.
January 22: Contracted by Marcel Breuer and the Bijenkorf department store to create a monumental outdoor sculpture in Rotterdam.

1956

Construction of Bijenkorf sculpture begun by Dutch ship building company under Gabo's guidance.
November: For Wallace K. Harrison, completed a bas-relief for lobby of an addition to U.S. Rubber Company building, Rockefeller Center, New York. (In 1976 the sculpture was moved to the new Celanese Corporation Building, also in Rockefeller Center).

1957

May 21: 85-foot high Bijenkorf construction unveiled by the burgomaster of Rotterdam.

Fig. 10 Gabo and Herbert Read, 1953 (with *Column*, cat. 11).

Publication of *Gabo: Constructions, Sculptures, Paintings, Drawings, Engravings* with introductions by Herbert Read and Leslie Martin.

1958

One-man exhibition, Boymans Museum, Rotterdam, and Stedelijk Museum, Amsterdam.

1959

Delivered the A. W. Mellon Lectures in the Fine Arts, National Gallery of Art, Washington, D.C. (Lectures published as *Of Divers Arts,* 1962).
Alexei Pevsner heard of Gabo through the catalogue of an American exhibition in Moscow and inquired as to his whereabouts, leading to renewed contact between Gabo and family members in Russia with whom he had been out of touch since 1936.

1960

May: Received Achievement Medal in 1960 Creative Arts Awards presented by Brandeis University, Waltham, Massachusetts. Charles Wilson, a graduate student in sculpture at Yale University, began working with Gabo as studio assistant.

1961

Participated in exhibitions of kinetic art held at the Stedelijk Museum, Amsterdam, and at the Moderna Museet, Stockholm.

1962

April 12: Antoine Pevsner died in Paris.
June: Visited brothers Mark, Jeremy, and Alexei, and sister Anna in Moscow and Leningrad.
Of Divers Arts published.
First visited Portugal, where he met the sculptor Antonio Duarte, who helped Gabo select stone at Portuguese quarries and whose studio later assisted Gabo in roughing out and finishing certain carvings.

1964

Publication of Alexei Pevsner's book, *A Biographical Sketch of my Brothers, Naum Gabo and Antoine Pevsner* (a French edition was published in 1968).

Fig. 11   Gabo and George Rickey, Middlebury, 1964.

1965

Elected to 250-member National Institute of Arts and Letters.

1965–66

April–April: Traveling retrospective exhibition held at Stedelijk Museum, Amsterdam; Kunsthalle, Mannheim; Wilhelm-Lehmbruck Museum, Duisburg; Kunsthaus, Zurich; Moderna Museet, Stockholm; and Tate Gallery, London.

1966

Elected to Royal Academy of Arts, Sweden.

1966–69

Lawsuit with Marlborough Gallery settled out of court.

Fig. 12   Gabo and Miriam at St. Thomas' Hospital for trials of *Fountain*, 1974/75.

1967

Awarded honorary doctorate at Royal College of Art, London. Awarded Grosser Kunstpreis des Landes Nordrhein-Westfalen for sculpture, Düsseldorf.

1968

Retrospective exhibition held at Albright-Knox Art Gallery, Buffalo, New York.
Alexei Pevsner visited Gabo in America, and would visit him again in London in 1972.

1969

May: Elected to American Academy of Arts and Sciences.

1970

At the instigation of Sir Norman Reid, Director of the Tate Gallery, *Torsion* fountain commissioned by Alistair McAlpine.

1970–72

Traveling retrospective exhibition held at Louisiana Museum, Humlebaek, Denmark; Sonja Henies og Niels Onstads Stiftelser, Høvikodden, Norway; Nasjonalgallereit, Oslo; Nationalgalerie, Berlin; Kunstverein, Hannover; Musée de Peinture et de Sculpture, Grenoble; Musée National d'Art Moderne, Paris; and Museu Calouste Gulbenkian, Lisbon.
Began writing an autobiography.

1971

Made an Honorary Knight Commander, Order of the British Empire, by Queen Elizabeth II.

1972

Film on Gabo made by John Read for the BBC.

1972–73

Torsion fountain produced by Stainless Metalcraft Ltd. of London and presented by McAlpine to the Tate Gallery (to be installed on long-term loan at the new St. Thomas' Hospital, London).

1975

Elected to 50-member American Academy of Arts and Letters.

1976

November 16: Opening of St. Thomas' Hospital and inauguration of *Torsion* fountain by Queen Elizabeth II.

1976–77

November–January: One-man exhibition at Tate Gallery, London.

1977

August 23: Died in Waterbury (Connecticut) Hospital after a long illness.

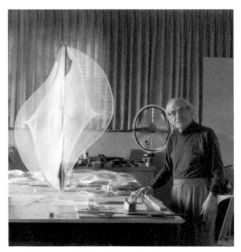

Fig. 13   Gabo in his studio, April 1977.

Catalogue

Constructed Head No. 1, 1915/reassembled 1985 (cat. 1)

Constructed Head No. 2, 1916/1923–24 (cat. 3)

Model for ›Constructed Torso‹, 1917/reassembled 1981 (cat. 6)

Monument for an Airport, c. 1932/1948 (cat. 21)

Construction: Stone with a Collar, 1933
(cat. 22)

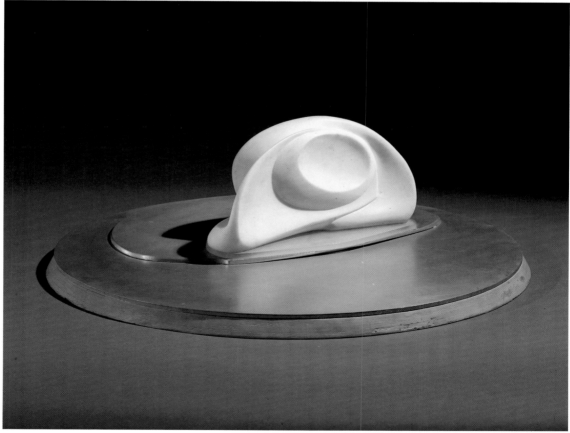

Repose, 1953
(cat. 48)

Construction in Space with Crystalline Center, 1938/1940 (cat. 33)

Linear Construction in Space No. 2, 1949/1972−73 (cat. 40)

Construction in Space, with Net, 1951/1952 (cat. 44)

Construction in Space: Arch No. 2, 1958/1963 (cat. 54)

Linear Construction in Space No. 1 (Variation), 1942–43/c. 1957–58 (cat. 38)

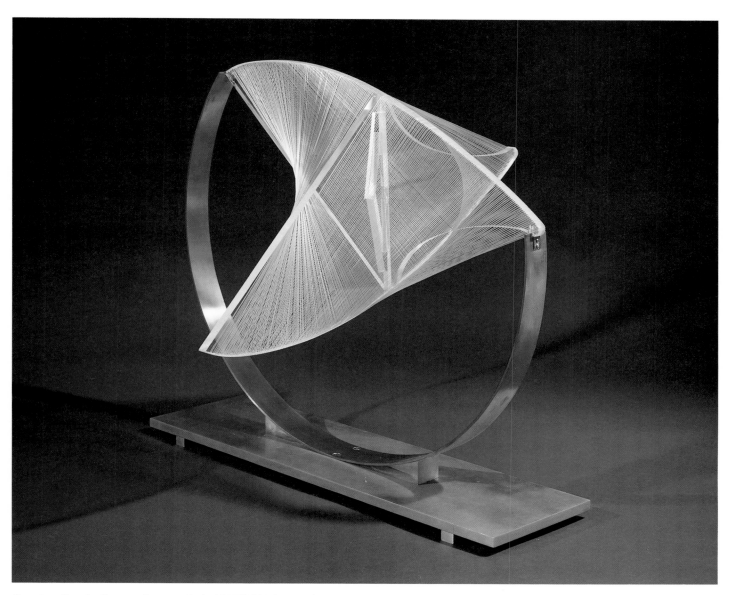

Construction in Space: Suspended, 1957/1965 (cat. 52)

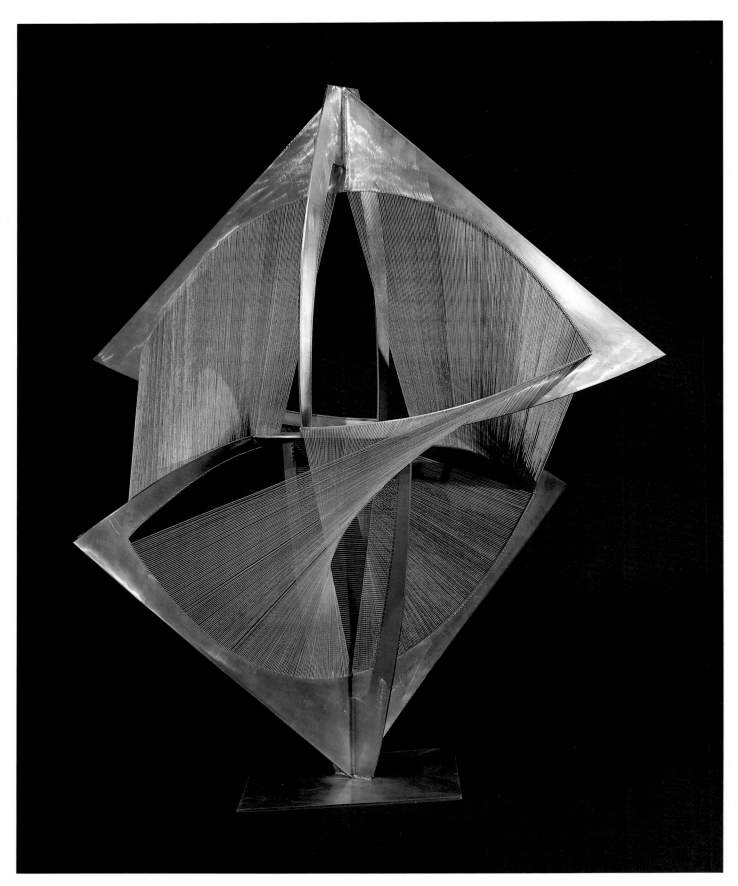

Torsion, Variation, 1962/1963 (cat. 55)

Torsion, Variation, 1962/c.1974–75 (cat. 56)

Vertical Construction No. 1, 1962/1967 (cat. 58)

Kinetic Stone Carving
1936–44 (cat. 23)

Red Stone, 1964–65
(cat. 60)

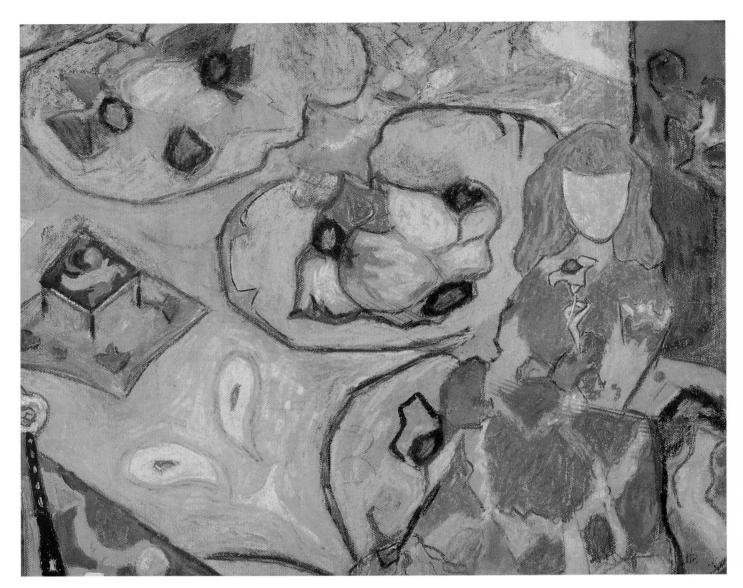

Christmas, c. 1910–12 (cat. 67)

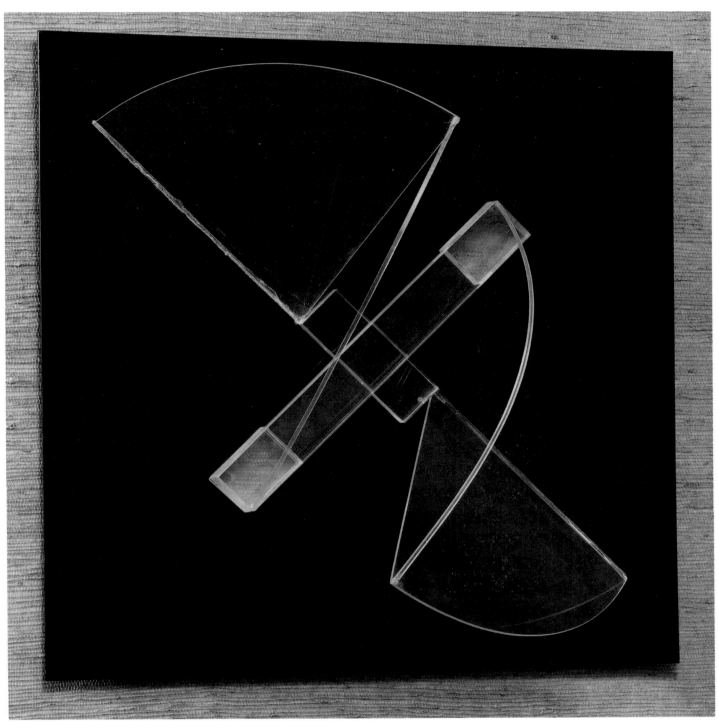

12
Square Relief
1920–21/1937
Perspex, on aluminum base
44.5 × 44.5 × c.16.5
Family Collection
S.-L. 12.2

11
Column
1922–23/1975
Glass, Perspex, and stainless steel, 193 h.
Family Collection
S.-L. 10.8

13 **Tower,** 1921–22
Celluloid, 12.5 h.; Yale University Art Gallery, Bequest of Katherine S. Dreier to the Collection of the
Société Anonyme; S.-L. 13

14
Model for a Fountain
1923–24/reassembled 1985
Glass (replaced) and enamelled
metal (repainted)
72.5 h.
Family Collection
S.-L. 17

15
**Model for ›Construction in Space
with Balance on Two Points‹**
c. 1924–25/reassembled 1978–79
Celluloid, on plastic base, 13.5 × 18.2
Family Collection
S.-L. 22.2

16
**Construction in Space with Balance
on Two Points**
1924–25/assembled 1982
Plexiglass, 27 × 37
Family Collection
S.-L. 22.6

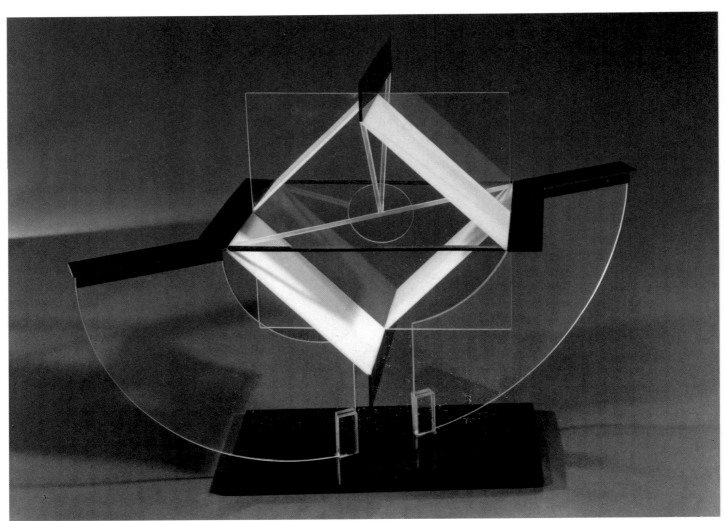

17   **Monument for an Airport,** 1924–26/reassembled 1985
Glass (replaced), enamelled brass and aluminum (repainted), and wood, on wood base, 49.5 × 73.3 × c.30
Family Collection; S.-L. 23.2

19 Construction in Space: Soaring, 1929–30/reassembled 1985
Brass painted black and white (repainted), plexiglass cones (replaced), 112 h.; Family Collection; S.-L. 29.2

18
Model for ›Construction in Space: Two Cones‹
1927/altered 1932–37
Celluloid, 8.3 × 12.4
The Tate Gallery, London
S.-L. 29.1

20
Construction in Space: Arch
1929/1937
Rhodoid with plexiglass substitutions,
on Perspex base, 46.4 × 76.2 × 21.6
Family Collection
S.-L. 33.2

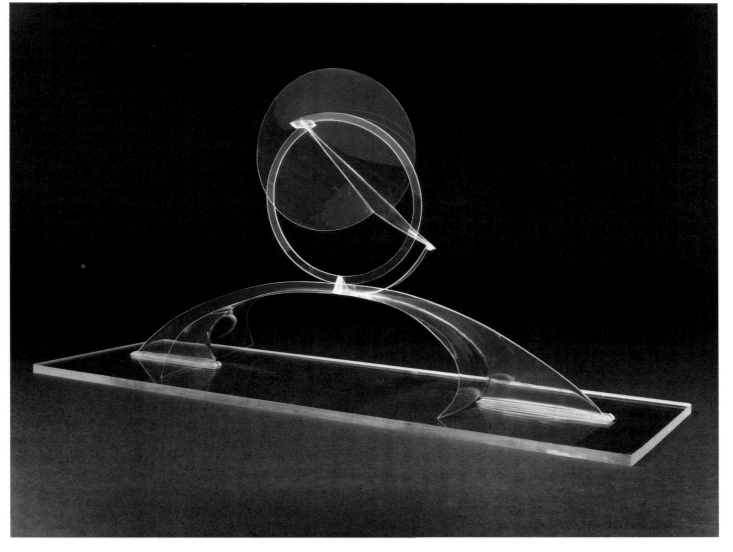

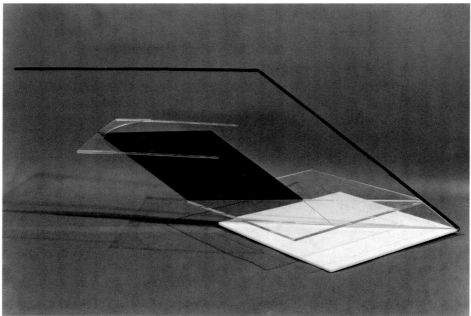

21
Monument for an Airport
c. 1932/1948
Perspex with brass painted black
41.6 × 108 × 57.5
Family Collection
S.-L. 35.4

22
Construction: Stone with a Collar
1933
Stone, ivory rhodoid, brass strip painted black,
on slate base, c.40 × c.72
Family Collection
S.-L. 34.3

23
Kinetic Stone Carving
1936–44
Portland stone
24 × 37
Family Collection
S.-L. 36

25 **Model for ›Spheric Construction: Fountain‹**
1937–38; Perspex, 9.5 h.
Family Collection; S.-L. 43.1

24 **Model for ›Spheric Theme‹,** 1936–37
Perspex, 10.2 diam.
Family Collection; S.-L. 37.2

27
Spheric Theme: Transparent Variation
c. 1937
Celluloid and Perspex, 21.5 diam.
Family Collection
S.-L. 37.7

26   **Spheric Theme: Black Variation,** 1937
Rhodoid and black celluloid, 42.5 diam.; Family Collection; S.-L. 37.6

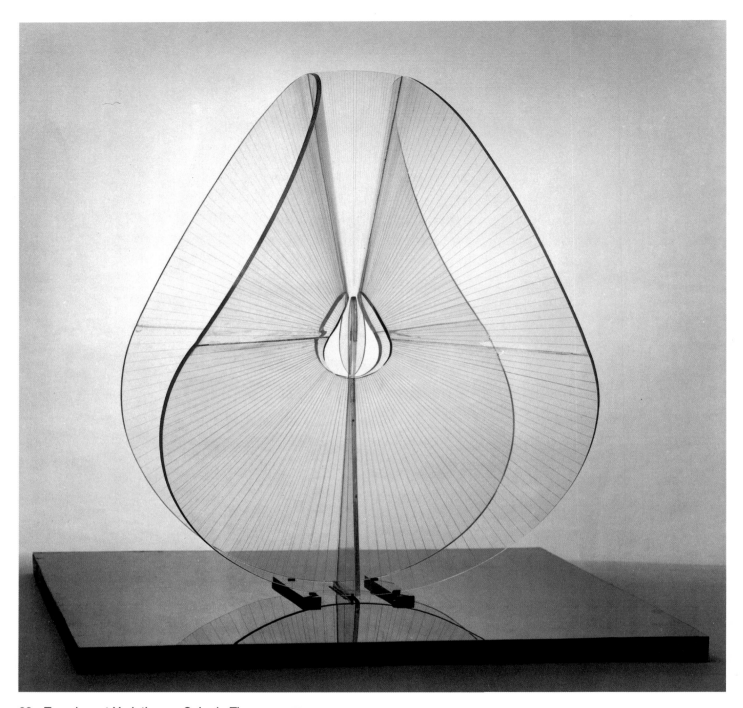

28 **Translucent Variation on Spheric Theme,** 1937/1951
Perspex, on Perspex base, 57.3 diam.; The Solomon R. Guggenheim Museum, New York; S.-L. 37.10

29 **Construction on a Plane,** 1937
Perspex and celluloid, on Perspex and wood base, 48 × 48 × c.19.6; Family Collection; S.-L. 39.2

30 **Construction on a Line,** 1937
Rhodoid and Perspex, 43.4 × 43.6 × 19.2; Family Collection; S.-L. 40.2

31
Model for ›Construction in Space: Crystal‹, 1937
Celluloid, 7.6 × 7.6 × 3.8
The Tate Gallery, London
S.-L. 41.1

32
Construction in Space: Crystal
1937/1939
Rhodoid, 22 × c.27 × c.18
Family Collection
S.-L. 41.5

33 **Construction in Space with Crystalline Center,** 1938/1940
Perspex and celluloid, 32.4 × 47; Family Collection; S.-L. 46.2

34
Marble Carving
1938/1966–67
Portugese marble,
mounted in Perspex,
on stainless steel base
107 × 76.4 × 10.4
Family Collection
S.-L. 47.6

35 Construction in Space with Rose Marble Carving (Variation No. 2), 1938/1969
Rose marble, mounted in Perspex, 81 × 81; Family Collection; S.-L. 47.7

36
**Linear Construction
in Space No. 1**
1942/1945–49
Perspex with nylon filament
61.3 × 61.3 × 13
Family Collection
S.-L. 48.10

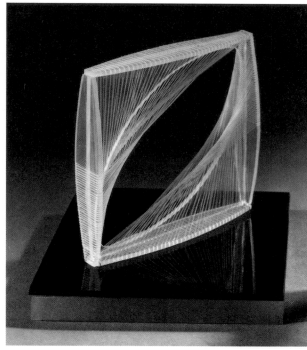

37
Linear Construction in Space No. 1
1942/c. 1970
Perspex with nylon filament, on Perspex base
10.2 × 10.2 × 2.5
Family Collection
S.-L. 48.17

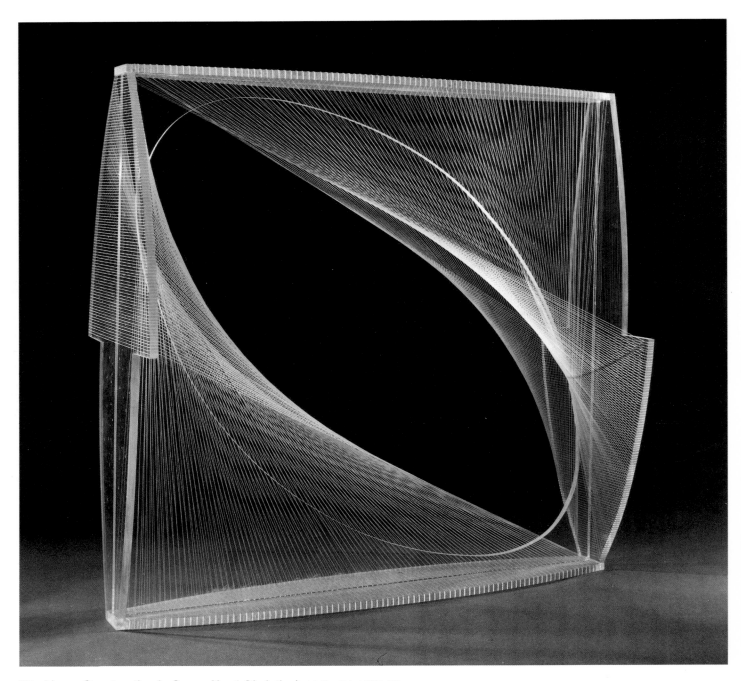

38   Linear Construction in Space No. 1 (Variation), 1942–43/c.1957–58
Perspex with nylon monofilament, 62.9 × 62.9 × 24.2;
Collection of Mr. and Mrs. Raymond D. Nasher, Dallas; S.-L. 53.7

39   **Linear Construction in Space No. 1 (Variation),** 1942–43/1976
Perspex with nylon monofilament, 21.9 × 21.9 × 10.1
Family Collection; S.-L. 53.11

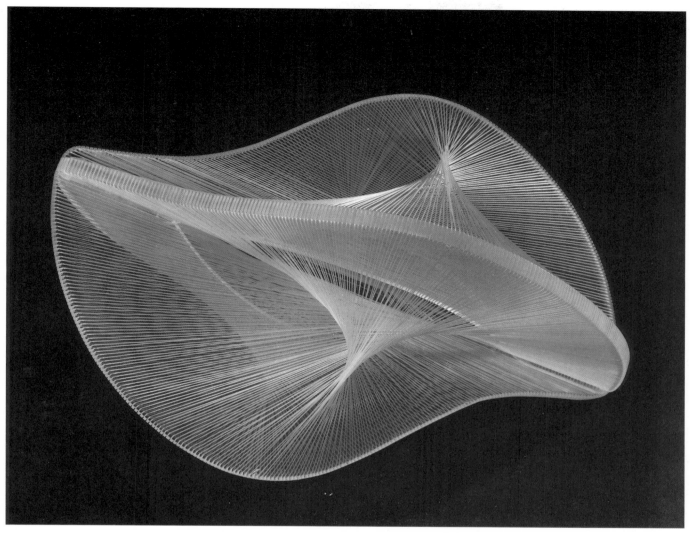

41 **Linear Construction in Space No. 2,** 1949/c. 1976
Perspex with nylon monofilament, on wood base, 38.1 long
Family Collection; S.-L. 55.25

40
Linear Construction in Space No. 2
1949/1972–73
Perspex with nylon monofilament, 92 h.
Family Collection
S.-L. 55.24

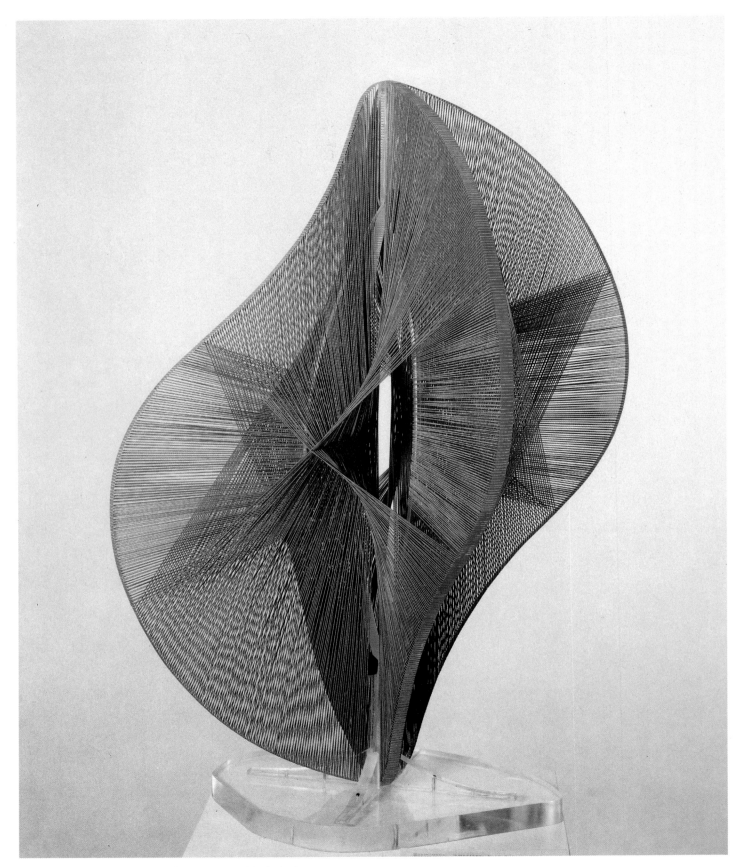

42   Linear Construction in Space No. 2 (Variation), 1949/1962–64; Perspex with a stainless steel spring-wire, on Perspex base, 78.7 h.; Albright-Knox Art Gallery, Buffalo, Gift of the Seymour H. Knox Foundation, Inc.; S.-L. 55.18

43 Optical Relief, 1951–67
Aluminum, plastic, stainless steel spring-wire, and paint, on wood base, c. 81 × 47 × 5.1; Family Collection; S.-L. 60

44   Construction in Space, with Net, 1951/1952
Phosphor-bronze wire mesh, aluminum, Perspex, and metal wire, on wood and aluminum base, 63.6 h.;
Family Collection; S.-L. 58.2

45 Model for a ›Monument to the Unknown Political Prisoner‹, 1952
Plastic with stainless steel wire mesh, on plastic and slate base, 41 h.
The Tate Gallery, London; S.-L. 61.2

46   **Model for ›Linear Construction in Space No. 3, with Red‹,** 1952
Plastic with nylon thread, 9.5 h.; The Tate Gallery, London; S.-L. 62.2

47
Linear Construction in Space No. 3, with Red
1952/1957–58
Perspex and stainless steel, with stainless steel spring-wire
and red paint, on aluminum and wood base, 152 h.
The Jeffrey H. Loria Collection, New York; S.-L. 62.4

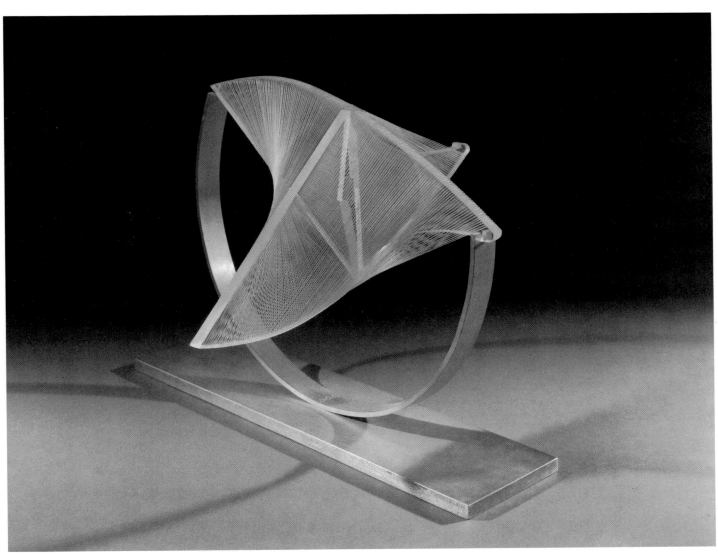

51
Construction in Space: Suspended, 1957/1962
Perspex, nylon monofilament, red and black paint,
gold-plated stainless steel cradle, on stainless steel base
30.5 × 28 × 28
Family Collection; S.-L. 70.10

50
Linear Construction in Space No. 4
1955/c.1970
Phosphor-bronze with stainless steel
and phosphor-bronze spring-wire,
on phosphor-bronze base, 78.7 h.
Family Collection
S.-L. 68.14

52
**Construction
in Space:
Suspended**
1957/1965
Perspex, nylon filament,
gilded phosphor-bronze cradle,
on aluminum base
51.3 × 61.6 × 52.7
Family Collection
S.-L. 70.12

53
**Construction in Space:
Suspended (Variation)**
1957/c. 1971
Perspex, nylon monofilament,
phosphor-bronze cradle,
on aluminum and Perspex base
53 × 61.9 × 55.9
Family Collection
S.-L. 70.13

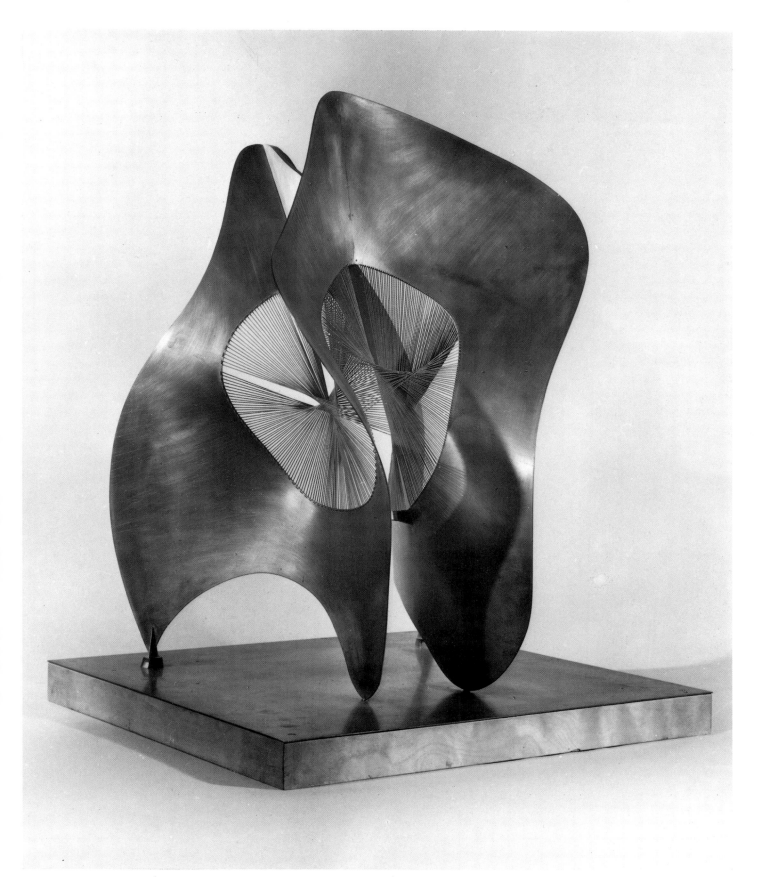

54   **Construction in Space: Arch No. 2,** 1958/1963
Phosphor-bronze, copper, and stainless steel spring-wire, on wood base, 82.6 h.; Family Collection; S.-L. 72.4

55
Torsion, Variation, 1962/1963
Phosphor-bronze with phosphor-bronze
and stainless steel spring-wires,
on wood base, 73.1 h.
Family Collection; S.-L. 77.2

56
Torsion, Variation
1962/c. 1974–75
Stainless steel with stainless
steel spring-wire, 136.5 h.
Family Collection; S.-L. 77.4

57 **Vertical Construction No. 1,** 1962/1964–65
Bronze with stainless steel spring-wire, on bronze and wood base, 103.2 h.
Collection of Marion and Nathan Smooke, Los Angeles; S.-L. 73.2

58
Vertical Construction No. 1
1962/1967
Phosphor-bronze with stainless steel
and black spring-wire, on wood base
203 h.; Family Collection; S.-L. 73.6

59 **Granite Carving,** 1964–65
Granite, 63.5 × 61; Family Collection; S.-L. 51.2

60   **Red Stone,** 1964–65
African red stone, 24 × 45
Family Collection; S.-L. 54.2

59

61
Torsion (Project for a Fountain)
1965
Bronze, 76.2 h.
The Tate Gallery, London
S.-L. 30.6

63
Model for ›Bronze Spheric Theme‹
c. 1966–67; Phosphor-bronze with stainless
steel spring-wire, 20.5 h.
Family Collection; S.-L. 42.6

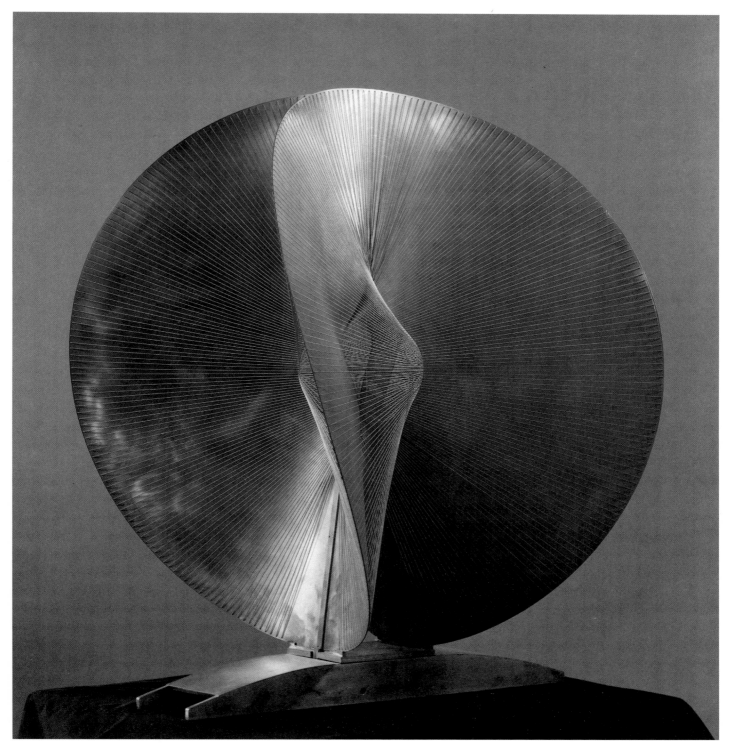

62 **Bronze Spheric Theme (Variation),** 1964–66
Phosphor-bronze with stainless steel spring-wire, on bronze base, c. 99 × c. 68; Family Collection; S.-L. 78

64   **Spheric Theme,** 1967/1969–71
Stainless steel and spring-wire, 246 h.; Berlin, Staatliche Museen Preußischer Kulturbesitz, Nationalgalerie; S.-L. 42.10
Not exhibited in North American tour.

65
Vertical Construction No. 2
1964–65/1969–70
Stainless steel with stainless
steel spring-wire, set into
motorized base, c. 292 h.
Family Collection; S.-L. 79.3

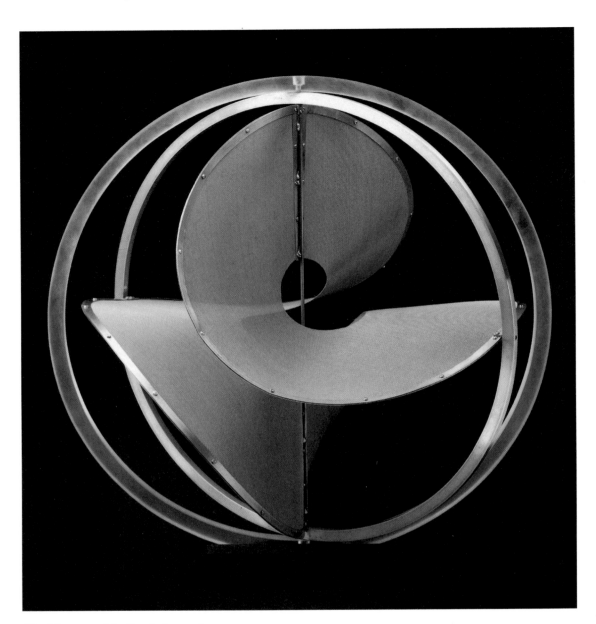

66   **Monument to the Astronauts,** started c. 1966
Brass, plastic, and stainless steel gauze, 54.3 h. × 54.7 w.
Family Collection; S.-L. 80.2

Linear Construction in Space No. 4, 1970
Aluminum with stainless steel spring-wire, 211.5 h.
Centre Georges Pompidou, Musée National d'Art Moderne, Paris
S.-L. 68.13
Not in the exhibition

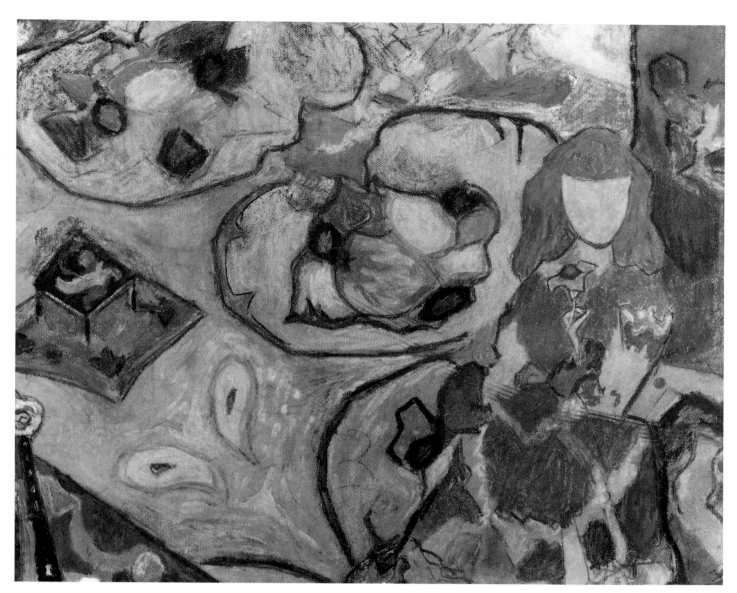

67 **Christmas,** c. 1910–12
Pastel, 36.3 × 45; Family Collection

68   **Hamlet,** 1912
Watercolor and pencil, 14.2 × 11. Inscribed on verso in Russian:
»To dear Nina Serafima I am giving you this watercolor painted
by your father Naum Gabo in the year 1912 and preserved by
me for 52 years. Your uncle Alexei Pevsner.« Family Collection

69   **Young Girl,** 1912
Watercolor and pencil, 17.9 × 13.9 (sight). Inscribed on verso in Russian:
»This watercolor was painted by my brother Naum Pevsner (Gabo) in the
year 1912 in the town of Bryansk, Alexei Pevsner«. And: »I certify that
this watercolor was painted by me. N. Gabo.« Family Collection

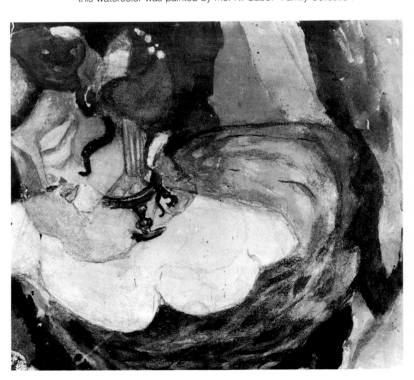

70
Girl in a Low Necked Dress, 1912
Watercolor and pencil, 16.6 × 18.3 (sight). Inscribed on verso in
Russian: »This watercolor was painted by my brother Naum Pevsner
(Gabo) in the year 1912 in the town of Bryansk. Alexei Pevsner.«
And: »I certify the authenticity of this painting as my work. N. Gabo.«
Family Collection

71   Kneeling Figure, c. 1915
Pencil and charcoal, 51 × 36 (irregular); Indecipherable stamp in Russian, lower left; Family Collection

72　Study for ›Head No. 1‹, 1915
Pencil, 19 × 17; Family Collection

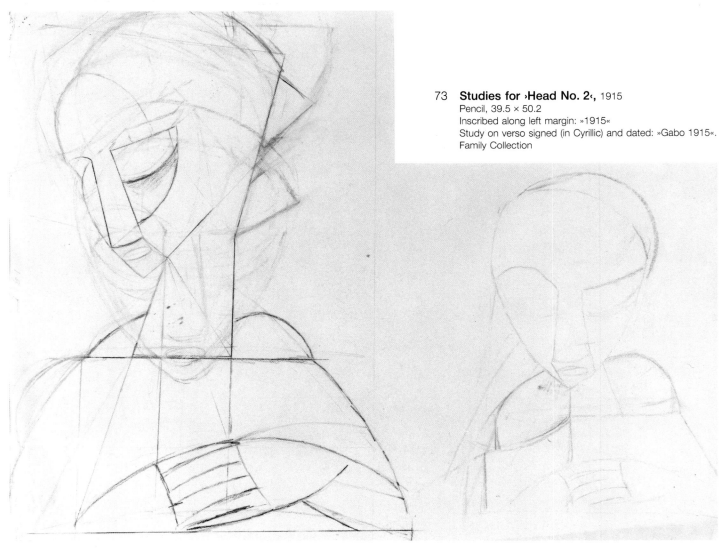

73　Studies for ›Head No. 2‹, 1915
Pencil, 39.5 × 50.2
Inscribed along left margin: »1915«
Study on verso signed (in Cyrillic) and dated: »Gabo 1915«.
Family Collection

74 **Study for ›Head No. 2‹,** 1915
Blue pencil, 18 × 11 (irregular)
Dated lower left: »15« and inscribed
in Russian ». . . Norvegia«
Family Collection

75
Studies for ›Head No. 2‹, 1915
Pencil, 43.5 × 34.5; Initialled (in Cyrillic) and
dated lower left: »G.1915«
Family Collection

76
Study for a Constructed Head, 1916
Pencil, 19 × 17 (irregular)
Signed (in Cyrillic) and dated
lower left: »N. Gabo/1916«
Family Collection

77
Sketch of a Nude, c. 1915–16
Pencil, 29 × 30
Family Collection

78
Sketch of a Figure, c. 1915–16
Ink, 21.8 × 14.1
Family Collection

79
Nude Study, c. 1915–16
Ink, 12.6 × 14.2
Family Collection

80   **Studies of Kneeling Figure,** 1916
Pencil, 39.5 × 50; Signed (in Cyrillic) and dated, lower left: »16./Gabo«; Family Collection

81 **Study for ›Torso‹,** 1916
Pencil, 42.2 × 33; Signed (in Cyrillic) and dated, lower right: »Gabo 16«; Family Collection

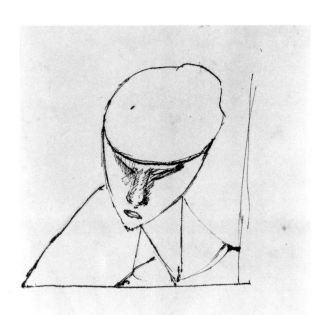

82
Study for ›Head in a Corner Niche‹
c. 1916–17; Ink, 14 × 12.5
Family Collection

83   **Studies of Mother and Child,** c. 1916–17
Pencil, 30 × 26.5 (irregular)
Inscribed in three places in Russian: »prodlavka«.
Signed twice (in Cyrillic), lower right: »Gabo«. Dated,
upper right (not Gabo's hand): »1914–15«
Family Collection

84 **Tower Project,** 1917
Charcoal and pencil, 41.2 × 31.5; Initialled (in Cyrillic) and dated, lower right: »G.17« Architectural scale, lower left; Family Collection

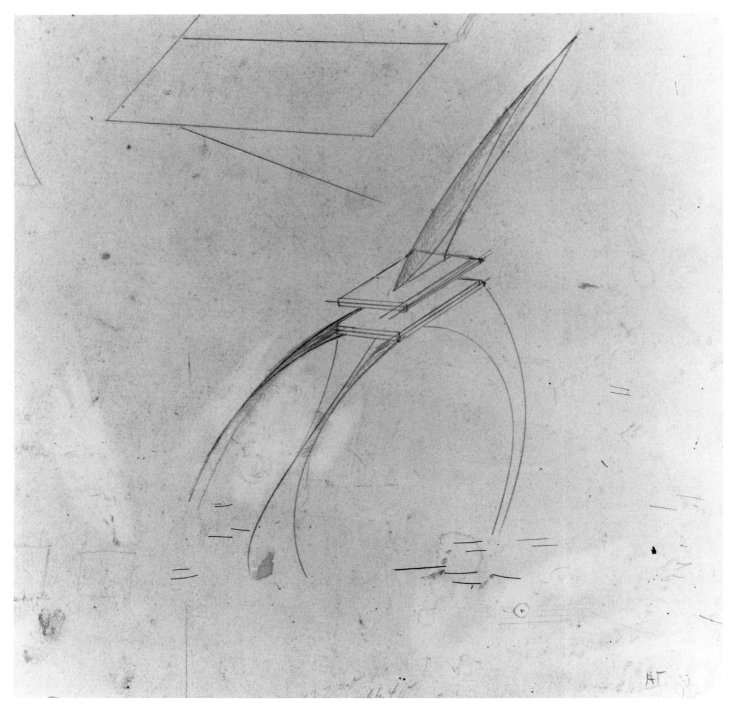

85
Study for an Outdoor Construction, 1917
Pencil, 23 × 23.5 (irregular); Initialled
(in Cyrillic) and dated, lower right: »N.G. 17«
Family Collection

86
Study for a Tower
c. 1917
Pencil, 40.3 × 28.5
Drawing on verso signed
and dated 1917
Family Collection

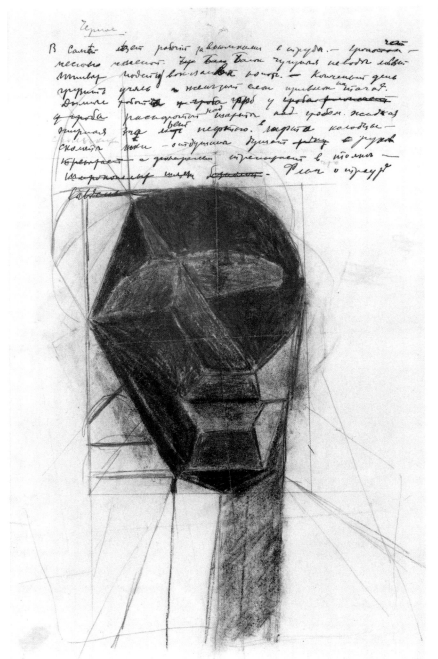

Study of a Head, c. 1917–18
Pencil and pastel, 35.8 × 22.2
For inscription at top see p.19, note 41.
Family Collection

89
Study for a Relief Construction, c. 1917–19
Pencil, 17.9 × 14.5; Signed (in Cyrillic)
and dated, lower right: »N. Gabo 1917«
The Tate Gallery, London

88   Study for a Relief, c. 1917–19
Pencil, 48 × 35; Signed (in Cyrillic), lower left: »Gabo«; Dated, lower right: »1914«; Family Collection

90 **Study for a Construction on a Stairway,** 1918
Pencil, 44 × 32; Initialled (in Cyrillic) and dated, lower right: »N.G. 1918«; Family Collection

91
Design for a Construction, 1918
Pencil, 40.5 × 27.3 (irregular)
Inscribed (in Russian) and dated, lower right:
»Serpukhov 1918. Feb.-March.«
Family Collection

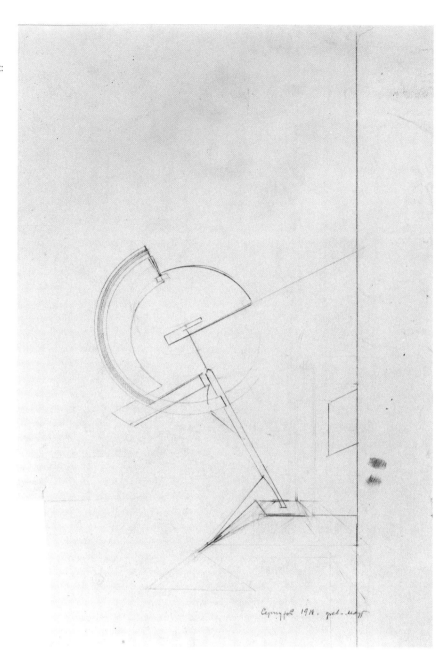

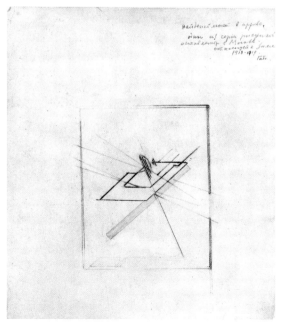

92
Sketch, c. 1918–1919
Pencil and crayon, 24.3 × 20.4
Inscribed (in Russian) and dated, upper right:
»Found by me in the archives, one of a series of drawings
left in Moscow relating to the winter 1918–19. Gabo«
The Tate Gallery, London

93 Sketch for a Square in Moscow, 1919
Pencil, 42 × 35; Architectural scale, lower right; Collection of Thomas P. Whitney

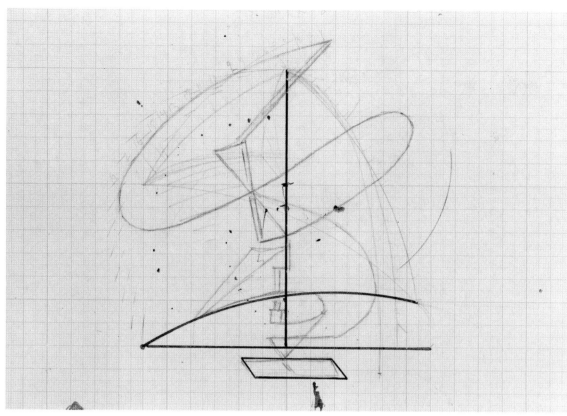

94 **Design for a Kinetic Construction,** c. 1922
Pencil and ink, 22 × 26.7 (irregular)
Family Collection

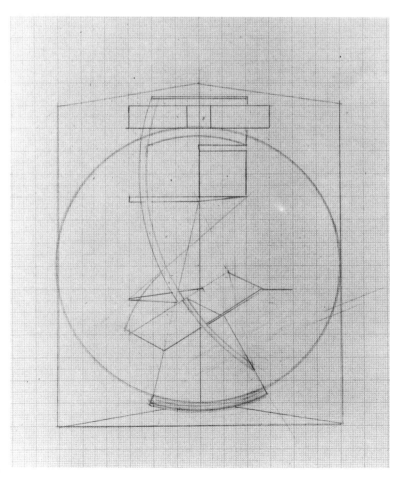

95
Study for a Relief
after 1922
Pencil, 25 × 21
Family Collection

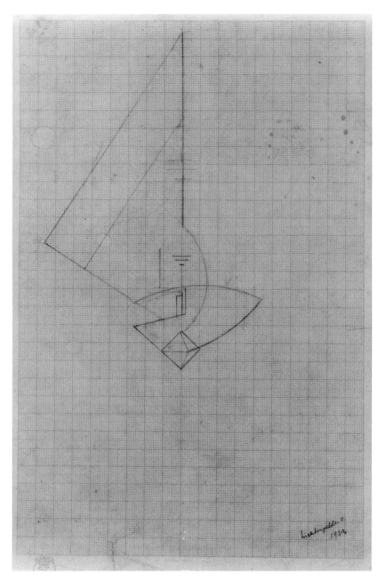

96   **Study for a Tower Construction,** 1923
Pencil, 34 × 22.2; Inscribed and dated,
lower right: »Lichterfelde O./1923«
Family Collection

97   **Study for ›Model for a Fountain‹,** c. 1923
Pencil, 21.5 × 16; Signed, lower right: »N. Gabo«; Family Collection

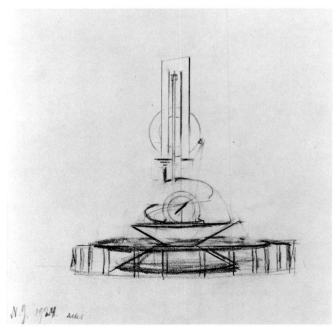

98
Study for a Tower Fountain
1924, Pencil, 20.5 × 21
Initialled and dated, lower left: »N.G. 1924«
Family Collection

99 Architectural Project, 1924
Pencil and charcoal, 65 × 50; Inscribed lower left by Gabo's daughter, per his information: »Berlin 1924«; Family Collection

100
Architectural Project
1925
Watercolor, ink, and pencil
22.6 × 40.2 (sight)
Signed and dated, lower right:
»N. Gabo 1925/Licht. O.«
Family Collection

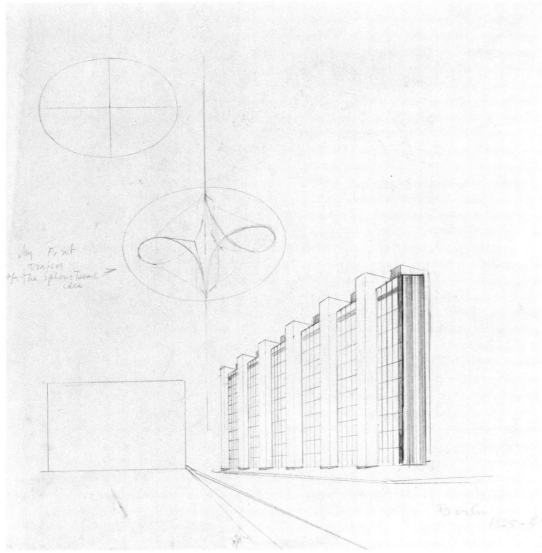

101
**Studies for Architecture
and ›Spheric Theme‹**
1925–26
Pencil, 54.7 × 50
Dated, lower right: »Berlin
1925–26.« And inscribed along left
margin: »My first traises [sic] of
the Spheric Theme idea.«
Family Collection

102
**Study for Stage
Set ›La Chatte‹**
1926, Charcoal,
34.3 × 39.5 (sight)
Family Collection

103 Study for Stage Set, ›La Chatte‹, 1926
Pencil, 22 × 28; Signed, lower left: »Gabo«; Family Collection

104 Costume Sketch for ›La Chatte‹, 1926
Pencil, 28.3 × 22 (irregular); Signed (in Cyrillic),
lower right: »Gabo«; Family Collection

105

106

105
Costume Sketch for ›La Chatte‹, 1926
Pencil and pastel, 26.7 × 21 (sight)
Inscribed, lower right (in Russian):
»Costume design/Gabo«
Family Collection

106
Costume Sketch for ›La Chatte‹, 1926
Pencil and pastel, 27.3 × 21.5
Inscribed, lower right (in Russian):
»Design for Spestsova [sic]/›La
Chatte‹ of Diaghilev/Gabo«
Family Collection

107
Costume Sketch for ›La Chatte‹, 1926
Pencil and pastel, 25.5 × 19 (sight)
Signed, lower right (in Cyrillic): »Gabo«
Family Collection

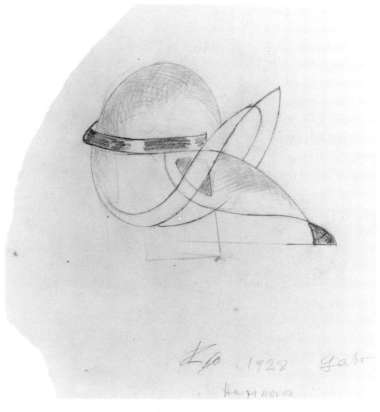

108   Sketch, Monte Carlo, 1926
Pencil and crayon, 26.7 × 20.3; Initialled and dated, lower right:
»N.G./1926/Mont [sic] Carlo«; Family Collection

109   Study for a Construction, 1928
Pencil, 28.7 × 25.5; Signed and dated, lower right:
»1928 Gabo/Hannover«; Family Collection

110
**Study for
›Arch No. 1‹**
1929
Pencil, 21 × 30
Initialled (in Cyrillic)
and dated, upper left:
»N.G. 1929«
Family Collection

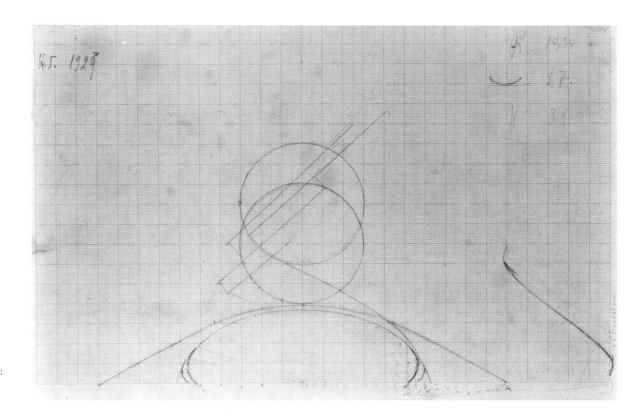

111
Sketch for a Carving in Stone, 1930
Crayon and gouache, 27.3 × 33.7 (sight)
Initialled (in Cyrillic) and dated, lower right: »N.G./Okt. 1930«
Family Collection

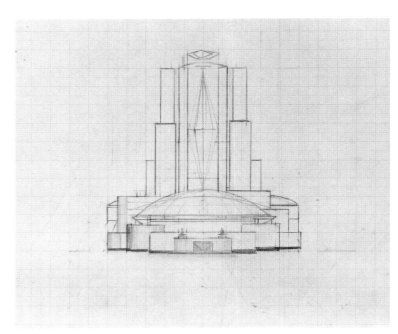

112
**Front Elevation of the Palace
of the Soviets,** 1931
Pencil, 23.2 × 26
Family Collection

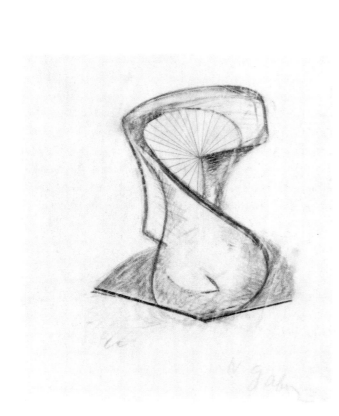

113
Sketch for a Stone Carving, 1933
Pencil and crayon, 16.5 × 15.2
Signed and dated, lower right: »N. Gabo 33«
Family Collection

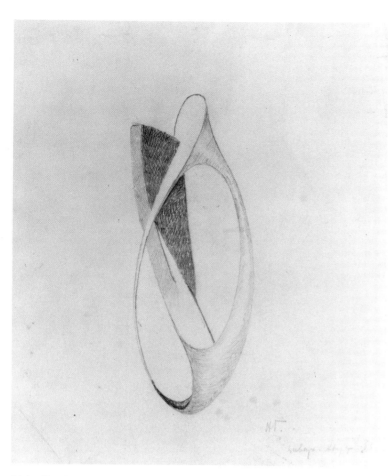

114   Study for ›Logan Rock (the Urn)‹, 1933
Pencil, 29 × 22.5; Initialled and dated (in Russian),
lower right: »N.G./Jan. – August 33«
Family Collection

115   **Untitled,** 1930s (?)
Crayon, 39.5 × 25.5; Initialled, lower right: »N.G.«
Family Collection

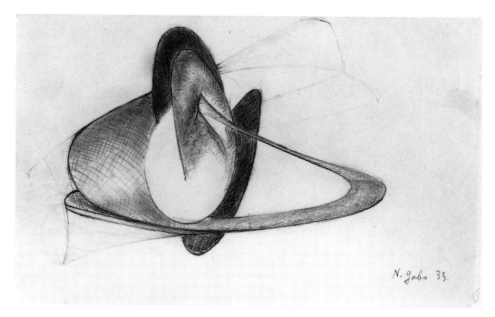

116

Sketch for a Stone Carving, 1933
Pencil, 14 × 22
Signed and dated, lower right: »N. Gabo 33«
The Tate Gallery, London

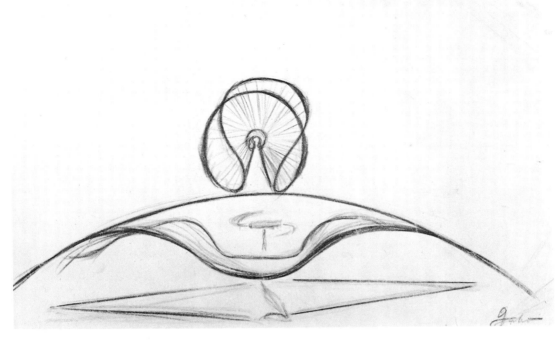

117
Sketch for ›Spheric Theme‹
c. 1935–37
Blue pencil, 19.7 × 32.2
Signed, lower right: »Gabo«
The Tate Gallery, London

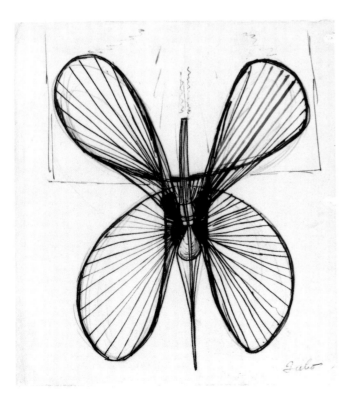

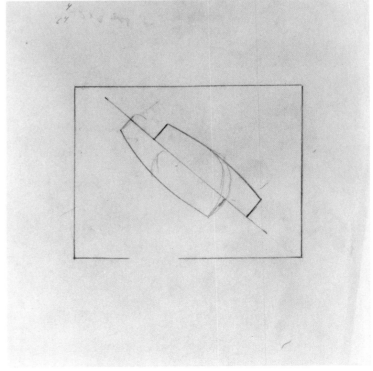

118   Sketch for ›Spheric Theme‹, c. 1937
Pencil and ink, 24 × 20.4; Signed, lower right: »Gabo«;
The Tate Gallery, London

119   Study for ›Construction on a Line‹, c. 1937
Pencil, 24 × 20.5; Family Collection

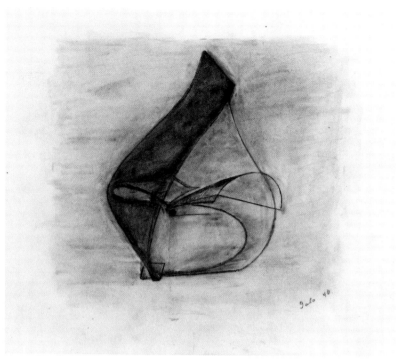

120 Study for ›Construction in Space: Crystal‹
c. 1937; Pencil, 24 × 20.5; Family Collection

121 Sketch, 1940
Crayon, 31 × 29; Signed and dated, lower right: »Gabo.40.«; Family Collection

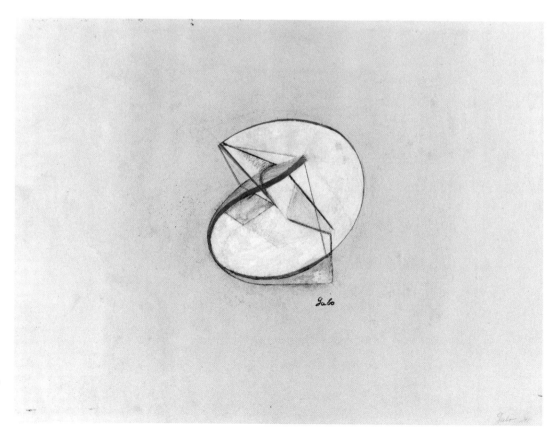

122
Study with Red, 1941
Mixed media, 27 × 34
Signed under image: »Gabo«
And signed and dated,
lower right: »Gabo 41«
Family Collection

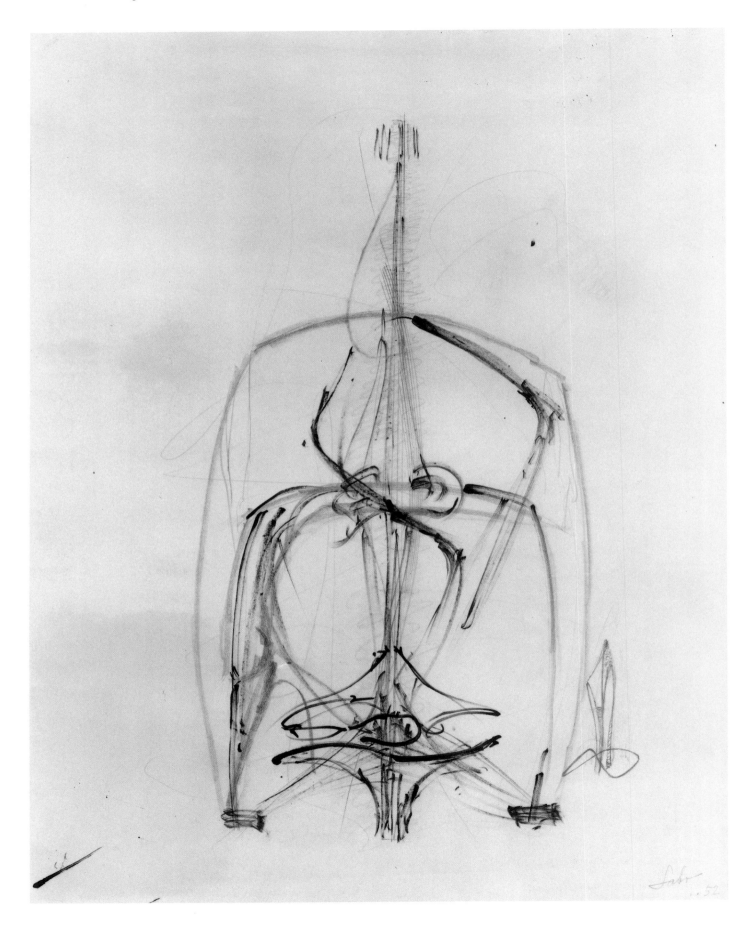

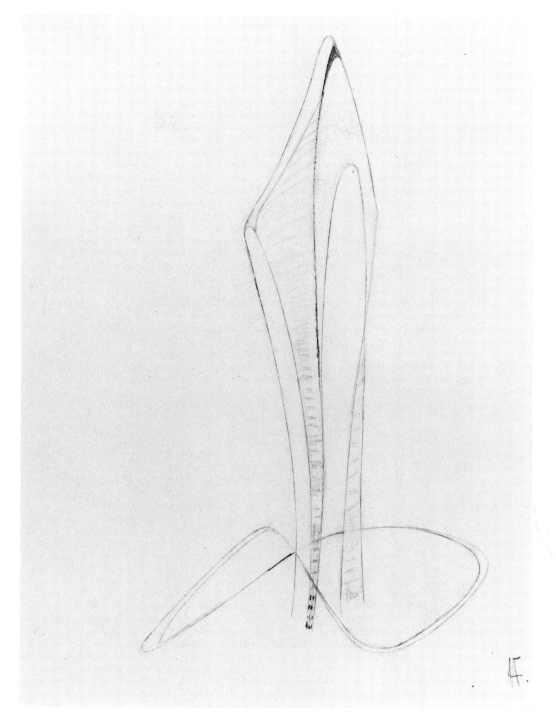

124 Sketch for a Vertical Composition, c. 1952
Pencil, 38 × 27; Initialled (in Cyrillic),
lower right: »N.G.«; Family Collection

123
Study for an Arch Monument, 1952
Pencil and felt pen, 48.5 × 39.5 (sight)
Signed and dated, lower right: »Gabo/.52«
Family Collection

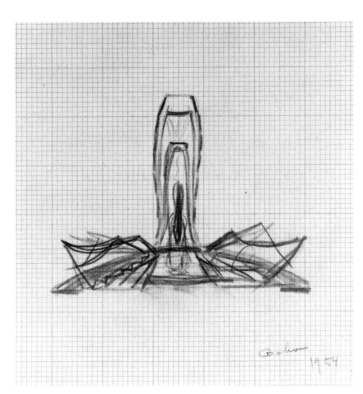

125
**Sketch of the ›Monument to the
Unknown Political Prisoner‹,** 1954
Pencil, 23.7 × 18.7
Signed and dated, lower right: »Gabo/1954«
Family Collection

126
Study for a Fountain, 1950s (?)
Pencil and crayon, 34.3 × 42.4 (sight)
Initialled (in Cyrillic), lower right: »N.G.«
Family Collection

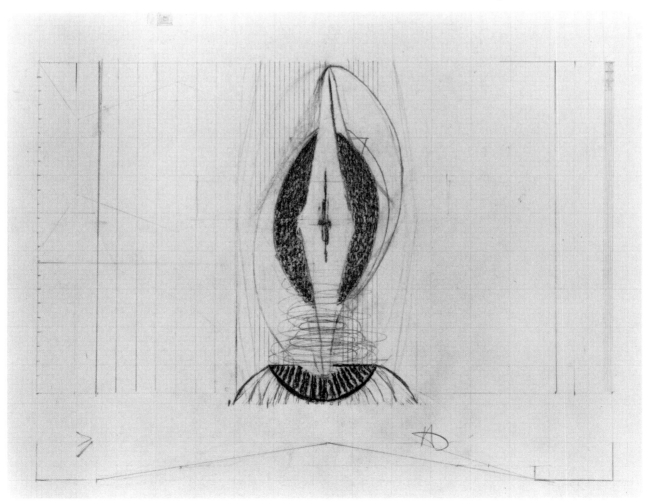

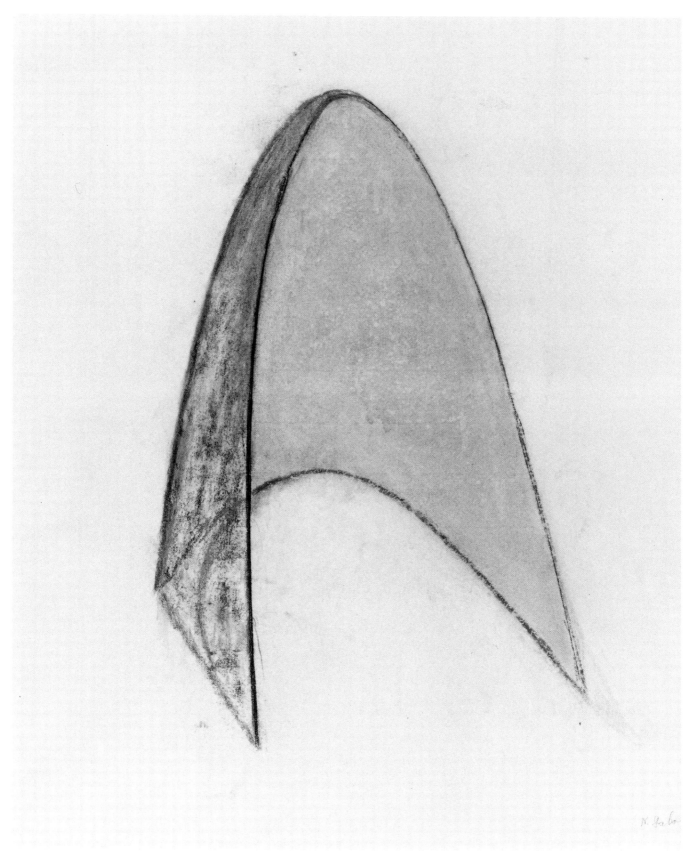

127   Project for a Color Lithograph, date unknown
Pastel, 58.5 × 47; Signed, lower right: »N. Gabo«; Family Collection

Paintings and Prints

128
Self Portrait, c. 1907–10
Oil on canvas, c. 24 × 17
Family Collection

129
Logan Rock (The Urn), 1938
Oil on board, 21.5 × 27
Inscribed (in Russian), lower left:
»from a drawing of 33«. And signed,
lower center: »Gabo«. Inscribed on
verso: »Written on back of panel in
Russian ›painted in the summer
of 1939 from a drawing of the year 1933.‹«

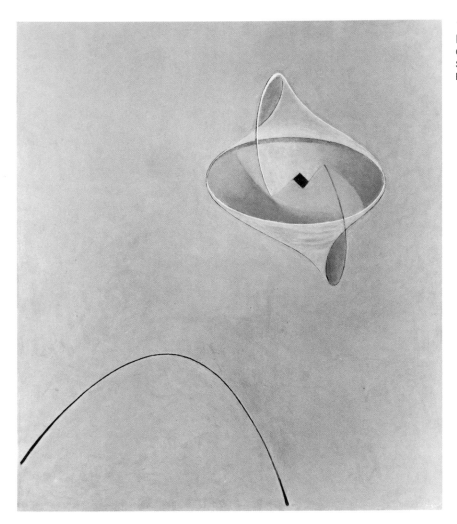

130
Hovering, 1940
Oil on board, 76 × 63.5
Signed, lower right: »Gabo«
Family Collection

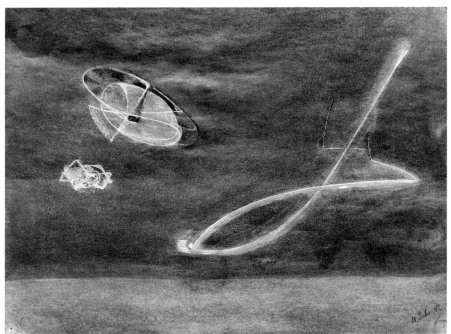

131   **The Pilot's View,** 1942
Oil on paper; 37 x 27.5 (sight); Signed and dated, lower right: »N. Gabo.42.«; Family Collection

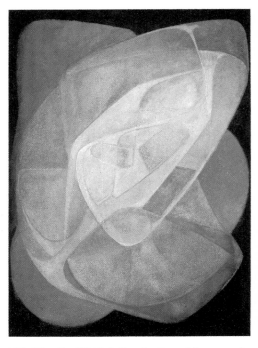

132 **Kinetic Oil Painting in Four Movements**
1943, oil on board, 26.5 × 19; Family Collection

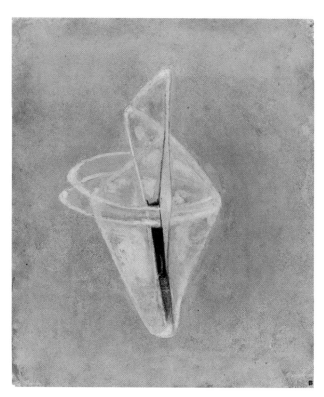

133 **Spinning,** 1944
Oil on paper, 19.5 × 15.5; Signed, lower right: »Gabo«
And inscribed on verso: »N. Gabo/Aug. 44«
Family Collection

135 **Turquoise,** 1945
Oil on board, mounted on motorized revolving disc, 20.2 × 23.2
Signed in one corner: »Gabo«; Family Collection

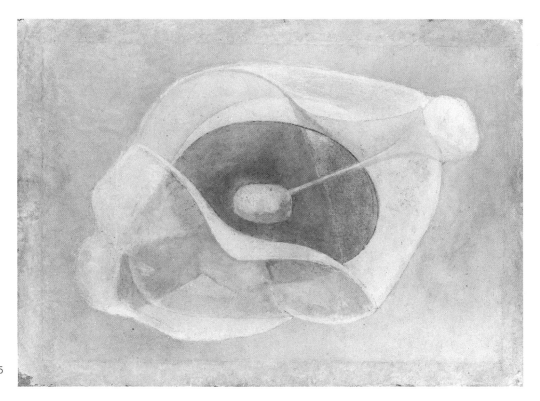

134
Strontium, 1945
Oil on cardboard, 22.5 × 29.5
Family Collection

136   **Portfolio of twelve wood engravings,** 1950 – mid 70s
Measurements vary; Family Collection

Opus 6

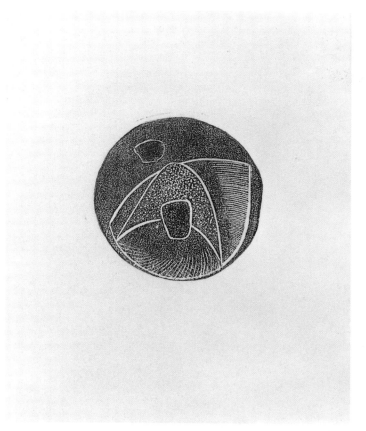

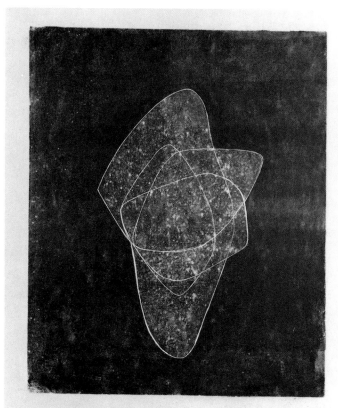

Opus 1

Opus 8

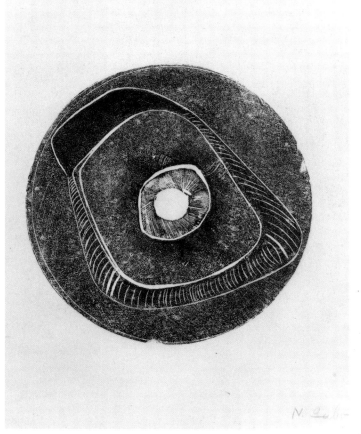

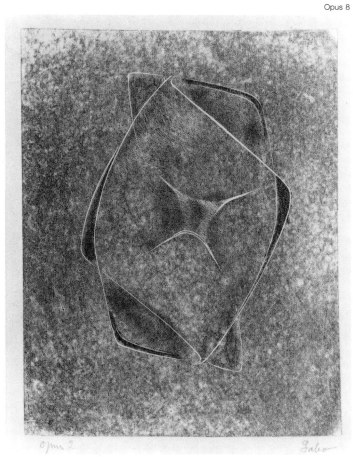

Opus 12

Opus 2

Catalogue Raisonné
of the Constructions and
Sculptures of Naum Gabo

Compiled by Colin C. Sanderson
Editor and Consultant: Christina Lodder

For Miriam Gabo

Contents

Preface

In his introduction to the 1957 monograph *Gabo: Constructions, Sculpture, Paintings, Drawings, Engravings,* Sir Herbert Read wrote the following:

»[Naum Gabo's] constructions . . . are images of a tradition that has still to be established – prototypes of an art that is emerging to give expression to the unformulated ideals and blind aspirations of a new age. New materials, new processes, a new technology of unknown potentiality, are waiting to be fused by the imagination of a new breed of artists into the monuments of a new civilization. Of this breed of artists Naum Gabo is the forerunner. This volume is an impressive record of the thought and experiment that he has devoted to the realization of a totally new conception of art, and in an age of experiment it is distinguished by the passion, the consistency, and the clarity of vision that have constantly inspired the artist.«

When Sir Herbert Read was writing Gabo still had twenty years of creative activity ahead of him. Today the 1957 monograph is sadly out of date and the need to present a fuller and more up-to-date view of Gabo's work has become pressing. A *catalogue raisonné* of Naum Gabo's work has long been overdue.

The fullest published listing of Gabo's works was compiled by the artist himself and included in the 1957 monograph. This list necessarily omitted almost twenty years of his work, yet it remained an essential work of reference and a starting point for subsequent research. Since 1980 Colin Sanderson has been indefatigable in tracing works and amassing data. The results of his research formed the basis for the first draft of this catalogue. At this stage there were still a large number of problems to be tackled: mainly in unravelling the complexities that are necessarily involved in chronicling the oeuvre of an artist whose work spanned more than sixty years, and at least five countries. Since October 1983 the compiler and editor have been working together, and have managed to solve some of these problems. The catalogue has been revised and largely rewritten, in an attempt to make some of the necessarily tortuous lines of argument accessible to those not so immersed in the details of Gabo's life and work.

No *catalogue raisonné* is the work of one person and this one is no exception. The many scholars, owners, gallery staff and librarians who have contributed to making this work as accurate as possible are thanked in the acknowledgements. I would like, however, to say a particular thank you to Miriam Gabo and Nina and Graham Williams. They have not only been constant sources of support and inspiration, they have also ransacked their memories and their archives on our behalf. Without their unswerving commitment and their continual help the initial compilation, subsequent revision, and ultimate production of this catalogue would not have been possible.

Gabo said: »My work represents not change but development.« Both Colin Sanderson and myself hope that some of the complexities and richness of that development will now be more apparent.

Christina Lodder

Acknowledgements

My first debt of thanks is to Miriam Gabo and Nina Williams (née Gabo) for asking me to undertake the catalogue, and then for suffering and answering innumerable questions over some four and a half years. My thanks, however, are also due to them and to Graham Williams for their commitment to seeing the catalogue in print.

Secondly I must thank Dr. Christina Lodder. Her detailed examination of the arrangement and content of the catalogue, and the experience she brought to the re-drafting of the notes, has both averted errors and contributed significantly to the content.

It is impossible to thank individually the scores of people, who, by providing information and hospitality, have helped in the compilation of this catalogue. My thanks go to them all, including those who wish to remain anonymous. Some particular debts, however, must be acknowledged personally.

In 1979, Gabo's younger brother, the late Alexei Pevsner, generously gave up part of his time in London to answer questions about Gabo's early years. Early in my research, Alan Bowness allowed me to work from his preliminary listings of Gabo's works and Ronald Alley kindly gave me access to proofs of his catalogue entries covering works in the Tate Gallery. Gabo's assistant, Charles Wilson, continuously provided much helpful information, and in Chicago in 1981 he showed me the works which were discovered in the attic of the Gabos' house in Middlebury in 1977.

At Yale, Professor Robert L. Herbert has been indefatigably helpful and encouraging, as were his colleagues, particularly Eleanor Apter and Ruth Bohan. At the Solomon R. Guggenheim Museum, Angelica Rudenstine, who also supplied information regarding the Peggy Guggenheim Collection, and subsequently Vivian Barnett and Lewis Kachur, have been most helpful. I would also like to acknowledge the research done at that museum by Susan Ferliger-Brades. In other museums, galleries and collections, I would also thank Celia Ascher, V. Beston, Erica Brausen, Judith Cousins, Courtney Donnell, Stephen Dunn, J. M. Joosten, Annely Juda, L. J. Kruger, and Brenda Richardson.

In my work on the papers in the Gabo Archive and in the Archive of the Société Anonyme, I owe a great deal to the efforts of Dr. David Schoonover and the staff at the Beinecke Rare Book and Manuscript Library, Yale University. I would also like to thank Sarah Fox-Pitt and the staff of the Tate Gallery Archive, London.

Many private individuals, including owners of works, have answered letters and given generous hospitality. Particularly I would thank the late Marcus and Mrs. Brumwell; Harold Diamond; Mr. and Mrs. Arthur Duckworth; Paul Feiler; Dr. and Mrs. Owen Franklin; Beverley Franklin; Margaret Gardiner; Professor and Mrs. George Heard Hamilton; Professor Gyorgy Kepes; Sir Leslie and Lady Martin; Benedict Read; Sir Norman and Lady Reid; Mr. and Mrs. George Rickey; Mr. and Mrs. Eugene Rosenberg; Katherine Ryan; Professor P. Sanders; Nathan Smooke; the late Dr. John and Mrs. Sisson; the late Dr. G. van der Wal; and Mr. Thomas P. Whitney.

I am indebted to Bernard Karpel's bibliography and list of exhibitions published in 1957 and 1961 (G28). Among the staff at many libraries I would particularly like to thank Clive Philpott and his staff at the Museum of Modern Art, New York. Thanks are also due to Carol Evans at the BBC's Data Enquiry Service, and Jane Ellison for help with the Filmography, and to Elizabeth Bode for checking several of the newspaper references.

My tutor at the Courtauld Institute of Art, Dr. Christopher Green, has given much patient and thoughtful advice, and friends and colleagues have also helped by providing information and unfailing encouragement: particularly Elizabeth Childs, Judi Freeman, Nigel Halliday, John Klein, Peter Nisbet, Mary Shepard, Charles Steiner, and David Thistlewood.

Christina Lodder would like her particular thanks to be extended to: Mr. and Mrs. Thomas P. Whitney, Ruth Israels, Sir Norman and Lady Reid, Professor and Mrs. George Heard Hamilton, Mr. Francis Cooke and the late Mrs. Cooke, Dr. and Mrs. Owen Franklin, Annely Juda; Mr. and Mrs. Eugene Rosenberg, and Dr. David Schoonover and the staff of the Beinecke Rare Book and Manuscript Library, Yale University.

Lastly I would like to thank my family and above all my lovely and long-suffering wife, Lynne. Without her practical and moral support, I feel sure that this catalogue would never have been.

Colin C. Sanderson

Introduction

Colin C. Sanderson

In 1977 Gabo's family asked Alan Bowness to revise Gabo's own list of works published in 1957. In 1980 Miriam and Nina Gabo (now Mrs. Graham Williams) asked me to continue the compilation. From this beginning I started to compile a complete list for a projected publication. As work progressed during the following three years, the scope of the intended list grew into a *catalogue raisonné*. In 1983 Dr. Christina Lodder was appointed by the family as Editor and Consultant. With the prospect of major retrospective exhibitions opening in the autumn of 1985, and with the family's commitment to publication, we embarked on the preparation of the manuscript for publication. In April 1984 the large collection of works belonging to the Gabo family, held in storage, was made available for examination. In the following summer I made the last of three visits to the USA to complete my researches there.

A concise *Guide to the Catalogue Raisonné Entries* has been provided for the reader. Certain problems underlying the compilation, and the decisions taken in establishing the criteria governing entries, require some elaboration.

The Scope of the Catalogue Raisonné

This catalogue is confined to Gabo's constructions and sculptures and comprises some 347 objects under 87 group headings. In addition to the finished works, studies, models and the few reconstructions are listed. Gabo also made objects which, although they are not sculptures, relate particularly to his constructions or demonstrate his sculptural ideas. When sufficient data exist, these objects are given their own entries (e.g. 2, 30.1). Otherwise they are noted in the text. Gabo's design works, such as the set and costumes for Diaghilev's ballet *La Chatte*, although often closely related to his constructions, are excluded. Significant drawings and templates are mentioned in the catalogue notes.

Gabo rejected any suggestion that his work could reasonably be divided into periods, but rather claimed that it demonstrated a continuous development. An attempt has been made to indicate the connections of form and structure between different works, sometimes in different media. Biographical and historical commentary has been kept to a minimum.

Models, Templates and Drawings

Although Gabo sometimes explored sculptural ideas on paper, he rarely made finished three-dimensional drawings before making a work. Indeed, of the more finished drawings, some may have been made after the construction or sculpture had been realised.

Gabo's statements about his working methods and the evidence of his surviving drawings and models, particularly those for his early figurative works, suggest that he sometimes proceeded directly from a complete mental image of a work to the production of a model in cardboard, or, for later works, in celluloid. For *Torso* (6), he also made an enlarged model in cardboard (6.2). This larger model was subsequently disassembled and the pieces used as templates for the finished work. 6.2 was clearly at one time constructed, it has therefore been entered as a »model« rather than as templates.

Several scale drawings on graph paper exist, representing on one sheet the several sections required to make the construction. The earliest of these are small, corresponding with the smaller versions, and probably date from the 1920s. Some are annotated with the colours and thicknesses of the materials to be used, and with a figure apparently indicating the extent to which the work was to be enlarged (see e.g. 20.1, 23.1). Other scale-drawings from a later period are far larger, corresponding with enlarged versions.

Gabo may have used these scale-drawings as guides in cutting the required shapes from transparent plastic sheets, and so the first constructed versions of works, whether on a small or a large scale, would appear quite highly finished. The question arises, therefore, should these works be considered as models for subsequent versions or as finished works in their own right? In the catalogue the degree of finish has been taken into account. Where there are several small versions of a work, it seems certain that some should be considered as finished works rather than as models (e.g. 52). Such distinctions must remain open to question, but an attempt has been made to differentiate in the titles, between studies, models and finished works. Some works, previously described as models due primarily to their small size, are more accurately classified as small finished works. Gabo intended many of his constructions to be enlarged for display in public places and considered several of his larger constructions as designs for still larger fountains. Therefore, some quite large finished works served in their turn as models for yet larger versions.

Titles of Works

Gabo's own preference was for titles which did not distract the viewer from the work itself. Miriam Gabo recalls that when she first met Gabo, he referred to most of his works simply as *Construction* or *Construction in Space* (the latter being Gabo's translation of the German *Raumkonstruktion*). Gabo later used the subtitle *Variation* with similar freedom, often implying simply that other versions of the works existed. These indeterminate titles created problems for galleries and shippers and so Gabo occasionally gave more distinctive titles. For some works, the proliferation of different titles has meant that no particular title can be regarded as authoritative.

Whilst giving priority to titles sanctioned by Gabo's own use, the titles have been chosen so that distinct reference can be made to each particular work or group of works. This policy has been followed consistently even where it meant adopting a name that had fallen into disuse. For example, *Construction in Relief*, 1920 (8), is entitled here *Construction in Space C [Raumkonstruktion C]*, a title which Gabo gave it in 1922. Where several titles were available, or where no title was published, the simplest possible title has been chosen. Where no alternative was available, indeterminate titles have been retained. In some cases, the group, and several individual members of the group, all bear the same title. Where Gabo used a distinguishing subtitle for one, this is retained. Where a second title was commonly used by Gabo for a particular work, it has been retained as a subtitle, for example, 5.1 is entitled *Constructed Head No. 3 (Head of a Woman)*. *Constructed Head No. 3* was the first specific title used by Gabo. Since 5.1 has also been known for many years as *Head of a Woman*, this has been incorporated as a subtitle.

Dates of Works

Gabo was concerned with developing his ideas, not with documenting them. Not surprisingly numerous inaccuracies occur even in major published sources.

Gabo dated his works variously. The dates he gave were either when the ›image‹ had originally formed in his mind; when he had made the first drawing or the first model; or when he had made the first finished work. For later versions of the same work, the date often referred to the original construction rather than to the later version. This led to inconsistencies of dating even in those sources which one might expect to be authoritative. An attempt has been made to give the date when a particular work, or version of a work, was constructed. The main reliance remains on dates which may be ascribed directly or indirectly to Gabo himself. In many cases it has only been possible to indicate a broad range of dates within which the individual work was made.

Inscriptions

Gabo did not always sign or date his works at the time he finished them; inscriptions were sometimes added many years later. The same holds true for the dates on drawings. The signatures vary from a simple initial ›G‹ to ›N. Gabo‹, which, occasionally on sculptures, but often on drawings, is in cyrillic.

Materials

Gabo used many different materials – cardboard, glass, plastics, metals and stone – and many varieties of some individual materials, particularly of plastics and alloys. Although they cannot be regarded as ›materials‹, Gabo considered space and time to be fundamental elements in his work.

Particularly for works that could not be examined personally, the identification of materials relies heavily on published sources and on information from the Gabo archives. Much of Gabo's correspondence with suppliers is preserved (Yale 1). Reference to these letters is extremely limited; only rarely can a specific order for materials be related with certainty to a particular work. Future physical and chemical analyses of Gabo's materials, particularly the plastics, will prove helpful in dating individual versions of works more precisely.

To differentiate between plastics, and particularly between analogues of the same plastic, visual inspection alone is unreliable. Until recently, little chemical or physical analysis has been carried out on the plastics used by artists, and only two of Gabo's works have been subjected to such examination (see 22.4, 29.3).

CELLULOID: Some of the plastics that Gabo used in early works were forms of celluloid, various forms of ›cellulose nitrate‹. These plastics proved unstable, eventually becoming yellowed and deformed or even distintegrating. The term ›celluloid‹ has also commonly been used to refer to ›cellulose acetate‹, which is not nearly so vulnerable to degradation. Although the early works which have yellowed most are probably composed of cellulose nitrate, this must remain inconclusive. Gabo later repaired several of his early works in more durable materials, including cellulose acetates, and it is often impossible to be certain of the materials originally used. The term ›celluloid‹ is used to cover both cellulose nitrates and acetates.

CELLON: Cellon was a cellulose acetate produced in Germany by Dynamit A.-G.[1] None of the works in this catalogue are known to have been made of Cellon. However as Gabo did use Cellon in the set for the ballet La Chatte in 1927[2] he may have used it in other constructions.

GALALITH AND TROLIT: Galalith (Galalit), was a casein plastic, produced in Germany before the First World War.[3] It has been described as »artificial horn produced by the action of formaldehyde on casein.«[4] Trolit (sometimes spelled Trolith or Trolite), was a cellulose acetate moulding powder. Gabo probably used Trolit F which was a nitrocellulose plastic, supplied as sheets, rods and tubes.[5] Only 11 has been said to have contained both these plastics, and 10.2 to have contained Galalith. Gabo may, however, have used them more often. In 1932 Ernst Kállai recorded Gabo's use of Galalith (A126), and in Plastics, in 1938, a review of Gabo's London exhibition stated that ›casein‹ was one of the plastics Gabo used (E6; A12).

RHODOID: Rhodoid was the trade-name for a form of cellulose acetate distributed in France by Société des Usines Chimiques Rhône-Poulenc, as sheets, rods or tubes.[6] It is not known when Gabo first encountered Rhodoid, but he continued to use it after he settled in London in 1936, where it was supplied by May and Baker Ltd.

Gabo used both clear and pigmented Rhodoid. Clear Rhodoid is said to have a slight bluish hue, but some of Gabo's works thought to be made of Rhodoid hardly show this trait, and it does not therefore appear to be a reliable characteristic. Some of the works entered here simply as celluloid may be made specifically of Rhodoid.

PERSPEX: Perspex is the trade-name for a plastic polymer, poly(methyl methacrylate), developed in Britain by Imperial Chemical Industries. Production of Perspex began in 1934,[7] and it was marketed in 1935.[8] According to Miriam Gabo, Marcus Brumwell introduced Gabo to Dr. John Sisson of ICI in late 1936 or early 1937.[9] Dr Sisson was then Works Manager of Mouldrite, later to become ICI Plastics Division, of which he became Chairman. Through this friendship Gabo had direct access to ICI materials and technical advice (see 48.14).

Subsequently analogues of Perspex were made under license in the USA by Rohm and Haas (Plexiglas), and by Du Pont (Lucite). After Gabo moved to the USA in 1946, it is rarely possible to be certain which analogue he used in any particular work. Dr Sisson continued to supply materials and Gabo sometimes bought them in England. Seldom is the distinction made between the analogues; the term Perspex is used to cover them all.

NYLON: The large-scale commercial production of nylon did not start until the end of 1939 in the USA; and British production under license,not until the 1940s.[10] In 1941 production in Britain was still described as ›imminent‹.[11] It is unlikely that Gabo used nylon filament before 1941, but it is certain that he used it in 1942 (48.2).

Some Intriguing Mysteries Remain

A number of references to Gabo's works, both published and unpublished, cannot be identified with a particular work. Although many of these references are apparently quite insignificant, others deserving attention are noted here.

Miss Katherine Dreier and Jane Heap exhibited several works in the USA in the mid-1920s (see B101). Jane Heap, joint-editor of The Little Review and organiser of the Little Review Gallery, exhibited several works in 1926 and 1927 (E4, E42). Miss Dreier, who with Marcel Duchamp founded the Société Anonyme in 1920, acquired several works from Gabo for her own collection and for the Société, and borrowed at least one work from Gabo for the Société's touring exhibition of 1926–7 (E38–41). Much of Miss Dreier's correspondence with Gabo and Jane Heap is preserved (Yale 1 and Yale 2). There are five constructions known or thought to have been in their possession at the time (6.1, 8, 13, 15, 16). But it remains difficult to correlate the references in their letters, and in the relevant exhibition catalogues, with specific works. For this reason, some of the identifications made in this catalogue remain speculative (e.g. see 14).

In the catalogue for the Hannover exhibition of 1930 (E5), amongst the owners of his works Gabo listed Tristan Tzara – Paris; Bornes – Chicago; Essel – Paris; Toorop – Amsterdam; Arch. Olsen – Oslo; and museums in Moscow and Smolensk. What belonged to Tristan Tzara is unknown and may perhaps have been a drawing rather than a construction. The reference to Bornes remains unexplained (see 32). ›Essel-Paris‹ must refer to the gallery owner Jos. Hessel (see 5.1). ›Toorop‹ refers to the Dutch artist, Charley Toorop, who is known from correspondence to have owned a work (probably a relief), but the construction remains untraced.[12] ›Arch. Olsen-Oslo‹, apparently an architect, may have acquired a work when Gabo was living in Norway in 1914–17. On the other hand, the reference might be to the Swedish artist, Axel Olson, who was in Berlin in the early 1920s studying with Archipenko (B157 p. 50). One of the works in Moscow or Smolensk must have been Con-

structed Torso (6.3), and Constructed Head No. 3 (5.2) was probably another. Neither of these works, however, has been traced.

In 1937 Gabo credited an illustration of Construction in Space: Two Cones (29.3), to ›Coll. Mrs Francis, London‹ (G12 p. 286). According to Miriam Gabo, Mrs Francis was interested in the ballet and knew Arthur Duckworth (see 12.4, 41.2), and Ernst Stern, the theatrical designer, both of whom were friends of Gabo. Miriam Gabo, however, clearly remembers that 29.3 was acquired directly from Gabo by A. E. Gallatin, whereas Mrs Francis, although she may have acquired a small version of Two Cones, probably had a version of Linear Construction in Space No. 1 (48). Exactly what work Mrs Francis owned remains unidentified.

In 1946 Alexander Dorner wrote to Gabo: ›For . . . the stone sculpture, you have to write to my successor. I left it in the basement in good condition. It will still be there I guess.‹[13] The building to which Dorner referred may have been the Hannover Landesmuseum, where Dorner was Director until 1936, but more likely the Museum of the Rhode Island School of Design, from which he retired in 1941. This work remains unidentified.

In 1942 Peggy Guggenheim listed two works by Gabo as belonging to her gallery ›Art of This Century‹ (B98). One, known only from the listing as Kinetic Construction, was not illustrated; later Peggy Guggenheim stated that the entry was an error and the work never existed.[14] The second, Model for a Fountain, was illustrated, but was subsequently destroyed. It remains unknown from whom she acquired this work (see 21).

Perhaps the most intriguing questions of all concern the history of the original Constructed Head No. 2 which was lost to Gabo for some thirty years (4.2). Where had it been, and how did it return to Gabo? This, the first full catalogue of Gabo's constructions and sculptures, cannot be the last word. Despite all efforts, some errors and omissions will no doubt be discovered and for these we apologise to the reader. It is hoped that it will aid and stimulate new research and, above all, promote the far wider appreciation of Gabo's work.

Notes:

1. Emil Ott, Harold M. Spurlin and Mildred W. Grafflin [eds] High Polymers. Vol. V. Cellulose and Cellulose Derivatives 2nd ed., New York etc., 1955, Part III, p. 1474.
2. Letter from Gabo to J. Wood, Albright-Knox Art Gallery, 31 Mar 1971, Yale 1, where Gabo refers to it as ›Celon‹.
3. F. Greenaway et al ›The Chemical Industry‹, in Trevor I. Williams (ed.) A History of Technology Vol. VI: The Twentieth Century, c. 1900 to c. 1950. Part I Oxford, 1978, p. 553.
4. Edward Chauncey Warden The Nitrocellulose Industry New York, 1911, Vol. 2, p. 763.
5. E. Ott et al, op. cit., Part III, p. 1479.
6. E. Ott et al, op. cit., Part III, p. 1478.
7. F. Greenaway et al, op. cit., p. 558.
8. W. J. Reader Imperial Chemical Industries: A History Oxford, 1975, Vol. 2, p. 346.
9. St. Ives 1939–64 London, Tate Gallery, 13 Feb–14 Apr 1985, p. 163.
10. J. Jewkes, D. Sawers and R. Stillerman The Sources of Invention London, 1958, pp. 336–7.
11. V. E. Yarsley and E. G. Couzens Plastics Harmondsworth, Pelican Books, 1941, p. 145.
12. Letter to Gabo from C. Toorop, 5 Apr 1930.
13. Letter to Gabo from A. Dorner, 25 Dec 1946.
14. Information from A. Z. Rudenstine, interview with Peggy Guggenheim 1977/8.

Guide to the Catalogue Raisonné entries

General Structure

The groups and the individual objects within each group are listed chronologically. Undated works are listed within the group to which they are related, or at the end of the catalogue (groups 82–87). Some information is only contained in the introductory notes to each group and the reader is advised to read the relevant introduction when consulting the entry for a specific work.

Photographs which appear in the front sections of this exhibition catalogue are not repeated here, but a cross reference, e.g *photo. Exhib. Cat. No. XX* is included after the provenance.

Entries

Each entry is numbered, and it comprises the title of the work, the date when it was made, whether or not it is inscribed, its materials and dimensions (if known), its present location and provenance, its exhibition history and publications in which it is illustrated or discussed. This is followed, where relevant, by notes relating to its history, its present condition, restoration or reconstruction, etc.

Titles

Usually the simplest distinctive title has been chosen. Alternative titles have been noted and Gabo's own distinguishing subtitles for specific works have been retained.

Dates

The following notation has been adopted:

/   Dates separated by an oblique indicate that the work was made at some time between the two dates.
–   Dates separated by a hyphen indicate that the work was started in the former and finished in the latter year.
( )   Dates in parentheses are more doubtful.
n.d.   Not dated.

E.G. »(1927)/1930–31« indicates that the work was started at sometime between 1927 and 1930 (probably closer to 1930), and was completed in 1931.

Materials

Materials are identified where known. Early plastics are identified where possible. Perspex is used as a generic term to cover analogues such as Plexiglas and Lucite. See the Compiler's Introduction for further discussion of materials.

Dimensions

Dimensions are given where known. Unless otherwise stated, they are given in centimetres: height x width x depth. For some works the relevance of width and depth measurements is questionable. For these only a single dimension is given such as height, or the height plus one other dimension such as diameter.

It has not always been possible to re-measure works. Dimensions provided by people other than the editor and compiler, which may have been taken with different criteria, are indicated by square brackets. Measurements converted from inches are given to the nearest millimetre, although the work may not originally have been measured with this accuracy. For incomplete works overall dimensions have been estimated from the measurements of the pieces which remain.

Present Location and Provenance

When the name of an institution changed after it acquired a work, the name given in the provenance is that in use at the time of acquisition. The current name is given under present location. The date of the change or transfer is indicated where known.

Bibliographic and Exhibition References

Full details of publications and exhibitions are provided in the following lists:

G – writings by Gabo
F – films and broadcasts
B – books
A – articles and essays
N – newspapers
S – sale catalogues
E – exhibitions

Each item in these lists is numbered. In the exhibition and literature listings for each entry, each item comprises a number prefixed by a letter; the surname of the author of a publication, or the place of an exhibition; the date; the number under which a work was exhibited, and/or the page and figure references. *Catalogue raisonné* numbers quoted in the notes have no prefix; all other reference numbers are preceded either by No., referring to an exhibition catalogue entry, or by the appropriate letters indicating the reference.

Only the first or significant edition of a publication is normally listed. In later or earlier editions there may be some variations in pagination and content and where relevant these are cited, e.g. B76 (1937) was later revised, and under 55.3 the 1960 edition is cited as B76 (1960).

In some exhibition catalogues and other publications, captions to illustrations do not correspond to the actual work illustrated. These captions have been ignored and the photograph noted only in the literature section under the work illustrated, not under the work exhibited or discussed.

Where a work is illustrated or discussed in an exhibition catalogue but was not exhibited, the reference is listed in the literature section. Where works were not numbered in catalogues no numbers are cited in the *catalogue raisonné*. For one man shows however, numbers have been given to the exhibits and are cited in square brackets.

Primary Sources and Archives

The sources for information provided in an entry are normally cited in parentheses at the end of the relevant sentence. Unless otherwise stated, information from Gabo's family and other named individuals was given in interview or correspondence with the compiler, or editor, between 1978 and 1985. Letters and other documents cited are usually in Yale 1 (see below). When material in other archives has been used this is indicated. When documents in a museum's file, relating to a work in that collection, are cited in discussion of that work only, the initials of the institution are given in the reference. Elsewhere the following abbreviations are used:

AAA – Archives of American Art, Smithsonian Institution, Washington, DC
FAL – Family Archive, London
GAP – Gabo Archival Papers, The Library, The Museum of Modern Art, New York
MoMA – The Museum of Modern Art, New York
PA – The J. C. Pritchard Archive, University of Newcastle-upon-Tyne
SRGM – The Solomon R. Guggenheim Museum, New York
TGA – The Tate Gallery Archive, London
UVBC – The Herbert Read Archive, McPherson Library, University of Victoria, British Columbia
Yale 1 – The Naum Gabo Archive, The Collection of American Literature, Beinecke Rare Book and Manuscript Library, Yale University, New Haven, Connecticut
Yale 2 – The Société Anonyme Archive, details as Yale 1 above

Square brackets are used in the catalogue to indicate information that remains uncertain.

The British Library system of transliteration from Russian and Greek is used in the catalogue.

Further details and discussion of the catalogue are included in the Compiler's Introduction.

1. HEAD OF A NEGRO

Winter 1912–13. Clay.
Lost 1914; presumed destroyed.

Lit: B162 Pevsner (1964) p. 8, fig. p. 9, as ›1912‹ :
G31 (1966) p. 127 : A76 Clay (1966) p. 56 : B47
Clay (1969) p. 84.

Gabo referred to this as ›. . . the head of *The
Slave* . . . which I made in the winter of
1912–13 . . .‹ (letter to R. Johnson, 13 May 1965).
He recalled: ›Once, in Munich, on the way to a
lecture, I passed a Negro. His face seemed full of
suffering. Somehow he gave me the impression of
being blind. I looked at his face again and again;
then I went straight home, took out some clay, and
built up that face‹ (G31). The rough model was
finished in twenty minutes (A76).‹

Although Gabo had carved pieces of wood as a
child, and had modelled a portrait of his father out
of a mixture of brick-dust and water, this remains
his earliest known sculpture and the only documented modelled work (B162, G31). Gabo left
Head of a Negro in Munich in 1914 when he went
to Norway, and it was never recovered (›Autobiographical Fragments‹, FAL).

2. TWO CUBES (DEMONSTRATING
     THE STEREOMETRIC METHOD)

These cubes were not conceived as works of art,
but were made to demonstrate the ›stereometric
method‹, derived from solid geometry, that Gabo
considered fundamental to his work. The method
formed one of the five main points of *The Realistic
Manifesto* of 1920: ›Here we take four planes and
we construct with them the same volume as of four
tons of mass‹. This is the earliest reference to the
cubes, and in his translation Gabo amended the
phrase to ›Here (in this exhibition) we take . . .‹,
suggesting that he had included a pair of cubes in
the 1920 exhibition (E30; G28 p. 152). Although
Gabo may have made his first cubes in Norway,
only two pairs have been documented by their inclusion in exhibitions.

2.1 Two Cubes (Demonstrating the
        Stereometric Method)

[1920] Lost; destroyed.

Exh: E30 Moscow (1920).

Lit: G1 (1920)

The precise dating for these is uncertain. Gabo may
have used them for his teaching in the Moscow
State Free Art Studios, but it seems probable that
he would have made a pair especially for the exhibition of 1920 (E30).

2.2 Two Cubes (Demonstrating the
        Stereometric Method)

1930. Painted plywood. 30.5 x 30.5 x 30.5,
each cube.
London, Tate Gallery (T02166).
Presented by the artist, 1977.

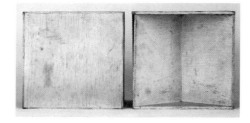

Exh: E5 Hannover (1930) No. 2a : E28 London
(1976–7) No. 5 : E255 Cambridge (1982) No. 5.

Lit: G12 (1937) pp. 106–7, fig. p. 103 : B184 Rickey (1967) p. 26, fig. 31 : B115 Krauss (1977)
pp. 57–8, fig. 42 : B3 Alley (1981) p. 242, fig.

These were apparently made especially for Gabo's
exhibition in Hannover in 1930 (E5; B3). There they
were exhibited with a contrasting pair of columnar
forms.

3. CONSTRUCTED HEAD NO. 1

This was the first work which Gabo made using the
›stereometric method‹ of construction. In the 1970s
Gabo told Ronald Alley that he considered that 3.2
had only been partially successful, and that he remained particularly dissatisfied with the lower section (B3 p. 263). This probably accounts for the fact
that Gabo did not exhibit this work after 1930 (E5;
see 3.2).

In 1957 Gabo listed a bronze version as owned
by the artist (G28). It is possible that Gabo had
planned to make such a version, but according to
Miriam Gabo, no metal variant was ever made.

3.1 Model for ›Constructed Head No. 1‹

1915. Cardboard.
Lost; presumed destroyed.

Lit: B3 Alley (1981) p. 263.

3.2 Constructed Head No. 1

1915. Triple-layered plywood. *c.* 54 high.
London, Family Collection.
See illus. p. 14, fig. 5, pp. 73 and 91

Exh: E1 Christiania (1916) : E2 Moscow (1917) :
E30 Moscow (1920) : E31 Berlin (1922) ex-cat. :
E32 Amsterdam (1923) ex-cat. : E5 Hannover
(1930) No. 4.

Lit: A11 (1931) p. 16, fig. 45 : G28 (1957) p. 182,
figs 1 and 2 : A152 Palme (1959) fig. p. 68 : B162
Pevsner (1964) p. 14, fig., as ›winter (1915–16)‹ :
A155 Ragon (1964) fig. p. 3 : B184 Rickey (1967)
p. 25, fig. 30 : B23 Besset (1976) fig. 25 : B9
Arnason (1977) fig. 393, : B115 Krauss (1977) figs
43a and 43b : E234 New York (1979) fig. 12 : B3
Alley (1981) p. 263 : B129 Lodder (1983) p. 35,
fig. 1.46.

In 1957 Gabo entered this work as ›in the USSR‹
(G28). In 1977, however, with the exception of one
piece on the shoulder and two curved pieces representing the breasts, all the pieces for this work
were found in the attic of the house in Middlebury
and entrusted to Charles Wilson for reconstruction.

Gabo listed this work as having been exhibited in
Berlin and Amsterdam in 1922–3 (E31, E32; G28).
Although there is no catalogue entry to confirm this,
Gabo was responsible for organising a section of
the exhibition and so could have exhibited 3.2 ex-
catalogue. When he exhibited 3.2 in 1930, Gabo
subtitled it ›First application of the stereometric
system in sculpture‹ [›*Erste Anwendung des stereo-
metrischen Systems in der Plastik*‹] (E5).

4. CONSTRUCTED HEAD NO. 2

This head, like *Constructed Head No. 1* (3), was
first made as a cardboard model and then enlarged
in more durable materials. According to Alexei
Pevsner, Gabo made *Constructed Head No. 2* in
Oslo in the early Autumn of 1916 (F17).

Gabo made several drawings which, although
mostly undated, can be related to the two early
heads, 3 and 4 (Family Collection). The drawing
closest to 4 is dated 1916 (G28, fig. 8). Another in
the group, apparently of a negro head, in which the
nose and the mouth are rendered as geometric
planes, may post-date 4, although the subject
clearly refers back to *Head of a Negro* (1).

4.1 Model for ›Constructed Head No. 2‹

1916. Cardboard.
Lost; presumed destroyed.

Lit: A201 (1972) p. 106 : B3 Alley (1981) p. 263.

4.2 Constructed Head No. 2

1916. Not inscribed.
Galvanised iron (originally covered with
yellow-ochre paint; paint removed 1962/3).
45 high; on wooden base 3.9 x 43.2 x 43.3.
London, Family Collection.
See illus. p. 15, fig. 6 and p. 92

Exh: E2 Moscow (1917) : E30 Moscow (1920) : E31 Berlin (1922) No. 543, as ›Konstruktiver Kopf, Nr 2, 1915‹, fig. 42, as ›1916 (Eisen)‹ : E32 Amsterdam (1923) as E31 : E20 Stockholm (1965–6) No. 55 : E22 Buffalo (1968) No. 1.

Lit: A221 Westheim (1922) fig. p. 495 : A172 (1923) fig. facing p. 65 : A123 Kállai (1924) p. 380 : E3 Paris (1924) fig.: A82 De Mély (1927) p. 417, fig. 1, as ›Cardboard Bust‹ : A69 Carter (1928) fig. p. 39 : B76 Giedion-Welcker (1937) fig. p. 129 : E9 New York (1948) fig. p. 22 : A176 Segi (1954) fig. p. 20, No. 1 : A153 Perilli (1954) fig. p. 73 : G28 (1957) p. 182, figs 3 and 4 : A196 Sylvester (1958) p. 168, fig. : [B204 Seuphor (1959) fig. p. 71] : B189 Rosenblum (1959) p. 264, fig. 197 : B76 Giedion-Welcker (1960) figs p. 176 : A225 Xagoraris (1962) p. 36, fig. 15 : B179 Read (1964) p. 293, fig. 98 : B162 Pevsner (1964) fig. p. 49 : E162 Milan (1964) fig. p. 33 : N23 Tucker (1964) fig. : E17 Amsterdam (1965) fig. : E18 Mannheim etc. (1965) fig. : E19 Zurich (1965) fig. : A103 Granath (1966) p. 11 : A224 Wolfram (1966) fig. p. 103 : B233 Zanini (1971) fig. 84 : A186 [Spar] (1975) fig. p. 47 : E234 New York (1979) fig. : E239 Milan (1979–80) fig. 149 : [B149 Mumford (1979) p. 236] : B151 Nakov (1981) fig. p. 34 *in situ* E32 : B3 Alley (1981) p. 263 : B129 Lodder (1983) p. 35, fig. 1.47 : E261 London (1983) fig. p. 14 *in situ* E32.

The pieces are soldered together and attached to the wooden base with four round-topped screws. Some surfaces, such as the curved piece of the right-hand shoulder, are abraded following the curve of the form. There is some very slight rusting.

In 1957 Gabo did not list this work as having been exhibited in Moscow in 1920 (G28), although he did include it in a later list (undated note, FAL). One photograph shows it bearing a label with a number corresponding to the catalogue entry for the 1922 exhibition (E31; G28 fig. 3).

According to Gabo, after the exhibition in Amsterdam in 1923 (E32), 4.2 was not returned to him in Berlin but was sent back to Russia by mistake (B3). Apparently Gabo had still hoped to recover 4.2 for the Vienna exhibition of 1924, because Kurt Ratke referred to Gabo's intention to show a head made of sheet-metal (E34; letter from K. Ratke, Gesellschaft zur Förderung Moderner Kunst in Wien, 21 Jul 1924). In the event Gabo exhibited 4.3.

De Mély illustrated 4.2 and implied that he had seen it in the Galerie Percier (A82 p. 417). Since 4.2 had been returned to Russia, he must have seen a different version (see 4.3).

A BBC film of 1981 included archival footage which suggested that 4.2, or a photograph of it, was shown in the exhibition *Decadent Art [Entartete Kunst]*, Munich, 1937 (F15). The shot of *Head No. 2*, however, was taken from an anti-Jewish propaganda film, ›The Wandering Jew‹ [›Der ewige Jude‹], made in 1940, and did not relate to the exhibition (Bundesarchiv, Filmarchiv, Koblenz, Mag. Nr. 3002). It is not known where or when this shot, possibly of a photograph, was taken.

Later, the pieces of 4.2 were mysteriously returned to Gabo in Middlebury, without his family knowing exactly how, when or whence they came. According to Miriam Gabo, 4.2 had been recovered before Gabo made 4.4. In 1957 Gabo listed 4.4 as a finished work, which would suggest that 4.2 had

been returned by then (G28). Yet Gabo did not list 4.2 as in his possession in 1957 (G28). According to Charles Wilson, Gabo may have started 4.4 before 1953; the slight differences between 4.4 and 4.2 indicate that Gabo had not recovered 4.2 before 4.4 was made. There is, therefore, no firm evidence to suggest that 4.2 was in Gabo's possession by 1957.

When 4.2 was returned, the covering of yellow ochre paint, which Gabo had applied to the construction before he left Norway, had deteriorated (M. Gabo, notes, 1982/3, FAL). At Gabo's insistence, it was stripped off by Charles Wilson who remembered helping Gabo to restore the work in 1962/3, by which date 4.2 had evidently been recovered. The process of restoration was evidently completed by November 1964 (N23), in time for 4.2 to be exhibited in Stockholm in 1965–6 (E20).

4.3   Constructed Head No. 2

1923/4. Inscribed in cyrillic on base at right: ›Gabo‹. Ivory Rhodoid, on wooden base. [43 high; on wooden base 2.9 high]. Dallas, Museum of Fine Arts (1981.35). From the artist's family, 1981. *See illus. pp. 74 and 93*

Exh: [E3 Paris (1924) No. 1] : E34 Vienna (1924) No. 149, as ›Konstruktiver Kopf. Zelluloid‹ : [E35 Paris (1925) No. 1276, as ›Construction Tête (1916)‹] : E9 New York (1948) [No. 1] : E68 Washington, DC (1948) : E11 Cambridge, Mass. (1951) [No. 11] : [E12 Chicago (1952) No. 7] : E88 Paris (1952) No. 120 : E89 London (1952) No. 101 : E14 Hartford (1953) No. 1.

Lit: A82 De Mély (1927) p. 417 : N24 (1948) fig. *in situ* E68 : N1 Adlow (1951) : G28 (1957) p. 182, n. 3 : A8 (1957) fig. p. 176 : B28 Bowness (1965) fig. p. 139 : B13 Bann (1974) fig. p. 5.

The original *Constructed Head No. 2* (4.2) was lost in 1923. At that time Gabo probably still had the original templates, although, according to Charles Wilson, the existing set of early templates may be a later replacement (Family Collection). 4.3 seems to have been made after 1922, because when it was damaged in 1952, Gabo stated that it had been made from Rhodoid, bought in Germany (letters to J. Sweeney, 28 Sep 1952, and to Mr Lenox, Topliss and Harding, 3 Oct 1952). 4.3 was evidently completed by September 1924, when Gabo substituted it for 4.2 in the Vienna exhibition (E34; see 4.2). It seems probable that Gabo made the plastic version after the loss of the original in 1923, and possibly for the Paris exhibition of 1924 (E3).

4.3 may have been shown in Paris in 1924 as No. 1, ›Construction Tête (1915)‹ (E3). The date suggests that *Constructed Head No. 1* (3.2) might have been shown, and in a copy of the catalogue No. 1 is annotated ›wood‹ (FAL). However, undue importance should not be attached to the date in E3 since the *Torso* of 1917 was also dated 1915 (see 6.1). More importantly, the original iron version of *Constructed Head No. 2* (4.2), was illustrated in the catalogue, implying that the head exhibited was a version of 4. In 1927 De Mély illustrated 4.2 as ›Cardboard Bust by Gabo‹, and stated that he had seen the work the previous year, in a studio on the corner of the Avenue Percier (A82). Unless Gabo

lent works to the Galerie Percier a second time, De Mély must have seen a version of 4 in the exhibition of 1924. The ›cardboard‹ in De Mély's caption suggests that 4.1 was shown at E3. It seems unlikely, however, that Gabo would have shown a cardboard model of 4 in addition to the cardboard model of *Torso* (6.1), when he was only showing eight works in all. It seems more likely that 4.3 was shown. (The Parisian shipping label on the base of 4.3 is inscribed ›120‹, and refers to E88, not E3).

4.3 was the version exhibited in Cambridge in 1951, as indicated in a review (E11; N1). Apparently the work was damaged in 1952, in transit to Paris for E88, and was repaired by Antoine Pevsner at Gabo's request (telegrams from and to J. Sweeney, 3 and 7 May 1952).

Bann illustrated 4.3 as in the Arensberg Collection, Philadelphia (B13). This location was provided by the Museum of Modern Art which had confused a photograph from the 1948 exhibition (E9), with slides of the Arensberg Collection, taken by the same photographer, Dr F. Block.

4.4   Constructed Head No. 2

1953/7. Inscribed twice in corner of base-plate with two overlapping signatures: ›Gabo‹. Phosphor-bronze; on wooden base. 44.4 high; on base 3.7 x 43.5 x 43.5 London, Family Collection.

Exh: E15 Rotterdam etc. (1958) No. 1 : E113 Amsterdam (1958) No. 70, fig. : E118 Frankfurt (1959) No. 48, fig. : E17 Amsterdam (1965) No. P1 : E18 Mannheim etc. (1965) No. 1, : E19 Zurich (1965) No. 1 : E21 London (1966) No. 1, fig. shows 4.2 : E22 Buffalo (1968) No. 2 : E23 Humlebaek etc. (1970–71) No. 1 : E24 Berlin (1971) No. 1 : E25 Hannover (1971) No. 1, fig. p. 107 : E26 Grenoble etc. (1971–2) No. 1 : E27 Lisbon (1972) No. 1, fig. p. 13 : E208 London (1973) No. 102a, photograph only : E234 New York (1979) No. 36 fig. p. 70 : E236 Paris (1979) p. 527, fig. p. 198 : E246 Los Angeles etc. (1980–81) No. 61, fig. p. 155 : E252 Saint Paul (1981) No. 74, fig. p. 102 : E 254 Madrid (1981) No. 43 : E261 London (1983) No. 17, fig. p. 99 : E268 Shiga (1984).

Lit: G28 (1957) p. 182, n. 3 : G30 (1962) figs 39a–d, screened fig. p. 110 : B116 Kuh (1962) fig. 45 : B202 Selz (1963) fig. 214 : B162 Pevsner (1964) fig. p. 17, as ›1916‹ : A219 Webb (1966) p. 660, fig. 1 : A31 (1967) colour fig. p. 99 : N2 Andreae (1968) fig. p. 9 : A54 Besset (1971) figs pp. 9, and 8 *in situ* E26 : B63 Elsen (1974) fig. 74.

4.4 was first listed by Gabo in 1957, and first exhibited in 1958 (G28; E15). According to Charles Wilson, Gabo may have started 4.4 before the family left Woodbury in 1953. According to Miriam Gabo, 4.4 was made in Middlebury and Gabo was helped by a welder, Mr Gembalsky. It seems probable, therefore, that Gabo planned or even cut pieces of bronze for 4.4 before 1953, although the work was not constructed until some time between 1953 and 1957.

Miriam Gabo believes that 4.4 was based on 4.2. According to Charles Wilson, however, 4.4 was made before the return of 4.2, and slight differences between the orientation of certain pieces in 4.4 and 4.2 indicate that Gabo did not base 4.4 on

4.2, but rather on the celluloid version (4.3). Moreover, the thickness of the material used in 4.4 is far closer to 4.3 than to 4.2.

4.5   Constructed Head No. 2

1965. Signed and dated on base: ›Gabo Christiania 1916‹.
Cor-ten steel. [95 high].
Oslo, University of Oslo, Mathematics Building.
From the artist, 1968.

Exh: E19 Zurich (1965) No. 90 : E20 Stockholm (1965–6) No. 54, fig. : E21 London (1966) No. 2.

Lit: N17 (1965) fig. : A70 Causey (1966) fig. p. 34 : A75 Clay (1966) fig. p. 116 *in situ* E20 : A103 Granath (1966) fig. p. 10 *in situ* E20 : A105 Gray (1966) fig. p. 49 *in situ* E19 : A219 Webb (1966) p. 660, fig. 2 : A222 Whitford (1966) fig. 1 : G31 (1966) fig. p. 128 : A93 Forge (1966) fig. p. 42.

According to Charles Wilson, 4.5 was direct-ly on 4.2. The University of Oslo decided to acquire this work in May 1968 (telegram from P. Palme, 22 May 1968). It was shipped in August and was un-veiled on 1 October 1968 (letter to P. Palme, 9 Aug 1968; invitation). The inscription, engraved after a signature provided by Gabo, refers to the fact that Gabo made the first version of this work (4.2), in 1916, when he was living in Christiania, now Oslo.

4.6   Constructed Head No. 2

1966. Not inscribed.
Cor-ten steel painted grey-green. 178 high, on wooden base 3.7 x 121.9 x 121.9.
London, Family Collection.
See illus. p. 94 and front cover

Exh: E23 Humlebaek etc. (1970–71) No. 17 : E24 Berlin (1971) No. 14 : E25 Hannover (1971) No. 14 : E26 Grenoble etc. (1971) No. 16 : E27 Lisbon (1972) No. 15.

Lit: B3 Alley (1981) p. 264.

4.6 is made of one-sixteenth inch steel plate (US Standard 16 gauge). According to Charles Wilson, Gabo was not completely satisfied with 4.6 and within a few months he decided to make 4.7 in a slightly thicker material. 4.6 was probably com-pleted by the summer of 1966, because Gabo stated that he had made 4.7 in the summer of that year (letter M. Gabo to J. Jeffreys, Tate Gallery, 21 Jun 1969). The date of 1966 for the completion of 4.6 has also been confirmed by Charles Wilson. Ronald Alley thought that 4.6 had been made after 4.7, and accordingly dated 4.6 ›1966–7‹ (B3).
4.6 was probably the version of 4 shown in the European touring exhibition of 1970–72, because 4.7 was by then on loan to the Tate Gallery (E23–7).
In 1974, 4.6 was painted with grey automobile primer, because the Cor-ten steel had not proved to be as resistant to corrosion as had been ex-pected. In 1983 the work was sandblasted and re-sprayed with two coats of matt grey, epoxy-resin paint, matching the original. It was also given a new base made from resin-bonded marine-ply to the ex-act dimensions of the original.

4.7   Constructed Head No. 2

1966. Not inscribed.
Cor-ten steel. [175.3 high].
London, Tate Gallery (T01520).
From the artist, May 1969, on loan to the Tate Gallery; 1972, purchased.

Exh: [E180 Montreal (1967) p. 117 : [E22 Buffalo (1968) No. 27] : E208 London (1973) No. 102, pp. 38–9, fig. : E28 London (1976–7) No. 1, figs. p. 27, frontispiece, as ›1964‹ and ›Iron‹.

Lit: [A129 Khalturin (1967) fig. p. 14, *in situ* E180] : [B36 (1968) frontispiece] : [A9 (1968) figs pp. 42–3 *in situ* E22] : A192 (1969) fig. p. 34 : B140 Merillat (1974) p. 148, fig. 49 : B130 (1975) fig. p. 22 : B53 Compton (1980) fig. p. 134 : B3 Alley (1981) pp. 263–4, fig.

According to Charles Wilson, Gabo was not com-pletely satasfied with the thickness of steel used in 4.6, and therefore slightly thicker plate (it appears to be US Standard gauge 13), was used in 4.7, which was made immediately after 4.6. In 1969 Gabo stated that 4.7 was made in the summer of 1966 (letter M. Gabo to J. Jeffreys, Tate Gallery, 21 Jun 1969). (See 4.6.)
It remains uncertain which version, 4.6 or 4.7, was sent to Montreal in 1967, but as Gabo was slightly dissatisfied with 4.6, it seems probable that 4.7 was exhibited there and subsequently at Buffalo (E180, E22). In April 1969 Gabo sent 4.7 on ex-tended loan to the Tate Gallery for exhibition out-side in the garden (loan receipt, 12 May 1969). Gabo specified that it should be mounted on a black base, so that the chin of the statue was level with, or slightly above, the eyes of the viewer (letter to N. Reid, 6 Feb 1969). Because of conservation difficulties, 4.7 was moved indoors on 24 Sept-ember 1971 (Tate Gallery records). The Tate finally acquired 4.7 in 1972 (letter M. Gabo to N. Reid, 8 Dec 1972).

4.8   Constructed Head No. 2

1975. Not inscribed.
Stainless steel. [183 high].
USA, Private Collection.
From the artist's family, 1981 on extended loan to the Fondation Maeght; Autumn 1982 returned to family collection; June 1983 to USA.

Exh: E234 New York (1979) ex-cat. : E252 Saint Paul (1981) No. 75, fig. p. 99 : E254 Madrid (1981) No. 44, fig.

According to both Miriam Gabo and Nina Williams, Gabo considered this to be the best large version of the Head.

5.   CONSTRUCTED HEAD NO. 3

The first title Gabo used for this work was *Con-structed Head No. 3* [*Konstruktiver Kopf Nr. 3*] (E31). He later listed it as *Head of a Woman* (G28), and the Museum of Modern Art's version is known by this title. It has been most frequently exhibited as *Head in a Corner Niche* (E17–22, E23–5, E27).

In the catalogue of the 1922 Berlin exhibition, for which Gabo was one of the organisers, this work is dated 1916 (E31). Alexei Pevsner captioned it ›Con-structed Head in a Niche, started in 1916, finished in 1917‹, which corresponds to the date Gabo gave it in 1957 (B162 p. 18; G28 fig. 7). Gabo may have made his first three-dimensional studies for this construction in Norway in 1916, although there is no reference to suggest that a cardboard model was made. The celluloid version was probably started after Gabo's return to Russia in 1917, be-cause, according to Alexei Pevsner, Gabo did not use plastics before then (F17).

In 1948 Gabo wrote to A. H. Barr, Jr., about the Museum of Modern Art's version: ›[it is] finished and complete and was, in fact, the original model which I always make before executing a work in a proper and solid material. In the case of this head, I told Hessel that the material was celluloid and therefore unstable, and I proposed to him that we should make it either in iron or in brass as the piece was done which the Soviet Government had bought. (Incidentally, I understand that this piece is lost, amongst others of my works which were in Russia.) But Hessel did not want to spend the money for it and was satisfied by having the mod-el . . . *Head No. 3* which is in your collection was made in brass also enamelled‹ (letter to A. H. Barr, 20 Jan 1948). In this statement Gabo did not con-tradict Barr's letter, which had recorded that Hessel had bought 5.1 at a Paris exhibition, presumably E3 of 1924 (letter from A. H. Barr, 16 Jan 1948).

In 1964 the Museum of Modern Art presented their records for Gabo's scrutiny. Gabo did not correct the Museum's statements that their version was made ›c. 1917–20 after a work of 1916‹, and that the original, made in iron in Norway in 1916, was remade in celluloid in Russia. Gabo did, how-ever, amend the Museum's record that the original iron version was ›in Russia‹ to read ›in the posses-sion of the artist's wife‹. Gabo seemed to be con-tradicting his statement of 1948 that the Museum's version was the original model (letter to A. H. Barr, 20 Jan 1948). Moreover, Miriam Gabo does not possess, and does not remember ever having seen a metal version of this work until Gabo made 5.3. It is possible that Gabo was confusing *Constructed Head No. 3* (5.1), with the original iron version of *Constructed Head No. 2* (4.2), which had been re-turned to him. Alternatively, Gabo may have been thinking of *Constructed Head No. 3* as a direct development from *Constructed Head No. 2* of 1916, made in galvanised iron (A. H. Barr, undated note, MoMA). This would be consistent with the title *Constructed Head No. 3*, and with the fact that Gabo only referred to a metal original for the cellu-loid *Head No. 3* in 1964, after the return of 4.2.

In accordance with this, there is no entry for a pre-1917 version, but there is an entry for the brass version which Gabo sold to the Soviet Government.

5.1   Constructed Head No. 3 (Head of a Woman)

1917/20. Signed lower right: ›Gabo‹.
Celluloid and metal on wood.
[62.2 x 69.2 x 34.6].
New York, Museum of Modern Art (397.38).
From the artist, June 1924 through Galerie Percier, Paris, to Galerie Jos. Hessel, Paris; 1938 to Museum of Modern Art.

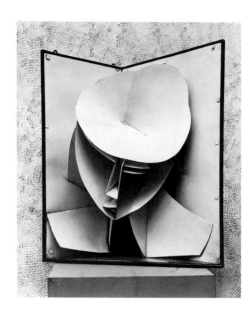

Exh: E30 Moscow (1920) : E31 Berlin (1922) No. 544, as ›*Konstruktiver Kopf, Nr. 3, 1916*‹ : E32 Amsterdam (1923) as E31 : E3 Paris (1924) ex-cat. : E54 Toledo (1939) : E197 Frankfurt etc. (1972) No. 7, fig. 56 : E234 New York (1979) No. 37, fig. p. 71 : E236 Paris (1979) p. 527, fig. p. 196.

Lit: E9 New York (1948) fig. p. 16 : A59 Blanc (1952) fig. p. 150 : B188 Roos (1954) p. 281, fig. A : B58 Dorazio (1955) fig. following p. 80 : A177 Seuphor (1955) fig. p. 38 : B176 Read (1956) fig. 214 : G28 (1957) p. 182, fig. 7 : B136 McCurdy (1958) p. 264, fig. D66 : B83 Gray (1962) p. 225, fig. 171 : B137 Maillard (1962) fig. p. 101 : B202 Selz (1963) fig. 216 : B162 Pevsner (1964) p. 18, fig. 18 : A51 Bekkers (1966) fig. following p. 32 : B123 Licht (1967) p. 335, fig. 243 : B93 Hammacher (1969) fig. 198 : G36 (1969) fig. p. 65 : B92 Hamilton (1970) fig. p. 236 : B195 (1972) fig. p. 65 : B63 Elsen (1974) p. 172, fig. 118 : B193 J. Russell (1975) fig. 19 : A114 Hilberry (1976) fig. 5 : B17 Barr (1977) pp. 543, 627, fig. p. 133 : B115 Krauss (1977) fig. 44 : B64 Elsen (1979) p. 82, fig. 82 : B128 Lloyd (1979) fig. 3 : B142 Milner (1979) fig. 30 : A49 Barron (1980) p. 71, fig. 8 : B151 Nakov (1981) fig. p. 34 *in situ* E32 : B129 Lodder (1983) p. 37, fig. 1.51 : E261 London (1983) fig. p. 14 *in situ* E32.

This piece was bought by Hessel from the Galerie Percier in June 1924 (A. H. Barr, undated note, MoMA). The catalogue for that exhibition contains no entry appropriate to this work, which suggests that 5.1 might have been shown ex-catalogue (E3). In 1957 Gabo listed it as an exhibit, although he gave the date of E3 as 1925 (G28).

Although listed and illustrated in the catalogue for the 1948 exhibition, 5.1 was not shown because it was in need of repair (E9). The illustration in the catalogue for E9 shows two pieces of celluloid missing, i. e., a thin strip running from the left-hand side to the chin, and one wedge-shaped piece from the neck (still in the Museum's possession). The illustration also shows that the work had been edged with a metal framing-strip. The work's earlier state is documented in G28.

5.2 Constructed Head No. 3

1920/22. Brass, covered with enamel.
Lost; probably in the USSR.
From the artist, 1920/22 to the Soviet Government.

The evidence for the existence of this lost version and its sale to the Soviet Government is Gabo's statement of 1948 (letter to A. H. Barr, 20 Jan 1948). 5.2 was probably started after the completion of 5.1, which Gabo described as the final model for 5, and which may not have been finished until 1920. Presumably Gabo completed and sold 5.2 before he left Russia in 1922.

5.3 Constructed Head No. 3 (Head in a Corner Niche).

1964. Phosphor-bronze [62.2 x 70 x 35].
London, Family Collection.
See illus. p. 95

Exh: E17 Amsterdam (1965) No. P2, fig. : E18 Mannheim etc. (1965) No. 2, fig. : E19 Zurich (1965) No. 2, fig. 2 : E20 Stockholm (1965–6) No. 56, fig. : E21 London (1966) No. 3, fig. 2 : E22 Buffalo (1968) No. 3 : E23 Humlebaek etc. (1970–71) No. 2, fig. p. 7 : E24 Berlin (1971) No. 2, fig. p. 10 : E25 Hannover (1971) No. 2, fig. p. 45 : E26 Grenoble etc. (1971–2), No. 2, fig. : E27 Lisbon (1972) No. 2, fig. p. 14 : E244 Basel (1980) fig. p. 70 : E252 Saint Paul (1981) No. 76, fig. p. 98 : E254 Madrid (1981) No. 45, fig. : E261 London (1983) No. 18, fig. p. 102.

This version is dated ›1954–64‹ in all the references. Gabo had borrowed the celluloid version from the Museum of Modern Art in 1948 and 1957. In January 1964 Gabo requested the loan again so that he could make a bronze version for the European touring exhibition (letter to A. H. Barr, 1 Jan 1964). Gabo may have started working on 5.3 in the 1950s, but it was evidently not completed until 1964. Charles Wilson remembers helping Gabo with this version in the early 1960s.

In accordance with the state of 5.1 after 1948, 5.3 has no wedge-shaped piece at the neck, but it does have the thin strip from the left-hand side to the chin, present in the original state of 5.1.

6. CONSTRUCTED TORSO

When the model for this work was exhibited in Paris in 1924 (E3), it was dated 1915, which would make it contemporaneous with *Constructed Head No. 1*. It seems unlikely that *Torso* was made before *Head No. 1* or *Head No. 2*, since Gabo repeatedly referred to these as his first constructed works. Later Gabo stated that the iron version of *Torso* was made in the ›winter of 1917–18‹ (letter to A. H. Barr, 20 Jan 1948). That date has been followed here. Presumably the cardboard versions were made just before the metal version (6.3).

6.1 Model for ›Constructed Torso‹

1917; reconstructed 1981.
Cardboard. 39.5 high.

London, Family Collection.
From the artist, *c.* 1924 on loan to Miss Jane Heap, date of return unknown.
See illus. pp. 75 and 96

Exh: E3 Paris (1924) No. 2, as ›*Construction torse (1915)*‹ : E4 New York (1926) No. 1 : E42 New York (1927) No. 361.

Lit: N3 (1926) fig. *in situ* E4.

This model, stored in pieces in Gabo's studio, was presumed lost until 1977. 6.1 was reconstructed by Charles Wilson in 1981, following the original glue marks which showed clearly that two pieces were missing. These were replaced with new card.

The entry for this work in a copy of the catalogue for the Paris exhibition of 1924 (E3), is annotated ›Jane Heap's‹ (FAL). This suggests that by 1924, 6.1 was in the possession of Jane Heap, organiser of the Little Review Gallery in New York. She probably knew Gabo through Miss Dreier, who had met him in Berlin in 1922. In spring 1924, before E3, Jane Heap illustrated the large version of *Torso* in *The Little Review* (6.3; A133). In 1926 and 1927 she exhibited the model in New York (6.1; E4, E42). The catalogue for E4 illustrated 6.3, but a photograph in a review indicates that 6.1 was shown (N3).

6.2 Maquette for ›Constructed Torso‹

Winter 1917–18. Cardboard. [*c.* 137 high].
London, Family Collection.
See illus. p. 97

This was discovered in pieces in Gabo's studio after his death. The surviving glue marks indicate that 6.2 had been constructed and subsequently disassembled. The scale suggests that the pieces of 6.2 were used as templates for 6.3. 6.2 was reassembled by Charles Wilson in 1984/5.

6.3 Constructed Torso

Winter 1917–18.
Sheet metal, covered in sand. [*c.* 137 high].
Lost; probably in the USSR.
From the artist, December 1920 to the Museum Bureau, Department of Fine Arts, the Peoples' Commissariat for Enlightenment, Moscow.
See illus. p. 17, fig. 10

Exh: E29 Moscow (1918) : E31 Berlin (1922) No. 545, as ›*Konstruktiver Torso*‹ : E32 Amsterdam (1923) as E31 : E208 London (1973) Nos 102 b-c, as photographs, fig. p. 52.

Lit: A217 Voskuil (1923) fig. p. 331 : A133 (1924) fig. following p. 16 : E42 New York (1927) fig. p. 35 : A69 Carter (1928) fig. p. 42 : G28 (1957) p. 182, figs 5, 6 *in situ* E31 : B162 Pevsner (1964) fig. 19 : G38 (1971) fig. p. 171 *in situ* E31 : E24 Berlin (1971) fig. p. 25 : E25 Hannover (1971) fig. p. 49 : E27 Lisbon (1972) fig. p. 44 : B63 Elsen (1974) p. 172, fig. 100 : E234 New York (1979) fig. 13 : B151 Nakov (1981) fig. p. 34 *in situ* E32 : B143 Milner (1983) fig. 134 : B129 Lodder (1983) p. 35, figs. 1.48, 8.1 : E261 London (1983) fig. p. 14 *in situ* E32.

According to Peter Nisbet, this work was acquired by the Museum Bureau of the Department of Fine Arts, the People's Commissariat for Enlightenment in 1920. The purchase is recorded in an inventory book as ›No. 2081, Gabo *Torso*‹. A further document is dated 14 December 1920 and another lists the work as made of iron (Museum Bureau papers, fond 665, ed. khr. 14, lists 5v, 84–5, Central State Archive for Literature and Art, Moscow).

When 6.3 was exhibited in Berlin and Amsterdam in 1922–3 (E31, E32), it already belonged to the State, and was consequently returned to Moscow after the exhibition closed in 1923. This confirms Gabo's entry of 1957: ›Original now in the USSR‹ (G28).

7. CONSTRUCTION EN CREUX

These two works may not be directly related to each other, but they are similar in conception, and 7.1 may be ›the first version in painted cardboard‹ which Gabo mentioned in 1957 (G28 p.182, n.18). Apparently Gabo made several of these reliefs in Russia which have since been lost (E28 p. 57).

Together with 8, they seem to comprise the first completely non-figurative constructions Gabo made. As in his figurative works, the ›stereometric method‹ reduces the physical solidity of the image, and the use of transparent materials enabled Gabo to avoid the visual solidity of works produced with opaque materials.

7.1 Construction en Creux: First Version

1919. Painted cardboard.
Lost; destroyed.
See illus. p. 18, fig. 11 and p. 20, fig. 21

Exh: E30 Moscow (1920) : E31 Berlin (1922) No. 549, as ›Relief encreux‹ : E32 Amsterdam (1923) as E31.

Lit: A86 (1922) fig. p. 8 : G28 (1957) p. 182, n. 18 : B162 Pevsner (1964) fig. p. 26, as ›*Construction in a Niche,* Moscow 1919‹ : B129 Lodder (1983), p. 37, fig. 1.49 : E261 London (1983) fig. p. 61.

This is only known from a photograph of 1919 published in 1922 (A86). Its similarity to 7.2 suggests that 7.1 should be identified with the cardboard version, which Gabo listed in 1957 as having been destroyed after the exhibition of 1922–3 (E30, E31; G28).

7.2 Construction en Creux: Second Version

1920/21. Plastic and wood.
Lost; presumed destroyed.
From the artist [1924/30] to Collection of the late Vicomte de Noailles, Paris.
See illus. p. 18, fig. 12

Exh: E3 Paris (1924) No. 3.

Lit: G12 (1937) p. 287, sculpture fig. 23, as ›*Bas Relief* 1920‹ : G28 (1957) p. 182, fig. 18, as ›1921‹ : B129 Lodder (1983) p. 37, fig. 1.50.

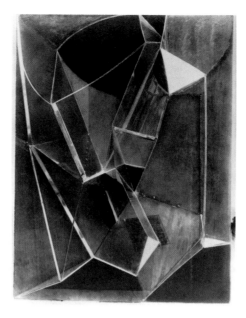

Gabo's listing of 1957 implies that although 7.1 was exhibited in Berlin and Amsterdam in 1922–3 (E30, E31), 7.2 was exhibited in Paris in 1924 (E3; G28). The title in the catalogue for E3, *Construction en creux,* could apply to either version.

In 1981 the late Vicomte de Noailles recalled: ›my wife and I had bought a large sculpture in a transparent »matière« made by »Gabo and Pevsner«. Some accident or other happened to it, and as far as I remember, the diverse pieces had to be thrown away.‹

This reference to its having been made by ›Gabo and Pevsner‹ suggests that it was bought from Gabo and Pevsner's Paris exhibition of 1924 (E3). The Noailles were balletomanes and may have met the brothers, or at least become acquainted with their work, through Diaghilev's production of *La Chatte,* for which Gabo and Pevsner designed the set. In the catalogue for the 1930 exhibition, Gabo listed Noailles as the owner of one of his works (E5). The sale had presumably been completed by then.

There is a drawing, dated 1918, which bears a strong resemblance to this construction (Tate Gallery T02152).

8. CONSTRUCTION IN SPACE C

1919/21. Plastic, or plastic and glass.
[c. 76 x c. 91.5].
Lost before 30 April 1938; presumed destroyed.
From the artist, 1922 to Miss Katherine S. Dreier, New York, for the Collection of the Société Anonyme, Museum of Modern Art.
See illus. p. 18, fig. 13

Exh: E31 Berlin (1922) No. 548, fig. 40, as ›Raumkonstruktion C, Modell einer Glas-Plastik‹ : [E4 New York (1926) No. 5, as ›Construction‹] : [E38 Brooklyn (1926–7) No. 183, as ›Construction 1920‹] : E5 Hannover (1930) No. 14, as photograph ›Glas-Plastik, oval. 1919/21‹ : E6 London (1938) No. 13, as photograph ›actual size‹ : E76 New Haven (1950) as photograph.

Lit: A127 Kassák (1922) fig. : A188 (1923) fig. p. 14 : A172 (1923) fig. facing p. 65 : A133 (1924) fig. following p. 16 : B132 Lozowick (1925) fig. p. 45 : B125 Lissitzky and Arp (1925) fig. 24, as ›Glaskonstruktion 1922‹ : A157 (1927) fig. p. 16 : A69 Carter (1928) fig. p. 42 : A36 (1928) fig. p. 46 : G12 (1937) p. 286, sculpture fig. 5 : A159 Read (1939) fig. p. 8 : E9 New York (1948) p. 19 : B90 Hamilton (1950) p. 17, fig. p. 15 : A177 Seuphor (1955) fig. p. 35 : G28 (1957) p. 182, fig. 17, as ›Construction in Relief 1920. Plastic.‹ : B181 Rice (1963) fig. 249 : B162 Pevsner (1964) fig. p. 27 : E162 Milan (1964) fig. p. 33 : B9 Arnason (1977) fig. 504 : B151 Nakov (1981) p. 187 n. 185, fig. p. 189 : B129 Lodder (1983) p. 38, fig. 1.52 : B101 Herbert *et al* (1984) No. 281, pp. 282–3, fig.

This work has been known variously as *Glas-plastik, oval, Oval Relief,* and most commonly as *Construction in Relief* (E5; G28).

Since this work is known only through a photograph, it is difficult to ascertain whether it was made of plastic, glass, or as Alexei Pevsner suggested in 1981, a combination of glass and plastic (F17). The title *Glas-plastik* is inconclusive since transparent plastics were often referred to as ›artificial glass‹. In 1948 it was described as ›clear celluloid‹ (E9). The curved pieces would be difficult to make from glass without more obtrusive fixtures, and although glass may have been used for the oval backplate, its weight would seem to preclude its use throughout the work.

Bought by Katherine Dreier from the Berlin exhibition of 1922 (E31), 8 was possibly not shown in Amsterdam, although it is not in the list of exhibits removed (E32 supplement). Since only four or five works by Gabo are known to have been in the USA in 1926, this work was probably amongst those shown then (E4). In 1938 Miss Dreier informed Gabo that 8 had been lost in storage in New York (letter from K. Dreier, 30 Apr 1938). The large photograph of 8 that Gabo donated to Yale was probably the one exhibited in 1930 and 1938 (E5, E6; letter from K. Dreier, 2 Dec 1949).

9. KINETIC CONSTRUCTION (STANDING WAVE)

9.1 Kinetic Construction (Standing Wave)

Winter 1919–20. Metal rod, with electric motor. [61.5 high, including steel rod 46.5 long].
London, Tate Gallery (T00827).
Presented by the artist, 1966, through the American Federation of Arts.

Exh: After the execution of the reconstructions 9.1a and 9.1b, there is no certainty as to which variant was exhibited. E30 Moscow (1920) : E31 Berlin (1922) No. 550 as ›*Kinetische Konstruktion (Zeit als neues Element der Plastischen Künste)*‹ : E36 Paris (1926) No. 1304, as ›*Construction kinétique (temps)*‹ : E5 Hannover (1930) No. 9, as ›1919/20‹ : E14 Hartford (1953) No. 2, fig. 8 : E134 Amsterdam (1961) No. 84, fig., as ›*Virtueel volume*‹ : E135 Stockholm (1961) No. 87, fig. : E166 Edinburgh etc. (1965) No. 6, as photograph : E17 Amsterdam (1965) No. P3 : E18 Mannheim etc. (1965) No. 3, fig. : E19 Zurich (1965) No. 3, fig. 3 : E20 Stockholm (1965–6) No. 57, fig. : E21 London (1966) No. 4, fig. 3a : E28 London (1976–7) No. 13.

Lit: A123 Kállai (1924) p. 380 : A124 Kállai (1927) p. 246 n., fig. p. 249 : B144 L. Moholy-Nagy (1929) fig. 141 : B104 Hildebrandt (1931) p. 451, fig. 499 : A99 Giedion-Welcker (1935) p. 200, fig. following p. 202 : B76 Giedion-Welcker (1937) p. 130, fig. : G12 (1937) fig. p. 112 : E9 New York (1948) p. 18, as ›*Kinetic Model*‹ : G28 (1957) p. 182, fig. 15 : B76 Giedion-Welcker (1960) fig. p. 177 : A166 Rickey (1963) fig. 20 : E162 Milan (1964) fig. p. 86 : A100 (1965) fig. p. 323 : A93 Forge (1966) fig. p. 40 : A167 Rickey (1967) fig. p. 67 : B221 Vallier (1967) fig. 99 : B184 Rickey (1967) p. 191, figs. p. 192 : B52 Compton (1967) fig. 11 : A197 (1967) pp. 27–8 : A179 Sharp (1968) fig. p. 336 : B31 Brett (1968) p. 22, fig. : B38 Burnham (1968) pp. 230–32, fig. 85 : E184 New York etc. (1968–9) p. 106, figs : A89 Fenton (1969) fig. p. 22 : G34 (1969) p. 5, fig. : G35 (1969) p. 89, figs : B22 Benthall (1972) pp. 102–4, fig. 64 : B73 Gardner (1975) p. 754, fig. 17.39 : A114 Hilberry (1976) p. 180, figs 7a,b : B9 Arnason (1977) fig. 503 : B115 Krauss (1977) p. 216, fig. 160 : B142 Milner (1979) fig. 32 : B3 Alley (1981) pp. 234–6, fig. : B143 Milner (1983) p. 167, fig. : B129 Lodder (1983) p. 40, fig. 1.53 : E261 London (1983) fig. p. 100.

This work is sometimes titled *Kinetic Sculpture,* and less frequently *Kinetic Model. Standing Wave* seems to have been adopted as a subtitle when 9.1 was acquired by the Tate Gallery in 1966 (A197).

9.1, like the stereometric cubes (2), was not conceived as a work of art, but was made to demonstrate the kinetic principle. In *The Realistic Manifesto* Gabo wrote: ›The realization of our perceptions of the world in the forms of space and time is the only aim of our pictorial and plastic art . . . We affirm . . . a new element, the kinetic rhythms of our perception of real time.‹ Gabo remained dissatisfied with 9.1, because the mechanism was rather crude (G35). Later he explained the reasons for creating 9.1:

›The standing waves had attracted my attention since my student days, in particular the fact that when you look at a standing wave, the image becomes three-dimensional. In order to show what I meant by calling for the introduction of kinetic rhythms into a constructed sculpture, I chose that standing wave as a good illustration of the idea – so I decided to construct a standing wave which would be vibrating on one fixed point and rigid enough to be indeed a »*standing* wave«.‹

›One must keep in mind that the year was the winter of 1919–1920. It was the height of civil war, hunger, and disorder in Russia. To find any part of machinery or to do any kind of work in a recently nationalized factory in Moscow – most of which were idle and impenetrable – was next to impossible. What I was looking for was the basic mechanism of an electric bell, but of a bell stronger than the usual household one – strong enough to produce enough vibration in a rigid rod.‹

›I knew that there was a mechanical workshop in the Polytechnicum Museum where apparatus was being made for the Scientists in Physics, and I visited that workshop and found that some of the workmen were still there and some work was still going on.‹

›I asked the director and was given permission to do my experiments in that workshop, which was a godsend. The mechanics there knew all the places in Moscow where odd, unused machinery was lying about. In one of them we found an old factory bell which was not in use because it had been replaced by a whistle. The only useful piece of that bell, for me, was a powerful electromagnet. To make the magnet work was a simple thing – we still had electricity.‹

›But the main task was to create with this a regular rhythmic wave. It was not difficult to arrange a horizontal iron bar which would vibrate when the electricity was on, but to join that bar with a mechanism which would let a vertical steel rod vibrate demanded a great deal of effort and inventiveness.‹

›After a lot of experimenting, what I did was to arrange the bar in such a way that at the base of it were two separate springs which would touch the spring on which the iron bar was fixed. I arranged the springs in such a way that together they would produce a rhythmic standing wave, co-ordinating each other's vibration.‹

›This was not at all simple as it sounds. I had to change a great many springs. I had to choose the length, strength, and elasticity of each one; I had to attach a kind of a brake to the main spring on which the bar was which would regulate the primary movement of the bar. I also had to balance out the steel rod so that the wave would be staying in the same dimensions and not jump out and divide itself into two waves.‹

›I solved the problem by fastening to the rod two balancing gadgets, one at the bottom of the rod and one at the top. At the bottom I made a ring, fixed into a particular point at the base of the rod, which produced the beginning of the wave. At the top of the rod, two small triangular pieces of plastic regulated the height of the wave. Later on, by choosing a stronger steel rod, this last arrangement proved to be unnecessary.‹

›This is how the thing was made . . . it took me almost three quarters of a year.‹

›When I showed it to the students, I made it emphatically clear that this was done by me in order to show them what I mean by »kinetic rhythms«. This piece is only a basic example of one single movement – nothing more‹ (G35).‹

Gabo listed 9.1 as one of the works exhibited in Moscow in 1920 (E30; undated note FAL; see also A124). Gabo stressed that although 9.1 had been shown in Berlin in 1922, it was not shown in Amsterdam in 1923 (E31-2; letter to R. Alley, 30 Sep 1975). In the 1930 Hannover catalogue, Gabo subtitled this work ›The creation of an immaterial spatial body through a material line (rod) moving in space‹ [›*Gestaltung eines immateriellen Raumkörpers durch eine sich im Raum bewegende materielle Linie (Stab)*‹] (E5).

9.1a Kinetic Construction (Standing Wave): Reconstruction

1968. Metal rod, with electric vibrator. [53.5 high].
New York, Museum of Modern Art, Study Collection (777.69).

Exh: E184 New York etc. (1968–9) p. 106 : E23 Humlebaek etc. (1970–71) No. 56 : E24 Berlin (1971) No. 52 : E25 Hannover (1971) No. 52 : E26 Grenoble etc. (1971–2) ex-cat. : E27 Lisbon (1972) ex-cat.

Lit: G34 (1969) p. 5, fig. : G35 (1969) p. 89.

This reconstruction was made with Gabo's approval, by Witt Wittnebert for the Museum of Modern Art on the occasion of E184 (1968).

9.1 b-d Kinetic Construction (Standing Wave): Reconstructions

1919–20/reconstructed 1985
Metal rod with electric motor.
[61.5 high].
London, Tate Gallery.
See illus. p. 98

Exh: E261 London (1983) No. 21 : E262 Paris (1983–4) No. eM20 : E265 Basle (1984) No. 72, fig.

Lit: B3 Alley (1981) p. 236.

The first of these reconstructions, 9.1 b, was made with Gabo's approval in 1974 by Ronald A. Woolner for the Tate Gallery. It did not work well, and in 1983 Miriam Gabo gave permission for a further two reconstructions to be made.

10. COLUMN

According to Gabo, this work was ›conceived in the winter of 1920–21, as a tiny model, and executed in the winter of 1922–23 in its big form‹ (letter to B. Hayes, 13 Mar 1949, Addison Gallery).

In 1957 Gabo explained: ›From the very beginning of the Constructive Movement it was clear to me that a constructed sculpture, by its very method and technique, brings sculpture very near to architecture. The *Project for a Radio Station* which I did in the winter of 1919–20, and Tatlin's model for the 3rd International done a year earlier, indicate the trend of our thought at that time. My works of this time, up to 1924 . . . are all in the search for an image which would fuse the sculptural element with the architectural element into one unit. I consider this *Column* the culmination of that search‹ (G28, fig. 26).

A number of pieces for different versions of the *Column* were found in the attic of the house in Middlebury in 1977. An old base, which has slots to take vertical sheets 8.2 cms wide, is conceivably the original base for 10.3. It has three tiers similar to the base of 10.2 (G28 fig. 26).

10.1 Model for ›Column‹

Winter 1920–21. Not inscribed.
Celluloid [and other plastic]. [14.4 high, including integral base, 9.4 diameter].
London, Tate Gallery (T02167).
Presented by the artist, 1977.
See illus. p. 99

Exh: E28 London (1976–7) No. 17, fig. p. 29.

Lit: A124 Kállai (1927) fig. p. 246 : B3 Alley (1981) pp. 236–7, fig.

This is presumably the model, made in the winter 1920–21, which Gabo mentioned in 1949 (letter to B. Hayes, 13 Mar 1949, Addison Gallery). Unlike the later versions, this has a red base.

10.2 Column

Winter, 1922–3; rebuilt 1937. Not inscribed.
Glass [galalith], painted metal and wood; most of the glass replaced with Perspex.

105.3 high, including integral base, 73.6 diameter.
New York, Solomon R. Guggenheim Museum (55.1429).
From the artist, 23 Aug 1938, on extended loan (EL38.2191) to the Museum of Modern Art, New York, until 7 May 1948; 1949 to The Addison Gallery of American Art, Phillips Academy, Andover, Mass. (1949.13), exchanged Jan 1952; from the artist, 1955 to the Guggenheim.
See illus. p. 23, fig. 26

Exh: [E3 Paris (1924) No. 5] : E5 Hannover (1930) No. 5, as ›Säule 1923 Glas‹ : E43 Hartford etc. (1935–6) No. 4 : E6 London (1938) No. 1 : E7 Hartford etc. (1938) No. 1, fig. : [E8 Poughkeepsie (1938)] : E56 New York (1939) No. 314, fig., repaired state : E58 New York (1940) : E59 New York (1940–41) : E64 New York (1944) p. 220, fig. p. 140 : E9 New York (1948) [No. 4], fig. p. 26 : E70 New York (1949) : E73 Andover (1949–50) : E11 Cambridge, Mass. (1951) [No. 13] : [E12 Chicago (1952) No., 5] : E90 Philadelphia etc. (1952–3) No. 34 : E14 Hartford (1953) No. 4 : E106 New York (1955) : E108 New York (1956) : E143 New York (1962) : E152 New York (1963) : E186 New York (1969) p. 120, fig. p. 121 : E220 New York (1977) No. 17, fig. : E224 New York (1977–8) No. 37, fig. : E234 New York (1979) No. 101, colour fig. p. 140 : E266 New York (1984) pp. 18–19 fig.

Lit: A50 (1929) fig. p. 19 : A56 Bier (1931) fig. p. 467 : A126 Kállai (1932) fig. p. 288 : G8 (1933) fig. p. 16 : E46 New York (1936) fig. 135 : G10 (1936) fig. p. 847 : A16 (1938) p. 88 : G14 (1938) fig. p. 3 : A10 (1945) fig. p. 121 : A185 Soby (1948) fig. p. 23 : B158 Osborn (1948) fig. 17 : B24 Biederman (1948) fig. 206 : E70 Goldwater *et al* (1949) p. 44, fig. p. 19 : B203 Seuphor (1949) fig. p. 58 : B185 Ritchie (1952) fig. p. 151 : B81 Goldwater *et al* (1953) p. 19, figs. pp. 19, 45 *in situ* E70 : B188 Roos (1954) fig. C, p. 282 : A176 Segi (1954) fig. p. 20 : B55 Damaz (1956) fig. p. 59 : G28 (1957) p. 183, fig. 26, in original state, but captioned ›Glass, plastic, metal, wood‹ : A8 (1957) fig. p. 176 : B136 McCurdy (1958) fig. D68 : B220 Trier (1961) fig. 14 : A225 Xagoraris (1962) pp. 35–6, fig. 13 : B202 Selz (1963) colour fig. 15 : B179 Read (1964) fig. 103 : B110 Huyghe (1965) fig. 888 : E17 Amsterdam (1965) fig. B : E20 Stockholm (1965–6) fig. : B139 Meilach *et al* (1966) fig. p. 17 : A87 Ernest (1966) fig. p. 150 : B11 Baldwin (1967) fig. p. 15 : B93 Hammacher (1969) fig. 194 : B155 (1970) pp. 124–5, colour fig. : B206 Seuphor *et al* (1971) fig. 33 : B29 Bowness (1972) fig. 175 : B39 Burnham (1973) pp. 94–5, fig. : B193 J. Russell (1975) fig. 20 : B9 Arnason (1977) pp. 323–4, fig. 505 : B115 Krauss (1977) pp. 60–63, fig. 46 : B64 Elsen (1979) p. 83, fig. 83 : B142 Milner (1979) fig. 33 : B14 Barnett (1980) pp. 254–6, fig. : B129 Lodder (1983) pp. 41–2, fig. 1.55.

Gabo stated that this version was made in the winter of 1922–3 ›. . . when it was first shown in Germany and then in Holland, in France and in America‹ (letter to B. Hayes, 13 Mar 1949, Addison Gallery). This implies that 10.2 was exhibited in Berlin and Amsterdam in 1922–3 (E31, E32). There is,

however, no catalogue entry to confirm this, and in 1957 Gabo did not indicate that 10.2 was exhibited ex-catalogue in E31 and E32 (G28). 10.2 may have been exhibited in 1924 in Paris as ›Construction 1923‹, although the title is inconclusive (E3, No. 5).

A note by Gabo on the verso of an early postcard of this work reads: ›exhibit in Museum of Modern Art New York. Material – Perspex + gallalite‹ (FAL). This suggests that Galalith was amongst the original materials used. The white horizontal and vertical planes are made of painted metal, and the black strip around the base is of painted brass. Justus Bier mentioned the artificial illumination of 10.2, and this seems to have been an important element in Gabo's work at the time (A56; A124).

In 1936 this work was severely damaged and consequently was not shown at E46, despite the catalogue entry. A photograph was taken to document the damage (MoMA No. S1333, see B14). The pieces were returned to Gabo in London, via Paris, in August 1937 (letter and bill from L. Lefebvre-Foinet, 13 Mar 1936, 29 Jan 1938). According to Miriam Gabo, Gabo rebuilt 10.2 in Cholmley Gardens in 1937 (M. Gabo, notes, 1982/3, FAL). The original state, documented in G28, shows that 10.2 initially had metal struts and a black ring; now both the struts and the ring are transparent. According to Angelica Rudenstine, the positions of the vertical supports and the slanted ring have been slightly changed. A photograph of Gabo with his works in the basement of the Wadsworth Atheneum in 1938 includes 10.2, and confirms that the *Column* had a transparent ring by then (FAL; *re* this photograph see 41.3).

The Addison Gallery acquired this piece in 1949, but in 1952 Gabo agreed to exchange it for *Linear Construction No. 2 (Variation No. 1)* (55.1).

If 10.2 was the version of *Column* shown in Chicago in 1952, it again sustained some unspecified damage (E12; letter to W. Eisendrath, Arts Club of Chicago, 18 Mar 1952).

10.3 Column

(1923)/1928; rebuilt [1938]. Not inscribed.
Celluloid; rebuilt in Perspex; on metal base. [27 high, including integral base, 18.5 diameter].
New Haven, Yale University Art Gallery, Collection of the Société Anonyme (1941.474).
From the artist [1929] to Miss Katherine S. Dreier for the Collection of the Société Anonyme, Museum of Modern Art; 1941 to Yale.

Exh: E60 New Haven (1942) No. 19 : E67 New Haven (1948) No. 36, as ›celluloid 1922–23‹ : E22 Buffalo (1968) No. 6, fig. p. 20, as ›Model Glass Fountain‹.

Lit: G22 (1949) fig. p. 46 : B90 Hamilton (1950) p. 17 : B231 Williams (1980) p. 96 : B101 Herbert *et al* (1984) pp. 282, 285–6, fig. 283, colour fig. 18.

The majority of works given to Yale University under the Deed of Gift of the Société Anonyme were received in October 1941 (receipt, 11 Oct 1941, ›1911 Ledger‹, Yale 2). Only one work by Gabo is listed, Société Anonyme No. 3, *Model for Glass Fountain* (›1911 Ledger‹, Yale 2). This entry cross-references to the acquisition number for 10.3 (Yale/SA Cross-Reference Lists, Yale 2). Miss Dreier's use of the title *Fountain* for 10.3 may have followed Gabo's suggestion, because he did inscribe an early drawing relating to the form of *Column*: ›column with a fountain‹ in Russian (Family Collection; see also 13, 16).

It is recorded that Miss Dreier bought this work from Gabo in 1927 (ledger, 1947, Yale 2; B90). Other evidence, however, suggests that Miss Dreier acquired this work later. In August 1928 she only possessed three works by Gabo (letter from K. Dreier, 1 Aug 1928). These must be 8, 16, and one which Gabo seems to have given to her (letter from K. Dreier, 1 Aug 1928). The work he gave has been tentatively identified as 13 (B101).

10.3 is now made of Perspex, so it must have been rebuilt sometime after 1936. This suggests that 10.3 is the unnamed work which Gabo sent to Miss Dreier for her consideration in 1929, ›very well packed‹ in a celluloid cylinder, and which arrived broken because it was ›*too well* packed‹ (letters to and from K. Dreier, 25 Jan, 27 Jul 1929, Yale 2).

In 1938 Miss Dreier wrote that she had already returned 16 to Gabo, and that she only had two models: ›One was forgotten to be returned when everything was shipped – and the other you sent me and it arrived in such a condition that I could not put it together – although all the pieces are there‹ (letter from K. Dreier, 30 Apr 1938). The first of these models has not been identified, but the second is taken to be 10.3 which may have been one of the works which Gabo restored for Miss Dreier in 1938 (letter from K. Dreier, 29 May 1938).

10.4 Column

1936/7. [Celluloid; on aluminium base].
[30.5 high, including integral base, 18.8 diameter].
Formerly Collection Mr and Mrs Leslie Martin; stolen, presumed destroyed.
From the artist, 1936/7.

Lit: N6 (1938) : N9 (1938).

The Martins met Gabo at the *Abstract and Concrete* exhibition in London, 1936 (E45; A83 p. 15). Afterwards at dinner they told Gabo that they would like to buy a work. Gabo suggested *Column*, and made it for them. Later, in January 1938, after 10.4 had been returned to Gabo for repair, it was stolen from his car. This theft was noted in the press, and one report stated that the work was made mainly of celluloid (N6).

10.5 Column

1938. Not inscribed.
Perspex; on aluminium base. 30.5 high, including integral base, 18.8 diameter.
England, Collection Sir Leslie and Lady Martin.
From the artist, 1938.

Exh: E21 London (1966) No. 6.

Lit: G28 (1957) p. 183, n. 26.

This was a replacement for 10.4, lost in January 1938.

10.6 Column

[*c.* 1947]. Inscribed, bottom right: ›N. GABO‹.
Perspex; on aluminium base. 28.2 high, including integral base, 19.2 diameter.
London, Family Collection.
See illus. p. 99

Exh: [E66 Cambridge, Mass. (1947)] : [E83 Boston (1951)] : E28 London (1976–7) No. 18 : E231 Paris (1978) No. 115, supplement p. 5 : E243 London (1980) No. 54 : E261 London (1983) No. 22, fig. p. 101.

This has a mended fracture that runs diagonally across the top of the right-hand front vertical and around the signature. According to Miriam Gabo, this version was made after the move to Middlebury in 1953. Two exhibition records, however, suggest that this version was made earlier. In 1947 Gabo lent a *Column*, 11 inches high with an aluminium base, to the Fogg Museum of Art (E66). In 1951 Gabo also lent a *Model for the Column* to the Margaret Brown Gallery (E83; letter from M. Brown, 18 Oct 1951). See also 10.8.

10.7 Column

1958. [Not inscribed].
Perspex; on aluminium base. [28.5 high, including integral base, 19 diameter].
Caracas, Venezuela: Collection the late Mr Carlos, and Mrs M. Villanueva.
From the artist, 1958.

Exh: E202 Caracas (1972) No. 23.

Lit: G28b (1961) p. 199, n. 26.

This version was apparently commissioned by Mr and Mrs Villanueva in 1958 (letter from C. Villanueva, 3 May 1958). The *Column* arrived with a small piece detached (letter from C. Villanueva, 2 Jul 1958).

10.8 Column

1975. Glass, Perspex and stainless steel. [193 high, including integral base, 156 diameter].
London, Family Collection.
See illus. p. 100

Exh: E252 Saint Paul (1981) No. 77: E254 Madrid (1981) No. 46, fig.

Correspondence between Gabo and Bo Boustedt in 1963–4 documents their attempts to produce three large versions of *Column*, each three metres high. For this purpose Gabo sent Boustedt a ›model‹ *c.* 33 cms high, probably 10.6. Gabo required a glass of optical quality in large thick sheets, and Orrefors Glass and Corning Glass were considered as suppliers. According to Miriam Gabo, the tendency of the glass to transmit light at its edges as green lines annoyed Gabo. Consequently the project fell through in October 1964, and Boustedt returned the model.

Knud Jensen, Director of the Louisiana Museum, discussed the project with Gabo in 1970 during Gabo's exhibition in Humlebaek (E23; letter K. Jensen to S. Ferliger, 6 Apr 1978, SRGM). By December 1971 Gabo had found the glass he needed, produced by Pilkington Brothers. He wrote to Jensen that he had ›never dreamt that such a beautiful, crystal-clear sheet of glass can be now produced.‹ He was so impressed with the quality and the price that he wrote ›I cannot miss the opportunity to make the *Column* for myself, at least six feet high‹ (letter to K. Jensen, 6 Dec 1971). Subsequently it was decided to make two enlarged versions; one for Humlebaek and one for Gabo.

In April 1973 Gabo sent 10.6 to Denmark to serve as the model (receipt from H. Buch, 13 Apr 1973). The glass (including two pieces 72 x 16 inches and four pieces 72 x 8 inches), came from Pilkington's whilst other parts were made to Gabo's specifications in Denmark (letter to R. Earle, Pilkington's, 16 Dec 1971, Yale 1; letter K. Jensen to S. Ferliger, 6 Apr 1978, SRGM). 10.8 was completed by March 1975, and 10.9 by June of the same year (letters from K. Jensen, 6 Mar, 12 Jun 1975).

10.8 is entered in the catalogue for the Moscow exhibition of 1979, but according to Miriam Gabo, 10.9 was shown (E236).

10.9 Column

1975. Not inscribed.
Glass, Perspex and stainless steel. [193 high, including integral base, 156 diameter].
Humlebaek, Denmark: Louisiana Museum (1/2).
From the artist, 1975.

Exh: E28 London (1976–7) No. 19, colour fig. on cover, fig. p. 29 : E236 Paris (1979) ex-cat., replaced 10.8 : E244 Riehen-Basel (1980) pp. 70–71, fig. : E250 Moscow (1981) Vol. 1, p. 312 : E263 Bern (1984) No. 38, fig. p. 23.

See 10.8.

11. CONSTRUCTION IN RELIEF

1921. Glass, Trolith, Galalith and celluloid; on black [metal] base.
Lost; presumed destroyed.

Exh: [E34 Vienna (1924) No. 150, as ›*Konstruktion*. Glas, Trolit, Galalit, Zelluloid‹].

Lit: [E9 New York (1948) p. 19] : G28 (1957) p. 183, fig. 34.

The date of this work is taken from an original photograph (FAL). According to Gabo, 11 was last known to be ›On loan to Koschak Esq. of Vienna, editor of *Maa*‹ (G28). This obviously refers to the Hungarian, Lajos Kassák, editor of the avant-garde magazine *MA*. In 1965 Gabo wrote to Kassák enquiring about the loan, but Kassák replied that he had only received photographs for publication, not a construction (letters to and from L. Kassák, 6 and 13 Sep 1965). In April 1977 Gabo told Alan Bowness that the work was multi-coloured, that it was lent to an exhibition in Hungary after 1922 and never returned. There is no evidence of an exhibition in Hungary, and it seems probable that Gabo sent this work to Vienna for the 1924 exhibition and that it went astray there (E34).

In 1957 Gabo listed this work as made of plastic and metal (G28). Later, however, Gabo wrote that it was ›made on a black board, of plastic and was constructed in different coloured materials‹ (letter to L. Kassák, 6 Sep 1965). In 1948 Olson and Chanin mentioned a ›construction of 1921‹ in which Gabo had ›used tubes of coloured fluids to catch lights‹ (E9). This may refer to the coloration of 11, although Gabo is not known to have used this particular technique.

12. SQUARE RELIEF

The original version of this work no longer exists, although two other versions which were constructed in the 1930s have survived. Of these, 12.2 appears to be a replica of the original, and 12.3 a variant.

12.1 Square Relief

> 1920/21. Celluloid, on black [metal] base.
> [44.5 x 44.5 x c. 16.5].
> Formerly collection of the artist; presumed destroyed.

Gabo consistently dated 12.2 as 1920 or 1921 (E9, G28). 12.2, however, is made from Perspex which Gabo did not use until 1936/7. The earlier dates, therefore, must refer to the original version, 12.1.

It seems that 12.1 had deteriorated to such an extent by the mid-1930s that Gabo decided to make a replica, 12.2. There are several early photographs which may show 12.1, but they are all extremely unclear (FAL).

12.2 Square Relief

> 1937; base 1950s. Signed on smaller central oblong: ›NG‹.
> Perspex, on anodised aluminium base.
> 44.5 x 44.5 x c. 16.5.
> London, Family Collection.
> *See illus. p. 101*

Exh: E9 New York (1948) [No. 3], fig. p. 24, as ›*Square Relief* 1920‹ : E10 Baltimore (1950) [No. 9] : [E11 Cambridge, Mass. (1951)] : E13 New York (1953) No. 1 : E14 Hartford (1953) No. 3 : E15 Rotterdam etc. (1958) No. 2, fig. : E17 Amsterdam (1965) No. P4, fig. : E18 Mannheim etc. (1965) No. 4, fig. : E19 Zurich (1965) No. 4, fig. 4 : E20 Stockholm (1965–6) No. 58, fig. : E21 London (1966) No. 5, fig. 3b : E256 London (1982) No. 25, fig. p. 31, as ›*Construction in a Square*‹.

Lit: [N1 Adlow (1951)] : G28 (1957) p. 182, fig. 19 : G31 (1966) fig. p. 130 : A93 Forge (1966) fig. p. 41 : A139 S. Moholy-Nagy (1966) fig. 16.

Made of Perspex, 12.2 seems to be a replica of 12.1. In 1957 Gabo listed 12.2 as the second version of 12 (G28). This suggests that 12.2 preceded 12.3, which was made in 1937 and exhibited in London in 1938 (E6; see 12.3). According to Miriam Gabo, the original base of 12.2 was later replaced

with one of anodised aluminium, made after the move to Middlebury in 1953. In 1965/6, 12.2 suffered some unspecified damage (memo from M. Gabo to C. Israels, 4 Jun 1966).

12.3 Square Relief

> 1937. [Perspex, on metal base].
> [44.5 x 44.5 x c. 16.5].
> New York, Private Collection.
> From the artist, [1938].

Exh: [E6 London (1938) No. 6] : [E7 Hartford etc. (1938) No. 6] : [E8 Poughkeepsie (1938)].

Lit: A12 (1938) fig. p. 51 : G14 (1938) fig. p. 6, as ›1928‹ : G28 (1957) p. 182, n. 19.

12.3 was probably shown in the London exhibition of 1938. Photographs taken at the gallery and reproduced in *Plastics* indicate that 12.3 was in the exhibition, probably as ›No. 6 *Relief* (variant of relief 1921) 1937‹ (E6; A12; letter to editor, n. d.). In 1938 in New York, 12.3 was shown as No. 6 under the same title (E7). In a copy of the catalogue, that entry is annotated with the present owner's surname (FAL). On this evidence, 12.3 is dated 1937 and its date of acquisition is taken to be 1938. The present owner before remembers buying 12.3, 1938, in which case the annotation could refer to its loan by the present owner for that exhibition.

In either case, the title and annotation imply that this was not the original version of 1920/21. In 1957 Gabo listed 12.3 as the first version and 12.2 as the second version (G28), but he reversed that order in 1966 when he referred to 12.3 as ›a second version‹ (E21).

The illustration in *Plastics* appears to show 12.3 mounted on a square sheet, possibly of Perspex, held at each corner by a bracket attached to the black base. The same photograph is reproduced in G14. 12.3 differs from 12.2 in being mounted on the transparent sheet and also in having more thin strips in the relief itself.

During the Second World War, probably c. 1942, the work was damaged at, or *en route* to, an exhibition in Cincinnati (letter from owner, 26 Apr [1942]). Gabo had supplied spare pieces for 12.3, and these were used to effect an immediate repair. Gabo later carried out a more extensive repair and reconstruction that was completed in November 1948 (letter to owner, 11 Nov 1948).

12.4 Square Relief

> 1937/8. Signed and inscribed on the back:
> ›To Arthur and Alice with love Gabo
> 22 [month unreadable] 38‹.
> Perspex. c. 10.8 x c. 10.8 x c. 3.2;
> in Perspex box, 11.7 x 11.6 x 6.8.
> England, Collection Arthur Duckworth, Esq.
> From the artist, 1938.

Exh: [E167 London (1965) No. 23, as ›*Construction c. 1936*. perspex . . . 11.8 x 11.8 x 5.4 cm‹].

The size of this work and the list of lenders to the exhibition implies that 12.4 was exhibited in London in 1965 (E167). Nevertheless, the dating of c. 1936

in the catalogue remains an anomaly, and the present owner is uncertain whether or not he lent this work.

In April 1978, 12.4 was cleaned and polished, a broken filament was renewed, and some of the original pieces that had become loose were reattached.

12.5 Square Relief

> 1937/9. [Perspex]. [c. 7.5 high].
> Present whereabouts unknown.
> Gift from the artist [1938/9] to Mrs Sybille Stephenson, London (latterly Mrs E. L. T. Mesens).

Gabo apparently gave this work to Sybille Stephenson while she was living at No. 6 Mall Studios with her husband, John Cecil Stephenson, whose work was illustrated in *Circle* (M. Gabo, notes, 1982/3, FAL; A163, G12). From 1938 to 1940 Mrs Stephenson worked for the London Gallery where Gabo exhibited in 1937 and 1938 (E49, E6). The Gallery was run by E. L. T. Mesens, who also edited the associated *London Bulletin* (see B1).

13. TOWER

> 1921–2. Not inscribed.
> Celluloid. [12.5 high].
> New Haven, Yale University Art Gallery, Collection of the Société Anonyme (1953.6.3): Bequest of Miss Katherine S. Dreier, 1953 [Gift] from the artist [1923/6] to Collection of Miss Katherine S. Dreier, USA; 1953 to Yale.
> *See illus. p. 102*

Exh: [E4 New York (1926) No. 3] : E92 New Haven (1952–3) No. 30, as ›*Construction* Yellow plastic, Height 5¼"‹.

Lit: G28 (1957) p. 183 as ›Amber plastic model about 6 in. high‹, fig. 23, as ›*Tower*‹ : B101 Herbert *et al* (1984) No. 282, pp. 282, 284–5, fig.

At some time, this piece was broken and reassembled incorrectly, with the baseplate at the top. In July 1978 Charles Wilson was commissioned to restore it. He replaced several pieces, reconstructed it, and mounted it on a Perspex base. The photograph in G28 shows the work without the small black pieces at the intersection of the two large vertical planes.

On account of its small size, this might be the work Miss Dreier mentioned in 1928 as ›the one which you gave me‹ (›die die Sie mir schenkten‹; letter from K. Dreier, 1 Aug 1928; B101; see 22.1). If this is correct, 13 was probably shown as ›Construction Fountain‹ in New York in 1926 (E4). Miss Dreier referred to her *Column,* (10.3), as the *Fountain,* and may equally have thought of 13 as a design for a fountain.

14. TOWER

1921–2. Bronze [and glass].
Present whereabouts unknown.
[From the artist, *c.* 1924 on loan to Jane Heap, New York].

Exh: [E4 New York (1926) No. 4] : [E38 Brooklyn (1926–7) No. 183, as ›Construction 1920‹] : [E42 New York (1927) No. 360, as ›Lighting Tower‹].

Lit: [N4 (1926) p. 9] : G28 (1957) p. 182, fig. 22.

In 1957 Gabo stated that 14 was in the USSR (G28). Unlike some works so designated then and later recovered from the attic of the house in Middlebury, no identifiable pieces of this work have been found. The only material Gabo cited was bronze, but it is clear from the photograph that it contained glass or some other transparent material.

It is possible that 14 was amongst those works which Gabo lent Jane Heap, and which she exhibited in 1926 and 1927 (E4, E42). A review of E4 referred to one of the works in the exhibition, presumably ›No. 4 *Construction Colonne d'Illumination*‹, as ›a street signal tower‹. It described this work as ›. . . a composition of glass and metal, which will take light and give it out again pleasantly and effectively, and it is skeletonized in its construction in a way aesthetically satisfactory to an expert in economics‹ (N4). This description fits 14 but could also be applied to 15. The latter, however, is taken to be the work collected by Miss Dreier from Gabo in Berlin in 1926, and therefore could not have been shown in E4.

If this hypothesis is correct, 14 might also be the unidentified work which Jane Heap lent to Miss Dreier for the Brooklyn exhibition of 1926–7 (E38; see 16).

15. CONSTRUCTION IN SPACE: DIAGONAL

1921/5. Signed in cyrillic and dated: ›Gabo 1919‹.
Glass, metal and celluloid. [62.2 high].
London, Family Collection.
From the artist [1926 on loan to Miss Katherine S. Dreier until 1928].

Exh: E38 Brooklyn (1926–7) No. 185, as ›Construction for an Observatory II‹ : E39 New York (1927) No. 109, as E38 : E40 Buffalo (1927) No. 116; as ›Construction for an Observatory I‹ : E41 Toronto (1927) No. 116, as E40 : E5 Hannover (1930) No. 15.

Lit: B59 Dreier (1926) fig. p. 75 : [A29 (1926) p. 3] : B144 L. Moholy-Nagy (1929) fig. 119 : A56 Bier (1931) fig. p. 466 *in situ* E5 : A11 (1931) fig. 47 : G28 (1957) p. 182, fig. 21, as ›Tower 1921–22‹ : B26 Bohan (1982) p. 141, fig. 16 *in situ* E38 : B101 Herbert *et al* (1984) fig. p. 12, *in situ* E38.

Gabo exhibited this work in Hannover in 1930 as ›Raum-Konstruktion, diagonal‹ (E5), and this title has been adopted here.

In 1957 Gabo listed 15 as in the USSR (G28). Yet, in 1977 most of the pieces were found in the attic of the house in Middlebury. These comprised the two lower circles together with the structure complete down to the black square at the base (mostly celluloid); the metal section from the middle up to the bottom of the crossed transparent rectangles; and the four glass discs from the centre of the work. An illustration of 1931 indicates that the long vertical strips were originally transparent and probably made of glass (A11). It may have been one of these strips that broke in transit in 1928, for which Miss Dreier sent Gabo 200 marks compensation (letter from K. Dreier, 1 Aug 1928). Subsequently Gabo may have replaced them with opaque vertical strips, as illustrated in G28. Pieces of brass which might have been suitable for this were found in 1977. Alternatively the photograph in G28 may simply have been retouched.

One piece is inscribed in cyrillic ›Gabo 1919‹, but this may have been done later. When exhibited in 1930, 15 was dated ›1925/1927‹ (E5). In 1957, however, Gabo dated it ›1921–22‹ (G28). The work may have been conceived as early as 1921/2, but not actually made until 1925, the date it was given in a review of E5 (A11). The reference to 1927 may

be discounted as the work was shown in Brooklyn at the end of 1926 (E38).

15 was illustrated in the book *Modern Art,* produced for the Brooklyn exhibition (B59). 15 also appears in an installation photograph of that show (B101), and its height accords well with the 24½ inches that Miss Dreier listed for No. 185 in the exhibition ledger (Yale 2). The title for No. 185, however, was ›Construction for an Observatory II‹, whilst No. 184 was titled ›Construction for an Observatory I‹. The latter has been identified with 16. When the exhibition moved to Buffalo and Toronto, 16 became No. 117, and was retitled ›Model for a Public Fountain (Model privately owned)‹ (E40; E41; see 16). This suggests that the entry for No. 116, ›Construction for an Observatory I‹, refers to 15.

15 was returned to Gabo in time for the Hannover exhibition of 1930 (E5), and it was probably sent in 1928. Miss Dreier did return a work with broken glass to Gabo in Europe, via Lefebvre-Foinet in Paris, in August 1928 (letter from K. Dreier, 1 Aug 1928). This was apparently the work about which Gabo had enquired in July 1928, stating that Miss Dreier had taken it with her from Berlin two years previously (letter to K. Dreier, 12 Jul [1928]). This work seems to have been finally returned to Gabo in December 1928 (letter from L. Lefebvre-Foinet, 21 Dec 1928).

15 was definitely exhibited in Hannover in 1930 (E5), as it is reproduced in a review with the exhibition catalogue number, 15, clearly visible on the base, and with the caption ›From the Kestner Gesellschaft exhibition‹ (A56).

A photograph shows 15 in Gabo's room at 23 rue des Volontaires, Paris, *c.* 1933/6 (FAL). Another photograph of 15 is drawn over with white ink or paint, and suggests that Gabo may have considered elaborating this piece (FAL).

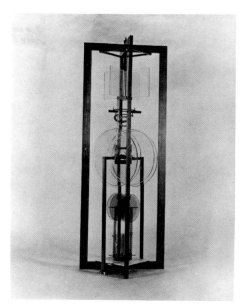

16. MODEL OF A MONUMENT FOR AN OBSERVATORY

1922. [Not inscribed].
Celluloid, metal and wood. [35.6 high].
London, Family Collection.
From the artist, 1924/6 to Jane Heap, USA;
1926 to Collection of Miss Katherine S.
Dreier, New York; [1930s] returned to Gabo
for repair.
See illus. p. 24, fig. 28

Exh: E3 Paris (1924) No. 4, as ›*Construction d'un monument pour une place d'observatoire*‹ : E4 New York (1926) No. 2 : E38 Brooklyn (1926–7) No. 184 : E39 New York (1927) No. 108, fig. p. 5 : E40 Buffalo (1927) No. 117, as ›*Model for Public Fountain* (Model privately owned)‹, fig. p. 5 : E41 Toronto (1927) No. 117, as E40.

Lit: A123 Kállai (1924) fig. p. 382 : A189 (1924/5) fig. p. 116 : [A29 (1926) p. 3] : A212 Tschichold (1926) fig. p. 2 : A84 Dreier (1927) p. 47, fig. p. 50 : N7 (1927) fig. p. 18 : A35 (1927) fig. p. 34 : B215 Teige (1928) fig. 14 : B144 L. Moholy-Nagy (1929) fig. 121 : B234 Zervos (1938) fig. p. 366 : E9 New York (1948) fig. p. 25 : G22 (1949) p. 26, fig. p. 29 : G28 (1957) p. 183, as ›14 in.‹, fig. 20, as ›*Monument for an Observatory*‹ : A208 Thompson (1966) fig. p. 137 : B221 Vallier (1967) p. 190, fig. 100 : B91 Hamilton (1972) pp. 353–4, fig. 211 : B26 Bohan (1982) pp. 55, 101, 141, figs 11 [16] : B101 Herbert *et al* (1984) p. 282, [fig. p. 12].

In 1957 Gabo listed this work as destroyed (G28), but a large part of the work was recovered in 1977. No metal or wooden parts survive and the thin celluloid is warped and discoloured. The complex lower portion and the pointer have been lost, but the rest of the structure, above the join of the two arched strips, is intact. The illustration of 16 in the catalogue for the 1927 exhibition in New York has possibly been retouched, but it shows the pointer

at the top missing, an extra piece at the centre, and the top disc and ring slightly bent (E39). 16 was probably returned to Gabo for repair in the 1930s (letter from K. Dreier, 30 Apr 1938; B101).

This work was first exhibited in 1924 (E3), as ›*Construction of a Monument for an Observatory*‹. It has also been subtitled ›for a square in St. Petersburg‹ (A123), and it is possible that Gabo knew of a suitable site there. Miss Dreier referred to the work as ›*Model for a Public Fountain*‹ (A84).

Apparently Jane Heap, organiser of the Little Review Gallery, brought this work to the USA and subsequently sold it to Miss Dreier. In March 1926 Miss Dreier made one payment for ›*The Observatory*‹, promising to pay the balance in August or October (letter from K. Dreier to J. Heap, 16 Mar 1926, Yale 2). In the same letter Miss Dreier listed it as the one Gabo (among other works), which she was borrowing from Miss Heap for exhibition in Brooklyn (E38), and which were to be credited ›courtesy of the Little Review Gallery‹. In the first printing of the catalogue, however, no such acknowledgement was made against any of the works by Gabo. Miss Heap complained, and in the second printing ›No. 183 *Construction 1920*‹ was credited to the Little Review Gallery (letter to K. Dreier, 27 Nov 1926, Yale 2). In the catalogue, ›No. 184 *Construction for an Observatory I*‹ must have been 16, because Miss Dreier annotated it ›not for sale‹ in her copy of the catalogue, and noted it in her ledger as 11¾ inches (Yale 2). Also, ›No. 185 *Construction for an Observatory II*‹ was for sale and its height accords with 15. If Miss Dreier's purchase of 16 had not been completed, the credit line should perhaps have been under No. 184. Alternatively the credit line was correct and Miss Heap lent a different work.

The New York show opened on 25 January 1927 (E39), and only two works by Gabo appear in the catalogue; the work credited to the Little Review Gallery apparently having been withdrawn. 16 was illustrated in the catalogue as ›*Model for a Public Fountain*‹, but was entered as ›*Construction for an Observatory I*‹. On the day before E39 closed, Miss Dreier returned ›1 Gabo, *The Fountain*‹ to Jane Heap along with other works (letter K. Dreier to J. Heap, and receipt from J. Heap, 4 Feb 1927, Yale 2). If Miss Dreier returned 16 because she had not completed the purchase, she would have had to have borrowed it again very soon because it was shown in E40. This exhibition opened on 25 February, and 16 was illustrated in the catalogue with the caption ›*Model for a Public Fountain*‹. Unfortunately, neither the completion of the purchase, nor a second loan is documented. The identity of the work loaned by Heap to E38 remains uncertain (see 14, and Introduction – Some Intriguing Mysteries Remain).

In 1928 it seemed possible that 16 might eventually be erected as a full-scale monument. Miss Dreier annotated a copy of a letter to Gabo, of 1 Aug 1928: ›Sent Mr Archibald's letter & [. . .] Mr Archibald wanted a fountain. Mrs an observatory. Arizona. (Both chose the *same model* which I bought from Jane Heap)‹ (Yale 2). Miss Dreier had earlier written to Mr Archibald Adams that his plan to enlarge 16 in New York would be wonderful, and that the Société Anonyme would make the model available to the artist (letter from K. Dreier to A. Adams, 5 Feb 1927, Yale 2). Gabo wrote to the other inquirer: ›You inform me that you seriously

intend to suggest the *Model of a Monument for an Observatory* which is to be erected by a Society in an Observatory in Arizona‹ (letter to unidentified lady, 23 Aug 1928). No more details are known about the proposed commissions, but apparently neither was pursued.

17. MODEL FOR A FOUNTAIN

1923/4. [Not inscribed].
Metal and glass, with enamel paint. 72.5 high, including integral base, 91.4 diameter.
London, Family Collection.
See illus. p. 103

Exh: E5 Hannover (1930) No. 8, as ›*Modell eines Springbrunnens. 1924*‹.

Lit: A126 Kállai (1932) fig. p. 288 : G28 (1957) p. 182, fig. 24, as ›1923‹ : B184 Rickey (1967) p. 83 n. 31, fig. 33.

Although listed in 1957 as ›Private collection, Dresden. Destroyed‹ (G28), this work was found in the attic of the house in Middlebury in 1977. Only the wedge-shaped piece of glass and most of the base were missing.

The photograph reproduced in A126 and G28 shows the work standing on a stand marked ›8‹, which must show it *in situ* at Hannover in 1930 (E5).

18. CONSTRUCTION IN SPACE: VERTICAL

1923/5. Glass, painted brass [and plastic]; on black painted wooden base. [c. 120 high, including integral base 2 x 60.5 x c. 53].
London, Family Collection.

Exh: [E5 Hannover (1930) No. 10, as ›*Raum-Konstruktion, vertikal. 1925*‹].

Lit: G7 (1932) fig. p. 14, as ›1923‹ : G28 (1957) p. 182, fig. 25, as ›48 in. high, 28 in. wide. Private Collection‹.

Although listed as ›Private Collection‹ in 1957 (G28), pieces of this work were found in the attic of the house in Middlebury in 1977. All of the long thin strips appear to be missing.

This work was probably shown in 1930 at Hannover (E5). The identification of the other exhibits at this show suggests that 18 was shown as No. 10. The photograph reproduced in G28 may have been taken at E5 because the stand of 18 resembles the stand for 17, which was probably photographed at E5 (G28 fig. 24; see 17).

19. MONUMENT FOR AN INSTITUTE OF PHYSICS AND MATHEMATICS

1923/5. Glass and bronze [and plastic].
[*c.* 44 high].
London, Family Collection.

Exh: E5 Hannover (1930) No. 13, as photograph.

Lit: A124 Kállai (1927) fig. p. 247 : B144 L. Moholy-Nagy (1929) fig. 120 : B124 Ligeti (1931) p. 222, fig. 287 : E9 New York (1948) fig. p. 25, as ›1925‹ : G28 (1957) p. 183, fig. 29, as ›24 in. high, in the USSR‹ : B179 Read (1964) p. 293, fig. 102 : E17 Martin (1965) fig. A : E20 Stockholm (1965–6) fig. : B123 Licht (1967) p. 335, fig. 245 : B66 Feldman (1967) fig. p. 364 : B233 Zanini (1971) fig. 89 : B66 Feldman (1973) pp. 480–81, fig. : B23 Besset (1976) fig. 128 : A214 Van Wijk (1978) fig. 7.

In 1957 Gabo listed this work as in the USSR (G28). In 1977 pieces of 19 were found in the attic of the house in Middlebury: the square-section brass tube and the arching brass strip, which together form the structural support for the bar and circular strip above, and the glass dodecahedron. The tube measures 19.2 x 2 cms. The faces of the dodecahedron are irregular, and the glass has been repaired with glue. The circular pieces at the centre of the work may have been made of celluloid.

Gabo stated that the drawing for this work was done in 1919, although the actual model was made in 1924 (letter to H. Read, 6 Jan 1942, UVBC). In 1930 it was dated 1923 (E5). The drawing Gabo mentioned is presumably *First Sketch for a Monument for an Institute of Physics and Mathematics‹*, dated 1919 (Tate Gallery, T02156).

20. CONSTRUCTION IN SPACE: SLIDING

This title was used in the catalogue for the Hannover exhibition of 1930 (E5). In its approach to linear and planar elements, this work can be related to *Construction in Space with Balance on Two Points* (22). The black parallelogram to suggest movement was also used in *Monument for an Airport* (23).

20.1 Model for ›Construction in Space: Sliding‹.

1924. Celluloid. Diameter of circles 7.3.
London, Family Collection.

Pieces of celluloid, found in the attic of the house in Middlebury in 1977, correspond well with a photograph and a scale-drawing for this work (FAL; Family Collection). The photograph, annotated ›Hannover Constr.‹, shows two circular discs with uneven edges (suggesting plastic), and a connecting central structure. The materials are apparently black, white and transparent plastic. The central vertical differs slightly from the final version (20.2).

The scale-drawing on orange graph paper depicts two circles of 9.5 and 7.2 cms in diameter,

representing respectively the base and the transparent discs. It also provides details of the central construction and notes colours and materials. The annotation ›x5‹ suggests that the model was to be enlarged five times.

20.2 Construction in Space: Sliding

1924. Glass and metal. Diameter of circles [*c.* 36.5].
Formerly Hannover, Museum für Kunst und Landesgeschichte; destroyed.
From the artist, 1930.
See illus. p. 28, fig. 32

Exh: E5 Hannover (1930) No. 7, as ›Raum-Konstruktion, gleitend. 1924‹.

Lit: N22 (1930) fig. [*in situ* E5] : A56 Bier (1931) p. 466 : G28 (1957) fig. 35 : B212 Steneberg (1969) p. 46, fig. 23.

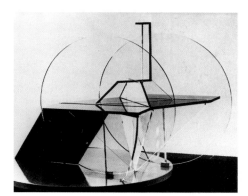

A review of the Hannover exhibition of 1930 illustrated 20.2 with the subtitle ›gleitend‹, indicating that 20.2 was No. 7 in that show (E5, N22). In 1930 Gabo stated that Alexander Dorner had bought a work for the Kunstmuseum, Hannover (letter to K. Dreier, 3 Dec 1930, Yale 2). In 1956 Gabo asked Dorner for a photograph of ›my Construction in Hannover, the one which you bought‹. Gabo added: ›I remember seeing a photo of it once at your home. Unfortunately I don't have any photo of it at all except a newspaper clipping from a Hannover paper with a bad reproduction and the publisher says it is useless‹ (letter to A. Dorner, 28 May 1956). Dorner supplied a slide from which a negative was made (letter to A. Dorner, 26 Dec 1956). The plate in G28, made from this negative, appears to be the same photograph as in N22. This suggests that 20.2 was probably the work bought for Hannover (see 22.4 and 23.2). Later Dorner told Gabo that he was sure that the construction had been destroyed by the Nazis during the Second World War (M. Gabo, notes, 1982/3, FAL).

21. MODEL FOR A FOUNTAIN

1924. [Celluloid].
Formerly Collection Peggy Guggenheim – Art of This Century; destroyed.
From the artist [through A. Pevsner or Galerie Charpentier, 1938/41].

Lit: B88 Guggenheim (1942) fig. p. 91, as ›*Model for a Fountain*, 1924‹.

There is no record that Peggy Guggenheim ever bought a work directly from Gabo, although he did exhibit at her gallery in London in May 1939 (E55). In 1940 Gabo understood from Antoine Pevsner that Peggy Guggenheim wanted to buy 39.4

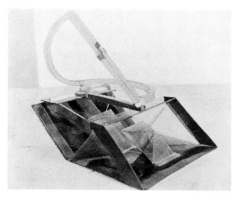

(stenographic notes, letters to P. Guggenheim, 24 Jan and 11 Feb [1940]). Apparently, however, she did not want 39.4, but another work which had been shown in E55, and which Gabo described as ›the most difficult which I ever made and I don't know if I will be able to repeat it‹ (stenographic notes, 11 Feb [1940]). There is no evidence that this sale was transacted. According to Angelica Rudenstine, 21 was not included in any listing of Peggy Guggenheim's collection before 1942. Yet, in 1942 Peggy Guggenheim published *Art of This Century* (B88), which illustrated 21. Later that year, she opened her gallery of the same name with a show that included works by Gabo and Pevsner (letter from J. Sweeney, 6 Nov 1942). If she did not buy 21 directly from Gabo, she may have bought it from the Galerie Charpentier exhibition of 1939 (E57). Alternatively, she may have acquired it (probably before she left for the USA in 1941), from Antoine Pevsner, with whom Gabo had left several early models when he moved to England in 1936. (See also Introduction – Some Intriguing Mysteries Remain).

22. CONSTRUCTION IN SPACE WITH BALANCE ON TWO POINTS

This work has been titled variously: *Raum-Konstruktion, schwebend*; *Construction on Two Points*; *Construction in Space, Balanced on Two Points*; and *Two Circles*. The title adopted here was that most consistently used by Gabo (e.g. E9, G28).

In 1936 Gabo described it as ›a pure plastic to be placed indoors‹ (G10). This does not, however, preclude the possibility that he may have regarded it as a potentially monumental form.

Early photographs of 22 are difficult to ascribe to particular versions, and some may show early celluloid versions which are not listed here (FAL; Yale 1). In particular, the photograph reproduced by Kállai in 1930 (A125 p. 19), seems to show neither a hole, nor circles of plastic at the centre of the square sheet. This does not correspond to either 22.1 or 22.2. Kállai's photograph may illustrate a version now lost or altered, but the photograph may also have been retouched. This photograph was also reproduced in the catalogue for the Hannover show of 1930, E5; G10 (1936) fig. p. 847; G12 (1937) p. 125, fig. 3; and in the first series of post-cards published by *Circle* in 1939.

22.1 Model for ›Construction in Space with Balance on Two Points‹

Winter 1924–5. White, black and transparent plastic. [13.3 high].
Formerly Collection Katherine S. Dreier, USA; lost, 1953.
From the artist [(1938)/1947].

Exh: E92 New Haven (1952–3) No. 29.

Lit: [N11 Bier (1930) fig.] : [A56 Bier (1931) fig. p. 465, as ›Raumplastik, schwebend 1924‹] : [A126 Kállai (1932) fig. p. 289] : [G28 (1957) p. 183, fig. 36] : B101 Herbert et al (1984) p. 282.

This model was probably made in the winter of 1924–5, just before the enlargement, 22.3.

By April 1938 Miss Dreier apparently had only two ›models‹ by Gabo (letter from K. Dreier, 30 April 1938). 8 had been lost, and 16 had apparently been returned to Gabo for repair. Therefore, unless 22.1 was the work Gabo gave her before August 1928, the two works still in Miss Dreier's possession must have been 10.3 and 13 (letter from K. Dreier, 1 Aug 1928). It would seem that Miss Dreier did not acquire 22.1 until after 1938, and probably not before Gabo arrived in the USA in 1946. It was photographed together with 13 in 1947 by William Miller Jr. (letter from K. Dreier, 21 Nov 1947; photographs, Yale 2).

In 1953 Lamont Moore, Director of Yale University Art Gallery, offered this model as part of a bequest from Miss Dreier to the Solomon R. Guggenheim Museum. Although accepted, this work was reported missing from the shipment delivered to the Museum in February 1953 (B101). In 1957 Gabo listed the original model belonging to Miss Dreier as lost (G28). In 1977 a similar model (22.2), was found in the attic of the house in Middlebury. This must be a duplicate model since 22.1 was not returned to Gabo (M. Gabo, notes, 1982/3, FAL). Indeed, although Miller's photographs are not entirely clear, they suggest that 22.1, unlike 22.2, did not have a hole at the centre, but had a circular piece of celluloid either side of the transparent square.

Since 22.1 is lost, it is impossible to establish whether the bibliographical references cited refer to it or to 22.2. The illustration in G28 is credited to Yale University, but it cannot have been taken by Miller, because the same photograph was published in 1930 and 1931 (N11, A56). The newspaper illustration clearly shows the second quarter-annular piece at the back, but in A56 and G28 only a black line appears: presumably the photograph used in A56 and G28 had been retouched. The illustration in N11 corresponds with Miller's photographs in so far as there are small rectangular cross-pieces between the quarter-annulars at the

base, and strips mounted on the lateral arms of the black angled pieces. This suggests that they are of the same model.

The illustration in a review of the 1930 Hannover exhibition (E5; N11), suggests that this model might have been shown, although in view of the importance of E5 it seems more likely that 22.3 was exhibited.

22.2 Model for ›Construction in Space with Balance on Two Points‹

[c. 1924/5]. [Signed on underside of base: ›N. Gabo‹].
Celluloid; on black plastic base. 13.5 x 18.2, including integral base 0.3 x 10 x 5.
London, Family Collection.
See illus. p. 104

Exh: E255 Cambridge (1982) No. 6, as ›c. 1925. Plastic and rhodoid; 12.7 high‹.

In 1977 this work was found in pieces in the attic of the house in Middlebury. One black angled piece was broken and one of the thin black struts was missing. It was subsequently reconstructed by Charles Wilson. The height of 22.2 is almost the same as that recorded for 22.1, which suggests that 22.2 was probably made from the same scale-drawing, soon after 22.1. The inscription on the base is not incised, but inscribed in paint or plastic solvent. It is not in Gabo's hand. It is possible that some of the bibliographical references given under 22.1 could apply to 22.2.

22.3 Construction in Space with Balance on Two Points

Winter 1924–5; altered 1951/3. Not inscribed.
Enamelled brass, glass, and plastic; wooden base. [67 x 127.6]
New Haven, Yale University Art Gallery (1956.23.1): Gift of H. Wade White in memory of Joseph M. Hirschman, 1956.
From the artist, 1955 to Collection H.Wade White; Nov 1955 on indefinite loan to Yale University Art Gallery (Loan No. 1.7.1955); Nov 1956, donated to Yale.
See illus. p. 28, fig. 31

Exh: E5 Hannover (1930) [No. 6 as ›Raum-Konstruktion, schwebend 1924‹, fig. of 22 but not 22.3] : E6 London (1938) No. 2 : E7 Hartford etc. (1938) No. 2 : E8 Poughkeepsie (1938) : E9 New York (1948) [No. 5] : E10 Baltimore (1950) [No. 8], as ›Two Circles‹ : E11 Cambridge, Mass. (1951) [No. 7] : [E12 Chicago (1952) No. 9] : E13 New York (1953) ex-cat. : E14 Hartford (1953) No. 5, fig. 8 : E15 Rotterdam etc. (1958) No. 3 : E21 London (1966) No. 7, fig. 4.

Lit: A12 (1938) figs pp. 51, 50 *in situ* E6 : N5 (1950) fig. *in situ* E10 : A28 (1957) fig. p. 14 : G28 (1957) p. 183, fig. 37 : B76 Giedion-Welcker (1960) fig. p. 369 *in situ* E13 : B137 Maillard (1962) fig. p. 102 : A7 (1967) fig. p. 344 : B38 Burnham (1968) p. 36, fig. 12 : B91 Hamilton (1972) p. 355,

fig. 212 : B152 Neilson (1972) No. 133, fig. : B142 Milner (1979) fig. 31.

The earliest identifiable photograph of this version shows it in Gabo's studio at 23 rue des Volontaires, Paris, between 1933 and 1936 (FAL). This photograph shows the work with white strips above the lateral arms of the black angled pieces, as in the models (22.1 and 22.2). These strips are present in the installation photograph of the 1951 show (E11, FAL), but are absent from the installation photograph of the 1953 exhibition (E13, B76). This suggests that the strips were lost or removed between 1951 and 1953. On top of each the lateral arms are three holes where they would have been mounted. The same change occurred in 22.4.

Gabo usually dated this version 1924 or 1925 (e.g. E5). In 1965 he stated that 22.3 was made in the winter of 1924–5 and recorded that it was exhibited in Hannover, Paris, London, New York, Hartford and Poughkeepsie, returning to London before the Second World War (letter to G. Hamilton, 3 Feb [1965]). Its inclusion in the London exhibition of 1938 (E6), is confirmed by the illustration in A12. The loan list for the Baltimore show of 1950 enters it as ›Two Circles‹ (E10), a title confirmed by Miriam Gabo and by the illustration in N5.

Gabo made substitute Perspex pieces to be used in place of the glass quarter-annulars when the piece was lent for exhibition. Wade White acquired the work in 1955 with the Perspex quarter-annulars (letter from M. Gabo to H. Wade White, 8 Dec 1955). In May 1978 the family donated the glass pieces to the Gallery (1956.23.1a, b, c).

22.4 Construction in Space with Balance on Two Points

c. 1925/6. Not inscribed.
Celluloid and Perspex. 25.6 x 34.9.
Cambridge, Mass: Harvard University, Busch-Reisinger Museum (1958.46) : Gift of Mrs Lydia Dorner in memory of Dr Alexander Dorner, 1958.
Gift from the artist, 1938 to Collection Alexander Dorner, Providence, R. I.; 1958 to Harvard.

Lit: G28 (1957) p. 183, n. 36 : B118 Kuhn (1967) No. 54, fig. : E201 Austin (1972) fig. p. 43 : E222 Berlin (1977) fig. 286 : E239 Milan (1979–80) fig. 478 : B40 (1980) figs pp. 64–5 : E257 Frankfurt am Main etc. (1982–3) fig. p. 175.

In 1958 Gabo wrote of 22.4: ›This is an old model of mine, actually done about 1925–26 and I don't know in what state it is. Being so old it was made in a very delicate material --- (it is not quite clear to me whether it belongs to the Fogg now or to some other Museum which has lent it for exhibition at the Fogg)‹ (letter to H. Wade White, 28 Jun 1958). Gabo was evidently confusing the Fogg with the Busch-Reisinger Museum, both at Harvard.

This version is made mostly from celluloid, although the central square is Perspex (K. Pasternak, ›Technical Examination‹, Jan 1985, Busch-Reisinger Museum). The use of celluloid is consistent with the date 1925/6 and the Perspex square was probably a later replacement. It must have been inserted either in 1937/8 before Gabo gave the work to Dorner, or after 1946 when Dorner informed Gabo that he had a plastic sculpture (presumably 22.4), which ›has to be cleaned and fixed (it has moved in itself, as this material seems to do and broke away from the glue)‹ (letter from A. Dorner, 25 Dec 1946).

In its present state 22.4 has no vertical strips above the black angled-pieces and no cross-pieces between the quarter-annulars. Glue or solvent marks on the work, however, suggest that these elements may have originally been present. Fractures in the horizontal black bars have also been repaired. These changes make the identification of bibliographical references difficult (see also 22.3).

Gabo probably first met Dorner in 1930 in connection with his exhibition at the Kestner-Gesellschaft of which Dorner was the President (E5). In his capacity as Director of the Hannover Landesmuseum, Dorner acquired a work from Gabo (20.2, see 23.2). After Dorner became Director of the Museum of the Rhode Island School of Design in January 1938, he bought two works for the Museum from the Julien Levy Gallery, New York (E7; 35.3, 41.3). Gabo apparently gave 22.4 to Dorner after the New York exhibition, possibly when he and Miriam visited Dorner in Providence in June 1938 (M. Gabo, notes, 1982/3, FAL; letters M. Gabo to K. Dreier, 8 and mid-Jun 1938).

22.4a Construction in Space with Balance on Two Points: Reconstruction

1967. Plexiglas, on painted wooden base. [25.6 x 34.9].
Cambridge, Mass.: Harvard University, Busch-Reisinger Museum (1967.53).

Exh: E201 Austin (1972) : E222 Berlin (1977) No. 1/509 : E239 Milan (1979–80) : E242 Washington, DC (1980) No. 24 : E247 New York (1980) No. 38 : E257 Frankfurt am Main etc. (1982–3) No. IX, 2.

This reconstruction was made for the Museum by Egan-De Young Associates of Brockton, Massachusetts, in April 1967.

22.5 Construction in Space with Balance on Two Points

[1936/46]. Plastic. [26 high].
Paris, Private Collection.
From the artist, [c. 1957] to Collection Mr and Mrs Bernard Reis, New York; c. 1978 to Harold Diamond, New York; 1978 to Paris.

Exh: E221 Münster (1977) fig., as ›1925‹ : E231 Paris (1979) No. 116, fig. p. 229, supplement p. 5 : E234 New York (1979) No. 102, fig., as ›Celluloid‹ : E250 Moscow (1981) Vol. 1, p. 312, fig. Vol. 2, captioned incorrectly as Pevsner.

Lit: G28 (1957) p. 183, n. 36.

This version is distinct from the others because the upper pair of slanting white sheets each join the

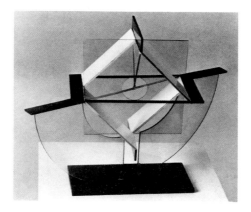

black angled pieces at the ends rather than at the angles, and there are no cross-pieces between the quarter-annulars at the base. These features identify 22.5 as the work in a photograph taken at Carbis Bay, probably by Barbara Hepworth, between 1939 and 1946 (FAL). This refutes the dating of ›1960s‹ given in E234. The thickness and clarity of the material suggest that the work is made of Perspex rather than celluloid. This is consistent with the dating 1936/46.

Miriam Gabo listed this work amongst others given to Bernard Reis between 1949 and 1964 (letter to C. Israels, 15 Feb 1967). It was clearly in Reis's possession by 1957 when he was listed as the owner (G28).

22.6 Construction in Space with Balance on Two Points

[1982]. Not inscribed.
Plexiglas. 27 x 37.
London, Family Collection.
See illus. p. 104

The pieces for this version were cut during Gabo's lifetime, and in 1982 the work was assembled by Charles Wilson at the family's request. The protective backing paper on the plastic showed it to be Plexiglas.

23. MONUMENT FOR AN AIRPORT

Gabo made two works with the same title within eight years of each other. This is the earlier of the two works (see also 35). Hildebrandt's caption ›Sculpture for an Airport as a Signal for Airmen‹ [›Plastik für einen Flughafen als Signal für Flieger‹] implies a utilitarian intention (B104 fig. p. 446). According to Miriam Gabo, the large version of 35 may have been intended to act as a weather-cock, although Gabo's title for 23 emphasises a monumental rather than a functional aim.

23.1 Model for ›Monument for an Airport‹

[1924/5]. [Not inscribed].
Celluloid. [c. 10 high].
London, Family Collection.

Lit: A124 Kállai (1927) fig. p. 244, without base : [A125 Kállai (1930) fig. p. 18] : [A56 Bier (1931) fig. p. 467, as ›1925/1926‹] : [B104 Hildebrandt (1931) pp. 446–7, fig.].

The main parts of this model, with the exception of the base, were found in the attic of the house in Middlebury in 1977. A scale-drawing of the model on orange graph paper is marked ›x 6‹, suggesting that it was to be enlarged six times (Family Collection). The size of the large version (23.2), however, is only about five times that of the model. In 1957 Gabo dated the enlargement ›1924–25‹ (G28), and presumably the model was also made at that time.

Most of the illustrations cited above are small and difficult to ascribe with certainty to 23.1. One reproduction shows obvious and heavy retouching (A125).

23.2 Monument for an Airport

1924/6. [Not inscribed].
Glass, black enamelled brass and aluminium, and wood; set into plywood base, painted white and covered with sand. 49.5 x 73.3 x c. 30, set into oval base 1.9 x 127.3 x 80.3.
London, Family Collection.
See illus. p. 105

Exh: E5 Hannover (1930) No. 19 as ›1925/26‹, fig. as ›1925‹ : E46 New York (1936) No. 73, p. 12, fig. 138.

Lit: A126 Kállai (1932) fig. p. 287, on oval base : G8 (1933) fig. p. 16 : G10 (1936) fig. p. 848 : E9 New York (1948) fig. p. 28 : B24 Biederman (1948) fig. 211 : A144 Mumford (1949) fig. p. 206 : G28 (1957) p. 183, fig. 30, as ›1924–25 Glass and metal‹ : B43 Cauman (1958) fig. p. 64 : A139 S. Moholy-Nagy (1966) fig. 15.

All the main parts of this work, with the exception of the glass planes and metal side-struts, were found in 1977 in the attic of the house in Middlebury. The metals used were brass and aluminium. The height of five feet given in the 1948 catalogue (E9) was a mistake. The measurements given here are based on those in the 1936 exhibition (E46).

In 1957 Gabo dated this work ›1924–25‹ (G28), although in 1930 he had dated it ›1925/26‹ (E5). The earlier date may refer to the conception of 23 or to the creation of the model (23.1).

According to Samuel Cauman, Alexander Dorner bought this work for the Hannover Museum in 1923 (B43). There is no evidence to confirm this, and only one work, 20.2, is known to have been sold to the Museum (M. Gabo, notes, 1982/3, FAL). Later, however, Dorner did buy 35.3 for the Museum of the Rhode Island School of Design, and Cauman may have been confusing the two works. Although 23.2 was illustrated in E9, it was not exhibited; 35.4 was shown.

24. ROTATING FOUNTAIN

24.1 Model for ›Rotating Fountain‹

> 1925. Metal, celluloid [and other plastics].
> [c. 54 x c. 35].
> London, Family Collection.

Exh: E37 Dresden (1926) No. 888, as ›Konstruk-
tion. Metall und Zelluloid, hoch 0,45 m‹ :[E5
Hannover (1930) No. 16, as ›Modell für rotierende
Springbrunnen – Konstruktion. 1925‹].

Lit: G28 (1957) p. 183, figs 27 and 28 : B127
Lissitzky-Küppers (1968) pp. 9, 76, figs. 187, 188
in situ E37 : B126 (1976) p. 37, fig. 5 : B228 Willett
(1978) fig. p. 136 *in situ* E37.

This model was found in pieces in the attic of the
house in Middlebury in 1977. Only the four black
feet at the base appear to be missing.

In the catalogue for the Dresden exhibition of
1926 (E37), Gabo is listed as Hungarian. 24.1, the
only work Gabo lent, was displayed in Lissitzky's
Exhibition Room (installation photographs, B127,
B228). 24.1 was damaged soon after the opening
and had to be withdrawn (letters to and from Herr
Probst, Neue Kunst Fides, Dresden, 19 Sep 1926,
6 Jan 1927).

24.2 Rotating Fountain

> c. 1925/7.
> Formerly Dresden, Private Collection;
> destroyed.
> From the artist.

Lit: G28 (1957) p. 183, n. 27 : A209 Thompson
(1977) p. 10.

In 1977 Gabo said of 24.2: ›it is a fountain in Dresden, but that was in a private garden. And it is
completely ruined now‹ (A209). 24.1 was shown in
Dresden in 1926, and the commission in Dresden
probably followed that exhibition.

25. CONSTRUCTION IN A HEMISPHERE

> 1925/7. Celluloid and metal. [Diameter 71.1].
> Lost; presumed destroyed.

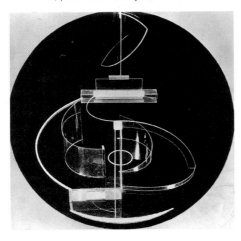

Exh: E5 Hannover (1930) No. 18, fig. on front, captioned on back cover, as ›Sphärische Konstruktion
1927‹.

Lit: A125 Kállai (1930) fig. p. 17 : G7 (1932) fig.
p. 14 : B76 Giedion-Welcker (1937) fig. p. 132, as
›Construction sphérique 1927 (celluloïde) London‹ :
G28 (1957) p. 183, fig. 31, as ›1925‹ : A7 (1967)
fig. p. 343.

In 1957 Gabo listed 25 as ›owned by the artist‹
(G28). Yet it was not found in Gabo's studio or attic
in 1977, and has presumably been lost.

Certain elements in 25, especially the transparent
square cross-sectioned tube, resemble components of 21 and Gabo's set-design for *La Chatte*
(for which part of the model is extant). One such
tube, made of celluloid, was found in 1977 and
may have belonged to 25.

26. CIRCULAR RELIEF

This work has also been called *Construction in
Space, Concave* [Raum-Konstruktion, konkav] (E5).

26.1 Model for ›Circular Relief‹

> 1925/(28). [Not inscribed].
> Celluloid. Diameter 10.
> London, Family Collection.

The black and transparent circles were the only
pieces of this model found in the attic of the house
in Middlebury in 1977. A drawing for 26.1 on
orange graph paper is partly drawn to scale (Family
Collection).

26.2 Circular Relief

> 1925/(28); rebuilt later. Signed on projecting
> plastic strip on wooden base: ›N. Gabo‹.
> Plastic; on circular wooden base.
> [23 deep x 50 diameter].
> London, Tate Gallery (T02142).
> Presented by the artist, 1977.

Exh: E5 Hannover (1930) No. 17, as ›1928‹ : E44
Oxford etc. (1936) No. 6 or 7, as ›Construction in
Relief‹ : E45 London (1936) No. 39 or 41, as ›Con-
struction‹ : E6 London (1938) No. 12, as ›Relief
1925‹ : E7 Hartford etc. (1938) No. 12 : [E8 Pough-
keepsie (1938)] : E9 New York (1948) [No. 6], figs.
pp. 14, 27 : E15 Rotterdam etc. (1958) No. 4 : E18
Mannheim etc. (1965) No. 5 : E19 Zurich (1965)
No. 5, fig. cover : E20 Stockholm (1965–6)
No. 59 : E28 London (1976–7) No. 22, fig. p. 30.

Lit: A126 Kállai (1932) fig. p. 289 : A39 (1936) fig.
p. 7 : G11 (1937) fig. p. 213 : A12 (1938) fig.
p. 51 : A153 Perilli (1954) fig. p. 72 : G28 (1957)
p. 183, figs 32 and 33, as ›Circular Relief 1925‹ :
B179 Read (1964) p. 293, fig. 104 : B3 Alley (1981)
pp. 238–9, fig. : E255 Cambridge (1982) fig. p. 20
in situ E45.

This work was made in celluloid or a similar plastic.
Its original state is shown in G28 (fig. 33). By 1938

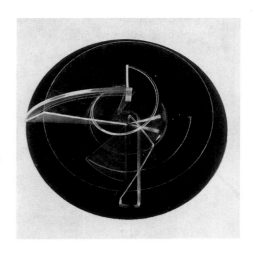

the piece with rounded corners (probably made
from tubing), that projected at the bottom of the
relief, had been replaced with a sharply angled
piece of Perspex (A12, G28 fig. 32). Further repairs
were carried out in 1965, in time for 26.2 to be
shown in Mannheim (E18; letter to G. Lloyd,
8 Mar 1965).

26.2 must have been exhibited in 1930 in
Hannover as No. 17 ›Construction in Space, Concave‹ [Raum-Konstruktion, konkav], because No.
18 ›Spheric Construction 1927‹ [Sphärische Konstruktion 1927] was illustrated, and can therefore
be identified with 25 (E5). The inclusion of 26.2 in
the exhibition at Oxford and elsewhere in 1936
(E44), is confirmed by A39, and its presence in
London in 1938 (E6), is suggested by the text and
illustration in A12.

27. MODEL FOR AN OVAL RELIEF

> [c. 1926]. Celluloid. [1.5 deep, including
> integral base 7 x 5.1].
> London, Family Collection.

This tiny model, probably incomplete, does not relate to any large-scale work. Its format, an oval dish
set against a rectangular background, is reminiscent of *Red Cavern* (28), and *Circular Relief* (26).
These similarities suggest the date given here.

28. RED CAVERN

> c. 1926. Inscribed on wooden backing:
> ›GABO‹.
> Celluloid and/or Rhodoid, glass, metal and
> cork, set into wooden box. [66 x 51.5 x 28].
> London, Tate Gallery (T02144).
> From the artist, 1938 on extended loan to the
> Museum of Modern Art, New York; 1977 pre-
> sented by the artist to the Tate.

Exh: E43 Hartford etc. (1935) No. 3 : E46 New
York (1936) No. 74, as ›Celluloid, glass and metal‹ :
E9 New York (1948) [No. 7], as ›1926. Rodoid,
plexiglas and metal‹ : E28 London (1976–7)
No. 26.

Lit: B24 Biederman (1948) fig. 204 : G28 (1957)
p. 183, fig. 40, as ›Construction Encreux‹ : B3 Alley
(1981) pp. 239 fig., 241.

In 1948 Gabo listed this work as made in 1926 (E9), although in 1976 it was dated ›1928–9‹ (E28). 28 was initially made of celluloid, glass and metal. The first indication of a change of materials is in the catalogue entry of 1948 where it is described as ›Rodoid [*sic.*], plexiglas and metal‹ (E9). Gabo may have used the Plexiglas in repairs prior to E9. The Museum of Modern Art's photograph (No. S1393, B24), shows the work in a damaged state: the elements inside the ellipse are askew – especially the horizontal strip. 28 was again repaired in April 1976 for inclusion in the London exhibition E28 (B3). There is a drawing for this work on orange graph paper (Family Collection).

29. CONSTRUCTION IN SPACE: SOARING, and CONSTRUCTION IN SPACE: TWO CONES

The dual title stems from the fact that the model for *Construction in Space: Soaring,* with its struts pointing upwards and to one side, was later used, with those same struts curving down on either side of the work, as the model for *Construction in Space: Two Cones* (see 29.1).

29.1 Model for ›Construction in Space: Soaring‹, later, Model for ›Construction in Space: Two Cones‹

1927; altered [1932/7]. Not inscribed.
Celluloid. [8.3 high].
London, Tate Gallery (T02169).
Presented by the artist, 1977.
See illus. p. 107

Exh: E28 London (1976–7) No. 23, fig. p. 31, as ›1927‹.

Lit: G28 (1957) fig. 44, as ›*Variation of Construction in Space*‹, n. d. : B3 Alley (1981) p. 239, fig.

This model has existed in two states, with the black struts up (G28), and with them turned down (B3,

E28). That these photographs do show the same model in different states is proved by a large print of the struts-up state, taken by Semo Flechine in Paris, 1933/6, which shows a tiny nick in the edge of the left-hand cone (FAL). This nick is visible in the model as it is today, i.e. in its struts-down state. Evidently 29.1 served as the model for both *Soaring* and *Two Cones.* There is no firm evidence of an enlarged *Two Cones* before 1937, so that the alteration to the model was probably effected between 1932 and 1937.

29.2 Construction in Space: Soaring

1929/30. Not inscribed.
Brass painted black and white, celluloid cones (lost); on black painted wooden base. 112 high.
London, Family Collection.
See illus. p. 106

Exh: E5 Hannover (1930) No. 21, as ›*Raum-Konstruktion, aufschwingend.* 1929/30‹ : [E48 Basel (1937) No. 130, as ›*Raumkonstruktion, aufschwebend*‹].

Lit: A11 (1931) fig. 46, as ›*Raum-Konstruktion aufschwingend* 1929‹ [*in situ* E5] : B212 Steneberg (1969) p. 46, fig. 22.

The four upswept struts; one vertical white support attached to these struts; and the two-part wooden base were found in the attic of the house in Middlebury in 1977. The celluloid cones are lost.

In 1930 Gabo dated this work ›1929/30‹ (E5). Steneberg dates it 1927 but also erroneously places the work in the Gallatin Collection, Philadelphia Museum of Art, and is presumably confusing 29.2 with 29.3 (B212).

29.2 was probably exhibited in Basel in 1937, although the entry could refer to a version of *Construction in Space with Balance on Two Points* (22; E48).

29.3 Construction in Space: Two Cones

(1927)/1937. Not inscribed.
Rhodoid [and other plastics]; on coloured and veined marble base. [25.4 high].
Philadelphia, Museum of Art (1952-61-27): A. E. Gallatin Collection.
From the artist, 1937 to Collection A. E. Gallatin, the Museum of Living Art, New York; 1952 to Philadelphia.

Lit: G12 (1937) p. 286, sculpture pl. 6, as ›1928‹ : B70 Gallatin (1940) No. 33, fig. : B24 Biederman (1948) fig. 138 : B71 Gallatin (1954) No. 51, fig., as ›1928. Rhodoid‹ : G28 (1957) p. 183, fig. 43, as ›1927‹ : A181 Siegl (1966) pp. 151–3, figs 21, 22 : B38 Burnham (1968) p. 127, fig. 41 : B3 Alley (1981) pp. 239–40.

When Gabo first published a photograph of 29.3 in *Circle* (1937), he dated it 1928. Later he amended this date to 1927 (G28), which he confirmed in 1968 (B3; receipt from T. Siegl, Conservator, Philadelphia Museum of Art, 5 Jun 1968). The

model for this version was 29.1 in its altered ›struts down‹ state, which was probably not effected before 1933 (see 29.1). 29.3 was probably made in the 1930s, and Gabo's date of 1927 may refer to the execution of 29.1.

By 1960 some of the plastic in 29.3 had disintegrated, although other elements remained intact, suggesting that they were made from a more stable plastic. Gabo stated that the material used was the same as that used in other works which were still in good order, such as *Construction on a Line* (40.6), and ›Mrs Gabo's construction‹ (probably 41.5), which was made of Rhodoid (letter to E. Turner, Philadelphia Museum of Art, 7 Apr 1968). 29.3 was returned to Gabo in January 1968, but he found any repair to be impossible (letters from A. d'Harnoncourt, 30 Jan 1968, and to E. Turner, 20 Apr 1968). Gabo speculated: ›The reason for the deterioration may be the complete air-tightness of the glass cover which kept the fumes inside where they re-acted on the material in a destructive way, or that certain parts of the material might have been older than the rest. I rather am inclined to think that my first guess is the right one‹ (letter to T. Siegl, 7 Apr 1968). On spectrographic analysis, the pieces of broken plastic were found to be either ›a regenerated cellulose or a methylcellulose‹ (spectrogram, 13 Feb 1968, and letter from R. Feller, National Gallery of Art Research Project, to T. Siegl, 5 Apr 1968). Feller added that such material was now known to be short-lived, but had been in production around 1927, the date he had been given for the construction. Nevertheless, Gabo may have made the work later than 1927, using some older materials.

In 1968 the museum commissioned a replica (29.3a), and Gabo also made a replica which he later presented to the Tate Gallery (29.4).

The reproduction of this work in *Circle* was captioned ›Coll. Mrs Francis, London‹ (G12). According to Miriam Gabo, however, Mr A. E. Gallatin acquired this work directly from Gabo when he visited them in Cholmley Gardens in 1937 (M. Gabo, notes, 1982/3, FAL; *re* Mrs Francis, see Introduction – Some Intriguing Mysteries Remain). Certainly it was in Gallatin's possession by 1938 because the catalogue for the London exhibition of that year (E6) mentions a work owned by his ›Museum of Living Art‹.

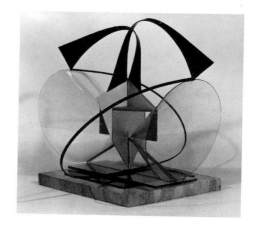

29.3a Construction in Space:
Two Cones: Reconstruction

1968. Plexiglas. [26.5 high, including integral base 1.5 high].
Philadelphia, Museum of Art.

This replica of 29.3 was made for the Museum by Arturo Cuetara, in conjunction with Rohm and Haas. It was made as a record for the Museum's use only and has not been exhibited or reproduced.

29.4 Construction in Space:
Two Cones

1968. Not inscribed.
Plastic; on white marble base. [26.7 high, including integral marble base 1.6 high].
London, Tate Gallery (T02143).
Presented by the artist, 1977.

Exh: E28 London (1976–7) No. 24.

Lit: B3 Alley (1981) pp. 239–40, fig.

Gabo made this version in 1968 as a replica of the original 29.3.

30. TORSION

This work demonstrates the subtlety with which Gabo developed a complex work from a simple geometric form, in this instance, a tetrahedron balanced on one of its edges. The cardboard study clearly shows this development (30.1).

The helical form suggested by this work can be traced backwards to the swinging S-curves of *Construction in a Hemisphere* (25), and forwards to works like *Sketch for a Stone Carving* of 1933 (A93 Forge, 1966, fig. p. 40), and much later to *Vertical Construction No. 1* (73).

30.1 Stereometric Tetrahedral Study
for ›Torsion‹

[1928/9]. Inscribed in ink: ›N. Gabo‹.
Cardboard, masking tape, with pencil markings. Sides each 11.8.
London, Tate Gallery Archive (Gabo 801).
Presented by the artist, 1977.

This ›skeletal‹ tetrahedron, constructed in the same way as the stereometric cubes (2), comprises six obtuse-angled isosceles triangles of card, the obtuse angles of which meet in the centre. The joints, originally glued, have been strengthened with masking tape. Pencil lines mark the curved elements to be removed in order to leave the basic form of *Torsion*. In the model (30.2), the curves are deeper.

30.2 Model for ›Torsion‹

(1928)/1929. Not inscribed.
Plastic. 8.9 x 9.5 diameter.
London, Tate Gallery (T02171).
Presented by the artist, 1977.

Exh: E28 London (1976–7) No. 34, as ›1929‹.

Lit: G12 (1937) p. 286, sculpture pl. 7, as ›1929‹ : A203 (1979) p. 56, fig., as ›c. 1928‹ : B3 Alley (1981) p. 240, fig., as ›c. 1929‹.

This model developed from the cardboard study (30.1). The addition of the curved elements at the top and bottom brought the basic form of the work closer to that of a spherical tetrahedron.

30.3 Model for ›Torsion‹

[(1928)/1929].
Formerly Paris, Collection the late Antoine and Mme Virginie Pevsner: present whereabouts unknown.
From the artist, c. 1929

Lit: B3 Alley (1981) p. 241.

According to Gabo, he gave his brother, Antoine Pevsner, a small model of *Torsion,* as an idea for Pevsner to develop in his work (B3). Presumably this model would have been similar in size, form, and date to 30.2. A few pieces for such a model were found in 1977, but there is no evidence to suggest that they were part of a complete model or of 30.3.

Apparently after receiving the model, Pevsner produced *Construction in Space (Project for a Fountain)* of 1929 (Kunstmuseum, Basel), and later other works, like *Bas-relief* (Solomon R. Guggenheim Museum, NY), which are clearly based on a similar tetrahedral form.

30.4 Model for ›Torsion‹

[c. 1929]. [Not inscribed].
Celluloid. [c. 35] x 39.5 diameter.
London, Family Collection; in pieces.

Gabo described 30.4 as an ›old model for *Torsion*‹ (Gabo's inscription on box, Family Collection). It is no longer intact and one curved element is missing. According to Miriam Gabo, 30.4 had almost perished by the mid-1930s, and Gabo made 30.5 in Perspex as a replacement (M. Gabo, notes, 1982/3, FAL).

30.5 Torsion

(1936)/1937; altered 1948/53; base added c. 1948. Not inscribed.
Perspex. [35.3 x 41 diameter].
London, Tate Gallery (T02146).
Presented by the artist, 1977.

Exh: E6 London (1938) No. 3 : E7 Hartford etc. (1938) No. 3 : [E8 Poughkeepsie (1938) no cat.] : E9 New York (1948) [No. 11], fig. p. 31, as ›13¾″ high‹ : E13 New York (1953) No. 2, as ›1928–36, Plastic, 17 x 28 x 22″‹ : E14 Hartford (1953) No. 6, fig. 9 : E15 Rotterdam etc. (1958) No. 5, fig. : E17 Amsterdam (1965) No. P5, fig. : E18 Mannheim etc. (1965) No. 6, fig. : E19 Zurich (1965) No. 6, fig. 5 : E20 Stockholm (1965–6) No. 60, fig. : E21 London (1966) No. 8, fig. 5 : E22 Buffalo (1968) No. 5 : E28 London (1976–7) No. 35, fig. p. 32.

Lit: A74 Chermayeff (1948) fig. 27 : G28 (1957) p. 183, figs. 53, 54 : A224 Wolfram (1966) fig. : A219 Webb (1966) fig. 3 : A222 Whitford (1966) fig. 7 : A105 Gray (1966) fig. p. 49 *in situ* E19 : A9 (1968) fig. p. 43 *in situ* E22 : A168 Rickey (1977) fig. p. 24 : B3 Alley (1981) pp. 240–41, fig.

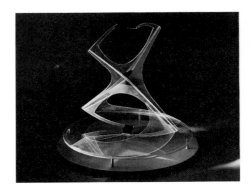

When Gabo first exhibited this work at the London Gallery in 1938, it was titled ›*Construction »Torsion«* (Variant of Construction 1929) 1937‹ (E6). In 1948 Gabo modified the date to ›1928–36‹ (E9). Presumably the earlier dates refer to the models (30.2–4).

In 1957 Gabo reproduced two photographs of 30.5, stating clearly that the two views were of one work (G28). One view showed 30.5 without black insets and on a simple base (fig. 53); the other showed 30.5 with black insets and a raised base (fig. 54). Fig. 53, showing 30.5 without the insets or special base, was taken in Cornwall by Barbara Hepworth, 1939/46. The first datable photograph which shows the special base is an installation shot of the 1948 exhibition (E9; FAL). In this photograph 30.5 has no black insets. These are first shown in conjunction with the new base in an installation photograph of the 1953 exhibition (E13; FAL). At present 30.5 does not have the special base, which was retained by Gabo, but it does have the black plastic inserts.

30.6 Torsion (Project for a Fountain)

(1960)/1965. Not inscribed.
Bronze [76.2 x 84.1 diameter].
London, Tate Gallery (T01171).
Presented by the artist, 1969, through the American Federation of Arts.
See illus. p. 142

Exh: E17 Amsterdam (1965) No. P22 : E18 Mannheim etc. (1965) No. 21 : E19 Zurich (1965) No. 21 : E20 Stockholm (1965–6) No. 79 : E21 London (1966) No. 26 : E22 Buffalo (1968) No. 16, fig. p. 22 : E28 London (1976–7) No. 36, fig. p. 32.

Lit: A75 Clay (1966) fig. p. 116 *in situ* E20 : A103 Granath (1966) fig. p. 13 *in situ* E20 : A93 Forge (1966) fig. p. 42 : A51 Bekkers (1966) p. 35, fig. following p. 32 : B184 Rickey (1967) pp. 192–3, fig. : A118 Hultén (1971) fig. p. 65 : B3 Alley (1981) p. 262, fig.

This version served as the model for the large fountain (30.7). Although 30.6 is usually dated ›1960–64‹ (E17-21), in 1966 Gabo stated that it was made in ›1964–5‹ (A51). A photograph of 30.6 was retouched by Gabo to show the effect that the water would create in the final fountain (A51).

30.7 Revolving Torsion, Fountain

1972–3. Not inscribed.
Stainless steel. [310 x 335 diameter].
London, Tate Gallery (T01754), installed outside St. Thomas's Hospital, London, 1975.
Presented by Alistair McAlpine, 1973.
See illus. p. 43, fig. 51

Exh: E28 London (1976–7) No. 37, as photograph, fig. p. 33.

Lit: A209 Thompson (1977) fig. p. 10 : A168 Rickey (1977) fig. p. 27 : B3 Alley (1981) p. 267.

Plans to construct this fountain were initiated by Sir Norman Reid in 1968 when he showed 30.6 to Alistair McAlpine who agreed to finance the work. Sir Robert McAlpine and Sons Ltd drew up the plans (TGA, Gabo 784), and the construction was carried out by Stainless Metalcraft Ltd of London in 1972–3. Eugene Rosenberg, the architect, energetically supported the installation of the fountain outside St. Thomas's Hospital. This was realised in late 1975 (E28 p. 7).

In 1977 Gabo wrote of the fountain: ›I had from the beginning an idea that this subject, called *Torsion*, has certain curves outside, that it should be connected with kinetics. This piece changes its image when it turns round . . . I thought the wings of the piece should also have a movement of their own in the form of water jets. Now these water jets should replace lines. At that time I was very much preoccupied making surfaces with lines, so I connected it with water . . . and the jets will give a certain kind of form by themselves. So the direction of the water is dictated by the form of the wings of the structure, and it goes round and then it becomes like a ball of water, and then it goes down . . . All these wings are provided with 140 jet holes and the jets go out and round and, when you [force] the water out more, they become a kind of ball. In ten minutes [it makes one revolution] . . . you stay there and look at the whole thing and then you suddenly see a totally different thing in the middle‹ (A209).

The fountain completes one revolution every ten minutes, and the water-pressure of the jets changes from minimum pressure to maximum, returning to minimum in a ten minute cycle. As George Rickey has emphasised, the partial surface created by the thin jets of water represents conceptually, as well as physically, an extension of Gabo's use of incised lines and nylon filament (A168; see e.g. 37, 48).

31. DOUBLE RELIEF IN A NICHE

This construction was designed for the house which the architect Eric Mendelsohn built for himself overlooking the Havelsee at Rupenhorn, Berlin, in 1929. A drawing for 31 shows the relief, about

three or four feet high, set into a wall above a sofa (TGA, file 7711). Another drawing, showing the left side only, is signed and dated ›1929‹. Nevertheless, Mendelsohn had not received the drawings by the autumn of 1930 (letter from E. Mendelsohn, 1 Sep 1930, TGA). According to Gabo, the project was not pursued because the glass-work was too expensive (F10 p. 18).

31.1 Model for ›Double Relief in a Niche‹

1929/30. Inscribed bottom right: ›N. Gabo‹.
Plastic, cork and cardboard.
[11.4 x 22.2 x 5.1, set in wood and plastic surround 28.2 x 36 x 6].
London, Tate Gallery (T02170).
Presented by the artist, 1977.

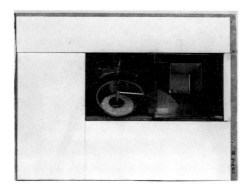

Exh: [E5 Hannover (1930) No. 20, ›*Konstruktive Raumgestaltung für eine Wandnische* 1930‹] : E28 London (1976–7) No. 25, fig. p. 31.

Lit: G28 (1957) p. 183, fig. 41, as ›*Construction in a Niche* 1930‹ : B3 Alley (1981) p. 241, fig.

This model shows the intended arrangement with the white plastic representing the wall. It is uncertain whether the model (31.1), or the enlargement (31.2), was shown at Hannover in November 1930 (E5). 31.1 was found in the attic of the house in Middlebury in April 1976 and repaired for inclusion in E28.

31.2 Construction in a Niche

1930. Inscribed on wooden backing: ›GABO‹.
Plastic, metals, and cork, set into wooden box. [61 x 28 x 58.5].
London, Tate Gallery (T02145).
Presented by the artist, 1977.

Exh: [E5 Hannover (1930) No. 20, as ›*Konstruktive Raumgestaltung für eine Wandnische* 1930‹] : [E6 London (1938) No. 5, as ›*Constructive Treatment for an Interior Niche*‹] : [E7 Hartford etc. (1938) No. 5] : E9 New York (1948) [No. 8] : E28 London (1976–7) No. 27, as ›1928–29‹.

Lit: G28 (1957) p. 183, fig. 42, as ›1930‹, shows it the wrong way round : A8 (1957) fig. p. 178 : B3 Alley (1981) pp. 241–2, fig.

This construction is an enlargement of the left-hand side of the model (31.1). Although it is possible that the model may have been exhibited in 1930 in Hannover (E5), it seems very probable that in later exhibitions Gabo would have shown the enlargement. 31.2 was repaired for the 1976–7 exhibition in London (E28). Perspex was then used to replace some elements.

32. CONSTRUCTION

1929/33. Metal and [glass or Rhodoid].
Lost.

Lit: B172 Read (1936) fig. 67 : B172 Read (1948) fig. 171 : B76 Giedion-Welcker (1937) fig. p. 133, in German ed. elaborated as ›*Konstruktion für Halle eines Schwimmbades in Chicago* 1932. (bewegliche Feder, die durch Wind rotiert)‹. : B87 Grohmann (1953) p. 263 : B67 Francastel (1954) p. 397, as ›*matière plastique bleue*‹ : B76 Giedion-Welcker (1960) fig. p. 178.

This lost work is known through a photograph, taken by Semo Flechine, which is annotated ›Design for Fountain '29 Rodoid [*sic*.]‹ (FAL). Giedion-Welcker captioned this piece: ›Construction for Chicago Swimming Pool 1932. Model in Metal and Glass, Maryland Club Gardens‹ (B76). This caption is so detailed, it seems unlikely to be totally speculative. However, neither the ›Maryland Club‹ in Chicago, nor its gardens have been traced. In the catalogue for the 1930 Hannover exhibition (E5), ›Bornes‹ of Chicago was listed as an owner of a work by Gabo, but no further details were provided and no connection has been established with 32.

33. CONSTRUCTION IN SPACE: ARCH

Gabo may have considered *Arch* as a potential structure for a fountain. The entry for *Arch* in a catalogue for the London exhibition of 1938 is annotated ›Model for a fountain‹ (E6, FAL). A sketch relating to this is discussed under 43.

33.1 Model for ›Construction in Space: Arch‹

> 1929/37. Not inscribed.
> Celluloid. [*c.* 10 high, in its present state].
> London, Tate Gallery (T02206).
> Presented by the artist, 1977.

Lit: B3 Alley (1981) p. 247, fig.

This model is badly distorted and the celluloid discoloured. A drawing for the model is initialled in cyrillic and dated ›NG 1929‹ (Family Collection). The length of the base in the drawing is 20 cms which corresponds with the model. Ronald Alley dates the model 1937 because this is the date of the large version of *Arch* (33.3; B3). In 1938 Gabo dated a version of *Arch* 1925 (G14). This seems too early, although the celluloid model is possibly closer in date to the drawing than to the enlargements.

33.2 Construction in Space: Arch

> (1929)/1937. Not inscribed.
> Rhodoid with Perspex substitutions; on Perspex base. [46.4 x 76.2 x 21.6; on base 1.3 x 90.2 x 30.5].
> London, Family Collection.
> *See illus. p. 107*

Lit: B3 Alley (1981) p. 247.

In 1957 Gabo did not list this version (G28 p. 183, n. 60). After 1936 Gabo replaced several pieces of Rhodoid with Perspex. Following damage in storage, Charles Wilson restored 33.2 in the winter of 1982–3. He straightened out some of the pieces, replaced the small circular element and reassembled the construction.

33.3 Construction in Space: Arch

> 1937. Not inscribed.
> Perspex. 47.5 x 81 x 24;
> on base 2 x 88.8 x 30.4.
> New York. Solomon R. Guggenheim Museum (47.1103).
> From the artist, 1947.

Exh: E6 London (1938) No. 16 : E7 Hartford etc. (1938) No. 15 : [E8 Poughkeepsie (1938)] E143 New York (1962) : E152 New York (1963) : E186 New York (1969) p. 119, fig. : E224 New York (1977–8) No. 38 : E266 New York (1984).

Lit: A12 (1938) fig. p. 50 : G14 (1938) fig. p. 6, as ›1925‹ : G28 (1957) p. 183, figs 60 and 61 : B133 Lukach (1983) p. 269.

A version of *Arch* was first exhibited in 1938 as ›Construction in Space 1937‹ (E6). A diagrammatic sketch against No. 16 in a copy of the catalogue, and a photograph of 33 in A12 confirm this (FAL, endorsed by Miriam Gabo). The photograph in A12 is identical to the photograph reproduced in 1957, and since Gabo only listed 33.3 then, this is presumably the version illustrated (G28 fig. 60, St. Ives Photo Studio). 33.3 was therefore probably the version shown in London and subsequently in the USA in 1938 (E6–7).
According to Ruth Israels, Gabo's sister-in-law, Solomon R. Guggenheim bought this work directly from Gabo in December 1946, soon after Gabo's arrival in the USA. The acquisition was completed in 1947 (cheque voucher, 28 Mar 1947, SRGM).

34. CONSTRUCTION IN SPACE : STONE WITH A COLLAR

Gabo apparently carved pieces of wood as a child, and one of his earliest memories was of trying to inscribe words on a stone (F11 J. Read 1972). Nevertheless, *Stone with a Collar* is the earliest known work by Gabo to contain a glyptic element.
The stone used in the various versions is often referred to as ›Portland‹ stone. It is, however, unlikely that Gabo had access to Portland stone before he settled in England in 1936, and the earlier versions of 34 were probably made of another type of limestone. According to Miriam Gabo, when she met Gabo in 1936, he was working on a middlesized version of 34 (probably 34.4 or 34.5), in Mr Gumbrill's mason's workshop (M. Gabo, notes, 1982/3, FAL).

34.1 Model for ›Stone with Collar‹

> 1930/32. Not inscribed.
> Stone, on black plastic; formerly with [cardboard collar and plastic strips].
> [4.6 high x 5, in its present state].
> London, Tate Gallery (T02172).
> Presented by the artist, 1977.

Exh: E28 London (1976–7) No. 43, fig. p. 47, centre of group.

Lit: A165 Richards (1937) fig. p. 161 : B3 Alley (1981) p. 243, fig.

Ronald Alley dated this tiny model ›1930–31‹ (B3), although earlier it had been dated ›1931–32‹ (A165). A photograph, taken by Semo Flechine while Gabo was in Paris in 1933–6, shows the model with a collar, possible of cardboard, and a thin black strip, probably of plastic (FAL, similar to A165).

34.2 Stone with Collar

> 1930/32. Not inscribed.
> Stone, on slate. [17.8 high x 15.2].
> London, Tate Gallery (T02147).
> Presented by the artist, 1977.

Exh: E28 London (1976–7) No. 44, as ›1930–31‹.

Lit: B3 Alley (1981) p. 243, fig.

34.2 is dated on the same basis as 34.1, although there is no indication that 34.2 originally had a collar and thin black strip. 34.2 may be a second model, but its size suggests that it is probably an unfinished work.

34.3 Construction: Stone with a Collar

> 1933. Inscribed at back of base at left: ›N. GABO‹, and back right: ›G‹.
> Stone [Ivory Rhodoid], brass strip painted black, on [slate]. *c.* 40 high x *c.* 72.
> London, Family Collection.
> *See illus. pp. 77 and 109*

Exh: [E7 Hartford etc. (1938) No. 11] : [E8 Poughkeepsie (1938)] : E9 New York (1948) [No. 10], as ›Construction 1933. Portland stone‹ : E10 Baltimore (1950) [No. 1] : E11 Cambridge, Mass. (1951) [No. 4] : [E12 Chicago (1952) No. 6] : E13 New York (1953) No. 3 : E14 Hartford (1953) No. 7 : E15 Rotterdam etc. (1958) No. 6 : E17 Amsterdam (1965) No. P6 : E18 Mannheim etc. (1965) No. 7, fig. : E19 Zurich (1965) No. 7, fig. 6 : E20 Stockholm (1965–6) No. 61 : E21 London (1966) No. 9, fig. 6a : E22 Buffalo (1968) No. 7 : E235 Buffalo etc. (1979) No. 19, fig. p. 85 : E252 Saint Paul (1981) No. 78, fig. p. 102 : E254 Madrid (1981) No. 47, colour fig. : E255 Cambridge (1982) No. 7, fig. p. 8 and cover.

Lit: G28 (1957) p. 183, fig. 51. stereoscopic colour fig. 105 : B76 Giedion-Welcker (1960) fig. p. 369 *in situ* E13 : A75 Clay (1966) fig. p. 116 *in situ* E20 : A222 Whitford (1966) fig. 5.

An early photograph shows that this work initially had transparent and black pieces of plastic which continued the sweep of the collar down to the base (G28 fig. 51). Two small pieces of black plastic suggest that at one time 33.3, like 33.4, also had a strip of plastic arching over the top of the stone. A brass plate, painted black and attached to the stone base, may have some connection with the plastic arch. The present arching strip is made of brass, painted black. The small blemish on the stone's surface was present when Gabo was making 34.3.
According to Miriam Gabo, this version was probably made before Gabo came to England. The collar appears to be of ivory Rhodoid which is compatible with the date of 1933 given in 1948 (E9).

34.4 Construction: Stone with a Collar

> (1933)/1937. Not inscribed.
> [Portland] stone and plastic, on slate.
> [20.3 high x 34.3].
> New York, Collection Judith Rothschild.
> From the artist, *c.* 1937 to Collection Winifred Dacre Nicholson, England; 1956/7, to Harold Diamond, New York; 1956/7 to Rose Fried Gallery, New York; 1956/7 to Collection Herbert and Nannette Rothschild, New York.

Exh: E48 Basel (1937) No. 131, fig., as ›Konstruktion, windend‹ : E126 New York (1960) p. 22, ex-cat. : E179 New York (1967) fig. p. 44.

Lit: G12 (1937) p. 286, sculpture pl. 8, as ›1933‹ : G14 (1938) fig. p. 6 : G13 (1939) fig. p. 46, as ›1938‹ : E9 New York (1948) fig. p. 29 : A176 Segi (1954) fig. p. 20 : G28 (1957) p. 183, fig. 50 : B79 Goldwater (1967) fig. p. 44.

Apparently this work was damaged sometime in the late 1950s (letter H. Diamond to M. Gabo, 25 Jan 1960). In 1981 Diamond confirmed much of the provenance. According to Judith Rothschild, 34.4 was exhibited in 1960 (E126).

34.5   Construction: Stone with a Collar

(1933)/1938. Inscribed on back: ›GABO‹.
Stone and plastic, on slate. [18 high x 33].
Paris, Private Collection.
From the artist, 1937/8 to Collection Lawrence Wright, England; 1961 to Collection Mr and Mrs E. Estorick, London; 6 Nov 1979 through Sotheby's to Paris.

Exh: [E49 London (1937) No. 8, as ›Construction 1933‹] : E6 London (1938) No. 11, as ›Construction in Space 1933‹ : E178 London (1967) No. 24 : E227 Münster only (1978) Gabo No. 2, fig. p. 154.

Lit: S6 New York (1979) No. 217, fig. : A20 (1980) p. 200, fig.

This version, like 34.4, may have been made in England of Portland stone. The stone, however, is not very grey and is probably another type of limestone. In 1961 the black arching strip was replaced by the painter, Paul Feiler, and the work was cleaned. In c. 1979 it again underwent some slight restoration.
   According to Lawrence Wright, he acquired 34.5 at an exhibition of Gabo's work at the London Gallery in the late 1930s. This could have been E49, but it is more likely to have been E6, which was a one-man show.
   Apparently the provenance given in S6 is inaccurate. According to Mr and Mrs Estorick, 34.5 was their personal property and not that of the Grosvenor Gallery. The Piccadilly Gallery never owned the work.

35.   MONUMENT FOR AN AIRPORT

This is sometimes referred to as a *Model* or *Monument for an Aerodrome*, although in 1957 Gabo titled it *Monument for an Airport* (G28). Confusion has occasionally arisen between this work and 23, which has the same title. In 1938 Gabo exhibited 35.3 as ›Model for an Airdrome (Variant of 1924) 1932‹ (E6). Presumably the ›Variant of 1924‹ refers to 23.
   According to Miriam Gabo, in 1937 Gabo suggested that 35 could be used for Imperial Airways advertising: on a small scale as a desk display, on a larger scale in a booking-hall, or as an outdoor monument (see 35.5). Apparently Gabo also considered mounting this work on a pivot to turn it

into a weather-cock, with the pointer indicating wind-direction (see 23).

35.1   Model for ›Monument for an Airport‹

c. 1932. Not inscribed.
Plastic. [6.3 x 12.7 x 7.6].
London, Tate Gallery (T02168).
Presented by the artist, 1977.

Exh: E28 London (1976–7) No. 21, as ›1923‹, fig. p. 28.

Lit: E9 New York (1948) fig. p. 28, as ›42½″ long‹ : B203 Seuphor (1949) fig. p. 295 : G28 (1957) p. 183, fig. 45, as ›glass and metal‹ : A208 Thompson (1966) fig. p. 136 : E25 Hannover (1971) fig. p. 88 : B3 Alley (1981) pp. 243–4, fig.

In 1948 Gabo dated this work 1932 (E9). The first photograph of 35.1 was taken by Semo Flechine while Gabo was living in Paris in 1933–6 (FAL; G28). This photograph bears the later annotation, ›Monument for an Airport 1924‹, which seems to confuse 35 with 23. Another photograph, taken in Paris, shows Gabo and Antoine Pevsner holding the two small models, 35.1 and 35.2 (B203).

35.2   Variation of Model for ›Monument for an Airport‹, with two cones

[c. 1932]. Not inscribed.
Celluloid with silvered paper. c. 5 x c. 12 x 9.
London, Family Collection.

Lit: B203 Seuphor (1949) fig. p. 295 : F11 J. Read (1972).

This model was found in the attic of the house in Middlebury in 1977. It appears in an early photograph of Gabo with Antoine Pevsner (see 35.1). The model's base is circular, but a square of silvered paper on the underside follows the alignment of pointer and base in 35.1. Apparently Gabo did not make any enlargements of 35.2.

35.3   Monument for an Airport

1932. Celluloid, steel and plywood.
33.3 x 74.3 x 47.
Providence, Rhode Island: Rhode Island School of Design, Museum of Art (83.061) : Gift of Mrs Murray S. Danforth, 1938.
From the artist, 1938 through the Julien Levy Gallery, New York.

Exh: E6 London (1938) No. 15 : E7 Hartford etc. (1938) No. 14 : [E8 Poughkeepsie (1938)] : E73 Andover (1949–50).

Lit: G28 (1957) p. 183, n. 45 : B3 Alley (1981) p. 243.

This piece was restored by Julius Ternbach in 1968, although the celluloid is seriously distorted. The transparent composite element on top of the black rhombus points backwards. In this 35.3 differs from all other versions, although the point of attachment at the front of the rhombus is the same as 35.1. The orientation of the composite element

may be a variation introduced by Gabo, or it may be the result of a mistake made during restoration.
   The Museum records indicate that 35.3 was bought from the Nierendorf Gallery, New York. Like 41.3, however, 35.3 was selected by the Museum's director, Dr Alexander Dorner, from the exhibition at the Julien Levy Gallery in 1938 (E7). Gabo later confirmed the date of acquisition as 1938 (letter to G. Washburn, 20 Feb 1949).

35.4   Monument for an Airport

1936/48. Not inscribed.
Perspex with brass painted black. 41.6 x 108 x 57.5.
London, Family Collection.
See illus. pp. 76 and 108

Exh: E9 New York (1948) [No. 9], fig. 28 shows 35.1 : E22 Buffalo (1968) No. 4, as ›1926‹.

Lit: A162 Read (1950) fig. p. 30, as ›1924‹.

This work may have been made by Gabo to show to Marcus Brumwell in 1937 (see 35.5). It was first exhibited in 1948 (E9).
   In this version the transparent cross-piece points forward, but is attached at the back of the black rhombus. The base stands on nine small hemispheres and one rectangle (at the back).
   An installation photograph of the 1948 exhibition indicates that this version was shown there on a large circular base, which is now separated from 35.4 (E9; FAL). At E9 it was also photographed in colour by Dr F. Block.

35.5   Monument for an Airport

c. 1937. Inscribed on edge of white square: ›GABO‹, and on front tip of black rod: ›Gabo‹.
Perspex. c. 10.2 x c. 26.7 x 14.
England, Collection the late Mr Marcus, and Mrs Brumwell.
From the artist, [1937/8].

Lit: B3 Alley (1981) pp. 243–4.

In 1936/7 Marcus Brumwell, of the Stuart Advertising Agency, suggested that Gabo design advertising and display materials for Imperial Airways (letter from M. Brumwell, 21 Jan 1937). Gabo apparently executed two designs: a ›circular display for inclusive tours‹ and a ›concave globe map‹ (letter from M. Brumwell, 1 Jul 1937). Neither of these can be identified with a version of 35, and the map relates to an entirely different design (drawing, Family Collection). There is no mention of 35 in the correspondence, and Gabo may not have suggested it or shown it to Brumwell immediately. It is not certain whether the version Gabo showed Brumwell was 35.5 or 35.4. Nothing came of the advertising project, although Brumwell acquired 35.5, which was probably made especially for him at this time.
   In 35.5 the transparent cross-piece is mounted as in the model, 35.1. 35.5 is unique, however, in having a tiny rectangle of white Perspex placed on the transparent sheet, at right-angles to the front end of the black rhombus. Apparently in 1948 the pointer snapped at the base, and Hans Erni repaired it (letter from M. Brumwell, 26 Nov 1948).

35.6   Monument for an Airport

c. 1937. [Perspex]. [*c.* 10.2 x *c.* 26.7 x 14].
Formerly, San Francisco, Collection Mrs
Miriam Wornum; lost late 1940s.
From the artist, *c.* 1937.

According to Mrs Wornum and Alan Bowness, this
version was made when Mr Grey Wornum was
working as the Decoration Architect on the S. S.
Queen Elizabeth – an appointment which com-
menced in October 1936 and continued after the
ship was launched in 1938. There is no photograph
of this version, but apparently it was the same size
as 35.5.

36.   KINETIC STONE CARVING

1936(– 44). Inscribed at one end: ›NG‹ (›N‹
barely legible).
Portland stone. 24 high x 37.
London, Family Collection.
See illus. pp. 87 and 109

Exh: E9 New York (1948) [No. 12], 4 figs. pp. 32–3 :
E69 New Haven (1949) No. 9, fig. : E10 Baltimore
(1950) [No. 2], as ›Grey Stone‹ : E11 Cambridge,
Mass. (1951) [No. 5] : E12 Chicago (1952) No. 2 :
E90 Philadelphia etc. (1952–3) No. 35 : E15
Rotterdam etc. (1958) No. 7, fig. : E17 Amsterdam
(1965) No. P7, fig. : E18 Mannheim etc. (1965)
No. 8, fig. : E19 Zurich (1965) No. 8, fig. 7 : E20
Stockholm (1965–6) No. 62, fig. : E21 London
(1966) No. 11, fig. 6 b : E22 Buffalo (1968) No. 8 :
E269 London (1985) No. 40, fig. p. 162.

Lit: A98 Gibson (1946) figs. following p. 64 : A150
(1946) fig. opp. p. 176 : A73 Chermayeff (1948) fig.
p. 56 : B4 Alvard *et al* (1952) fig. p. 124 : A176
Segi (1954) figs. p. 21 : G28 (1957) p. 183, figs.
55–6 as ›1936‹, stereoscopic colour fig. 108 : A81
Davies (1982) fig. p. 56 : B56 Davies (1984) fig. 11.

According to Miriam Gabo, this work was started in
1936 and Gabo continued to work on it for several
years. It was evidently completed by 1944 when it
appears in the background of a photograph of
Gabo and Bernard Leach, taken that year at St.
Ives (A81).
    The loan receipt list for the Baltimore exhibition of
1950 (E10), is annotated ›(smaller one) Eng. limestone‹, presumably to differentiate it from *Stone
with a Collar* (34.3), which is also listed.

37.   SPHERIC THEME

In 1957 Gabo wrote:
    ›The *Spheric Theme* is the result of many years
of research for a constructive method of transferring my perception of space in terms of visual experience of it . . . I felt that the visual character of
space is not angular: that to transfer the perception
of space into sculptural terms, it has to be spheric.
I was looking for some kind of an indication in the
scientific world, where a method of spheric structure could be found. I found no answer in graphic
terms in science which would satisfy my vision of
space. I consider that in this work of mine there is

a satisfactory solution to that problem. Instead of
indicating space by an angular intersection of
planes, I enclose the space in one curved continuous surface . . . I have used this system since
1936 . . . There is an immense variety of images
which . . . can be executed with the help of this
system‹ (G28, text to figs 64, 65).
    Later Gabo explained the importance of this
work:
    ›Being done in 1936, it served me as a basis for
a great part of my later constructions. Many . . . like
*The Arch, The Monument for the Unknown Political
Prisoner,* the Bijenkorf structure and others would
not be, I think, produced by me without my first
invention of this work.
    ›I call it an »invention« advisedly, as a contrast to
the Heads which, in the constructive principle, are
not my invention. I introduced in them a stereometric principle well-known in stereometry [i. e. solid
geometry] but this *Spheric Theme* structure, I claim
as my invention and, in fact, some scientists did
consider it as such‹ (letter to N. Reid, 10 May
1966).
    There are two undated drawings relating to later
variations of *Spheric Theme* (Tate Gallery, T02161,
T02162; see 43). Ronald Alley dates the former ›*c.*
1935–7‹ (B3 pp. 245–6). Gabo's dating of *Spheric
Theme* as 1936, suggests that he had completed
his first studies by then (G28).
    The basic structure of the work may be the result
of working directly with paper or card discs. Several
examples of such models were in Gabo's studio.
They comprise two circular discs of card from the
centre of which a small concentric disc has been
removed. The rings are cut radially, twisted and
then joined together along the edges to produce
the basic structure of *Spheric Theme* (see B38
p. 141). Alternatively *Spheric Theme* may have
been the result of a process of reduction from a
sphere (see 37.1).
    Spheric Theme is directly related to several of
Gabo's later works, particularly: *Spheric Theme:
Metal Versions* (42), *Bas-Relief on a Circular Surface, Semi-Spheric* (44), *Bronze Spheric Theme
(Variation)* (78), and *Monument to the Astronauts*
(80).

37.1   Spherical Study

Not inscribed.
Ivory. 4.1 diameter.
London, Family Collection.

This ivory carving, made from a billiard ball, under-
lines the fact that the outside edge of *Spheric
Theme* follows the same line as that formed by the
seam on the surface of a tennis ball. *Spherical
Study* is formed by the removal of the material between the convolutions of this line, producing two
interlocking concave surfaces. The extension of this
process might produce models such as 37.2 and
37.3, where the surface of the sphere is indicated
by the edges of the planes created by the solid
material. It is impossible to date 37.1, or to determine whether it pre- or post-dates the other
models.

37.2   Model for ›Spheric Theme‹

1936/7. Inscribed by one join: ›Gabo‹, and
by the opposite join: ›NG‹.
Transparent Perspex; on black Perspex
base.
10.2 diameter; on base 1.3 x 15.9 x 15.9.
London, Family Collection.
See illus. p. 110

Exh: E28 London (1976–7) No. 52.

This model has a hole at the centre of *c.* 5 mm
in diameter, although unlike 37.3 it has no incised
lines.

37.3   Model for ›Spheric Theme‹

1936/7. Inscribed across join: ›NG‹ [the G in
cyrillic], and at centre: ›Gabo‹.
Transparent Perspex. 10.2 diameter.
London, Family Collection.
Gift from the artist [early 1950s] to Collection Yves Tanguy, Woodbury; *c.* 1963 by
bequest to Mattatuck Museum, Waterbury;
late 1960s, returned to the artist.

Exh: E230 London (1978) No. 55.

A photograph of this model is inscribed: ›Photo.
Roger Franklin *Model for Spheric Theme.* Naum
Gabo. 1937. 8 cm x 10 cm, Plastic, signed NG.
Cat. No. 55 *The Non-Objective World 1914–39.*
June 28-Sept. 30 1978‹ (FAL).
    According to Nina Williams, this model was
broken at the Mattatuck Museum and returned to
Gabo who repaired it. It is constructed from four
quarters, one of which is now made of two separate pieces, presumably representing the repaired
section. One of the complete quarters is incised
with radiating lines. Like 37.2, this model also has a
small hole at the centre, *c.* 5 mm in diameter.

37.4   Model for ›Spheric Theme‹

c. 1937. Not inscribed.
Celluloid. 12 diameter.
London, Tate Gallery (T02173).
Presented by the artist, 1977.

Exh: E28 London (1976–7) No. 50, fig. p. 35, as
›*c.* 1937‹.

Lit: B3 Alley (1981) p. 247, fig.

This model is more complex than 37.2 or 37.3, and
was probably made later. Like 37.6, for which it
might have been the model, 37.4 has a double
›skin‹ of celluloid, supported by a four-pointed star
shape. Gabo abraded the celluloid to create a less
transparent surface.

37.5   Study for one quarter of ›Spheric
Theme: Black variation‹

1937. Not inscribed.
Black and transparent Perspex.
27.5 x 43 x *c.* 25.
London, Family Collection.

This study is directly related to 37.6.

37.6 Spheric Theme: Black Variation

1937. Not inscribed.
Transparent Rhodoid and black [celluloid].
42.5 diameter.
London, Family Collection.
See illus. p. 111

Exh: E67 New Haven (1949) No. 38, as ›1936‹.

Lit: G28 (1957) p. 184, figs 72, 73 : B179 Read (1964) p. 293, fig. 108, miscaptioned.

The curving planes of black and transparent plastic in this version are held apart by a central four-pointed star shape into which the transparent plane is slotted (see 37.4, 37.5).

37.7 Spheric Theme: Transparent Variation

[*c.* 1937]. Inscribed at edge, across join: ›NG‹.
Celluloid and Perspex. 21.5 diameter.
London, Family Collection.
See illus. p. 36, fig. 42 and p. 110

This medium sized version is incised with radiating lines. The Perspex piece in the middle lends rigidity to the celluloid which is fastened to the Perspex with two iron bolts *c.* 5 mm long. It is uncertain whether 37.7 was made before or after 37.8, but the mixture of materials and the size suggest that 37.7 may be the earlier version. In outline, the Perspex piece is reminiscent of *Vertical Construction No. 2* which can be related to *Spheric Theme* (see 79).

37.8 Translucent Variation on Spheric Theme

1937. Transparent Perspex; on black Perspex base. [56.8 diameter; on base 3.5 high].
Formerly, New York, Solomon R. Guggenheim Museum (48.1174); destroyed 1950.
From the artist, 1948.

Exh: E9 New York (1948) [No. 16], fig. p. 38.

Lit: G22 (1949) fig. p. 59, set upright : B4 Alvard *et al* (1952) fig. p. 123 : G28 (1957) p. 184, fig. 70 : B76 Giedion-Welcker (1960) figs pp. 180–81 : A183 Sjöberg (1960) fig. p. 188 : A225 Xagoraris (1962) fig. 7 : [A184 Sjöberg (1964) fig. p. 22] : A51 Bekkers (1966) figs following p. 32 : B133 Lukach (1983) pp. 269, 340 n. 1.

Although entitled *Translucent Variation,* 37.8 was in fact made of transparent plastic. 37.8 was acquired by the Solomon R. Guggenheim Museum in 1948 (cheque voucher, 23 Jun 1948, SRGM). In 1950 it was completely destroyed, and a replica was made (letter to Mr Thiel, 6 Apr 1950; see 37.10).

37.9 Spheric Theme

1941–2. Translucent plastic.
[57 diameter].
Lost *c.* 1964; presumed destroyed.

Exh: E9 New York (1948) [No. 15], as ›1937‹ : E10 Baltimore (1950) [No. 4], as ›opaque plastic‹ : E11 Cambridge, Mass. (1951) [No. 6] : E13 New York (1953) No. 7, as ›*Construction in Space (Continuity)* 1941–42‹ : E14 Hartford (1953) No. 13, fig. 11 : E15 Rotterdam etc. (1958) No. 11, fig. P9.

Lit: B175 Read (1955) fig. 85, as ›1941–42‹ : G28 (1957) p. 184, fig. 69 : B76 Giedion-Welcker (1960) fig. p. 369 *in situ* E13 : B179 Read (1964) p. 293, fig. 109 : E17 Amsterdam (1965) No. P9, fig. : E18 Mannheim etc. (1965) No. 10 : E19 Zurich (1965) No. 10 : G31 (1966) fig. p. 132 : B123 Licht (1967) p. 335, fig. 246, miscaptioned : E25 Hannover (1971) fig. p. 101 : A118 Hultén (1971) fig. p. 69.

According to Gabo, 37.9 was stolen from Middlebury before the European touring exhibitions of 1965–6 (statement to Supreme Court of the State of New York, 28 Jul 1966). It was listed in the catalogues, so it must have been stolen *c.* 1964 (E17–19). Miriam Gabo has confirmed that it was never recovered. Although the material is always cited as ›opaque plastic‹, according to Miriam Gabo, 37.9 was made of abraded plastic.

37.10 Translucent Variation on Spheric Theme

1951 (base 1937). Not inscribed.
Transparent Perspex; on black Perspex base. 57.3 diameter; on base 2.5 x 61.3 x 61.3.
New York, Solomon R. Guggenheim Museum (48.1174).
From the artist, 1951.
See illus. p. 112

Exh: E100 Toronto (1954) No. 14 : E103 Vancouver (1954) No. 9, fig. : E104 Montreal (1955) No. 11, fig. : E15 Rotterdam etc. (1958) No. 10, fig. : E116 Flushing (1959) : E121 Boston (1959) : E127 Chicago (1960) No. 12, fig. : E143 New York (1962) : E152 New York (1963) : E20 Stockholm (1965–6) No. 64, fig. : E186 New York (1969) p. 123, fig. : E266 New York (1984).

Lit: G28 (1957) fig. 71, as ›1937‹ : A8 (1957) fig. p. 177 : B154 (1959) fig. 180 : A77 Cleaver (1963) p. 236, fig. 9 : B110 Huyghe (1965) p. 328, fig. 889 : E17 Martin (1965) fig. D : B184 Rickey (1967) p. 106, fig. 2 : A14 (1967) fig. p. 349 : B38 Burnham (1968) p. 141, fig. 50 : B179 Read (1964) p. 107, fig. 110 : B8 Argan (1970) p. 548, fig. 593 : E25 Hannover (1971) fig. p. 105 : B140 Merillat (1974) p. 149, fig. 58 : B115 Krauss (1977) p. 62, fig. 48.

This version was commissioned in April 1950 as a replacement for 37.8 (letter from C. Hunt, 14 Apr 1950, SRGM). It was delivered to the Museum on 14 February 1951 (letter to R. Bullis, 20 Feb 1951).

38. QUARTZ STONE CARVING

38.1 Quartz Stone Carving

1937/40; finished 1961/2. Not inscribed.
White quartz. 16 high x 25.
London, Tate Gallery (T02148).
Presented by the artist, 1977.

Exh: E28 London (1976–7) No. 45.

Lit: B3 Alley (1981) p. 249, fig.

The catalogue for the London exhibition of 1966 mentioned a small carving made in ›1961/2‹ of which 38.2 is an enlargement (E21). In 1977, however, 38.1 was dated ›1936–40‹ (E28). According to Miriam Gabo, the stone may have been acquired on a trip to Ireland, probably in the spring of 1937. Although Gabo worked on 38.1 before he left England in 1946, the finishing touches may have been added in 1961/2, before the work was enlarged.

38.2 Quartz Stone

November 1964(-65). Inscribed ›G‹.
Portuguese marble. 80 high x 60.3.
London, Family Collection.

Exh: [E17 Amsterdam (1965) No. P25] : [E18 Mannheim etc.(1965) No. 22] : [E19 Zurich (1965) No. 22] : E20 Stockholm (1965–6) No. 80] : E21 London (1966) No. 27 : E22 Buffalo (1968) No. 19 : E23 Humlebaek etc. (1970–71) No. 9, fig. p. 18 : E24 Berlin (1971) No. 8, fig. p. 24 : E25 Hannover (1971) No. 8, figs p. 65, and p. 13 *in situ* E23 : E26 Grenoble etc. (1971) No. 9, fig. *in situ* E23 : E27 Lisbon (1972) No. 8, fig. p. 18.

Lit: A103 Granath (1966) fig. p. 13 *in situ* E20 : A70 Causey (1966) fig. p. 34 *in situ* E21 : A105 Gray (1966) fig. p. 49 *in situ* E21 : A9 (1968) fig. p. 43 *in situ* E22 : A118 Hultén (1971) fig. p. 70 *in situ* E21, as ›*Sculpture cinétique*, 1963–64‹.

38.1, titled *Kinetic Sculpture in Quartz Stone,* was received for enlargement in Portugal by Antonio Duarte in September 1964 (receipt from A. Duarte, 16 Sep 1964). Work on 38.2 apparently started in November 1964, but was probably not completed until January 1965 when Gabo asked for the sculpture to be sent to him (letters from and to R. and A. Duarte, 30 Nov 1964, 20 Jan 1965). According to Miriam Gabo, although 38.2 was entered in the catalogues for the European exhibition tour of 1965–6 (E17–20), it was only shown in London (E21).

39.   CONSTRUCTION THROUGH A PLANE

This work has been called both *Construction through a Plane* and *Construction on a Plane*, and these two titles have been used interchangeably. The coloured plastic form at the centre of the work is technically an ›astroid‹ or ›hyperboloid of four cusps‹.

39.1   Model for ›Construction through a Plane‹

1937. Not inscribed.
Celluloid, set into integral Perspex base.
[15.2 x 15.2 x 3.1].
London, Tate Gallery (T02177).
Presented by the artist, 1977.

Exh: E28 London (1976–7) No. 58, fig. p. 38.

Lit: B3 Alley (1981) p. 245, fig.

A sketch for this work is signed and inscribed ›On a Plane Construction, drawing, final to be made‹ (Tate Gallery, T02163). When the enlargement was first exhibited it was dated ›1935–37‹ (39.2; E6). According to Miriam Gabo, this model and 40.1 were the first works Gabo made after they moved to Cholmley Gardens in April 1937. This suggests that the date of 1935 relates to the drawing or conception of the image.
  This model, which has a black centre, is slightly distorted. The illustration in B3 shows the model incorrectly mounted, having been turned anti-clockwise through ninety degrees.

39.2   Construction on a Plane

1937. Inscribed on Perspex sheet, bottom right: ›N. Gabo‹.
Perspex and celluloid, set into integral Perspex and wooden base. 48 x 48 x *c.* 19.6; set into base 8.4 x 59.7 x 21.6.
London, Family Collection.
Anniversary gift from the artist 17 Oct 1947 to Miriam Gabo.
See illus. p. 113

Exh: [E6 London (1938) No. 9, as ›*Construction through a Plane* 1935–37‹] : [E7 Hartford etc. (1938) No. 9] : [E8 Poughkeepsie (1938)] : [E52 London (1939) No. 6] : [E9 New York (1948) [No. 14], as ›*Construction on a Plane* 1937‹, [fig. p. 34] : E10 Baltimore (1950) [No. 7] : E11 Cambridge, Mass. (1951) [No. 10] : E12 Chicago (1952) No. 10 : E13 New York (1953) No. 4 : E14 Hartford (1953) No. 9 : E15 Rotterdam etc. (1958) No. 8 : E17 Amsterdam (1965) No. P8, fig. : E18 Mannheim etc. (1965) No. 9 : E19 Zurich (1965) No. 9 : E20 Stockholm (1965–6) No. 63 : E21 London (1966) No. 12 : E256 London (1982) No. 26, fig. p. 32.

Lit: [E52 London (1939) p. 57, fig. p. 14, miscaptioned *Construction* 1938‹] : B171 Ramsden (1953) fig. 102 b *in situ* E9 : G28 (1957) p. 183, figs [57], 58 *in situ* E9 : A75 Clay (1966) fig. p. 116 *in situ* E20 : [B23 Besset (1976) fig. 134].

39.2 is very difficult to distinguish from 39.3, because they are the same size and both have black centres. The stands now differ, since 39.2 was remounted in 1948 (E9), and in 1972/4, when Charles Wilson replaced a few pieces and reassembled the construction. 39.2 is made of Perspex, except for the central cone, which is celluloid.

39.3   Construction through a Plane

[*c.* 1937]. Inscribed: ›N Gabo‹.
Perspex. [48.2 x 48.2 x 21.6].
England, Collection Sir Leslie and Lady Martin.
From the artist [late 1930s].

Exh: E28 London (1976–7) No. 59.

Lit: G28 (1957) p. 183, n. 57 : B94 Harrison (1981) fig. 145.

39.4   Construction on a Plane

1937/9. Inscribed lower right: ›N. Gabo‹.
Perspex. 48 x 48 x 23.5; set into Perspex feet on wooden base 4.4 x 61 x 30.6.
New York, Solomon R. Guggenheim Museum (47.1102).
From the artist, 1947.

Exh: E127 Chicago (1960) No. 11 : E143 New York (1962) : E152 New York (1963) : E186 New York (1969) p. 119, fig. : E266 New York (1984).

Lit: G28 (1957) p. 183, n. 57 : B3 Alley (1981) p. 245 : B133 Lukach (1938) p. 269.

This version sustained some slight damage in June 1969 and was repaired. The plastic is crazed in some areas.
  39.4 differs from the other versions of 39 in having a white centre. According to Miriam Gabo, it was the last to be made and was completed in Cholmley Gardens between April 1937 and September 1939.
  According to Ruth Israels, Gabo's sister-in-law, Solomon R. Guggenheim bought this work directly from Gabo in December 1946, soon after Gabo's arrival in the USA. The acquisition was completed in 1947 (cheque voucher, 28 Mar 1947, SRGM).

40.   CONSTRUCTION ON A LINE

Construction on a Line is clearly allied to *Construction through a Plane* (39). Both models (39.1 and 40.1), were apparently made in 1937 and it is impossible to establish which was made first. They may have been conceived at the same time as a contrasting pair.

40.1   Model for ›Construction on a Line‹

1937. Not inscribed.
[Celluloid]. [10.8 x 10.1 x 3.8].
London, Tate Gallery (T02178).
Presented by the artist, 1977.

Exh: E28 London (1976–7) No. 60, fig. p. 39.

Lit: B3 Alley (1981) pp. 246–7, fig.

This is probably made of celluloid. Gabo's dating of ›1935–37‹ for the first enlargement suggests that the model was made within this period (40.2; G28). According to Miriam Gabo, 40.1 and 39.1 were the first works Gabo made after they moved to Cholmley Gardens in April 1937.

40.2   Construction on a Line

1937. Inscribed: ›N. GABO‹.
Rhodoid and Perspex. 43.4 x 43.6 x 19.2.
London, Family Collection.
See illus. p. 114

Exh: [E11 Cambridge, Mass. (1951)].

Lit: E9 New York (1948) fig. p. 30 : [N1 Adlow (1951)] : G28 (1957) p. 183, fig. 59.

Two Perspex struts in 40.2 appear to be replacement parts. The signature is inscribed on the back of the rear curving sheet so that it reads correctly from the front.
  A review suggests that a *Construction on a Line* was exhibited in 1951 (E11; N1). This is not confirmed by the documentation for E11, but if a version of 40 was shown, it must have been 40.2.

40.3   Construction on a Line

1937. Inscribed bottom left of flat sheet: ›N. GABO‹.
Celluloid [or Perspex]. [45 x 43 x 9].
London, Tate Gallery (T03054) : Grant-in-aid.
From the artist, 1938 to Collection Mrs Dorothea Ventris, London; 1940 to Collection Michael Ventris; 1956 to Collection Mrs Lois Ventris, London; June 1971 on loan (L00021) to the Tate Gallery; 1979 purchased.

Exh: E6 London (1938) No. 10, as ›*Construction on a Line in Space* 1937‹ : [E51 London (1938) addendum] : E61 London (1942) 0 : E167 London (1965) No. 26, fig. : E21 London (1966) No. 10, as ›1935–37‹ : E28 London (1976–7) No. 61.

Lit: [A131 Le Corbusier (1938) figs pp. 114, 115] : B171 Ramsden (1953) figs 102 c, 103 : G28 (1957) p. 183, n. 59 : B3 Alley (1981) pp. 246–7 : A217 (1981) p. 94, fig.

Mrs Dorothea Ventris bought this work at the London exhibition of 1938 (annotated copy of catalogue E6, FAL; letter from D. Ventris, 23 Sept 1938). Marcel Breuer had advised her on furnishings for her flat at Highpoint, and may have suggested the purchase of 40.3. Gabo later visited her to advise on its display.
  40.3 may also have been shown in the MARS Exhibition which opened a week after E6 (E51). The addendum to the catalogue for E51 thanks ›the London Gallery for the Construction by Gabo in the living room‹, and photographs of the living-room at E51 seem to show a *Construction on a Line* (A131). The London Gallery may have had more

than one version of 40 available, because 40.1, 40.4 and 40.5 were probably made in 1937. If 40.3 was shown, however, it must have been removed from E6, with Mrs Ventris's consent, before the exhibition closed.

Mrs Ventris's son, Michael Ventris, who deciphered the Creto-Mycenaean Linear B script, became a close friend of Gabo, and after Michael's death in 1956 in a car accident, Gabo dedicated 40.3 to his memory.

40.4 Construction on a Line in Space

1937. [43.5 x 43.8 x *c*. 9].
Formerly Hartford, Wadsworth Atheneum (38.269); destroyed.
From the artist, 1938.

Exh: E7 Hartford etc. (1938) No. 10 : [E8 Poughkeepsie (1938)] : E12 Chicago (1952) [No. 3].

Between November 1951 and January 1952 Gabo repaired this work, replacing the ›missing and broken parts‹ (letters to Wadsworth Atheneum, 6 Nov 1951; Wadsworth Atheneum to Arts Club of Chicago, 22 Jan 1952, WA).

In 1952, 40.4 was lent to Chicago (E12). On 22 Jan 1952 Gabo telephoned the museum to request its loan for the Chicago show, and offered to take it to Chicago himself as it was already in his studio (letter from Wadsworth Atheneum to Arts Club of Chicago, 22 Jan 1952, WA). 40.4 may have been shown as ›No. 3 *Construction in Space* 1937‹, but the exhibition opened on 29 January and, as a late inclusion, 40.4 may have been shown ex-catalogue (see 41.6).

In Chicago 40.4 was broken beyond repair and was returned to Hartford on 14 Mar 1952 (E12; records, WA). Gabo made a replacement for the Wadsworth Atheneum (40.6), but was very distressed by the damage to 40.4 and to 10.2 at the same exhibition (letter to W. Eisendrath, 18 Mar 1952).

40.5 Construction on a Line

1937. [Not inscribed].
Perspex. [43.2 x 43.2 x *c*. 9].
New York, Collection James Johnson Sweeney.
From the artist, [late 1940s].

Exh: E9 New York (1948) [No. 13], as ›*Construction on a Line, No. 1 1935–37*‹.

Lit: G22 (1952) fig. p. 8 *in situ* E9 : G28 (1957) p. 183, n. 59, as ›Collection James J. Sweeney‹ : A31 (1967) colour fig. p. 98 : B3 Alley (1981) p. 246.

It is probable that 40.5 was bought by James Johnson Sweeney before 1948, since it was ›lent anonymously‹, and not by Gabo, to the 1948 exhibition (E9). Sweeney was Director of the Houston Museum of Fine Arts, 1961–7, which may explain the incorrect attribution of 40.5 to the Museum in A31. In 1968 the work was damaged in transit from Houston and in 1969 Gabo made a ›perfunctory‹ repair (letters from W. S. Budworth and Sons, 3 Dec 1968, and to J. Sweeney, 4 Mar 1969).

40.6 Construction on a Line in Space

1953. Not inscribed. Plastic [43.5 x 43.8 x *c*. 9].
Hartford, Wadsworth Atheneum (38.269) : Henry and Walter Keney Fund.
From the artist, 1953.

Exh: E14 Hartford (1953) No. 8, as ›*Construction on a Line No. 1*‹ : E155 Hartford (1963) No. 6, fig. : E176 New Britain (1966) No. 4 : E218 Hartford (1977).

In 1953 Gabo made this version as a replacement for 40.4. In 1966 this replacement was damaged at E176 and ›five pieces of plastic detached‹ (Museum records, WA). There was a further repair in 1978. By 1984, however, 40.6 had seriously deteriorated.

41. CONSTRUCTION IN SPACE: CRYSTAL

Anthony Hill has shown that this work is related to a mathematical model in the Institut Poincaré: an ›[oscillating] developable of a cubic ellipse‹ (A115 p. 144). This model had been shown in May 1936 in the *Exposition Surréaliste d'Objets. Chez Charles Ratton* (see B1 p. 322). Although Gabo's passport shows that he was in England in May 1936, he may have seen it earlier. Gabo was interested in mathematics and wrote that ›[while] in Paris . . . I advised [Antoine] to study the subject of descriptive geometry and not to be discouraged by its mathematics‹ (annotation, 14 Mar 1957, in *Antoine Pevsner*, Paris, Musée National d'Art Moderne, 1956–7, FAL). Gabo explained to Hill that ›his idea [in *Crystal*] was to take this complicated formula and change its realization to prove that what was basically a fantasy (the intuition of the mathematician) could be seen through the intuition of an artist . . . he was attracted to this model as it was totally asymmetric and . . . few other models have interested him‹ (A115 p. 144).

41.1 Model for ›Construction in Space: Crystal‹

1937. Inscribed on base: ›N. GABO‹.
Celluloid. [7.6 x 7.6 x 3.8].
London, Tate Gallery (T02179).
Presented by the artist, 1977.
See illus. p. 115

Exh: E28 London (1976–7) No. 62 : E240 London (1979–80) No. 6.64.

Lit: B3 Alley (1981) p. 247, fig.

According to Miriam Gabo, 41.1 was made in Cholmley Gardens in 1937, after 39.1 and 40.1. This corresponds with the ›1937‹ inscribed on the first enlargement, 41.2. It is possible, however, that Gabo conceived this work earlier, in 1934, since in 1938 he exhibited the second enlargement as ›*Construction in Space* 1934–37‹ (41.3; E6). He also later dated 41.6, 1935 (stenographic notes, letter to J. Israels, 24 Jan/11 Feb 1940). This dating suggests that ›1934‹ and ›1935‹ relate to the conception of 41.

41.2 Construction in Space: Crystal

1937. Inscribed on bottom: ›No.1 TO MR DUCKWORTH MADE BY MYSELF N. GABO 9.6.37‹.
Rhodoid or Perspex. 22.9 x 27.3 x *c*. 20.3.
England, Collection Arthur Duckworth Esq.
Gift from the artist, 1937.

Exh: E167 London (1965) No. 22.

Lit: B3 Alley (1981) p. 247.

The ›No. 1‹ in the inscription may indicate that this was the first enlargement of 41.1 to be made. The plastic has a distinct bluish tinge which suggests that 41.2 is made of Rhodoid, as is 41.3.

Arthur Duckworth, who became a close friend of the Gabos, was MP for Shrewsbury, 1929–45, and was introduced to Gabo by Wilfrid Roberts MP, brother of Winifred Dacre Nicholson. Roberts and Duckworth helped Gabo in his application for a British residency permit. Mr Duckworth clearly remembers that this work was exhibited in 1965 (E167).

41.3 Construction in Space: Crystal

1937. Not inscribed.
Rhodoid. 48.9 x 67.9 x 45.1.
Providence, Rhode Island: Rhode Island School of Design, Museum of Art (38.062): Gift of Mrs Murray S. Danforth.
From the artist, 1938 through Julien Levy Gallery, New York.
See illus. p. 35, fig. 38

Exh: E49 London (1937) No. 7 : E50 Paris (1937) ex-cat. : E6 London (1938) No. 8 : E7 Hartford etc. (1938) No. 8 : E73 Andover (1949–50) : E75 Providence (1950) fig. 1 *in situ*, fig. 3 : E193 Ithaca etc. (1971) No. 33, fig.

Lit: A26 (1937) fig. p. 131 : A16 (1938) fig. p. 87, as in E6 : A12 (1938) fig. p. 51 : N19 Murray (1938) : E9 New York (1948) fig. p. 14 : A73 Chermayeff (1948) fig. p. 58 : B4 Alvard *et al* (1952) fig. p. 125 : A176 Segi (1954) fig. p. 19 : G28 (1957) p. 183, n. 52 : B43 Cauman (1958) fig. p. 155.

In 1968 Julius Ternbach restored this piece, although the surface is still pitted and some of the parts are warped.

Miriam Gabo dated this version ›1937–38‹ (annotation on letter from A. Dorner, 17 Nov 1953). This work was exhibited in London in 1937, so it had evidently been completed by then (E49, A26). According to Miriam Gabo, 41.3 was the only work shown in Paris in 1937, although the one catalogue entry for Gabo reads ›No. 154 *Construction sur mur* 1936‹ (E50).

Dr Dorner selected this work for the Museum from the New York show of 1938 (E7; letter to G. Washburn, 20 Feb 1949). The Museum files refer to the Nierendorf Gallery, but there is no record that they handled any work by Gabo.

41.3 was the version of *Crystal* exhibited in London in 1938 (E6), as is confirmed by the illustrations in A16 and A12. It was probably shown as ›No. 8 *Construction in Space* 1934–37‹, because the only other appropriate entry, ›No. 16 *Construction in*

Space 1937‹, has been identified as *Construction in Space: Arch* (33.3). The date ›1934‹ in the entry probably refers to the conception of 41 rather than to this enlargement (see 41.1).

The illustration in the catalogue for the 1948 exhibition (E9), is captioned ›Gabo in his studio 1935‹, but according to Miriam Gabo this shows the basement of the Wadsworth Atheneum in 1938. This is confirmed by N19 of 1938, where this photograph was first published. When reproduced in A176 the photograph was cut; the full version shows 10.2 on the left (FAL).

41.4   Construction in Space: Crystal

1938. Inscribed bottom right: ›N. GABO‹.
Rhodoid; on painted white wooden base.
[22.2 x 22.2 x 18.7; on base 6.3 x 26.7 x 12.7].
Poughkeepsie, New York: Vassar College Art Gallery (38.10): Gift of Mrs Gilbert Harrison (Nancy Blaine, '40) Vassar College Trustee, 1960–68.
From the artist, 1938 through Julien Levy Gallery, New York.

Exh: E8 Poughkeepsie (1938) : E63 Basel (1944) No. 42, fig. p. 37, as photograph : E130 Cleveland (1960) No. 107, fig. : E171 Williamstown (1966) : E172 Albuquerque (1966) No. 19, fig.

Lit: G14 (1938) fig. p. 5 : B223 (1939) p. 65, fig. 79, as ›1937‹ : B145 Moholy-Nagy (1947) fig. 306 : B24 Biederman (1948) fig. 173 : B185 Ritchie (1952) fig. p. 152 : G28 (1957) p. 183, fig. 52 : A115 Hill (1966) fig. p. 144 : B224 (1967) p. 84, fig. p. 169 : A114 Hilberry (1976) fig. 6 b.

This work has undergone several repairs. The thin curving element has a fracture which extends from the front centre to the lower left-hand corner, and the circular laminated layers of the Rhodoid in the front right-hand corner have separated. The present base is not original, but was provided by the Cleveland Museum of Art in 1960.

41.4 was bought by Vassar at the New York exhibition of 1938 (E7; letter form C. Israels, 9 Nov 1938). 41.4 was not exhibited there; 41.3 had been exhibited in London in 1938 (E6), and it was also shown in New York (E7). According to Miriam Gabo, 41.4 was made by Gabo while he was in the USA in 1938 especially for Vassar. B224 states that 41.4 was made in 1937, but this could refer to the first enlargement (41.2), rather than to 41.4.

41.5   Construction in Space: Crystal

1937/9. Inscribed in cyrillic front left, on base: ›N. Gabo‹; and bottom left, under base: ›N. GABO‹; and bottom right, under base: ›N GABO N. 3‹.
Rhodoid [and celluloid]. 22 x *c.* 27 x *c.* 18.
London, Family Collection.
Anniversary gift from the artist, 17 Oct 1947 to Miriam Gabo.
See illus. p. 115

Exh: E61 London (1942) M, as ›Construction in Space 1939‹: [E62 Leicester (1942) ex-cat.].

Lit: G28 (1957) p. 183, n. 52, as ›rhodoid‹ : E17 Amsterdam (1965) fig. P10 : E20 Stockholm (1965–6) fig.

41.5 is apparently made of two different plastics. The frame is probably Rhodoid, although the inner elements are yellowed as if made of celluloid.

The inscription ›N. 3‹ may indicate that 41.5 was the third enlargement to be made. As 41.2 was the first enlargement, this would suggest that 41.5 pre-dated 41.4. Alternatively, the inscription may imply that 41.5 was the third version to be made in this size. In this case it would post-date 41.4, and this would explain why it was dated 1939 when it was exhibited in 1942 (E61).

That 41.5 was exhibited at the London Museum in 1942 (E61), is suggested by a revised list of works to be shown, drawn up by Gabo, mentioning ›the big *Crystal*‹ (stenographic notes, letter to M. Eates and H. Ramsden, 17 Mar [1942]). One of Gabo's works from the London exhibition was shown in Leicester in 1942 (E62; letter from M. Eates, 4 Jun 1942). This seems to have been 41.5 because *Spiral Theme* had been returned damaged, *Construction on a Line in Space* had been returned to Ventris, and Miss Eates had the *Alabaster Constructive Carving* (letters from M. Eates, 17 May, 23 Jun 1942).

41.6   Construction in Space: Crystal

1938/9. Not inscribed.
Perspex. [57.2 x 57.2 x 46].
Cologne, Museum Ludwig (SK270).
From the artist, 1940–48 on loan to the Art Institute of Chicago; 1960 to Otto Gerson Gallery, New York; 1963 to Marlborough-Gerson Gallery, New York; 1969 to Samm-lung Ludwig, Wallraf-Richartz Museum, Cologne; 1976 to Museum Ludwig.

Exh: E53 San Francisco (1939) No. 762, fig. p. 89 upside down, as exhibited : E67 New Haven (1948) No. 39, as ›Construction in Space 1936‹ : E10 Baltimore (1950) [No. 3] : E11 Cambridge, Mass. (1951) [No. 9] : [E12 Chicago (1952) No. 3] : [E90 Philadelphia etc. (1952–3) ex-cat. probably Chicago only] : E13 New York (1953) No. 5, as ›Crystallic Image‹ : E14 Hartford (1953) No. 10, fig. 10 : E15 Rotterdam etc. (1958) No. 12, as ›Crystalline Construction‹ : E128 Zurich (1960) No. 60 : E141 New York (1961–2) No. 11 : E17 Amsterdam (1965) No. P10 : E20 Stockholm (1965–6) No. 65, fig.

Lit: N8 (1939) fig. : A13 (1948) p. 25 : G28 (1957) p. 183, stereoscopic colour fig. 111 : A208 Thompson (1966) colour fig. p. 134 : B93 Hammacher (1969) fig. 200 : A128 Keller (1969) p. 324, fig. 242 : A220 Weiss (1969) p. 1048, fig. : A24 (1970) p. 207, fig. : B8 Argan (1970) p. 545, colour fig. 119 : B35 Budde *et al* (1973) pp. 24–5, fig. 40 : B50 (1979) pp. 232–3, colour fig. : B101 Herbert *et al* (1984) fig. p. 26 *in situ* E67.

This work was repaired while in the possession of the Marlborough Gallery.

41.6, the only Perspex version of 41, was probably made after Gabo's return to England in 1938. It is distinctive in having small areas at the centre of

the work abraded to make the surface white. This is not visible in the earliest published photograph (E53), and may have been done in the late 1940s.

This version was probably shown in San Francisco in 1939 (E53). Its display at E53, upside-down, produced some publicity (N8, A13). When E53 closed, 41.6 was apparently sent to Josef Israels II, Gabo's brother-in-law (stenographic notes, letter to J. Israels, 24 Jan/11 Feb 1940).

In 1940 Gabo lent a work to the Art Institute of Chicago (loan receipt No. 7061, 25 Mar 1940, Loan No. 15.40, AIC). The work was returned to Gabo in 1948 (letter M. Gabo to Mr Meyer, 17 Feb 1948, AIC). This work was probably 41.6. Gabo did write to Josef Israels about the ›Construction in Space, 1935‹ shown upside-down in E53, and the possibility of lending it to an exhibition at the Institute (stenographic notes, 24 Jan/11 Feb 1940).

An installation photograph (FAL), confirms that 41.6 was shown in Cambridge, Mass., in 1951 (E11). It may also have been shown in Chicago in 1952, although the only appropriate catalogue entry, ›No. 3 Construction in Space 1937‹, may apply to 40.4. A photograph showing 41.6, on a long table set for dinner, is annotated ›Chicago April 1953‹ (FAL). According to Miriam Gabo, this was probably a meeting of the College Art Association. The work may then have been shown ex-catalogue in *Sculpture in the Twentieth Century* (E90), subsequently kept in Chicago and borrowed by the Association as a centrepiece.

This work was sold to Otto Gerson and the Fine Art Associates in 1960 (letter to O. Gerson, 7 Apr 1960).

42.   SPHERIC THEME: METAL VERSIONS

The metal versions of *Spheric Theme* are a direct continuation of the earlier plastic versions of *Spheric Theme* (37). However, to present a clearer picture of the development of the metal variants the two groups have been separated.

42.1   Model for ›Spheric Theme, "with centre"‹

[*c.* 1937]. Not inscribed.
Tin-plate. 10.2 high.
London, Tate Gallery (T02174).
Presented by the artist, 1977.

Exh: E28 London (1976–7) No. 51, as ›c. 1937‹.

Lit: B3 Alley (1981) p. 248, fig., as ›Tin‹.

In 1976 Gabo dated this metal model as ›c. 1937‹ (E28).This suggests that from an early date Gabo had considered making metal versions of *Spheric Theme*. Gabo also dated 42.3-6, which were made in 1960s, as ›c. 1937‹.This date could either apply to the execution of 42.1, or refer back to the date of the original plastic models for *Spheric Theme* (37). It is possible that 42.1 was made just before the first enlargement in 1960 (42.2).

One seam, slightly rusted, shows no evidence of soldering and was possibly glued. The other seam has been soldered, although this might be a later repair.

42.2 Bronze Spheric Theme

1960/(65). Not inscribed.
Bronze with bronze spring-wire; on wooden motorised turntable. [92 high].
London, Tate Gallery (T00826): Grant-in-aid. From the artist to Collection Miriam Gabo; 1966 through Marlborough-Gerson Gallery, New York, to the Tate.

Exh: E17 Amsterdam (1965) No. P21, as ›c. 1960‹ : E18 Mannheim etc. (1965) No. 20, fig. : E19 Zurich (1965) No. 20, fig. 12, as ›Slg. Miriam Gabo‹ : E20 Stockholm (1965–6) No. 78, fig. : E21 London (1966) No. 25, fig. 10 : E28 London (1976–7) No. 56, fig. p. 37.

Lit: [N23 Tucker (1964) fig.] : A103 Granath (1966) fig. p. 13 in situ E20 : A197 (1967) pp. 26–7, fig. : B180 Read (1969) p. 172, fig. 52 : N13 Bruce-Milne (1971) fig. p. 8 : B3 Alley (1981) p. 261, fig.

In the catalogue for the Amsterdam exihibition of 1965, Gabo dated this version ›c. 1960‹ (E17). Gabo himself neither welded, nor did he do heavy soldering work, and until Charles Wilson became his assistant in early 1960, those constructions which required such work were done with the help of casual labour. It is therefore unlikely that 42.2 was completed before 1960, although it was obviously finished in time for exhibition in 1965 (E17). 42.2 may be the work, apparently unfinished, shown on Gabo's work-bench in November 1964 (N23). The work illustrated, however, could also be Bronze Spheric Theme (Variation) (78), before it was strung or mounted.

42.3 Spheric Theme (Penetrated Variation).

1963/5. Not inscribed.
Bronze. [33 high].
London, Tate Gallery (T02176).
Presented by the artist, 1977.

Exh: E28 London (1976–7) No. 55, fig. p. 36, as ›c. 1937‹ : E253 London (1981) No. 163.

Lit: B3 Alley (1981) p. 248, fig.

According to Charles Wilson, this work was made between 1963 and 1965 when Gabo was considering having the large versions of Spheric Theme cast. Gabo was unhappy about the philosophical implications of casting, and had earlier deplored ›the falsity of such a technique for a truly constructive work‹ (letter to H. Read, 10 Mar 1955, UVBC). 42.3 was constructed for the purpose of making plaster moulds: the inserted plate made it easier to remove them.

42.4 Model ›Bronze Spheric Theme‹

c. 1966/7. Not inscribed.
Phosphor-bronze. 30.4 high.
London, Family Collection.

This version is made from two discs of phosphor-bronze. The base plate has three small holes drilled in it for mounting on a base. According to Charles

Wilson, 42.4–6 were made, probably towards the end of the 1960s, as experiments for the construction of the large versions of Spheric Theme. This has been confirmed by Sir Norman Reid.

42.5 Model ›Bronze Spheric Theme‹

c. 1966/7. Inscribed on bronze at bottom edge: ›Gabo‹.
Bronze; on wooden base. 15.2 high; on base 5 x 8.9 x 8.5.
London, Private Collection.
From the artist, 1970.

Exh: E28 London (1976–7) No. 54, as ›Spheric Theme (Variation)‹.

In a letter dated 13 Nov 1970, the owner of 42.5 wrote to Gabo referring to the acquisition of an unnamed work. This is taken to be 42.5. (See also 42.4).

42.6 Model ›Bronze Spheric Theme‹

c. 1966/7. Not inscribed.
Phosphor-bronze with stainless steel spring wire. 20.5 high.
London, Family Collection.
See illus. p. 142

Correspondence between Gabo and the Earl of Shannon indicates that Gabo had explicitly referred to this model in his discussions with Lord Shannon concerning possible methods of treating the surface of 42.7 (letter to Earl of Shannon, Starkie Gardner Ltd, 12 Mar 1967). Subsequently Gabo received from Lord Shannon a photograph of 42.6, annotated on the verso ›Mar '67‹ (letter to Earl of Shannon, 12 Mar 1967; see 42.4).

42.7 Spheric Theme

1967–8. [Not inscribed].
Metallised Cor-Ten steel. [243.8 high].
Formerly Oslo, Munch Museet; destroyed 1969.
Commissioned from the artist, Dec 1967; Sep 1968 installed.

Discussions concerning this commission were probably prompted by the European touring exhibition of 1965–6. In February 1967 Gabo presented his model to the board of ›The Legacy to the Benefit of Improving the Appearance of the City of Oslo‹ (contract, 22 Dec 1967). This model was probably either 42.6, or 42.2 which had been exhibited in Stockholm in 1965–6 (E20). In the contract Gabo reserved the right to metallise the surface of 42.7. He was considering using this process, and finally decided to employ it (letter to P. Hougen, 13 Aug 1968; see also 42.6).

In March 1969 Mrs R. Stang, the Director of the Museum, reported trouble with the spring-wires which had been repeatedly broken by visitors (letter from R. Stang, 4 Mar 1969). Gabo offered to restring the work with stronger spring-wire (letter to R. Stang, 14 Mar 1969).

Later, problems also arose with the metallised surface, and in September 1969 Gabo agreed to its

being sanded (letter to R. Stang, 7 Sep 1969). On a visit to Oslo in November of the same year, Gabo decided that 42.7 was in such poor condition that it should be destroyed, and he agreed to make a replacement in stainless steel (minutes of meeting, and agreement, 8 Nov 1969; see 42.9).

42.8 Spheric Theme

1969. Not inscribed.
Outer body: stainless steel with stainless steel spring-wire. Central structure and base: Cor-Ten steel. [243.8 high].
Albany, New York: The Governor Nelson A. Rockefeller Empire State Plaza Art Collection.
From the artist, to Collection Miriam Gabo; 18 Sep 1969 to Albany.

Lit: A108 Hand (1979) fig.

The Art Commission for the Empire State Plaza, Albany, was set up in 1965 at the instigation of Nelson A. Rockefeller, then Governor of New York. Wallace K. Harrison was chairman, and other members included Seymour H. Knox, Dorothy C. Miller and René d'Harnoncourt (see B141 pp. 25–6). In 1966 Gabo was approached to contribute to the large art collection that was being assembled (letter to H. Read, 23 Dec 1966).

In September 1969 Gabo was informed of the Commission's decision to buy 42.8 (letter from R. Doty, The Art Commission for the South Mall Project in Albany, 16 Sep 1969). It was delivered and installed soon after (bill of lading, 25 Sep 1969).

Nelson A. Rockefeller was one of Gabo's most important American patrons, and the Albany project was the last of a series of major projects which he commissioned from Gabo. Since the 1930s Rockefeller had worked closely with the architect, Wallace Harrison, and in New York it was their partnership which commissioned Gabo's Project for the Esso Building of 1949 (56), and the large Bas-Relief for the U.S. Rubber Company Building installed in 1956 (69.2). In 1953 Nelson Rockefeller also acquired Gabo's Linear Construction in Space, with Red (62.3).

42.9 Spheric Theme

1969–70. Not inscribed.
Stainless steel with stainless steel spring-wire. [242 high].
Oslo, Munch Museet.
From the artist, 1970.

Lit: A118 Hultén (1971) fig. p. 66, as ›bronze‹ : A120 Johnsrud (1973) pp. 59, 18–19 figs, fig. on back cover.

Gabo made this version to replace 42.7 (minutes of meeting and agreement with R. Stang, 8 Nov 1969). Gabo described the refinements he introduced: ›This work has been made in stainless steel and the stainless-steel springs are much stronger than those used before. All dimensions and all parts of it are exactly the same with the exception of the central frame, in black, which has been improved by shortening the ends around the wings. This improvement is to eliminate the resistance to the flow of air‹ (letter to R. Stang, 30 Apr 1970).

42.9 was finished by March 1970 (letter to R. Stang, 27 Mar 1970). It was installed outside the Munch Museet in May 1970, but the springs were again partially vandalised, and it was moved into the atrium of the Museum (letter from R. Stang, 2 Jun 1970).

42.10   Spheric Theme

1969/71. Not inscribed.
Stainless steel. [246 high].
Berlin, Nationalgalerie (NG3/72).
From the artist, 1972.
See illus. p. 143

Lit: A106 Haftmann (1972) pp. 272–3, fig. 78 : A216 Von Rohr (1973) p. 313, fig. : B109 Honisch (1979) p. 371, fig. 340.

Dr Werner Haftmann, Director of the National-galerie, Berlin, approached Gabo about the possi-bility of acquiring a work for the Museum in April 1971 during the Berlin exhibition (E24; letter from W. Haftmann, 27 Apr 1971). Gabo suggested 42.10, which he finished in November 1971. He pointed out that the Nationalgalerie was designed by Mies van der Rohe, who had been President of the Arts Club of Chicago when a version of *Spheric Theme* had been exhibited there, probably in 1952 (E12; letter to W. Haftmann, 14 Nov 1971). 42.10 was delivered to Berlin in spring 1972 (letter from H. Bock, 2 Mar 1972).

42.11   Spheric Theme

1972/73–1974. Not inscribed.
Stainless steel. [244 high].
Princeton, New Jersey; University of Princeton, The John B. Putnam, Jr., Memorial Collection.
From the artist, 1974.
See illus. p. 44, fig. 52

Lit: B111 Kelleher (1982) pp. 20–21, 48–51, 126–7, fig. p. 50, colour fig. p. 49.

In 1971 Princeton University approached Gabo, who suggested that ›the large *Spheric Theme*‹ would be particularly suitable for an outdoor site (letter to P. Kelleher, 23 Apr 1971, Princeton Art Museum). In March 1972 Gabo informed Kelleher that he had sold 42.10 to Berlin, and it would take him 3 to 5 months to make another version (letter to P. Kelleher, 29 Mar 1972). In May 1973 the commission was confirmed and 42.11 was com-pleted by May 1974 (letters from and to J. Farring-ton, 4 and 26 May 1973, and receipt, 8 May 1974, PAM).

The work suffered from handling by visitors and from weathering. The thinner spring-wire, of the two gauges used, was particularly prone to breaking; one spot-weld failed; and the black paint peeled. In 1979, 42.12 was removed from its site. After resto-rations, which included restringing with a thicker gauge of spring-wire, 42.12 was installed in the En-gineering Quadrangle (B111 pp. 126–7, fig. p. 49).

42.12   Spheric Theme

c. 1974–6. Not inscribed.
Stainless steel with stainless steel spring-wire. [244 high].
Kanagawa-ken, Japan; Hakone Open-Air Museum.
From the artist, to Collection Miriam Gabo; 1979 to Hakone.

Lit: B201 Segawa (1979) colour fig. p. 66, fig. p. 209.

According to Miriam Gabo, this was the last version of 42 which Gabo made, and it was completed in 1976. It was acquired by the Hakone Museum in 1979 and was unveiled in August of that year.

43.   SPHERIC CONSTRUCTION: FOUNTAIN

A sketch for this work is dated ›*c.* 1937‹ (Tate Gallery T02162). It shows a jet for water coming up through the centre of the work, but it is possible that water would also have issued from the radial spokes. This would have resulted in the form being extended as a diaphanous spray, in the same way as Gabo extended the form of *Revolving Torsion, Fountain* (30.7). This drawing and the different ver-sions of *Spheric Theme* illustrate a development from incised lines to linear members of plastic or metal filaments, and eventually to jets of water (A168 Rickey p. 26).

Another sketch appears to show a different idea for a fountain developed from *Spheric Theme* (Tate Gallery T02161; see 37). Under the convex pedes-tal there appears to be a revolving spray with two jets. This design also relates to the image of *Con-struction in Space: Arch* (33.).

A band of Perspex, representing the contour of 43.3, was made by Gabo as ›a guide for the firm who were going to execute the large-scale work‹ (letter to B. Allea, Rohm and Haas, 9 Sep 1965). The Family Collection contains at least one such band which is not entered here.

43.1   Model for ›Spheric Construction: Fountain‹

(1937)/1938. Not inscribed.
[Perspex]. 9.5 high.
London, Family Collection.
See illus. p. 110

Lit: A185 Soby (1948) fig. p. 22 : B44 Chipp (1968) fig. p. 327.

This model is in poor condition. The delicate struts have come unstuck in many places and some appear to have been repaired rather haphazardly.

In June 1938 Miriam Gabo wrote that ›[Harrison] asked Gabo to make him two models for world's fair project and Gabo is working days and nights to get them done quickly.‹ (letter to K. Dreier, n. d., [mid-Jun 1938]; see 43.2). According to Miriam Gabo, these two models were 43.1 and 43.2.

The only photograph showing this work is a shot of Gabo's studio taken in Cornwall in December

1944 (FAL). When this photograph was reproduced in A185 and B44, it was cropped, obscuring the model.

43.2   Model for ›Spheric Construction: Fountain‹

1938. [Perspex]. [*c.* 41 high].
Present whereabouts unknown.
From the artist, 1938 to Collection Wallace K. Harrison, New York.

Lit: E9 New York (1948) figs pp. 40–41, four views : B203 Seuphor (1949) fig. p. 59 : A176 Segi (1954) figs pp. 22 and 25, No. 1 : B58 Dorazio (1955) figs following p. 96, two views : B176 Read (1956) pp. 101 and 202 : G28 (1957) p. 183, figs 67 and 68 : B217 Thwaites (1957) fig. 12 : A79 Courthion (1959) fig. p. 34.

A double photograph of 43.2 (identical to G28, plates 67, 68) is signed by Wallace K. Harrison and annotated: ›This is a photo of the model which Naum Gabo proposed to me in 1938, during his exhibition in New York, as a project for a monu-ment at the World's Fair. It was accepted for the project (and acquired by me) to be built on a large scale but due to lack of space on the grounds of the Fair, it was not executed‹ (FAL). The phrase in parentheses has subsequently been blocked out, an alteration possibly prompted by the transference of the model to the contractor, and its subsequent loss.

In 1947 Gabo sent Herbert Read a photograph of 43.2, annotated on the verso: ›Gabo. *Construc-tion in Space*. Project for a monument 1937 Lon-don.‹ Gabo explained: ›I made that work *in 1937 before* going to USA in February 1938. I am send-ing you this photo for your orientation. It has never been published. Unfortunately it is in the collection of the Architect Harrison here in NY. He bought it in the beginning of 1938 when I was in the US with my exhibition. He wanted to build it in his pavilion at the international exhibition. Nothing came of it‹ (letter to H. Read, 8 Sep 1947, UVBC). The full-scale construction was to have been made by Kenneth Lynch of Long Island (letter from K. Lynch to K. Dreier, 5 Oct 1938, Yale 2). The project apparently fell through after January 1939 when Harrison had informed Gabo that ›The sculpture for the Electric Utilities goes along fine‹ (letter from W. Harrison, 20 Jan 1939).

In 1957 two views of 43.2 were captioned ›Two models for *Spheric Construction, Fountain*‹, and the dimension given as 16 inches diameter (G28).

43.3 Spheric Theme (2nd Variation)
1937/8. [Not inscribed].
Perspex. *c.* 43.5 high.
London, Family Collection.

Exh: E9 New York (1948) [No. 17], as ›22¼″ high‹ : [E69 New Haven (1949) No. 10, as ›*Spheric Theme, Variation II*‹]

The Perspex of the outer band has been abraded to produce a matt surface. In the centre, there is a small black version of *Spheric Theme, c.* 10 cms in diameter, made from four semi-circular pieces of Perspex. This resembles 43.1. 43.3 was probably made in 1938, after Gabo's return to England. Although it was dated 1937 in the 1948 catalogue (E9), there is no evidence that Gabo showed this version to Wallace Harrison in 1938. An installation photograph shows 43.3 at E9, where it was also photographed in colour by Dr Fred Block (FAL).

44. BAS-RELIEF ON A CIRCULAR SURFACE, SEMI-SPHERIC
1938. Inscribed on the reverse.
Plastic. [45.7 diameter].
Paris, Private Collection.
Gift from the artist, 1938 to Collection Wallace K. Harrison, New York; date unknown to Paris.

Exh: E9 New York (1948) [No. 18], as ›*Spheric Relief Construction* 1937‹, fig. p. 42 : E15 Rotterdam etc. (1958) No. 9, fig. : E227 Münster etc. (1978) Gabo No. 1, fig. p. 155, as ›en celluloid‹.

Lit: A73 Chermayeff (1948) fig. p. 56, as ›*Spirit Relief Construction,* 1937‹ : G28 (1957) p. 183, figs 65 and 66 : A139 S. Moholy-Nagy (1966) fig. 17.

Some of the radial spokes in this work are now slightly deformed. Although this work is usually dated 1937, Gabo told Alan Bowness in 1977 that he had made this work during his visit to the USA in 1938. The date of 1937 may refer to the origin of *Spheric Construction: Fountain,* to which this work is related (43). In August 1938, on Gabo's departure from the USA, he left this work with Josef Israels II, his brother-in-law, as a gift for Harrison (letter from B. O'Toole to J. Israels, 12 Sep 1938; letter from Mrs E. Harrison, 15 Oct 1938).

45. ALABASTER CARVING: ›THE BOBBIN‹

The epithet used in the title here is a family nickname used to distinguish this work from *Construction with Alabaster Carving* (47).

45.1 Alabaster Carving: ›The Bobbin‹
1938. Not inscribed.
Alabaster. 2.5 high x 15.7.
London, Family Collection.

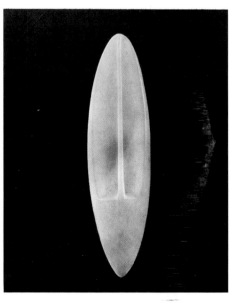

Lit: G28 (1957) p. 183, fig. 64.

According to Miriam Gabo, this work was accidentally broken when a cast was being taken for the bronze version (45.2; M. Gabo, notes, 1982/3, FAL). It was subsequently repaired with glue.

45.2 Bronze Cast of ›Alabaster Carving: »The Bobbin«‹
1972. Not inscribed.
Bronze. 2.5 high x 15.7.
London, Family Collection.

It is known that bronze casts were taken from five of Gabo's stone sculptures (45.1, 47.1, 51.1, 74.1, and 83.1). One cast was made by a student of Charles Wilson, Gabo's assistant (51). The other four works were cast for Gabo by Antonio Duarte in Lisbon in 1966/7, and by the Morris Singer Foundry in London in 1972.

Correspondence between Gabo and Duarte does not list the titles of the work, or works, that he cast (telegram from A. Duarte 4 Nov 1966; letter from A. Duarte, 10 Jan 1967; see 47.4).

In February 1972 Gabo asked Singer's to make ten casts each of three different works, referred to as ›Shield‹, ›Seed‹, and ›M‹ (letter from Morris Singer Foundry, 10 Feb 1972). Later Gabo added a fourth work ›Double Image‹ (letter to E. Gibbard, 10 Feb 1972).

According to Miriam Gabo, the nickname ›Seed‹ probably refers to *The Bobbin* (45.1); ›M‹ refers to the nickname ›Madonna Stone‹ used for *White Stone* (74); and ›Double Image‹ to *Round Stone* (83; M. Gabo, notes, 1982/3, FAL). The nickname ›Shield‹ refers to the *Alabaster Carving* (47.1). Only one cast is known to have been taken of 45, and so it was probably cast by Singer's.

In 1972 Gabo wrote to Singer's: ›I am very anxious to see what they will look like cast in metal. I would like to talk to you about the kind of metal you intend to use for the first cast. I think the light alloy of bronze would be right. I do not like too much copper‹ (letter to E. Gibbard, 21 Feb 1972). In August 1972 Gabo received the four cast proof pieces (letter to E. Gibbard, 20 Aug 1972). Later he decided to retain only one cast of each of the four works, asking Singer's to destroy the other 36 casts and the moulds (letter from E. Gibbard, 29 Nov 1972).

46. CONSTRUCTION IN SPACE WITH CRYSTALLINE CENTRE

The two large versions of this work are particularly difficult to differentiate in photographs. The work bears some relationship to a sketch of 1917 (Tate Gallery T02149), and to *Construction on a Line* (40).

46.1 Model for ›Construction in Space with Crystalline Centre‹
(1938)/1940. Not inscribed.
Plastic. [10.1 high x 15.6].
London, Tate Gallery (T02180).
Presented by the artist, 1977.

Exh: E28 London (1976–7) No. 63, fig. p. 39.

Lit: B3 Alley (1981) p. 249, fig.

The large versions of this work have been consistently dated 1938. According to Miriam Gabo, however, 46.1 was probably made in Cornwall, where she and Gabo were living after September 1939 (M. Gabo, notes, 1982/3, FAL).

46.2 Construction in Space with Crystalline Centre

(1938)/1940. Not inscribed.
Perspex and celluloid. 32.4 high x 47.
London, Family Collection.
See illus. pp. 78 and 116

Exh: E9 New York (1948) [No. 19], fig. p. 36 [and p. 37] : E10 Baltimore (1950) [No. 6] : E11 Cambridge, Mass. (1951) [No. 1] : E12 Chicago (1952) No. 4 : E13 New York (1953) No. 6 : E14 Hartford (1953) No. 11 : E15 Rotterdam etc. (1958) No. 13, fig. : E17 Amsterdam (1965) No. P11 : E18 Mannheim etc. (1965) No. 11 : E19 Zurich (1965) No. 11 : E20 Stockholm (1965–6) No. 66.

Lit: G20 (1944) figs following p. 64, top [and bottom] : [A98 Gibson (1946) fig. following p. 64] : [A73 Chermayeff (1948) fig. p. 57] : A175 Seeley (1950) fig. p. 163 : B171 Ramsden (1953) fig. 102 a : G28 (1957) figs 74 and 75, stereoscopic colour fig. 107, as ›1938‹ : B76 Giedion-Welcker (1960) fig. p. 188 : G30 (1962) fig. 1 : A208 Thompson (1966) colour fig. p. 134 : B31 Brett (1968) fig. p. 19 : B3 Alley (1981) p. 249 : A81 Davies (1982) fig. p. 56 : B56 Davies (1984) fig. 10.

This work was probably made in 1939/40 (see 46.1). Although 46.2 could be a later version, a completion date of 1944 may be discounted (A98). A photograph of this work, taken by Barbara Hepworth during the Second World War, shows 46.2 against the background of the sea at Carbis Bay, Cornwall (G28 fig. 74).
  Sometimes *Crystalline* in the title has been understood as referring to the material, therefore there are references to 46 being made of ›Crystaline‹, ›Crystalline‹, or ›Crystalloid‹.

46.3 Construction in Space with Crystalline Centre

(1938)/1940. Inscribed at bottom:
›N. GABO‹.
Perspex. *c.* 33 x *c.* 46.
London, Margaret Gardiner.
From the artist, [1938/9].

Lit: B3 Alley (1981) p. 249.

This version was damaged *c.* 1946 and repaired in September 1977 with pieces cut by Gabo.

47. CONSTRUCTION WITH ALABASTER CARVING

One plaster cast of a small *Rose Marble Carving*, and two unmounted carvings of the *Rose Marble*, are not entered here (Family Collection).

47.1 Construction with Alabaster Carving

1938/(40); mounted in 1946/8. Inscribed lower right: ›N. Gabo‹.
Alabaster, mounted in Perspex, on black base. [21.5 x 15.2 x 4; within mount 39.4 x 35.6 x 17.8; on base 4.4 x 45.7 x 27.9].
Baltimore, Museum of Art (51.380): Saidie A. May Collection.
From the artist, 1 May 1949 to Collection Saidie A. May, Baltimore: 1951 to Baltimore Museum.

Exh: E61 London (1942) N, as ›Constructive Carving in Ellipse‹ : E9 New York (1948) [No. 20], fig. p. 35 : E74 Baltimore (1950) : E11 Cambridge, Mass. (1951) [No. 12] : E15 Rotterdam etc. (1958) No. 14.

Lit: A73 Chermayeff (1948) fig. p. 59, as ›1939‹ : A185 Soby (1948) fig. p. 24, as ›1¼ feet high‹ : A42 (1950) p. 26, No. 118 : A43 (1951) fig. p. 4 : B4 Alvard etc. (1952) fig. p. 127 : A176 Segi (1954) fig. p. 22 : B12 (1955) p. 85 : G25 (1956) fig. 57 : G28 (1957) pp. 183–4, figs 62 and 63 without mount, fig. 79 with mount, stereoscopic colour fig. 109 : A208 Thompson (1966) colour fig. p. 134 : A45 (1972) fig. p. 47.

This carving was dated 1940 when it was first exhibited in 1942 (E61; letter from M. Eates, 23 Jun 1942). Later, however, Gabo dated it ›1938–39‹ (G28). The Perspex frame was added in time for exhibition in 1948 (E9).

47.2 Plaster Cast of the Alabaster in ›Construction with Alabaster Carving‹

1965. Inscribed in pencil on one side:
›Gabo‹.
Plaster. [21.5 x 15.2 x 4].
London, Tate Gallery (T02204).
Presented by the artist, 1977.

Lit: B3 Alley (1981) p. 249, fig.

In July 1965 Gabo made 47.2–3 from 47.1, which he had on loan from the Baltimore Museum (receipts to and from Baltimore Museum, 14 and 24 Jul 1965).

47.3 Cast of one side of the Alabaster in ›Construction with Alabaster Carving‹

1965. Inscribed on front surface near centre [possibly not by the artist]: ›Gabo‹.
Plaster. [21.5 x 15.2 x 4].
London, Tate Gallery (T02205).
Presented by the artist, 1977.

Lit: B3 Alley (1981) p. 249, fig.

47.4 a-f Bronze Casts of the Alabaster in ›Construction with Alabaster Carving‹

1966. Bronze. 21.4 x 15.5 x 4.2.
Locations: a) London, Collection Dr and Mrs Owen Franklin; b) Chicago, Collection Charles Wilson; c) USA, Collection George Rickey; d)-f) London, Family Collection.

According to Charles Wilson who cleaned some of them, these were almost certainly amongst the works cast in Portugal by Antonio Duarte. These were probably the bronzes which Duarte told Gabo would be ready by ›20 October‹ 1966 (telegram from A. Duarte, 4 Oct 1966). One of the six casts, however, was probably made by the Morris Singer Foundry in 1972. (See 45.2).

47.5 Construction in Space with Rose Marble Carving

1966. [Not inscribed].
Rose marble, mounted in Perspex. 68.6 x 68.6 x 15.2, including stone *c.* 44 x *c.* 33.5 x *c.* 10.
London, Family Collection.

Exh: E22 Buffalo (1968) No. 26, fig. p. 26 : E23 Humlebaek etc. (1970–71) No. 15, fig. p. 19 : E24 Berlin (1971) No. 12, fig. p. 21 : E25 Hannover (1971) No. 12, fig. p. 17 miscaptioned : E26 Grenoble etc. (1971–2) No. 14 : E27 Lisbon (1972) No. 13, fig. p. 22 : E268 Shiga (1984).

The illustration in the Buffalo catalogue of 1966 suggests that this version was made in that year (E22). It is distinguished from 47.7 and 47.8 by the Perspex ›globe‹ form which surrounds the carving, and in this it resembles 47.1 and 47.6.

47.6 Marble Carving

1966/7. [Not inscribed].
Portuguese marble, mounted in Perspex on stainless steel base. 107 x 76.4 x 10.4, including stone 89 x 66 x *c.* 19; set into base 5 x 77.5 x 60.8.
London, Family Collection.
See illus. p. 117

Lit: A210 Thurston (1976) fig. p. 18 in studio, Middlebury, colour fig. p. 18 : B3 Alley (1981) p. 249.

This is a greatly enlarged version of 47.1, made for Gabo by Antonio Duarte. Regine Duarte was probably referring to this work when she informed Miriam Gabo in April 1967 that ›the big marble sculpture‹ was finished (letter from R. Duarte, 12 Apr 1967).

47.7 Construction in Space with Rose Marble Carving (Variation No. 2)

1969. Rose marble, mounted in Perspex. [Frame 81 high x 81].
London, Family Collection.
See illus. p. 118

Exh: E23 Humlebaek etc. (1970–71) No. 18 : E24 Berlin (1971) No. 15 : E25 Hannover (1971) No. 15 E26 Grenoble etc. (1971–2) No. 17, fig. miscaptioned : E27 Lisbon (1972) No. 16.

47.8 Construction in Space with Rose Marble Carving

[late 1960s]. Not inscribed.
Rose Marble, mounted in Perspex.
35.5 x 35.7 x 4.2, including stone
21.6 x 15.9 x 4.2; on base
1.9 x 50.4 x 14.
London, Family Collection.

48. LINEAR CONSTRUCTION IN SPACE NO. 1

Until Gabo made *Linear Construction in Space No. 2* (55), this series was referred to simply as *Linear Construction* or *Linear Construction in Space*.

The technique of stringing was first used by Gabo in this construction. According to Miriam Gabo, the first model was made with red thread and was about 3 or 4 inches square. There is, however, no further evidence of such a model and it is not entered here. The first known version is a larger model made of celluloid, strung with silk and elasticated thread. It is most unlikely that Gabo used nylon before the early 1940s (see Introduction – Materials). A version described as a ›model‹, dated 1941, was shown by the Société Anonyme in 1948 (E67). Although Gabo would probably have shown a nylon-strung version, he may have exhibited 48.1.

This is one of the most numerous groups, and the individual versions were made over a period of many years. Most were probably made to order, but it is often impossible to date a version precisely.

48.1 Model for ›Linear Construction in Space No. 1‹

(1938)/1942. Not inscribed.
Celluloid with silk and elasticated [cotton] thread. 30 x 30 x 5.9.
London, Family Collection.

Exh: [E67 New Haven (1948) No. 40].

This version has 60 notches down each side. The celluloid frame is in fair condition, although the elasticated thread has now perished and the silk has sagged. In one corner, the pieces of the frame are joined with two very tiny screws, a method not used in any other version and possibly indicating a repair. This model is also distinctive in that two strips of plastic are attached to the edge of the elliptical hole in the middle: one is fixed with three pins, the other is glued.

This work may have been made as early as 1938. An annotation to *Linear Construction in Space No. 1,* on a list of works to be sent on the European touring exhibition of 1965–6, states ›First model '38 Rhodoid‹. In 1948 Gabo exhibited a version described as a ›model‹ with the date 1941 (E67). He also inscribed 48.2 ›1942‹, which suggests that 48.1 was completed by then.

48.2 Linear Construction in Space No. 1

1942. Inscribed at corner: ›GABO 1942‹.
Perspex with Nylon monofilament.
29.8 x 29.8 x 5.9.
England, Collection Nicolete Gray.
From the artist, April 1943 to Collection Helen Sutherland, England; 1965 by bequest to Gray.

Exh: [E167 London (1965) No. 24, fig. p. 27, as ›c. 1939‹] : E191 London (1970–71) No. 8, fig., not shown at other venues.

Lit: G28 (1957) p. 184, n. 76 : B169 Raine (1975) p. 130.

This is the only known version of 48 which is inscribed with a date. Helen Sutherland purchased 48.2 in March 1943, but it arrived broken (letters from H. Sutherland, 28 Mar, 1 Apr 1943). Gabo subsequently repaired 48.2, returning it by Easter (letter from H. Sutherland, Easter 1943). By January 1945 the stringing had collapsed, and Gabo returned it in March, after restringing it with a different nylon (letters from H. Sutherland, 7 Jan, 2 Mar 1945; stenographic notes, letter to H. Sutherland, 4 Apr [1945]).

In the early 1960s the nylon filament snapped, and 48.2 was restrung by Philip Ward. In c. 1968 the frame broke and was repaired. 48.2 remains warped.

48.2 was probably exhibited in London in 1965 (E167). The work illustrated has 59/60 notches on each side, and of the lenders who owned versions of 48 in 1965, only Miss Sutherland had a version with 60 notches. 48.2 is inscribed ›1942‹ and the catalogue dating is presumably an error.

48.3 Linear Construction in Space No. 1

1942/3. Not inscribed.
Perspex with nylon monofilament; on base of black Perspex and wood, and with Perspex cover. [30.5 x 30.5 x 6; on base 2 x 38 x 48].
Düsseldorf, Galerie Denise René-Hans Mayer.
From the artist [1943] to Collection Mr and Mrs Leslie Martin; summer 1956 to Harold Diamond, New York; 12 Oct 1956 to Collection Dr and Mrs Israel Rosen, Baltimore; 1960/61 to Otto Gerson Gallery, New York; [1962] to Collection Arnold H. Maremont, Chicago; 1 May 1974 through Sotheby Parke-Bernet to Düsseldorf.

Exh: E16 Waltham (1960) No. 4 : [E141 New York (1961–2) No. 12] : E165 Washington (1964) : E221 Münster (1977) fig. : E233 Paris (1978).

Lit: E196 Chetham et al (1971) p. 419 : S2 New York (1974) No. 40, fig. : S10 New York (1984) No. 613, fig.

This version has 60 notches down each side. It is now attached to a base with two small pieces of Perspex, so that it is turned ninety degrees from its

normal orientation. According to Miriam Gabo, this was probably not done by Gabo.

In 1944 Jack Pritchard mentioned having seen a ›full size‹ version of 48 at Leslie Martin's (letter from J. Pritchard, 20 Mar 1944). Gabo and Pritchard had visited the Martins in mid-August 1943, but it is unclear whether Pritchard saw 48.3 then (letter to J. Pritchard, 20 Aug 1943, PA). The evidence suggests that this version was acquired sometime in the second half of 1943, and the date ›1942–3‹ usually given to the piece, is probably correct.

According to Harold Diamond, he bought this work from the Martins in the summer of 1956 (letter from M. Gabo to A. Bowness, 6 Jun 1978). He subsequently sold it to Dr and Mrs Israel Rosen and it was later acquired by the Otto Gerson Gallery (letter I. Rosen to O. Gerson, 18 Feb 1961; letter from O. Gerson, 23 Mar 1962).

48.4 Linear Construction in Space No. 1

1942/3. Inscribed bottom left, on edge: ›GABO‹.
Perspex with nylon monofilament.
20.8 x 20.8 x 5.5.
New York, Marlborough Gallery.
From the artist, 1943/4 to Collection J. C. Pritchard, England; November 1963 to Marlborough Fine Art, London.

Exh: E167 London (1965) No. 25, fig. p. 27, as ›Linear Construction 1938‹ : E228 New York (1978) No. 20, fig. p. 23.

Lit: A93 Forge (1966) fig. p. 41.

This version, which has 41 notches, is slightly warped, and some of the Perspex is crazed. It is unusual in that notches are cut along the entire length of each of the side pieces, although only half the notches are used. This suggests that it is an early version, probably 1942/3.

The date of 1938, given to this work by Marlborough in its exhibition of 1965 (E167), and subsequently repeated elsewhere, may derive from the annotation on the list of exhibits for the European touring exhibition of 1965–6 (see 48.1).

By March 1944 Jack Pritchard apparently had already had the work in his possession for some time (letter from J. Pritchard, 20 Mar 1944). It seems to have been returned to Gabo in early 1946, possibly for repair (letter from J. Pritchard, 17 May 1946).

48.5 Linear Construction in Space No. 1

1942/3. Not inscribed.
Perspex with nylon monofilament.
[21 x 21 x 5.6].
Stromness, Orkney, The Pier Gallery: Presented by Margaret Gardiner.
From the artist, early 1940s to Margaret Gardiner, London; May 1978 to Orkney.

Exh: E232 London (1978) not shown at other venues.

Lit: G28 (1957) p. 184, n. 76 : [A184 Sjöberg (1964) fig. p. 23] : B97 Havelock-Allan (1978) p. 21 No. 11, fig. p. 20 : B54 Cross (1984) pp. 54–5, colour fig. 33.

This version has 41 notches down each side. According to Margaret Gardiner, she acquired this work from Gabo during the Second World War.

48.6   Linear Construction in Space No. 1

Summer 1944. Inscribed: ›GABO‹.
Perspex with nylon monofilament.
10.6 x 10.6 x 2.1.
England, Private Collection.
From the artist, 1944.

According to the present owner, one corner of this work was damaged in the mid-1960s and repaired in *c.* 1972.

48.7   Linear Construction in Space No. 1

1944. Not inscribed.
Perspex with nylon monofilament.
[30 x 30 x 6].
England, Collection C. F. Reddihough.
From the artist, 1944.

Lit: G28 (1957) p. 184, n. 76.

This version has 60 notches down each side, and was restrung in the spring of 1978.

48.7 was probably in Mr Reddihough's possession by July 1944 (letter from C. Reddihough, 8 Jul [1944]). According to Mr Reddihough, he acquired it from Gabo when the letter was visiting Yorkshire in connection with his work for Jowett Cars. At the time, Reddihough understood from Gabo that it had been made very recently. Gabo had planned to visit Jowett's just after Easter 1944, and this may be when he delivered 48.7 (letter from H. Read, 28 Mar 1944). By August, the Jowett project was losing impetus and it is unlikely that Gabo made another visit (letter to H. Read, 9 Aug 1944).

In the summer of 1944 the joints of 48.7 parted, and Gabo repaired them, returning 48.7 in September (letters from C. Reddihough, 8 Jul, 29 Sep [1944]).

48.8   Linear Construction in Space No. 1

(1944)/1945. Not inscribed.
Perspex with nylon monofilament.
30.4 x 30.4 x 6.2.
Cambridge, England: University of Cambridge, Kettle's Yard (NG2): Gift of Mrs Joy Finzi, in memory of Frank and Vera Strawson, 1969. From the artist, *c.* July 1945, to Collection Frank and Vera Strawson, England; 1969 bequeathed by Vera Strawson to Mrs Joy Finzi.

Exh: E269 London (1985) No. 47, colour fig. p. 63.

Lit: G28 (1957) p. 184, n. 76 : B187 Robinson (1970) fig. NG2 : A66 (1980) fig. p. 4.

The Strawsons received this work in July 1945 (letter from F. and V. Strawson, 15 Jul 1945). Gabo described it as the ›fifth copy‹ he had made (stenographic notes, letter to Frank [Strawson], 17 July [1945]). This must refer to the versions in this size, comprising 48.1, 48.2, 48.3 and 48.7. Gabo suggested that black glass would make a good background for the work, and sent a piece of black Rhodoid (letter from F. Strawson, 19 Aug 1945).

48.9   Linear Construction in Space No. 1

[*c.* 1945/6]. Inscribed on edge of frame, bottom right: ›GABO‹.
Perspex with nylon monofilament.
45.6 x 45.6 x 9.7.
New York, Solomon R. Guggenheim Museum (47.1101).
From the artist, 1947.
See illus. p. 37, fig. 43

Exh: [E14 Hartford (1953) No. 14] : E121 Boston (1959) : E143 New York (1962) : E152 New York (1963) : E186 New York (1969) No. 47.1101, fig. p. 122 : E224 New York (1977–8) No. 39 : E266 New York (1984).

Lit: A98 Gibson (1946) fig. following p. 64 : A150 (1946) fig. following p. 176 : A73 Chermayeff (1948) fig. p. 59 : B24 Biederman (1948) figs 188 and 198 : B4 Alvard *et al.* (1952) fig. p. 126 : G28 (1957) p. 184, fig. 76 : B154 (1959) p. 203, fig. 179 : A225 Xagoraris (1962) p. 35, fig. 12 : B38 Burnham (1968) p. 141, fig. 49 : B206 Seuphor (1972) p. 186, fig. 93 : B14 Barnett (1980) p. 257, fig. : B133 Lukach (1983) p. 269.

This version has 90 notches down each side. Gabo had evidently completed 48.9 before he left England in 1946. According to Ruth Israels, Gabo's sister-in-law, Solomon R. Guggenheim bought this work directly from Gabo in December 1946, soon after Gabo's arrival in the USA. The acquisition was completed in 1947 (cheque voucher, 28 Mar 1947, SRGM).

Judging by the measurements, this was the version of 48 shown at Hartford in 1953, although there is no record of the loan (E14).

48.10   Linear Construction in Space No. 1

1945/9. Inscribed in one corner, circumscribed with a triangle: ›N. GABO N2 of TWO‹, and on the edge of the frame opposite this corner: ›N. Gabo‹.
Perspex with nylon monofilament.
61.3 x 61.3 x 13.
London, Family Collection.
See illus. p. 119

Exh: E17 Amsterdam (1965) No. P12 : E18 Mannheim etc. (1965) No. 12 : E19 Zurich (1965) No. 12 : E20 Stockholm (1965–6) No. 67 : E21 London (1966) No. 15 : E252 Saint Paul (1981) No. 79 : E254 Madrid (1981) No. 48.

Lit: G31 (1966) fig. p. 130.

This version has 95 notches down each side and is unique in that it is double-strung, i.e., the notches carry two thin nylon filaments rather than one thicker filament.

The date of 1945/9 is derived from a list of works to be shown in the European touring exhibition of 1965–6. This describes the version of 48 to be shown as ›of the late 40's.‹

The inscription, ›N2 of TWO‹, suggests that the dimensions of this work are identical to those of another version. 48.9, although closest in size to 48.10, is 15.7 cms smaller. In 1957 Gabo had erroneously listed 48.9 as ›24 inches high‹ (G28 p. 184). This may explain the inscription on 48.10. Alternatively, the inscription may merely indicate that 48.10 was made soon after 48.9.

48.11   Linear Construction in Space No. 1

1946. Inscribed on base: ›Gabo‹.
Perspex with nylon monofilament, on Perspex base; all mounted on wooden base, which may not have been made by Gabo. 30.9 x 30.8 x 6.4, mounted diagonally on Perspex 0.5 x 30.4 x 30.7; on wood 1.9 x 32.8 x 33.1.
Washington, DC: Hirshhorn Museum and Sculpture Garden, Smithsonian Institution (66.1976).
From the artist, [1946] to Collection Ashley Havinden, England; summer 1958 to Harold Diamond, New York; 19 Sep 1958 to Collection Joseph H. Hirshhorn, New York; by 1974 to Museum.

Exh: E117 Detroit (1959) No. 81, fig. p. 39, not shown at other venues : E151 New York (1963) No.161, fig. p. 93 : E213 Washington, DC (1974–5) No. 464.

Lit: B171 Ramsden (1953) p. 45, fig. 101 : A173 Saltmarche (1959) p. 352 : B66 Feldman (1967) fig. p. 363 : B89 Hale (1969) p. 184, fig. : B46 Clapp (1970) p. 411 : B66 Feldman (1973) pp. 479–80, fig. p. 480 : E213 Lerner (1974) p. 693, fig. : B194 S. Russell (1975) fig. 15.14 : A21 (1974) fig. p. 112.

This version has 60 notches down each side. The date of 1946 is taken from Ramsden (B171). Ashley Havinden probably acquired this work before Gabo went to the USA in 1946. Harold Diamond acquired and resold this work in 1958 (letter M. Gabo to A. Bowness, 6 Jun 1978, FAL).

48.12   Linear Construction in Space No. 1

[*c.* 1950]. Not inscribed.
Perspex with nylon monofilament; on black Perspex base. [5.7 x 21 x 21; on base *c.* 0.6 x 30.5 x 30.5].
Cambridge, Mass.: Collection Alexis Morgan.
From the artist, 1951 through the Margaret Brown Gallery, Boston, to Mr and Mrs Patrick Morgan, Cambridge, Mass.; by gift.

Exh: E83 Boston (1951).

This version has 40 notches down each side, and is slightly warped. It is at present displayed lying flat, rather than standing. A label under the base, presumably attached by a gallery, is inscribed ›X5668 L40‹.

Mr and Mrs Morgan bought this work on 22 Oct 1951 (›customer card‹, Papers of the Margaret Brown Gallery, Reel 663, Frame 295, AAA). This was the only sale from ›a small selection‹ of Gabo's works exhibited in Boston in 1951 (E83; letter from M. Brown, 13 Jun 1955).

48.13 Linear Construction in Space No. 1

[Early 1950s]. Inscribed at bottom of the vertical piece of frame, on outside: ›N. Gabo‹.
Perspex with nylon monofilament.
30.8 x 30.8 x 6.2.
Japan, Private Collection.
From the artist, 1954 to Collection Dr and Mrs Owen Franklin, London; 1982 to Japan.

This version has 63 notches down each side. The frame was slightly damaged in 1957 and was mended by Dr Franklin, Gabo's stepson (letter from O. Franklin, 11 Jun [1957]). In 1982, following the instructions he had previously received from Gabo, Dr Franklin restrung this work.

48.14 Linear Construction in Space No. 1

[Early 1950s]. Inscribed bottom of one side: ›N. Gabo‹, and again on edge of frame: ›N. GABO‹.
Perspex with nylon monofilament.
21 x 21 x 5.5.
New York, Collection Jeffrey H. Loria.
Gift from the artist *c.* 1954 to Dr John Sisson; 26 Mar 1984 through Christie's to Loria.

Lit: S8 London (1984) No. 34, colour fig. p. 62.

This version has 40 notches down each side. In its present state two notches on one side and one on the opposite side are not strung. On the side with one notch unused, there is a faintly incised line without the usual corresponding pair of notches. The frame is slightly warped. According to Mrs M. Sisson, Dr Sisson acquired this work in *c.* 1954.

48.15 Linear Construction in Space No. 1

[1955/6]. Inscribed bottom of one vertical piece of frame, on outside: ›N. Gabo‹.
Perspex with nylon monofilament.
30.8 x 30.8 x 6.2.
London, Marlborough Fine Art.
From the artist [1956] to Collection E. C. Gregory; 4 Nov 1959 through Sotheby's to David Gibbs, London; to Collection Sir Edward and Lady Hulton; on loan to the Art Gallery of Ontario, Toronto; 1981 to Marlborough.

Exh: E188 London (1970) : E199 London etc. (1972) No. 65, fig. p. 77, as ›1940‹ : E206 London etc. (1973) No. 47, fig. p. 77 : E211 London (1974) No. 54, p. 154, fig. p. 101.

Lit: S1 London (1959) No. 92 : E230 London (1978) fig. p. 33.

This version has *c.* 64 notches down each side. 48.15 was in Mr Gregory's possession by July 1956 (letter to E. Gregory, 4 Jul 1956). Mr Gregory was managing director of Lund Humphries, who published Gabo's monograph in 1957 (G28). Gabo probably made this version for Mr Gregory in 1955/6, and not in the 1940s as has been suggested (letter from A. Juda, 19 Mar 1971).

48.16 Linear Construction in Space No. 1

Before 1965. Not inscribed.
Perspex with nylon monofilament; on transparent Perspex base.
[30.3 x 30.3 x 6.4; on base 2.6 x 30.3 x 30.3].
Atherton, California: Collection Mr and Mrs Harry W. Anderson.
From the artist [1969] to Marlborough Gallery, New York; January 1974 to Anderson.

Lit: E17 Amsterdam (1965) fig. : E20 Stockholm (1965-6) fig. : E252 Saint Paul (1981) fig. p. 101.

This version is unusual for its size in having 67 notches down each side. The base, listed above, was made for Mr Anderson, to support a protective Perspex cover. This work was probably one of the pieces the Marlborough Gallery acquired in 1969 in the settlement of the law-suit between Gabo and themselves.

48.17 Linear Construction in Space No. 1

[*c.* 1970]. Inscribed top right corner of inner sheet: ›NG‹, and underneath top section of frame: ›FOR NINA‹.
Perspex with nylon monofilament; on base of black and transparent Perspex.
10.2 x 10.2 x 2.5; on base 1.7 x 12.6 x 12.5.
London, Family Collection.
See illus. p. 119

Exh: E28 London (1976-7) No. 70, as ›1942-43‹.

48.17 has 39 notches down each side. According to Nina Williams, this was the last version Gabo made.

49. OWEN'S STONE

1939. Inscribed in 1949: ›Gabo‹.
Stone (two pebbles). *c.* 4 x 9.2 x 5.2.
London, Collection Dr and Mrs Owen Franklin.
From the artist, 1949.

Exh: E167 London (1965) No. 27, fig. p. 27, as ›Carving 1939 Cornish stone 4 x 2½ x ¾ in/10.2 x 6.4 x 1.9 cm‹.

Gabo never gave a title to this work: the title used here has been established by family usage.

50. NEGATIVE VOLUME

1940. Not inscribed.
Oil paint on gourd. 14.5 x 22.8 x 6.
London, Family Collection.

Exh: E21 London (1966) No. 13, fig. p. 8, as ›1940‹.

Lit: A93 Forge (1966) fig. p. 41.

During the Second World War, Gabo bought a dried gourd from an antique shop in St. Ives. From this he made *Negative Volume,* which he dated 1940 (E21). In 1978 Miriam Gabo recollected that in 1941 Gabo had also carved a ›Möbius strip‹ from a gourd (see E238 p. 11).

51. GRANITE CARVING

According to Charles Wilson, one of his students at Yale University took a plaster cast from 51.1 and cast it in bronze. According to both Miriam Gabo and Nina Williams, Gabo was so dissatisfied with the result that he defaced it with the intention of destroying it. It was subsequently destroyed.

51.1 Granite Carving

c. 1940. Not inscribed.
Tintagel stone. 12.3 high x 12.
London, Family Collection.

Exh: E28 London (1976-7) No. 47, fig. p. 34.

Lit: B56 Davies (1984) p. 22.

According to Miriam Gabo, 51.1 was made from Polyphant stone, from the Trevillet Slate Quarries at Tintagel, Cornwall. In 1945 Gabo did discuss Polyphant stone with these quarries (letter to E. Hughes, 19 Oct 1945). Polyphant stone, a type of Cornish potstone, is soft and usually greenish or iron-grey in colour, but 51.1 is hard and has a reddish tinge. It has been described as serpentine stone (B56), but the less specific term ›Tintagel stone‹ is used here (E28).

51.2 Granite Carving (large version)

1960/61-5. Not inscribed.
Granite. 63.5 high x 61.
London, Family Collection.
See illus. pp. 140 and 141

Exh: E173 Cleveland (1966) p. 200, fig. 162, as ›Pennsylvania Granite‹.

Lit: A118 Hultén (1971) fig. p. 68.

When exhibited in 1966, 51.2 was dated ›1964–5‹ (E173). According to Nina Williams and Charles Wilson, it was begun slightly earlier, in 1960/61.

52. SPIRAL THEME

The available information about this group is confusing and often inconsistent concerning the provenance, the number, and the order of the versions that were made.

In 1964 Gabo stated that he had made two large and three small versions of this work (letter to D. Miller, MoMA, NY, 25 Jan 1964). Of the two large versions (52.3 and 52.4), it is now accepted that 52.3 was made first (B3 pp. 250–51).

There do, however, appear to be four and not three small versions. In 1958 Gabo wrote that before he made 52.3, he had ›made a very tiny one, about three inches wide, a tiny model‹ (letter to R. Alley, 13 Aug 1958). This probably refers either to 52.1, now in the Tate Gallery, or to 52.2, which was sold to Margaret Gardiner in January 1942 (letter from M. Gardiner, 19 Jan [1942]). A third apparently went to Wilhelmina Barns-Graham, and a fourth to Mr and Mrs Leslie Martin.

Subsequently, W. Barns-Graham and the Martins sold theirs to Harold Diamond of New York. In 1958 Diamond approached Gabo with a damaged version (letter from H. Diamond, 25 Jun 1958). Gabo was presumably referring to this version, when he told Dorothy Miller that he had refused to undertake the repair. In 1981 Diamond recollected that he had sold one model to Mrs Kay Hillman, but he could not remember the purchaser of the other model. Having examined a photograph of Mrs Hillman's version, Gabo stated that he believed it to have been reconstructed (letter to D. Miller, 31 Mar 1964).

It may be that the Tate's model was in fact a ›working model‹ and, as such, would not necessarily have been included in Gabo's reckoning when he said he had made three small versions. The Tate's model is now in rather poor condition, and it is impossible to ascertain whether it was originally highly finished.

Early in 1942 an unspecified model had been irreparably broken while on exhibition in Lewes, and in claiming compensation Gabo valued the work at £25, the price he was charging for small versions of *Spiral Theme* (stenographic notes, letter to [C.] Lucas, 20 Feb [1942]). This might have been the model now in the Tate Gallery, and if so could explain its poor condition, and the reason why Gabo did not include it among the versions he listed for Dorothy Miller.

A small version was made in April 1942, so that Margot Eates could have it available for sale during the London Museum exhibition, where the large version 52.3 was on display (E61; stenographic notes, letter to Margot [Eates], 21 Apr [1942]; letter from M. Eates, 27 Apr 1942). It has not been identified.

This work attracted Herbert Read's warm praise. In 1942 he stated: ›the art represented . . . by Gabo's *Spiral Theme,* is the highest point ever reached by the aesthetic intuition of man . . . Creation is a much abused word, applied loosely to imitations and logical constructions: it is justified only

for that absolute lyricism we call »pure poetry«, for music, for certain branches of mathematics, and for constructivism in the plastic arts (which includes architecture). But even within this absolute world there is an hierarchy, and at the summit I would place this spatial construction of Gabo's, (A160 p. 269; Read qualified this statement in a later revision of the essay, B173).

52.1 [Model for] ›Spiral Theme‹

[1941]. Not inscribed.
Celluloid. [6.3 high x 17.2].
London, Tate Gallery (T02181).
Presented by the artist, 1977.

Exh: E28 London (1976–7) No. 68 : E269 London (1985) No. 42, fig. p. 163.

Lit: B3 Alley (1981) p. 250, fig.

This version may have been a ›working model‹, or it may have been the work broken while on exhibition in Lewes (see introduction to 52). In either case it now lacks a vertical piece at one side.

52.2 Spiral Theme

1941. Inscribed in corner of base:
›N. GABO‹.
Celluloid on black Perspex base.
c. 6.5 high x *c.* 17; on base 0.2 x 15.9 x 15.6.
London, Margaret Gardiner.
From the artist, Jan 1942 to Margaret Gardiner, given to J. D. Bernal.

Margaret Gardiner acquired this work from Gabo in January 1942, as a birthday present for Desmond Bernal who greatly admired Gabo's work (letter from M. Gardiner, 19 Jan [1942]).

52.3 Spiral Theme

1941. Inscribed in one corner: ›NG‹ in monogram.
Plastic. [14 high x 24.4].
London, Tate Gallery (T00190): Presented by Miss M. Pulsford, 1958.
From the artist, 1946 to Collection Miss Madge Pulsford, Woking; 1958 to the Tate.

Exh: E61 London (1942) L : E21 London (1966) No. 14 : E28 London (1976–7) No. 69, fig. p. 40 : E269 London (1985) No. 43, colour fig. p. 64.

Lit: A151 Newton (1942) fig. : A97 Gibson (1942) fig. p. 42 : A140 Morris (1943) fig. : A143 Mumford (1944) fig. XII : G20 (1944) fig. opp. p. 65 : B24 Biederman (1948) fig. 205 : B172 Read (1948) fig. 178 : A102 Goffin (1949) fig. p. 58 : G22 (1949) fig. on dust jacket credited wrongly MoMA, NY : B174 Read (1952) fig. 15 : B171 Ramsden (1953) p. 17, fig. 23c : G28 (1957) p. 184, fig. 80 : E15 Rotterdam etc. (1958) fig. : B2 Alley (1959) p. 84, fig. 29f : B52 Compton (1967) fig. 12 : B134 Lynton (1980) fig. 108 : B3 Alley (1981) pp. 250–51, fig. : B54 Cross (1984) p. 54, fig. 32.

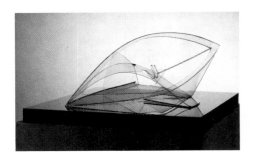

A large version of *Spiral Theme*, dated 1941, was exhibited in 1942 (E61; stenographic notes, letters to M. Eates, early March, 21 Apr 1942; letter from M. Eates, 27 Apr 1942). The illustration in Eric Newton's review shows a version with 9 incised lines between the lower backward pointing angle and the piece on the left (A151). This identifies it firmly as 52.3. While on exhibition in 1942, 52.3 suffered some unspecified damage (E61). Evidently Gabo repaired 52.3 before it was purchased by Miss Pulsford in March 1946 (letter from M. Pulsford, 14 Mar 1946). In his correspondence with Miss Pulsford, Gabo stated that the work was made in 1941 and had been exhibited at E61 (draft letter to M. Pulsford, n. d.; see also B3).

52.4 Spiral Theme

(1941)/1946. Inscribed at unfastened point of spiral, near base: ›Gabo‹.
Plastic; on two-tiered black plastic base. 14 x 33.6 x 23.7; on composite base 5.1 x 61 x 61.
New York, Museum of Modern Art (7.47): Advisory Committee Fund.
From the artist, 1947.

Exh: E9 New York (1948) [No. 22], fig. p. 39 : E14 Hartford (1953) No. 12 : E15 Rotterdam etc. (1958) No. 15.

Lit: A73 Chermayeff (1948) fig. p. 58 : A148 (1948) fig. p. 6 : B185 Ritchie (1952) fig. p. 153 : B16 Barr (1954) p. 127, fig. : A176 Segi (1954) fig. p. 22: B218 Trier (1955) fig. 86 : B176 Read (1956) fig. 219 : B218 Trier (1961) fig. 162 : B131 Lowry (1961) p. 269, fig. 155 : B80 Goldwater (1969) pp. 67 figs., 69, 143 : B17 Barr (1977) pp. 133 fig., 543 : B64 Elsen (1979) pp. 83–4, fig. 84.

In 1958 Gabo stated that 52.4 was a duplicate of 52.3 made ›afterwards for the Museum of Modern Art‹ (letter to R. Alley, 13 Aug 1958; B3 p. 250). By August 1944 James Thrall Soby had approached Gabo with a view to buying *Spiral Theme* for the Museum (letter to H. Read, 9 Aug 1944). Gabo, however, decided not to send the work at his own risk during the Second World War. Gabo did not sell 52.3 until March 1946, so that 52.3 was probably the version that he discussed with Soby. This suggests that Gabo made 52.4 after the sale of 52.3 and before he left England for the USA in November 1946. In 1964 Gabo made some statements which suggested that although 52.3 was made before 52.4, both works had been made in the winter of 1941 (letters to D. Miller, 25 Jan, 31 Mar 1964). There is, however, no other evidence to indicate that 52.4 was made in 1941.

This version differs from 52.3 in having a two-tiered base, and ten, rather than nine, incised lines between the lower backward-pointing angle and the vertical piece on the left. References which give the height of 52.4 as 24 inches are confusing the height with the size of the base.

52.5 Spiral Theme

[1942]. Present whereabouts unknown.
From the artist [before 1946] to Collection Mr and Mrs Leslie Martin, England; summer 1956 to Harold Diamond, New York.

For a discussion of this version, see introduction to 52.

52.6 Spiral Theme

[1942]. New York, Collection Mrs Kay Hillman.
From the artist [before 1946] to Collection Wilhelmina Barns-Graham, England; to Harold Diamond, New York.

Exh: E145 Newark (1962) No. 72, as ›*Spiral Theme (Study Model)* Plastic 8½″ h., 8½″ w. Lent by Kay Hillman‹.

According to Miriam Gabo, Harold Diamond stated that the version belonging to W. Barns-Graham had passed to Mrs Hillman (letter M. Gabo to A. Bowness, 6 Jun 1978, FAL). Although this has not been confirmed, it has been followed here (see introduction to 52).
Mrs Hillman's version was exhibited in 1962 (E145), and listed as ›8½″ h., 8½″ w.‹ These dimensions must be wrong, because they suggest a third large version, whereas Gabo described Mrs Hillman's version as ›a miniature model of *Spiral Theme*‹ (letter to D. Miller, 25 Jan 1964).

53. LINEAR CONSTRUCTION IN SPACE NO. 1 (VARIATION)

This variation differs only slightly from the original *Linear Construction in Space No. 1* (48), in having ›steps‹, of varying width, on two of the four sides. Versions of 53 also differ in size, the thickness of Perspex used, and the number of notches carrying nylon filament. It is not always possible to establish the precise dates when they were made.

53.1 Linear Construction in Space No. 1 (Variation)

Winter 1942–3. Not inscribed.
Perspex with nylon monofilament.
[34 x 34.9 x 9].
London, Tate Gallery (T00191): Presented by Miss M. Pulsford.
From the artist, 1946 to Collection Miss M. Pulsford, Woking; 1958 to the Tate.

Exh: E28 London (1976–7) No. 71, fig. p. 41 : E253 London (1981) No. 164 : E269 London (1985) No. 44, fig. p. 164.

Lit: G28 (1957) p. 184, n. 76 : B2 Alley (1959) p. 84, fig. 17 : B28 Bowness (1965) fig. p. 141 : B198 Scharf (1968) fig. 200 : E196 Chetham *et al* (1971) fig. p. 421 : B52 Compton (1974) [p. 6], fig. 13 : B3 Alley (1981) pp. 251–2, fig.

53.1 has 70 notches down each side and, compared with later versions, a very shallow step. Miss Pulsford acquired this work at the same time as 52.3 in 1946 (letter from M. Pulsford, 14 Mar 1946). Gabo told her that it was made in ›1942–1943‹ (letter to M. Pulsford, n. d.).

53.2 Linear Construction in Space No. 1 (Variation)

(1942–3)/1948. Not inscribed.
Perspex with nylon monofilament.
[61.3 x 61.3 x 24.9].
Washington, DC, Phillips Collection.
From the artist, December 1948.

Exh: E9 New York (1948) [No. 23], figs pp. 44–5 : E68 Washington (1948) : E169 Washington (1965).

Lit: A211 (1948) p. 72, fig. p. 97 : N14 (1948) : B45 Cirlot (1949) fig. opp. p. 64 : B208 Seymour (1949) fig. p. 58 : B164 (1952) p. 40, fig. 243 : A178 Seymour (1954) fig. 11 : A176 Segi (1954) fig. p. 23 : B112 Kepes (1965) fig. [p. 19] : B150 Myers (1957) pp. 659–60, fig. 545 : B165 Phillips (1970) p. 329, figs pp. 236, 306 : A67 Campbell (1971) fig. p. 20 : B182 Richardson [1973], fig. 303 : B9 Arnason (1977) p. 324, fig. 507 : B197 Sarff *et al* (1979) fig. p. 72 : B42 Canaday (1980) p. 192, fig. 60.

Marjorie Phillips gave the date of acquisition as 1943 (B165). This is an error. According to the Museum's records, the work was acquired in 1948 through the Institute of Contemporary Arts, Washington, DC, presumably from their exhibition of that year (E68).
53.2 has slightly slanted steps, c. 120/22 notches down each side, and is strung right down to the step. Therefore it is not the version illustrated in G28 (figs. 77, 78, p. 184). The records of the Phillips Collection state that 53.2 is ›strung with nylon on a base of ringlite‹. Ringlite, however, has not been traced.

53.3 Linear Construction in Space No. 1 (Variation)

[1940s]. Perspex with nylon monofilament.
[47.5 x 47.5 x 15].
Japan, Kawamura Collection.
From the artist to Private Collection, USA; 1979 to Annely Juda Fine Art, London; 1979 to Japan.

Exh: E230 London (1978) No. 56, fig. shows 48.15.

A photograph of this version shows c. 88 notches down each of the stepped sides and c. 128 along the unstepped sides. This produces an unusual arrangement of the filaments. On the unstepped sides they are strung through groups of three notches each, with one notch missed out between

each of these groups. Several notches at the ends are left unused. Miriam Gabo thinks that 53.3 must have been restrung at some time. This does not, however, explain the unequal number of notches on the different sides. Moreover, one version of *Linear Construction in Space No. 2* is also strung with every other notch unused (55.3). The stringing of 53.3 may therefore have been an intentional variation by Gabo.
Unfortunately, the paucity of information available makes it impossible to reconstruct the history of this piece. According to Annely Juda, the anonymous private collector stated that it was made in the 1940s.

53.4 Linear Construction in Space No. 1 (Variation)

1946/50. Inscribed at bottom of one side: ›Gabo‹.
Perspex with nylon monofilament.
[45.4 x 45.4 x 17.8].
Portland, Oregon: Portland Art Museum (78.15): Evan H. Roberts Memorial Sculpture Collection.
From the artist, (1947)/1950 to Collection Benny Goodman, Stamford, Conn.; 17 May 1977 through Christie's to William Pall Gallery, New York; 5 Oct 1977 to Waddington and Tooth Galleries, London; June 1978 to Portland.

Lit: N16 Henry (1950) :[G28 (1957) figs 77 and 78] : [E15 Rotterdam etc. (1958) fig.] : [A183 Sjöberg (1960) fig. p. 189] : [A2 Alvard (1962) fig. p. 5] : S4 New York (1977) No. 88, colour fig. : [E235 Buffalo etc. (1979) fig. 78] : A6 (1980) p. 529, fig. 103.

After moving to the USA, the Gabos probably contacted Alice and Benny Goodman in November 1947 (letter from A. Duckworth, 9 Nov 1947). According to Miriam Gabo, 53.4 had been recently completed when Alice Goodman bought it for her husband. A newspaper article shows that Goodman had acquired this work by June 1950, although it also states erroneously that Goodman owned two works by Gabo (N16).
53.4 has 90 notches down each side. It is very similar to 53.7, and, although different in size, to 53.8. This makes precise identification in photographs particularly difficult. Gabo apparently restrung 53.4 twice. In 1974 it was sent to Gabo again for restringing, but Gabo was unable to find a sufficiently fine nylon, and returned it to Goodman in June without completing the work (letters to and from B. Goodman, 22 Feb, 8 Jun 1974). Goodman subsequently had 53.4 restrung. The uprights are crazed.

53.5 Linear Construction in Space No. 1 (Variation)

1950. Inscribed on bottom part of frame, upper side, next to internal vertical: ›GABO‹.
Perspex with nylon monofilament.
60.6 x 60.6 x 24.5.
England, Private Collection.
From the artist 22 Nov 1969 to Collection Bo Boustedt, Sweden; 1971/2 to England.

Exh: E23 Humlebaek etc. (1970–71) No. 3, fig. p. 16, as ›1950‹ : E24 Berlin (1971) No. 54 : E25 Hannover (1971) No. 54, figs. pp. 91, 93, 94, 95 detail, 11 *in situ* E23 : E26 Grenoble etc. (1971–2) No. 3, fig. *in situ* E23 : E203 London (1973) No. 36, as ›ex collection Bo Boustedt‹.

Lit: A54 Besset (1971) figs. p. 8 *in situ* E26, p. 10.

This version has *c.* 115 notches down one side, and is strung down to the step. According to Miriam Gabo, it was made in 1950 and acquired by Bo Boustedt in 1969 (letter M. Gabo to B. Boustedt, 8 Apr 1970; letter to B. Boustedt, 23 Nov 1969).

53.6   Linear Construction in Space No. 1 (Variation)

c. 1956/7. Inscribed bottom corner of interior vertical: ›Gabo‹.
Perspex with nylon monofilament.
45.3 x 45.3 x 17.9.
London, Collection Dr and Mrs Owen Franklin.
From the artist, 1957.

This version has 89/90 notches down each side. According to Dr Franklin, Gabo's stepson, he acquired it in 1957 soon after it had been completed. His ownership was mentioned by Gabo in 1958 (letter to R. Alley, 13 Aug 1958).

53.7   Linear Construction in Space No. 1 (Variation)

c. 1957/8. Inscribed: ›N. Gabo‹.
Perspex with nylon monofilament.
62.9 x 62.9 x 24.2.
USA, Collection Mr and Mrs Raymond D. Nasher.
From the artist's family, 1985.
See illus. pp. 82 and 120

Exh: E15 Rotterdam etc. (1958) No. 16 : E235 Buffalo etc. (1979) No. 20.

According to Miriam Gabo, 53.7 was probably finished just before its exhibition in 1958 (E15). It has 92 notches down each side.

53.8   Linear Construction in Space No. 1 (Variation)

1958. Inscribed at bottom, on outside of vertical side: ›Gabo 58‹.
Perspex with nylon monofilament.
21.8 x 21.8 x 9.5.
London, Private Collection.
From the artist, 1958.

This version has 52 notches down each side. According to Miriam Gabo, 53.8 was acquired by the present owner in 1958.

53.9   Linear Construction in Space No. 1 (Variation)

[*c.* 1959]. Inscribed top left at end: ›Gabo‹.
Perspex with nylon monofilament.
[61 x 61 x 25.4].
St. Louis, Washington University Gallery of Art, Steinberg Hall (4285): Gift of Louise and Joseph Pulitzer, Jr., 16 Dec 1965.
From the artist, 6 Dec 1959 to Fine Art Associates, New York; 9 Dec 1959 to Collection Louise and Joseph Pulitzer, Jr., St. Louis.

Exh: E133 St. Louis (1961) fig. : E181 St. Louis (1968) No. 94, fig. : E196 Cambridge, Mass., etc. (1971–2) No. 173.

Lit: A53 Bernier (1967) fig. p. 38 : E196 Chetham *et al* (1971) pp. 418–20, No. 173, fig. p. 420.

This version has *c.* 192 notches down each side and is strung almost to the steps. Gabo sold this piece on 6 Dec 1959 (purchase agreement, O. Gerson, C. B. Haim, 6 Dec 1959). It was purchased by the Pulitzers three days later (letter from O. Gerson, 13 Jan 1960).

53.10   Linear Construction in Space No. 1 (Variation)

[(1960)/1964]. Inscribed on end at bottom of frame: ›N. Gabo‹.
Perspex with nylon monofilament.
[46 x 45.7 x 17.9].
Hamburg, Kunsthalle.
From the artist, 25 Feb 1964 to Marlborough-Gerson Gallery, New York; 1981 to the Kunsthalle.

Exh: E17 Amsterdam (1965) No. P13, fig. : E18 Mannheim etc. (1965) No. 13, fig. : E19 Zurich (1965) No. 13, fig. 8 : E20 Stockholm (1965–6) No. 68, fig. : E21 London (1966) No. 16, fig. on cover: E209 New York (1974) No. 18, fig.

Lit: [B123 Licht (1967) p. 335, fig. 247].

This version has deep steps, and, like 53.2, is strung right down to the steps. Unlike 53.2, however, it has 134 notches down each side and the steps are straight, not slanted.

It was bought by the Marlborough-Gerson Gallery in 1964, and was retained by Marlborough until its sale to Hamburg in 1981 (receipt, 25 Feb 1964; letter from B. Reis, 6 Jul 1965).

53.11   Linear Construction in Space No. 1 (Variation)

1976. Inscribed top left edge of vertical frame: ›FOR MIRIAM/Gabo [in cyrillic]‹, and bottom left edge ›GABO‹.
Perspex with nylon monofilament.
21.9 x 21.9 x 10.1.
London, Family Collection.
See illus. p. 121

Lit: [E28 London (1976–7) fig. p. 48].

This version has 66 notches down each side, 65 of which carry strings. According to Miriam Gabo, 53.11 was completed in 1976. It is possibly the incomplete version shown in a photograph of Gabo's work-bench, which was taken in 1976 and reproduced in the 1976 catalogue (E28). 53.11 is probably the last work Gabo completed.

54.   RED STONE

54.1   Model for ›Red Stone‹

1949/(51). 24.4 [or *c.* 15.2] diameter.
New York, Collection the late Mr Bernard J., and Mrs Reis.
From the artist, before or in 1962.

Lit: G30 (1962) p. xvi, fig. 40, two views : A184 Sjöberg (1964) fig. p. 26.

In 1962 Gabo dated this work 1949, although later it was ascribed to 1951 (G30; A184). Miriam Gabo included it as ›*Carved Stone*, small version‹ in the list of works Gabo gave Bernard Reis between 1949 and 1964 (letter M. Gabo to C. Israels, 15 Feb 1967). It was certainly in Reis's possession by 1962 (G30).

54.2   Red Stone

1964–5. [Not inscribed].
African Red Stone. 24 high x 45.
London, Family Collection.
See illus. pp. 87 and 141

Exh: [E17 Amsterdam (1965) No. P14] : [E18 Mannheim etc. (1965) No. 15] : [E19 Zurich (1965) No. 15] : [E20 Stockholm (1965–6) No. 70] : E21 London (1966) No. 18, as ›1963–4‹ : E22 Buffalo (1968) No. 20.

Lit: A51 Bekkers (1966) fig. following p. 32 : A103 Granath (1966) fig. p. 13 *in situ* E20 : A105 Gray (1966) fig. p. 52, as ›1965‹.

This work was apparently made in 1964 in Portugal by Antonio Duarte, working from a plaster model of 54.1, under Gabo's supervision. In the summer of 1964 Miriam Gabo and Regine Duarte discussed the search for a ›pink stone‹, presumably for 54.2 (letters from M. Gabo and R. Duarte, 13 Jul, 5 Aug 1964). In November 1964 Regine Duarte stated that ›the enlargement of the red stone‹, again presumably 54.2, was finished (letter from R. Duarte, 30 Nov 1964). The sculpture was sent by air to the USA in early spring 1965 (letters from Cohen and Powell, 20 Jan 1965; from A. Duarte, 8 Feb 1965). Miriam Gabo recollects that Gabo put the final finish on 54.2 prior to sending it to Europe. However, according to Miriam Gabo, although 54.2 was entered in the catalogues for the other venues of the European tour (E17–20), it was only shown in London (E21).

55. LINEAR CONSTRUCTION IN SPACE NO. 2

No original model for this work has been traced. According to Miriam Gabo, the only surviving small versions of 55 (which Gabo included in the Project for the Lobby of the Esso Building in New York), were made in 1949, after and not before 55.1 (see 56.6 and 56.7).

This is one of the most numerous groups, comprising 26 versions, one of which is now destroyed. Similarities between the different versions are so strong that it is often difficult to make precise identifications from photographs.

Gabo produced a variation of 55 (63), and developed the general format of two similar intersecting planes strung with nylon or spring-wire in *Linear Construction No. 3, with Red* (62); and *Linear Construction No. 4* (68); which in turn led to *Construction in Space: Suspended* (70).

55.1 Linear Construction in Space No. 2 (Variation No. 1)

1949. Perspex with nylon monofilament.
[53.3 long].
Andover, Massachusetts: Phillips Academy, Addison Gallery of American Art (1952.19).
From the artist, January 1952.

Exh: E10 Baltimore (1950) [No. 5] : [E78 Worcester, Mass. (1951) No. 94] : E80 Andover etc. (1951) No. 24 : E11 Cambridge, Mass. (1951) [No. 8] : E87 Andover (1952) : E96 Minneapolis (1953) No. 44, fig. p. 31.

Lit: N16 Henry (1950) fig. : [A14 (1951) fig. p. 22, as ›1948‹] : A110 Hayes (1952) p. 508, fig. 2, as ›1950‹, shown mounted on slotted base : A141 Morris (1953) fig. p. 26 : B98 Hayes (1955) fig. p. 102 : G25 (1956) fig. p. 60, as ›*Linear Construction in Space No. 3*‹.

This version has no black insets. A photograph of 55.1 bears a statement of originality, signed by Miriam Gabo, witnessed by a Notary Public, and dated ›November 1, 1949‹ (FAL). 55.1 was first exhibited in spring 1950 (E10). The loan receipt for that exhibition lists it as ›*String Construction* (made 1949)‹, and a review evidently illustrates 55.1, since size and the lack of black insets correspond to this version (N16).

Gabo first used this title, *Linear Construction in Space No. 2 (Variation No. 1)*, in 1951, but did not use it again (letter to Addison Gallery, 22 May 1951). The subtitle probably refers to the fact that 55.1 was the first version of this work to be made (see Introduction – Titles).

The Addison Gallery acquired 55.1 in 1952, when Gabo agreed to exchange it for the *Column* now in the Solomon R. Guggenheim Museum (10.2). 55.1 is usually exhibited lying horizontally, although it has also been shown vertically.

55.2 Linear Construction in Space No. 2

1949/50. [Not inscribed].
Perspex with nylon monofilament.
[101.6 high].

Chicago, Art Institute of Chicago (1971.879): Gift of Florene M. Schoenborn, formerly Mrs Samuel A. Marx, 1971.
From the artist, 1951/(52) to Collection Mr and Mrs Samuel A. Marx, Chicago; Dec 1962 on loan to the Art Institute of Chicago; 1971 donated to the Institute.

Exh: E79 New York (1951) No. 18 : [E82 Springfield, Mass. (1951)] : [E84 Chicago (1951) No. 57].

Lit: G28 (1957) p. 184, n. 87 : B140 Merillat (1974) p. 149, fig. 56 : B197 Sarff *et al* (1979) fig. p. 73.

This version is suspended and has two black plastic insets. Gabo dated it 1949, although this may be the date of its inception rather than of its completion (letter to A. Speyer, Art Institute, 11 Mar 1967). 55.2 was first exhibited in the spring of 1951 at the Whitney Annual (E79, catalogue annotation ›large *Linear* [*No. 2*] shown first time,‹ FAL).

55.2 was almost certainly the version of 55 exhibited later that year in Chicago, where it was priced in the catalogue (E84). Samuel Marx, who was a Trustee of the Art Institute of Chicago, probably acquired 55.2 at the exhibition or soon after. E84 closed on 16 December 1951, and 55.2 was certainly in Marx's possession by early 1952, when Gabo mentioned seeing it in Marx's home (letter to S. Marx, 4 Feb 1952). Before its acquisition by Marx, 55.2 was probably exhibited in Springfield in 1951 (E82; installation photograph, Yale 2).

55.3 Linear Construction in Space No. 2

1950; base *c.* 1952. Not inscribed.
Perspex with nylon monofilament; on circular tiered base of transparent Perspex.
[*c.* 40.5 high, including integral base *c.* 2.5 high].
New York, The Lydia and Harry Winston Collection (Dr and Mrs Barnett Malbin).
From the artist, Dec 1951 to Rose Fried Gallery, New York; 1 May 1952 to Winston.

Exh: E85 New York (1952) No. 6 : E97 Bloomfield Hills (1953) No. 59 : E107 Ann Arbor (1955) No. 21, fig., on base : E110 Detroit etc. (1957–8) No. 42, fig. p. 50 : E125 Toledo (1960) : E212 Detroit (1974) No. 84, fig. p. 113.

Lit: A107 Hamilton (1954) fig. p. 20 : G28 (1957) p. 184, fig. 86, without base : A8 (1957) fig. p. 177 : B204 Seuphor (1959) fig. p. 72 : B76 Giedion-Welcker (1960) figs pp. 182–3 : A206 Taylor (1963) fig. p. 301 : B117 Kuh (1965) pp. 111, 136, fig. 76 : A51 Bekkers (1966) figs. following p. 32 : B91 Hamilton (1967) fig. p. 137 : B148 Mumford (1971) opp. p. 341, fig. 30 : A48 Baro (1971) fig. p. 185 : B128 Lloyd (1979) fig. 5 : E239 Milan (1979–80) fig. 166.

This is the only version in which every other notch carries nylon filament. The base for 55.3 was not made by Gabo, although he did suggest certain elements of its design (letters R. Fried to L. Winston, n. d., Winston Collection Papers, D220, frames 1219–22, AAA). The base was added after 1952 when the work was acquired by Lydia Win-

ston, and before 1955 when 55.3 was first exhibited with a base (E107).

In 1950 Rose Fried approached Gabo with a view to acquiring a work for Mrs Winston (letters from R. Fried, 17 May, 24 Sep 1950). According to Miriam Gabo, Marcel Duchamp was instrumental in persuading Gabo to contribute to Miss Fried's exhibition of 1952 (E85). In December 1951 Miss Fried accepted 55.3 for inclusion in E85 (receipt, 14 Dec 1951), and she bought it during the exhibition. In 1952 Gabo told Marcel Duchamp that he did not want the work to be sold to a museum, as he ›would be very badly represented . . . with such a tiny model‹ (letter to M. Duchamp, 27 Feb 1952). Mrs Winston acquired 55.3 on 1 May 1952 (note, n. d., Winston Collection Papers, D220, frame 1202, AAA).

55.4 Linear Construction in Space No. 2

1950/51; base added 1958/9. Not inscribed.
Perspex with nylon monofilament; on irregular transparent Perspex base. 40.6 high, including integral base 2.5 high.
Massachusetts, USA: Private Collection.
From the artist, 1951.

Exh: E101 New Haven (1954) No. 10, fig., as ›Lucite and nylon‹.

Lit: G28 (1957) p. 184, n. 86 : B73 Gardner (1959) p. 760, fig. 22.14.

This version was commissioned in July 1950 and completed by March 1951 (letters from present owner, 17 Jul 1950, 22 Mar 1951). According to the owner, Gabo made the irregular base in 1958/9. The supports and the square piece were added later by the Williamstown Regional Conservation Laboratory.

55.5 Linear Construction in Space No. 2

1949/52. Not inscribed.
Perspex with nylon monofilament.
[91.4 high].
Amsterdam, Stedelijk Museum (BA320).
From the artist, May 1955 on loan to the Stedelijk Museum, Amsterdam; 30 Sep 1958 acquired by the Museum.

Exh: E105 Amsterdam (1955) fig. on cover: E109 Paris (1956) No. 33, fig. : E15 Rotterdam etc. (1958) No. 17, fig. : E119 Amsterdam (1959) No. 59, fig. : E136 Recklinghausen (1961) No. A213 : E138 Amsterdam (1961) No. A46 : E139 Humlebaek (1961) No. 115 : E142 Stockholm (1961–2) No. 114 : E17 Amsterdam (1965) No. P17.

Lit: B4 Alvard *et al* (1952) fig. p. 129 : B57 (1955) fig. 125 : G28 (1957) p. 184, fig. 87 : B196 Sandberg *et al* (1961) fig. 88 : A184 Sjöberg (1964) fig. p. 23 : E18 Mannheim etc. (1965) fig. : E19 Zurich (1965) fig. 9 : E20 Stockholm (1965–6) fig. : [E21 London (1966) fig. 7] : A41 Baljeu (1966) fig. p. 37 : B122 Leymarie *et al* (1971) p. 180, fig. 170 : A186 [Spar] (1975) fig. p. 49.

This version is suspended and has black insets. Although 55.5 was illustrated in the catalogue for the *Documenta* exhibition of 1955, Gabo was not listed as a contributor (B57). Furthermore, 55.5 could not have been shown, because it was on exhibition in Amsterdam at the time (E105). It is possible that a photograph, or a different version of 55 was exhibited.

55.6 Linear Construction in Space No. 2

1953. Not inscribed.
Perspex with nylon monofilament.
[113 high].
Grenoble, Musée de Peinture et de Sculpture (MG 3397).
From the artist, to Collection Miriam Gabo; 1972 to Grenoble.

Exh: E18 Mannheim etc. (1965) No. 14 : E19 Zurich (1965) No. 14 : E20 Stockholm (1965–6) No. 69 : E21 London (1966) No. 17 : E22 Buffalo (1968) No. 9 : E23 Humlebaek etc. (1970–71) No. 4, fig. p. 8 : E24 Berlin (1971) No. 3 : E25 Hannover (1971) No. 3, fig. pp. 11 *in situ* E23, and 75 : E26 Grenoble etc. (1971–2) No. 4, fig. and fig. *in situ* E23 : E27 Lisbon (1972) No. 3 : E226 Paris (1978) No. 101, p. 147, fig.

Lit: B110 Huyghe (1965) p. 256, fig. 666 : A70 Causey (1966) figs pp. 34, 35 *in situ* E21 : A219 Webb (1966) p. 661, fig. 4 : A222 Whitford (1966) fig. 3 : A105 Gray (1966) fig. p. 49 *in situ* E19 : A187 Spencer (1967) fig. p. 21 : N2 Andreae (1968) p. 9, fig. : B180 Read (1969) p. 172, fig. 53.

This version is suspended and has black insets. When 55.6 was first exhibited in the European tour of 1965–6, it was dated ›1949–53‹ (E18–21). In the list of proposed exhibits for the tour, 55 is annotated ›Version shown 1953‹.

55.7 Linear Construction in Space No. 2

1954. Inscribed: ›G (in cyrillic) 1954 Gabo‹.
Perspex with nylon monofilament.
[38.7 high].
New York State, Collection Mr and Mrs G. Rickey: 1980 on loan to the Neuberger Museum, State University of New York, Purchase, New York.
From the artist, 1954 to Collection Helen McAuslan, McLeod, Montana; August 1970 by bequest to Mr and Mrs De Weese, Bozeman, Montana; December 1974 on loan (No. TR. 1848) to the Los Angeles County Museum of Art; May 1979 to Asher-Faure Gallery, Los Angeles; 4 January 1980 to Rickey.

Exh: E241 Purchase (1980).

Helen McAuslan commissioned this version in April 1954, and Gabo dispatched the completed work in July of that year (letters from and to H. McAuslan, 16 Apr, 30 Jul 1954). In 1957 Gabo listed the owner of this version erroneously as ›Miss McLeod‹ (G28). Further details of the provenance have been confirmed by George Rickey.

55.8 Linear Construction in Space No. 2

1954. Inscribed at bottom of one plane: ›Gabo 1954‹.
Perspex with nylon monofilament.
[38.1 high].
London, Collection Mr and Mrs Eugene Rosenberg.
From the artist Dec 1954 to Collection V. N. Buchanan, England; Nov 1960 to Hanover Gallery, London; 1962 to Rosenberg.

Lit: G28 (1957) p. 184, n. 86 : A191 (1966) fig. on cover.

This version is suspended and has black insets. Gabo stated that it was made of Perspex, bought in England (letter to J. Buchanan, 14 Nov 1954). Mr Buchanan probably saw it in the studio at Middlebury in November 1954, and it arrived in Britain in December of that year (letter from J. Buchanan, 17 Nov, 26 Dec 1954). In 1966 Eugene Rosenberg informed Gabo that he had acquired 55.8 (letter, 2 Feb 1966).

55.9 Linear Construction in Space No. 2

(1949)/1955. Not inscribed.
Perspex with nylon monofilament.
[38.1 high].
Washington, DC: Hirshhorn Museum and Sculpture Garden, Smithsonian Institution (66.1977).
From the artist Feb 1958 to Harold Diamond, New York; by Oct 1958 to G. David Thompson, Pittsburgh; [through Harold Diamond, New York]; 10 Oct 1962 to Collection Joseph H. Hirshhorn, New York; by 1974 to Museum.

Exh: E150 Stamford (1962) No. 3 : E213 Washington (1974–5) p. 693, No. 656 : E216 Washington (1976) No. 174, fig. p. 355.

The records concerning this work are confusing. In February 1958 Gabo sold a version of 55 to Mr and Mrs Harold Diamond. He described this as ›16″ x 8½″ [40.6 x 21.6 cms], made of plastic and nylon thread, and signed by me‹ (purchase agreement, 23 Feb 1958). This is not exactly the same size as 55.9. By October 1958 this work had passed to Mr Thompson (letter from H. Diamond, 4 Oct 1958). According to the Museum records, however, Thompson bought their version from Gabo in 1956, and it passed to Diamond in 1962. This suggests that initially Thompson may have considered Diamond as his agent rather than as an owner, and was mistaken about the date. Mr Hirshhorn definitely bought 55.9 from Diamond in 1962 (Museum records).

In 1978 Diamond stated that Gabo had sold 55.9 to him in 1955, a date he might have communicated to Thompson (letter M. Gabo to A. Bowness, 6 Jun 1978, FAL). Diamond told the Museum that it was signed at the centre, as stated in the purchase agreement of 1958. However, no signature is visible. Diamond is only known to have handled one version of 55, and this suggests that there is only one version involved in these transactions, and that the discrepancies are the result of human error.

55.10 Linear Construction in Space No. 2

c. 1955. Perspex with nylon monofilament.
c. 76 long.
London, Collection Mr and Mrs Roger Franklin.
From the artist *c.* 1955/6.

According to Miriam Gabo, this was made shortly before it was acquired by the present owners.

55.11 Linear Construction in Space No. 2

(1956)/1957. Not inscribed.
Perspex with nylon monofilament; on wooden base. 43.2 high, on integral base 3.2 x 30 x 30.
Schiedam, Holland: Collection Prof. and Mrs Piet Sanders.
Commissioned from the artist, 1957.

Exh: E111 Paris (1958) : E15 Rotterdam etc. (1958) No. 18 : E124 Schiedam (1960) No. 194.

This version has black insets (installation photograph of E111, FAL). Professor and Mrs Sanders commissioned this version after having seen 55.5 in the Stedelijk Museum, Amsterdam (letter from Prof. P. Sanders, 29 Nov 1956). 55.11 arrived in Holland in October 1957 (letter from M. Sanders, 26 Oct 1957). The Sanders asked Gabo to suggest a design for a base, which Gabo sent in November (letters from and to M. Sanders, 26 Oct, 4 Nov 1957). The base was made in Schiedam.

55.12 Linear Construction in Space No. 2

c. 1957/8. Inscribed: [›GABO‹ and ›Gabo‹].
Perspex with nylon monofilament.
[38 high].
Caracas, Venezuela: Collection the late Mr Carlos, and Mrs M.Villanueva.
From the artist, 1958.

Exh: E140 Caracas (1961) : E202 Caracas (1972) No. 22.

This version has black plastic insets. In December 1957 Mr Villanueva approached Gabo about acquiring a sculpture (letter from C. Villanueva, 8 Dec 1957). Gabo sent him a selection of photographs, including one of 55 (letter, 22 Dec 1957). 55.12 was evidently in Villanueva's possession by May 1958, when he informed Gabo that the nylon had stretched (letter from C. Villanueva, 3 May 1958).

55.13 Linear Construction in Space No. 2

1957/8. Not inscribed.
Perspex with nylon monofilament.
[39.4 high].
England, Collection the late Sir Herbert, and Lady Read.
Gift from the artist, Apr 1958.

Lit: G28 (1961) p. 200, n. 86.

From their first meeting in *c.* 1936 and for thirty years until his death in 1968, Herbert Read was one of Gabo's closest friends and his most constant advocate. In 1936 when Gabo settled in London, at 11 Lawn Road, Herbert Read was living nearby in No. 3 The Mall. Although Gabo and Read shared many philosophical and political interests, Read was as involved with Surrealism as he was with ›constructive‹ art. In 1942, Read warmly praised Gabo's *Spiral Theme* (52). The following year, as Director of the Design Research Unit, Read entrusted Gabo with one of the first major commissions, a car design for the Jowett car company.

After Gabo moved to the USA in 1946, Read continued his support. He wrote introductions for the major exhibition catalogues of 1948 and 1966, and contributed an introductory essay to Gabo's monograph published in 1957 (E9, E21, G28). Despite occasional misunderstandings, they maintained a steady and lengthy correspondence (UVBC, Yale 1). In 1956 Gabo wrote to Read: ›Needless to say that I don't know anyone who could give a more comprehensive account of what I have done in my work and make clear to the public what I am aiming at. May I add that I don't know anybody else amongst my contemporaries to whom I would be as near spiritually as I am to you‹ (letter to H. Read, 10 Jan 1956, UVBC).

Read was delighted with Gabo's gift of 55.13 in 1958 (letter from H. Read, 27 Apr 1958). In 1969 Gabo made another version of 55 as his personal memorial to Read (see 55.21 and 55.23).

55.14   Linear Construction in Space No. 2

1958. Inscribed one end, at intersection of planes: ›Gabo‹.
Perspex with nylon monofilament; on black Perspex base. 38 long, on base
2.5 x 50.7 x 35.4.
New York, Solomon R. Guggenheim Museum (78.2455): Gift of Mr and Mrs Marcel Breuer, 1978.
From the artist [1958] to Collection Mr and Mrs Marcel Breuer, New York; 1978 to Guggenheim.
See illus. p. 41, fig. 49

Exh: E266 New York (1984).

This version is displayed horizontally. The base was apparently made by the Museum.

Marcel Breuer probably acquired 55.14 in 1958. The Guggenheim's letter accepting this gift in 1978, dated the work 1958 (letter, 18 Dec 1978, SRGM). This presumably followed information supplied by Breuer. According to Miriam Gabo, Gabo made 55.14 as a gift for Breuer following the completion of the Bijenkorf project in 1957 (see 67).

55.15   Linear Construction in Space No. 2

c. 1959. Perspex with nylon monofilament; mounted on a pivot on Perspex base.
[38.1 high].
Chicago, Collection Mrs Lillian Florsheim.
From the artist, 6 Dec 1959 to Otto Gerson Gallery, New York, in association with Galerie Claude Bernard, Paris; 1961 to Florsheim.

Otto Gerson and Claude Bernard Haim purchased a version of 55, cited as ›15″ x 8¼″ x 8½″‹, from Gabo in 1959 (purchase agreement, 6 Dec 1959). This work was probably the version of 55, described as ›15 inches high‹, that Mrs Florsheim bought from Gerson in 1961 (letter from M. Schmierer, 22 Sep 1966). Gabo stated that this work had a Plexiglas base and was mounted on a pivot (letter to M. Schmierer, 19 Oct 1966).

55.16   Linear Construction in Space No. 2

1959. Perspex, aluminium, and stainless steel spring-wire. [48 high, including irregular base].
Zollikon, Switzerland: Collection Dr W. A. Bechtler.
From the artist, Dec 1959 to Otto Gerson Gallery, New York in association with Galerie Claude Bernard, Paris; Nov 1960 to Bechtler.

Exh: E131 Saint-Etienne (1960) No. 86, fig. 37 : E19 Zurich (1965) No. 93, as ›1959‹.

Lit: G28 (1961) p. 200, n. 86 : A27 (1975) fig. p. 27.

This version has been called *Construction en matière plastique, aluminium et fils d'acier* (E131). It is strung with stainless steel springs, with some of the central notches omitted.

Otto Gerson and Claude Bernard Haim bought this work from Gabo in December 1959 (purchase agreement, 6 Dec 1959). It was subsequently sold through the Galerie Claude Bernard, which had previously exhibited another version of 55 (E111; 55.11).

55.17   Linear Construction in Space No. 2

[1959/60]. Not inscribed.
Perspex with nylon monofilament. 79.5 high, on irregular base.
Duisburg, Wilhelm-Lehmbruck-Museum der Stadt Duisburg.
From the artist [1960] to Otto Gerson Gallery, New York; [1963] to Marlborough Fine Art, London; July 1963 to Galerie Wilhelm Grosshennig, Düsseldorf; 1963 to Duisburg.

Exh: E141 New York (1961–2) No. 13, as ›36″ H.‹ : E148 Düsseldorf (1962) fig., as ›91,5 cm, lent by Otto Gerson‹ : E182 Düsseldorf (1968) : E259 Marl (1982–3).

Lit: B60 (1964) p. 11, fig. p. 47.

In 1960 Gabo sold Otto Gerson a third version of 55 (see 55.15 and 55.16). The purchase agreement records neither the materials nor the size of the work, but the price paid indicates that it was a large version and therefore must be identified with 55.17 (letter to O. Gerson, 7 Apr 1960). In 1963 Marlborough Fine Art sold 55.17 to the Galerie Wilhelm Grosshennig (letter from F. Lloyd, 17 Jul 1963).

55.18   Linear Construction in Space No. 2

1962–4. Not inscribed.
Perspex with stainless steel spring-wire; on Perspex base. 78.7 high, including base.
Buffalo, Albright-Knox Art Gallery (65:15): Gift of the Seymour H. Knox Foundation Inc., 1965.
From the artist, Dec 1964 to Marlborough-Gerson Gallery, New York; 25 Jun 1965 to Knox Foundation.
See illus. p. 124

Exh: E175 Buffalo (1966) No. 146, fig. p. 69, as ›1962–65‹ : E22 Buffalo (1968) No. 18, fig. on cover : E200 Buffalo (1972) No. (47).

Lit: N23 Tucker (1964) fig. : A119 Johnson (1967) p. 52, fig. : A164 Read (1968) fig. p. 10 : A30 (1968) p. 94, fig. : B37 (1972) pp. 182–3 and 415, fig. p. 183.

Although 55.18, like 55.16, has metal springs, it is strung differently. In stringing 55.16 Gabo evidently encountered the problem of the springs bunching in the middle, and hence omitted the central notches. In 55.18 he wound some of the springs through the central aperture, rather than around the outer edges of the verticals. This is a unique arrangement.

Marlborough-Gerson bought this in December 1964, and sold it in 1965 (receipt, 3 Dec 1964; letters from and to B. Reis, 6 Jul, 30 Jun 1965).

55.19   Linear Construction in Space No. 2

1964. Inscribed on top at intersection of planes: ›Gabo‹, and on edge of base: ›N.G.‹.
Perspex with nylon monofilament; on Perspex base. 81.9 high, including integral base 2.9 high.
England, Private Collection.
From the artist, 1968 to Collection Bo Boustedt, Sweden; *c.* 1970 to England.

Exh: E23 Humlebaek etc. (1970–71) No. 12, fig. p. 2.

Lit: E25 Hannover (1971) figs. pp. 73, 35 detail.

This version has two black plastic insets. It was acquired by Bo Boustedt in 1968 and shipped to him in the autumn of that year (letter M. Gabo to B. Boustedt, 3 Sep 1968).

55.20   Linear Construction in Space No. 2

1966–7. Not inscribed.
Perspex with nylon monofilament.
[48.2 high].
Saskatoon, University of Saskatchewan Permanent Art Collection (74–360).
From the artist, 1967.

Exh: E204 Saskatoon (1973) fig. p. 33.

Lit: A104 Gray (1968) fig. p. 44 : B21 Bell (1980) fig. p. 67.

This version has black plastic insets. It was stolen in August 1977, but was recovered undamaged in 1978.

55.21 Linear Construction in Space No. 2

1968–9. Not inscribed.
Perspex with nylon monofilament.
[114.9 high].
Formerly London, Tate Gallery (T01105); destroyed 1970.
Presented by the artist, 1969 through the American Federation of Arts to the Tate, in memory of Sir Herbert Read.

Lit: A5 (1970) p. 339, fig. 97 : A200 (1970) p. 82, fig. p. 20 : N13 Bruce-Milne (1971) p. 8, fig.

Sir Herbert Read was one of Gabo's closest friends (see 55.13). After Read died on 12 Jun 1968, Norman Reid, Director of the Tate Gallery, invited Gabo, Barbara Hepworth, Ben Nicholson, and Henry Moore, each to donate one work to the Tate as a memorial to Read (letter from N. Reid, 17 Dec 1968; for Gabo's tribute, see G33). Gabo chose *Linear Construction in Space No. 2* because he knew that Read ›was very fond of that image‹. He added: ›I made it all white, without the black inlay in the center because I felt that in order to keep the serenity of Herbert, no black should be in it‹ (letter to R. Alley, 26 Aug 1969). 55.21 was finished by the beginning of February and arrived at the Tate in April 1969 (letters to and from N. Reid, 6 Feb, 11 Apr 1969).

In 1970, 55.21 was broken. A report and photograph were sent to Gabo, who accepted the news philosophically and promised to make a replacement (letters from and to Sir N. Reid, n. d., 12 Aug 1970; for replacement, see 55.22).

55.22 Linear Construction in Space No. 2

1969. [Inscribed at top ›Gabo‹.]
Perspex with nylon monofilament.
[45 high, including integral base 4 high.]
Sweden, Private Collection.
From the artist, 1969 to Collection Professor Erik Andreason, Copenhagen; 1983 to Sweden.

Exh: E256a Copenhagen (1982).

Professor Andreason met Gabo in Denmark in 1968 and discussed with him the possibility of acquiring a *Linear No. 2* (letters from and to E. Andreason, 30 Dec 1968, 9 Jan 1969, FAL). 55.22 had evidently been completed and was in Professor Andreason's possession by 30 January 1970 (letter from E. Andreason, 30 Jan 1970, FAL).

55.23 Linear Construction in Space No. 2

1970–71. Not inscribed.
Perspex with nylon monofilament.
[114.9 high].
London, Tate Gallery (T01105).
Presented by the artist, 1971 through the American Federation of Arts to the Tate, in memory of Sir Herbert Read.

Exh: E28 London (1976–7) No. 86, fig. p. 43.

Lit: B130 (1975) fig. p. 34 : A169 Roberts (1976) p. 878, fig. : A210 Thurston (1976) fig. p. 18 : B3 Alley (1981) p. 266, fig.

Gabo made this version to replace the broken 55.21, which was returned to Gabo in September 1970 (letter M. Gabo to N. Reid, 21 Sep 1970). 55.23 was finished by April 1971 and arrived in London by 1 June (letters from B. Sainsbury, 19 Apr 1971, and from N. Reid to A. Kaplan, American Federation of Arts, 1 June 1971). Like 55.21, 55.23 has no black insets.

55.24 Linear Construction in Space No. 2

1972/3. Perspex with nylon monofilament.
92 high.
London, Family Collection.
See illus. pp. 79 and 122

Lit: A168 Rickey (1977) fig. p. 25.

This version is suspended and has black insets which come to the very edge of the transparent Perspex. It initially had a base (A168), which according to Miriam Gabo, was found to be unsatisfactory for the weight of the work and was removed almost immediately.

55.25 Linear Construction in Space No. 2

c. 1976. [Inscribed: ›G.‹].
Perspex with nylon monofilament; resting on side on wooden base, stained black.
38.1 long, on base 1.9 x 45.5 x 32.9.
London, Family Collection.
See illus. p. 123

According to Miriam Gabo, this was the last *Linear Construction in Space No. 2* that Gabo made.

55.26 Linear Construction in Space No. 2

Date unknown. Inscribed on top at intersection of the planes: ›Gabo‹.
Perspex with nylon monofilament; mounted on a pivot on ›kidney-shaped‹ Perspex base. 40.6 high, including integral base 2.5 high.
London, Marlborough Fine Art.
Provenance unknown.

This version has no black insets. 55.26 is supported by a metal pivot and four small blocks between the vertical planes. A thin disc of Perspex lies between the blocks and the base. No documentation relating to 55.26 has been traced, nor has Marlborough Fine Art provided any provenance.

56. PROJECTED CONSTRUCTIONS FOR THE LOBBIES OF THE ESSO BUILDING, ROCKEFELLER CENTER, NEW YORK

In 1950, in a letter to Herbert Read, Gabo described this project:
›The project was for two lobbies of the Esso Building, Radio-City facing on to 51st and 52nd St. The lobbies are different in space arrangement but the two walls* both face the respective streets. The difference in their arrangement influenced the theme of both constructions.‹
›The one on 52nd St. is larger and the wall is nearer to the entrance, and therefore the theme was on a larger scale. The background walls were faced with marble slabs and as the one on the 52nd. St. side was nearer to the street, it was proposed to cover this wall with a brass wire mesh as a background to the bar-relief construction on this wall, which is made of divers materials, metal, plastic and stainless steel-wire. It was proposed to make a fountain, sunk in to the ground in this lobby and also standing sculptures above the rotating entrance doors, which would rotate on their bases by the movement of the doors (the rate being one revolution of the sculpture to 20 of the door), and casting shadows on the side walls.‹
›The lobby on 51st St. represents a long corridor with the big wall at the end of it, therefore the elongated structure of the sculpture on this wall.‹
›This is all that I can tell you in addition to what you already know, i.e., that because of the unusual character of the project, the contracting firms were unwilling to cooperate and sabotaged the whole affair by demanding a price out of all proportion to the work.‹
* The size of the wall is 18′ x 30′.
›P. S. The two photos of the 52nd Street wall need some explanation: I think you saw the one with the basin on the floor; the other was an attempt of mine to cut down the cost by eliminating some parts and simplifying the structure without greatly impeding the main theme of the design – it did not help me much. The difference in cost was negligeable‹ (letter to H. Read, 20 Jan 1950, UVBC).

In December 1948 the architects for the Esso Building, Carson and Lundin, sent Gabo a sample of the Roman Travertine Marble used in the building (letter from R. Carson, 3 Dec 1948). In January 1949, Woodcote Associates of Woodbury, Connecticut, started making the architectural models of the lobbies (letter from H. Soper, 19 Jan 1949). Estimates for the final construction and installation of Gabo's designs were ready in July (letters from G. Brennan, 6 and 27 Jul 1949). According to Gabo, he worked on the models for six months, completing them for delivery in August (memorandum from D. Miller to D. Dudley, 6 Feb 1953, MoMA). By November 1949, the project had been abandoned for financial reasons (letter from N. Rockefeller to M. Gabo, 3 Nov 1949).

Although the individual components of the models for this project are entered separately, the bibliography, exhibition references, and history of the complete models are entered under 56.3 for the 51st Street entrance, and under 56.8 for the 52nd Street entrance.

Two sets of templates for the models are not entered here (Family Collection).

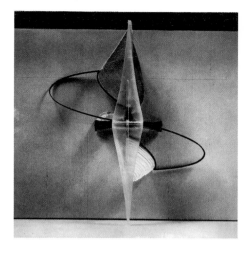

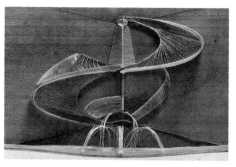

56.1 Model for a Construction for the 51st Street Entrance, Esso Building, Rockefeller Center, New York.

1949. Not inscribed.
Plastic with gold wire mesh.
[8.9 x 12.7 x 5.1].
London, Tate Gallery (T02184).
Presented by the artist, 1977.

Exh: E28 London (1976–7) No. 77, as ›1949–52‹.

Lit: B3 Alley (1981) pp. 252–3, fig., as ›Model for the Esso Project, Radio City, New York‹.

A photograph shows that this relief was originally mounted on the architectural model with its central axis horizontal (FAL).

56.2 Maquette for Sculpture of plastic and wire mesh for 51st Street Entrance, Esso Building, Rockefeller Center, New York

1949. Not inscribed.
Plastic and metal. [22.2 x 18.4].
New York, Museum of Modern Art (13.53.1).
Presented by the artist, 1953.

See 56.3.

56.3 Architectural Model of 51st Street Entrance, Esso Building, Rockefeller Center, New York

1949. Not inscribed.
Plywood. [38.1 x 112 x 88.3].
New York, Museum of Modern Art (13.53.2).
Presented by the artist, 1953.

Exh: E11 Cambridge, Mass. (1951) [No. 2] : E94 New York (1953) : E15 Rotterdam etc. (1958) No. 19a : E17 Amsterdam (1965) No. P15/1 : E18 Mannheim etc. (1965) No. 16a : E19 Zurich (1965) No. 16a : E20 Stockholm (1965–6) No. 71 : E21 London (1966) No. 19.

Lit: A193 Sweeney (1951) pp. 34–5, 61–2, fig. p. 34 : B4 Alvard *et al* (1952) fig. p. 128 : A149 (1953) p. 43, No. 1009 : A46 [Banham] (1955) p. 203 fig. 1 : G28 (1957) p. 184, fig. 88 : B204 Seuphor (1959) fig. p. 266 : B76 Giedion-Welcker (1960) fig. p. 179 : A118 Hultén (1971) fig. p. 71 : B206 Seuphor (1972) fig. 94 : B17 Barr (1977) p. 543, fig. p. 133.

The architectural models for both the entrances (56.3 and 56.8), were damaged during the European touring exhibition of 1965–6. They were returned to Gabo, who found the damage to be considerable, especially in the wall of the 52nd Street entrance: ›Certain parts are lost and will have to be made anew and others are broken‹ (letters to D. Miller, 14 Feb, 16 Jul 1967). In the 51st Street entrance, 56.2 had become detached from 56.3 (report, 11 May 1966, MoMA). Gabo repaired the models and returned them to the Museum in April 1968 (letter M. Gabo to D. Miller, 23 Apr 1968).

A complete view of 56.3 has never been reproduced. All the illustrations listed above show 56.2 only.

56.4 Model for Fountain in 52nd Street Lobby, Esso Building, Rockefeller Center, New York

[1949]. Not inscribed.
Perspex with rolled-gold wire.
4.8 x 16.9 x 10.7. Internal models 7.6 long.
London, Family Collection.

Lit: G28 (1957) fig. 90.

Gabo had attempted to reduce the cost of the project by relinquishing the ›basin‹ in the 52nd Street lobby (see introduction to 56). 56.4 is presumably the model he removed.

At the centre of the bowl are two constructions which are almost identical in size and form to the tiny model, *Linear Bas-Relief (Duplicate Part of the Model for the First Bijenkorf Project)*, 66.6. The fountain constructions, however, have larger supports than 66.6. Strips of white are attached to the edges of these supports, which rest on a white rectangle. There is a lozenge of black plastic between the two models, and two holes in the base of the bowl.

56.5 Maquette for Construction against centre wall for 52nd Street Entrance, Esso Building, Rockefeller Center, New York

1949. Not inscribed.
Plastic and wire. [16.5 x 22.9 x 3.5].
New York, Museum of Modern Art (14.53.1).
Presented by the artist, 1953.
See illus. p. 40, fig. 48

See 56.8.

56.6 Maquette for Construction over revolving doors at left side of 52nd Street Entrance, Esso Building, Rockefeller Center, New York

1949. Not inscribed.
Plastic and wire; on plastic base. [8.1 high, including integral base 0.5 x 7 x 4.5].
New York, Museum of Modern Art (14.53.2).
Presented by the artist, 1953.

See 56.8.

56.7 Maquette for Construction over revolving doors at right side of 52nd Street Entrance, Esso Building, Rockefeller Center, New York

1949. Not inscribed.
Plastic and wire; on plastic base. [8.1 high, including integral base 0.5 x 7 x 4.5].
New York, Museum of Modern Art (14.53.3).
Presented by the artist, 1953.

See 56.8.

56.8 Architectural Model of 52nd Street Entrance, Esso Building, Rockefeller Center, New York

1949. Not inscribed.
Plywood. [43.2 x 78.7 x 88.6].
New York, Museum of Modern Art (14.53.4).
Presented by the artist, 1953.

Exh: E11 Cambridge, Mass. (1951) [No. 3] : E94 New York (1953) : E15 Rotterdam etc. (1958) No.

19b : E17 Amsterdam (1965) Nos P15/2–4 : E18 Mannheim etc. (1965) Nos 16b-d : E19 Zurich (1965) Nos 16b-d : E20 Stockholm (1965–6) Nos 72–4 : E21 London (1966) Nos 20a-c : E28 London (1976–7) No. 78, as photograph, miscaptioned, fig. p. 42.

Lit: A193 Sweeney (1951) pp. 34–5, 61–2, fig. p. 35 : A149 (1953) fig. p. 43, No. 1009 : A46 [Banham] (1955) p. 203, fig. 2, 56.4 : G28 (1957) p. 184, figs. 89–90 : B17 Barr (1977) p. 543, fig. p. 133.

The original schema for the 52nd Street entrance, including the basin (56.4), is shown in G28 (fig. 90). Although to reduce costs Gabo altered 56.8 and removed the complex ›basin‹, he did retain a drastically simplified fountain in the final design (see A193). 56.8 was damaged during the European touring exhibition of 1965–6 (see 56.3).

57.   THE BALTIMORE ›CONSTRUCTION SUSPENDED IN SPACE‹

This work was Gabo's first major public commission to be realised. Donated by Mrs Saidie A. May to the Baltimore Museum of Art, the construction was commissioned in May 1950 (contract, 18 May 1950). It was to be hung in the stairwell of the new children's wing. Gabo explained how he exploited this location: ›In effect, the spiral movement of the ascending or descending spectator, if it is incorporated in[to] the conception of the structure, would give an imaginary movement to the sculpture . . .‹ (G24, B3).

The skeletal form which is attached to the ceiling in 57 is clearly related to the frame of *Linear Construction in Space No. 4* (68).

57.1   Model for the Baltimore ›Construction Suspended in Space‹

1950. Not inscribed.
Plastic; in two sections. [21.5 high].
London, Tate Gallery (T02182).
Presented by the artist, 1977.

Exh: E28 London (1976–7) No. 74, lower section only.

Lit: B3 Alley (1981) p. 253, fig.

This model was accepted by Mrs May and by the architects, Wrenn, Lewis and Jencks, in November 1950 (letters from S. May, 3 Nov 1950, and W. Casey, Treasurer, Baltimore Museum of Art, 14 Nov 1950). Like the final construction, this model comprises two sections, one of which is attached to the ceiling and the other suspended from it.

57.2   Study for the middle section of the Baltimore ›Construction Suspended in Space‹

1950. Inscribed at one end: ›Gabo‹.
Transparent plastic, with rolled-gold wire.
20.5 long x 4.4.
New York, Solomon R. Guggenheim Museum (55.1416): Gift of Alfred J. Jensen, in memory of Saidie A. May, 1955.
Gift from the artist, Oct 1950 to Collection Mrs Saidie A. May, Baltimore; 1951 bequeathed to Alfred J. Jensen; 1953 on loan to the Solomon R. Guggenheim Museum; 1955 donated to the Museum.

This model is marked with red [wax crayon] in two places, to indicate where the black saddle-shaped piece would be in the final construction. Details of provenance were provided by Alfred Jensen (letters from A. Jensen, 16 Jun 1951, 11 Jul 1955).

57.3   The Baltimore ›Construction Suspended in Space‹

1950–51. [Not inscribed].
Aluminium (baked black), phosphor-bronze mesh, stainless steel wire, rolled-gold wire, and plastic. [c. 457 high x c. 114].
Baltimore, The Baltimore Museum of Art (51.148): Gift of Mrs Saidie A. May, 1951.
Commissioned from the artist, 1950; 4 Nov 1951 unveiled.
See illus. p. 40, fig. 47

Exh: E28 London (1976–7) No. 75, as photograph.

Lit: N16 Henry (1950) p. 3 : A44 (1951) p. 4 : G23 (1951) pp. 3–4, fig. : G24 (1952) six figs : A178 Seymour (1954) fig. p. 24 : B102 Heron (1955) pp. 44–5 : A46 [Banham] (1955) pp. 203–4, three figs : B176 Read (1956) p. 101, figs 220–23 : G28 (1957) p. 184, figs 81–5, stereoscopic colour fig. 110, as ›1951–52‹ : B10 Baldinger et al (1960) p. 159, figs. 5.20, 5.21a–b : A183 Sjöberg (1960) fig. p. 190 : G30 (1971) fig. on cover : B213 Sylvester (1965) fig. p. 233 : A208 Thompson (1966) colour fig. p. 135 : A51 Bekkers (1966) four figs following p. 32 : B184 Rickey (1967) fig. 36 : B9 Arnason (1968) pp. 317–18, fig. : B233 Zanini (1971) fig. 87 : A118 Hultén (1971) fig. p. 72 : A45 (1972) p. 48, fig.

57.3 was evidently completed by October 1951 when it was delivered to the Museum (letters to J. Foster, 30 Sep 1951, and to W. Casey, 31 Oct 1951). At the formal unveiling, which took place on 4 November 1951, Gabo delivered a short address, in which he said:

›In my career I have designed several monumental works but this is the first I have been given the opportunity to execute. Looking back over the year and a half during which I worked on it, I see myself in a state of an intense vitality which I have not experienced before and, looking at the result, I don't find anything in it for which I could reproach myself or which I would have liked to change; and that is the greatest degree of gratification which an artist can ever hope to experience‹ (G23).

Unfortunately Mrs May died in June 1951, before the construction was competed, and in his closing remarks, Gabo dedicated this work as a memorial to her.

In January 1978 the construction was removed during renovation work in the Museum, and was not replaced until the late summer of 1982.

58.   CONSTRUCTION IN SPACE, WITH NET

This work is often titled simply *Construction in Space*. It is clearly related to *Spheric Theme* (37), and less directly to *Linear Construction in Space No. 3* and *Linear Construction in Space No. 4* (62 and 68).

58.1   Study for ›Construction in Space, with Net‹

1951. Not inscribed.
Wire-mesh, [Perspex], celluloid, and stainless steel wire. 8.8 high.
London, Family Collection.

Lit: E90 Philadelphia etc. (1952–3) fig. p. 19 : B185 Ritchie (1952) fig. p. 203 : B75 Gertz (1955) p. xxiii, fig. p. 164.

The term *Study* in the title (identical in all three references) presumably indicates that Gabo did not consider that this was a fully finished model. Although the study may have undergone some subsequent changes, it contains several elements which are not present in the final work (58.2). It differs from 58.2 in several respects. The arched strips are notched, indicating that Gabo may have considered stringing the work. The wires linking the notched black strip and the wire-mesh reinforce this hypothesis. In addition, two wire struts cross at the centre; the wire-mesh is lined with celluloid; and additional pieces of plastic and mesh, added to the base, provide a flat edge for standing.

The wire-mesh may be made of brass (B185), of bronze, or possibly of rolled-gold wire which Gabo often used in small models at this time. Although the references cited give the height as 15.2 cms, 58.1 was undoubtedly the version illustrated.

58.2   Construction in Space, with Net

1952. Not inscribed.
Phosphor-bronze wire-mesh, aluminium, Perspex and metal wire; on base of aluminium, and wood painted grey. 63.6 high, including integral two-tiered base 4.4 high x 81.5 diameter.
London, Family Collection.
See illus. pp. 80 and 126

Exh: E90 Philadelphia etc. (1952–3) No. 36, as ›c. 42 x 30"‹ : E14 Hartford (1953) No. 17 : [E99 New York (1954) No. 19, as ›1953‹] : E112 Brussels (1958) No. 96, fig. p. 201 : E120 Kassel (1959) Gabo No. 1, fig. p. 72 : E21 London (1966) No. 23 : E22 Buffalo (1968) No. 11 : E23 Humlebaek etc. (1970–71) No. 5, fig. p. 9, colour fig.

p. 11 : E24 Berlin (1971) No. 4, fig. p. 24, colour fig. p. 18 : E25 Hannover (1971) No. 4, figs pp. 11 *in situ* E23, 77, 78, colour fig. p. 79 : E26 Grenoble etc. (1971–2) No. 5, two figs, one *in situ* E23 : E27 Lisbon (1972) No. 4, fig. p. 15.

Lit: G28 (1957) p. 184, fig. 95, stereoscopic colour fig. 106 : N12 Bollman (1957) fig. p. 6 : E112 Langui (1959) fig. 96 : A208 Thompson (1966) colour fig. p. 135 : A105 Gray (1966) fig. p. 53 *in situ* E21 : A54 Besset (1971) fig. p. 10.

In this version, blackened pieces of wire mesh cover the vertices of the curved aluminium elements.

58.3 Construction in Space, with Net

1963. Not inscribed.
Phosphor-bronze wire-mesh, aluminium, Perspex, and stainless steel spring-wire; on aluminium base. 83.5 high, including integral base 1 x 98.7 diameter.
New York, Marlborough Gallery.
From the artist, *c.* 1969 to Marlborough-Gerson Gallery, New York.

Exh: E228 New York (1978) No. 22, fig. p. 22 : E267 New York (1984) No. 22, fig.

Lit: A38 (1977) fig. p. 5.

This version, unlike 58.2, has no black pieces at the vertices of the curved aluminium elements. Although it has been dated 1953 (E228), Gabo dated it 1963 in an agreement with Frank Lloyd (memorandum agreement, 15 Dec 1965).
In December 1964 it was delivered to the Marlborough-Gerson Gallery, to be sold on commission (receipt, 4 Dec 1964; letter to B. Reis, 6 Jul 1965). It became the property of the Marlborough Gallery *c.* 1969.

59. MODEL FOR SHADOW PIECE

1951–2. Not inscribed.
Bronze, with pencil drawing on squared paper. [10.8 high x 22.2].
London, Tate Gallery (T02183).
Presented by the artist, 1977.

Exh: E28 London (1976–7) No. 76.

Lit: B3 Alley (1981) p. 256, fig.

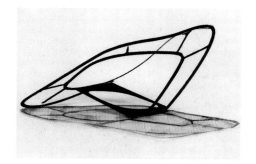

The drawing is not part of the construction, but merely indicates the shadows cast by the work (B3). Gabo never made an enlargement of this model, although its skeletal structure shows some similarity to the Baltimore *Construction Suspended in Space* (57).

60. OPTICAL RELIEF

1951–67. [Not inscribed].
Aluminium, plastic, with stainless steel spring-wire on wooden base painted white. *c.* 81 x 47 x 5.1, set on integral base 2.5 x 53.2 x 36.8.
London, Family Collection.
See illus. p. 125

Exh: [E13 New York (1953) No. 8] : E22 Buffalo (1968) No. 10, fig. p. 20 : E23 Humlebaek etc. (1970–71) No. 16, fig. p. 18 : E24 Berlin (1971) No. 13 : E25 Hannover (1971) No. 13, fig. p. 21 : E26 Grenoble etc. (1971–2) No. 15 : E27 Lisbon (1972) No. 14 : E245 Münster (1980) No. 122, fig. p. 209, as ›1951–61‹.

When this work was exhibited in 1968, Gabo dated it ›*c.* 1951–1967‹ implying that he had made substantial changes to it over that period (E22). No model for 60 has apparently survived, although one was probably made *c.* 1951. 60 may have been exhibited in 1953 as ›Relief. 1953. Plastic, metal, mesh, aluminium base. 32 x 18″‹ (E13). The title and dimensions are appropriate to 60, but the materials differ slightly. The aluminium frame of this work is anodised black.

61. MODEL FOR A MONUMENT TO THE UNKNOWN POLITICAL PRISONER

Gabo made this work as his entry for the international competition for a Monument to the Unknown Political Prisoner, announced in January 1952 by the Institute of Contemporary Arts, London (E95). Gabo heard of the competition from Herbert Read in February (letter from H. Read, 8 Feb 1952). The number of entries received by the closing date of December 1952, was so enormous (three thousand five hundred entries from fifty-seven countries), that it was necessary to hold elimination contests. Gabo was one of eleven entrants selected in the USA (E93). Reg Butler was given the first prize, and Gabo was one of five artists awarded a second prize. Gabo's design anticipates his Bijenkorf construction in Rotterdam (67).
In January 1953 Gabo explained to Herbert Read the major considerations that had inspired him:
›. . . I have actually only worked on that maquette during the last three months . . . There are two ways to look at this tragic fact of our times---the political imprisonment---one is compassion and condolence for the suffering of the imprisoned, and the other is awe and admiration. I did not hesitate for a moment to see that it is the latter feeling which I have for those who let themselves be imprisoned---who stand up and fight and take the consequences, no matter what suffering it entails. »Glory to them who go to the stake and vanquish

the pain of torture for the sake of their belief.« I wrote it down on my table---banal as it is---in order to have it before me---and that was my guidance.
›The mental conditions for my image to appear were prepared and then I only let it come and waited, quite relaxed, for its conception. And then one morning, in twenty minutes the image was done.‹
›I must tell you that I feel that, since the first *Column* in 1922–23, this work is the height of my thirty years striving towards an image which would combine sculpture and architecture in one entity‹ (letter to H. Read, 4 Jan 1953, UVBC).
Read later explained that the symmetry of Gabo's entry and the absence of any humanistic element had dissatisfied some members of the jury (letter from H. Read, 19 Mar 1953). Gabo defended his use of symmetry, describing it as ›the spine and core of everything created by man . . . what is not there as formal symmetry, you will find in the symmetry of balance‹ (letter to H. Read, 1 Apr 1953, UVBC).
Some drawings and cardboard patterns, made at twice the scale of 61.2, may have been preparatory studies for the larger model that Gabo had considered making (TGA, Gabo 8117; letter to H. Read, 11 May 1953). These studies emphasise the similarity between the outline of 61 and the frame of *Linear Construction in Space No. 1* (48).

61.1 First model for a ›Monument to the Unknown Political Prisoner‹

1952. Not inscribed.
Plastic, with wire-mesh. [12.7 high].
London, Tate Gallery (T02186).
Presented by the artist, 1977.

Exh: E28 London (1976–7) No. 81.

Lit: B3 Alley (1981) p. 257, fig.

Although this has been dated 1953 (E28), it was clearly made before the closing date of the competition in December 1952.

61.2 Model for a ›Monument to the Unknown Political Prisoner‹

1952. Not inscribed.
Plastic, with stainless steel wire-mesh; on base of slate and plastic. 41 high, including integral base 3 high.
London, Tate Gallery (T02187).
Presented by the artist, 1977.
See illus. p. 127

Exh: E93 New York (1953) No. 6, fig. : E95 London (1953) No. 30, fig. : E22 Buffalo (1968) No. 13 : E23 Humlebaek etc. (1970–71) No. 7, colour fig. p. 12 : E24 Berlin (1971) No. 6, colour fig. p. 18 : E25 Hannover (1971) No. 6, fig. p. 63, colour fig. p. 61 : E26 Grenoble etc. (1971–2) No. 7 : E27 Lisbon (1972) No. 6, fig. p. 16 : E28 London (1976–7) No. 82.

Lit: A95 Geist (1953) fig. p. 9 : A135 McBride (1953) fig. p. 21 : A195 Sylvester (1953) p. 478 : B75 Gertz (1955) p. xxiii, fig. p. 165 : B76 Giedion-Welcker (1956) fig. p. 163 : B161 Petersen (1956)

p. 118, fig. 100 : G28 (1957) p. 184, figs 91–3 : A8 (1957) fig. p. 178 : B204 Seuphor (1959) fig. p. 73 : E17 Martin (1965) fig. E : E20 Stockholm (1965–6) fig. : B3 Alley (1981) pp. 257–8, fig. : B77 Glozer (1981) fig. p. 185.

62. LINEAR CONSTRUCTION IN SPACE NO. 3, WITH RED

This work has been titled variously *Construction in Space, Linear Construction* (with Red), and *Kinetic Construction.* The title *Construction in Space X* or *No. 10* is an error derived from the catalogue number of the 1953 exhibition (E13).

A. L. Chanin, writing about this work in 1953, illustrated several drawings as preliminary sketches (A72). Although contemporary with the evolution of 62, these actually relate to other works. One is clearly a finished sketch for the *Bas-Relief for the U.S. Rubber Company Building, New York* (69). Although there is some similarity between the centre of this *Bas-Relief* and half of 62 (strengthened by the common use of red), there is an even stronger similarity between the central portion of 62 and the central sections of the *Bijenkorf Construction* (67.5), and the large versions of *Spheric Theme* (e.g. 42.12).

The substantial use of colour, albeit a single primary colour, makes 62 unusual amongst Gabo's constructions.

62.1 Model for ›Linear Construction in Space No. 3, with Red‹

1952. [Plastic with nylon thread]. Lost; presumed destroyed.

Lit: A72 Chanin (1953) fig. p. 36.

See 62.2.

62.2 Model for ›Linear Construction in Space No. 3, with Red‹

1952. Not inscribed. Plastic with nylon thread. [9.5 high]. London, Tate Gallery (T02185). Presented by the artist, 1977. *See illus. p. 128*

Exh: E28 London (1976–7) No. 79, as ›1953‹.

Lit: A72 Chanin (1953) fig. p. 36 : B3 Alley (1981) p. 257, fig.

62.2 and 62.1 were the two models illustrated by Chanin in 1953 (A72). The smaller model, 62.1, has subsequently been lost.

62.3 Linear Construction in Space No. 3, with Red

1952/3. Not inscribed. Plexiglas with nylon monofilament; mounted on a pivot on an aluminium base. [75.2 high, including integral irregular base 2.2 x 33.7 x 55.2].

New York, Museum of Modern Art (954.79): Nelson A. Rockefeller Bequest, 1979. From the artist, Oct 1953 through Pierre Matisse Gallery, New York, to Collection Nelson A. Rockefeller, New York; 1979 to MoMA.

Exh: E13 New York (1953) No. 10, fig. on cover : E14 Hartford (1953) No. 16, fig. 7 and on cover : E15 Rotterdam etc. (1958) No. 21, fig. : E160 London (1964) No. 15 : E185 New York (1969) p. 130, fig. p. 67.

Lit: A68 [L. Campbell] (1953) fig. : A96 Geist (1953) fig. p. 15 : A91 Fitzsimmons (1953) fig. p. 8 : A72 Chanin (1953) four figs p. 37 : G28 (1957) p. 184, fig. 96, colour fig. 97 : A130 Lassaw et al (1957) fig. p. 86 : B177 Read (1957) fig. 3 : B136 McCurdy (1958) p. 265, fig. D70 : E112 Langui (1959) fig. 97 : B204 Seuphor (1959) fig. p. 74 : B76 Giedion-Welcker (1960) fig. p. 369 *in situ* E13 : A55 (1961) fig. 13 : B179 Read (1964) fig. 111 : A208 Thompson (1966) colour fig. p. 135 : A224 Wolfram (1966) fig. on cover : B119 Kultermann (1968) fig. 166 : E25 Hannover (1971) fig. p. 70 : B233 Zanini (1971) fig. 88 : B206 Seuphor (1972) fig. 92 : B141 Miller (1982) colour fig. p. 152.

This work was sold to Nelson A. Rockefeller in October 1953 (letter from Pierre Matisse Gallery, 1 Oct 1953).

62.4 Linear Construction in Space No. 3, with Red

1957–8. Not inscribed. Perspex and stainless steel, with stainless steel spring-wire and red paint; on aluminium and wood base. [152 high]. New York, The Jeffrey H. Loria Collection. From the artist, to Collection Miriam Gabo; 1980 to Loria. *See illus. p. 129 and back cover*

Exh: E112 Brussels (1958) No. 96, fig. p. 202 : E120 Kassel (1959) Gabo No. 2 : E132 New York (1960–61) No. 28, fig. p. 16 : E17 Amsterdam (1965) No. P19 : E18 Mannheim etc. (1965) No. 18, fig. : E19 Zurich (1965) No. 18, fig. 10 : E20 Stockholm (1965–6) No. 76 : E21 London (1966) No. 22, fig. 8 : E22 Buffalo (1968) No. 12 : E23 Humlebaek etc. (1970–71) No. 6, colour fig. on cover : E24 Berlin (1971) No. 5, colour fig. on cover : E25 Hannover (1971) No. 5, figs p. 71 (detail), p. 11 *in situ* E22 : E26 Grenoble etc. (1971–2) No. 5 : E27 Lisbon (1972) No. 5.

Lit: N12 Bollman (1957) fig. p. 6 : B33 (1959–62) fig. p. 32 : G30 (1962) colour fig. 37 : E160 London (1964) fig. : A103 Granath (1966) fig. p. 13 *in situ* E20 : A219 Webb (1966) fig. 5 : A208 Thompson (1966) colour fig. p. 134 : A105 Gray (1966) figs p. 55, p. 53 *in situ* E21 : A9 (1968) fig. p. 43 *in situ* E22 : A54 Besset (1971) fig. p. 11 : A 210 Thurston (1976) colour fig. p. 16.

The base of this version differs from 62.3 in having wood beneath the aluminium. Although it is usually dated 1953, 62.4 may have been started in 1957. A photograph, probably taken in December 1957, shows Gabo doing some preliminary work on 62.4 (N12). It was clearly finished by April 1958 for inclusion in the Brussels exhibition (E112).

63. LINEAR CONSTRUCTION IN SPACE NO. 2 (VARIATION)

This variation of *Linear Construction in Space No. 2* (55) has been listed separately because the basic form, the shape of the two intersecting Perspex planes, is quite different. A piece of plastic similar in shape to one of these planes is visible in a photograph reproduced by Chanin in 1953 (A72, lower fig. p. 36). From this piece of plastic, Gabo seems to have cut an element for a tiny model of *Linear Construction in Space No. 2* (55).

The two drawings visible in the same illustration also show how 63 can be related to *Monument to the Astronauts* (80), and to *Model for a Hanging Construction* (65). 65 developed from the drawing shown on the left of the illustration, whilst 80 is related to both drawings. A paper model (Family Collection), resembling the model for *Monument to the Astronauts,* has a curved section excised and is marked with pencil, so that when the model is flattened it conforms with the outline of the left-hand drawing which represents the basic form of 63 (A72 p. 36).

Michael Mazur has compared elements in Gabo's wood-engraving *Opus 5* of 1950, with *Spiral Theme,* 52 (A138 p. 150; for *Opus 5,* see G28 fig. 130). However, in the form and orientation of the two intersecting planes, *Opus 5* seems closer to 63.

63.1 Linear Construction in Space No. 2 (Variation)

[1953]. Not inscribed. Perspex with nylon monofilament. [22.1 long]. Lexington, Massachusetts: Private Collection. Gift from the artist [1953].

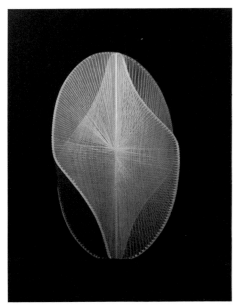

In an undated letter the present owners referred to their recent acquisition of 63.1 and to the Gabos' new home in Middlebury. This suggests that they acquired 63.1 in late 1953.

63.2 Linear Construction in Space No. 2 (Variation)

1954/5. Perspex with nylon monofilament. Formerly, Connecticut, Collection Mr and Mrs Henry F. Miller; destroyed 1955/61. From the artist, (1954)/1955.

Gabo made this work in 1954/5 (letters to and from H. Miller, 27 Feb 1954, 11 Jul 1955). This work was accidentally and irreparably damaged sometime after 1955, and in *c.* 1961 Gabo used the pieces to make a new construction, *Linear Bas-Relief* (66.7).

64. REPOSE

1953. Inscribed faintly, at back: ›G‹. Carrara marble; on base of Perspex, aluminium and wood. *c.* 19 high x 60 diameter, including stone *c.* 15 high x 30. London, Family Collection. *See illus. pp. 77 and 130*

Exh: E14 Hartford (1953) No. 15, fig. 12 : E102 Boston (1954) : E15 Rotterdam etc. (1958) No. 20, fig. : [E162 Milan (1964) No. 3, fig. p. 32] : E17 Amsterdam (1965) No. P18 : E18 Mannheim etc. (1965) No. 17 : E19 Zurich (1965) No. 17 : E20 Stockholm (1965–6) No. 75, fig. : E21 London (1966) No. 21 : E22 Buffalo (1968) No. 14.

Lit: G28 (1957) p. 184, fig. 94 : B116 Kuh (1962) fig. 46 : G31 (1966) fig. p. 132 : A103 Granath (1966) fig. p. 13 *in situ* E20.

65. MODEL FOR A HANGING CONSTRUCTION

c. 1953/5. Not inscribed. [Rhodoid]. 11.1 high x 19.7. London, Tate Gallery (T02193). Presented by the artist, 1977.

Exh: E28 London (1976–7) No. 88, as ›c. 1955‹.

Lit: B3 Alley (1981) pp. 260–61, fig.

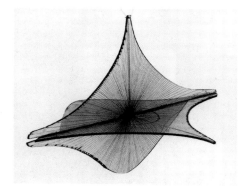

This model has a slight bluish tinge, which suggests that it may be made of Rhodoid. Incised in the centre of one of the planes of 65 is a circle, similar to the circles in Gabo's wood-engraving *Opus 5* (see also 63).

66. LINEAR RELIEF CONSTRUCTION FOR THE BIJENKORF BUILDING, ROTTERDAM
(NOT EXECUTED)

Gabo's construction for the Bijenkorf Building in Rotterdam was the largest public commission he ever received (67). The department store, designed by Marcel Breuer and A. Elzas, was a major investment for the company, NV Koninklijke Bijenkorf Beheer KBB, and for the City of Rotterdam it represented an important element in post-war reconstruction. Not surprisingly therefore the overall project was not completed without some difficult negotiations, and at times Gabo doubted that his construction would ever be completed.

The Town-Planning Department of Rotterdam stipulated that a large projection should be added to the façade of the Bijenkorf on the Coolsingel, and it was suggested that this effect could be achieved with a sculpture (letter to H. Read, 19 Nov 1954, UVBC). At this point the architects and Dr G. Van der Wal, Director of the Bijenkorf, approached Gabo with whom they discussed the project in London on 2 June (telegram from G. Van der Wal, 29 May 1954). Two weeks later Gabo was commissioned to produce a scale model (1 : 100), for a construction to be attached to the side of the building. On acceptance of this model, Gabo would be required to make a larger model and to supervise the final fabrication and installation (letter from M. Breuer, 21 Jun 1954). The final construction was ›to fill out a space 60 feet high, 45 feet wide and 12 feet deep‹ (letter to H. Read, 19 Nov 1954, UVBC).

Gabo delivered the model to Amsterdam in September 1954 (telegram from G. Van der Wal, 4 Sep 1954). Designed to extend upwards from the first storey, it comprised five elements: a central con-

struction (66.5), surrounded by four ›linear forms‹ (66.1–4). These five pieces, constituting one work, are now dispersed and are therefore entered separately. The complete design was recorded in a series of photographs of the plans and of the model (album, n. d., Yale 1).

This first design, however, was rejected by the Town-Planning Department, on the grounds that it did not balance another projection from a building further down the street (letter to H. Read, 19 Nov 1954, UVBC). For Gabo's final solution, see 67.

66.1 Linear Form (Part of the Model for the First Bijenkorf Project)

1954. Not inscribed. Plastic with metal wire. 6.8 long. London, Tate Gallery (T02189). Presented by the artist, 1977.

Exh: E28 London (1976–7) No. 87, as one of ›Three Untitled Models (Variations on a Theme) *c.* 1953‹.

Lit: B3 Alley (1981) pp. 258–9, fig.

66.2 Linear Form (Probably Part of the Model for the First Bijenkorf Project)

1954. Not inscribed. Plastic with metal wire. 5.9 long. London, Tate Gallery (T02190). Presented by the artist, 1977.

Exh: E28 London (1976–7) No. 87.

Lit: B3 Alley (1981) p. 259, fig.

66.3 Linear Form (Possibly Part of the Model for the First Bijenkorf Project)

1954. Not inscribed. Plastic with metal wire. 5.7 long. London, Tate Gallery (T02191). Presented by the artist, 1977.

Lit: B3 Alley (1981) p. 259, fig.

66.4 Linear Form (Part of the Model for the First Bijenkorf Project)

1954. [Plastic with metal wire]. Formerly in the possession of the artist; lost, presumed destroyed.

66.5 Linear Bas-Relief (Part of the Model for the First Bijenkorf Project)

1954. [Plastic with metal wire]. [Size as 66.6]. Formerly in the possession of the artist; lost, presumed destroyed.

66.6 Linear Bas-Relief (Duplicate Part of the Model for the First Bijenkorf Project)

1954. Not inscribed.
Plastic with rolled-gold wire. 7.5 x 5.9 x 3.
London, Family Collection.

66.6 was found in 1984. It does not appear to be the original model for this central element, because it does not have the hole in the back which is shown in photographs of the complete model. It is probably a duplicate.

Although the first Bijenkorf Project was rejected, Gabo enlarged this central section as *Linear Bas-Relief* (66.7), and this is the title used here. 66.6 is very similar to the central elements in the *Model for a Fountain in 52nd Street Lobby, Esso Building, Rockefeller Center, New York* (56.4). 66.6 has a shorter support than the elements in 56.4, which suggests that 66.6 was not made for the Esso Project.

66.6 is related to *Linear Construction in Space No. 2* (55), and to the *Variation* (63). The first version of 63 predated the Bijenkorf commission by about a year.

Judging from photographs of the complete model, 66.5 was to be mounted directly on to the wall of the building, within a frame formed by cutting a hexagonal hole in an octagonal sheet. This design linked the construction with the hexagonal blocks of the façade.

66.7 Linear Bas-Relief

c. 1961. Inscribed bottom left: ›Gabo‹.
Perspex with nylon monofilament; on black Perspex base. 39.5 x *c.* 29 x *c.* 16.5,
on integral black Perspex sheet
40 x 40 x [*c.* 2].
London, Marlborough Fine Art.
From the artist, Aug 1962 to Otto Gerson Gallery, New York; 1963 to Marlborough-Gerson Gallery, New York; to London.

Exh: E245 Münster etc. (1980) No. 121, fig. p. 208.

This title was used by Otto Gerson in 1962 when he acquired 66.7 (letter from O. Gerson, 31 Aug 1962). According to Miriam Gabo, 66.7 was made from the pieces of 63.2. The hole at the top of the relief, from which the original construction was suspended, is still visible at the back. 66.7 was not made in connection with the Bijenkorf commission, but is included here because it is an enlargement of 66.5. In late 1962 it was repaired (letter from O. Gerson, 9 Oct 1962).

67. CONSTRUCTION FOR THE BIJENKORF BUILDING, ROTTERDAM

In November 1954, after Gabo's first design for the Bijenkorf had been rejected (66), Marcel Breuer discussed with Gabo and the City authorities, the possibility of erecting a free-standing construction (telegram from Dr Van der Wal to M. Breuer, 26 Nov 1954). Gabo was commissioned to make a small scale-model (1 : 100), to be followed by a large scale-model ›about 6 ft.‹ high (agreement, 1 Jan 1955). These models were accepted, and the monument was constructed under Gabo's supervision, by the engineering firm Hollandia of Rotterdam.

In January 1956 Gabo wrote to Herbert Read about this construction:
›The organic structure in the world of plants provided for me the solution for the new conception which I needed. There in the world of plants, in the structure of a tree . . . there lies a structural principle which was, as far as I know, neglected, yet which could be with great advantage applied to many a structural task. In particular, I felt it was there that I had to look for a solution of my structural problem and once this principle became evident to me, the image of the whole sculpture evolved out of it naturally. I conceived it as a tree, the trunk, the roots and the branches . . .‹ (letter to H. Read, 10 Jan 1956, UVBC).

This work has attracted various nicknames: ›the Flower‹, ›the Tree‹, and even the title ›Herbium bicovium Gaboï‹ (A33). Occasionally it has been implied that the work is situated in Amsterdam, probably because the head office of the Bijenkorf group is there.

67.1 Linear Form (Curved)

[1954/5]. Not inscribed.
Plastic with metal wires. 8.6 high.
London, Tate Gallery (T02192).
Presented by the artist, 1977.

Exh: E28 London (1976–7) No. 87, as one of ›Three Untitled Models (Variations on a Theme) *c.* 1953‹.

Lit: B3 Alley (1981) p. 259, fig. as ›1954‹.

This small model is entered here because it seems to relate to the lower central element in the final construction. It resembles the structure used in the centre of *Linear Construction in Space No. 3, with Red* of 1953 (62), but the latter has straight sides, and the points of the interlocking triangles are not truncated.

67.2 Model for a Construction outside the Bijenkorf Building, Rotterdam

1954/5. Not inscribed.
Plastic. 25.1 high.
London, Tate Gallery (T02188).
Presented by the artist, 1977.

Exh: E28 London (1976–7) No. 84, fig. p. 44.

Lit: B222 Van Traa (1955) fig. p. 159 : B3 Alley (1981) pp. 259–60, fig., as ›1955‹.

Gabo made two models in this size, the original model constructed in 1954/5, and a duplicate made between July and September 1955 (67.2–3). Gabo presented his first model for approval by the Board of the Bijenkorf in May 1955 (minutes of meeting, 23 May 1955). This original model included a collar around the base, to give additional support to the long vertical elements. In July 1955 Van der Wal asked Gabo to make a duplicate small

model, to facilitate discussion of the project in Holland. In September 1955 Gabo reported that the duplicate was nearing completion, and that he had decided to eliminate the collar (letter to G. Van der Wal, 23 Sep 1955). This suggests that the duplicate model was made without a collar, although it is not known whether Gabo also removed the collar from the original model.

There is no record of when the duplicate model was completed and delivered to Rotterdam in 1955, or when it was returned to Gabo. On 26 June 1957, after the unveiling of 67.5, Gabo sent a 1 : 100 scale model to Rotterdam to be displayed beside the architectural model (letter from R. 't Hooft, 29 May 1957, with M. Gabo annotation). It is uncertain whether Gabo sent the original model or the duplicate. Presumably the model that Gabo sent had no collar to conform with 67.5. It seems probable that if Gabo had the duplicate, he would have sent it, whether or not the original model still had its collar.

The original model has been tentatively identified with 67.2 on the assumption that the collar had been removed by 1977, when Gabo presented 67.2 to the Tate Gallery. Although the Tate model shows no marks to indicate that a collar was initially fixed to its base, the collar may have been attached in such a way that no marks remained. It is possible, however, that the collar was not removed from the original model, in which case, it is the original model which has been lost, and the model in the Tate is the duplicate, which must have been returned to Gabo from Rotterdam.

The illustration in B222 shows the original model (with collar), *in situ* on an architectural model of the building.

67.3 Duplicate Model for a Construction outside the Bijenkorf Building, Rotterdam

1955. [Plastic]. [25.1 high].
Formerly N. V. Koninklijke Bijenkorf N. V., Amsterdam; present whereabouts unknown.
From the artist, June 1957.

See 67.2.

67.4 Final Model for the Bijenkorf Construction, Rotterdam

1955. Not inscribed.
Brass, copper, and steel; on black marble base. [145 high; on base 50 x 64 x 34].
Amsterdam, Headquarters of N. V. Koninklijke Bijenkorf Beheer KBB.
From the artist, Oct 1955.

Exh: E120 Kassel (1959) Gabo No. 3 : E149 Vienna (1962) No. 206, fig.

Lit: A47 [Banham] (1956) fig. : G28 (1957) p. 184, figs 98–9 : A19 (1957) fig. p. 18 : B3 Alley (1981) pp. 259–60.

After 67.2 had been approved by the Rotterdam authorities in May 1955, the task of constructing the large scale model was entrusted to the modelmaker Joseph F. Reed, Jr., of Omega Inc., Litchfield, Connecticut (letter M. Breuer to J. Reed,

19 Jul 1955). A photograph (FAL), shows Gabo and Reed with a wooden form which was used to bend parts of the model (Family Collection).

Apparently Gabo did the work on the inner structure of the large model (letters to G. Van der Wal, 21 Jul, 11 and 23 Sep 1955). As the work progressed, Gabo decided to eliminate the collar (letter to G. Van der Wal, 23 Sep 1955). Dr Van der Wal was concerned that this might entail a new round of negotiations, but assured Gabo of his support (letter, 30 Sep 1955).

In October 1955 the large model was shipped to Amsterdam (letters to Keating's, 11 Oct 1955, and to G. Van der Wal, 16 Oct 1955). The deadline had prevented Gabo and Mr Reed from finishing the inner structure as well as Gabo would have liked (letters to G. Van der Wal and to M. Breuer, 16 Oct 1955). In transit a few soldered joints came apart. These were resoldered in Holland, and thin pins were added (telegram from G. Van der Wal, 18 Oct 1955; letter from C. Eweg, 21 Oct 1955).

This altered model was accepted by the Board of the Bijenkorf (letter from G. Van der Wal, n. d., M. Gabo annotation, 4 Nov 1955). The official acceptance by the Rotterdam authorities arrived in January 1956 (letter from G. Van der Wal, 27 Jan 1956).

The structure was examined by the Institut T.N.O. voor Bouwmaterialen en Bouwconstructies, Amsterdam. 67.4 and an expendable model, constructed in Holland from stainless steel, was subjected to a series of wind-tunnel tests at the National Luchtvaart Laboratorium (minutes of meeting between Ir. Burkey and De Jager of Hollandia, Ir. Bouma and Ir. Bouwkamp of TNO, Gabo and Van der Wal, 13 Oct 1956; A34). The reports were sent to Gabo in February 1957 (Reports Nos B-56−778, B-57−188, letter from J. Bouwkamp, 27 Feb 1957).

In September 1956 Gabo requested the return of the inner structure, to enable him to make some adjustments (letter to G. Van der Wal, 17 Sep 1956). The large model had also been damaged and required repair, for which Gabo agreed to send some bronze springs (letter from G. Van der Wal, 26 Sep 1956; minutes of meeting, 13 Oct 1956).

67.5   The Bijenkorf Construction

1956−7. Pre-stressed concrete, steel ribs, stainless steel, bronze wire, and marble.
[*c.* 25 metres high].
Rotterdam, outside the building of N. V. Magazijn De Bijenkorf on the Coolsingel.
Commissioned from the artist, 1 Jan 1955; 21 May 1957 unveiled.
See illus. p. 42, fig. 50

Exh: E122 Washington etc. (1959) as photograph : E28 London (1976−7) No. 85, as photograph, fig. p. 45.

Lit: G27 (1956) p. 24 : G28 (1957) pp. 8, 10, 184, fig. 100, fig. p. 186 : B177 Read (1957) fig. 4 : A174 Schweicher (1957) pp. 27−32, six figs : A145 Mumford (1957) pp. 91−8 : A8 (1957) figs pp. 169, 171, 175, colour fig. on cover : N12 Bollman (1957) figs p. 6 : A52 Berger (1958) pp. 724−5 : B204 Seuphor (1959) p. 211 : A152 Palme (1959) fig. p. 67 : B76 Giedion-Welcker (1960) figs pp. 184−5 : A183 Sjöberg (1960) fig. p. 191 : B220 Trier (1961)

figs 212−13 : B116 Kuh (1962) p. 100, fig. 44 : B137 Maillard (1962) fig. p. 103 : A2 Alvard (1962) fig. p. 4 : A225 Xagoraris (1962) fig. 14 : B186 Robb *et al* (1963) fig. 353 : E21 London (1966) fig. 14 : A208 Thompson (1966) p. 136, fig. p. 133 : A51 Bekkers (1966) p. 35, fig. following p. 32 : B123 Licht (1967) fig. 248 : B146 Moore (1967) pp. 93−5, fig. : B184 Rickey (1967) pp. 31−2, figs 34−5 : B221 Vallier (1967) fig. 101 : A31 (1967) colour fig. p. 98 : B38 Burnham (1968) pp. 37−8, fig. 14 : B119 Kulterman (1968) fig. 254 : A89 Fenton (1969) fig. p. 23 : B93 Hammacher (1969) figs 199, 201 : B233 Zanini (1971) fig. 90 : E25 Hannover (1971) figs pp. 58−9 : B13 Bann (1974) fig. p. 255 : B206 Seuphor (1974) fig. 316 : A114 Hilberry (1976) figs 12a−b : B9 Arnason (1977) figs 508−9.

In July 1956 Hollandia sent Gabo examples of materials with various finishes, and by November Gabo had selected one for 67.5 (letter from Hollandia to M. Breuer, 10 Jul 1956; letter from M. Breuer, 16 Nov 1956). A photograph shows the main beams being twisted through 90 degrees along their length (G28 p. 186).

The structure was finally erected in May 1957 and unveiled by the burgomaster of Rotterdam, Dr. G. E. van Walsum, on 21 May (invitation to ceremony).

In the summer of 1958 the monument had to be repaired because of cracking and corrosion, perhaps resulting from the speed with which the construction had been made, and particularly from the intensive grinding which had been necessary to give it a good finish (letter from J. Bons, 26 Jul 1959). The repairs continued into the summer of 1960, when a fire in the scaffolding caused further damage (letter from J. Bons, 23 May 1960). The springs were destroyed, the marble socle was damaged, and the bronze and plastic coating affected (letters to H. Isaac, 27 May 1960; from J. Bons, 30 Sep 1960). By November 1961 the necessary repairs had been completed, the welded seams renewed, and the steel plates covered with coats of zinc, bronze and plastic (letters from J. Bons, 27 Jun, 10 Nov 1961).

In addition to the references cited, 67.5 has been illustrated in Bijenkorf publications and Rotterdam tourist brochures.

68.   LINEAR CONSTRUCTION IN SPACE NO. 4

The frame of this work is based directly on the form attached to the ceiling in the Baltimore *Construction Suspended in Space* of 1952 (57). In addition to the versions listed here, patterns and one plastic frame for 68 are in the Family Collection.

Gabo planned to attach a motor to 68, or at least to 68.3 (B116 Kuh, p. 96). He did not do this, but he did mount some versions on a pivot so that the piece could be rotated to alter the viewpoint.

Several versions of 68 are strung with spring-wire made from two different metals. In these works, the difference between the metal shows clearly that the centre of 68 contains the form of *Construction in Space: Suspended* of 1957 (70). The centres of two versions (68.9, 68.13), also contain the form of *Vertical Construction No. 1* (73).

68.1   Model for ›Linear Construction in Space No. 4‹

(1954)/1955. Formerly in the possession of the artist; now lost.

In 1960 Gabo stated that the first model for 68 was completed in 1955 (questionnaire, 22 Sep 1960, Whitney Museum). Earlier, Gabo had dated 68.5 ›1954−58‹ (letter to F. Sweet, Art Institute of Chicago, 24 Aug 1959). However, since 68.5 is known to have been made in 1958−9, the date of 1954 must refer either to the conception of 68 or to the date Gabo started making 68.1 According to Miriam Gabo, 68.1 has been lost.

68.2   Linear Construction in Space No. 4

1957. Inscribed: ›Gabo Fecit 1957‹.
Anodised aluminium [stainless steel or beryllium] spring-wire; on aluminium base.
49.5 high, including integral irregular base 1 high.
London, Collection Dr and Mrs Owen Franklin.
From the artist, 1961.

Exh: E166 Edinburgh etc. (1965) No. 31.

Lit: N12 Bollman (1957) fig. p. 6.

A photograph, showing Gabo at work on 68.2, was taken in December 1957 by Don A. Coviello (FAL, reproduced N12). Gabo inscribed the *verso* of this photograph ›1955 *Linear Constr. N4.* (first version)‹. Not all the notches in the frame have been used in the stringing, perhaps because Gabo was not certain of the number required for this, in the first enlargement of 68.

68.3   Linear Construction in Space No. 4

1957−8. Not inscribed.
Perspex with stainless steel spring-wire; on aluminium base. [101.6 high].
New York, Whitney Museum of American Art (58.61): Gift of the Friends of the Whitney Museum.
From the artist, 1958.

Exh: E114 New York (1958−9) No. 12 : E144 New York (1962) No. 30, fig. 32 : E146 New York (1962) fig. : E161 New York (1964) No. 37, fig. p. 63 : E164 New York (1964) No. 4, fig. : E174 New York (1966) No. 317, fig. p. 123.

Lit: G28 (1961) p. 200, fig. 105 : A3 (1959) p. 88, fig. p. 90 : B116 Kuh (1962) p. 96, fig. 43 : A2 Alvard (1962) fig. p. 5 : B92 Hamilton (1970) fig. 226 : B156 (1974) p. 189, fig. p. 115 : A114 Hilberry (1976) fig. 8 : B103 Hibbard (1977) fig. p. 232, colour fig. 120.

Gabo dated this work ›1957−58‹ and stated that it was completed in November 1958 (G28b; questionnaire, 22 Sep 1960, WM). That month, Gabo had explained to Herbert Read that he had not written because he had been busy finishing this

version for the Whitney Annual (E114; letter to
H. Read, 13 Nov 1958, UVBC). This version, like
68.6, has an additional carved Perspex piece in the
centre.

68.4 Linear Construction in Space No. 4

[1957/8]. Not inscribed.
Phosphor-bronze with stainless steel and
phosphor-bronze spring-wire. *c.* 52.5 high,
including integral base 0.3 high.
London, Family Collection.

68.4 is one of the earliest versions of 68 strung
with metal springs in two contrasting tones, and it
was possibly the prototype for later versions strung
in this way, the first of which, 68.5, is dated
1958–9.

68.5 Linear Construction in Space No. 4, in Black and Grey

1958–9. Inscribed on top edge of frame at
centre bottom: ›Gabo‹.
Anodised aluminium with stainless steel
spring-wire. [96.5 high].
Chicago, Art Institute of Chicago
(1958.526): Gift of Mrs Eugene A. Davidson,
formerly Mrs Zurcher.
Commissioned from the artist, 1958; delivered 1959.
See illus. p. 131

Exh: E123 Chicago (1959–60) No. 33, as
›1954–59‹.

Lit: A194 [Sweet] (1960) fig. : G28 (1961) p. 200,
figs 103–4, as ›1959‹ : G30 (1962) colour fig. as
frontispiece, as ›1955‹ : A184 Sjöberg (1964) fig.
p. 24 : B139 Meilach *et al* (1966) fig. 13 : A208
Thompson (1966) colour fig. p. 139 : A51 Bekkers
(1966) fig. following p. 32 : A105 Gray (1966) fig.
p. 51 : B49 Clifford (1968) colour fig. vii : A122
Jürgen-Fischer (1970) fig. p. 20 : B121 M. Levy
(1970) colour fig. ii : B153 Newman (1975) fig.
p. 228 : A114 Hilberry (1976) fig. 9 : B197 Sarff *et
al* (1979) fig. p. 82.

This work was commissioned by the Art Institute of
Chicago, on behalf of Mrs Davidson, in November
1958 (telegram from F. Sweet, AIC, 26 Nov 1958).
Gabo had started working on 68.5 by November
1958, but did not complete it until August 1959
because he was writing his Mellon Lectures (letters
to F. Sweet, 28 Nov 1958, 24 Aug 1959). 68.5 is
usually dated ›1954–58‹, in accordance with
Gabo's note (letter to F. Sweet, 24 Aug 1959; see
also 68.1). There is, however, no evidence that
Gabo started 68.5 before 1958. The sub-title, ›*in
Black and Grey*‹, refers to the two tones of spring-
wire used in 68.5.

68.6 Linear Construction in Space No. 4

1959. Perspex with stainless steel spring-
wire; mounted on a pivot on a black base.
[48 high].
Caracas, Venezuela: Collection the late Mr
Carlos, and Mrs M. Villanueva.
From the artist, 1959/60.

Exh: E140 Caracas (1961) : E202 Caracas (1972)
No. 21.

Lit: G28 (1961) p. 200, n. 105 as ›Vitta Nuova,
Caracas‹ : G30 (1962) colour fig. 41, p. xvi miscaptioned ›Whitney Museum‹ : A208 Thompson (1966)
colour fig. p. 138 : B225 Waddington (1969) colour
fig. 17.

In March 1959 Mr Villanueva bought this work, on
the understanding that it would be completed and
delivered by January 1960 (agreement, 25 Mar
1959). Gabo finished 68.6 in December 1959 (letter
to C. Villanueva, 6 Dec 1959).
    This version is similar to 68.3 in that it is made of
Perspex and has two carved pieces inserted between adjacent edges of the frame. It differs, however, from 68.3 in that it is smaller; has fewer
notches along each edge; the black Perspex base
is rectangular, not kidney-shaped; and the attachment to the base is much less obtrusive.
    A plaster mould of the carved Perspex pieces
was made in case Gabo wanted to repeat this version (dimensions 6.3 x 23.5 x 10.2). In 1978 Miriam
Gabo presented the mould and a wooden carving
for 68.6 (*c.* 3½ inches high), to the Whitney
Museum, which owns 68.3.

68.7 Linear Construction in Space No. 4

1959. Not inscribed.
Aluminium with stainless steel spring-wire;
on aluminium base. [48.3 high].
Los Angeles, Los Angeles County Museum
of Art (M79.14): Gift of Anna Bing Arnold.
From the artist, Apr 1961 to Otto Gerson
Gallery, New York with Claude Bernard
Haim, Paris; 1963 to Marlborough-Gerson
Gallery, New York; July 1963 to E. J.
Power, London; [early 1970s] to William Pall
Gallery, New York; [1976] to Mitchell C.
Shaheen, Brett Mitchell Collection Inc.
Lyndhurst, Ohio; 31 Oct 1978 through
Christie's to Los Angeles.

Exh: E148 Düsseldorf (1962) as ›1960‹ : E154
London (1963) No. 31, fig. : E207 London (1973)
fig. on cover.

Lit: A51 Bekkers (1966) fig. following p. 32 : B48
[1977], figs p. 5, on cover : S5 New York (1978)
No.. 55, colour fig. p. 119 : A49 Barron (1980)
pp. 71, 74–7, figs 6, 7, 10–11 : A32 (1980) pp.
86–7, fig.

The Museum's title for 68.7 is simply *Linear Construction No. 4*. 68.7 was probably purchased by
Otto Gerson in April 1961 (letter from O. Gerson,
20 Apr 1961). In July 1963 it was sold to E. J.
Power (letter from F. Lloyd, 26 Jul 1963).

68.8 Linear Construction in Space No. 4

1959. Inscribed on base: ›Gabo‹.
Bronze with phosphor-bronze wires.
[101.6 high].
Zurich, Private Collection.
From the artist, 1963 to Marlborough-Ger-
son Gallery, New York; Jan 1964 to Zurich.

Exh: E19 Zurich (1965) No. 92, as ›97 cm‹.

This version was purchased by the Marlborough-
Gerson Gallery in 1963, and the materials were described as ›brass and phosphorbronze‹ (letter from
F. Lloyd, 5 Oct 1963). It was sold to Zurich in 1964
(letter from B. Reis, 30 Jun 1965).

68.9 Linear Construction in Space No. 4

1959–61. Bronze with bronze and stainless
steel spring-wire. [52 high].
Paris, Private Collection.
From the artist [1969] to Marlborough Fine
Art, London; before 1981 to Paris.

Exh: E198 London (1972) No. 25, colour fig. p. 51,
as ›*Model for Linear Construction No. 4 1959–61*‹.

68.9 was probably acquired by Marlborough in
1969 as part of the settlement of the lawsuit with
Gabo. It was subsequently sold to Paris.

68.10 Linear Construction in Space No. 4

1959–61. Inscribed back lower centre:
›Gabo‹.
Aluminium with stainless steel spring-wire.
[99.1 high].
Washington, DC: Hirshhorn Museum and
Sculpture Garden, Smithsonian Institution.
From the artist 1962 to Fine Art Associ-
ates, New York; 13 Nov 1962 to Collec-
tion Joseph H. Hirshhorn, New York; by
1974 to Museum.

Exh: E147 New York (1962) No. 3, fig. : E155 Hartford (1963) No. 7 : E173 Cleveland (1966) No.
139 a, fig. : E213 Washington (1974–5) : E216
Washington (1976) No. 175, fig. p. 357.

Lit: E213 Lerner (1974) p. 693, fig. 655 : B140
Merillat (1974) p. 149, fig. 57 : A114 Hilberry (1976)
fig. 10 : A168 Rickey (1977) fig. p. 25.

Otto Gerson and Claude Bernard Haim purchased
this version in 1962 (letter from O. Gerson, 7 Mar
1962).

68.11 Linear Construction in Space No. 4

1962. Not inscribed.
Bronze with stainless steel spring-wire;
set in a rectangular limestone base.
[128.3 high].

Detroit, Institute of Arts (72.437) : Gift of
W. Hawkins Ferry, 1972.
From the artist, before 1965 to Collection
Miriam Gabo; 1972 to Detroit.

Exh: E17 Amsterdam (1965) No. P23 : E18 Mann-
heim etc. (1965) No. 23 : E19 Zurich (1965) No. 23 :
E20 Stockholm (1965–6) No. 81 : E21 London
(1966) No. 28, fig. 11 : E22 Buffalo (1968) No. 17 :
E190 Pittsburg (1970–71) No. 66, fig., as ›1964‹ :
E205 Detroit (1973) fig. 12.

Lit: A103 Granath (1966) fig. p. 13 *in situ* E20 : A70
Causey (1966) fig. p. 35 *in situ* E21 : A75 Clay
(1966) fig. p. 116 *in situ* E20 : A222 Whitford (1966)
fig. 4 : A105 Gray (1966) fig. p. 49 *in situ* E19 : A37
Arkus (1970) fig. p. 308 : E25 Hannover (1971) fig.
p. 67 : A114 Hilberry (1976) p. 178, figs 1, 11 :
B197 Sarff *et al* (1979) fig. p. 72.

When this work was first exhibited in 1965, it was
dated 1962 (E17). The centre of 68.11 originally
contained *Vertical Construction No. 1* (73.1), as
shown in photographs of 68.11 in exhibitions in
1966 (e.g. A70). Subsequently, during alterations to
68.11, Gabo and Charles Wilson removed 73.1.

68.12 Linear Construction in Space No. 4 (Variation No. 2)

Completed 1963. Not inscribed.
Phosphor-bronze, brass with stainless
steel spring-wire. [51.8 high, including in-
tegral base 3.5 high].
Los Angeles, Collection Frederick Weis-
man Company.
From the artist, 1963 to Marlborough-
Gerson Gallery, New York; Sept 1964 to
Los Angeles.

Lit: B28 Bowness (1965) fig. p. 137, as ›1962–64‹ :
[A76 Clay (1966) colour fig. p. 57] : A49 Barron
(1980) p. 79, n. 33.

This work is strung with stainless steel springs in
the centre and brass strings on the periphery. Marlborough bought this work in 1963, as ›*Linear Construction in Space No. 4 (Variation No. 2)*‹ (letter
from F. Lloyd, 5 Oct 1963).

68.13 Linear Construction in Space No. 4

1970. Not inscribed.
Aluminium with stainless steel spring-wire.
[211.5 high].
Paris, Centre Georges Pompidou, Musée
National d'Art Moderne (AM1973–35).
From the artist, 1973 to Musée National
d'Art Moderne, Paris.
See illus. p. 147

Exh: E23 Humlebaek etc. (1970–71) No. 20, colour
fig. p. 13 : E24 Berlin (1971) No. 17, colour fig.
p. 15 : E25 Hannover (1971) No. 17, fig. p. 9 *in situ*
E23, colour fig. p. 7 : E26 Grenoble etc. (1971–2)
No. 19, fig. : E27 Lisbon (1972) No. 18, fig. p. 24.

Lit: F12 Littlewood (1973) fig. : B69 Futagawa
(1977) fig. p. 24.

The base of this version, like that of 68.14, consists
of two arches, which intersect at right-angles, and
rest on an irregularly shaped flat plate. The similarity
of the bases suggests that 68.13 and 68.14 were
probably made at approximately the same time.

68.14 Linear Construction in Space No. 4

[c. 1970]. Phosphor-bronze with stainless
steel and phosphor-bronze spring-wire; on
phosphor-bronze base. 78.7 high, including integral base 0.3 high.
London, Family Collection.
See illus. p. 132

This is strung with stainless steel springs in the
centre and phosphor-bronze springs on the
periphery. The phosphor-bronze is quite reddish,
implying a high copper content. The base is similar
to 68.13.

69. BAS-RELIEF FOR THE U.S. RUBBER COMPANY BUILDING, NEW YORK

A drawing, reproduced by A. L. Chanin in
November 1953 indicates that Gabo had conceived
the form of 69 by then (A72 p. 36). It is not known
precisely when Gabo was first approached for this
commission, but it was evidently before March
1955 (see 69.1). It is possible that Gabo proposed
an already existing design, as he had done for
Monument for an Airport (35).
    The central portion of this construction has been
compared with *Linear Construction in Space No. 3,
with Red*, 62 (A72). The design also resembles the
wood-engraving *Opus 6*, of which Gabo wrote: ›I
made *Opus 6* . . . about 1955–56 as a sketch for
the bas-relief which I did for the lobby of the U.S.
Building in Radio City, NY‹ (B3 p. 260). It seems
that both the print and the relief were derived from
the drawing of 1953 (A72).

69.1 Model for the ›Bas-relief for the U.S. Rubber Company Building, New York‹

(1954)/1955. Not inscribed.
Red and white plastic with nylon and wire,
on black marble. [66 high x 55.9].
Zurich, Marlborough Galerie.
From the artist, 1955/6 to Collection Nelson
A. Rockefeller, New York; to Marlborough.

Exh: E15 Rotterdam etc. (1958) No. 22.

In March 1955 Gabo stated that he did not expect
remuneration for the little ›sketch model‹ that he
had shown Wallace Harrison, but that he would
expect payment if a larger scale model, ›showing
the structure and materials‹, was required (letter to
W. Harrison, 13 Mar 1955). In December 1955
Gabo received a slab of marble that had broken in
transit. He wrote: ›I don't know yet whether I will be
able to use it for the model. I may think about
some other means of presenting my sketch for the

sculpture‹ (letter to W. Harrison, 1 Dec [1955]). It is
not clear whether this ›sketch‹ was the model presented in March 1955, or a second, larger model.
69.1 appears to show the materials and structure
of the final work, but since it is the only model
known, and Gabo continually referred to it as a
›sketch‹, it may have been the only model executed. The marble slab may have been supplied
merely for the presentation of the ›sketch‹, rather
than to make a new model.

69.2 Bas-relief for the US Rubber Company Building, New York

1956. Signed with aluminium cut-out:
›Gabo‹.
Cast aluminium covered with translucent
plastic, phosphor-bronze and plastic.
[305 diameter x 45.7].
New York, Celanese Building, Avenue of the
Americas.
From the artist, 1956, commissioned by the
architects, Harrison and Abramowitz, for the
US Rubber Company Building, New York;
10 Dec 1956 unveiled; 1976/7 to Celanese
Building.

Exh: E126 New York (1960) No. 49, as photograph,
fig. p. 33 : E28 London (1976–7) No. 80, as photograph.

Lit: G28 (1957) p. 184, fig. 101 : A19 (1957) fig.
p. 20 : A8 (1957) fig. p. 178.

In January 1956 it was agreed that Gabo should
execute the full-scale work, and receive payment
for the ›sketch model‹ which he had left with
Wallace Harrison for Mr Nelson Rockefeller to ex-
amine (letter to W. Harrison, 26 Jan 1956).
    The construction was unveiled on 10 December
1956. The task of bonding the plastic on to the
metal was completed by Dura Plastics in September 1956, using ›Acryloid 13.7‹, a glue made by
Rohm and Haas (letters from Dura Plastics, 25 Sep
1956; to Dr J. Sisson, 16 Oct 1957).

70. CONSTRUCTION IN SPACE: SUSPENDED

This work corresponds to an element in the centre
of *Linear Construction in Space No. 4* (see introduction to 68). In addition to the normal listing of
size and materials, certain distinctive features present in some versions of 70, e.g. the presence of
Perspex supports to the cradle, square as opposed
to rounded cradle-ends, and the presence of feet
on the base, are noted where known.

70.1 Model for ›Construction in Space: Suspended‹

1957/(65). Not inscribed.
Perspex with nylon monofilament.
10.3 x 10.1 x 4.
London, Tate Gallery (T02196).
Presented by the artist, 1977.

Exh: E28 London (1976–7) No. 91.

Lit: B3 Alley (1981) p. 262, fig.

When the first enlargement of 70 was exhibited in 1963, it was dated 1957, and the same date was given to an unidentified version of 70 exhibited in 1964 (70.3; E156; E159). In 1966 Gabo stressed that the original version of 70 was made in 1957 (letter to G. Lloyd, 26 Feb 1966). Gabo may have been referring to the fact that the form of 70 was already present in the central sections of *Linear Construction in Space No. 4*, the first enlargement of which was made in 1957 (68.2). Nevertheless, it seems probable that Gabo would have made a model before he made the first enlargement of 70 in 1957 (70.3). Yet, when 70.1 was exhibited in 1976–7, it was dated 1965 (E28). It is possible that 70.1 is not the original model and was made in 1965. However, it is the only such model known to have been made and it seems more likely that it was made in 1957.

70.2 Model for Variation of ›Construction in Space: Suspended‹

1957/(65). Not inscribed.
Perspex with cotton thread.
4.3 x 10.4 x 10.
London, Tate Gallery Archive (Gabo 801).
Presented by the trustees of the estate of the artist, 1980.

Lit: B3 Alley (1981) p. 262.

This model differs from 70.1 in the way it is strung. The two planes of 70.2 are each made from three pieces of Perspex glued together. The middle piece of each plane has notches cut along both edges, and these form holes at the junction with the straight edges of the outer pieces. Although there are notches cut across the top of each plane, the stringing only runs through the interior holes. This creates a virtual surface around the centre of the model only. There is no large version like this, although it is possible that Gabo was contemplating making a version with a double, inner and outer, form of stringing.

There is no documentary evidence for dating 70.2, but the use of cotton thread and the crazing of the plastic suggest that it is an early model.

70.3 Construction in Space: Suspended

1957. Inscribed.
Perspex, nylon monofilament; on aluminium base. [55 high x 61].
Formerly Basel, Galerie Beyeler; irreparably damaged 1970/71.
From the artist, 1963 to Collection Bo Boustedt, Sweden; 1970 to Basel.

Exh: E156 Stockholm (1963) No. 24, four figs pp. 22–3, as ›1957‹ : E157 Stockholm (1963–4) No. 88, fig. p. 46 : E158 Oslo etc. (1964–5) No. 24, three figs.

Lit: E25 Hannover (1971) figs pp. 25 and 27, miscaptioned : E27 Lisbon (1972) fig. p. 21.

This version was bought by Bo Boustedt in February 1963, and was delivered by Gabo personally in April of that year (letters from and to B. Boustedt, 15 Feb, 12 Mar 1963; passport entry). In 1971 at the Galerie Beyeler, 70.3 was accidentally dropped and the Perspex section was broken. In February 1971 Boustedt, presumably acting on behalf of the gallery, returned 70.3 to Gabo, who said that the work was irreparably damaged but offered to make him a new one (invoice, 5 Feb 1971, indicating that 70.3 was signed; letter to B. Boustedt, 14 Mar 1971). Boustedt agreed to this and Gabo made a replacement (70.3a; letter from B. Boustedt, 9 Apr 1971).

70.3a Construction in Space: Suspended: Reconstruction

1971. Not inscribed.
Perspex, nylon monofilament, phosphor-bronze cradle; on aluminium base.
[48.5 x 60.2 x 54.8, on integral base 60.7 x 19.1].
USA, Private Collection.
Commissioned from the artist, 1971 by Bo Boustedt for the Galerie Beyeler, Basel; 1975 to USA.

Exh: [E194 Basel (1971) ex-cat.].

Bo Boustedt commissioned this work in April 1971, following the irreparable damage to 70.3 (letter from B. Boustedt, 9 Apr 1971). 70.3a was apparently completed by May 1971 (letter from B. Boustedt, 22 May 1971). Gabo described the replacement as a reconstruction rather than as a restoration (bill, 27 May 1971). On that basis it has been entered here as 70.3a, although it is possible that Gabo may have reused some elements from 70.3.

70.3a has square cradle-ends and the base stands on two recessed but irregularly shaped feet. Although not entered in the catalogue for E194, 70.3a may have been shown since Gabo was listed in the catalogue and 70.3a had been finished and acquired by the gallery in time for the opening.

70.4 Construction in Space: Suspended

1957/64. Inscribed on base: ›Naum Gabo‹.
Perspex, stainless steel spring-wire, phosphor-bronze cradle; on aluminium base.
[Perspex 55.8 x 55.8 x 43, on integral base 1.9 x 68.6 x 20.3].
New Orleans, Museum of Art (64.13): Gift of Mrs Edgar B. Stern, 1964.
From the artist, Feb 1964 to Marlborough-Gerson Gallery, New York; 18 Aug 1964 to New Orleans.

Lit: A4 (1964) fig. p. 392 : B41 Caldwell (1980) p. 91, fig.

70.4 was probably the version of 70 received on commission by the Marlborough-Gerson Gallery in February 1964 (receipts 24 and 25 Feb 1964). It was sold to Mrs Stern on 6 May 1964 (letter from B. Reis, 30 Jun 1965). According to Marlborough, however, this invoice was cancelled, and on 18 August 1964, 70.4 was sold directly to the Museum.

The cradle of this version is supported by two Perspex blocks, the ends of which are slanted, approximately at right-angles to the cradle (see 70.7).

70.5 Construction in Space: Suspended

1957/64; altered c. 1966. Inscribed on top: ›Gabo‹.
Perspex, beryllium spring-wire, phosphor-bronze cradle; on aluminium base.
53 x 62.2 x c. 57, on integral base 1.3 x 68.6 x 19.
New York, Marlborough Gallery.
From the artist, Dec 1964 to Marlborough-Gerson Gallery, New York; 16 Jan 1965 to Collection Mrs Lillian H. Florsheim, Chicago; c. 1966 substantially damaged and reconstructed; c. 1966 directly or indirectly to Marlborough Gallery, New York.

Exh: E228 New York (1978) No. 21, as ›Construction in Space – Suspended Version I 1957–66‹, ›45 x 57 x 60.5 cm‹, fig. p. 23 : E267 New York (1984) No. 23, as ›Version II‹.

This version was acquired by the Marlborough-Gerson Gallery in December 1964 (receipt, 4 Dec 1964; letter to B. Reis, 6 Jul 1965). It was subsequently sold to Mrs Lillian H. Florsheim on 16 January 1965 (letter from B. Reis, 30 Jun 1965).

According to Mrs Florsheim, 70.5, in need of repair, was shipped to one of Gabo's assistants. Unfortunately it was damaged in transit, and was subsequently reconstructed. According to the Marlborough Gallery, this task was probably undertaken by Mr Julius Ternbach.

Apparently, during restoration 70.5 was changed in two ways. First, the Perspex construction was reversed in its cradle, so that the angle of the transverse Perspex piece changed. Secondly, Perspex blocks were introduced under the cradle to provide greater support; these blocks each consist of three separate pieces of Perspex (see E228). These changes are documented by two photographs, both taken by O. E. Nelson and with labels of the ›Marlborough-Gerson Gallery‹ and ›Marlborough Gallery‹ respectively. The first photograph, described on the label as ›Collection: Florsheim‹, shows the work in its original state, with 260 notches across the top of the work, and no supporting Perspex blocks. The second photograph, also of a work with 260 notches, records the two changes made during reconstruction. Both photographs show a few small scratch marks, as if made by a vice, on the edge of the cradle where it meets the base. These similarities suggest that the two photographs show the one work in two different states. 70.5, now in the possession of Marlborough, remains in the state documented by the second photograph, except that the Perspex blocks have since been removed (E267).

Although 70.5 was exhibited in 1978 as ›Version I‹, in 1984 it was shown as ›Version II‹ (E228, E267). The measurements given in the catalogues differ, although the measurements in E267 correspond to those on the first photograph. The measurements given in E228 do not correspond to those on the second photograph, and presumably both sets are inaccurate. The work shown in both instances has to be 70.5, since the only other version of 70 belonging to the Marlborough Gallery still has distinctive Perspex supports under the cradle (70.7). In both catalogues 70.5 was dated ›1957–66‹. Presumably 1957 refers to the first enlargement of this work (70.3), and 1966 to the date of the reconstruction of 70.5.

70.6 Construction in Space: Suspended

(1957)/1964. Inscribed at one end: ›Gabo‹. Perspex, nylon monofilament, yellow paint; on metal base. [*c.* 24.1 x *c.* 29.2 x *c.* 26.7, on integral base *c.* 1.3 x 34.3 x 8.9]. Washington, Conn.: Collection Thomas P. Whitney. From the artist (1957)/1964 to Collection Bernard J. Reis, New York, 6 Nov 1981; sold from his estate through Sotheby Parke Bernet.

Lit: S7 New York (1981) No. 399, colour fig.

In 1967 this work was listed amongst those acquired by Bernard Reis (letter from M. Gabo to C. Israels, 15 Feb 1967). In the centre it contains two small pieces of Perspex, painted yellow.

70.7 Construction in Space: Suspended

(1957)/1966. Inscribed on top and at edge of cradle: ›Gabo‹. Perspex, beryllium spring-wire, bronze cradle; on aluminium base. 46.4 x 57.8 x *c.* 57.2, on integral base 1.3 x 64 x 16. New York, Marlborough Gallery. From the artist, 1966 to Marlborough-Gerson Gallery, New York.

In March 1966 the Marlborough-Gerson Gallery bought a version of 70, which Gabo described as ›signed on the bronze part of the base‹, ›22 x 22 x 7 inches high‹, and made from ›plastic, beryllium springs, bronze, [on] aluminium base‹ (letter to G. Lloyd, 26 Feb 1966; receipt, 4 Mar 1966). This describes 70.7, except that 70.7 is 18⅓ inches high, suggesting that Gabo's figure of 7 inches is an error. The Gallery noted that there were a few notches missing which allowed the wire to slip out of place (receipt, 4 Mar 1966). The cradle rests on a single piece of Perspex, which is cut to the curve of the cradle, and the ends of which almost form a tangent to that curve.

70.8 Construction in Space: Suspended

1959; modified 1969. Not inscribed. Perspex, nylon monofilament, gilded metal cradle; on aluminium base. 24.1 x 29.3 x 26.7, on integral base 1 x 34.2 x 9.9. London, Collection Dr and Mrs Owen Franklin. From the artist, 1964.

Exh: E170 London (1965) fig. on cover.

Lit: A182 (1965) fig. p. 1.

Dr Franklin acquired this work in 1964 (letter from O. Franklin, 1 Aug 1964). According to Dr Franklin, in 1969 Gabo replaced the original beryllium spring-wire with nylon.

70.9 Construction in Space: Suspended

[1961/2]. Not inscribed. Perspex, nylon monofilament, phosphor-bronze cradle; on aluminium base. [49 x 58 x 49, on integral base 2.2 x 60.4 x 19]. Amsterdam, W. Sandberg Collection, Stedelijk Museum (BA545). Presented by the artist, 1962.

Exh: E17 Amsterdam (1965) No. P16, fig. : E219 Treigny (1977) No. 50.

According to Miriam Gabo, it is possible that Gabo met Willi Sandberg in Europe before the Second World War, although they definitely met at Miss Dreier's in the late 1940s or early 1950s. In 1953, as Director of the Stedelijk Museum, Sandberg was a member of the jury which awarded Gabo second prize for his *Monument to the Unknown Political Prisoner* (61.2). Later, Sandberg warmly supported Gabo's project for the Bijenkorf (67), and the large retrospective which opened in Rotterdam in 1958 also travelled to the Stedelijk (E15). In 1962 Sandberg retired as Director, and 70.9 was among other works donated to the Museum's Sandberg Collection, formed in his honour.
The base of 70.9 rests on two bars which are recessed. The cradle has square corners and has been varnished. When 70.9 was exhibited in 1965, it was dated 1949 (E17). This error possibly derived from a list, drawn up by Miriam Gabo in 1965, of works to be sent for the European touring exhibition.

70.10 Construction in Space: Suspended

1962. Inscribed: ›FOR NINA FROM/ PAPA [in cyrillic]/Gabo‹. Perspex, nylon monofilament, red and black acrylic paint, gold-plated [stainless steel] cradle; on stainless steel base. [30.5 x 28 x 28]. London, Family Collection. *See illus. p. 133*

Exh: E28 London (1976–7) No. 92.

70.11 Construction in Space: Suspended

1965. Perspex, nylon monofilament, phosphor-bronze cradle; on aluminium and Perspex base. [57 high]. Formerly in the possession of the artist; damaged and presumed destroyed, 1971.

Exh: E23 Humlebaek etc. (1970–71) No. 14, colour fig. p. 12.

Lit: E24 Berlin (1971) colour fig. p. 27 : E25 Hannover (1971) colour fig. pp. 28–9.

The cradle of 70.11, which had rounded ends, rested on a single piece of Perspex with sloping ends, cut to fit the curve of the cradle. The base was formed from a sheet of Perspex bonded to a sheet of aluminium with a bevelled edge.
While on display at Høvikodden in 1971 (E23), the transverse sheet of this work was broken (letter from O. Moe, 2 Mar 1971; photographs). Gabo found it to be beyond repair, and 70.11 became the subject of an insurance claim (telegram, 14 Apr 1971). If Gabo retained 70.11, it is possible that he reused the cradle and base in 70.13. At subsequent venues on the 1971 exhibition tour (E24, E25), another version of 70, probably 70.12, was substituted.

70.12 Construction in Space: Suspended

[1965]. Inscribed on top of intersection: ›N. Gabo‹, and on tip of the cross-plane: ›Gabo‹. Perspex, nylon monofilament, gilded phosphor-bronze cradle; on aluminium base. 51.3 x 61.6 x 52.7, on integral base 3.2 x 68.5 x 19.1. London, Family Collection. *See illus. pp. 83 and 134*

Exh: E21 London (1966) No. 32 : E22 Buffalo (1968) No. 24 : [E24 Berlin (1971) No. 11] : [E25 Hannover (1971) No. 11] : E26 Grenoble etc. (1971–2) No. 13 : [E27 Lisbon (1972) No. 12] : E268 Shiga (1984).

Lit: N2 Andreae (1968) fig. *in situ* E22 : A54 Besset (1971) fig. p. 8, and on cover *in situ* E26.

The base of 70.12 rests on two long bars, which are slightly recessed. The nylon filament has been repaired with thread at the uppermost edge of the Perspex, near the cradle.
70.12 was probably the version of 70 exhibited in Buffalo in 1968 (E22), because it is the only version of 70 still belonging to Gabo in 1968 that accords with the materials and base of the work shown *in situ* at E22 (N2). It was probably also shown in 1966 in London (E21). In 1971, after 70.11 was broken, Gabo had to substitute another version of 70 in the touring exhibition. As 70.12 was definitely the version shown at Paris in 1971–2 (E26; A54), it seems most probable that it was also shown at the other venues on the tour.

70.13   Construction in Space: Suspended (Variation)

[*c.* 1971]. Not inscribed.
Perspex, nylon monofilament, phosphor-bronze cradle; on aluminium and Perspex base. 53 x 61.9 x 55.9, on integral base 2.5 x 64.1 x 17.8.
London, Family Collection.
See illus. p. 134

This variation is strung in reverse so that the stringing forms concave rather than convex surfaces. This gives 70.13 a distinctive appearance. The base, of aluminium bonded to Perspex; and the phosphor-bronze cradle, with rounded ends, supported by a single piece of Perspex, resemble those used in 70.11. This suggests that Gabo may have reused these elements from his broken construction to make 70.13. If this is correct, 70.13 was probably made [*c.* 1971].

70.14   Construction in Space: Suspended

[*c.* 1971/2]. Inscribed on top edge of transverse sheet: ›Gabo‹.
Perspex, stainless steel spring-wire, gilded phosphor-bronze cradle; on aluminium base. *c.* 26.8 x *c.* 31.1 x *c.* 26.8, on integral base 2.5 x 32 x 9.
London, Private Collection.
From the artist, 1972.

This work was acquired by the present owner in 1972 (letter to Gabo, 17 Mar [1972]).

70.15   Construction in Space: Suspended

[1970s]. Inscribed on corner of base: ›FOR MIRIAM. GABO‹.
Perspex, nylon monofilament, phosphor-bronze cradle; on aluminium base. 27.2 x 31.1 x 27.6, on integral base 2.5 x 32 x 8.9.
London, Family Collection.

The base of 70.15 rests on bars, the ends of which are flush with the edge of the base.

70.16   Construction in Space: Suspended

[1970s]. Inscribed on cradle, beside bolt-heads: ›N. Gabo‹.
Perspex, stainless steel spring-wire, phosphor-bronze cradle; on aluminium base. 27 x 30.5 x 27.5, on integral base 2.5 x 32 x 8.9.
London, Family Collection.

The base of 70.16 rests on bars, the ends of which are flush with the edge of the base. One tip of the cross-plane is slightly chipped, and there is a crack across one angle of the longitudinal plane.

70.17   Construction in Space: Suspended

[1970s]. Inscribed in the upper angle of the longitudinal Perspex plane: ›Gabo‹.
Perspex, stainless steel spring-wire, phosphor-bronze cradle; on aluminium base. 51.8 x 60.3 x 55.2, on integral base 3.2 x 68.5 x 19.1.
London, Family Collection.

Although 70.17 is strung with stainless steel spring-wire, in other respects, it is similar to 70.12. The bars supporting the base are slightly recessed. One of the screws attaching the Perspex to the cradle at the uppermost end is broken.

70.18   Construction in Space: Suspended

[1970s]. Inscribed on top edge of cross-plane; ›Gabo‹.
Perspex, nylon monofilament, phosphor-bronze cradle; on aluminium base. 52.9 x 61.9 x 56.5, on integral base 2.5 x 64 x 17.8.
London, Family Collection.

The cradle of 70.18, which has squared ends, is supported by two Perspex blocks with ends perpendicular to the base. The base is supported by bars, the ends of which are flush with the edge of the base.

70.19   Construction in Space: Suspended

[1970s]. Not inscribed.
Perspex, nylon monofilament; on aluminium base. 52.5 x 62.5 x 55.5, on integral base 2.2 x 68.6 x 19.1.
London, Family Collection.

71.   MODEL FOR HANGING PIECE

c. 1957. Not inscribed.
Plastic. 15.2 high x 8.2.
London, Tate Gallery (T02194).
Presented by the artist, 1977.

Exh: E28 London (1976–7) No. 89.

Lit: B3 Alley (1981) p. 261, fig.

According to Gabo, he made this model in *c.* 1957 but never made an enlargement (B3). The shapes excised from the rounded outer surfaces of this model are similar to the planes of *Linear Construction in Space No. 2* (55).

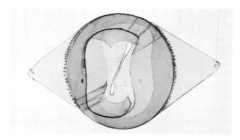

72.   CONSTRUCTION IN SPACE: ARCH NO. 2

The ›*No. 2*‹ of the title is obviously referring to *Construction in Space: Arch* (33) as ›Arch No. 1‹.

A photograph shows an unidentified version of 72, signed ›Gabo‹, with surfaces which are incised with lines radiating outwards from each hole, and a completely metal base (FAL). The work is dated 1960 and its height is given as ›15½″‹ on the verso of the photograph. This version is not entered separately here, because it probably represents the unfinished state of one of the versions listed.

Although Gabo probably made a small, finished model for 72, the only small model known, made of Perspex and in poor condition, may be a later experiment (Family Collection). It is not entered here.

72.1   [Model for] ›Construction in Space: Arch No. 2‹

[1958/60]. [Not inscribed].
Phosphor-bronze. 40 high.
London, Family Collection.

72.1 and 72.2 are probably models, although it is possible that they are unfinished works. If so, they may have been made later than suggested here. 72.1 is not strung, and unlike 72.2, has no holes drilled for stringing. It is made of a redder phosphor-bronze than 72.2.

72.2   [Model for] ›Construction in Space: Arch No 2‹

[1958/60]. [Not inscribed].
Phosphor-bronze. *c.* 40 high.
London, Family Collection.

Lit: B179 Read (1964) p. 293, colour fig. 112 : A210 Thurston (1976) colour fig. p. 17.

72.2 like 72.1, may not be a model, but a later, unfinished work. Markings »B« and »B'« (probably in red crayon), indicate the edges that were to be joined together. Although it is not strung, there are holes for stringing.

Herbert Read reproduced 72.2, but he captioned it incorrectly as 18 inches high, and as belonging to the Marlborough-Gerson Gallery (B179). The only version of 70.2 known to have been through that Gallery now belongs to the Peter Stuyvesant Foundation (72.3). The photographs reproduced by Read and Thurston are identical, and the latter gives the correct height of 84 cms (A210).

72.3   Construction in Space: Arch No. 2

(1958)/1960. Not inscribed.
Bronze. [39 high, on integral base 46 x 45.5].
Amsterdam, The Netherlands: Collection the Peter Stuyvesant Foundation, Liechtenstein.
From the artist [to Otto Gerson Gallery, New York]; [1963] to Marlborough-Gerson Gallery, New York; June 1966 to Stuyvesant Foundation.

Lit: B199 Scheepmaker (1969) p. 71, colour fig.

72.4 Construction in Space: Arch No. 2

(1958)/1963. Not inscribed.
Phosphor-bronze [copper], and stainless
steel spring-wire; on wooden base.
[82.6 high, including integral wooden base
5 x 61 x 61].
London, Family Collection.
See illus. pp. 81 and 135

Exh: E17 Amsterdam (1965) No. P20, fig. : E18
Mannheim etc. (1965) No. 19, fig. : E19 Zurich
(1965) No. 19, fig. 11 : E20 Stockholm (1965–6)
No. 77, fig. : E21 London (1966) No. 24, fig 9 : E22
Buffalo (1968) No. 15, fig. p. 21 : E23 Humlebaek
etc. (1970–71) No. 8, colour fig. p. 11 : E24 Berlin
(1971) No. 7, colour fig. p. 6 : E25 Hannover (1971)
No. 7, colour fig. pp. 40–41, fig. p. 11 *in situ* E23 :
E26 Grenoble etc. (1971–2) No. 8, as ›H. 68 cm‹ :
E27 Lisbon (1972) No. 7, fig. p. 17.

Lit: A184 Sjöberg (1964) fig. p. 25 : A208 Thomp-
son (1966) fig. p. 133 : A93 Forge (1966) fig. p. 42 :
A105 Gray (1966) fig. p. 53 *in situ* E21 : A54
Besset (1971) p. 11, fig. 5.

72.4 is usually dated ›1958/63‹ (e.g. E21). It
seems, however, that it was made in 1963, because in Miriam Gabo's list of works to be exhibited in the European tour of 1965–6, *Arch No. 2*
is annotated ›one shown 1963‹.
    In 72.4, two of the points are mounted on small
hoof-shaped feet, made of layered phosphor-
bronze, possibly interleaved with copper. The other
two points are slotted into round-headed screws.

72.5 Construction in Space: Arch No. 2

(1958)/1964. Phosphor-bronze.
New York, Collection the late
Mr Bernard J., and Mrs Reis.
From the artist, before 1964.

This version was acquired by Bernard Reis sometime before 1964 (letter M. Gabo to C. Israels,
15 Feb 1967). Although the exact dimensions are
unknown, 72.5 is apparently a small version.

**73. VERTICAL CONSTRUCTION
NO. 1**

Until the creation of *Vertical Construction No. 2*
(79), this was known simply as *Vertical
Construction*.
    This group is entered here in the chronological
sequence because the image of 73 was first realised in three dimensions in 1959/61, as the central
element in a version of *Linear Construction in
Space No. 4* (68.9). Gabo later used the same image in a further two versions of *Linear Construction
in Space No. 4* (68.11, 68.13). The model for 73
(73.1), was made in 1962 (see 73.1).

**73.1 Model for ›Vertical Construction
No. 1‹**

1962; after a form of 1959/61. Not inscribed.
Bronze with stainless steel spring-wire; set
in plastic base. [11.6 high, set into base 1.1
high].
London, Tate Gallery (T02195).
Presented by the artist, 1977.

Exh: E28 London (1976–7) No. 90, as ›1964–65‹.

Lit: B3 Alley (1981) pp. 261–2, fig. p. 261.

73.1 formerly constituted the central part of a version of *Linear Construction in Space No. 4* (68.11),
which was made in 1962. 73.1 was removed in
c. 1966, after Gabo had already made the first four
large versions of *Vertical Construction No. 1*
(73.2–5).

73.2 Vertical Construction No. 1

1964/5. Inscribed: ›Gabo‹.
Bronze with stainless steel spring-wire; on
base with bronze plate on light-coloured
wood. [103.2 high, including integral base
4.2 x 26.8 x 26.8].
Los Angeles, Collection Marion and Nathan
Smooke.
From the artist's family, 1983.
See illus. p. 138

Exh: E26 Grenoble etc. (1971–2) No. 12 : E27 Lisbon (1972) No. 11.

73.2 is distinctive in that the wooden stand, on
which the base-plate rests, has arched sides.

73.3 Vertical Construction No. 1

1964–5. Inscribed at base: ›Gabo‹.
Phosphor-bronze with stainless steel spring-
wire, and aluminium; on base with brass
plate on light-coloured wood. [107 high,
including integral base 4 x 27 x 27].
Kobe, Japan: Hyogo Prefectural Museum of
Modern Art.
From the artist, 1967 to Collection Bo
Boustedt, Sweden; 2 May 1974 through
Sotheby Parke Bernet, New York, to Galerie
Denise René-Hans Mayer, Düsseldorf;
15 July 1982 to Seibu Department Stores,
Tokyo; 1984 to Kobe.

Exh: E23 Humlebaek etc. (1970–71) No. 13, fig.
p. 21 : E203 London (1973) No. 37, as ›ex collection Bo Boustedt‹.

Lit: E22 Buffalo (1968) fig. p. 25 : E25 Hannover
(1971) figs. pp. 23, 11 *in situ* E23 : E26 Grenoble
etc. (1971–2) fig. *in situ* E23 : A118 Hultén (1971)
fig. p. 67 : E27 Lisbon (1972) fig. p. 20 : F12 Littlewood (1973) fig. : S3 New York (1974) No. 290,
colour fig. : A186 [Spar] (1975) fig. p. 54.

Bo Boustedt received this work from Gabo in
March 1967 (receipt, 31 Mar 1967). The wooden
stand of 73.3 has grooves cut in its sides.

73.4 Vertical Construction No. 1

1964–5. Inscribed on base: ›Naum Gabo‹.
Phosphor-bronze, stainless steel spring-
wire; on brass base. [99.7 high].
Washington, DC: Hirshhorn Museum and
Sculpture Garden, Smithsonian Institution
(72.122).
From the artist, 28 Nov 1967 to Collection
Joseph H. Hirshhorn, New York; by 1974 to
Museum.

Exh: [E19 Zurich (1965) No. 91, as ›99 cm‹] : [E20
Stockholm (1965–6) No. 84, as ›91 cms‹] : E21
London (1966) No. 31, fig. 13 : E213 Washington
(1974–5) : E216 Washington (1976) No. 176, fig.
p. 358.

Lit: A105 Gray (1966) figs pp. 52, 53 *in situ* E21 :
G31 (1966) fig. p. 132 : A93 Forge (1966) fig. p. 41 :
A164 Read (1968) fig. p. 11 : E213 Lerner (1974)
p. 693, fig. 921.

There are no bronze ›fins‹ at the foot of 73.4, and
the square base-plate does not rest on a wooden
stand.

**73.5 Vertical Construction No. 1
(Variation)**

1964/6. Inscribed on base: ›Gabo‹.
Phosphor-bronze with stainless steel spring-
wire; on [brass] base. [103 high, on base of
side 15.2].
Maryland, USA: Collection Mr and Mrs
Robert H. Levi.
From the artist, 1966 to Marlborough
Gallery, New York; 3 May 1971 to Mary-
land.

Exh: E192 New York (1971) No. 15, fig. p. 33.

The Marlborough-Gerson Gallery acquired this work
in 1966 (receipt, 4 Mar 1966). The metal base plate
of 73.5 stands on four metal cubes. E192 states
incorrectly that 73.5 was exhibited in London in
1966 (E21). An installation photograph shows clearly that the version exhibited was 73.4 (FAL).

73.6 Vertical Construction No. 1

1967. Inscribed on base: ›N. Gabo‹.
Phosphor-bronze with stainless steel and
black spring-wire; on wooden base.
203 high, including integral wooden base
5.7 x 39 x 39.
London, Family Collection.
See illus. pp. 86 and 139

Exh: E22 Buffalo (1968) No. 28, as ›Enlarged 1967‹.

Lit: N2 Andreae (1968) fig. p. 9 : A9 (1968) fig.
p. 43 *in situ* E22.

The metal base-plate of 73.6 is attached to a
wooden block, from which sections have been
removed, leaving four cuboid feet on which the
work stands. 73.6 was shown in Buffalo in 1968,
although 73.3 is illustrated in the catalogue and incorrectly captioned ›Vertical Construction No. 2,
Kinetic with Motor‹ (E22 p. 25).

74. WHITE STONE

This has sometimes been referred to as the
›Madonna Stone‹.

74.1 Model for ›White Stone‹

[1960]. Inscribed on the underside:
›FOR MIRIAM N. GABO 3.4 [60]‹.
Alabaster. 5.5 high x 7.3.
London, Family Collection.

Exh: [E28 London (1976–7) in No. 93, fig. p. 47 in
foreground].

74.1 was probably one of ›Ten miniature carvings‹
exhibited in London in 1976–7 dated ›1960–70‹
(E28; see also 75). The date inscribed on 74.1 is
probably ›3.4.60‹, although it is extremely faint.

74.2 White Stone

1963–4. Inscribed: ›G‹.
Grey marble on black marble with white
veining. 46 high x 59, on integral base
6.8 high x 71.5.
London, Family Collection.

Exh: [E17 Amsterdam (1965) No. P26] : [E18 Mann-
heim etc. (1965) No. 25] : [E19 Zurich (1965)
No. 25] : [E20 Stockholm (1965–6) No. 83] : E21
London (1966) No. 30.

This was one of three works enlarged in Portugal
by Antonio Duarte, under Gabo's supervision, between 1963 and 1965 (see 38.2, 54.2). The three
works were delivered to Gabo in early spring 1965,
and subsequently sent for exhibition in Europe
(receipt, Cohen and Powell, 20 Jan 1965; letter
M. Gabo to R. Duarte, 26 Mar 1965). According
to Miriam Gabo, although 74.2 was entered in the
catalogues for the European touring exhibition of
1965–6 (E17–20), it was only shown in London
(E21).

74.3 Bronze Cast of ›Model for White Stone‹

1972. Bronze. *c.* 5.5 high x 7.3.
London, Family Collection.

According to Miriam Gabo, 74.3 is the cast listed
as ›M‹, made by the Morris Singer Foundry in 1972
(memo from Singer's, [10 Feb 1972]).

75. MINIATURE STONE CARVINGS

Gabo was an incorrigible collector of stones and
pebbles; most of them he picked up himself from
beaches, others were gifts from friends. According
to Miriam Gabo, in 1946 they took a weighty collection with them to the USA. Occasionally Gabo
carved a stone, and a few were later used as models for enlargement. The majority, however, were
only lightly worked and have not been entered here.
   Gabo selected ten small stones to be exhibited in
London in 1976–7 (E28). These definitely included,

the *Model for ›Blue Marble‹* (76.1), and the six
stones which were donated to the Tate Gallery, on
the basis of having been in that exhibition (75.1–6).
The other three stones exhibited were probably
Model for ‹White Stone› (74.1), and two stones
which remain in the Family Collection (75.7–8). The
catalogue for E28 illustrated a selection of small
stones, including *Model for ›Construction in Space:
Stone with a Collar‹* (34.1), which was catalogued
separately as No. 43.
   Many of the stones were probably worked on
repeatedly over a number of years, and according
to Miriam Gabo, the date range of ›1960/70‹ given
in E28 should be treated with caution.

75.1 Carving

c. 1960/70. Not inscribed.
Plaster. [6 high x 12.7].
London, Tate Gallery (T02197).
Presented by the artist, 1977.

Exh: E28 London (1976–7) in No. 93.

Lit: B3 Alley (1981) p. 264, fig.

75.2 Carving

c. 1960/70. Not inscribed.
Stone. [2.5 high x 11.7].
London, Tate Gallery (T02198).
Presented by the artist, 1977.

Exh: E28 London (1976–7) in No. 93.

Lit: B3 Alley (1981) p. 264, fig.

75.3 Carving

c. 1960/70. Not inscribed.
Stone. [3.8 high x 10.5].
London, Tate Gallery (T02199).
Presented by the artist, 1977.

Exh: E28 London (1976–7) in No. 93.

Lit: B3 Alley (1981) p. 264, fig.

75.4 Carving

c. 1960/70. Not inscribed.
Stone. [5.1 high x 15.6].
London, Tate Gallery (T02200).
Presented by the artist, 1977.

Exh: E28 London (1976–7) in No. 93.

Lit: B3 Alley (1981) p. 264, fig.

75.5 Carving

c. 1960/70. Not inscribed.
Stone. [1.9 high x 8.3].
London, Tate Gallery (T02201).
Presented by the artist, 1977.

Exh: E28 London (1976–7) in No. 93, fig. p. 47 at
front left of group.

Lit: B3 Alley (1981) pp. 264–5, fig. p. 264.

75.6 Carving

c. 1960/70. Not inscribed.
Stone. [3.8 high x 4.1].
London, Tate Gallery (T02202).
Presented by the artist, 1977.

Exh: E28 London (1976–7) in No. 93, fig. p. 47
[at back right of group].

Lit: B3 Alley (1981) p. 265, fig.

75.7 Miniature Carving

c. 1960/70. Not inscribed.
White stone. 1.6 high x 4.
London, Family Collection.

Exh: [E28 London (1976–7) in No. 93, fig. p. 47 at centre right of group].

75.8 Miniature Carving
c. 1960/70. Not inscribed.
Black stone. 2.3 high x 3.7.
London, Family Collection.

Exh: [E28 London (1976–7) in No. 93].

76. BLUE MARBLE

76.1 Model for ›Blue Marble‹
c. 1960/70. Not inscribed.
Stone. [6.7 high x 4.2].
London, Tate Gallery (T02203).
Presented by the artist, 1977.

Exh: E28 London (1976–7) in No. 93, fig. p. 47 at centre left.

Lit: B3 Alley (1981) p. 265, fig.

According to Nina Williams, this model may have been carved slightly later than the date given here, which is taken from E28.

76.2 Maquette for ›Blue Marble‹
[1965/70]. Not inscribed.
Plaster. 6.7 high x c. 4.4.
London, Family Collection.

76.3 Plaster enlargement for ›Blue Marble‹
[1967/73]. Plaster.
London, Family Collection.

Gabo visited Lisbon every year between 1965 and 1970, and also in 1972 and 1973. According to Charles Wilson, 76.3 was probably enlarged in Portugal in the late 1960s, from the small stone (76.1). Miriam Gabo also suggests that 76.3 was executed in the late 1960s or early 1970s.

76.4 Blue Marble
1977. Not inscribed.
Marble. 50 high x 30.5.
London, Family Collection.

This work was carved by Charles Wilson, from the large plaster (76.3), in accordance with Gabo's instructions.

77. TORSION, VARIATION

This work is sometimes known as *Torsion Variation No. 3*, or *Variation Torsion II*. The title, *Torsion – Bronze Variation* which has been used, is potentially confusing, as it could refer to 30.6, entered here as *Torsion (Project for a Fountain)*.

Torsion, Variation is made from elements reminiscent of the original *Torsion* (30). In 30, the upper and lower parts consist of basically triangular forms (each with one curved edge), which are derived from a tetrahedron. In 77, similar triangular forms are inverted and set at right-angles to each other, providing a basic frame, which no longer relates directly to a tetrahedron. The stringing of 77 creates a diaphanous curved surface, as do the water jets in *Revolving Torsion, Fountain* (30.7).
In 1969 a version of 77 was used to illustrate the cover of P. B. Medawar's *The Art of the Soluble* (Pelican Books).

77.1 Torsion, Variation
1962. Not inscribed.
Bronze with stainless steel spring-wire; on wooden base painted black. [73.4 high, including integral wooden base 4.4 high].
New Orleans, Longue Vue House and Gardens.
From the artist, Dec 1964 to Marlborough-Gerson Gallery, New York; 1966 to Collection Mrs Edgar B. Stern, New Orleans; 1980 to Longue Vue.

Exh: E168 Dallas (1965) No. 27, fig. p. 13 : E195 New Orleans (1971–2) No. 69, fig., as ›Variation Tortion II‹.
This work was acquired by Marlborough-Gerson in 1964 (receipt, 3 Dec 1964; letter from B. Reis, 6 Jul 1965). In 1980 Mrs Stern bequeathed Longue Vue House, its contents, and gardens to New Orleans, as a museum.

77.2 Torsion, Variation
1963. Inscribed bottom centre: ›NG‹ monogram.
Phosphor-bronze with phosphor-bronze and stainless steel spring-wire; on wooden base. 73.1 high, including integral wooden base 3.8 high.
London, Family Collection.
See illus. pp. 84 and 136

Exh: E23 Humlebaek etc. (1970–71) No. 10, colour fig. p. 14 : E24 Berlin (1971) No. 9, colour fig. on back cover : E25 Hannover (1971) No. 9 : E26 Grenoble etc. (1971–2) No. 10 : E27 Lisbon (1972) No. 9, colour fig. on cover.

Lit: A54 Besset (1971) figs p. 8 : A210 Thurston (1976) colour fig. p. 18.

77.3 Torsion, Variation
1963/4. Signed on base.
Gold-plated bronze with stainless steel spring-wire. [62 high].
New York, McCrory Corporation.
From the artist, 1972.

Exh: E17 Amsterdam (1965) No. P24 : E18 Mannheim etc. (1965) No. 24, fig. : E19 Zurich (1965) No. 24, fig. 13 : E20 Stockholm (1965–6) No. 82, fig. : E21 London (1966) No. 29, fig. 12, as ›Torsion (Variation No. 3)‹ : E22 Buffalo (1968) No. 21, fig. p. 23 : E217 Düsseldorf (1976) : E225 Humlebaek (1978) No. 48, fig. p. 23 : E229 Geneva (1978) No. 52, fig. : E237 Buffalo etc. (1979–81) No. 58, fig. p. 61.

Lit: G31 (1966) fig. p. 132 : A93 Forge (1966) fig. p. 42 : A105 Gray (1966) fig. p. 49 *in situ* E19 : N2 Andreae (1968) fig. *in situ* E22 : A164 Read (1968) fig. p. 12 : B191 Rotzler (1977) p. 266, No. 175, fig. p. 225, as ›Torsion – Bronze Variation‹ : A170 Rotzler (1978) fig. p. 23.

This version has no small pieces of bronze supporting the vertical structure where it is attached to the base-plate. In 1972, Gabo referred to 77.3 as ›Construction in Space, »Torsion, Variation«‹ (invoice to McCrory Corporation, 11 Apr 1972). Gabo supplied a plastic cover for 77.3 (receipt, 6 May 1972, also detailing materials). According to Miriam Gabo, the work is signed on the metal base (letter to C. Ascher, 7 May 1972).

77.4 Torsion, Variation
c. 1974/5. Not inscribed.
Stainless steel with stainless steel spring-wire. 136.5 high, including integral base 0.5 high.
London, Family Collection.
See illus. pp. 85 and 137

According to Charles Wilson, this work was made c. 1974/5. Although holes have been drilled for stringing, the upper central portion of this version is not strung.

78.   BRONZE SPHERIC THEME (VARIATION)

1964/6. [Not inscribed].
Phosphor-bronze with stainless steel spring-wire; on bronze base. *c.* 99 high, including integral base 7.5 high.
London, Family Collection.
See illus. p. 143

Exh: E22 Buffalo (1968) No. 23, fig. p. 24 : E23 Humlebaek etc. (1970–71) No. 11, fig. p. 19 : E24 Berlin (1971) No. 10, fig. p. 21 : E25 Hannover (1971) No. 10, figs pp. 31, 33 : E26 Grenoble etc. (1971–2) No. 11 : E27 Lisbon (1972) No. 10, fig. p. 19.

Lit: A9 (1968) fig. p. 43 *in situ* E22 : A54 Besset (1971) p. 10, fig. 3.

This is probably the work which Gabo mentioned in 1966, in a letter to Carlos Israels: ›*Spheric Theme,* variation, bronze. This is the *new* one which you saw in the studio yesterday. It has never been exhibited . . .‹ (letter, 18 Sep 1966). According to Charles Wilson, it may have been made as early as 1962, although when exhibited it was dated 1964 (E22).

79.   VERTICAL CONSTRUCTION NO. 2

This work is sometimes titled *Vertical Construction No. 2 (Kinetic with Motor),* (E23–5).
    There is no complete model for 79. The inner form is related to the central element of the Baltimore *Construction Suspended in Space* (57); and it can also be seen as a variation on *Spheric Theme* (e. g. 37.10), with the structure oriented to rest on one edge rather than two. Gabo used this orientation of a modified *Spheric Theme* in a painting of 1941 (G28 fig. 126), and later in *Monument to the Astronauts* (80).

79.1   Vertical Construction No. 2

1964–5. Phosphor-bronze with stainless steel spring-wire; motorised. [205.7 high].
Lund, Sweden: Town Hall: Gift of the Sparbanken i Lund, 1968.
From the artist, 1968.

Lit: A71 Celsing (1968) fig. p. 4.

In 1966 Professor P. Sandblom approached Gabo in connection with acquiring a sculpture for Lund's new Town Hall, designed by Klaus Anshelm (letter from P. Sandblom, 24 May 1966). Several works were discussed, but 79.1 was finally selected (letter from P. Sandblom, 15 Mar 1968, citing date and materials). Gabo confirmed the height as ›81 inches‹, and the work was sent by air in May 1968 (letter to P. Sandblom, 19 Mar 1968; receipt, Cohen and Powell, 24 May 1968). The work was donated to the town by Sparbanken i Lund (letter to Sparbanken i Lund, 25 Apr 1968). Gabo visited Lund for the unveiling, which took place on 12 June 1968 (letter to P. Hougen, Munch Museet, 6 May 1968; passport entry).

79.2   Vertical Construction No. 2

1965–6. Not inscribed.
Bronze with stainless steel spring-wire.
[205.7 high].
Hartford, Wadsworth Atheneum: On loan from the Julia F. Whitney Foundation (TL.60.1972).
From the artist, to Collection Miriam Gabo; June 1970, to the Julia A. Whitney Foundation; 1972 to Hartford.

Exh: E21 London (1966) No. 33 : E22 Buffalo (1968) No. 25 : E23 Humlebaek etc. (1970–71) No. 19 : E24 Berlin (1971) No. 16 : E25 Hannover (1971) No. 16, figs pp. 13 *in situ* E23, 15 : E26 Grenoble etc. (1971–2) No. 18, figs, one *in situ* E23 : E27 Lisbon (1972) No. 17, fig. p. 23.

Lit: A219 Webb (1966) fig. 6 : A105 Gray (1966) fig. p. 52 : A9 (1968) fig. p. 43 *in situ* E22 : B115 Krauss (1979) fig. 190.

The Julia A. Whitney Foundation, set up by Thomas P. Whitney, acquired this work in June 1970 (annotated photograph, FAL; see also 87).

79.3   Vertical Construction No. 2

1969–70. [Not inscribed].
Stainless steel with stainless steel spring-wire, set into motorised hemi-spherical black base. *c.* 292 high, set into integral base *c.* 12.7 high.
London, Family Collection.
See illus. p. 145

80.   MONUMENT TO THE ASTRONAUTS

An alternative title for this work, *Kinetic Spheric Theme* (file, FAL), emphasises the relationship between 80 and *Spheric Theme,* which can be traced through Gabo's painting of 1941 (G28 fig. 126), and an undated drawing (A72 p. 36, bottom fig.), to the lower element in *Sketch for a Monument* of 1952 (E25 fig. p. 113). In 1976 Gabo dated 80.1 ›*c.* 1937‹, which suggests that he may have considered making a rotating version of *Spheric Theme* in the 1930s. Earlier, in 1925, he had used a spindle mounting for *Rotating Fountain* (24). (See also 63 and 79.)

80.1   Model for ›Monument to the Astronauts‹

c. 1966–8. Not inscribed.
Plastic, plastic-coated paper, and pencil.
[8.9 high x 7.6].
London, Tate Gallery (T02175).
Presented by the artist, 1977.

Exh: E28 London (1976–7) No. 53, fig. p. 36, as ›*c.* 1937‹.

Lit: B3 Alley (1981) p. 265, fig., as ›*c.* 1966–8‹.

Pencil lines on this model suggest that Gabo may have considered excising four almond-shaped sections, which, if removed, would have left a modified form of *Spheric Theme,* similar to that depicted in a painting of 1941 (G28, colour fig. 126).

80.2   Monument to the Astronauts

Started *c.* 1966.
Brass, plastic and stainless steel gauze.
London, Family Collection.
See illus. p. 146

Lit: E28 London (1976–7) fig. p. 48.

A photograph, probably taken in 1976, shows this work in its present state in Gabo's studio at Middlebury (E28). Gabo applied for copyright on the design of 80 in July 1975. This suggests that the design was fully formulated by then, although according to Charles Wilson, Gabo never quite resolved the interior form, and the central rod was only temporary. According to Ronald Alley, Gabo wished to build this work on a monumental scale, with neon tubes highlighting the curved edges of the rotating form (B3 p. 265).

81.   STONE CARVING

1967/(73). Not inscribed.
Portuguese stone. *c.* 13 high x *c.* 24.
England, Collection Sir Leslie and Lady Martin.
Gift from the artist, 1967/(73).

Gabo visited Portugal every year from 1965 to 1970, and also in 1972 and 1973. On one of these visits, after seeing the stone at the Martins' house, Gabo carved 81 with tools bought locally. The stone, originally taken from the beach, had been used as a door-stop. Sir Leslie Martin has a photograph of Gabo carving this piece outside his house, probably in 1967.

UNDATED WORKS

82. MODEL FOR A STANDING CONSTRUCTION

No date. Not inscribed.
Plastic. 11.3 high, including integral base
10.5 diameter.
London, Family Collection.

Traces of black on the transparent fan-shape (across the top and on the inside), suggest that a strip of black plastic may have been attached to it. The fan-shape is built up of several triangular pieces of plastic, joined edge to edge, in a way that is reminiscent of Antoine Pevsner's technique. The black base is rather roughly cut.

The plastic used in 82 could be either celluloid or Perspex. If it is celluloid, 82 might date from the early 1930s when Gabo's works became less rectilinear. Alternatively, 82 may have been made in the 1950s when Gabo was investigating vertical themes in *Monument to the Unknown Political Prisoner* and the *Bijenkorf Construction* (61, 67). A drawing of *c.* 1952 shows a vertical construction which is similar to 82, but which is more curved at the top (Family Collection).

83. ROUND STONE

83.1 Round Stone

Inscribed on bottom: ›Gabo‹.
Red-coloured stone. 4.4 high x 9.5.
London, Family Collection.

According to Miriam Gabo, 83.1 could have been carved at any time after 1939. It was obviously finished before 1972 when it was cast in bronze (see 83.2 a–b).

83.2 a-b Bronze casts of ›Round Stone‹

Bronze. 4.4 high x 9.5.
a) Inscribed on bottom: ›Gabo/FOR NINA WITH LOVE‹.
London, Family Collection.
b) Inscribed on bottom: ›Gabo Fecit‹.
London, Private Collection.
Gift from the artist, 1975.

According to Miriam Gabo, 83.2 was cast by the Morris Singer Foundry in 1972, and was referred to as ›Double Image‹ (memo from Singer's, [10 Feb 1972]). Gabo prepared 83.1 for casting, using a filler to smooth the surface (letter to E. Gibbard, Singer's, 21 Feb 1972). Gabo received the proofs in August 1972, but was so dissatisfied with the results that he retained only one proof-cast of 83.1 (letters to and from E. Gibbard, 20 Aug, 29 Nov 1972). Since there are now two casts (83.2 a-b), one was probably made by Antonio Duarte. (See also 45.2).

84. SOMERSAULT STONE

Stone. 2.5 high x 5.1.
London, Family Collection.

Gabo carved away parts of this small stone so that when positioned at a particular angle and allowed to fall over freely, its momentum carried it through a further half roll. This gave rise to the nickname, which has been adopted here as the title.

85. IMBEDDED STONE

Inscribed on bottom: ›N. Gabo‹.
Two stones, one imbedded in the other, fixed with [nylon]. 5.1 high x 8.9.
London, Family Collection.

Exh: E269 London (1985) No. 41, as ›Carved Pebbles 1939–46‹.

85 appears to be an alabaster stone, imbedded in granite. The stones were probably bonded together by heating the plastic.

86. STONE CARVING

Not inscribed.
Red stone. 5.7 high x 6.9.
London, Family Collection.

87. STONE CARVING

Black stone. 2.8 high x 3.2.
Washington, Conn., Collection Thomas P. Whitney.
Gift from the artist, *c.* 1967.

Gabo met Thomas Whitney *c.* 1964, and they became very close friends. They shared many interests, including a love of the Russian language, literature and art. Gabo probably gave 87 to Whitney in the late 1960s.

Bibliography, Film and Exhibition listings

GENERAL INTRODUCTION

The Bibliography, Film and Exhibition lists have been compiled primarily as references for the *catalogue raisonné*. At the same time, they are intended to provide a comprehensive coverage of Gabo's life and work. Although there is a predominance of items concerning Gabo's sculpture and constructions, some items only relate to Gabo's work in other fields, such as painting, printmaking, and design.

The lists of books and periodicals are intended to be fairly comprehensive. In an attempt to provide easily accessible sources in several languages, some commonly available text-books and general articles have been included. Others, containing only passing references to Gabo, have been omitted. The lists of films and newspapers are deliberately selective. In each list the more important items have been highlighted in bold type. The abbreviations used are identical to those listed in the *Guide to the Catalogue Raisonné Entries*.

WRITINGS BY GABO

This list contains all Gabo's published writings, including those produced in collaboration with others. It is arranged in chronological order.

G1. ***Realisticheskii Manifest*** [*The Realistic Manifesto*], Moscow, 2nd State Printing House, 1920. Written by Gabo, and signed by him and by his brother, Antoine Pevsner, as ›Noton [sic.] Pevzner‹. 5 Aug 1920. For translations: English, G28a, G31, B14, B29, B45, E28; French G28b, E26; German G28c, E19, E24, E25; Danish E23; Hungarian A86. The Russian broadsheet is reproduced in G28a-c. For Camilla Gray's translation and Gabo's reaction, see A104 and G36.

G2. ›Thesen: Aus dem realistischen Manifest. Moskau 1920‹ *G: Material zur elementaren Gestaltung* (Berlin) No. 1, Jul 1923, p. 4.

G3. Letter to the editors of *L'Esprit Nouveau*, May 1927, in *Seuphor*, B204, 1977, p. 69.

G4. ›Gestaltung?‹, *Bauhaus* (Dessau) Vol 2, No. 4, 1928, pp. 2–6.

G5. Marianne Brandt and Naum Gabo ›Bauhausstil (Polemik zwischen M. Brandt u. N. Gabo)‹, *Bauhaus* (Dessau) Vol. 3, No. 1, 1929, p. 21.

G6. Two letters to Will Grohmann, Jan 1932, in Karl Gutbrod, ed. *Künstler schreiben an Will Grohmann*. Cologne, Verlag M. Du Mont Schauberg, 1968, pp. 133–4.

G7. Statements by Naum Gabo and Antoine Pevsner, *Abstraction-Création: Art non-figuratif* (Paris) No. 1, 1932, pp. 14, 27. Reprinted Arno Press, New York, 1968.

G8. Statement, *Abstraction-Création: Art non-figuratif* (Paris) No. 2, 1933, p. 16. Reprinted Arno Press, New York, 1968.

G9. ›Fragment del manifest constructivista de Gabo i Pevsner, Moscu, 1920‹, *D'Aci i d'alla* (Barcelona) Vol. 22, No. 179, Dec 1934, p. 28.

G10. ›Constructive Art‹, *The Listener* (London) Vol. 16, No. 408, 4 Nov 1936, pp. 846–8. Reprinted in E255.

G11. Laszlo Moholy-Nagy, Naum Gabo, Eileen Holding, and Herbert Read. ›Modern Art and Architecture: Reports of the Principal Speakers at the Informal General Meeting on Wednesday, 9 December 1936‹, *Journal of the Royal Institute of British Architects* (London) Vol. 44, 9 Jan 1937, pp. 213–15. Revised as G14.

G12. J. Leslie Martin, Ben Nicholson, and Naum Gabo, eds. ***Circle: International Survey of Constructive Art.*** London, Faber and Faber, 1937; 1971. Contains:
a) ›The Constructive Idea in Art‹, pp. 1–10. Reprinted in B14, B100, and G28a; in French in G28b; in German in G28c, E24 and E25; in Danish in E23.
b) ›Sculpture: Carving and Construction in Space‹, pp. 103–12. Reprinted in G28a and B45; in French in G28b; and in German in G28c and E25. (For reviews of *Circle*, see E255).

G13. ›Gabo and Pevsner: And Constructive Realism: Extract from a Letter by Gabo and Pevsner‹, *XXe Siècle* (Paris) Vol. 1, Nos 5/6, 1939, pp. 45–7. Translated from ›Auszug aus einem Brief von Gabo and Pevsner‹, *Das Werk* (Zurich) Vol. 25, No. 8, Aug 1939, p. 255. Reprinted as ›Extraits d'une lettre de Gabo et Anton Pevsner‹, *Réalités Nouvelles* (Paris) No. 1, 1947, pp. 63–4. Reprinted in B182, and *XXe Siècle* (Paris) Vol. 21, No. 13, Christmas 1959, pp. 44–5.

G14. ›Toward a Unity of the Constructive Arts‹ *Plus* (New York) No. 1, Dec 1938, pp. 3–6, and *Architectural Forum* (New York) Vol. 69, Dec 1938, pp. 435–8 (marked as pp. 3–6). G11 revised; reprinted in G28, and in German in E25.

G15. E. J. Carter and Naum Gabo ›Frank Lloyd Wright‹, *Focus* (London) No. 4, Summer 1939, pp. 49–52. Contributions to discussion of Wright's lectures at RIBA.

G16. Extracts from Gabo's Diaries 1939–45, in E269, p. 100.

G17. Eric Newton, William Coldstream, and Naum Gabo. ›The Artist in the Witness Box: Centre Party v. Left Wing‹, *The Listener* (London) Vol. 23, No. 576, 25 Jan 1940, pp. 163–5, 191. Report of F1.

G18. ›The Concepts of Russian Art‹, *World Review* (London) Jun 1942, pp. 48–53. Reprinted in E19. Cover photomontage by Naum Gabo.

G19. ›Prepare for Design‹, *World Review* (London) Apr 1943, pp. 43–9.

G20. Naum Gabo and Herbert Read. ›Constructive Art: An Exchange of Letters', *Horizon* (London) Vol. 10, No. 55, Jul 1944, pp. 57–65. Reprinted in G28, B170; sections reprinted in B14, B187.

G21. Untitled note, *Kurt Schwitters*. New York, The Pinacotheca, 19 Jan-Feb 1948.

G22. ›A Retrospective View of Constructive Art‹, or ›On Constructive Realism‹, in Katherine S. Dreier, James J. Sweeney, and Naum Gabo. *Three Lectures on Modern Art*. New York, Philosophical Library, 1949, pp. 63–87. Lecture of 19 Mar 1948, for the Thomas Rutherford Trowbridge Lecture Foundation at Yale University. Reprinted in *Architect's Year Book* (London) No. 4, 1952, pp. 8–14; also in G28a, B14, B222; in French in G28b, B4; and in German in G28c, E25.

G23. ›Memorial to Sadie [sic.] A. May‹, *Baltimore Museum of Art News* Vol. 15, No. 3, Dec 1951, pp. 3–4. Address delivered 4 Nov 1951.

G24. ›A New Construction for Baltimore‹, *Magazine of Art* (New York) Vol. 45, No. 2, Feb 1952, pp. 71–4.

G25. ›Art and Science‹, in G. Kepes, ed. *The New Landscape: In Art and Science*. Chicago, Paul Theobald, 1956, pp. 60–63. Reprinted in G28, in English, French and German; and in E23, in Danish.

G26. Letter to Alexander Dorner, 8 Oct 1953, reprinted in B44, p. 60.

G27. Naum Gabo, Nina Franchina, and Ugo Sissa. ›Due monumenti a Rotterdam e a Taranto‹, *Civiltá delle macchine* (Rome) Vol. 4, No. 3, May-Jun 1956, pp. 24, 101–2.

G28a. *Gabo: Constructions, Sculpture, Paintings, Drawings, Engravings.* London, Lund Humphries, and Cambridge, Mass., Harvard University Press, 1957. Essays by Herbert Read (reprinted in B173; and in Dutch in E15), and Leslie Martin (in Dutch in E17). Contains G1, G12a-b, G14, G20, G22, G25, and ›»Image« (An Explanatory Note)‹, plus interview from A130. Bibliography by Bernard Karpel.

G28b. *Naum Gabo: Constructions, sculpture, peinture, dessins, gravures.* Neuchâtel, Editions du Griffon, 1961. G28a revised.

G28c. *Naum Gabo: Bauten, Skulptur, Malerei, Zeichnungen, Graphik.* Neuchâtel, Editions du Griffon, 1961. As G28b.

G29. Statement, *L'Oeil* (Paris) No. 28, Apr 1957, p. 61. Gabo's response to ›Propos d'un sculpteur – Interview d'Antoine Pevsner par Rosamond Bernier‹. *L'Oeil* (Paris) No. 23, Nov 1956, pp. 28–35.

G30. *Of Divers Arts.* Bollingen Series XXXV.8, Princeton University Press, 1962; 1971. The A. W. Mellon Lectures in Fine Arts, National Gallery of Art, Washington, DC, 1959.

G31. ›Naum Gabo Talks about His Work‹ and ›The Realistic Manifesto 1920‹, *Studio International* (London) Vol. 171, No. 876, Apr 1966, pp. 126–32.

G32. Winifred Nicholson, Barbara Hepworth, Miriam Gabo, Herbert Read, Ben Nicholson, and Naum Gabo. ›Reminiscences of Mondrian‹, *Studio International* (London) Vol. 172, No. 884, Dec 1966, pp. 286–92.

G33. Roland Penrose, Ben Nicholson, Naum Gabo, and Peter du Sautoy. ›Tributes to Herbert Read 1893–1968‹, *Studio International* (London) Vol. 177, No. 907, Jan 1969, pp. 2–4.

G34. Naum Gabo and Witt Wittnebert. ›Naum Gabo's »Kinetic Sculpture«: Construction and Reconstruction‹, *Techne* (New York) Vol. 1, No. 1, 14 Apr 1969, p. 5.

G35. ›The »Kinetic Construction of 1920«‹, *Studio International* (London) Vol. 178, No. 914, Sep 1969, p. 89.

G36. Naum Gabo and Eli Bornstein. ›An Exchange of Letters with Naum Gabo‹, *The Structurist* (Saskatoon) No. 9, 1969, pp. 64–5. Gabo's response to Camilla Gray's translation of *The Realistic Manifesto*, A104.

G37. Tribute, *Mark Tobey*. Basel, Galerie Beyeler, Dec 1970–Feb 1971.

G38. ›The 1922 Soviet Exhibition‹, *Studio International* (London) Vol. 182, No. 938, Nov 1971, p. 171.

G39. ›Introduction‹ in Andrew Causey. *Peter Lanyon: His Painting*. Henley-on-Thames, Aidan Ellis, 1971.

FILM AND AUDIO-VISUAL MATERIAL

The entries in the *catalogue raisonné* do not include detailed references to Gabo's works reproduced or discussed in film or in sound recordings. The catalogue notes, however, do cite significant evidence derived from film or from recorded interviews with Gabo. The following list is arranged chronologically. It is not comprehensive, covering mainly British radio and television.

F1. ›The Artist in the Witness Box (6). The Centre Party v. The Left Wing‹ BBC Home Service, 15 Jan 1940. Speakers: William Coldstream, Naum Gabo and Eric Newton. Postponed from 6 Nov 1939. Reported in G17.

F2. ›Coventry: A Test Case of Planning‹ BBC Third Programme, 6 Apr 1958. Written and presented by Percy Johnson-Marshall. BBC recording. Re 67. Reported in *The Listener* (London) Vol. 59, No. 1516, 17 Apr 1958, pp. 653–5.

F3. Interview with Billy Klüver. Recorded for E135 at Moderna Museet, Stockholm, 1961.

1 sided 8″ disc; 45 rpm. Includes Gabo reading excerpts from the *The Realistic Manifesto* in Russian.

F4. ›Monitor: The Frozen Frame‹ BBC1 Television, 1 Jun 1965. Produced by Nancy Thomas, Christopher Burstall. Edited by Jonathan Miller. Includes Gabo interviewed by Susan Sontag. Reported in William Trevor ›The Arts‹, *The Listener* (London) Vol 73, No. 1891, 24 Jun 1965, pp. 950–51.

F5. ›The Thirties in Britain. Art: Innovation and Commitment‹ BBC Third Programme, 2 parts, 25 Nov and 2 Dec 1965. BBC recording. Produced by Leonie Cohn. Gabo *inter alia*, talking to Andrew Forge.

F6. Statement recorded for E166 at National Gallery of Scotland, Edinburgh, 1965.

F7. ›The Critics‹ BBC Home Service, 27 Mar 1966. Chairman: Philip Hope-Wallace. BBC recording. Produced by Carl Wildman. Reviews E21.

F8. ›»We Are Poets« Said Pythagoras: Naum Gabo Talks about his Sculptural Constructions‹, in ›The Lively Arts‹ BBC Home Service 27 Mar 1966. Introduced by Derek Hart. BBC recording. Produced by Jocelyn Ferguson and Udi Eichler.

F9. ›Naum Gabo‹ BBC Third Programme, 10 Apr 1966. BBC recording. Interview with Andrew Forge, recorded 22 Oct 1965. See A93.

F10. Interview with S. Frederick Starr and Kenneth Frampton ›Russian Art in Revolution and Emigration: An Interview with Naum Gabo‹ 1969. Tape, S. F. Starr; unedited and edited transcripts, Yale 1; letter from Starr, 18 Aug 1970.

F11. ›The New Masters (9): Naum Gabo‹. BBC2 Television with Time-Life Films, New York, 8 Aug 1972. Written and Produced by John Read. (Transcript of the soundtrack, edited by Nina Williams née Gabo, Yale 1, 59 pp.).

F12. Interview with Susan Littlewood, September 1973. (Recording, FAL; transcript, Yale 1). Published in edited form as ›The Home Forum: Naum Gabo‹, *The Christian Science Monitor* (Boston), 14 Nov 1973, [p. 19], and 15 Nov 1973, [p. 23].

F13. ›Naum Gabo‹ BBC Radio 3, 16 Nov 1976. Interview with David Thompson. (Tape, FAL). Reported in A209.

F14. ›The Shock of the New (2): The Powers That Be‹. BBC2 Television with RM Productions, Munich, and Time-Life Films, New York, 28 Sep 1980. Written and Presented by Robert Hughes. Produced by Lorna Pegram. Includes interview with Gabo.

F15. ›The Great Art Dictator‹ BBC2 Television, 14 Dec 1981. Written and Narrated by Norman Stone. Produced by David Wallace. (Shows 4.2).

F16. Recorded interview with Miriam Gabo by David Lewis and Sarah Fox-Pitt, 28 May

1981, for ›Modern Movement in Cornwall 1935–75‹, Tate Gallery Archive with the Carnegie Institute, Pittsburgh. (Recording and transcription, TGA).

F17. Interview with Alexei Pevsner by Colin C. Sanderson, 9 and 14 Nov 1979. (Transcript, FAL).

SEE ALSO: interviews in B47, B116, A51, A83, A130, A209, N2 and E23.

BOOKS AND BROCHURES

This list also includes catalogues for exhibitions to which Gabo was not a contributor. Page references are given for guidance only and are not exhaustive.

B1. Ades, Dawn. *Dada and Surrealism Reviewed*. London, Arts Council of Great Britain, 11 Jan–27 Mar 1978. pp. 322, 346–57. (Re the *London Bulletin*).

B2. Alley, Ronald. *The Tate Gallery Catalogues: The Foreign Paintings, Drawings and Sculpture*. London, Tate Gallery, 1959. pp. 83–4.

B3. Alley, Ronald. *Catalogue of the Tate Gallery's Collection of Modern Art: Other than Works by British Artists*. London, Tate Gallery with Sotheby Parke Bernet, 1981. pp. xvii–xviii, 231–67, 585–7, 786, 788.

B4. Alvard, J. and R. V. Gindertael, eds. *Témoignages pour l'art abstrait, 1952*. Paris, Editions ›Art d'Aujourd'hui‹, 1952. pp. 114, 123–9. (Contains G22).

B5. Amberg, George. *Art in Modern Ballet*. New York, Pantheon, 1946. pp. 47–8.

B6. Andersen, Troels. *Moderne Russisk Kunst 1910–1930*. Copenhagen, Borgens Ferlag, 1967.

B7. Andersen, Troels. *Malevich*. Amsterdam, Stedelijk Museum, 1970. pp. 13, 28, 58 n. 6.

B8. Argan, Giulio C. *L'Arte moderna 1770–1970*. Florence, Sansoni, 1970. pp. 547–8.

B9. Arnason, H. H. *A History of Modern Art: Painting, Sculpture, Architecture*. New York, Abrams, 1968. Revised London, Thames and Hudson, 1977. pp. 239–40, 315, 323–6, 412–13, *et passim*.

B10. Baldinger, Wallace, S. and Harry B. Green. *The Visual Arts*. New York, Holt Rinehart and Winston, 1960. p. 159.

B11. Baldwin, John. *Contemporary Sculpture Techniques: Welded Metal and Fibreglass*. New York, Rheinhold, 1967. p. 15.

B12. [Baltimore Museum of Art] *A Picture Book: 200 Objects in the Baltimore Museum of Art*. Baltimore, 1955. p. 85.

B13. Bann, Stephen, ed. *The Tradition of Constructivism*. The Documents of 20th-Century Art, New York, Viking Press and London,

Thames and Hudson, 1974. pp. xxvi–xxvii, xxxi–xxxii, xxxvii, xlii–xlv, 3–11, 204–20, 234–48. (Contains G1, G12a, G20, G22).

B14. Barnett, Vivian E. *Handbook: The Guggenheim Museum Collection 1900–1980*. New York, Solomon R. Guggenheim Foundation, 1980. pp. 254–7.

B15. Barr, Alfred, H., Jr. *Cubism and Abstract Art*. New York, Museum of Modern Art, 1936; reprinted London, Secker and Warburg, 1975. pp. 12, 60, 103, 130, 133, 136, 138–9, 209–10, *et passim*. Published for E46.

B16. Barr, Alfred H., Jr. *Masters of Modern Art*. New York, Museum of Modern Art, 1954. p. 127.

B17. Barr, Alfred, H., Jr. *Painting and Sculpture in the Museum of Modern Art, 1929–1967*. New York, Museum of Modern Art, 1977. pp. 133, 543. Revision of 1948 and 1958 catalogues. For updated checklist, see Alicia Legg, ed. *Painting and Sculpture in the Museum of Modern Art: With Selected Works on Paper: Catalog of the Collection, January 1, 1977*. New York, Museum of Modern Art, 1977.

B18. Barros, Tomas. *Los Procesos abstractivos del arte contemporáneo: Nociones para una concepcion dialectica de los estilos*. Osedo-Coruña, Ediciones del Castro, 1965. p. 79.

B19. Beaumont, Cyril W. *Complete Book of Ballets*. London, Putnam, 1937; revised 1949, 1951, 1956. pp. 972–3.

B20. Beaumont, Cyril, W. *The Diaghilev Ballet in London*. London, A. and C. Black, 1940; 3rd ed., 1951. pp. 272–7, 281, 291.

B21. Bell, L. S. *University of Saskatchewan Permanent Art Collection*. Saskatoon, University of Saskatchewan, 1980. p. 67.

B22. Benthall, Jonathan. *Science and Technology in Art Today*. London, Thames and Hudson, 1972. 102–4, 117.

B23. Besset, Maurice. *Art of the Twentieth Century*. London, Weidenfeld and Nicolson, 1976. pp. 12, 30, 128–30, 132–4. (Translation of *20. Jahrhundert*. Belser Stilgeschichte Band XI. Stuttgart, Chr. Belser Verlag, 1971).

B24. Biedermann, Charles. *Art as the Evolution of Visual Knowledge*. Red Wing, Minnesota, Charles Biedermann, 1948. pp. 391, 537, 567, 587, 606, 610, 625.

B25. Blanshard, Frances B. *Retreat from Likeness in the Theory of Painting*. New York, Columbia University Press, 2nd ed. 1949. pp. 4, 9, 119–21, 143–7.

B26. Bohan, Ruth, L. *The Société Anonyme's Brooklyn Exhibition: Katherine Dreier and Modernism in America*. Ann Arbor, Mich., UMI Research Press, 1982. pp. 55–7, 100–101, 141, 219 n. 42, 230 n. 2. (*Re* E38).

B27. Bowlt, John E., ed. *Russian Art of the Avant-Garde: Theory and Criticism 1902–1934*. The Documents of 20th-Century Art. New York, Viking Press, 1976. pp. 152, 208–14, 305 n. 1. (Contains G1).

B28. Bowness, Alan. *Modern Sculpture*. London, Studio Vista, 1965. pp. 136–41.

B29. Bowness, Alan. *Modern European Art*. London, Thames and Hudson, 1972. pp. 182–4, 196.

B30. Brederoo, Nico J. *Charley Toorop: Leven en Werken*. Amsterdam, 1982. p. 70.

B31. Brett, Guy. *Kinetic Art: The Language of Movement*. London, Studio Vista, 1968. pp. 18–20, 22.

B32. Brion, Marcel, *L'Art abstrait*. Paris, Editions Albin Michel, 1956. pp. 162–5, *et passim*.

B33. [Brussels] *Exposition Universelle et Internationale de Bruxelles 1958: Vol. 5: Les Arts*. Brussels, 1960. (After E112). p. 32.

B34. Buckle, Richard. *Diaghilev*. London, Weidenfeld and Nicolson, 1979. pp. 482–8, 491, 507, 531, 580–81.

B35. Budde, Rainer and Evelyn Weiss. *Kataloge des Wallraf-Richartz-Museums: Band IX. Bildwerke und Objekte. Neuzugänge Seit 1965*. Cologne, 1973. pp. 24–5.

B36. [Buffalo: Albright-Knox Art Gallery] *Plus by Minus: Today's Half-Century* Buffalo, 3 Mar–14 Apr 1968. (See E22).

B37. Buffalo: Albright-Knox Art Gallery] *Contemporary Art 1942–72: Collection of the Albright-Knox Art Gallery*. New York, Praeger, 1972. pp. 182–3, 415.

B38. Burnham, Jack. *Beyond Modern Sculpture*. New York, George Braziller, 1968; 1975. pp. 34–9, 112–13, 118, 130, 140–44, 150, 155, 226, 230–32, *et passim*.

B39. Burnham, Jack. *The Structure of Art*. New York, George Braziller, 1971; revised, 1973, pp. 94–5.

B40. *The Busch-Reisinger Museum, Harvard University*. New York, Abbeville Press, 1980. pp. 64–5.

B41. Caldwell, Joan G. *Handbook of the Collection*. New Orleans, Museum of Art, 1980. p. 91.

B42. Canaday, John. *What is Art?* London, Hutchinson, and New York, Alfred A. Knopf, 1980.

B43. Cauman, Samuel. *The Living Museum: Experiences of an Art Historian and Museum Director – Alexander Dorner*. New York University Press, 1958. pp. 60, 155. Reprinted as *Das lebende Museum*. Hannover, Fackelträger Verlag, 1960.

B44. Chipp, Herschel B., ed *Theories of Modern Art: A Source Book by Artists and Critics*. Berkeley and Los Angeles, University of California Press, 1968, pp. 312, 325–37, 588. (Contains G1, G12b).

B45. Cirlot, Juan E. *Diccionario de los ismos*. Barcelona-Buenos Aires, Argos, 1949. pp. 58–60.

B46. Clapp, Jane. *Sculpture Index*. Metuchen, NJ, Scarecrow Press, 1970. 3 volumes. pp. 409–12.

B47. Clay, Jean. *Visages de l'art moderne*. Paris, Editions Rencontre, 1969. pp. 79–120. Interview with Gabo.

B48. [Cleveland: Brett Mitchell Collection Inc.] *Twentieth Century Masters*. [1977]. p. 5.

B49. Clifford, Derek. *Art and Understanding: Towards a Humanist Aesthetic*. London, Evelyn, Adams and Mackay, 1968.

B50. [Cologne: Museum Ludwig] *Handbuch Museum Ludwig*. Cologne, 1979. pp. 232–3.

B51. Comfort, Alex. *Art and Social Responsibility: Lectures on the Ideology of Romanticism*. London, Falcon Press, 1946. p. 10. fig.

B52. Compton, Michael. *Optical and Kinetic Art*. London, Tate Gallery, 1967; 1974.

B53. Compton, Michael, ed. *Toward a New Art: Essays on the Background to Abstract Art 1910–1920*. London, Tate Gallery, 1980. pp. 19, 86, 134.

B54. Cross, Tom. *Painting the Warmth of the Sun: St Ives Artists 1939–1975*. Newmill, Alison Hodge with Guildford, Lutterworth Press, 1984. pp. 47–8, 51–6, 59, 66–7, 78, 82–3, 85, 126–7, 148, *et passim*.

B55. Damaz, Paul F. *Art in European Architecture: Synthèse des arts*. New York, Reinhold Publishing, 1956. pp. 30, 59.

B56. Davies, Peter. *The St Ives Years: Essays on the Growth of an Artistic Phenomenon*. Wimborne, Dorset, The Wimborne Bookshop, 1984. pp. 14, 20–23, 25–7, 29, 31–2, 34, 38–9.

B57. *Documenta: Kunst des XX. Jahrhunderts*. Kassel, Museum Fridericianum, 15 Jul–18 Sep 1955. p. 28. (55.5 illustrated).

B58. Dorazio, Piero. *La Fantasia dell'arte nella vita moderna*. Rome, Polveroni e Quinti, 1955. pp. 77–83.

B59. Dreier, Katherine S. *Modern Art*. New York, Société Anonyme-Museum of Modern Art, 1926. pp. 70, 74–5. Published for E38. Reprinted in B209.

B60. [Duisburg: Wilhelm-Lehmbruck-Museum] *Katalog der Lehmbruck-Sammlung. Band II. Katalog der Sammlungen: Ausgenommen Wilhelm Lehmbruck: Bildhauer-Maler*. Recklinghausen, Verlag Aurel Bongers, 1964. pp. 11, 47.

B61. Ede, Jim. *A Way of Life: Kettle's Yard*. Cambridge University Press, 1984. pp. 174–5, 177.

B62. Elgar, Frank. *Mondrian*. London, Thames and Hudson, 1968. p. 175.

B63. Elsen, Albert, E. *Origins of Modern Sculpture: Pioneers and Premises*. London, Phaidon, 1974; 1978. pp. 54, 78, 96–7, 102, *et passim*. Revision of E208.

B64. Elsen, Albert, E. *Modern European Sculpture 1918–1945: Unknown Beings and Other Realities*. New York, George Braziller, 1979. pp. 78–9, 82–5, 176–7. Catalogue for E235.

B65. Farr, Dennis. *English Art 1870–1940*. Oxford University Press, 1978. pp. 277, 288.

B66. Feldman, E. B. *Art as Image and Idea*. New York, Prentice-Hall, 1967. p. 365. Revised as *Varieties of Visual Experience: Art as Image and Idea* New York, Prentice-Hall with Abrams, 1973, pp. 479–81, 506–7.

B67. Francastel, Pierre. *Les sculptures célèbres*. Paris, Lucien Mazenod, 1954. p. 397.

B68. Franke, Herbert W. *Kunst und Konstruktion: Physik und Mathematik als fotografisches Experiment*. Munich, Verlag F. Bruckmann, 1957. p. 74.

B69. Futagawa, Yukio. *Global Architecture: Piano and Rogers: Centre Beaubourg, Paris, France, 1972–1977*. Tokyo, ADA Edita, 1977. p. 24.

B70. *The Gallatin Collection*. New York, Museum of Living Art, 1940. p. 29.

B71. *A. E. Gallatin Collection: Museum of Living Art*. Philadelphia Museum of Art, 1954. pp. 8, 34, 82.

B72. Gardiner, Margaret. *Barbara Hepworth: A Memoir*. Edinburgh, Salamander Press, 1982. pp. 28, 41–6, 51.

B73. Gardiner, Helen. *Art through the Ages*. New York, Harcourt, Brace and Co., 4th ed. 1959; revised 1970, 1975, 1980.

B74. Gee, Malcolm. *Dealers, Critics, and Collectors of Modern Painting: Aspects of the Parisian Art Market between 1910 and 1930*. New York/London, Garland Editions, 1982.

B75. Gertz, Ulrich. *Contemporary Plastic Art: Plastik der Gegenwart*. Berlin, Rembrandt, 2nd ed. 1955. pp. iv, xviii–xix, 164–5, 256.

B76. Giedion-Welcker, Carola. *Modern Plastic Art*. Zurich, Girsberger, 1937. pp. 14, 128–30, 132–3. Translation of *Moderne Plastik*, 1937. Revised as *Contemporary Sculpture: An Evolution in Volume and Space*. London, Faber and Faber, 1956, 1961; and New York, George Wittenborn, 1960, pp. 176–86, 188.

B77. Glozer, Laszlo. *Westkunst: Zeitgenössische Kunst seit 1939*. Cologne, Du Mont Buchverlag, 1981. p. 185, *et passim*.

B78. Goldsmith, Maurice. *Sage: A Life of J. D. Bernal*. London, Hutchinson, 1980. p. 87.

B79. Goldwater, Robert. *Space and Dream*. New York, Walker, with M. Knoedler, 1967. pp. 21, 23–4, 44. Published for E179.

B80. Goldwater, Robert. *What is Modern Sculpture?* New York, Museum of Modern Art, 1969. pp. 66–7, 69, 143.

B81. Goldwater, Robert with René d'Harnoncourt. *Modern Art in Your Life*. New York, Museum of Modern Art, 2nd ed. 1953. pp. 19, 45. Revision of E70.

B82. Goldwater, Robert and Marco Treves. *Artists on Art*. New York, Pantheon, 1945. pp. 454–5. (Contains extracts from G1).

B83. Gray, Camilla. *The Great Experiment: Russian Art 1863–1922*. London, Thames and Hudson, 1962. pp. 219–21, 225, 243, 245, 246. Reprinted as *The Russian Experiment in Art 1863–1922*. London, Thames and Hudson, 1971.

B84. Gray, Cleve, ed. *Hans Richter by Hans Richter*. New York, Holt, Rinehart and Winston, 1971. pp. 40, 42, 56.

B85. Green, Chistopher. ›Naum Gabo in England‹ M. A. Thesis, Courtauld Institute of Art, University of London, 1967.

B86. Gregor, Joseph and René Füllöp-Miller. *The Russian Theater*. Philadelphia, J. B. Lippincott, 1930. figs. 336–9.

B87. Grohmann, Will. *Bildende Kunst und Architektur*. Berlin, Suhrkamp Verlag, 1953. pp. 128, 169, 262–3, 450.

B88. Guggenheim, Peggy, ed. *Art of This Century*. New York, Art of This Century, 1942. pp. 89, 91, 138.

B89. Hale, William H. *The World of Rodin: 1840–1917*. Amsterdam, Time-Life International, 1969, 1972. p. 184.

B90. Hamilton, George, H., ed. *Collection of the Société Anonyme: Museum of Modern Art, 1920*. New Haven, Yale Associates in the Fine Arts, 1950. pp. 15–17. Compiled and planned by Katherine S. Dreier and Marcel Duchamp.

B91. Hamilton, George H. *Painting and Sculpture in Europe 1880–1940*. Harmondsworth and New York. Penguin Books, 1967; revised 1972. pp., 135–7, 230–33.

B92. Hamilton, George H. *19th and 20th Century Art*. New York, Abrams, 1970. pp. 236, 238.

B93. Hammacher, Arno M. *The Evolution of Modern Sculpture: Tradition and Innovation*. London, Thames and Hudson, 1969. pp. 175, 178–84, *et passim*.

B94. Harrison, Charles. *English Art and Modernism 1900–1939*. London, Allen Lane; and Bloomington, Indiana University Press, 1981. pp. 256, 259–60, 274, 276, 282–9, 304–5, 377.

B95. Hart, Walker W., Veryl Schult, and Henry Swain. *New Plane Geometry and Supplements*. Boston, D. C. Heath, 1964. p. 10.

B96. [Hartford, Conn., Wadsworth Atheneum] *The Serge Lifar Collection of Ballet Set and Costume Designs*, 1965. pp. 46–7.

B97. Havelock-Allan, Lucy. *The Pier Gallery, Stromness, Orkney*. Kirkwall, Orkney, The Pier Centre Trust, 1978. pp. 8, 10, 20–21. Essays by Sir Norman Reid, Patrick Heron, and Alan Bowness. Published for E232.

B98. Hayes, Bartlett H., Jr. *The Naked Truth and Personal Vision*. Andover, Mass., Addison Gallery of American Art, Phillips Academy, 1955. pp. 102–3. Published following E87.

B99. Hepworth, Barbara. *A Pictorial Autobiography*. 1970; reprinted Bradford-on-Avon, Moonraker Press, 1977. pp. 33, 37–9, 41, 45–6, 49.

B100. Herbert, Robert L., ed. *Modern Artists on Art: Ten Unabridged Essays*. Englewood Cliffs, NJ, Prentice-Hall, 1964. pp. 103–13. (Contains G12a).

B101. Herbert, Robert L., Eleanor S. Apter, and Elsie K. Kenney, eds. *The Société Anonyme and the Dreier Bequest at Yale University: A Catalogue Raisonné*. New Haven and London, Yale University Press, 1984, pp. 12, 26, 281–6, 758, 764, 767, 771.

B102. Heron, Patrick. *The Changing Forms of Art*. London, Routledge and Kegan Paul, 1955. pp. 43–5, 69–70, *et passim*.

B103. Hibbard, Howard. *Masterpieces of Western Sculpture*. London, Thames and Hudson, 1977. p. 232.

B104. Hildebrandt, Hans. *Die Kunst des 19. and 20. Jahrhunderts*. Wildpark-Potsdam, Akademische Verlagsgesellschaft Athenaion, M.B.H. [1931]. pp. 318, 428, 432, 446–7, 451. (Publication date, p. 453).

B105. Hirdina, Heinz. *Neues Bauen, Neues Gestalten: Das Neue Frankfurt, die neue Stadt: eine Zeitschrift zwischen 1926 und 1933* Berlin, Elefanten Press, 1984. pp. 295. 310–11.

B106. Hodin, Joseph P. *Modern Art and the Modern Mind*. Cleveland and London, Case Western Reserve University Press, 1972.

B107. Hofman, Werner. *Die Plastik des 20. Jahrhunderts*. Frankfurt, Fischer Bücherei, 1958.

B108. Hofman, Werner. *Grundlagen der Modernen Kunst*. Stuttgart, Alfred Kröner Verlag, 1966. pp. 448, 483, *et passim*

B109. Honisch, Dieter. *Die Nationalgalerie Berlin*. Recklinghausen, Verlag Aurel Bongers, 1979. pp. 304, 371.

B110. Huyghe, René, ed. *Art and Mankind: Larousse Encyclopedia of Modern Art*. London, Paul Hamlyn, 1965. pp. 256, 328.

B111. Kelleher, Patrick J. *Living with Modern Sculpture: The John B. Putnam, Jr., Memorial Collection, Princeton University*. The Art Museum, Princeton University, 1982. pp. 48–51, 122, 126–7, 130–31.

B112. Kepes, Gyorgy, ed. *Structure in Art and in Science*. New York, George Braziller; and London, Studio Vista, 1965. p. 19.

B113. Kochno, Boris. *Diaghilev and the Ballets Russes*. London, Allen Lane, The Penguin Press, 1971. pp. 248–53.

B114. Kostelanetz, Richard, ed. *Moholy-Nagy*. London, Allen Lane, The Penguin Press, 1971. pp. 111–13, 200, 215, 217.

B115. Krauss, Rosalind E. *Passages in Modern Sculpture*. London, Thames and Hudson, 1977. pp. 4, 56–63, 131–2, 143–4, 157, 161, 207, 216, 221, 253–4, *et passim*.

B116. Kuh, Katherine. *The Artist's Voice: Talks with 17 Artists*. New York, Harper and Row, 1962. pp. 94–104. Interview with Gabo.

B117. Kuh, Katherine. *Modern Art Explained*. London, Cory, Adams and Mackay, 1965. pp. 110–11. Published in the USA as *Breakup: The Core of Modern Art* Greenwich, Conn., New York Graphic Society, 1965.

B118. Kuhn, Charles, L. *German Expressionism and Abstract Art: The Harvard Collections: A Supplement to the 1957 Catalogue of Twentieth Century German Art at Harvard*. Cambridge, Mass., Busch-Reisinger Museum, 1967. [9, 64].

B119. Kultermann, Udo. *The New Sculpture: Environments and Assemblages*. London, Thames and Hudson, 1968, and New York, Frederick A. Praeger, 1968. pp. 113, 120, 158, 160–61.

B120. Levy, Julien. *Memoir of an Art Gallery*. New York, G. P. Putnam's Sons, 1977. pp. 136, 145, 203.

B121. Levy, Mervyn. *Drawing and Sculpture*. Bath, Somerset, Adams and Dart, 1970. pp. 102–11.

B122. Leymarie, Jean, ed. *Abstract Art since 1945*. London, Thames and Hudson, 1971. p. 182, *et passim*. Published in the USA as *Art Since Mid-Century: The New Internationalism: Volume 1. Abstract Art*. Greenwich, Conn., New York Graphic Society, 1971.

B123. Licht, Fred S. *Sculpture 19th and 20th Centuries*. London, Michael Joseph, and Greenwich, Conn., New York Graphic Society, 1967. p. 335.

B124. Ligeti, Paul. *Der Weg aus dem Chaos: Eine Deutung des Weltgeschehens aus dem Rhythmus der Kunstentwicklung*. Munich, Verlag Georg D. W. Callwey, 1931. fig. 287.

B125. Lissitzky, El and Hans Arp. *Die Kunstismen: Les ismes de l'art: The Isms of Art*. Zurich, Munich and Leipizig: Eugen Rentsch Verlag, 1925. fig. p. 5.

B126. *El Lissitzky*. Cologne, Galerie Gmurzynska, 9 Apr–30 Jun 1976. p. 37.

B127. Lissitzky-Küppers, Sophie. *El Lissitzky: Life, Letters, Texts*. London, Thames and Hudson; and Greenwich, Conn., New York Graphic Society, 1968. pp. 8–9, 24, 76, 338, figs 187–8. Translation of *El Lissitzky: Maler, Architekt, Typograf, Fotograf: Erinnerungen, Briefe, Schriften*. Dresden, VEB Verlag der Kunst, 1967.

B128. Lloyd, Christopher. *A Picture History of Art.* Oxford, Phaidon, 1979. p. 282.

B129. Lodder, Christina. *Russian Constructivism.* New Haven and London, Yale University Press, 1983. pp. 34–43, 228, 230, 236, 242–3, 272–3, 282, 285, 298, 302–3.

B130. [London: Tate Gallery] *Guide to the Collections of the Tate Gallery.* London, 1975; 1978. p. 22, 34.

B131. Lowry, Bates. *The Visual Experience: An Introduction to Art.* London, Prentice-Hall, 1961. p. 202.

B132. Lozowick, Louis, *Modern Russian Art.* New York, Museum of Modern Art – Société Anonyme, 1925. p. 45. Reprinted in B209.

B133. Lukach, Joan M. *Hilla Rebay: In Search of the Spirit in Art.* New York, George Braziller, 1983. pp. 110, 158–9, 232, 252–3, 262, 269–70, 340.

B134. Lynton, Norbert. *The Story of Modern Art.* Oxford, Phaidon, 1980. pp. 120–22, *et passim.*

B135. McCoy, Garnett. *Archives of American Art: A Dictionary of Resources.* New York and London, R. R. Bowker, 1972. p. 85.

B136. McCurdy, Charles, ed. *Modern Art: A Pictorial Anthology.* New York, Macmillan, 1958. pp. 233, 264–5.

B137. Maillard, Robert, ed. *A Dictionary of Modern Sculpture.* London, Methuen, 1962. pp. 101–3.

B138. Martin, J. Leslie and S. Speight. *The Flat Book.* London, William Heinemann, 1939. pp. 58–9.

B139. Meilach, Dona Z. and Don Seiden. *Direct Metal Sculpture: Creative Techniques and Appreciation.* London, George Allen and Unwin, 1966. pp. 13, 17.

B140. Merillat, Herbert C. *Modern Sculpture: The New Old Masters.* New York, Dodd Mead, 1974. pp. 43–4, 47–50, 65, 82, 120, 122–3, *et passim.*

B141. Miller, Dorothy C., ed. *The Nelson A. Rockefeller Collection: Masterpieces of Modern Art.* London, Orbis Publishing, 1982. pp. 23, 152.

B142. Milner, John. *Russian Revolutionary Art.* London, Oresko Books, 1979. pp. 25–6, 29–31, 40–41.

B143. Milner, John. *Vladimir Tatlin and the Russian Avant-Garde.* New Haven and London, Yale University Press, 1983. pp. 128, 130, 167.

B144. Moholy-Nagy, László. *The New Vision: From Material To Architecture.* New York, Brewer, Warren and Putnam, 1930. Translated from *Von Material zu Architektur* Munich, A. Langen, 1929. Reprinted 1968. pp. 135–7, 156, 162–3, 217.

B145. Moholy-Nagy, László. *Vision in Motion.* Chicago, Paul Theobald, 1947; 8th ed. 1969. pp. 226, 238.

B146. Moore, Lamonte. *The Sculptured Image.* New York, Franklin Watts, 1967. pp. 93–5.

B147. *Alistair Morton and Edinburgh Weavers: Abstract Art and Textile Design 1935–46.* Edinburgh, Scottish National Gallery of Modern Art, 29 Apr–29 May 1978. pp. 23, 32–3, *et passim.*

B148. Mumford, Lewis. *The Pentagon of Power.* London, Secker and Warburg, 1971. pp. 31–2.

B149. Mumford, Lewis. *My Works and Days: A Personal Chronicle.* New York and London, Harcourt Brace Jovanovich, 1979. pp. 178, 212, 235, 236–7, 408, 503, 507.

B150. Myers, Bernard S. *Art and Civilisation.* New York, McGraw-Hill, 1957. pp. 659–60.

B151. Nakov, Andrei B. *Abstrait/Concret: Art non-objectif Russe et Polonais.* Paris, Transédition, 1981. pp. 183–90.

B152. Neilson, Katherine B. *Selected Paintings and Sculpture from the Yale University Art Gallery.* Yale University Press, 1972. No. 133.

B153. Newman, Jay H. and Lee S. Newman. *Wire Art.* New York, Crown Publishers, 1975. p. 228.

B154. [New York: Solomon R. Guggenheim Museum] *A Handbook to the Solomon R. Guggenheim Collection.* New York, 1959. pp. 202–3. Revised as B14.

B155. [New York: Solomon R. Guggenheim Museum] *Selections from the Guggenheim Museum Collection: 1900–1970.* New York, 1970.

B156. [New York: Whitney Museum of American Art] *Catalogue of the Collection.* New York, 1974. pp. 115, 189.

B157. O'Konor, Louise, *Viking Eggeling 1880–1925: Artist and Film-Maker: Life and Work.* Stockholm, Almqvist and Wiksell, 1971. pp. 8, 14, 45, 49, 51, 76, 250 n. 20.

B158. Osborn, Elodie C. *Teaching Portfolio Number One: Modern Sculpture.* New York, Museum of Modern Art, [1948]. pp. [9–10].

B159. Osborne, Harold. *Abstraction and Artifice in Twentieth Century Art.* Oxford University Press, 1979. pp. 82, 125–6, 130, 171, 174.

B160. Ozenfant, Amedée. *Foundations of Modern Art.* London, John Rodker, 1931, p. 124; revised ed. New York, Dover, 1952. Translation of *Art* Paris, 1928.

B161. Petersen, V. Bjerke. *Konkret Konst.* Stockholm, Rabén and Sjögren, 1956. pp. 83, 118, 133.

B162. Pevsner, Alexei. *A Biographical Sketch of my Brothers, Naum Gabo and Antoine Pevsner.* Amsterdam, Augustin and Schoonman, 1964; French ed. 1968; Norwegian ed. 1971. (Reviewed in A155).

B163. *Antoine Pevsner.* Paris, Galerie René Drouin, 1947.

B164. *The Phillips Collection: A Museum of Modern Art and Its Sources: Catalogue.* Washington, DC, 1952. p. 40.

B165. Phillips, Marjorie. *Duncan Phillips and His Collection.* Boston, Little, Brown and Co., 1970. pp. 236, 306, 329.

B166. Popper, Frank. *Origins and Development of Kinetic Art.* London, Studio Vista, 1968. Translation of *Naissance de la cinétique.* Paris, Gauthier-Villars, 1967.

B167. Pritchard, Jack. *View from a Long Chair.* London, Routledge and Kegan Paul, 1984. pp. 21, 22, 92.

B168. Propert, W. A. *The Russian Ballet, 1921–9.* London, Allen Lane, 1931. pp. 52–5.

B169. Raine, Kathleen. *The Land Unknown.* London, Hamish Hamilton, 1975. p. 130.

B170. Ramsden, E. H. *An Introduction to Modern Art.* Oxford University Press, 1940; 1949. pp. 18, 22–3.

B171. Ramsden, E. H. *Sculpture: Theme and Variations.* London, Lund Humphries, 1953. pp. 17, 44–6, 47–8, 51–2.

B172. Read, Herbert. *Art Now.* London, Faber and Faber, 2nd ed. 1936, fig. 67; revised 1948, 1960, 1963, 1968.

B173. Read, Herbert. *The Politics of the Unpolitical.* London, Routledge, 1943. pp. 81–92, 124–31. (Contains A158 and A160 revised).

B174. Read, Herbert. *The Philosophy of Modern Art: Collected Essays.* London, Faber and Faber, 1952; revised 1964, 1969, 1975. pp. 51–2, 93–5, 226–45, *et passim* (Contains G20, A162, and Read's essay for E9).

B175. Read, Herbert. *Icon and Idea.* Cambridge, Mass., Harvard University Press; and London, Faber and Faber, 1955. pp. 133–5, 152.

B176. Read, Herbert. *The Art of Sculpture.* Bollingen Series XXXV.3, Princeton University Press, 1956. pp. 43, 98–9, 101–2, 112. The A. W. Mellon Lectures in the Fine Arts, 1954, National Gallery of Art, Washington, DC.

B177. Read, Herbert. *The Tenth Muse: Essays in Criticism.* London, Routledge and Kegan Paul, 1957. (Essay No. 6, pp. 32–58, was also Read's introduction to G28).

B178. Read, Herbert. *The Forms of Things Unknown: Essays towards an Aesthetic Philosophy.* London, Faber and Faber, 1960. pp. 148, 163–5, 196.

B179. Read, Herbert. *A Concise History of Modern Sculpture.* London, Thames and Hudson, 1964; 1974. pp. 93–7, 100–102, 105–14, 228.

B180. Read, Herbert. *Art and Alienation: The Role of the Artist in Society.* New York, Viking Press, 1969. pp. 156–64, 172. (Contains essay in E21).

B181. Rice, Tamara T. *A Concise History of Russian Art.* London, Thames and Hudson, 1963. p. 265.

B182. Richardson, John A. *Art: The Way it Is.* Englewood Cliffs, NJ, Prentice-Hall; and New York, Abrams, [1973]; 1980.

B183. Richter, Hans. *Köpfe und Hinterköpfe.* Zurich, Arche, 1967. pp. 22, 97–8.

B184. Rickey, George. *Constructivism: Origins and Evolution.* New York, George Braziller, 1967. pp. 21, 23, 25–34, 37, 41, 84–5, 106–7, 111, 191–3, *et passim.*

B185. Ritchie, Andrew C. *Sculpture of the Twentieth Century.* New York, Museum of Modern Art, 1952. pp. 44, 151–3, 203. (Contains G13).

B186. Robb, David M. and J. J. Garrison. *Art and the Western World.* New York and Evanston, Harper and Row, 4th ed. 1963. p. 407.

B187. Robinson, Duncan and Elizabeth Robinson. *An Illustrated Handlist of the Paintings, Sculptures and Drawings.* Cambridge, Kettle's Yard, University of Cambridge, 1970. fig.

B188. Roos, Frank J. *An Illustrated Handbook of Art History.* New York, Macmillan, 1954.

B189. Rosenblum, Robert. *Cubism and Twentieth Century Art.* New York, Abrams, 1959; revised 1976. pp. 294, 299.

B190. Rothenstein, Michael. *Looking at Paintings.* London, Routledge, 1947. p. 63.

B191. Rotzler, Willy. *Constructive Concepts: A History of Constructive Art from Cubism to the Present: Collection McCrory Corporation, New York.* Zurich, ABC Edition, 1977. pp. 46, 50, 171, 225, 233, 266, *et passim.*

B192. Rudenstine, Angelica Z., ed. *Russian Avant-Garde Art: The George Costakis Collection.* New York, Abrams; and London, Thames and Hudson, 1981. pp. 41, 206, 223.

B193. Russell, John. *The Meanings of Modern Art. Vol. 8. A World Remodeled.* New York, Museum of Modern Art, 1975. p 17.

B194. Russell, Stella P. *Art in the World.* San Francisco, Holt, Rinehart and Winston, 1975. p. 306.

B195. *Russian Avant-Garde (1908–1922).* New York, Leonard Hutton Galleries, 16 Oct 1971–29 Feb 1972. pp. 64–5, 94–5.

B196. Sandberg, Willem and Hans L. C. Jaffé. *Pioneers of Modern Art in the Museum of the City of Amsterdam.* New York, McGraw-Hill, 1961. figs. 87–8. Translation of *Kunst van Heden in het Stedelijk.* Amsterdam, Stedelijk Museum, 1961.

B197. Sarff, Laura and Jan Harem. *Symmography: Linear Thread Design.* Worcester, Mass., Davis, 1979. pp. 72–3, 82.

B198. Scharf, Aaron. *Art and Photography.* London, Allen Lane The Penguin Press, 1968. p. 209.

B199. Scheepmaker, H. J., ed. *Adventure in Art: An International Group of Art Collections in Industrial Environments.* New York, Abrams, 1969. p. 71.

B200. Schmied, Wieland, *Wegbereiter zur Modernen Kunst: 50 Jahre Kestner-Gesellschaft.* Hannover, Schmidt-Küster, 1966. pp. 254, 262, 274, 287.

B201. Segawa, S., ed. *The Hakone Open-Air Museum.* Tokyo, Hakone Open Air Museum, 1979. pp. 66, 209.

B202. Selz, Jean. *Modern Sculpture: Origins and Evolution.* London, Heinemann, 1963. pp. 239, 246.

B203. Seuphor, Michel. *L'Art abstrait: Ses origines, ses premiers maîtres.* Paris, Maeght, 1949. pp. 52–60, 87, 294–5.

B204. Seuphor, Michel. *The Sculpture of This Century: Dictionary of Modern Sculpture.* Neuchâtel, Editions du Griffon, 1959. pp. 72–4, 211, 266–7, 360.

B205. Seuphor, Michel. *Cercle et carré.* Paris, Pierre Belfond, 1971. p. 14.

B206. Seuphor, Michel and Michel Ragon. *L'Art abstrait.* 4 vols, Paris, Maeght, 1971–74. Vol. 1, pp. 34, 39, 58, 62; Vol. 2, pp. 23–4, 40, 97, 185–7, 206; Vol. 4, p. 212.

B207. *Seuphor.* Paris, Musée National d'Art Moderne. 1977. pp. 69, 305–6, 345.

B208. Seymour, Charles, Jr. *Tradition and Experiment in Modern Sculpture.* Washington, DC, American University Press, 1949. p. 58.

B209. *Société Anonyme: Selected Publications. Vol. 1. Documents.* New York, Arno Press, 1972. (Contains B59, B132).

B210. *Some New Forms of Beauty 1909–36.* Springfield, Mass., G.W.V. Smith Art Gallery, 9 Nov–17 Dec 1939. pp. 15, 19–20. (*Re* Société Anonyme).

B211. Steinitz, Kate T. *Kurt Schwitters: A Portrait from Life.* University of California Press, 1968. pp. 78, 91.

B212. Steneberg, Eberhard. *Russische Kunst Berlin 1919–1932.* Berlin, Gebr. Mann Verlag, 1969. pp. 12, 19, 21, 22, 24–5, 33–7, 46, 53, 63, 68.

B213. Sylvester, David, ed. *The Book of Art. Vol. 8 Modern Art from Fauvism to Abstract Expressionism.* New York, Franklin Watts, 1965.

B214. Tasalov, V. *Prometei ili Orfei [Prometheus or Orpheus].* Moscow, 1967. pp. 237–45.

B215. Teige, Karel. *Sovetská kultura [Soviet Culture].* Prague, Odeon, 1928. pp. 59, 61, 84.

B216. Thistlewood, David. *Herbert Read: Form and Formlessness.* London, Routledge and Kegan Paul, 1984. pp. 85–96, 101–4, 139–40, 165–6, 191, *et passim.*

B217. Thwaites, John A. *Ich hasse die Moderne Kunst!* Krefeld und Baden-Baden, Agis-Verlag, 1957. fig. 12.

B218. Trier, Eduard. *Moderne Plastik: Von Auguste Rodin bis Marino Marini.* Frankfurt-am-Main, Büchergilde Gutenberg, 1955. pp. 73–5, 86–7.

B219. Trier, Eduard. *Zeichner des XX. Jahrhunderts.* Berlin, Gebr. Mann Verlag, 1956. p. 100.

B220. Trier, Eduard. *Form and Space.* London, Thames and Hudson, 1961.

B221. Vallier, Dora. *L'Art abstrait.* Paris, Livre de Poche, 1967. pp. 186–95.

B222. Van Traa, Ir. C., ed. *Rotterdam: De Geschiedenis van Tien Jaren Wederopbouw.* Rotterdam, Ad. Donker, 1955. pp.158–9.

B223. *Vassar College Art Gallery, 1939.* Poughkeepsie, NY, 1939. pp. 65, 123.

B224. *Vassar College Art Gallery: Selections from the Permanent Collection.* New York, Clarke and Way, 1967. pp. 84, 169.

B225. Waddington, C. H. *Behind Appearance: A Study of the Relations between Painting and the Natural Sciences in This Century.* Edinburgh University Press, 1969. pp. 45–50, 113, 115, 213–14, *et passim.*

B226. Wagar, W. Warren, ed. *Science, Faith, and Man: European Thought Since 1914.* New York, Walker, 1968. pp. 193–205. (Contains G22).

B227. *»Was die Schönheit Sei, Das Weiss Ich Nicht«: Künstler-Theorie-Werk: Katalog zur Zweiten Biennale.* Nürnberg 1971. pp. 223–5.

B228. Willett, John. *The New Sobriety: Art and Politics in the Weimar Period 1917–1933.* London, Thames and Hudson, 1978. pp. 39, 76, 79, 136, 171.

B229. Williams, Robert C. *Culture in Exile: Russian Emigrés in Germany, 1881–1941.* Ithaca, NY, Cornell University Press, 1972. pp. 305–9, 311, 364.

B230. Williams, Robert C. *Artists in Revolution: Portraits of the Russian Avant-Garde 1905–1925.* Bloomington, Indiana University Press, 1977; London, Scolar Press, 1978. pp. 141–2, 158, 195.

B231. Williams, Robert C. *Russian Art and American Money 1900–1940.* Cambridge, Mass., Harvard University Press, 1980. pp. 90, 95–6.

B232. Wingler, Hans M. *The Bauhaus: Weimar, Dessau, Berlin, Chicago.* Cambridge, Mass., M.I.T. Press, 3rd ed. 1976. pp. 276, 629.

B233. Zanini, Walter. *Tendências da escultura moderna.* São Paulo University, Museu de Art Contemporánea, 1971. pp. 212–24, *et passim.*

B234. Zervos, Christian. *Histoire de l'art contemporaine.* Paris, Editions Cahiers d'Art, 1938. p. 366.

B235. Zygas, K. Paul. *Form Follows Form: Source Imagery of Constructivist Architecture 1917–1925.* Ann Arbor, Mich., UMI Research Press, 1981.

ARTICLES, ESSAYS AND PERIODICAL PUBLICATIONS

Where the place of publication is clearly indicated by the title of a periodical, it is not repeated.

A1. Alvard, Julien. ›Le manifeste constructiviste‹, *Cimaise* (Paris) No, 4, Feb-Mar 1954, pp. 20–21.

A2. Alvard, Julien, ›Gabo le réaliste‹, *Aujourd'hui: Art et architecture* (Paris) Year 7, No. 39, Nov 1962, pp. 4–5.

A3. [Anon.] ›Accessions of American and Canadian Museums, October-December, 1958‹, *Art Quarterly* (Detroit) Vol. 22, No. 1, 1959, pp. 78–92. (*Re* 68.3, pp. 88, 90).

A4. [Anon.] ›Accessions of American and Canadian Museums, April-June, 1964‹, *Art Quarterly* (Detroit) Vol. 27, No. 3, 1964, pp. 370–92. (*Re* 70.4, pp. 378, 392).

A5. [Anon.] ›Acquisitions of Modern Art by Museums‹, *The Burlington Magazine* (London) Vol. 112, No, 806, May 1970, pp. 337–46. (*Re* 55.21, pp. 339, 343).

A6. [Anon.] ›Acquisitions of Twentieth Century Art by Museums‹, *The Burlington Magazine* (London) Vol. 122, No. 928, Jul 1980. (*Re* 53.4, pp. 529, 533).

A7. [Anon.] ›Antologia critica‹, *L'Arte moderna* (Milan) Vol. VI, No. 54, 1967, pp. 322–86.

A8. [Anon.] ›An Architecture for Day or Night‹ and ›Art, Artists and Architecture: Sculpture by Naum Gabo‹, *The Architectural Record* (New York) Vol. 122, No. 5, Nov 1957, pp. 167–74, 175–8.

A9. [Anon.] ›Art: Exhibitions‹, *Time* (New York) 15 Mar 1968, pp. 42–5. (Reviews E22).

A10. [Anon.] ›The Artist Looks at Plastics‹, *Modern Plastics* (New York) Vol. 23, No. 4, Dec 1945, pp. 120–27.

A11. [Anon.] ›Bemerkungen‹, *Das Neue Frankfurt* Vol. 5, No. 1, Jan 1931, pp. 16–17. Reprinted in B105. (*Re* E5).

A12. [Anon.] ›Constructions in Space: Naum Gabo's Work in Plastics‹, *Plastics* (London) Vol. 2, No. 9, Feb 1938, pp. 50–51. (Reviews E6).

A13. [Anon.] ›Constructivist‹, *The New Yorker*, 20 Mar 1948, pp. 25–6. (Reviews E9).

A14. [Anon.] ›Contemporary Art in the United States‹, *Worcester Art Museum: News Bulletin and Calendar* (Worcester, Mass.) Vol. 16, No. 5, 1951. pp. 19–20, 22. (*Re* E78).

A15.   [Anon.] ›Design Review‹, *The Architectural Review* (London) Vol. 96, No. 571, Jul 1944. pp. 24–6.

A16.   [Anon.] ›Events and Comments‹, *The Architect and Building News* (London) Vol. 153, No. 3605, 21 Jan 1938, pp. 87–8. (Reviews E6, E51).

A17.   [Anon.] ›Full Marks for the Hawkes Coat-Hanger‹, *Plastics* (London) Vol. 2, No. 14, Jul 1938, p. 232.

A18.   [Anon.] ›Gabo on »Sculpture and Architecture«‹ *The Architects' Journal* (London) Vol. 87, 16 Mar 1938, pp. 468–9. (Reports Gabo's speech to the Architectural Association School, 17 Feb 1938).

A19.   [Anon.] ›Integration des arts dans l'architecture‹, *Aujourd'hui: art et architecture* (Paris) Year 2, No. 11, Jan 1957, pp. 12–22.

A20.   [Anon.] ›Kunsthandel‹, *Pantheon* (Munich) Vol. 38, No. 2, Apr-Jun 1980, p. 200. (*Re* 34.5).

A21.   [Anon.] ›Le Musée Hirshhorn‹, *Connaissance des arts* (Paris) No. 272, Oct 1974, pp. 110–13.

A22.   [Anon.] ›Naum Gabo ontwierp Monument voor Rotterdam‹ [›Naum Gabo designed Monument for Rotterdam‹], *Bijenkorf: Personeelorgaan van de Bijenkorf* (Amsterdam) Year 20, No. 211, Mar 1956, pp. 52–3. (*Re* 67.5).

A23.   [Anon.] ›Netherlands Department Store Rebuilds‹, *The Architectural Record* (New York) Vol. 117, No. 5, May 1955, pp. 206–7. (*Re* Bijenkorf store).

A24.   [Anon.] ›Neuerwerbungen der Museen‹, *Kunstjahrbuch* (Hannover) No. 1, 1970, p. 207.

A25.   [Anon.] ›Queer Bolshevist Art in Berlin‹, *Arts and Decoration* (New York) Vol. 18, No. 6, Apr 1923, p. 87. (Reviews E31).

A26.   [Anon.] ›Round the Exhibitions‹, *The Listener* (London) Vol. 18, No. 445, 21 Jul 1937, p. 131. (*Re* E49).

A27.   [Anon.] ›Die Sammlung der Brüder ***‹, *Du* (Zurich) Year 35, No. 2, 1975, pp. 17–58.

A28.   [Anon.] ›A Sculpture – Naum Gabo‹, *Bulletin of the Associates in Fine Arts at Yale University* (New Haven) Vol. 23, Nos 1/2, Feb 1957, pp. 13–14. (*Re* 22.3).

A29.   [Anon.] ›Société Anonyme's Exciting Show‹, *The Art News* (New York) Vol. 25, No. 8, 27 Nov 1926, pp. 1, 3. Reprinted in *Brooklyn Museum Quarterly* Vol. 14, No. 1, Jan 1927, pp. 20–22. (Reviews E38).

A30.   [Anon.] ›Some Old Soldiers Live . . .‹, *The Architectural Forum* (New York) Vol. 128, No. 3, Apr 1968, p. 94. (Reviews E22).

A31.   [Anon.] ›Suprematisti e Construttivisti in Russia‹, *L'Arte moderna* (Milan) Vol. VI, No. 48, 1967, pp. 81–120.

A32.   [Anon.] ›Three Decades of Collecting: Gifts of Anna Bing Arnold‹, *Los Angeles County Museum of Art Bulletin*, Vol 26, 1980, pp. 6–95. (*Re* 68.7, pp. 86–7).

A33.   [Anon.] ›Veertig ton »bloem« nu bijna aaneengesmeed‹, [›Forty ton »flower« now almost welded together‹] *Bijenkorf: Personeelorgaan van de Bijenkorf* (Amsterdam) Year 21, No. 221, Feb 1957, p. 37. (*Re* 67.5).

A34.   [Anon.] ›Een Voorbeeld van Modelonderzoek‹ [›An Instance of the Investigation of a Model‹],

IBC: Mededelingen (Delft) Vol. 5, No. 4, Oct 1957, pp. 104–22. (*Re* structural tests for 67).

A35.   *Architecture Vivante* (Paris) [No. 1], Spring and Summer 1927, fig. p. 34.

A36.   *Architecture Vivante* (Paris) [No. 2], Autumn and Winter 1928, fig. p. 46.

A37.   Arkus, L. A. ›Expressing the Spirit of the Times: 1970 Pittsburgh International Exhibition of Contemporary Art, Opening October 30‹, *Carnegie Magazine* (Pittsburgh) Vol. 44, No. 8, 1970, pp. 305–8. (Reviews E190).

A38.   *Art International* (Lugano) Vol. 21, No. 6, Dec 1977, fig. p. 5.

A39.   *Axis* (London) No. 5, Spring 1936. Issue devoted to ›International Exhibition of Abstract Painting, Sculpture and Construction‹ (E44–5).

A40.   Baljeu, Joost. ›The Problem of Reality with Suprematism, Constructivism, Proun, Neoplasticism and Elementarism‹, *Lugano Review* Vol. 1, No. 1, 1965, pp. 105–28.

A41.   Baljeu, Joost. ›The Hegelian Romantic Negation in Modern Plastic Art‹, *Art International* (Lugano) Vol. 10, No. 2, Feb 1966, pp. 24–8, 37–9. Reprinted in Swedish in E20.

A42.   *Baltimore Museum of Art News* Vol. 13, No. 6, Mar 1950. (Catalogue of the Saidie A. May Collection).

A43.   *Baltimore Museum of Art News* Vol. 15, No. 1, Oct 1951, fig. p. 4.

A44.   *Baltimore Museum of Art News* Vol. 15, No. 2, Nov 1951, p. 4. (*Re* 57.3).

A45.   *The Baltimore Museum of Art Record* Vol. 3, No. 1, 1972. Special issue titled *Saidie A. May Collection,* cataloguing the collection. Introduction by Jane H. Cone. (*Re* 47.1, p. 47; *re* 57.3, p. 48).

A46.   B[anham], P. R[ayner]. ›Two Works by Naum Gabo‹, *Architectural Review* (London) Vol. 117, Mar 1955, pp. 203–4.

A47.   B[anham], P. R[ayner]. ›Gabo in Rotterdam‹. *Architectural Review* (London) Vol. 119, May 1956, p. 270.

A48.   Baro, Gene. ›Futurism Preserved: Lydia Winston Malbin‹, in Jean Lipman, ed. *The Collector in America* (London), Macdonald and Co., 1971, pp. 180–89.

A49.   Barron, Stephanie. ›Two Recent Acquisitions: A Painting by Paul Klee and a Sculpture by Naum Gabo‹, *Los Angeles County Museum of Art Bulletin*, Vol. 25, 1980, pp. 66–79. (*Re* 68).

A50.   *Bauhaus* (Dessau) Vol. 3, No. 4, Oct–Dec 1929, fig. p. 19.

A51.   Bekkers, Ludo. ›Gesprek met Naum Gabo‹ [›Talk with Naum Gabo‹], *Streven* (Amsterdam) Year 20, Part 1, No. 1, Oct 1966, pp. 29–35.

A52.   Berger, John. ›The Engineer as Prophet‹, *New Statesman* (London) Vol. 55, No. 1421, 7 Jun 1958, pp. 724, 726. (*Re* 67.5. Revised as ›Naum Gabo‹, in Berger, *Permanent Red: Essays in Seeing.* London, Methuen, 1960, pp. 58–64).

A53.   Bernier, Rosamond. ›Une collection du Middle West‹, *L'Oeil* (Paris) No. 156, Dec 1967, pp. 30–39.

A54.   Besset, Maurice. ›Gabo et l'abstraction scientifique‹, *L'Oeil* (Paris) No. 203, Nov 1971, pp. 8–11, cover fig. Reprinted from E26.

A55.   *La Biennale di Venezia* (Venice) Year 11, Nos 44/45, Dec 1961, fig. p. 13.

A56.   Bier, Justus. ›Gabo‹, *Die Form* (Berlin) Year 6, No. 12, 15 Dec 1931, pp. 465–7.

A57.   Bill, Max. ›Über konkrete Kunst‹, *Das Werk* (Bern) Vol. 25, No 8, Aug 1938, pp. 250–56.

A58.   Bird, Paul. ›Sculptures Provide Main Interest at Whitney Annual‹, *Art Digest* (New York) Vol. 25, No. 13, 1 Apr 1951, p. 9.

A59.   Blanc, Peter. ›The Artist and the Atom‹, *Magazine of Art* (Washington, DC) Vol. 44, No. 4, Apr 1951, pp. 145–52. Reprinted in *Smithsonian Institution Annual Report 1951* 1952, pp. 427–39.

A60.   Bouillon, Jean-Paul. ›Le Cubisme et l'avant-garde Russe‹, *Travaux IV: Le Cubisme.* Université de Saint-Etienne, Centre Interdisciplinaire d'Etudes et de Recherche sur l'Expression Contemporaine, 1973, pp. 153–223.

A61.   Bouillon, Jean-Paul ›Le Retour à l'ordre en U.R.S.S., 1920–1923‹, *Travaux VIII: Le Retour à l'ordre dans les arts plastiques et l'architecture, 1919–1925.* Université de Saint-Etienne, Centre Interdisciplinaire d'Etudes et de Recherche sur l'Expression Contemporaine, 1975, pp. 167–202.

A62.   Buckley, C. E. ›Mobiles and Constructions – Alexander Calder and Naum Gabo‹, *Wadsworth Atheneum Bulletin* (Hartford, Conn.) No. 42, Oct 1953, p. 2. (Reviews E14).

A63.   Buckley, C. E. ›Blue Construction in Space (Kinetic)‹, *Wadsworth Atheneum Bulletin* (Hartford, Conn.) No. 47, Mar 1954, p. 1.

A64.   Byard, S. ›Constructivist Art‹, *The Listener* (London) Vol. 16, No. 410, 18 Nov 1936, p. 966.

A65.   Calvacoressi, Richard. ›Public Sculpture in the 1950s‹, in Sandy Nairne and Nicholas Serota, eds. *British Sculpture in the Twentieth Century.* London, Whitechapel Art Gallery, 1981, pp. 135–53.

A66.   *Cambridge: The Magazine of the Cambridge Society,* No. 6, 1980, fig. p. 4.

A67.   Campbell, H. J. ›Pleasure Seeking Brains: Artificial Tickles, Natural Joys of Thought‹, *Smithsonian* (Washington, DC) Vol. 2, No. 7, Oct 1971, pp. 14–23.

A68.   C[ampbell], L[arry]. ›Naum Gabo‹, *Art News* (New York) Vol. 52, May 1953, p. 52. (Reviews E13).

A69.   Carter, Huntley. ›Russian Art Movements since 1917‹, *Drawing and Design* (London) Vol. 4, No. 20, Feb 1928, pp. 37–42.

A70.   Causey, Andrew. ›Gabo Sees »Endless Possibilities« for Constructivist Arts‹, *The Illustrated London News*, 19 Mar 1966, pp. 34–5. (Reviews E21).

A71.   Celsing, Peter. ›Stadshallen i Lund‹ [›Town Hall in Lund‹], *Arkitektur* (Stockholm) Year 68, No. 12, Dec 1968, p. 4.

A72.   Chanin, A. L. ›Gabo Makes a Construction‹, *Art News* (New York) Vol. 52, No. 7, Nov 1953, pp. 34–7, 46.

A73.   Chermayeff, Serge. ›Naum Gabo‹, *Magazine of Art* (Washington, DC) Vol. 41, Feb 1948, pp. 56–9, cover fig. (Reviews E9).

A74.   Chermayeff, Serge. ›Painting toward Architecture‹, *Arts and Architecture* (Los Angeles) Vol. 65, No. 6, Jun 1948, pp. 24–31.

A75. Clay, Jean. ›»Art . . . Should Change Man«: Commentary from Stockholm‹, *Studio International* (London) Vol. 171, No. 875, Mar 1966, pp. 116–19. (Reviews E20).

A76. Clay, Jean. ›The Gift of Gabo‹, *Réalités* (Paris) No. 188, Jul 1966, pp. 56–61. Translation of ›Gabo le précurseur‹, *Réalités* (Paris) No. 242, Mar 1966, pp. 84–9.

A77. Cleaver, Dale. ›The Concept of Time in Modern Sculpture‹, *Art Journal* (New York) Vol. 22, No. 4, Summer 1963, pp. 232–6, 245.

A78. Cornford, Christopher. ›Tanker ved den retrospektive Gabo-udstilling, Tate Gallery 1966‹ [›Thoughts on the Retrospective Gabo-Exihibition at the Tate Gallery, 1966‹], *Louisiana Revy* (Humlebaek) Year 11, No. 2, Nov 1970, p. 15. (Reviews E21).

A79. Courthion, Pierre. ›Prenez-garde à la sculpture‹, *XXe Siècle* (Paris) Year 21, No. 13, Christmas 1959, pp. 33–41.

A80. D[avidson], M[artha]. ›Gabo: Constructions in Space‹, *Art News* (New York) Vol. 36, No. 29, 16 Apr 1938, pp. 14–15. (Reviews E7).

A81. Davies, Peter. ›St. Ives in the Forties‹, *Artscribe* (London) No. 34, 31 Mar 1982, pp. 55–7.

A82. De Mély, F. ›Le Cubisme à travers les ages‹, *La Renaissance de l'Art Français et des Industries de Luxe* (Paris) No. 9, Sep 1927, pp. 417–24.

A83. De Sausmarez, Maurice. ›Naum Gabo Talking to Maurice De Sausmarez‹ in *Ben Nicholson: A Studio International Special* (London) 1969, pp. 15–16, 21.

A84. Dreier, Katherine S. ›Explaining Modern Art‹, *The American Art Student and Commercial Artist* (New York) Vol. 10, No. 7, Mar 1927, pp. 44–50.

A85. E., J. L. ›The Way beyond Kinsey or Aesthetic Behaviour in the Harvard Architect‹, *GSD Bulletin* (Cambridge, Mass.) Vol. 1, No. 9, 12 Aug 1948. (*Re* student responses to Gabo's teaching at Harvard).

A86. *Egység* (Vienna) No. 2, 1922, pp. 3–4, fig. p. 8. (Contains first translation of G1, without acknowledgement of authorship).

A87. Ernest, John. ›Constructivism and Content‹, *Studio International* (London) Vol. 171, No. 876, Apr 1966, pp. 148–56.

A88. Evans, Myfanwy. ›Order, Order!‹, *Axis* (London) No. 6, Summer 1936, pp. 4–8. Reprinted in E255. (Reviews E44, E47).

A89. Fenton, Terry. ›Constructivism and its Confusions‹, *Artforum* (New York) Vol. 7, Jan 1969, pp. 22–32.

A90. Field, Maurice E. ›Realist versus Abstract Art‹, *The Listener* (London) Vol. 23, No. 577, 1 Feb 1940, p. 230.

A91. Fitzsimmons, James. ›Art‹, *Arts and Architecture* (Los Angeles) Vol. 70, No. 6, Jun 1953, pp. 6–8, 12–14. (Reviews E13).

A92. Fletcher, Richard. ›The Arena of the Modern Artist‹, *Artwork* (London) No. 11, Sep-Nov 1927, pp. 182–6.

A93. Forge, Andrew. ›Naum Gabo at the Tate‹, *Artforum* (New York) Vol. 4, No. 10, Jun 1966, pp. 39–42. (Reviews E21).

A94. Freemantle, C. E. ›Constructivist Sculptures at the Museum of Modern Art‹, *Studio* (London) Vol. 136, Jul 1948, p. 28. (Reviews E9).

A95. Geist, Sidney. ›Monumental Contest: US entries‹, *Art Digest* (Hopewell, NJ) Vol. 27, No. 9, Feb 1953, p. 9. (Reviews E93).

A96. Geist, Sidney. ›Two Pure‹, *Art Digest* (Hopewell, NJ) Vol. 27, No. 15, May 1953, pp. 15–16. (Reviews E13).

A97. Gibson, William. ›Sculpture: A Comparison‹, *World Review* (London) Aug 1942, pp. 40–46.

A98. Gibson, William. ›Notes sur six artistes qui travaillent en Angleterre‹, *Choix* (London) Vol. 2, No. 12, Jan 1946, pp. 61–8.

A99. Giedion-Welcker, Carola. ›New Roads in Modern Sculpture‹, *Transition* (Paris) No. 23, Jul 1935, pp. 198–203.

A100. *Glaube und Tat* (Kassel) Year 16, No. 11, Nov 1965, fig. p. 323.

A101. Glazebrook, Mark, ›John Tunnard‹, *John Tunnard*. London, Arts Council Exhibition, 1977, pp. 13–36. (*Re* meeting Gabo p. 21).

A102. Goffin, Peter. ›Images of Movement‹, *Image: A Quarterly of the Visual Arts* (London) No. 2, Autumn 1949, pp. 51–63.

A103. Granath, Olle. ›Oändligheten som Form‹ [›Infinity as Form‹], *Konstrevy* (Stockholm) Year 42, No. 1, 1966, pp. 8–15. (Reviews E20).

A104. Gray, Camilla. ›A New Translation of the Realistic Manifesto‹, *The Structurist* (Saskatoon) No. 8, 1968, pp. 43–7. (For Gabo's reaction see G36).

A105. Gray, Cleve. ›Naum Gabo Talks about Constructivism‹, *Art in America* (New York) Vol. 54, No. 6, Nov–Dec 1966, pp. 48–55.

A106. Haftmann, Werner. ›Neuerwerbungen der Nationalgalerie im Jahre 1972‹, *Jahrbuch der Preussischer Kulturbesitz* (Berlin) Vol. 10, 1972, pp. 267–73.

A107. Hamilton, George H. ›Object and Image‹, *Art News* (New York) Vol. 53, No. 3, May 1954, pp. 18–21, 58–9.

A108. Hand, Jon R. ›Modern Art: Naum Gabo Expands Constructivism‹, *Kite* (Albany, NY) 7 Nov 1979.

A109. Harrison, Charles. ›Sculpture and the New »New Movement««, in Sandy Nairne and Nicholas Serota, eds. *British Sculpture in the Twentieth Century.* London, Whitechapel Art Gallery, 1981, pp. 102–11.

A110. Hayes, Bartlett, H., Jr. ›Time and No Decay‹, *Antiques* (New York) Vol. 61, No. 6, Jun 1952, pp. 508–11. (*Re* E87).

A111. Henry, Sara L. ›Form-Creating Energies: Paul Klee and Physics‹, *Arts Magazine* (New York) Vol. 52, No. 1, Summer 1977, pp. 118–21.

A112. Heron, Patrick. ›The Visual Arts‹, *Architect's Year Book* (London) No. 3, 1949, pp. 20–31.

A113. Hess, Thomas, B. ›Invited Guests of the Whitney‹, *Art News* (New York) Vol. 49, No. 8, Dec 1950, pp. 32–3, 63. (Reviews E77).

A114. Hilberry, Susanne, F. ›Naum Gabo: A Constructivist Sculptor‹, *Bulletin of the Detroit Institute of Arts*, Vol. 54, No. 4, 1976, pp. 175–83. (*Re* 68).

A115. Hill, Anthony. ›Constructivism – the European Phenomenon‹, *Studio International* (London) Vol. 171, No. 876, Apr 1966, pp. 140–47.

A116. Hinks, Roger. ›Reason and Imagination in Art‹, *The Listener* (London) Vol. 16, No. 394, 29 Jul 1936, pp. 224–6.

A117. Hodin, J. P. ›From Cornwall‹, *Art and Artists* (London) Vol. 11, No. 3, Jun 1976, pp. 16–21.

A118. Hultén, K. G. ›Om Gabos Første Skulpturer‹ [›On Gabo's First Sculptures‹] *Louisiana Revy* (Humlebaek) Year 11, No. 2, Nov 1970, pp. 7–9. Reprinted from E20. Reprinted in *XXe Siècle* (Paris) Vol. 33, No. 37, Dec 1971, pp. 65–73, and in German in E24.

A119. Johnson, Charlotte B. ›Gabo‹, *School Arts* (Boston) Vol. 66, No. 6, Feb 1967, p. 52.

A120. Johnsrud, Even H. ›Noen Nyere Utsmykninger i Oslo‹ [›Some Recent Examples of Decorative Art in Oslo‹], *Kunsten Idag* (Oslo) 1973, pp. 5–56; English text, pp. 57–64.

A121. Jordan, Jim M. ›The Structure of Paul Klee's Art in the Twenties: From Cubism to Constructivism›, *Arts Magazine* (New York) Vol. 52, Summer 1977, pp. 152–7.

A122. Jürgen-Fischer, K. ›Nachwirkungen des Jugendstils‹, *Das Kunstwerk* (Baden-Baden) Vol. 23, Nos 7–8, Apr–May 1970, pp. 13–43.

A123. Kállai, Ernst. ›Konstruktivismus‹, *Jahrbuch der Jungen Kunst* (Leipzig) Vol. 5, 1924, pp. 374–84.

A124. Kállai, Ernst. ›Der Plastiker Gabo‹, *i 10* (Amsterdam) Year 1, No. 7, 1927, pp. 244–50. Reprinted in Arthur Lehning and Juriaan Schrofer, eds. *De Internationale Avant-garde tussen de twee Wereldoorlogen: een Kuize uit de Internationale Revue i 10 [The International Avant-garde between the two World Wars: A Selection from the International Review i 10]* Den Haag, Bert Bakker, 1963.

A125. Kállai, Ernst. ›Der Raumplastiker Gabo‹, *Das Neue Frankfurt*, Vol. 4, No. 1, Jan 1930, pp. 17–19. Revised as A126.

A126. Kállai, Ernst. ›Der Raumplastiker Gabo‹, *Forum* (Bratislava) Nos 11–2, 1932, pp. 287–9. Revision of A125.

A127. Kassák, Lajos. ›A Berlini orosz kiállitáshoz‹ [At the Berlin Russian Exhibition‹], *MA* (Vienna) Vol. 8, Nos 2–3, 25 Dec 1922 [pp. 7–10]. (Reviews E31).

A128. Keller, Horst. ›Berichte aus Westdeutschen Museen: Wallraf-Richartz-Museum Köln›, *Wallraf-Richartz-Jahrbuch* (Cologne) Vol. 31, 1969, pp. 320–24.

A129. Khalturin, A. ›Sovetskaya kultura na mezhdunarodnoi vystavke v Monreale‹ [›Soviet Culture at the International Exhibition in Montreal‹], *Iskusstvo* (Moscow) No. 11, 1967, pp. 10–15. (Reviews E180).

A130. Lassaw, Abram and Ilya Bolotowsky. ›Russia and Constructivism‹, in American Abstract Artists, eds. *The World of Abstract Art.* New York, Wittenborn; and London, Alec Taranti, 1957, pp. 86–101, *et passim.* Reprinted in G28. Interview with Gabo.

A131. Le Corbusier. ›The Mars Group Exhibition of the Elements of Modern Architecture: A Pictorial Record‹, *The Architectural Review* (London) Vol. 83, No. 496, Mar 1938, pp. 109–16. (Reviews E51).

A132. Lewis, Adrian. ›British Avant-Garde Painting 1945–1956: Part I‹, *Artscribe* (London) No. 34, 31 Mar 1982, pp. 17–33.

A133. *The Little Review* (New York and London) Vol. 10, No. 1, Spring 1924, figs following p. 16.

A134. Lozowick, Louis. ›A Note on Modern Russian Art‹, *Broom: International Magazine of the Arts* (Berlin etc.) Vol. 4, No. 3, Feb 1923, pp. 200–204.

A135. McBride, Henry. ›Unknown Political Monument‹, *Art News* (New York) Vol. 51, No. 10, Feb 1953, pp. 20–21. (Reviews E93).

A136. *MA* (Vienna) Vol. 10, 1925, cover fig.

A137. Mashek, Joseph. ›Max Bill: An Assessment‹, *Arts Magazine* (New York) Vol. 50, No. 1, Sep 1975, pp. 53–5.

A138. Mazur, Michael. ›The Monoprints of Naum Gabo‹ *Print Collector's Newsletter* (New York) Vol. 9, No. 5, 1978, pp. 148–51.

A139. Moholy-Nagy, Sibyl. ›Constructivism from Kasimir Malevich to Laszlo Moholy-Nagy‹, *Arts and Architecture* (Los Angeles) Vol. 83, No. 5, Jun 1966, pp. 24–8.

A140. Morris, George L. K. ›Art Chronicle: English Abstract Painting‹, *Partisan Review* (New York) Vol. 10, No. 3, 1943, pp. 224–6.

A141. Morris, George L. K. ›A Note on the Classical Tradition‹ *Everyday Art Quarterly* (Minneapolis) No. 27, 1953, pp. 26–30. (Reviews E96).

A142. Mumford, Lewis. ›The Art Galleries: The Course of Abstraction‹, *The New Yorker*, Vol. 12, No. 5, 21 Mar 1936, pp. 61–2. Reprinted in Mumford, *Findings and Keepings: Analects for an Autobiography*. New York, Harcourt Brace Jovanovich, 1975, pp. 346–9. (Reviews E46).

A143. Mumford, Lewis. ›The Future of Sociology‹, *World Review* (London) Aug 1942, pp. 33–9. Reprinted as ›Looking Forward‹, in J.R.M. Brumwell, ed. *This Changing World*. London, George Routledge, 1944, pp. 83–95.

A144. Mumford, Lewis, ›Monumentalism, Symbolism and Style: Part I‹, *Magazine of Art* (Washington, DC) Vol 42, No. 6, Oct 1949, pp. 202–7, 227–8.

A145. Mumford, Lewis. ›The Sky Line: The Cave, the City and the Flower‹, *The New Yorker* Vol. 33, No. 36, 2 Nov 1957, pp. 85–98. Reprinted in Mumford, *The Highway and the City*. New York, Harcourt Brace and World, 1963, pp. 41–52.

A146. Mumford, Lewis. ›Naum Gabo 1890–1977‹, *Proceedings of the American Academy of Arts and Letters, 1977* (New York) No. 28, 1978, pp. 65–70.

A147. Munro, Eleanor. ›Explorations in Form: Some Recent American Sculpture‹, *Perspectives USA* (New York) No. 16, Summer 1956, pp. 160–72.

A148. *The Museum of Modern Art Bulletin* (New York) Vol. 15, No. 4, 1948, p. 6. (*Re* E9).

A149. *The Museum of Modern Art Bulletin* (New York) Vol. 20, Nos 3–4, Summer 1953, p. 43. (*Re* 56).

A150. *New Road: Directions in European Art and Letters* (London) No. 4, 1946, figs. following p. 176.

A151. Newton, Eric. ›Contemporary Art at the London Museum‹, *The Listener* (London) Vol. 27, No. 688, 19 Mar 1942, p. 376. (Reviews E61).

A152. Palme, Per. ›Nutida Skulptur‹ [›Contemporary Sculpture‹], *Paletten* (Göteborg) Vol. 20, No. 3, 1959, pp. 67–81.

A153. Perilli, Achille. ›Gabo e Pevsner‹, *Civiltà delle macchine* (Rome) Vol. 2, No. 6, Nov 1954, pp. 72–3.

A154. Piper, Myfanwy. ›Back in the Thirties‹, *Art and Literature* (Lausanne) No. 7, Winter 1965, pp. 136–61.

A155. Ragon, Michel. ›Le Sculpteur Pevsner, a-t-il pillé son frère cadet Gabo?‹, *Arts: lettres, spectacles, musique* (Paris) No. 967, 17 Jun 1964, p. 3. (Reviews B162).

A156. Ragon, Michel. ›Le Constructivisme de Pevsner et Gabo‹, *Jardin des arts* (Paris) No. 130, Sep 1965, pp. 18–23.

A157. *Ray: Art Miscellany* (London) No. 1, 1927, p. 16.

A158. Read, Herbert. ›What is Revolutionary Art?‹, in Betty Rea, ed. *5 on Revolutionary Art*. London, Wishart, 1935, pp. 11–22. (Revised in B173, pp. 124–31; and in Read, *To Hell with Culture and Other Essays on Art and Society*. London, Routledge and Kegan Paul, 1963, pp. 126–34).

A159. Read, Herbert. ›An Art of Pure Form‹, *London Bulletin* No. 14, 1 May 1939, pp. 6–9.

A160. Read, Herbert. ›Vulgarity and Impotence: Speculations on the Present State of the Arts‹, *Horizon* (London) Vol. 5, No. 28, Apr 1942, pp. 267–76. Revised in B173, pp. 81–92.

A161. Read, Herbert. ›The Present Situation of Art in Europe‹, *Hudson Review* (New York) Vol. 1, No. 1, Spring 1948, pp. 50–64.

A162. Read, Herbert. ›Realism and Abstraction in Modern Art‹, *Eidos* (London) No. 1, May–Jun 1950, pp. 26–37. Reprinted in B174, pp. 88–99.

A163. Read, Herbert. ›A Nest of Gentle Artists‹, *Apollo* (London) Vol. 76, No. 7, Sep 1962, pp. 536–40. Reprinted in E167.

A164. Read Herbert. ›Naum Gabo‹, *The Art Gallery Magazine* (New York) Vol. 11, No. 6, Mar 1968, pp. 10–11.

A165. Richards, J. M. ›Construction – Dead and Alive‹, *Transition* (New York) No. 26, 1937, pp. 195–208, fig. p. 161.

A166. Rickey, George. ›The Morphology of Movement: A Study of Kinetic Art‹, *Art Journal* (New York) Vol. 22, No. 4, Summer 1963, pp. 220–31.

A167. Rickey, George. ›Origins of Kinetic Art‹, *Studio International‹* (London) Vol. 173, No. 886, Feb 1967, pp. 65–9.

A168. Rickey, George. ›Naum Gabo: 1890–1977‹, *Artforum* (New York) Vol. 16, No. 3, Nov 1977, pp. 22–7.

A169. Roberts, Keith. ›Current and Forthcoming Exhibitions: London‹, *The Burlington Magazine* (London) Vol. 118, No. 885, Dec 1976, pp. 875–9.

A170. Rotzler, Willy. ›Nogle Aspekter af Konstruktiv Kunst‹ [›Aspects of Constructive Art‹], *Louisiana Revy* (Humlebaek) Year 18, No. 2, Jan 1978, pp. 18–24. Reprinted in French in E229; and in English in E237.

A171. Rubin, William. ›Painting and Sculpture‹, in *The Museum of Modern Art, New York*, New York, Museum of Modern Art with Abrams; and London, Thames and Hudson, 1984, pp. 43–6.

A172. *Russkoe Iskusstvo* (Moscow) No. 1, 1923, fig. facing p. 65.

A173. Saltmarche, K. ›Notes on Special Exhibitions: Sculpture in Our Time‹, *Art Quarterly* (Detroit) Vol. 22, No. 4, Winter 1959, pp. 350–55. (Reviews E117).

A174. Schweicher, Curt. ›Das Warenhaus »De Bijenkorf«‹, *Form: Internationale Revue* (Cologne) No. 1, 1957, pp. 27–33.

A175. Seeley, Carol. ›On the Nature of Abstract Painting in America‹, *Magazine of Art* (Washington, DC) Vol. 43, No. 5, May 1950, pp. 163–8.

A176. Segi, S. [›Constructivism and Naum Gabo‹], *Mizue* (Tokyo) No. 588, Aug 1954, pp. 19–25.

A177. Seuphor, Michel. ›Au temps de l'avant-garde‹ *L'Oeil* (Paris) No. 11, Nov 1955, pp. 24–39. Reprinted as ›Russia and the Avant-Garde‹ in Georges and Rosamond Bernier, eds. *The Selective Eye 1956/1957*. New York, Reynal, 1956, pp. 78–89.

A178. Seymour, Charles, Jr. ›Ideas on Sculpture‹, *Baltimore Museum of Art News*, Vol. 17, No. 4, Apr 1954, pp. 1–24.

A179. Sharp, Willoughby. ›Luminism and Kineticism‹, in Gregory Battcock, ed. *Minimal Art: A Critical Anthology*. New York, E. P. Dutton, 1968, pp. 317–58.

A180. Sidorov, A. ›V vystavke‹ [›On Exhibition‹], *Tvorchestvo* (Moscow) No. 5–6, 1920. p. 19.

A181. Siegl, Theodor. ›Conservation‹, *Bulletin of the Philadelphia Museum of Art*, Vol. 62, No. 291, Autumn 1966.

A182. *Signals Newsbulletin* (London) Vol. 1, No. 8, Jun-Jul 1965, pp. 1, 4, 7, 16.

A183. Sjöberg, Leif. ›Naum Gabo‹, *Konstrevy* (Stockholm) Year 36, No. 5–6, 1960, pp. 186–91.

A184. Sjöberg, Leif. ›Gabo und die konstruktive Idee‹, *Das Kunstwerk* (Baden-Baden) Vol. 17, No. 9, Mar 1964, pp. 20–28.

A185. Soby, James T. ›The Constructivist Brotherhood‹, *Art News* (New York) Vol. 47, No. 1, Mar 1948, pp. 22–5, 57–9. (*Re* E9).

A186. S[par], F[rancis]. ›Explorez la sculpture‹, *Connaissance des arts* (Paris) No. 276, Feb 1975, pp. 46–59.

A187. Spencer, Charles. ›The Plastics Medium‹, *Art and Artists* (London) Vol. 2, No. 6, Sep 1967, pp. 20–23.

A188. *Stavba* (Prague) Year 2, No. 2, 1923, fig. p. 14.

A189. *Stavba* (Prague) Year 3, No. 6, 1924–5, fig. p. 116.

A190. Sterenberg, D. ›Die künstlerische Situation in Russland‹, *Das Kunstblatt* (Berlin) Vol. 6, No. 11, Nov 1922, pp. 485–92.

A191. *Studio International* (London) Vol. 171, No. 876, Apr 1966. Special Issue devoted to Gabo. (Contains G1, G31, A87, A115 and A208.)

A192. *Studio International* (London) Vol. 178, No. 913, Jul-Aug 1969, fig. p. 34.

A193. Sweeney, James J. ›Construction Unconstructible?‹, *Art News* (New York) Vol. 50, No. 1, Mar 1951, pp. 34–5, 61–2.

A194. S[weet], F.[A.] ›A Modern Construction‹, *Art Institute of Chicago Quarterly*, Vol. 53, Feb 1960, p. 13. (*Re* 68.5).

A195. Sylvester, David. ›The Unknown Political Prisoner‹, *The Listener* (London) Vol. 49, No. 1255, 19 Mar 1953, p. 478. (Reviews E95).

A196. Sylvester, David. ‹A Systematic Sculptor‹, *The Listener* (London) Vol. 60, No. 1531, 31 Jul 1958, p. 168. (Reviews G28).

A197. *The Tate Gallery Report 1966–67* (London) 1967, pp. 14–44. (*Re* 42.2, pp. 26–8, 75).

A198. *The Tate Gallery 1967–68* (London) 1968, pp. 33–76. (*Re* five wood-engravings, p. 58).

A199. *The Tate Gallery: Acquisitions 1968–9* (London) 1969, pp. 5–28 (*Re* 55.21, p. 11).

A200. *The Tate Gallery 1968–70* (London) 1970, pp. 18–23, 24–9, 61–108. (*Re* 30.6, pp. 24, 82; *re* 55.21, Herbert Read Memorial, pp. 18–23, 82).

A201. *The Tate Gallery 1970–72* (London) 1972, pp. 49–214. (*Re* 4.6 and two wood-engravings, pp. 35, 104–6).

A202. *The Tate Gallery 1972–74: Biennial Report and Illustrated Catalogue of Acquisitions* (London) 1975, pp. 49–256. (*Re* 30.7, pp. 138–9).

A203. *The Tate Gallery 1976–8: Illustrated Catalogue of Acquisitions* (London) 1979, pp. 27–140. (*Re* 65 works, pp. 50–73. For revised entries see B3).

A204. *The Tate Gallery 1978–80: Illustrated Biennial Report* (London) 1980, pp. 61–3, 81–93. (*Re* E238, pp. 61–2; *re* 40.3, p. 88).

A205. *The Tate Gallery 1978–80: Illustrated Catalogue of Acquisitions* (London) 1981, pp. 55–175. (*Re* 40.3, p. 94).

A206. Taylor, Joshua C. ›Harry Lewis Winston: Futurist and Other Twentieth-Century Art‹, in Douglas Cooper, ed. *Great Private Collections*. London, Weidenfeld and Nicolson, and New York, Macmillan, 1963, pp. 292–303.

A207. Thistlewood, David. ›Herbert Read's Aesthetic Theorizing 1914–1952‹, *Art History* (London) Vol. 2, No. 3, Sep 1979, pp. 339–54.

A208. Thompson, David. ›Outlines for a Public Art‹, *Studio International* (London) Vol. 171, No. 876, Apr 1966, pp. 133–9.

A209. Thompson, David. ›Naum Gabo Talks to David Thompson‹, *Art Monthly* (London) No. 4, Feb 1977, pp. 10–13. (Reports F13).

A210. [Thurston, Laura B.] ›V gostyach u Nauma Gabo‹ [›A Visit to Naum Gabo‹], *Amerika: America Illustrated* (Washington, DC) No. 241, Dec 1976, pp. 16–19.

A211. *The Tiger's Eye* (Westport, Conn.) Vol. 1, No. 4, Jun 1948, fig. p. 97.

A212. Tschichold, Iwan. ›Die Neue Gestaltung‹, *ABC: Beiträge zum Bauen* (Basel) Series 2, No. 2, 1926, pp. 1–3.

A213. ›Ulen‹. ›Die Ausstellungen in Russland‹, *Veshch/Gegenstand/Objet* (Berlin) Nos 1/2, 1922, p. 19.

A214. Van Wijk, Kees. ›Internationale Revue i 10‹ [›International Review i 10‹], *Nederlands Kunsthistorisch Jaarboek 1977* (Haarlem) No. 28, 1978, pp. 1–54.

A215. *Virginia Museum of Fine Arts: Members Bulletin* (Richmond) Vol. 10, No. 3, Nov 1949, [p. 3]. (*Re* Gabo's lecture at E71, 4 Nov).

A216. Von Rohr, Alheidis. ›Aus der Arbeit der Museen‹ *Pantheon* (Munich) Vol. 31, No. 3, 1973, p. 313.

A217. Voskuil, Jan. ›De Tentoonstelling van Russische Kunst te Amsterdam‹ [›The Exhibition of Russian Art in Amsterdam‹] , *Eigen Haard* (Haarlem) Year 49, No. 20, 19 May 1923, p. 331. (Reviews E32).

A218. Warnod, A. ›Les Peintres et les ballets russes‹, *La Revue musicale* (Paris) Year 11, No. 110, Dec 1930, pp. 78–89.

A219. Webb, Michael. ›Sculpture of Space and Time‹, *Country Life* (London) Vol. 139, No. 3603, 24 Mar 1966, pp. 660–61. (Reviews E21).

A220. Weiss, Evelyn. ›Dreizehn Stacheln‹ *Weltkunst* (Munich) Vol. 39, No. 19, Oct 1969, p. 1048.

A221. [Westheim, Paul]. ›Die Ausstellung der Russen‹ *Das Kunstblatt* (Berlin) Vol. 6, No. 11, Nov 1922, pp. 493–8.

A222. Whitford, Frank, ›Gabo and Constructivism‹, *Architectural Review* (London) Vol. 139, No. 832, Jun 1966, pp. 469–72.

A223. Whyte, Lancelot L. ›The Unity of the Visual Experience‹, *Bulletin of the Atomic Scientists* (Chicago) Vol. 15, No. 2, Feb 1959, pp. 72–6. Reprinted in Walter Kern, ed. *J. P. Hodin: European Critic*. London, Cory, Adams and Mackay, 1965, pp. 73–81. (*Re* 37).

A224. Wolfram, Eddie. ›Gabo as Matchmaker at the Tate‹, *Arts Review* (London) Vol. 18, No. 5, 19 Mar 1966, p. 103. (Reviews E21).

A225. Xagoraris, Pantelis. ›Teleia Sterea kai Sugchrone Plastike‹ [›Perfect Solids and Contemporary Sculpture‹], *Zugos* (Athens) Vol. 7, No. 80, Jul 1962, pp. 29–37.

NEWSPAPERS

This section lists only newspaper references which document entries in the *catalogue raisonné* or in the bibliography.

N1. Adlow, Dorothy. ›Sculpture Exhibition by Gabo: Novel Constructions Shown at MIT Hayden Memorial‹, *The Christian Science Monitor* (Boston) 19 Nov 1951, p. 4. (Reviews E11).

N2. Andreae, Christopher. ›My Sculpture is a Living Thing‹, *The Christian Science Monitor* (Boston) 1968, Second Section, p. 9.

N3. [Anon.] ›Art and Artists across the Sea‹, *The Chicago Evening Post*, Jun 1926. (Reviews E4; *Re* 6.1).

N4. [Anon.] ›Art of Two Constructionists: Work of Gabo and Pevsner Reveals Artistic Tendencies of New Russia‹, *The New York Sun*, 1 May 1926, p. 9. (Reviews E4).

N5. [Anon.] ›Constructivism is Optimistic, Gabo Tells Museum Audience‹, *The Sun* (Baltimore) 15 Apr 1950, p. 6. (*Re* 22.3).

N6. [Anon.] ›The Londoner's Diary. The Lost Dimension.‹ *Evening Standard* (London) 14 Jan 1938, p. 6, (*Re* loss of 10.4).

N7. [Anon.] ›Puzzle Pictures by Great Modernists to be Seen Soon at Art Gallery of Toronto‹, *Toronto Evening Telegram*, 5 Mar 1927, p. 18.

N8. [Anon.] ›Upside Down? Is it? Isn't It? Do You Care?‹, *San Francisco Chronicle*, 4 Aug 1939. (*Re* 41.6).

N9. [Anon.] ›Yard's Queer Hunt‹, *News Chronicle* (London), 15 Jan 1938, p. 3. (*Re* loss of 10.4).

N10. Bertram, Anthony ›Art in the Abstract‹, *The Tablet*, Vol. 216, No. 6394 (London) 8 Dec 1962, p. 1196 (Reviews G30).

N11. Bier, [Dr Justus] ›Raumplastik von Gabo-Ausstellung in der Kestner-Gesellschaft‹, *Hannoverscher Anzeiger*, No. 263, Erste Beilage, 8 Nov 1930. (Reviews E5).

N12. Bollman, Robert B. ›Middlebury Sculptor's Art Acclaimed in Europe‹, *Waterbury Sunday Republican*, 15 Dec 1957, p. 6.

N13. Bruce-Milne, Marjorie ›The Home Forum‹, *The Christian Science Monitor* (Boston) 22 Jul 1971, p. 8.

N14. Crane, Jane W. ›Gabo has no Use for Tradition‹, *The Washington Post*, 17 Oct 1948, p. 6L. (*Re* 53.2 in E68).

N15. *The Hartford Times*, 31 Oct 1953, fig. p. 20. (Gabo and Herbert Read at E14).

N16. Henry, Frank ›An Engineer's Dreams Tap at Art's Door‹ *The Sunday Sun* (Baltimore) 11 Jun 1950, Section A, p. 3.

N17. Malice ›Rymden Ledmotiv på Storexpo‹, *Dagens Nyheter* (Stockholm) 5 Dec 1965. (*Re* E20).

N18. Mumford, Lewis ›The Moderns: International Exhibition of Modern Art at the Brooklyn Museum‹, *The New Republic* (New York) Vol. 49, No. 632 12 Jan 1927, pp. 221–2. (Reviews E38).

N19. Murray, Marian ›Constructivist Exhibits Sculpture at Avery Memorial‹, *The Hartford Times*, 22 Mar 1938, p. 18. (Reviews E7).

N20. Newton, Eric ›The Galleries. A Visit to Mars: The Modern Architect's Case‹, *The Sunday Times* (London) 16 Jan 1938, p. 11. (Reviews E51, E6).

N21. *Nieuwe Rotterdamse Courant*, 12 May 1960, fig. p. 1. (*Re* fire at Bijenkorf store).

N22. [SA] ›Neues Weltbild, Neue Kunst‹, [*Hannoverscher Kurier*], 18 Nov 1930. (Reviews E5).

N23. Tucker, Jean ›Gabo Started a New Art Form‹, *The Hartford Courant*, 22 Nov 1964, Part B, [p. 1].

N24. *Washington Daily News*, 9 Oct 1948, p. 5. (*Re* 4.3 in E68).

SALE CATALOGUES

Sales are listed in chronological order and they comprise all auctions which have included works by Gabo.

S1. *Modern British Drawings, Paintings and Sculpture*. London, Sotheby's, 4 Nov 1959, Lot No. 92. (48.15).

S2. *Important 20th Century Paintings, Drawings, and Sculpture, from the Collection of Arnold H. Maremont*. New York, Sotheby Parke Bernet, 1 May 1974, Lot No. 40, fig. (48.3).

S3. *Important 19th and 20th Century Paintings and Sculpture*. New York, Sotheby Parke Bernet, 2 May 1974, Lot No. 290, colour fig. (73.3).

S4. *Impressionist and Modern Paintings, Drawings and Sculpture*. New York, Christie's, 17 May 1977, Lot No. 88, colour fig. (53.4).

S5. *Impressionist and Modern Paintings, Drawings and Sculpture*. New York, Christie's, 31 Oct 1978, Lot No. 55, colour fig. (68.7).

S6. *Russian and European Avant-Garde Art and Literature 1905–1930.* New York, Sotheby Parke Bernet, 6 Nov 1979, Lot No. 217, fig. (34.5).

S7. *Modern Paintings and Sculpture.* New York, Sotheby Parke Bernet, 6 Nov 1981, Lot No. 399, colour fig. (70.6).

S8. *Impressionist and Modern Painting and Sculpture.* London, Christie's 26 Mar 1984, Lot No. 34, colour fig. p. 62. (48.14).

S9. *Ballet Material and Manuscripts from the Serge Lifar Collection.* London, Sotheby's, 9 May 1984. Lots Nos 51–4.

S10. *Impressionist and Modern Painting and Sculpture.* New York, Christie's, 14 Nov 1984, (Part 2), Lot No. 613, fig. p. 139. (48.3).

EXHIBITIONS

This list includes all exhibitions which took place before the end of February 1985. A major retrospective touring exhibition will open in Dallas in autumn 1985 and visit Toronto, New York, Berlin, Düsseldorf and London. It is envisaged that this will produce a series of important catalogues.

Gabo's first two exhibitions (E1 and E2) seem to have been informal displays of his works in his studios in Christiania (1916), and Moscow (1917). The first public exhibition for which there is any documentary evidence is the open-air exhibition of 1920, held in a bandstand on Tverskoi Boulevard, Moscow. This included works by Gabo, Pevsner, Gustav Klutsis and students from the State Free Art Studios (A213). There are no known photographs of the installation, but *The Realistic Manifesto* was printed and distributed to accompany the exhibition.

In this list, the data for each exhibition comprises the total number of sculptures shown, including works shown as photographs. The number of works in other media is given in parentheses. Sculptures known to have been exhibited are identified according to their numbers in the *catalogue raisonné*. If the particular version shown is unknown, only the group number is given. Square brackets indicate uncertainty of identification and further explanation will usually be found in the *catalogue raisonné* notes for that particular work. If sources other than published exhibition catalogues have provided the information listed, these sources are cited. Reviews listed in the bibliography are cross-referenced.

Travelling exhibitions are entered separately if separate catalogues were issued for each venue and slightly different selections of works were shown. If the catalogues were identical, or contained only very minor changes relative to Gabo's works (e.g. numbering), the various venues are listed under one entry.

The list of exhibitions has been divided so that group exhibitions are listed separately from one-man shows and exhibitions where Gabo exhibited with one other artist. This division has been adopted because Gabo frequently insisted that his works be exhibited together with those of his brother Antoine Pevsner.

ONE-MAN EXHIBITIONS

E1. Christiania studio, 1916. No catalogue. 3.2 (G28).

E2. Moscow studio, 1917. No catalogue. 3.2, 4.2 (G28).

E3. *Constructivistes Russes: Gabo et Pevsner,* Galerie Percier, Paris, 19 Jun–5 Jul 1924. 8 works, plus 1 ex-cat.: [4.3], 5.1 ex-cat., 6.1, 7.2, [10.2], 16. Preface by Waldemar George. First exhibition in France.

E4. *Gabo and Pevsner: Russian Constructionists,* Little Review Gallery, New York, 28 Apr–12 May 1926. 5 works: 6.1, [8], [13], [14], 16. Reviews N3, N4.

E5. *Gabo: Konstruktive Plastik,* Kestner-Gesellschaft, Hannover, 6–23 Nov 1930. 15 works (plus 5 drawings, 4 models and 1 photograph): 2.2, 3.2, 9.1, 10.2, 15, 17, [18], 20.2, 22.3, 23.2, [24.1], 25, 26.2, 29.2, 31.1 or 31.2; 8 and 19 as photographs. Preface by [Dr Justus] Bier. Reviews A11, N11, N22.

E6. *Constructions by Naum Gabo,* London Gallery, London, 5–29 Jan 1938. 15 works (plus photograph, and drawings): 10.2, [12.3], 22.3, 26.2, 30.5, [31.2], 33.3, [34.5], 35.3, [39.2], 40.3, 41.3; 8 as photograph. Reviews A12, A16, N20.

E7. *Constructions in Space: Gabo,* Wadsworth Atheneum, Hartford, Conn., 22–30 Mar 1938; Julien Levy Gallery, New York, 5 Apr–1 May 1938. 14 works (plus photograph and drawings): 10.2, [12.3], 22.3, 26.2, 30.5, [31.2], 33.3, [34.3], 35.3, [39.2], 40.4, 41.3. Reviews A80, N19.

E8. [*Naum Gabo*], Vassar College, Poughkeepsie, NY, 1938. No catalogue. [10.2], [12.3], 22.3, [26.2], [30.5], [33.3], [34.3], [35.3], [39.2], [40.4], 41.4. (According to Miriam Gabo, E8, planned as part of E7, was smaller since some works sold from E7 were omitted).

E9. *Naum Gabo-Antoine Pevsner,* Museum of Modern Art, New York, 1948. 22 works (plus 5 drawings and a photograph): 4.3, 5.1 not shown because damaged, 10.2, 12.2, 22.3, 26.2, 28, 30.5, 31.2, 34.3, 35.4, 36, 37.8, 37.9, 39.2, 40.5, 43.3, 44, 46.2, 47.1, 52.4, 53.2. Essays by Herbert Read (reprinted in B174); Ruth Olson; and Abraham Chanin (reprinted in Danish in E23). Catalogue reprinted in *Five European Sculptors.* New York, Arno Press, 1969. Reviews A13, A73, A94, A148, A185. Gabo's first major show after moving to the USA.

E10. *Naum Gabo Constructions,* Baltimore Museum of Art, 1950. 9 works (plus 8 paintings and drawings): 12.2, 22.3, 34.3, 36, 37.9, 39.2, 41.6, 46.2, 55.1. No catalogue. (Annotated loan receipt list, BMA).

E11. *Works by Naum Gabo.* Charles Hayden Memorial Library, Massachusetts Institute of Technology, Cambridge, Mass., 24 Oct–24 Nov 1951. [No catalogue]. [15 works (plus paintings, prints and drawings)]: 4.3, 10.2, [12.2], 22.3, 34.3, 36, 37.9, 39.2, [40.2], 41.6, 46.2, 47.1, 55.1, 56.2–3, 56.5–8. (Insurance list of 13 works, draft list, and press release, M.I.T. Museum; installation photograph, FAL; review N1). First exhibition of prints.

E12. *Two Exhibitions: Naum Gabo and Josef Albers,* Arts Club of Chicago, 29 Jan–28 Feb 1952. 11 works (plus 8 paintings, drawing, and 5 wood-engravings): [4.3], [10.2], [22.3], [34.3], 36, 39.2, 40.4, [41.6], 46.2.

E13. *Gabo: Space and Kinetic Constructions,* Pierre Matisse Gallery, New York, 21 Apr–16 May 1953. 10 works, plus 1 ex-cat. (plus 5 paintings): 12.2, 22.3 ex-cat., 30.5, 34.3, 37.9, 39.2, 41.6, 46.2, [60], 62.3. Preface by George Heard Hamilton. Installation photograph, B76. Reviews A68, A91, A96.

E14. *Alexander Calder, Mobiles – Naum Gabo, Kinetic Construction and Constructions in Space,* Wadsworth Atheneum, Hartford, Conn., 16 Oct–28 Nov 1953. 17 works (plus 8 paintings and a drawing): 4.3, 9.1, 10.2, 12.2, 22.3, 30.5, 34.3, 37.9, 39.2, 40.6, 41.6, 46.2, [48.9], 52.4, 58.2, 62.3, 64. Preface by C. E. B[uckley]. Reviews A62, N15.

E15. *Gabo,* Boymans Museum, Rotterdam, 12 Apr–18 May 1958; Stedelijk Museum, Amsterdam, 24 May–23 Jun 1958. 22 works (plus 11 paintings, 3 drawings and 6 wood engravings): 4.4, 12.2, 22.3, 26.2, 30.5, 34.3, 36, 37.9, 37.10, 39.2, 41.6, 44, 46.2, 47.1, 52.4, 53.7, 55.5, 55.11, 56.2–3, 56.5–8, 62.3, 64, 69.1. Preface by Herbert Read, reprinted from G28.

E16. *Exhibition of Sculpture by the Brandeis University Creative Arts Awards Recipients, Naum Gabo and James Rosati,* Wren Faculty Center, Brandeis University, Waltham, Mass., 15 May–15 Jun 1960. 1 work: 48.3.

E17. *Naum Gabo,* Stedelijk Museum, Amsterdam, 23 Apr–8 Jun 1965. 26 works (plus 23 paintings and 42 drawings): 4.4, 5.3, 9.1, 12.2, 30.5, 30.6, 34.3, 36, [38.2], 39.2, 41.6, 42.2, 46.2, 48.10, 53.10, [54.2], 55.5, 56.2–3, 56.5–8, 62.4, 64, 68.11, 70.9, 72.4, [74.2], 77.3. Essay by Sir Leslie Martin reprinted from G28.

E18. *Naum Gabo,* Kunsthalle, Mannheim, 23 Jun–8 Aug 1965; Wilhelm-Lehmbruck-Museum der Stadt Duisburg, 21 Aug–3 Oct 1965. 25 works (plus 22 paintings and 42 drawings): 4.4, 5.3, 9.1, 12.2, 26.2, 30.5, 30.6, 34.3, 36, [38.2], 39.2, 42.2, 46.2, 48.10, 53.10, [54.2], 55.6, 56.2–3, 56.5–8, 62.4, 64, 68.11, 72.4, [74.2], 77.3. Preface by Heinz Fuchs, reprinted in E19.

E19. *Naum Gabo,* Kunsthaus, Zurich, 30 Oct–1 Dec 1965. 29 works (plus 26 paintings and 38 drawings): 4.4, 4.5, 5.3, 9.1, 12.2, 26.2, 30.5, 30.6, 34.3, 36, [38.2], 39.2, 42.2, 46.2, 48.10, 53.10, [54.2], 55.6, 55.16, 56.2–3, 56.5–8, 62.4, 64, 68.8, 68.11, 72.4, [73.4], [74.2], 77.3. Essays by Heinz Fuchs (reprinted from E18), and R. Wehrli. Also contains G1 and G18 in English.

E20. *Den Inre och den Yttre Rymden,* Moderna Museet, Stockholm, 26 Dec 1965–13 Feb 1966. 29 works (plus 23 paintings and 42 drawings): 4.2, 4.5, 5.3, 9.1, 12.2, 26.2, 30.5, 30.6, 34.3, 36, 37.10, [38.2], 39.2, 41.6, 42.2, 46.2, 48.10, 53.10, [54.2], 55.6, 56.2–3, 56.5–8, 62.4, 64, 68.11, 72.4, [73.4], [74.2], 77.3. Essays by Joost Baljeu (reprint of A41), and K. G. Hultén, ›Om Naum Gabos första skulpturer‹ [›On Naum

Gabo's First Sculptures‹] (reprinted in A118). Reviews A75, A103, N17.

E21.   *Naum Gabo,* Arts Council at the Tate Gallery, London, 15 Mar–15 Apr 1966. 33 works (plus 33 paintings and 42 drawings): 4.4, 4.5, 5.3, 9.1, 10.5, 12.2, 22.3, 30.5, 30.6, 34.3, 36, 38.2, 39.2, 40.3, 42.2, 48.10, 50, 52.3, 53.10, 54.2, 55.6, 56.2–3, 56.5–8, 58.2, 62.4, 64, 68.11, 70.12, 72.4, 73.4, 74.2, 77.3, 79.2. Preface by Herbert Read, reprinted in B180. Reviews A70, A78, A93, A219, A224.

E22.   *Naum Gabo,* Albright-Knox Art Gallery, Buffalo, 2 Mar–14 Apr 1968. 28 works (plus 33 paintings, 42 drawings and 2 photo-prints): 4.2, 4.4, 4.7, 5.3, 10.3, 30.5, 30.6, 34.3, 35.4, 36, 38.2, 47.5, 54.2, 55.6, 55.18, 58.2, 60, 61.2, 62.4, 64, 68.11, 70.12, 72.4, 73.6, 77.3, 78, 79.2. Essay by Christopher Cornford, ›A Letter to the Visitors‹. Reviews A10, A30. E22 was a sub-section of *Plus by Minus: Today's Half-Century,* Buffalo Festival of Arts Exhibition, 3 Mar–14 Apr 1968 (catalogue B36).

E23.   *Naum Gabo,* Louisiana Museum, Humlebaek, 28 Nov 1970–17 Jan 1971; Sonja Henies og Niels Onstadts Stiftelser, Høvikodden, 26 Feb–28 Mar 1971. 21 works (plus 6 paintings, 15 drawings, and 14 wood-engravings): 4.4, 4.6, 5.3, 9.1a, 38.2, 47.5, 47.7, 53.5, 55.6, 55.19, 58.2, 60, 61.2, 62.4, 68.13, 70.11, 72.4, 73.3, 77.2, 78, 79.2. Catalogue in *Louisiana Revy,* Year 11, No. 2, Nov 1970. Essays by R. Olson and A. Chanin (reprinted from E9), and Knud W. Jensen, ›Gabo-udstillingen på Louisiana‹ [›Gabo Exhibition at Louisiana‹]. **Interview by Gunnar Jespersen ›Mode med en Pioner‹** [›Meeting with a Pioneer‹]. Contains G1, G12a, G25, A118.

E24.   *Naum Gabo,* Nationalgalerie, Berlin, Apr-May 1971. 19 works (plus 7 paintings, 14 drawings, and 14 wood-engravings): 4.4, 4.6, 5.3, 9.1a, 38.2, 47.5, 47.7, 53.5, 55.6, 58.2, 60, 61.2, 62.4, 68.13, [70.12], 72.4, 77.2, 78, 79.2. Essay by Werner Haftmann. Contains G1, G12a, A118.

E25.   *Naum Gabo,* Kunstverein, Hannover, 19 Jun–25 Jul 1971. 19 works (plus 7 paintings, 14 drawings, and 14 wood-engravings): 4.4, 4.6, 5.3, 9.1a, 38.2, 47.5, 47.7, 53.5, 55.6, 58.2, 60, 61.2, 62.4, 68.13, [70.12], 72.4, 77.2, 78, 79.2. Essays by Manfred de la Motte; and D. Sterenberg, reprinted from E31. Contains G1, G12a–b, G14, G22.

E26.   *Naum Gabo,* Musée de Peinture et de Sculpture, Grenoble, Sep–Oct 1971; Musée National d'Art Moderne, Paris, 10 Nov 1971–3 Jan 1972. 19 works, plus 1 ex-cat. (plus 6 paintings, and 15 drawings): 4.4, 4.6, 5.3, 9.1b ex-cat., 38.2, 47.5, 47.7, 53.5, 55.6, 58.2, 60, 61.2, 62.4, 68.13, 70.12, 72.4, 73.2, 77.2, 78, 79.2. Essay by Maurice Besset (reprinted in A54). Contains G1.

E27.   *Naum Gabo,* Calouste Gulbenkian Foundation, Galeria de Exposições Temporárias, Lisbon, Jan–Feb 1972. 18 works, plus 1 ex-cat. (plus 6 paintings and 15 drawings): 4.4, 4.6, 5.3, 9.1b ex-cat., 38.2, 47.5, 47.7, 55.6, 58.2, 60, 61.2, 62.4, 68.13, [70.12],

72.4, 73.2, 77.2, 78, 79.2. Essay by Leslie Martin ›A Obra de Naum Gabo‹ [›On the Work of Naum Gabo‹].

E28.   *Naum Gabo: The Constructive Process,* Tate Gallery, London, 3 Nov 1976–16 Jan 1977. 69 works (plus 7 paintings, 32 drawings, and 2 photographs of ›La Chatte‹): 2.2, 4.7, 9.1, 10.1, 10.6, 10.9, 26.2, 28, 29.1, 29.4, 30.2, 30.5, 30.6, 31.1, 31.2, 34.1, 34.2, 35.1, 37.2, 37.4, 38.1, 39.1, 39.3, 40.1, 40.3, 41.1, 42.1, 42.2, 42.3, 42.5, 46.1, 48.17, 51.1, 52.1, 52.3, 53.1, 55.23, 56.1, 57.1, 59, 61.1, 61.2, 62.2, 65, 66.1, 66.2, 67.1, 67.2, 70.1, 70.10, 71, 73.1, 75.1–6, [75.7–8], 76.1, 80.1, (30.7, 56.5–8, 57.3, 67.5, 69.2, as photographs). Preface by Sir Norman Reid, essay by Teresa Newman, ›Naum Gabo‹. Contains G1.

GROUP EXHIBITIONS
1916–1935

E29.   State Free Art Studios, Moscow, 1918. No catalogue. 6.2 (G28).

E30.   **Open-air exhibition,** Tverskoi Boulevard, Moscow, 6 Aug 1920. No catalogue. 2.1, 3.2, 4.2, 5.1, 7.1, 9.1 (G1, G28, A213; undated note, RLA; letter Gabo to R. Alley, 30 Sep 1975).

E31.   **Erste Russische Kunstausstellung,** Galerie Van Diemen, Berlin, 15 Oct 1922. 8 works, plus 1 or 2 ex-cat. (plus 1 drawing): 3.2, 4.2, 5.1, 6.3, 7.1, 8, 9.1. Prefaces by Dr E. Redslob and A. Holitscher. Essay by D. Sterenberg (reprinted in E25; excerpt in G28). Reviews A25, A127. (G28; opening date from *Izvestiya,* 19 Oct 1922, E261 p. 67; installation photograph E261, p. 68). First major Russian exhibition in the West after the Revolution.

E32.   *Eerste Russische Kunsttentoonstelling,* Stedelijk Museum, Amsterdam, 29 Apr–28 May 1923: 3.2, 4.2, 5.1, 6.3, 7.1. Catalogue for E31 used with supplementary list. (G28; installation photograph B151, p. 34). Review A217.

E33.   *Société Anonyme 30th Exhibition.* [*Modern Russian Artists*], Galleries of the Société Anonyme, New York, 13 Feb–6 Mar 1924. No catalogue. 1 work. (B101 p. 777).

E34.   *Internationale Kunstausstellung,* Gesellschaft zur Förderung moderner Kunst in Wien, Vienna, 11 Sep–20 Oct 1924. 2 works: 4.3, [11].

E35.   *36ème Exposition de la Société des Artistes Indépendants,* Palais de Bois, Paris, 21 Mar–3 May 1925. 2 works: [4.3].

E36.   *37ème exposition de la Société des Artistes Indépendants.* Palais de Bois, Paris, 20 Mar–2 May 1926. 2 works: 9.1

E37.   *Internationale Kunst Ausstellung,* Dresden, Jun-Sep 1926. 1 work: 24.1. Exhibited in Lissitzky's ›Raum der Abstrakten‹ (installation photograph B127).

E37a. *Novembergruppe,* Berlin, 1926. 2 works.

E38.   **The International Exhibition of Modern Art, Assembled by the Société Anonyme,** Museum of Arts and Sciences, Brooklyn,

19 Nov 1926–1 Jan 1927. 3 works: [8 or 14], 15, 16. Prefaces by W. H. Fox and K. S. Dreier. Reviews A29, N18; installation photographs, B26, B101; see also B59.

E39.   *The International Exhibition of Modern Art, Assembled by the Société Anonyme,* The Anderson Galleries, New York, 25 Jan–25 Feb 1927. 2 works: 15, 16.

E40.   *The International Exhibition of Modern Art, Assembled by the Société Anonyme,* Buffalo Academy of Fine Arts, The Albright Art Gallery, Buffalo, 25 Feb–20 Mar 1927. 2 works: 15, 16.

E41.   *The International Exhibition of Modern Art Assembled by the Société Anonyme,* Art Gallery of Toronto, 1–24 Apr 1927. 2 works: 15, 16. Shown together with *The Canadian Society of Graphic Art and Historical Paintings and Drawings.* (See N7).

E42.   *Machine Age Exposition,* 119 West 57th Street, New York, 16–28 May 1927. Organized by the Little Review Gallery, *et al.* 2 works: 6.1, [14].

E43.   *Abstract Art of Gabo, Pevsner, Mondrian, and Domela,* Wadsworth Atheneum, Hartford, Conn., 22 Oct–17 Nov 1935; Arts Club of Chicago, 3–25 Jan 1936. 4 works: 10.2, 28.

1936–1946

E44.   **Abstract and Concrete,** Oxford Arts Club, 41 St. Giles, Oxford, 15–22 Feb 1936; School of Architecture, Liverpool, 2–14 Mar 1936; Cambridge Arts Club, Gordon Fraser's Gallery, Cambridge, 28 May–13 Jun 1936. 2 works: 26.2. Catalogue published for Oxford only. (Dates from A39). Review A88.

E45.   **Abstract and Concrete,** Lefevre Gallery, London, Apr 1936. 2 works: 26.2. (As E44. Installation photograph E255, p. 20).

E46.   **Cubism and Abstract Art,** Museum of Modern Art, New York, 2 Mar–19 Apr 1936. 3 works (plus 4 drawings): 23.2, 28, 10.2 (not shown, because arrived damaged). Catalogue reprinted as B15. Review A142.

E47.   *Modern Pictures for Modern Rooms: An Exhibition of Abstract Art in Contemporary Settings,* Duncan Miller Ltd., London, Apr 1936. 1 work. Review A88.

E48.   *Konstruktivisten,* Kunsthalle, Basel, 16 Jan–14 Feb 1937. 2 works: [29.2], 34.4. Preface by Georg Schmidt.

E49.   *Exhibition of Constructive Art,* London Gallery, London, 12–31 Jul 1937. 2 works: [34.5], 41.3. Forewords by J. L. M[artin] and S. Giedion. Review A26.

E50.   *Origines et développement de l'art international indépendant,* Musée du Jeu de Paume, Paris, 30 Jul–31 Oct 1937. 1 work: 41.3. (According to Miriam Gabo, catalogue entry ›Construction sur mur 1936‹ inaccurate).

E51.   *New Architecture: An Exhibition of the Elements of Modern Architecture Organized by the MARS (Modern Architectural Research) Group,* New Burlington Galleries, London, 11–29 Jan 1938. 1 work: [40.3]. Reviews A16, A131, N20.

E52. *Living Art in England,* London Gallery, London, 18 Jan–11 Feb 1939. 2 works: [39.2]. Catalogue in *London Bulletin* Nos 8–9, Jan–Feb 1939, pp. 14, 57.

E53. *Decorative Arts,* Golden Gate International Exposition, San Francisco, [18 Feb–29 Oct] 1939. 1 work, fig. upside-down: 41.6.

E54. *Five Centuries of Realism,* Toledo Museum of Art, Toledo, Ohio, 2–30 Apr 1939. No catalogue. 1 work: 5.1. (Pamphlet; shipping document, 27 May 1939; TMA).

E55. *Abstract and Concrete Art,* Guggenheim Jeune, London, 10–27 May 1939. 2 works. Catalogue in *London Bulletin* No. 14, 1 May 1939, pp. 2–3. (Dates from *London Bulletin* Nos 15/16, May 1939, facing p. 1).

E56. *Art in Our Time: An Exhibition to Celebrate the Tenth Anniversary of the Museum of Modern Art and the Opening of its New Building,* Museum of Modern Art, New York, 10 May–30 Sep 1939. 1 work: 10.2.

E57. *Réalités Nouvelles,* Galerie Charpentier, Paris, 30 Jun–15 Jul 1939. Works not listed. More than 1 work. (B133 pp. 110, 329 n. 13; letters from ›Renaissance Plastique‹ at Galerie Charpentier, 20 Apr 1939, and Nelly Van Doesburg, 2 Jun 1939, and from L. Lefebvre-Foinet, 18 Jul 1939, indicate that Gabo sent works to this exhibition).

E58. *Painting and Sculpture from the Museum Collection,* Museum of Modern Art, New York, 12 Jan–3 Mar 1940. [No catalogue]. [1 work]: 10.2. (B155, p. 124).

E59. *We Like Modern Art,* Museum of Modern Art, New York, 27 Dec 1940–12 Jan 1941. No catalogue. [1 work]: 10.2. (B155, p. 124; arranged by student jury, see *Bulletin of the Museum of Modern Art* Vol. 8, No. 2, Dec–Jan 1940–41).

E60. *The Exhibition of the Collection of the Société Anonyme – Museum of Modern Art: 1920,* Yale University Art Gallery, New Haven, 14 Jan–22 Feb 1942. No catalogue. 1 work: 10.3. Artists listed, with preface by G. H. H[amilton] in *Bulletin of the Associates in Fine Arts at Yale University* Vol. 10, No. 3, Dec 1941. (Checklist, Yale 2).

E61. *New Movements in Art: Contemporary Work in England,* London Museum, 18 Mar–9 May, 1942. 4 works (plus drawings): 40.3, 41.5, 47.1, 52.3. Review A151.

E62. *New Movements in Art Exhibition,* Leicester Museum and Art Gallery, 23 May–21 Jun 1942. 1 work ex-cat. (plus 4 drawings): [41.5]. (Letter from M. Eates, 4 Jun 1942).

E63. *Konkrete Kunst,* Kunsthalle, Basel, 18 Mar–16 Apr 1944. 1 work as photograph: 41.4. Forewords by M. Bill and J. Arp.

E64. *Art in Progress,* Museum of Modern Art, New York, 24 May–15 Oct 1944. 1 work: 10.2.

1946–1977

E65. *The White Plane,* The Pinacotheca, New York, 19 Mar–12 Apr 1947. 1 work.

E66. *Modern Sculpture,* Fogg Art Museum, Cambridge, Mass., 12 May–5 Jun 1947. 1 work: [10.6].

E67. *Painting and Sculpture by the Directors of the Société Anonyme, 1920–48,* Yale University Art Gallery, New Haven, Mar 1948. 5 works (plus 2 paintings): 10.3, 37.6, 41.6, [48.1]. Catalogue in *Bulletin of the Associates in Fine Arts at Yale University* (New Haven) Vol. 16, No.1, Mar 1948. Preface by G. H. H[amilton]. (Installation photograph, B101 p. 26).

E68. Institute of Contemporary Arts, Washington, DC, 9 Oct–Nov 1948. [No catalogue] At least 2 works: 4.3, 53.2. (Figs in N14, N24).

E69. *Sculpture since Rodin,* Yale University Art Gallery, New Haven, 14 Jan–13 Feb 1949. 2 works: 36, [43.3]. Catalogue in *Bulletin of the Associates in Fine Arts at Yale University* (New Haven) Vol. 17, No. 1, Jan 1949. Preface by L. Moore.

E70. *Modern Art in Your Life,* Museum of Modern Art, New York, 5 Oct–4 Dec 1949. 1 work: 10.2. Catalogue by Robert Goldwater and René d'Harnoncourt in *Museum of Modern Art Bulletin* Vol. 17, No. 1, 1949, pp. 1–48; revised as B81.

E71. *Calder and Sculpture Today,* The Virginia Museum, Richmond, 28 Oct 1949. No catalogue. At least 1 work. (Invitation, GAP; re Gabo's lecture on 4 Nov, see A215).

E72. *Contemporary Connecticut Art,* Town Hall, Woodbury, Conn., under the auspices of the Woman's Club of Woodbury. 5–6 Nov 1949. 1 work.

E73. *Material and Immaterial,* Addison Gallery of American Art, Phillips Academy, Andover, Mass., 1949–50. No catalogue. 3 works: 10.2, 35.3, 41.3. (letter B. Hayes to F. Abbot Goodhue, 28 Mar 1949, Addison Gallery; letter to G. Washburn, 20 Feb 1949, and loan record, 4 Feb–13 Mar 1949, Rhode Island School of Design).

E74. *Saidie A. May Collection of Modern Paintings and Sculpture,* Baltimore Museum of Art, 17 Mar–16 Apr 1950. 1 work: 47.1.

E75. *A Century of Sculpture 1850–1950,* Museum of Art, Rhode Island School of Design, Providence, 30 Mar–18 May 1950. 1 work (plus 2 drawings): 41.3. Catalogue in *Museum Notes* Vol. 7, No. 5, May 1950, pp. 1–4. Essay by John Alford.

E76. *An Exhibition Commemorating the 30th Anniversary of the Société Anonyme: Museum of Modern Art 1920,* Yale University Art Gallery, New Haven, 30 Apr 1950. No catalogue. 1 work: (8 as photograph). (Mimeographed guide, and invitation, Yale 2).

E77. [Whitney Annual]. Whitney Museum of American Art, New York, 1950. 1 painting. Review A113.

E78. *Contemporary Art in the United States,* Art Museum, Worcester, Mass., 25 Jan–4 Mar 1951. [No catalogue]. 1 work: [55.1]. (See A14). Gabo, Reginald Marsh and Ben Shahn participated in an informal discussion chaired by George L. Stout, 18 Feb 1950.

E79. *1951 Annual Exhibition of Contemporary American Sculpture, Watercolors, and Drawings,* Whitney Museum of American Art, New York, 17 Mar–6 May 1951. 1 work: 55.2.

E80. *New England Sculptors,* Addison Gallery of American Art, Phillips Academy, Andover, Mass., 30 Mar–30 Apr 1951; Hartford,

Wadsworth Atheneum, 5 May–3 Jun 1951. 1 work: 55.1.

E81. *Some Areas of Search, 1913 to 1951,* Rose Fried Gallery, New York, 2 May–8 Jun 1951. (Invitation, FAL).

E82. *Eastern States Show: Connecticut Building,* Springfield, Mass., 16–22 Sep 1951. 1 work: [55.2]. No catalogue. (Installation photographs, FAL, Yale 2).

E83. [Untitled] Margaret Brown Gallery, Boston, 18 Oct–24 Nov 1951. No catalogue. At least 3 works: [10.6], 48.12, 55. (Receipt from M. Brown, 18 Oct 1951; ›customer card‹, Papers of the Margaret Brown Gallery, Reel 663, Frame 295, AAA).

E84. *60th Annual American Exhibition,* Art Institute of Chicago, 25 Oct–16 Dec 1951. 1 work: [55.2].

E85. *Coincidences,* Rose Fried Gallery, New York, 16 Jan–27 Feb 1952. 1 work: 55.3. (Winston Collection Papers, Roll D220, Frame 1202, AAA).

E86. *Contemporary Drawings from 12 Countries 1945–1952,* Art Institute of Chicago, 1952; Toledo Museum of Art, Ohio; Wadsworth Atheneum, Hartford, Conn.; San Francisco Museum of Art; Los Angeles County Museum; Colorado Springs Fine Arts Center, Colo.; J. B. Speed Art Museum, Louisville, Ky., 1952. 1 drawing.

E87. *The Naked Truth,* Addison Gallery of American Art, Phillips Academy, Andover, Mass., Jan–Oct 1952. No catalogue. 1 work: 55.1. (B98, p. 5; Review A110).

E88. *L'Oeuvre du XXe siècle,* Musée National d'Art Moderne, Paris, May–Jun 1952. 1 work: 4.3.

E89. *XXth Century Masterpieces,* Tate Gallery, London, 15 Jul–17 Aug 1952. 1 work: 4.3.

E90. *Sculpture of the Twentieth Century,* Philadelphia Museum of Art, 11 Oct–7 Dec 1952; Art Institute of Chicago, 22 Jan–8 Mar 1953; Museum of Modern Art, New York, 29 Apr–7 Sep 1953. 3 works, plus 1 excat.: 10.2, 36, [41.6 ex-cat.], 58.2.

E91. *Exhibition of Painting and Sculpture,* Art Gallery, Washington Depot, Conn., 20 Oct–2 Nov 1952. [No catalogue]. (Flysheet, GAP).

E92. *In Memory of Katherine S. Dreier 1877–1952: Her Own Collection of Modern Art,* Yale University Art Gallery, New Haven, 15 Dec 1952–1 Feb 1953. 2 works: 13, 22.1. Catalogue in *Bulletin of the Associates in Fine Arts at Yale University* (New Haven) Vol. 20, No. 1, Dec 1952.

E93. *International Sculpture Competition: The Unknown Political Prisoner,* Museum of Modern Art, New York, 28 Jan–8 Feb 1953. 1 work: 61.2. Reviews A95, A135.

E94. *New Acquisitions,* Museum of Modern Art, New York, 11 Feb–15 Mar 1953. 2 works: 56.2–3, 56.5–8.

E95. *The Unknown Political Prisoner,* Tate Gallery, London, 14 Mar–30 Apr 1953. 1 work: 61.2. Review A195. Showed winners of the competition sponsored by the Institute of Contemporary Arts, London.

E96. *The Classical Tradition in Contemporary Sculpture,* Walker Art Center, Minneapolis, Apr–Jun 1953. 1 work: 55.1. Review A141.

E97. *First Biennial Exhibition, American Painting, Sculpture,* Cranbrook Academy of Art, Bloomfield Hills, Michigan, 2 Oct–1 Nov 1953. [No catalogue] 1 work: 55.3. (Winston Collection Papers; Roll D220, frames 1202, 1215–16, AAA).

E98. *Acquired in Three Years,* Wadsworth Athenaeum, Hartford, Conn., 9 Jan– 7 Feb 1954. 1 painting.

E99. *1954 Annual Exhibition of American Sculpture, Watercolors, and Drawings,* Whitney Museum of American Art, New York, 17 Mar–18 Apr 1954. 1 work: [58.2].

E100. *A Loan Exhibition of Paintings from the Solomon R. Guggenheim Museum New York,* Art Gallery of Toronto, 2 Apr–9 May 1954. 1 work: 37.10.

E101. *Object and Image in Modern Art and Poetry,* Yale University Art Gallery, New Haven, 30 Apr–14 Jun 1954. 1 work: 55.4. Essay by George H. Hamilton, ›Object and Image: Aspects of the Poetic Principle in Modern Art‹.

E102. *Flowers in Art and Decoration,* Massachusetts Horticultural Society, Boston, 24 Oct– 4 Nov 1954. [No catalogue] 1 work: 64. (Letter to Mrs. Warner, Mass. Hort. Soc., 11 Oct 1954).

E103. *The Solomon R. Guggenheim Museum: A Selection from the Museum Collection,* Vancouver Art Gallery, 16 Nov–12 Dec 1954. 1 work: 37.10.

E104. *Selection from the Solomon R. Guggenheim Museum New York,* Montreal Museum of Fine Arts, 4 Jun–3 Jul 1955. 1 work: 37.10.

E105. *Moderne Kunst; Nieuw e Oud,* Stedelijk Museum, Amsterdam, 26 Jul–3 Oct 1955. 1 work: 55.5.

E106. *Selection V,* Solomon R. Guggenheim Museum, New York, 27 Jul–9 Oct 1955. 1 work: 10.2. (Dates from annotated catalogue, SRGM).

E107. *Twentieth Century Painting and Sculpture: The Winston Collection,* University of Michigan, Museum of Art, Ann Arbor, 30 Oct– 27 Nov 1955, 1 work: 55.3.

E108. *Selection VI,* Solomon R. Guggenheim Museum, New York, [24 Jan–1 May 1956]. 1 work: 10.2. (Dates from annotated catalogue, SRGM).

E109. *Exposition internationale de sculpture contemporaine,* Musée Rodin, Paris, [Summer] 1956. 1 work: 55.5.

E110. *Collecting Modern Art: Paintings, Sculpture and Drawings from the Collection of Mr and Mrs Harry Winston,* Detroit Institute of Arts, 27 Sep–3 Nov 1957; Virginia Museum of Art, Richmond, 13 Dec 1957–5 Jan 1958; San Francisco Museum of Art, 23 Jan– 13 Mar 1958; Milwaukee Art Institute, Wisc., 11 Apr–12 May 1958. 1 work: 55.3.

E111. *Sculpture,* Galerie Claude Bernard, Paris, 6 Feb 1958. [No catalogue] 1 work: 55.11. (Record, and installation photograph, FAL).

E112. *50 ans d'art moderne,* Palais International des Beaux-Arts, Exposition Universelle et Internationale de Bruxelles, Brussels, 17 Apr–21 Jul 1958. 2 works: 58.2, 62.4. Essay by Emile Langui. Catalogue revised as Emile Langui. *50 Years of Modern Art.* London, Thames and Hudson, 1959. See B33.

E113. *De Renaissance der XXe Eeuw,* Stedelijk Museum, Amsterdam, 4 Jul–29 Sep 1958. 1 work: 4.4.

E114. *Annual Exhibition 1958,* Whitney Museum of American Art, New York, 19 Nov 1958– 4 Jan 1959. 1 work: 68.3.

E115. *Leven met Beelden.* Stedelijk Museum, Amsterdam, Dec 1958–Jan 1959. 5 prints.

E116. [Student Exhibition], Paul Klapper Library, Queens College, Flushing, NY, Apr–May 1959. No catalogue. 1 work: 37.10. (Loan records 8 Apr and 20 May 1959, SRGM).

E117. *Sculpture in Our Time: Collected by Joseph H. Hirshhorn,* Detroit Institute of Arts, 5 May–23 Aug 1959. 1 work: 48.11. Review A173.

E118. *Beitrag der Russen zur Modernen Kunst,* Karmeliterkloster, Frankfurt-am-Main, 3 Jul–9 Aug 1959. 1 work (plus 3 woodengravings): 4.4. Essay by E. Steneberg.

E119. *50 Jaar Verkenningen,* Stedelijk Museum, Amsterdam, 4 Jul–28 Sep 1959. 1 work: 55.5.

E120. *Documenta '59. Kunst nach 1945. Internationale Ausstellung,* Fridericianum Museum, Kassel, 11 Jul–11 Oct 1959. 3 works: 58.2, 62.4, 67.4.

E121. *A Loan Exhibition from the Solomon R. Guggenheim Museum,* Museum of Fine Arts, Boston, 29 Oct–13 Dec 1959. 2 works: 37.10, 48.9.

E122. *Form Givers at Mid-Century,* Corcoran Gallery of Art, Washington, DC; Metropolitan Museum of Art, New York; Boston Museum of Fine Arts; Carnegie Institute, Pittsburgh; Minneapolis Institute of Arts, Minn.; Virginia Museum of Fine Arts, Richmond, 1959. Organized and Sponsored by *Time* magazine for the American Federation of Arts. 1 work as photograph, listed under Marcel Breuer: 67.5.

E123. *Sixty-Third American Exhibition,* Art Institute of Chicago, 2 Dec 1959–31 Jan 1960. 1 work: 68.5.

E124. *Schiedammers Tonen hun Kunstbezit,* Stedelijk Museum, Schiedam, 18 Dec 1959–16 Feb 1960. 1 work: 55.11.

E125. *What is Modern Art?,* Toledo Museum of Art, Ohio, 6–27 Mar 1960. 1 work: 55.3. (Winston Collection Papers, Roll D220, frames 1202, 1234, 1237, 1241, AAA).

E126. *Business Buys American Art,* Whitney Museum of American Art, New York, 17 Mar–24 Apr 1960. 1 work, plus 1 ex-cat.: 34.4 ex-cat., 69.2 as photograph.

E127. *Sculpture and Drawings by Sculptors from the Solomon, R. Guggenheim Museum,* The Arts Club of Chicago, 19 Apr–19 May 1960. 2 works: 37.10, 39.4.

E128. *Konkrete Kunst: 50 Jahre Entwicklung,* Helmhaus, Zurich, 8 Jun–14 Aug 1960. 1 work: 41.6.

E129. *Sculpture-Ceramics,* Otto Gerson Gallery, New York, Sep 1960. No listing of works. First exhibition with Gerson.

E130. *Paths of Abstract Art,* Cleveland Museum of Art, 4 Oct–13 Nov 1960. 1 work: 41.4. Catalogue by Edward B. Henning.

E131. *Cent sculpteurs de Daumier à nos jours,* Musée d'Art et d'Industrie, Saint-Etienne, 1960. 1 work: 55.16.

E132. *Annual Exhibition 1960, Sculpture and Drawings,* Whitney Museum of American Art, New York, Dec 1960–Jan 1961. 1 work: 62.4.

E133. *A Galaxy of Treasures from St. Louis Collections,* St. Louis City Art Museum, 18 Jan– 12 Feb 1961. 1 work: 53.9.

E134. *Bewogen Beweging,* Stedelijk Museum, Amsterdam, 10 Mar–17 Apr 1961. 1 work: 9.1.

E135. *Rörelse i Konsten,* Moderna Museet, Stockholm, May–Sep 1961. 1 work: 9.1. (see F3).

E136. *Polarität: Das apollonische und das dionysische,* Städtische Kunsthalle, Recklinghausen, 2 Jun–16 Jul 1961. 1 work: 55.5.

E137. *Drawings by Sculptors,* Smithsonian Institution circulating exhibition, [June] 1961–1962. 2 drawings. (letter from Otto Gerson Gallery, 26 Apr 1961).

E138. *Polariteit: Het apollinische en het dionysische in de Kunst,* Stedelijk Museum, Amsterdam, 22 Jul–18 Sep 1961. 1 work: 55.5.

E139. *Stedelijk Museum besøger Louisiana,* Louisiana Museum, Humlebaek, 28 Oct– 3 Dec 1961. 1 work: 55.5.

E140. *De Rodin a nuestros dias,* Fundación Eugenio Mendoza, Caracas, 1961. 2 works: 55.12, 68.6.

E141. *Spotlight on Sculpture 1880–1961,* Otto Gerson Gallery, New York, 13 Dec 1961– 21 Jan 1962. 3 works: 41.6, [48.3], 55.17.

E142. *Stedelijk Museum Amsterdam besøker Moderna Museet Stockholm,* Moderna Museet, Stockholm, 26 Dec 1961–28 Jan 1962. 1 work: 55.5.

E143. *Sculpture from the Museum Collection,* Solomon R. Guggenheim Museum, New York, 9 Jan–25 Feb 1962. No catalogue. 5 works: 10.2, 33.3, 37.10, 39.4, 48.9. (Wall list, SRGM).

E144. *Geometric Abstraction in America,* Whitney Museum of American Art, New York, 20 Mar–13 May 1962. 1 work: 68.3.

E145. *A Survey of American Sculpture: Late 18th Century to 1962,* Newark Museum, N. J., 10 May–20 Oct 1962. 1 work: 52.6.

E146. *The First Five Years: Acquisitions by the Friends of the Whitney Museum of American Art 1957–1962,* Whitney Museum of American Art, New York, 16 May–17 Jun 1962. 1 work: 68.3.

E147. *Monumental Sculpture,* Otto Gerson Gallery, New York, Jun–Jul 1962. 1 work: 68.10.

E148. *Ausstellung Auserlesener Meisterwerke des 19. und 20. Jahrhunderts,* Galerie Wilhelm Grosshennig, Düsseldorf, Jun–Aug 1962. 2 works: 55.17, 68.7.

E149. *Kunst von 1900 bis Heute,* Museum des 20. Jahrhunderts, Vienna, 21 Sep–4 Nov 1962. 1 work: 67.4.

E150. *Art Exhibition: Loans from Private Collections,* Stamford Museum, Conn., 3–11 Nov 1962. 1 work: 55.9.

E151. *Modern Sculpture from the Joseph H. Hirshhorn Collection,* Solomon R. Guggenheim Museum, New York, 3 Oct 1962–6 Jan 1963. 1 work: 48.11.

E152. *Museum Collection, Spring 1963,* Solomon R. Guggenheim Museum, New York, [19] Apr–[2 Jun] 1963. 5 works: 10.2, 33.3, 37.10, 39.4, 48.9.

E153. *Sculpture Exhibition,* Otto Gerson Gallery, New York, 18 May–15 Jun 1963. 1 work.

E154. *Aspects of Twentieth Century Art,* Marlborough Galleries, London, Jul–Aug 1963. 1 work: 68.7.

E155. *11 New England Sculptors,* Wadsworth Atheneum, Hartford, Conn., 18 Jul–15 Sep 1963. 2 works (plus 4 drawings): 40.6, 68.10.

E156. *Skulptur: Bo Boustedts Samling,* Moderna Museet, Stockholm, Oct–Nov 1963. 1 work: 70.3.

E157. *Onskemuseet,* Moderna Museet, Stockholm, 26 Dec 1963–16 Feb 1964. 1 work: 70.3.

E158. *Skulptur: Bo Boustedts Samling,* Kunstnernes Hus, Oslo, 7–30 Mar 1964; Stedelijk Museum, Amsterdam, 1 May–7 Jun 1964; Dommuseum, Lübeck, 4 Jul–2 Aug 1964; Museum am Ostwall, Dortmund, May 1965. 1 work: 70.3.

E159. *Twentieth Century Art: Loans from the Wellesley Alumnae and other Sources,* Art Museum, Jewett Art Center, Wellesley College, Wellesley, Mass., 6 Apr–3 May 1964. 1 work: 70. (Gallery list, FAL).

E160. *Painting and Sculpture of a Decade '54–'64,* Calouste Gulbenkian Foundation at the Tate Gallery, London, 22 Apr–28 Jun 1964. 1 work: 62.3.

E161. *Between the Fairs: 25 Years of American Art, 1939–1964,* Whitney Museum of American Art, New York, 24 Jun–23 Sep 1964. 1 work: 68.3.

E162. *Il Contributo Russo alle avanguardie plastiche,* Galleria del Levante, Milan, [Oct] 1964. [1 work: 64].

E163. *Beeldend Experiment op de Planken,* Stedelijk van Abbemuseum, Eindhoven, 10 Oct–22 Nov 1964. 4 drawings, plus 1 photograph of the set for *La Chatte.* Catalogue by Denis Bablet.

E164. *The Classic Spirit in 20th Century Art,* Sidney Janis Gallery, New York, 1964. 1 work: 68.3.

E165. *Treasures of Twentieth Art from the Maremont Collection,* Washington Gallery of Modern Art, Washington, DC, 1964. 1 work: 48.3.

E166. *Art and Movement,* Scottish Arts Council at the Royal Scottish Academy, Edinburgh, 6–28 Feb 1965; Art Gallery and Museum at Kelvingrove, Glasgow, 8–28 Mar 1965. 2 works: 9.1, 68.2. (See F6).

E167. *Art in Britain 1930–40, Centred around Axis, Circle, Unit One,* Marlborough Fine Art, London, 12 Mar–15 Apr 1965. 6 works: [12.4], 40.3, 41.2, [48.2], 48.4, 49. Reprints A163.

E168. *Sculpture: Twentieth Century,* Dallas Museum of Fine Arts, May–Jun 1965. 1 work: 77.1.

E169. Festival of Arts, The White House, Washington, DC, 14 Jun 1965. 1 work: 53.2. (Phillips Collection records).

E170. *Soundings Two,* Signals Gallery, London, 22 Jul–22 Sep 1965. 1 work: 70.8.

E171. *Williams-Vassar Exchange Exhibition,* Williams College Museum of Art, Williamstown, Mass., 28 Feb–18 Mar 1966. No catalogue. 1 work: 41.4. (Documentation, Vassar College).

E172. *Twentieth Century Sculpture,* University Art Museum, Albuquerque, New Mexico, 25 Mar–1 May 1966. 1 work: 41.4.

E173. *Fifty Years of Modern Art 1916–1966,* Cleveland Museum of Art, Ohio, 14 Jun– 31 Jul 1966. 2 works: 51.2, 68.10. Catalogue by Edward B. Henning.

E174. *Art of the United States: 1670–1966,* Whitney Museum of American Art, New York, 28 Sep–27 Nov 1966. 1 work: 68.3.

E175. *Contemporary Art – Acquisitions 1962–1965,* Albright-Knox Art Gallery, Buffalo, 30 Sep–30 Oct 1966. 1 work: 55.18.

E176. *The Innermost Eye,* Museum of Art, New Britain, Conn., 5–30 Nov 1966. 1 work: 40.6.

E177. *Avantgarde Osteuropa 1910–1930,* Kunstverein und Akademie der Künste, Berlin, Oct–Nov 1967. (B13, p. 313).

E178. *Aspects of Russian Experimental Art 1900–1925,* Grosvenor Gallery, London, 24 Oct–18 Nov 1967. 1 work: 34.5.

E179. *Space and Dream,* Knoedler Galleries, New York, 5–29 Dec 1967. 1 work: 34.4. Catalogue B79.

E180. *International Exhibition of Contemporary Sculpture,* Expo. '67, Montreal. 1 work: 4.7. Review A129.

E181. *Works of Art of the Nineteenth and Twentieth Centuries: Collected by Louise and Joseph Pulitzer, Jr.,* St. Louis City Art Museum, 23 Jan–24 Mar 1968. 1 work: 53.9.

E182. *Kunsthandel – Düsseldorf,* Galerie Wilhelm Grosshennig, Düsseldorf, Apr 1968. 1 work: 55.17. (Gallery records).

E183. *Drawings by Members,* National Institute of Arts and Letters, New York, Nov 1968–Feb 1969.

E184. *The Machine as Seen at the End of the Mechanical Age,* Museum of Modern Art, New York, 25 Nov 1968–9 Feb 1969; University of St. Thomas, Houston, 25 Mar–18 May 1969; San Francisco Museum of Art, 23 Jun–24 Aug 1969. 1 work: 9.1a. Catalogue by K. G. Pontus Hultén.

E185. *Twentieth Century Art from the Nelson Aldrich Rockefeller Collection,* Museum of Modern Art, New York, 26 May–1 Sep 1969. 1 work: 62.3.

E186. *Selected Sculpture and Works on Paper,* Solomon R. Guggenheim Museum, New York, 8 Jul–14 Sep 1969. 5 works: 10.2, 33.3, 37.10, 39.4, 48.9.

E187. *Sammlung Etzold,* Kunstverein, Cologne, 19 May–19 Jul 1970. 1 lithograph.

E188. *The Non-Objective World 1914–1924,* Annely Juda Fine Art, London, 30 Jun–30 Sep 1970. 1 work: 48.15.

E189. *Constructivist Tendencies: From the Collection of Mr and Mrs G. Rickey,* University of California, Santa Barbara, 5 Jan–14 Feb 1971; toured USA, 30 Aug 1970–15 Apr 1972. 2 prints.

E190. *1970 Pittsburgh International: Exhibition of Contemporary Arts,* Carnegie Institute, Museum of Art, Pittsburgh, 30 Oct 1970–10 Jan 1971. 1 work: 68.11. Review A37.

E191. *Helen Sutherland Collection: a pioneer collection of the 1930s,* Arts Council at the Hayward Gallery, London, 10 Dec 1970–10 Jan 1971. 1 work: 48.2.

E192. *Masters of the 20th Century,* Marlborough Galleries, New York, 1971. 1 work: 73.5.

E193. *Russian Art of the Revolution,* Andrew Dickson White Museum of Art, Cornell University, Ithaca, NY, 25 Feb–25 Mar 1971; Brooklyn Museum of Art, 14 Jun–25 Jul 1971. 1 work (plus reconstruction of *La Chatte* set): 41.3.

E194. [*America,* Basel Art Fair, Galerie Beyeler, 24–29 Jun 1971. 1 work ex-cat.: 70.3a].

E195. *New Orleans Collects,* New Orleans Museum of Art, 1971–1972. 1 work: 77.1.

E196. *Modern Painting, Drawing and Sculpture: Collected by Louise and Joseph Pulitzer, Jr.,* Fogg Art Museum, Cambridge, Mass., 15 Nov 1971–3 Jan 1972; Wadsworth Atheneum, Hartford, Conn., 2 Feb–19 Mar 1972. 1 work: 53.9. Catalogue by Charles S. Chetham *et al, Modern Painting, Drawing and Sculpture: Collected by Louise and Joseph Pulitzer, Jr.: Vol. III* Fogg Art Museum, 1971.

E197. *Kunst in der Revolution,* Kunstverein, Frankfurt, 14 Apr–11 Jun 1972; Württemberger Kunstverein, Stuttgart, 30 Jun–27 Aug 1972; Kunsthalle, Cologne, 28 Oct 1972–21 Jan 1973. 1 work: 5.1.

E198. *Masters of the 19th and 20th Centuries,* Marlborough Fine Art, London, summer 1972. 1 work: 68.9.

E199. *The Non-Objective World, 1939–1955,* Annely Juda Fine Art, London, 6 Jul–8 Aug 1972; Galerie Liatowitsch, Basel, 20 Sep–26 Oct 1972; Galleria Milano, Milan, 14 Nov–30 Dec 1972. 1 work: 48.15. Essay by George Rickey.

E200. *Continental Painting and Sculpture, 1942–1972, in the Albright-Knox Art Gallery,* Albright-Knox Art Gallery, Buffalo, 21 Jul–27 Aug 1972. 1 work: 55.18.

E201. *Not So Long Ago: Art of the 1920s in Europe and America,* University Art Museum, Austin, Texas, 15 Oct–17 Dec 1972. 1 work: 22.4a.

E202. *Colecciones privadas en Venezuela No. 7,* Museo de Bellas Artes, Caracas, 1972. 3 works: 10.7, 55.12, 68.6.

E203. *Master Sculptors of the 20th Century,* Gimpel Fils, London, 30 Jan–3 Mar 1973. 2 works: 53.5, 73.3.

E204. *Structure in Art,* University of Saskatchewan, Saskatoon, 12 Feb–2 Mar 1973. 1 work: 55.20. Essay by E. Bornstein.

E205. *Art in Space: Some Turning Points,* Detroit Institute of Arts, 15 May–24 Jun 1973. 1 work: 68.11.

E206. *The Non-Objective World, 1914–1955,* Annely Juda Fine Art, London, 5 Jul–22 Sep 1973; University Art Museum, Austin, Texas, 14 Oct–15 Dec 1973; Galerie Liatowitsch, Basel, [1974]. 1 work: 48.15. Essay by Margit Staber.

E207. *Sculpture,* Waddington Galleries, London, 10 Jul–4 Aug 1973. 1 work: 68.7.

E208. *Pioneers of Modern Sculpture,* Arts Council at the Hayward Gallery, London, 20 Jul–23 Sept 1973. 3 works: 4.7, (4.4 and 6.3 as photographs). Essay by Albert E. Elsen (revised as B63).

E209. *Masters of the 19th and 20th Centuries,* Marlborough Gallery, New York, 1974. 1 work: 53.10.

E210. *Less is More,* Lowe Art Museum, University of Miami, Miami, Fla., 7 Feb–10 Mar 1974. (list, Stedelijk Museum, Amsterdam).

E211. *Vordemberge-Gildewart Remembered,* Annely Juda Fine Art, London, 4 Jul–14 Sep 1974. 1 work: 48.15.

E212. *Cobra and Constrasts: The Lydia and Harry Lewis Winston Collection. Dr and Mrs Barnett Malbin,* Detroit Institute of Arts, 25 Sep–17 Nov 1974. 1 work: 55.3.

E213. *Inaugural Exhibition,* Hirshhorn Museum and Sculpture Garden, Smithsonian Institution, Washington, DC, 4 Oct 1974–15 Sep 1975. 4 works: 48.11, 55.9, 68.10, 73.4. Catalogue by A. Lerner, ed. *The Hirshhorn Museum and Sculpture Garden, Smithsonian Institution,* New York, Abrams, 1974.

E214. *Hampstead in the Thirties: A Committed Decade,* Camden Arts Centre, London, 29 Nov 1974–19 Jan 1975. 1 work: 48. Essay by J. P. Hodin.

E215. *A Tribute to Herbert Read 1893–1968,* Bradford Art Galleries and Museums at the Manor House, Ilkley, 25 May–22 Jun 1975. 1 wood-engraving and 1 photograph.

E216. *The Golden Door: Artists-Immigrants of America, 1876–1976,* Hirshhorn Museum and Sculpture Garden, Smithsonian Institution, Washington, DC, 20 May–22 Jun 1976. 3 works: 55.9, 68.10, 73.4.

E217. *Die reine Form: Von Malewitsch bis Albers,* Kunstmuseum, Düsseldorf, 15 Oct–28 Nov 1976. 1 work: 77.3.

E218. *Materials of Art: Plastics,* University of Hartford, Art School, Hartford, Conn., 9–25 Feb 1977. 1 work: 40.6.

E219. *Espace-lumière dans des sculptures du cubisme à aujourd'hui,* Château de Ratilly, Treigny, Yonne, 18 Jun–18 Sep 1977. 1 work: 70.9.

E220. *Forty Modern Masters,* Solomon R. Guggenheim Museum, New York, 1 Jul–11 Sep 1977. 1 work: 10.2.

E221. *Skulptur: Ausstellung in Münster,* Westfälisches Landesmuseum, Münster, 3 Jul–13 Nov 1977. 2 works: 22.5, 48.3.

E222. *Tendenzen der Zwanziger Jahre,* Neue Nationalgalerie, Berlin, 14 Aug–16 Oct 1977. 2 works: 22.4a.

POSTHUMOUS EXHIBITIONS 1977–1983

E223. *Les Ballets Russes de Diaghilev 1909–1929,* Centre Culturel du Marais, Paris, 29 Nov 1977–17 Mar 1978. 3 drawings.

E224. *Forty Modern Masters,* Solomon R. Guggenheim Museum, New York, 16 Dec 1977–5 Feb 1978. 3 works: 10.2, 33.3, 48.9, on show until March 1978.

E225. *Konstruktiv Kunst: McCrory Samlingen New York,* Louisiana Museum, Humlebaek, 21 Jan–27 Mar 1978. 1 work: 77.3. Catalogue in *Louisiana Revy* Year 18, No. 2, Jan 1978. Essay by W. Rotzler, reprint of A170.

E226. *L'Art moderne dans les musées de Province,* Grand Palais, Paris, 3 Feb–24 Apr 1978. 1 work: 55.6.

E227. *Abstraction-Création 1931–1936,* Westfälisches Landesmuseum, Münster, 2 Apr–4 Jun 1978; Musée d'Art Moderne de la Ville de Paris, 16 Jun–17 Sep 1978. 2 works: 34.5, 44.

E228. *Masters of Modern Sculpture,* Marlborough Gallery, New York, 6 May–17 Jun 1978. 3 works: 48.4, 58.3, 70.5.

E229. *Tendances constructivistes au XXe siècle: Collection McCrory Corporation New York,* Musée Rath, Geneva, 17 Jun–5 Sep 1978. 1 work: 77.3. Essay by W. Rotzler, reprint of A170.

E230. *The Non-Objective World, Twenty-Five Years, 1914–1939,* Annely Juda Fine Art, London, 28 Jun–30 Sep 1978. 2 works (plus 2 drawings): 37.3, 53.3.

E231. *Paris – Berlin,* Musée National d'Art Moderne, Centre Georges Pompidou, Paris, 12 Jul–6 Nov 1978. 2 works: 10.6, 22.5.

E232. *The Pier Gallery: Collection of the Pier Arts Centre, Stromness, Orkney,* Tate Gallery, London, 1978. 1 work; not shown at other venues: 48.5. Catalogue B97.

E233. *Foire internationale d'art contemporaine,* Grand Palais, Paris, Galerie Denise René display, 1978. No catalogue. 2 works: 48.3. (Installation photograph, FAL).

E234. *The Planar Dimension: Europe, 1912–1932,* Solomon R. Guggenheim Museum, New York, 9 Mar–6 May 1979. 4 works, plus 1 ex-cat.: 4.4, 4.8 ex-cat., 5.1, 10.2, 22.5. (Revised wall list, SRGM).

E235. *Modern European Sculpture 1918–1945: Unknown Beings and Other Realities,* Albright-Knox Art Gallery, Buffalo, 12 May–24 Jun 1979; Minneapolis Institute of Arts, Minn., 22 Jul–2 Sep 1979; San Francisco Museum of Modern Art, 5 Oct–18 Nov 1979. 2 works: 34.3, 53.7. Catalogue B64.

E236. *Paris – Moscou,* Musée National d'Art Moderne, Centre Georges Pompidou, Paris, 31 May–5 Nov 1979. 3 works (plus 3 drawings): 4.4, 5.1, 10.9 (replaced 10.8). See E250.

E237. *Constructivism and the Geometric Tradition: Selections from the McCrory Corporation Collection,* Albright-Knox Art Gallery, Buffalo, 14 Oct–25 Nov 1979; Dallas Museum of Fine Arts, 16 Jan–24 Feb 1980; San Francisco Museum of Modern Art, 14 Mar–27 Apr 1980; Museum of Contemporary Art, La Jolla, Cal., 23 May–8 Jul 1980; Seattle, Art Museum, 30 Jul–14 Sep 1980; Museum of Art, Carnegie Institute, Pittsburgh, 30 Oct 1980–4 Jan 1981; William Rockhill Nelson Gallery and Atkins Museum of Fine Arts, Kansas City, 23 Jan–15 Mar 1981; Detroit Institute of Arts, 22 Apr–1 Jun 1981; Milwaukee Art Center, Wisc., 14 July–26 Aug 1981. 1 work: 77.3. Essay by W. Rotzler, reprint of A170.

E238. *Archive Display 1979–1980: Artists International Association; Naum Gabo; Paul Nash; Richard Long,* Tate Gallery, London, 1979–80. 17 wood blocks and prints. Essay by Sarah Fox-Pitt. For installation see A204.

E239. *Origini dell'astrattismo: Verso altri orizzonti del reale 1885–1919,* Palazzo Reale, Milan, 18 Oct 1979–18 Jan 1980. 1 work: 22.4a.

E240. *Thirties: British Art and Design before the War,* Arts Council at the Hayward Gallery, London, 25 Oct 1979–13 Jan 1980. 1 work: 41.1.

E241. *The Spirit of Constructivism,* Neuberger Museum, Purchase, NY, 3 Feb–Nov 1980. 1 work: 55.7.

E242. *Busch-Reisinger Museum: The Twentieth Century Collection,* National Gallery of Art, Washington, DC, 15 Jun–1 Sep 1980. 1 work: 22.4a.

E243. *Abstraction 1910–1940,* Annely Juda Fine Art, London, 1 Jul–27 Sep 1980. 1 work (plus 6 drawings): 10.6.

E244. *Skulptur im 20. Jahrhunderts,* Wenkenpark, Riehen-Basel, 10 May–14 Sep 1980. 2 works: 5.3, 10.9.

E245. *Reliefs: Formprobleme zwischen Malerei und Skulptur im 20. Jahrhundert,* Westfälisches Landesmuseum für Kunst und Kulturgeschichte, Münster; Kunsthaus, Zurich, 1980. 2 works: 60, 66.7.

E246. *The Avant-Garde in Russia 1910–1930: New Perspectives,* Los Angeles County Museum of Art, 8 Jul–28 Sep 1980; Hirshhorn Museum and Sculpture Garden, Washington, DC, 20 Nov 1980–15 Feb 1981. 1 work (plus 2 drawings and 1 document): 4.4.

E247. *Busch-Reisinger Museum of Harvard University from the Twentieth Century Collection,* Wildenstein Gallery, New York, 23 Sep–24 Oct 1980. 1 work: 22.4a.

E248. *Invention and Tradition. Selected Works from the Julia A. Whitney Foundation and the Thomas P. Whitney Collection of Modernist Russian Art,* University of Virginia, Art Museum, Charlottesville, 19 Oct–19 Nov 1980. 1 print, 1 document (plus 1 drawing ex-cat.).

E249. *Spotlight: Four Centuries of Ballet Costume,* Victoria and Albert Museum, London, 8 Apr–26 Jul 1981. 1 drawing.

E250. *Moskva – Parizh,* Pushkin Museum of Fine Arts, Moscow, 3 Jun–4 Oct 1981. 2 works: 10.9, 22.5. See E236.

E251. *Configuration 1910–1940,* Annely Juda Fine Art, London, 1 Jul–26 Sep 1981. 4 drawings and 2 paintings.

E252. *Sculpture du XXe siècle 1900–1945: Tradition et rupture,* Fondation Maeght, Saint-Paul, 4 Jul–4 Oct 1981. 6 works: 4.4, 4.8, 5.3, 10.8. 34.3, 48.10.

E253. *British Sculpture in the Twentieth Century. Part One: Image and Form 1901–50,* Whitechapel Art Gallery, London, 11 Sep–1 Nov 1981. 2 works: 42.3, 53.1. Checklist only. See also A65, A109.

E254. *Medio siglo de escultura 1900–1945,* Fundacion Juan March, Madrid, Nov–Dec 1981. 6 works: 4.4, 4.8, 5.3, 10.8, 34.3, 48.10.

E255. *Circle: International Survey of Constructive Art,* Kettle's Yard Gallery, University of Cambridge, 20 Feb–28 Mar 1982. 4 works: 2.2, 22.2, 34.3. Catalogue by Jeremy Lewison, ed. *Circle: Constructive Art in Britain 1934–40.* Contains essays by Sir Leslie Martin, Jane Beckett, Nicholas Bullock, John Gage; reviews of *Circle;* A88 and G10.

E256. *Collages and Reliefs 1910–1945,* Annely Juda Fine Art, London, 30 Jun–2 Oct 1982. 2 works: 12.2, 39.2.

E256a. *[Abstract Art in a Danish Private Collection],* Glyptotek, Copenhagen, 18 Sept–31 Oct 1982. 1 work: 55.22.

E257. *Deutsche Kunst des 20. Jahrhunderts aus dem Busch-Reisinger Museum, Harvard University, Cambridge, USA,* Städtische Galerie, Frankfurt am Main, Oct 1982–Jan 1983; Bauhaus Archiv, Museum für Gestaltung, Berlin, Feb–Apr 1983; Kunstmuseum, Düsseldorf, May–Jun 1983. 1 work: 22.4a.

E258. *Art and Dance: Images of the Modern Dialogue, 1890–1980,* Institute of Contemporary Art, Boston, 9 Nov 1982–8 Jan 1983; Toledo Museum of Art, Toledo, Ohio, 6 Mar–24 Apr 1983. 3 drawings.

E259. *Fragile Skulpturen,* Skulpturenmuseum, Marl, 28 Nov 1982–23 Jan 1983. 1 work: 55.17.

E260. *Drawing in Air: An Exhibition of Sculptors' Drawings 1882–1982,* Sunderland Arts Centre, Ceolfrith Gallery, Sunderland, 11 Jul–20 Aug 1983; Glynn Vivian Art Gallery and Museum, Swansea, 3 Sep–5 Nov 1983; Leeds City Art Gallery and Henry Moore Study Centre, 13 Jan–19 Feb 1984. 2 drawings.

E261. **The First Russian Show: A Commemoration of the Van Diemen Exhibition Berlin 1922.** Annely Juda Fine Art, London, 15 Sep–3 Dec 1983. 4 works (5 plus drawings): 4.4, 5.3, 9.1b, 10.6.

E262. *Electra,* Musée d'Art Moderne de la Ville de Paris, Dec 1983–Feb 1984. 1 work: 9.1c.

E263. *Die Sprache der Geometrie,* Kunstmuseum, Bern, 16 Mar–13 May 1984. 1 work (plus 2 drawings): 10.9.

E264. *The Modern Art of the Print: Selections from the Collection of Lois and Michael Torf,* Williams College Museum of Art, Williamstown, Mass., 1984; Boston Museum of Fine Arts, 1984. 21 wood-engravings.

E265. *Skulptur im 20 Jahrhundert,* Merian-Park, Basle, 3 Jun–10 Sep 1984. 1 work: 9.1c.

E266. *From Degas to Calder: Sculpture and Works on Paper from the Guggenheim Museum Collection,* Solomon R. Guggenheim Museum, New York, 20 Jul–8 Sep 1984. 6 works: 10.2, 33.3, 37.10, 39.4, 48.9, 55.14. (Supplementary checklist, pp. 10–11).

E267. *Masters of Modern Art and Contemporary Sculpture,* Marlborough Gallery, New York, 8 Nov–4 Dec 1984. 2 works: 58.3, 70.5.

E268. Museum of Modern Art, Shiga, Japan, 1984. 3 works: 4.4, 47.5, 70.12.

E269. **St. Ives 1939–64,** Tate Gallery, London, 13 Feb–14 Apr 1985. 6 works (plus 3 paintings): 36, 48.8, 52.1, 52.3, 53.1, 85. (Contains G16, extracts from Gabo's diaries).

Photo credits